Readings in Church History

READINGS
in Church History

Edited by COLMAN J. BARRY, O.S.B.

PRESIDENT, ST. JOHN'S UNIVERSITY
COLLEGEVILLE, MINNESOTA

Volume Three

THE MODERN ERA
1789 TO THE PRESENT

NEWMAN PRESS
Paramus, N.J.   New York, N.Y.

Imprimi potest: BALDWIN W. DWORSCHAK, O.S.B.
Abbot, St. John's Abbey

Nihil obstat: JOHN A. EIDENSCHINK, O.S.B.
Censor deputatus

Imprimatur: PETER W. BARTHOLOME
Bishop of St. Cloud
July 6, 1965

Published by Newman Press
Editorial Office: 1865 Broadway, New York, N.Y. 10023
Business Office: 400 Sette Drive, Paramus, N.J. 07652

Contents

Contents

PART TWO:

The Church and the Contemporary Scene, 1917—

PART I

The Church and the Liberal Society
1789-1917

I. *Church and State Relations*

THE culmination of the currents of the Enlightenment, Deism, Rationalism, and Romanticism in the French Revolution of 1789 swept away the old order of absolute dynastic regimes. In North America the English colonists had revolted in 1776 and established the democratic republic of the United States whose basic ideas were rooted not only in Deism but also in traditional Judaeo-Christian concepts of the dignity of the individual. On the other hand, the French Revolution and the other European revolts that it ignited were an open challenge to Christianity. The ideology and program of French thinkers and revolutionists was a secularized, national version of an ideal human society, a "liberal state" based on the political dogma of popular sovereignty. This movement of "Liberalism" placed authority not in God but in the people. A self-sufficient national life was the final and practical source of authority.

The French Revolution destroyed the traditional fabric of Catholicism in that nation. Church-owned property, comprising roughly one-fifth of the domain of France, was confiscated; monasteries were dissolved; the last vestige of the medieval supremacy of the Church was swept away; and the state now claimed the right even to regulate the internal life of the Church. Gallican lawyers of the National Assembly drew up a law which was passed on 12 July 1790 wiping out the legal position, privileges, and exemptions of the Church in France: THE CIVIL CONSTITUTION OF THE CLERGY (*No. 1*). Bishops and parish priests were to be elected by all citizens, salaries were to be paid to the clergy by the government, the pope was to have no administrative control over the Church, while diocesan boundaries became synonymous with civil departments or divisions. A policy of delay was employed by Pope Pius VI who tried vainly to treat the cataclysm as a passing phenomenon. French Catholics were further confused by the position of their bishops who, fearing that France would be lost to the Church, advised Louis XVI to sign the decree. But then the pope acted, condemned the constitution, and prohibited the taking of the oath. The majority of French ecclesiastics remained loyal to the Church while about one-third of the parish clergy and seven bishops complied. The non-juring Catholics now suffered deportation, imprisonment, and even death in the Reign of Terror. The constitutional church created a secular Deist cult of reason, while the old Church was set against the Revolution, creating a division in French society and in large parts of Europe which persisted for the next eighty years.

With the advent of Napoleon, and the establishment of the French Empire, the more blatant anti-Catholic aspects of the revolutionary regime were mitigated. Napoleon, a nominal Catholic at most, perceived practical advantages in recognizing the Catholic sympathies of the majority of the citizens, and determined to use the Church for the ends of the state. With the election in 1800 of the Benedictine monk, Gregorio Chiaramonti, Bishop of Imola, as Pius VII (1823), the possibility of a *rapprochément* appeared, because the new pope had previously declared that Catholicism was compatible with democratic forms of government. It appeared that the traditional alignment of the papacy with the *ancien régime* might be altered as Cardinal Consalvi, the able papal secretary of state (a cleric but not a priest), and Talleyrand, ambivalent French bishop and Napoleon's representative, entered into negotiations. On 15 July 1801 a CONCORDAT BE- TWEEN THE HOLY SEE AND THE FRENCH REPUBLIC *(No. 2),* was concluded which set the pattern for relations between Rome and a number of European states throughout the century. Bishops and priests were required to take an oath of allegiance to the government; the Church's claim to previously alienated property was renounced; existing bishops resigned their sees in favor of new appointees; the state was to nominate and could veto bishops to be appointed by the pope; the diocesan clergy, appointed by the bishops, were to be paid state salaries. Protestants were given religious freedom and also clerical salaries from the state. In the following year Napoleon added several more restrictive articles concerning the publishing of papal documents, assembling of ecclesiastical synods, number and appointment of pastors, and seminary rules and clerical dress. He also supported the teaching of the famed Gallican Declaration of 1682. Pius VII rejected these so-called *Organic Articles;* nonetheless, they remained in French law until 1905.

Pius VII and Napoleon then entered upon an extended struggle, reminiscent of the titanic medieval struggles of papacy and empire, in which Napoleon tried to enforce papal support of his imperial aims. The Papal States were incorporated into the French Empire; monasteries were suppressed and Church properties confiscated in lands of Napoleonic conquest; and the clergy were hindered in their work both in Europe and in the missions. The pope was imprisoned and Napoleon, in turn, was excommunicated. Napoleon's purpose, in the spirit of all dictators, was to make the Church an instrument of his ambition. But with his final defeat Pius VII returned in triumph to Rome.

The Church was now faced with the problem which seriously divided Catholics throughout the nineteenth century, namely, what should be the attitude of Christians to the new order that was taking form. As conservatives and liberals fought a see-saw battle for political power, two groups of Gallicans and Liberals in the Church wrestled with the problem of how much good was in the new regimes and how much could be utilized. Conservatives held that the new liberties were dangerous as advancing a secular society which was non-Christian and untraditional. Liberals maintained that the new freedoms of speech, press, and religion actually aided the Church. The CATHOLIC EMANCIPATION ACT OF GREAT BRITAIN AND IRELAND (*No. 3*) of 1829 indicated what privileges could be gained, under courageous leadership such as that furnished by Daniel O'Connell, by minorities in a liberal government such as England's.

In France, Catholic thinkers like Lamennais, Montalembert, Lacordaire, and later Dupanloup, advocated a favorable attitude toward this new age in which the Church, free at last of entanglements with the state, could exert the fullness of its mission. The brilliant Abbé Félicité de Lamennais (1854) led the liberal front, and in the newspaper *L'Avenir* he organized a romantic democratic movement, with the motto "God and liberty," in defense of universal suffrage, separation of Church and State, and freedom of conscience and press. The French bishops had again aligned themselves with the restored Bourbon monarchy and were alarmed by the propagation of such ideas. Lamennais' FIRST PUBLIC LETTER TO THE ARCHBISHOP OF PARIS (*No. 4*) indicates the position of the Bourbon prince-archbishop of Paris in opposition to one of the most gifted of nineteenth-century French churchmen, whose document also reveals a certain naivetè, self-righteousness, and penchant for oversimplification.

Thus, when Lamennais tried to obtain papal approval of his position from Gregory XVI (1846) the French government and bishops intervened, and the pope in the *Encyclical "Mirari Vos"* of 1832 (*No. 5*) condemned the principles and techniques of *L'Avenir* which the bishops censured: unqualified advocacy of separation of Church and State, liberal ideals, and freedom of religion. Lamennais and his collaborators were not mentioned by name, possibly out of consideration for their active defense of the Holy See against Gallicanism. The three editors submitted, but Lamennais apparently lacked the flexibility, spiritual depth and maturity (even well into his fifties) to see his dreams crushed. He left the Church and, despite repeated efforts to restore this serious loss, died without the sacraments of the Church he had fought so vigorously and with such foresight to defend.

The liberal democratic movement of nineteenth-century Europe developed simultaneously with a resurgent nationalism that often dominated the liberal standards of liberty, equality, and fraternity. When Pope Pius IX (1878) ascended the papal throne in 1846 he at first inaugurated a series of liberal experiments in the Papal States which Metternich ridiculed as the work of "the reforming pope." When his liberal policies failed in execution, Pius IX dissociated himself after 1848 from the revolutionary movements. There now followed a series of disasters for the papacy as Italy, without and against the pope, was united under the House of Savoy by the unscrupulous Cavour and the revolutionists. The last of the Papal States were forcibly occupied in 1870 and the age-old temporal sovereignty of the Holy See came to an end. The new Italian government attempted to legalize the confiscation of the Church's properties and its general position over against the Pope in the ITALIAN LAW OF GUARANTEES (*No. 6*) of 13 May 1871. The Holy See refused to ratify this unilateral law, and Pope Pius IX retired into the Vatican palace as a voluntary prisoner, making himself dependent upon the offerings of Catholics throughout the world (Peter's Pence). The question of the temporal sovereignty of the pope preoccupied Catholics throughout the nineteenth and into the twentieth century, but for all practical purposes the major powers no longer recognized the pope as a temporal sovereign. The Vatican continued to protest against the seizure of the Papal States; after 1868 Catholics were directed not to participate in Italian elections. As a result Catholic influence on political life was seriously impeded.

Pius IX also had to combat the anti-Catholic policies of Prussia during the last years of his life. After the union of Germany under Prussian leadership in 1870, Prince Otto von Bismarck set about reducing German Catholicism to a position subordinate to state aims, as the LAW ON THE APPOINTMENT OF THE CLERGY (*No. 7*) of 21 May 1874 shows. This law was part of the *Kulturkampf* waged under Bismarck in the name of strident German nationalism. It was met with courageous and effective opposition by the hierarchy and the Catholic *Centrum Partei* under the skillful leadership of Ludwig von Windthorst. Finally Bismarck, anxious to secure Catholic support against the growing power of the Socialists, "went to Canossa" in 1887 and obtained a *modus vivendi* from the Holy See.

During the nineteenth century France underwent three more political revolutions while the Catholics, by continuing their division between Gallicans and Ultramontanes over state policy, alienated republican supporters from the Church. The anti-clerical, Freemason, and persecuting wing of the nineteenth-century doctrinaire liberals gained an upper hand in the Third Republic. Despite the desire and efforts of Pius IX's successor, Pope Leo XIII, to effect a *rapprochément* with France, while protecting the vital spiritual interests of the Church, the secular liberals pushed through the LAW OF SEPARATION OF CHURCH AND STATE (*No. 8*) of 9 December 1905. This law is a classic example of the nineteenth-century "persecuting liberal" state. It marked the final abolition of the agreement between Church and State that had been reached in 1801. The state now assumes exclusive rights to education, religious orders are expelled, and church buildings become the property of the state. Even religious ceremonies are to come under the surveillance of the state, and the Church in France is to be administered by local associations of laymen. The Holy See on 11 February 1906 unequivocally rejected this attempt to undermine the Christian concept of society by placing absolute control of religious matters in the hands of a secular state. The state was then forced to retreat from its extreme position, but discontinued financial support of the clergy. The Catholic majority of France continued into modern times in this anomalous extra-legal position, and Catholic life was reconstructed apart from the state. While the royalist position of French Catholics gradually diminished in modern times, the anti-clerical tradition of the Republic persisted in limiting the free religious life of this predominantly Catholic nation.

An early Catholic lay pioneer was the German merchant and political figure Peter Paul Cahensly of Limburg an der Lahn. He courageously worked in both the Church and state to better the condition of Catholic emigrants who were moving from Europe in such large numbers to the freedom of America, as his PETITION TO PRESIDENT ULYSSES S. GRANT FOR INTERNATIONAL LEGISLATION ON IMMIGRATION (*No. 9*) reveals. Though his motives were misunderstood and interpreted in some American quarters as a species of pan-Germanism, his stature as far seeing internationalist and social leader emerges with time.

1. *The Civil Constitution of the Clergy, 12 July 1790*

Reprinted with permission of The Macmillan Co. from *A Documentary Survey of the French Revolution* by John Hall Stewart, pp. 172-181. Copyright 1951, The Macmillan Company.

I. 1) EACH and every department shall constitute a single diocese, and each and every diocese shall have the same extent and limits as the department. ...

4) No church or parish of France, and no French citizen, may, under any circumstances or on any pretext whatsoever, acknowledge the authority of

an ordinary bishop or archbishop whose see is established under the name of a foreign power, or that of its delegates residing in France or elsewhere; without prejudice, however, to the unity of faith and communion, which shall be maintained with the visible head of the universal Church as hereinafter provided.

5) When the diocesan bishop in his synod has pronounced a decision on matters within his competence, appeal may be brought to the archbishop, who shall make his decision in the metropolitan synod.

6) A new organization and division of all parishes of the kingdom shall be undertaken immediately, upon the advice of the diocesan bishop and the district administrations; the number and extent thereof shall be determined according to rules to be established.

7) The cathedral church of each and every diocese shall be restored to its original status by the suppression of parishes and the redistribution of dwellings which it is deemed suitable to unite thereto, and it shall be at one and the same time the parochial and the episcopal church.

8) The episcopal parish shall have no other immediate pastor than the bishop. All priests established therein shall be his vicars, and shall perform the duties thereof.

9) There shall be sixteen vicars of the cathedral church in cities of more than 10,000 inhabitants, but only twelve where the population is fewer than 10,000 inhabitants.

10) In each and every diocese one seminary only shall be preserved or established for preparation for orders, without intending any prejudice for the present with regard to other houses of instruction and education.

11) The seminary shall be established near the cathedral church whenever possible, and even within the precincts of the buildings intended for the dwelling of the bishop.

12) For the direction and instruction of young pupils received into the seminary there shall be a superior vicar and three directing vicars subordinate to the bishop.

13) The superior and directing vicars shall be required to be present with the young ecclesiastics of the seminary at all offices of the cathedral parish, and to perform therein all duties with which the bishop or his first vicar shall see fit to entrust them.

14) The vicars of cathedral churches, together with the superior and directing vicars of the seminary, shall constitute the customary and permanent council of the bishop, who may perform no act of jurisdiction with respect to the government of the diocese and the seminary until he has deliberated therewith. The bishop may issue, however, in the course of his visits, such provisional ordinances as are necessary.

15) In all cities and towns of not more than 6,000 inhabitants there shall be only one parish; other parishes shall be suppressed and united with the principal church.

16) In cities of more than 6,000 inhabitants every parish may include a greater number of parishioners, and as many parishes shall be preserved or established as the needs of the people and the localities require.

17) The administrative assemblies, in concert with the diocesan bishop, shall indicate to the next legislature the parishes and annexes or chapels of ease in town and country which it is fitting to preserve, extend, establish, or suppress; and they shall indicate the limits thereof according to the needs of the people and the different localities, and as befits the dignity of religion. . . .

20) All titles and offices, other than those mentioned in the present consti-

tution, dignities, canonries, prebends, half prebends, chapels, chaplaincies, in both cathedral and collegiate churches, and all regular and secular chapters of either sex, abbeys and priories, regular or *in commendam,* of either sex, and all other benefices and *prestimonies* in general, of whatever kind and under whatever denomination, are abolished and suppressed dating from the day of publication of the present decree, and similar ones may never be established. . . .

24) Endowments for masses and other services now performed in parochial churches by the *curés* and by priests attached thereto, without being provided with their places in perpetual title of benefice, shall continue provisionally to be maintained and paid as heretofore; nevertheless, in churches where societies of priests not provided with perpetual titles of benefice are established . . . those who die or retire may not be replaced.

25) Endowments for the education of relatives of the founders shall continue to be administered in conformity with the provisions stated in the articles of foundation; and with regard to all other pious endowments, the interested parties shall present statements to the departmental assemblies, in order that, upon their advice and that of the diocesan bishop, the legislative body may make laws concerning the preservation or replacement.

II. 1) Dating from the day of publication of the present decree, appointments to bishoprics and cures are to be made by election only.

2) All elections shall be by ballot and absolute majority or votes.

3) The election of bishops shall take place according to the form prescribed by, and by the electoral body designated in, the decree of 22 December 1789, for the appointment of members of the departmental assembly.

4) As soon as the departmental *procureur-général-syndic* receives news of a vacancy in an episcopal see, owing to death, resignation, or other cause, he shall notify the district *procureurs-syndics* to convoke the electors who effected the last election of members of the administrative assembly; and at the same time he shall indicate the day on which the election of the bishop shall take place, which shall be not later than the third Sunday after his letter of notification.

5) If the vacancy in the episcopal see occurs during the last four months of the year in which the election of members of the departmental administration is to take place, the election of the bishop shall be deferred and assigned to the next assembly of electors.

6) The election of the bishop may take place or be initiated only on a Sunday, in the principal church of the chief town of the department, following the parochial mass, at which all electors are required to be present.

7) To be eligible for a bishopric, one must have performed for at least fifteen years the duties of ecclesiastical ministry in the diocese, in the capacity of *curé,* officiating minister or vicar, or as superior or directing vicar of the seminary.

8) Bishops whose sees are suppressed by the present decree may be elected to bishoprics now vacant, as well as to those which become vacant hereafter or which are established in some departments, even if they have not been in office fifteen years.

9) *Curés* and other ecclesiastics who, as a result of the new division of dioceses, find themselves in a new diocese, shall be considered to have performed their duties in such diocese, and accordingly shall be considered eligible there, provided that, in addition, they have fulfilled the requirement of tenure specified above.

10) Present *curés* who have been in office for ten years in a living of the

diocese may also be elected, even though they have not previously performed the duties of vicar.

11) The same rule shall apply with regard to *curés* whose parishes have been suppressed by virtue of the present decree, and the interval since the suppression of their cure shall be counted towards their period of tenure.

12) Missionaries, vicars-general of bishoprics, ecclesiastics officiating in hospitals or in charge of public education shall likewise be eligible when they have performed their duties for fifteen years, dating from their promotion to the priesthood.

13) All dignitaries, canons, or generally all incumbents and titularies obligated to residence or performing ecclesiastical duties, and whose benefices, titles, offices, or employments are suppressed by the present decree, are likewise eligible if they have been in office for fifteen years, computed as in the case of *curés* in the preceding article.

14) Proclamation of those elected shall be made by the president of the electoral assembly, in the church where the election was held, in the presence of the people and the clergy, and before beginning the solemn mass which is to be celebrated on such occasion.

15) The *procès-verbal* of the election and of the proclamation shall be sent to the king by the president of the assembly of electors to inform his majesty of the choice that has been made.

16) Not later than a month subsequent to his election, the bishop-elect shall present himself in person to his metropolitan bishop; and if elected to the metropolitan see, to the oldest bishop of the *arrondissement,* with the *procès-verbal* of the election and proclamation, and shall request him to grant canonical confirmation.

17) The metropolitan or the senior bishop shall have the right to examine the bishop-elect, in the presence of his council, concerning his doctrine and morals. If he considers him qualified, he shall give him canonical institution; if he believes it his duty to refuse, the reasons for such refusal shall be given in writing, signed by the metropolitan bishop and his council, reserving to the interested parties the right to appeal by writ of error as provided hereinafter.

18) The bishop from whom confirmation is requested may not exact of the bishop-elect any oath other than profession of the Catholic, Apostolic, and Roman religion.

19) The new bishop may not apply to the pope for confirmation, but shall write to him as the visible head of the universal Church, in testimony of the unity of faith and communion which he is to maintain therewith.

20) The consecration of a bishop may be performed only in his cathedral church by his metropolitan or, failing him, by the oldest bishop in the *arrondissement* of the metropolitan see, assisted by the bishops of the two nearest dioceses, on a Sunday, during the parochial mass, in the presence of the people and the clergy.

21) Before the ceremony of consecration begins, the bishop-elect shall take a solemn oath, in the presence of the municipal officials, the people, and the clergy, to watch with care over the faithful of the diocese entrusted to him, to be faithful to the nation, to the law, and to the king, and to maintain with all his power the constitution decreed by the national assembly and accepted by the king.

22) The bishop shall have the liberty of choosing the vicars of his cathedral church from among all the clergy of his diocese, provided that he names only priests who have performed ecclesiastical duties for at least ten years. He may remove them only upon the advice of his council, and by a resolu-

tion decided by majority vote and with full knowledge of the circumstances.

23) *Curés* at present established in any cathedral churches, as well as those from parishes which have been suppressed in order to be united with the cathedral church and constitute the jurisdiction thereof, shall be, without need of sanction, the first vicars of the bishop if they so desire, each one according to order of seniority in pastoral functions.

24) The superior and directing vicars of seminaries shall be appointed by the bishop and his council, and may be removed only in the same manner as vicars of the cathedral church.

25) The election of *curés* shall be conducted according to the forms prescribed by, and by the electors designated in, the decree of 22 December 1789, for the election of members of the district administrative assembly.

26) The assembly of electors for appointment to livings shall constitute itself annually at the time of the formation of the district assemblies, even if there be only one living vacant in the district; for which purpose the municipalities shall be required to notify the district *procureur-syndic* of all vacancies of livings occurring in their *arrondissement* through death, or resignation, or otherwise.

27) In convoking the assembly of electors, the *procureur-syndic* shall send each and every municipality the list of all livings to which appointments are to be made.

28) The election of *curés* shall be effected by a separate balloting for each vacant living.

29) Each and every elector, before depositing his ballot in the ballot box, shall take oath to vote only for that person whom he has chosen in his soul and conscience as the most worthy, without having been influenced therein by gifts, promises, solicitations, or threats. Such oath shall be taken for the election of bishops as well as for that of *curés*.

30) The election of *curés* may be held or initiated only on a Sunday, in the principal church of the chief town of the district, at the close of the parish mass, at which all electors are required to be present.

31) The announcement of those elected shall be made by the president of the electoral body, in the principal church, before the solemn mass which is to be celebrated for such purpose, and in the presence of the people and the clergy.

32) In order to be eligible to a living, it shall be necessary to have performed the duties of vicar for at least five years in a parish, or in a hospital or other house of charity of the diocese.

33) *Curés* whose parishes have been suppressed in execution of the present decree may be elected, even if they have not served five years in the diocese.

34) All those above declared eligible to bishoprics, provided they have also served five years, likewise shall be eligible to livings.

35) Whoever has been proclaimed elected to a living shall present himself in person to the bishop, with the *procès-verbal* of his election and proclamation, for the purpose of obtaining canonical institution therefrom.

36) The bishop shall have the privilege of examining the *curé-elect,* in the presence of his council, concerning his doctrine and morals; if he deems him competent, he shall bestow canonical institution; if he believes it his duty to refuse it, the reasons for refusal shall be given in writing signed by the bishop and his council, reserving to the parties recourse to civil authority as hereinafter provided.

37) In examining the *curé-elect* who requests canonical instituiton from him, the bishop may not require any

oath other than profession of the Catholic, Apostolic, and Roman religion. . . .

40) Bishoprics and livings shall be considered vacant until those elected have taken the oath above mentioned.

41) During the vacancy of the episcopal see, the first or, failing him, the second vicar of the cathedral church, shall replace the bishop both in his curial duties and in acts of jurisdiction which do not require episcopal authority; but he shall be required to follow the advice of the council in all matters.

42) During the vacancy of a living, the parish administration shall be entrusted to the first vicar, except for the establishment of an additional vicar if the municipality requires it; and in case there is no vicar in the parish, an officiating minister shall be established therein by the bishop.

43) Each and every *curé* shall have the right to choose his vicars, but he may choose only priests ordained or admitted to the diocese by the bishop.

44) No *curé* may dismiss his vicars except for legitimate cause determined by the bishop and his council.

III. 1) Ministers of religion, performing the primary and most important functions of society, and obliged to reside continuously in the place of service to which the confidence of the people has called them, shall be maintained by the nation.

2) All bishops, *curés*, and officiating ministers in annexes and chapels of ease shall be furnished with suitable dwellings, on condition, however, that they make all repairs for which tenants are liable, without intending for the present to introduce anything new with regard to parishes where the priest now receives money instead of a dwelling, and reserving to the departments cognizance of demands made by parishes and *curés;* moreover, salaries shall be assigned to all as indicated hereinafter. . . .

7) The monetary stipend of ministers of religion shall be paid in advance, every three months, by the district treasurer, under penalty of arrest on ordinary summons; and in case the bishop, *curé,* or vicar dies or resigns before the end of the last quarter, no claim for recovery of money may be made against him or his heirs.

8) During vacancies in bishoprics, livings, and all ecclesiastical offices maintained by the nation, the accumulations of stipend attached thereto shall be deposited in the district treasury to provide for the expenditures stated hereinafter.

9) *Curés* who are no longer able to attend to their duties because of old age or infirmity shall inform the departmental directory of such fact, which [directory], upon instructions from the municipality and the district administration, shall give them the choice, if need be, of taking another vicar, who is to be paid by the nation on the same basis as other vicars, or of retiring on a pension equal to the stipend of said vicar.

10) Upon establishing their status in the manner above prescribed, vicars, almoners of hospitals, superiors of seminaries, and others holding public office also may retire on a pension equal to their stipend, provided it does not exceed the sum of 800 *livres.*

11) The rate established above for the payment of ministers of religion shall become effective dating from the day of publication of the present decree, but only for those who henceforth are to be provided with ecclesiastical offices. The stipend of present titularies, both those whose offices or employments are suppressed and those whose titles are preserved, shall be established by special decree.

12) In view of the stipend assured them by the present constitution, bishops, *curés* and their vicars shall per-

form their episcopal and curial duties gratis.

IV. 1) The law of residence shall be strictly observed, and all who are invested with an ecclesiastical office or function shall be subject thereto without distinction or exception.

2) No bishop may absent himself from his diocese for more than fifteen consecutive days during any year, except in case of real necessity and with the consent of the directory of the department in which his see is located.

3) Likewise, *curés* and vicars may not absent themselves from the place of their duties beyond the term established above, except for serious reasons; and even in such cases the *curés* shall be required to obtain the consent of both their bishop and their district directory, the vicars that of their *curés*.

4) If a bishop or a *curé* deviates from the law of residence, the municipality shall inform the departmental *procureur-général-syndic*, who shall summon him in writing to return to his duty, and after a second warning shall bring suit against him to have his stipend declared forfeit for the entire period of his absence.

5) Bishops, *curés*, and vicars may not accept positions, functions, or commissions which oblige them to leave their dioceses or parishes, or which will take them away from the duties of their ministry; and those at present so encumbered shall be required to make their choice, within three months of the notification made to them of the present decree by the *procureur-général-syndic* of their department; otherwise, and after the expiration of said period, their office shall be considered vacant, and a successor shall be appointed according to the forms above provided.

6) Bishops, *curés,* and vicars may be present at the primary and electoral assemblies as active citizens. They may be appointed electors, deputies to the legislatures, elected members of the general council of the commune and of the district and departmental administrative councils; but their functions are declared incompatible with those of mayor and other municipal officials, and of members of the district and departmental directories; and if elected thereto they shall be required to make their choice.

7) The incompatibility mentioned in article six shall be effective only henceforth; and if any bishops, *curés,* or vicars have been summoned by the will of their fellow citizens to the office of mayor or to other municipal offices, or appointed members of the district or departmental directories, they may continue to perform the duties thereof.

2. *Concordat Between the Holy See and the Republic of France, 15 July 1801*

From Mary H. Allies, *Pius the Seventh (1800-1823)* (London: Burns and Oates, 1897), pp. 53-57.

THE government of the Republic recognizes that the Catholic Apostolic and Roman religion is the religion of the great majority of French citizens.

His Holiness likewise recognizes that the said religion has received, and further at this time expects the greatest good and the greatest honor from the establishment of the Catholic worship in France, and from the particular profession of it made by the consuls of the Republic.

Consequently, after this mutual recognition, they have agreed upon what follows as well for the good of religion as for the maintenance of internal tranquillity.

1) The Catholic, Apostolic, and Roman religion shall be freely exercized in France. Its worship shall be public, but in conformity with the rules of police which the government shall judge necessary for public tranquillity.

2) A new circumscription of French dioceses shall be made by the Holy See in concert with the government.

3) His Holiness shall declare to the titularies of the French sees, that he expects of them with a firm confidence every sort of sacrifice, even that of their sees, for the good of peace and unity.

After this exhortation, should they refuse this sacrifice required by the good of the Church, a refusal nevertheless which His Holiness does not expect, provision shall be made by new titularies for the government of the bishoprics of the new circumscription, as follows:

4) The First Consul of the Republic shall name, within the three months following the publication of the bull of His Holiness, archbishops and bishops of the new circumscription. His Holiness will confer canonical institution according to the forms established in respect of France before the change of government.

5) Nominations to bishoprics, which afterwards become vacant, shall also be made by the First Consul, and canonical institution shall be given by the Holy See, in conformity with the preceding article.

6) The bishops, before entering upon their office, shall make direct to the First Consul the oath of fidelity which was in use before the change of government, as follows:

'I swear and promise to God, upon the holy gospels, to maintain obedience and fidelity to the government established by the constitution of the French Republic. I promise likewise not to hold any communication, not to be present at any design, nor to enter into any engagement, whether within or without, which is contrary to the public tranquillity; and if in my diocese or elsewhere I learn of any design to the prejudice of the State, I will make it known to the government.'

7) Ecclesiastics of the second order shall make the same oath to the civil authorities designated by the government.

8) The following prayer shall be recited at the end of the divine office in all the Catholic churches of France: "Domine, salvam fac rempublicam; Domine, salvos fac consules."

9) The bishops shall make a new circumscription of the parishes of their dioceses, which shall not take effect until it has received the consent of the government.

10) The bishops shall appoint the *curés*. Their choice can only fall on persons accepted by the government.

11) The bishops may have a chapter for their cathedral, and a seminary for their diocese, without obligation on the part of the government to endow them.

12) All metropolitan, cathedral, parochial, and other churches not alienated, which are necessary for worship, shall be put at the disposition of the bishops.

13) His Holiness, for the good of peace and the happy re-establishment of the Catholic religion, declares that neither he nor his successors shall in any way trouble those who have acquired alienated ecclesiastical goods, and that in consequence the property of these goods, the rights and revenues attached to them, shall remain unchanged in their hands and in those of their representatives.

14) The government will assure a

suitable support to the bishops and the *curés* whose dioceses and cures shall be comprised in the new circumscription.

15) The government will likewise take measures in order that French Catholics may, if they choose, make endowments in favor of the churches.

16) His Holiness recognizes in the First Consul of the French Republic the same rights and prerogatives as the old government enjoyed in regard to the Holy See.

17) It is agreed between the contracting parties that in case any one of the successors of the actual First Consul should not be Catholic, the rights and prerogatives mentioned in the article above and the appointment of bishops shall be regulated in respect to him by a new convention.

3. *The Question of Catholic Emancipation in Britain and Ireland, 1812-1829*

From Sister M. F. Cusack, *Life of Daniel O'Connell* (New York: D. J. Sadlier Co., 1872), pp. 278-284, 556-557; Reprinted with permission of The Macmillan Company from *Select Documents of English Constitutional History* by George Adams & H. Morse Stephens, pp. 510-513. Copyright 1920, The Macmillan Co.

A. DANIEL O'CONNELL: SPEECH TO PARLIAMENT ON CATHOLIC EMANCIPATION, 4 JULY 1812

THE opposition to Catholic emancipation has assumed a new shape; bigotry and intolerance have been put to the blush, or covered with ridicule; everybody laughs at Jack Giffard and Paddy Duignan; and their worthy compeer and colleague in England, Sir William Scott, does no longer venture to meet, with adverse front, the justice of our cause.

He may, indeed, talk of setting our question at rest; he may declaim upon the moral inferiority of the Irish Catholic; but let him rest assured that, so long as his children—if he has any—so long as the swarthy race of his Scotts are placed, by law, on any superiority to the Irish Catholic, so long will it be impossible to put the question to rest. It never can—it never shall—rest, save in unqualified, unconditional emancipation. As to the moral inferiority, I shall not dispute the point with him; but I trust no Catholic judge will ever be found in this country with such an accommodating disposition as to decide the precise same question in two different ways, as we are told that learned gentleman has done with the question of "paper blockades." Let him, I am sure I consent, direct his sapient opposition, in his present prudent course of retarding the discussion of the right and justice of our claims, by introducing other topics. The points of delay—the resting-places—are obvious. And when the present are exhausted, I rely on the malignity of our oppressors to invent new terms for this purpose.

First, there was the veto. That, indeed, was soon put down by the unanimous voice of the Catholic people, who besides other reasons really could not see—in the actual selection made by the Irish government of persons to fill the offices belonging by right to them —anything to tempt them to confer on that government the nomination of upwards of thirty other offices of emolument and honor. If hostility to the Irish people be a recognized recommendation to all other employments, is it likely that, in one alone, virtue and moral fitness should obtain the appointment? It was too gross and glaring a presumption in an administration, avowing its abhorrence for everything Irish, to expect to be allowed to interfere with the religious discipline of the Irish Catholic Church.

Driven from any chance of the veto, our enemies next suggested "the arrangement," as it was called, but this half measure had but few supporters. It was not sufficiently strong for thh zealous intolerants; its advantages were not so obvious to the profligate. It was met by this plain reply—that we knew of no real inconvenience that could possibly arise from the present system of the government of our Church, but if any existed, it were fitter to be treated of by the venerable prelates of that Church, who understood the subject best, than by ministers who wish to turn everything into an engine of state policy.

"The arrangement" was then soon forgotten, and now, my lord, we have new terms stated—these are "sanctions and securities." We are now told we cannot be emancipated without "sanctions and securities." What are "sanctions"? They are calculated, I presume, to do a great deal of mischief, because they are quite unintelligible. As to "securities," indeed I can understand that word, and I am quite ready to admit that "securities" are necessary. They are necessary against the effects upon a passive, but high-minded people —of continued insult and prolonged oppression. They are necessary in a sinking state against the domestic disturbances and organized disaffection which prevail in England—against the enormous and increasing power of the enemy—against dilapidated resources, expiring commerce, depreciated currency, and accumulating expenditure —against the folly, the incapacity, the want of character of the administra-

tion—against all those evils of which there is courage to speak—against that domestic insult, respecting which it is prudent to be silent. Against all these, "securities" are necessary, and they are easy to be found. They are to be found in conciliation and emancipation, their rectitude and justice. The brave, the generous, the enthusiastic people of Ireland are ready to place themselves in the breach that has been made in their country. They claim the post of honor, that is, the post of utmost danger; they are ready to secure the throne and the constitution. And all they require in return is to be recognized as men and human beings, in this their native land.

Do not, then, I would say to any minister, do not presume to insult them, by attempting to treat them as maniacs, to be "secured" only by ropes and chains. Alas, their only insanity is their devotion to you. Tell them not that the more they are free, the less will they be grateful; tell them not that the less you have to fear from their discontent, the more strictly will you bind them. Oppress them if you please. But hesitate before you deem it prudent thus to insult their first, their finest feelings.

Having disposed of veto, arrangement, sanctions, and securities, there remains but one resource for intolerance: the classic Castlereagh has struck it out. It consists in—what do you think? Why in "hitches."

Yes, "hitches" is the elegant word which is now destined to protract our degradation. It is in vain that our advocates have increased; in vain have our foes been converted; in vain has William Wellesley Pole become our warm admirer. Oh, how beautiful he must have looked advocating the Catholic cause! And his conversion, too, has been so *satisfactory* . . . he has accounted for it upon such philosophic principles. Yes, he has gravely informed us that he was all his life a man detesting committees. You might see by him that the name of a committee discomposed his nerves, and excited his most irritable feelings; at the sound of a committee he was roused to madness. Now, the Catholics had insisted upon acting by a committee. The naughty Papists had used nothing but profane committees, and, of course, he proclaimed his hostility. But in proportion as he disliked committees, so did he love and approve of aggregate meetings—respectable aggregate meetings! Had there been a chamber at the castle large enough for an aggregate meeting, he would have given it. Who does not see that it is quite right to dote upon aggregate meetings and detest committees—by law, logic, philosophy, and science of legislation? All recommend the one and condemn the other. And, at length, the Catholics have had the good sense to call their committee a board, to make their aggregate meetings more frequent. They, therefore, deserve emancipation. And, with the blessing of God, he, Mr. Pole, would confer it on them!

But, seriously, let us recollect that Wellesley Pole is the brother of one of our most excellent friends, of Marquis Wellesley, who had so gloriously exerted himself in our cause, who had manfully abandoned one administration because he could not procure our liberty, and rejected power under any other unless formed on the basis of emancipation, and who had, before this hour in which I speak, earned another unfading laurel, and the eternal affection of the Irish people, by his motion in the house of lords. The eloquence and zeal and high character of that noble marquis seemed all that was wanting to insure, at no remote period, our success. He knows little of the Irish heart who imagines that his disinterested services will ever be forgotten. No, they are graved on the soul of Irish gratitude, and will ever live in the memory of the finest people on the earth.

Lord Castlereagh, too, has declared in our favor, with the prudent reserve of the "hitches." He is our friend, and has been so these last twenty years. Our *secret friend.* As he says so, upon his honor as a gentleman, we are bound to believe him. If it be a merit in the minister of a great nation to possess profound discretion, this merit Lord Castlereagh possesses in a supereminent degree. Why, he has preserved this secret with the utmost success. Who ever suspected that he had such a secret in his keeping? The Whole tenor of his life, every action of his, negatived the idea of his being our friend. He spoke against us. He voted against us. He wrote and he published against us. And it turns out now that he did all this merely to show how well he could keep a secret. Oh, admirable contriver! Oh, most successful placeman! Most discreet and confidential of ministers! . . .

Our legal persecutors, who hunt us with a keenness only increased by their disappointment, and rendered more rancorous by our prospect of success—good and godly men, all—are at this moment employed in projecting fresh scenes of prosecution. Every part of the press that has dared to be free will surely be punished, and public spirit and liberality will, in every case that can be reached by the arts of state persecution, expiate its offense in a prison. Believe me, my prophetic fears are not vain: I know the managers well, and place no confidence in their holy seeming. Again England affords another opportunity of extending the "hitches," under the pretense of making laws to prevent rebellion there. The administration will suspend the *habeas corpus,* for the purpose of crushing emancipation here—and thus will illustrate the contrast between the very words which it would require twelve simpletons to swear meant the same thing.

The new laws occasioned by English rioters will pass harmless over their heads, and fall only upon you. It would be inconsistent if Castlereagh, the worthy successor of Clare and John Foster, used another plan towards Ireland. The "hitches," the "hitches," plainly mean all that can be raised of venal outcry against us, and all that can be enacted of arbitrary law, to prevent our discussions.

Still, still we have resources. We have rich resources in those affectionate sentiments of toleration which our Irish Protestant brethren have proudly exhibited during the present year. The Irish Protestants will not abandon or neglect their own work. It is they who have placed us on our present elevation. Their support has rendered the common cause of our common country triumphant. Our oppressors, yielding an unwilling assent to the request of the Protestants of Ireland, may compensate themselves by abusing us in common. They may style us agitators —Mr. Canning calls us "agitators with ulterior views"—but those Protestant agitators are the best friends to the security and peace of the country. *And* to us, Popish agitators. For I own it, my lord, I am an agitator, and we solemnly promise to continue so until the period of unqualified emancipation, until "the simple repeal." As to us, agitators among the Catholics, we are become too much accustomed to calumny to be terrified by it. But how have we deserved reproach and obloquy? How have we merited calumny? Of myself, my lord, I shall say nothing. I possess no talents for the office —but no man shall prevent the assertion of my rigid honesty. I am, it is true, the lowliest of the agitators, but there are, among them, men of first-

rate talents, and of ample fortunes, men of the most ancient families and of hereditary worth, men of public spirit and of private virtue, and, above all, men of persevering, undaunted, and unextinguishable love of their country, of their poor, degraded, insulted country. To that country, will I say of all the agitators, with the exception of my humble self: "Boast, Erin, boast them tameless, frank, and free."

Out of the hands of those agitators, however, the government is desirous to take the people, and the government is right. Out of the sphere of your influence, my lord, the people can never be taken, for reasons which, because you are present, I shall not mention, but which are recognized by the hearts of the Irish nation. But out of our hands the people may easily be taken. They are bound to us only by the ties of mutual sympathies. We are the mere straws which are borne upon the torrent of public wrongs and public griefs. Restore their rights to the people, conciliate the Irish nation—which is ready to meet you more than half-way—and the power of the agitators is gone in an instant.

I do certainly feel the alarm expressed at the agitation of the question of Catholic rights as a high compliment. It clearly points out the course we ought to pursue. Let us rouse the Irish people, from one extreme to the other of the island, in this constitutional cause. Let the Catholic combine with the Protestant, and the Protestant with the Catholic, and one generous exertion sets every angry feeling at rest, and banishes, forever, dissension and division. The temptation to invasion will be taken away from the foreign enemy. The pretext and the means of internal commotion will be snatched from the domestic foe. Our country, combined in one great phalanx, will defy every assault, and we shall have the happiness of obtaining real security by that course of conciliation which deserves the approbation of every sound judgment, and must insure the applause of every feeling heart. We shall confer an honor on ourselves, and insure the safety of our country.

B. THE DUKE OF WELLINGTON: SPEECH TO PARLIAMENT IN FAVOR OF CATHOLIC EMANCIPATION, 2 APRIL 1829

It is already well known to your Lordships, that of the troops which our gracious sovereign did me the honor to entrust to my command at various periods during the war, a war undertaken expressly for the purpose of securing the happy institutions and independence of the country, that at least one-half were Roman Catholics. My lords, when I call your recollection to this fact, I am sure all further eulogy is unnecessary. . . . We must also confess that, without Catholic blood and Catholic valor, no victory could ever have been obtained, and the first military talents in Europe might have been exerted in vain at the head of an army.

My lords, if on the eve of any of those hard-fought days, on which I had the honor to command them, I had thus addressed my Roman Catholic troops: "You well know that your country either so suspects your loyalty, or so dislikes your religion, that she has not thought proper to admit you among the ranks of her citizens. If on that account you deem it an act of injustice on her part to require you to shed your blood in her defense, you are at liberty to withdraw"—I am quite sure, my lords, that, however bitter the recollections which it awakened, they would have spurned the alternative with indignation. For the hour of danger and glory is the hour in which the gallant, the generous-hearted Irishman best knows his duty, and is most determined to perform it. But if, my

lords, it had been otherwise; if they had chosen to desert the cause . . . the remainder of the troops would undoubtedly have maintained the honor of the British arms, yet, as I have just said, no efforts of theirs could ever have crowned us with victory.

Yes, my lords, it is mainly to the Irish Catholics that we owe our proud pre-eminence in our military career; and that I personally am indebted for the laurels with which you have been pleased to decorate my brow, for the honors which you have so bountifully lavished on me, and for the fair fame (I prize it above all other rewards) which my country, in its generous kindness, has bestowed upon me.

I cannot but feel, my Lords, that you yourselves have been chiefly instrumental in placing this heavy debt of gratitude upon me, greater, perhaps, than has ever fallen to the lot of any individual. And however flattering the circumstance, it often places me in a very painful position. Whenever I meet (and it is almost an everyday occurrence) with any of those brave men, who, in common with others, are the object of this bill, and who have so often borne me on the tide of victory —when I see them still branded with the imputation of a divided allegiance, still degraded beneath the lowest menial, and still proclaimed unfit to enter within the pale of the constitution, I feel almost ashamed of the honors which have been lavished upon me.

C. THE CATHOLIC EMANCIPATION ACT, 13 APRIL 1829

1. Whereas by various acts of parliament certain restraints and disabilities are imposed on the Roman Catholic subjects of his majesty, to which other subjects of his majesty are not liable: and whereas it is expedient that such restraints and disabilities shall be from henceforth discontinued:

and whereas by various acts certain oaths and certain declarations, commonly called the declaration against transubstantiation, and the invocation of saints and the sacrifice of the mass, as practiced in the Church of Rome, are or may be required to be taken, made, and subscribed by the subjects of his majesty, as qualifications for sitting and voting in parliament, and for the enjoyment of certain offices, franchises, and civil rights: be it enacted by the king's most excellent majesty, by and with the advice and consent of the lords spiritual and temporal, and commons, in this present parliament assembled, and by the authority of the same, that from and after the commencement of this act all such parts of the said acts as require the said declarations, or either of them, to be made or subscribed by any of his majesty's subjects, as a qualification for sitting and voting in parliament, or for the exercize or enjoyment of any office, franchise, or civil right, be and the same are (save as hereinafter provided and excepted) hereby repealed.

2. And be it enacted, that from and after the commencement of this act it shall be lawful for any person professing the Roman Catholic religion, being a peer, or who shall after the commencement of this act be returned as a member of the house of commons, to sit and vote in either house of parliament respectively, being in all other respects duly qualified to sit and vote therein, upon taking and subscribing the following oath, instead of the oaths of allegiance, supremacy, and abjuration:

"I, N.N., do sincerely promise and swear, that I will be faithful and bear true allegiance to his majesty King George the Fourth, and will defend him to the utmost of my power against all conspiracies and attempts whatever, which shall be made against his person, crown, or dignity; and I will do my utmost endeavor to disclose and make known to his majesty, his heirs and successors, all treasons and traitorous conspiracies which may be formed against him or them: and I do faithfully promise to maintain, support, and defend, to the utmost of my power, the succession of the crown, which succession, by an act, entitled "An Act for the further Limitation of the Crown, and better securing the Rights and Liberties of the Subject," is and stands limited to the princess Sophia, electress of Hanover, and the heirs of her body, being Protestants; hereby utterly renouncing and abjuring any obedience or allegiance unto any other person claiming or pretending a right to the crown of this realm: and I do further declare, that it is not an article of my faith, and that I do renounce, reject, and abjure the opinion, that princes excommunicated or deprived by the pope, or any other authority of the see of Rome, may be deposed or murdered by their subjects, or by any person whatsoever: and I do declare, that I do not believe that the pope of Rome, or any other foreign prince, prelate, person, state, or potentate, hath or ought to have any temporal or civil jurisdiction, power, superiority, or preeminence, directly or indirectly, within this realm. I do swear, that I will defend to the utmost of my power the settlement of property within this realm, as established by the laws: and I do hereby disclaim, disavow, and solemnly abjure any intention to subvert the present church establishment, as settled by law within this realm: and I do solemnly swear, that I will never exercize any privilege to which I am or may become entitled, to disturb or weaken the Protestant religion or Protestant government in the united kingdom: and I do solemnly, in the presence of God, profess, testify, and declare, that I do make this declaration, and every part thereof, in the plain and ordinary sense of the words of this oath, without any evasion, equivocation, or mental reservation whatsoever. So help me God."

3. And be it further enacted, that wherever, in the oath here appointed and set forth, the name of his present majesty is expressed or referred to, the name of the sovereign of this kingdom for the time being, by virtue of the act for the further limitation of the crown and better securing the right and liberties of the subject, shall be susstituted from time to time, with proper words of reference thereto.

4. Provided always, and be it further enacted, that no peer professing the Roman Catholic religion, and no person professing the Roman Catholic religion, who shall be returned a member of the house of commons after the commencement of this act, shall be capable of sitting or voting in either house of parliament respectively, unless he shall first take and subscribe the oath hereinbefore appointed and set forth, before the same persons, at the same times and places, and in the same manner as the oaths and the declaration now required by law are respectively directed to be taken, made, and subscribed; and that any such person professing the Roman Catholic religion, who shall sit or vote in either house of parliament, without having first taken and subscribed, in the manner aforesaid, the oath in this act appointed and set forth, shall be subject to the same penalties, forfeitures, and disabilities, and the offense of so sitting or voting shall be followed and attended by and with the same consequences, as are by law enacted and provided in the case of persons sitting or voting in either house of parliament respectively, without the taking, mak-

ing, and subscribing the oaths and the declaration now required by law.

5. And be it further enacted, that it shall be lawful for persons professing the Roman Catholic religion to vote at elections of members to serve in parliament for England and for Ireland, and also to vote at the elections of representative peers of Scotland and of Ireland, and to be elected such representative peers, being in all other respects duly qualified, upon taking and subscribing the oath hereinbefore appointed and set forth, instead of the oaths of allegiance, supremacy, and abjuration, and instead of the declaration now by law required, and instead also of such other oath or oaths as are now by law required to be taken by any of his majesty's subjects professing the Roman Catholic religion, and upon taking also such other oath or oaths as may now be lawfully tendered to any persons offering to vote at such elections. . . .

9. And be it further enacted, that no person in holy orders in the Church of Rome shall be capable of being elected to serve in parliament as a member of the house of commons; and if any such person shall be elected to serve in parliament as aforesaid, such election shall be void; and if any person, being elected to serve in parliament as a member of the house of commons, shall, after his election, take or receive holy orders in the Church of Rome, the seat of such person shall immediately become void; and if any such person shall, in any of the cases aforesaid, presume to sit or vote as a member of the house of commons, he shall be subject to the same penalties, forfeitures, and disabilities as are enacted by an act passed in the forty-first year of the reign of King George the Third, entitled "An Act to remove Doubts respecting the Eligibility of Persons in Holy Orders to sit in the House of

Commons"; and proof of the celebration of any religious service by such person, according the rites of the Church of Rome, shall be deemed and taken to be *prima facie* evidence of the fact of such person being in holy orders, within the intent and meaning of this act.

10. And be it enacted, that it shall be lawful for any of his majesty's subjects professing the Roman Catholic religion to hold, exercize, and enjoy all civil and military offices and places of trust or profit under his majesty, his heirs or successors, and to exercize any other franchise or civil right, except as hereinafter excepted, upon taking and subscribing, at the times and in the manner hereinafter mentioned, the oath hereinbefore appointed and set forth, instead of the oaths of allegiance, supremacy, and abjuration, and instead of such oath or oaths as are or may be now by law required to be taken for the purpose aforesaid by any of his majesty's subjects professing the Roman Catholic religion.

11. Provided always, and be it enacted, that nothing herein contained shall be construed to exempt any person professing the Roman Catholic religion from the necessity of taking any oath or oaths, or making any declaration, not hereinbefore mentioned, which are or may be by law required to be taken or subscribed by any person on his admission into any such office or place of trust or profit as aforesaid.

12. Provided also, and be it further enacted, that nothing herein contained shall extend or be construed to extend to enable any person or persons professing the Roman Catholic religion to hold or exercize the office of guardians and justices of the united kingdom, or of regent of the united kingdom, under whatever name, style, or title such office may be constituted; nor to enable any person, otherwise than as he is now by law enabled, to hold or enjoy the office of lord high chancellor, lord keeper or lord commissioner of the great seal of Great Britain or Ireland; or the office of lord lieutenant, or lord deputy, or other chief governor or governors of Ireland; or his majesty's high commissioner to the general assembly of the Church of Scotland.

4. *Félicité de Lamennais: First Letter to Archbishop Hyacinth Louis de Quélen of Paris, 10 March 1829*

From *Première Lettre à Monseigneur L'Archevêque de Paris par L'Abbé F. de Lamennais* (Paris: J. Gratiot, 1829), pp. 1-60. Trans. by Janet Knight.

FOR several years now, enough works have appeared in which the doctrines of Christianity, the general faith of mankind, and all the principles of religious and civil society have been openly attacked, delivered to mockery, and presented to the people as inventions of priests, who are occupied unceasingly with deceiving the people, to make them slaves. You have, I have no doubt, wept in secret at these excesses and others no less alarming, which each day sadden Christian souls. But your zeal there has not seen sufficient cause to warn the faithful against seduction, and your sadness is sealed up in a silence which I respect. Something more was necessary to awaken your pastoral solicitude. It was necessary, I say, that a priest try to defend

Catholic truth, the learning of the Church and of the Holy See, and to recall souls to the way of order with words of peace and conciliation.

However, during your repose, you have judged that the time to be silent has passed, the time to speak has come, and you have publicly accused this priest of proclaiming doctrines subversive to the order which Jesus Christ established on earth, which would result in nothing less than the rocking of our whole society to its foundations.

Certainly, one could not imagine graver imputations. Before they issue from the lips of a bishop it would seem that justice and at least prudence would insist that they be justified by a serious examination, and by a discussion following the book on which you based these odious accusations. At least he should be very certain that the exactitude of this résumé, more brief than substantial, could not be reasonably contested. You have released yourself from this discussion, and as for the exactitude of the résumé, I dare to assure you beforehand that, having read the letters to which you have put me under the necessity of replying, more to maintain the doctrine of the authority of the Church, which you revoke in doubt of the tradition of all essential points, than for my own justification, the most charitable thought which could be conceived, which I hesitate to embody here, is that—weighed down by the cares of a vast administration—you have not even opened the work of the author you censure so bitterly. It will remain, it is true, after that, to explain the censure itself. But this, my lord, does not concern me in any fashion.

I will begin by quoting in its entirety the passage in your mandate where you paint me in such black colors, for I am too sure of the defense to dread in the least the publication of this accusation to the world:

While we believe that we need not fear the audacity or the traps of our declared enemies, who neither leave us nor come to terms with us, nor relax their efforts, it is here the spirit of the system, sad and dangerous to the most gifted, is introduced, and we are menaced by an interior war. Not content with the vast field of innocent disputes, the very truth of which leaves the people free to undertake them, but the limits of truth they are forbidden to overstep, he wishes to insert his own opinions into dogma and to accuse us, unjustly, of overstepping the boundaries which have been defined by the infallible authority of the Church. Not content with holding up to censure those whose character and intentions he should at least respect, he has made himself strenuously the detractor of one of our greatest kings and the most learned of our popes. He proclaims, without authority and without mission, in the name of heaven, doctrines subversive to the order which Jesus Christ has established on earth, by sharing his sovereign power between two distinct powers, each independent of the other, each in the order which has been confided to them. These doctrines, in the natural sense in which they are presented, tend to nothing less, despite the most praiseworthy intentions, than to rock the whole of society to its very foundations, by destroying the love of obedience in the hearts of the people, and sowing in the hearts of the sovereigns defiance toward their subjects. These doctrines, far from serving religion, can only result in persecutions of all kinds, being represented there as a restless, jealous domination, which brings the crowds to his feet. These doctrines, besides, are supported by no solid proof, of which we find no successive and enduring monuments in antiquity, which carry nothing with them of the character of universality which distinguishes the faith of the Church from that of any other sect. We have received these doctrines neither from Jesus Christ nor from his apostles. They carry neither the authority of Scripture nor of tradition. Consequently, we weep to hear these doctrines announced, whether it be by the most gifted writer, the most profound publicist, the greatest genius or, if we dare to say it, quoting St. Paul, even by an angel descended from heaven. We are forced to arrest these doctrines, by our silences as by our reiterated and public protestations. Finally, we repulse these doctrines with all the loyalty of a French heart, without fearing to lose by that any of the integrity of a Catholic soul.

These, my lord, are serious accusations, and assertions of such a nature that they demand, according to the common ideas of equity, to be supported at least by some proofs. You have judged otherwise of this, to such an extent that, not knowing even on which precise point you accuse me of departing from the doctrine of the Catholic Church, which you are pleased to call a "sect," I am forced to put before you the total principles which I have maintained, both to justify them in themselves, and to show them to be in accord with tradition. For this, it is necessary to consider first what is the end which I propose to myself.

That the world, tormented by a heavy anxiety, is agitated by a general spirit of revolution. . . . That the European monarchies are tottering on their ancient foundations and menaced almost to sinking under the blows which rain incessantly on them. . . . That the Catholic Church, attacked with an unexampled violence in its dogmas, disciplines, and constitutions, should fear very soon attacks to which she has never before been submitted: these are facts so glaring that no one would dare to contest them. Contemplating this frightful social dissolution, I asked myself, or better than that, I asked of history and of religion, what could be its cause, and what could be done to remedy it. Both have taught me that this cause should be sought in the spiritual order, in the doctrines, in the opinions which alone determine in this manner the destinies of society. Tran-

quil or troubled according to the nature of the maxims which prevail, her interior state is never anything but the image of the state of her mind.

So, even though opinions today are divided almost to infinity, they amount altogether, in spite of the sands of difference, to two general and primitive doctrines: the doctrine called *Liberal* and the doctrine called *Gallican*. These doctrines correspond to two political parties which they characterize, the one having for its aim the establishment of liberty, the other the conservation of power. Considered under this point of view, one can recognize in each true and just beliefs. For the order on which the existence of society depends, the essential and fundamental order is, in fact, only the union of power and liberty.

But dogmatic liberalism, founding its social theories on an anti-Christian philosophy, rejects all divine revelation and denies that there exists any rapport between God and man. It is led, as I have shown, to despotism and anarchy, and that in two ways: in reversing any possible notion of right and of duty, and substituting for the only true and legitimate power a purely human power, that is to say, confounding sovereignty with blind force.

Gallicanism, which in the name of God frees the sovereign from any rule of justice which is obligatory to him, also condones despotism. For despotism is nothing else than the reign of a will independent in its action from the universal law of justice. And as despotism can never manifest itself among peoples whom Christianity has raised to the knowledge of the right, it follows clearly that Gallican doctrine leads to anarchy by revolutions. It has yet another effect, which is to alienate the people from the Christian religion and from the Church, which represents for them the ally and the natural result of arbitrary power, and of which the name is almost synonymous for them with the idea of slavery.

It follows from this that the liberal system which would destroy power to establish liberty, and the Gallican system which would destroy liberty to establish power, are equally incompatible with the existence of a regular and stable society. The first leads inevitably to despotism by anarchy; the second, to anarchy by despotism. There is no hope for order and peace, either for the Church or for the state, while the world is run only by their action.

But is there a possible means of affirming power without sacrificing liberty, and of assuring liberty without overthrowing the basis of power? Liberalism has asked this question; it has sought to find out how the accord of these two conditions could be conceived for an enduring society. Nothing, certainly, merits more serious attention than the theory at which it has arrived.

According to this theory, there exists no absolute and eternally legitimate sovereign power except in God, from whom the laws of reason, truth, and justice arise. Human power, whence inferior sovereignty is derived, is only that of the minister of God, who possesses of himself only conditional rights, legitimate when he governs according to reason, verity, and justice; without authority when he violates what supposes the existence of an infallible means of discerning truth and justice, namely the true law, the divine law, by which the minister of God should govern.

This is the idea which liberals have formed of a perfect society. They find in the society thus conceived the right to command, the duty to obey, an immutable law, a rule common to the sovereign and to his subjects, in fact order and liberty. But liberalism declares at the same time that this beautiful society is impossible to realize,

because they do not know of the existence on earth of any infallible authority. They conclude from this that these cannot exist any sovereignty of right either.

The consequence of this doctrine is that it is necessary, either to abolish all society, or to submit it to a sovereignty deprived of right, which constitutes slavery, or to recognize an authority which infallibly proclaims the universal law of justice and truth, the divine law, and to maintain its execution. Admitting this authority, one instantly sees born that which heretofore one searched for in vain, all that is called, according to liberals and royalists, a liberty so perfect that it covers the human condition, and a legitimate and stable power without which any order is impossible.

But it appears, in fact, that the theory which I have just expounded as the concept of liberalism and that which it presents, is only an exact summing up of the Catholic doctrine of society. What, in fact, does the Church teach? She distinguishes two powers, but without dividing society which is essentially one. Jesus Christ is the supreme head of it. As the pontiff, successor of Peter, is his vicar in the spiritual order, so the king is his vicar, his minister, in the temporal order. For this society supposes two things, an eternal law of justice and truth, and an immutable law, founded on and ruled by rights and duties; and a strength which constrains the wills which rebel against submitting themselves to this law. Here we have two swords, to speak the language of the Church: the sword of the spirit, which restrains error, of which the use belongs to the one pontiff; and the material sword, the use of which belongs to the one prince. But as strength which is not directed toward justice and truth is in itself the greatest evil, and perhaps nothing but a cause of disorder and ruin, the material sword must necessarily be subordinated to the sword of the spirit, as the body should be subordinated to reason. Otherwise it would be necessary to admit of two independent powers, one the conserver of justice and truth, the other blind and at the same time destructive by its nature of truth and justice. Well now, what is this unless it is to deliver the world to the empire of two principles, the one good, the other bad, and to constitute a veritable social Manichaeism? Nevertheless, says the Church, man or nation, adopt this monstrous error [Manichaeism], and you will go out by it from the way of salvation.

It is not yet the moment to prove that this is effectively the doctrine of the Church. At the same time, that which you choose to call "the system," and you appear to attribute to me the invention of this "system," I feel bound to bring to your attention that the entire passage which you have just read is nothing else than a faithful analysis of a papal bull, the text of which I have cited in my book *Justificatory Pieces*. And if you would say, with Bossuet, that this bull of Boniface VIII was revoked by his successor, Clement V, I would reply to you that, on the contrary, Clement V renewed it and caused it to be inserted into the body of canon law. He went so far as to declare, to please Philip the Fair, that which he understood only by virtue of this bull, that the king of France and his royalty were placed in very close dependence on the Holy See, which was where he had stood formerly. And in case you would add, again with Bossuet, that the doctrine of Boniface VIII was fought, even in Italy, by Aegidius, I would add again that this writer denied only that France depended in the temporal order upon the pope, like a slave dependent upon his sovereign lord, a ridiculous pretension, proudly

disavowed by Boniface VIII. For the rest, Aegidius, authorizing himself by a decretal of Innocent III, admitted fully the maxims established in the bull *Unam sanctam,* maxims which no one contested in France at this time, which would be easy for me to prove by contemporary documents, if you still have any doubt in this regard.

However that may be, in exposing the Catholic doctrine on society, I have taken care to avoid, whenever I could in a work so short, either the complete development of it, not to surround it with proofs, which are only, for the most part, I said, those of the general tradition of mankind, and of the particular tradition of the Christian Church. It was useless, besides, to produce these proofs, first because the facts are not contested by liberalism, and in the second place because they have no force in opposing the belief not only of Christianity in general, but also the authority of the Church. And as for the Gallicans, it is sufficient to make clear that their maxims on this point, summed up in the first article of 1682, were reproved by the Holy See. If anything astonishes me, my lord, it is that this proof of their opposition to Catholic truth has not been sufficient for you: because, on the one hand, the doctrine of Rome is so little doubted that Gallicanism has had to search for a century and a half to justify itself in combatting it; on the other, we know by the tradition of all the churches, and particularly that of France, that contrary to the Roman Church, it has ceased to be one of its members and goes in the ranks of the enemies of Christ.

Thus when you accuse me, my lord, of "proclaiming doctrines subversive to the order which Jesus Christ has established on earth, which would result in nothing less than the rocking of our whole society to its foundations," it is not I who accuses you but the

Apostolic See, the universal Church, which has professed them by its teaching and by its conduct during a long succession of ages, at least since 1615 when Cardinal Du Perron, a very learned prelate, defended them in the name of the clergy and of the nobility, showing that they rest on a tradition constantly maintained for eleven centuries. I do not know at which point it can be edifying any more to teach the faithful that the Church is deceiving herself, or has deceived the world for eleven hundred years, on points which tend to nothing less than the ruin of Christianity and of society. Perhaps it would be possible to find things more suitable to confirm them in the faith, and a more natural development of the creed: I believe in the Church. Perhaps also the assertions, so little respectful to the Roman pontiffs, could above all be better placed than in a mandate dedicated to the memory of one of these pontiffs, whose virtues of learning and spirit are eulogized. This confusion of eulogy for his person and of censure for the unchanging doctrine of the Holy See, penetrates the soul with, I cannot tell you how much, indefinable sadness. Forgive me, my lord, that I express what I feel and all true Catholics with me, who would not know how to be consoled—that on this occasion, not content to be the man of God, it has not been possible for you to be a little less the man of the times.

You reproach me with having spoken "without authority and without mission." But is the authority of the Apostolic See nothing in your eyes? And has not every priest a mission to proclaim what he knows? I declare that I have only wished to expose these doctrines. Show me in what I have set aside any of them. Cite a single word which has been in opposition to any of them. I will disavow them publicly. But you have never attempted this.

You will never attempt it. It has seemed easier to you to affirm in general that these doctrines, stated in pontifical bulls, "have neither the authority of Scripture nor of tradition in themselves." This is clear and decisive, even if lacking respect for the vicars of Jesus Christ. It is necessary to prove, then, my lord, that you have not even taken the trouble to consult this tradition, interpreted infallibly from Scripture. It is necessary to develop it, not from one's own understanding, that which is culled from books, but from that which has been the principle from earliest days until now. This will be the subject of the following letters which I shall have the honor to address to you. But for the present I wish to refute some particular imputations and to reply to several observations presented by the partisans of the opinions which you take under your protection.

"Not content," you say, "with holding up to bitter censure those of whom one should at least respect the character and the intentions, he has strenuously made himself the detractor of one of our greatest kings and the most learned of our pontiffs."

In all good faith, my lord, what has this to do with the question? Even if I had fully committed the wrong which you attribute to me, what result could it have on the doctrines which I have maintained? But it is still necessary to be exact when one is accused. In speaking of Louis XIV I have simply enunciated a fact which no one denies. I said that he had substituted despotism for the ancient constitutional monarchy of royalty. What is there in that which shocks you? And what is this strange "respect" which after fifteen hundred years seeks to impose silence on history? Religion neither flatters nor denies. She says what is true, and troubles herself little with interfering with the proud delicacy of the powerful of the earth. Would you care to know what Fenelon dared to write to the "great king" himself?

For about thirty years your principal ministers have shaken and overthrown almost all the ancient maxims of the state, to show forth your authority, which had become theirs, because they were in your hands. One no longer speaks of the state nor of laws; one only speaks of the king and his good pleasure. They have pushed your revenues and your expenses sky high. They have raised you to the heavens for having effaced, they say, the grandeur of all your predecessors in order to introduce to the court a monstrous and incurable luxury. They have wished to raise you up on the ruins of all the conditions of the state—as if you wished to be great by ruining all your subjects, on which your grandeur is founded. It is true that you have been jealous of authority, perhaps even too much in exterior things. But fundamentally each minister has been master in the area of his administration. You have been believed to govern because you have set the limits between those who govern. They have shown their power very clearly to the public, and it has been very much felt. They have been hard, haughty, unjust, violent, and in bad faith. They have known no other rule, neither for the administration in the state itself nor for foreign negotiations, than to threaten, to wipe out, to annihilate, all who resist them. You are scrupulous over trifles and indulgent to terrible evils. You bring everything to you, as if you were the God of the earth, and all the rest were created only to sacrifice themselves for you. On the contrary, it is you whom God has put on the earth for your people. But alas, you never understand these truths; how do they taste to you?

Would there be enough anathemas available, if such words had been mine?

You will not forgive me, either, my lord, for what I have said about Bossuet. What have I said, however? That he had declared the declaration of 1682 disproved, broken, and annulled by the Holy See. But these are still two

public facts, and it is not my fault, I think, if on this occasion the Roman pontiffs have judged as dangerous and false the doctrine of the most learned of our bishops. You will continue to hold to that, and I will submit myself to the other. Is it then so grave a wrong to prefer the authority of the vicar of Jesus Christ to the authority of the bishop of Meaux? No, you will reply, because I like to believe that you will condescend thus far. But you must at least respect his character and his intentions.

That is true. See now the terms in which I express myself:

At least to modify the sense [the natural sense of the declaration], as the Gallicans are obliged to do, that which they present is not only erroneous but heretical, than which nothing could be more opposed to the intention of the pious bishop who repeated it or the prelates who undersigned it.

My Lord, it would sometimes be useful to read *before* censuring!

I pass to another grievance, which I hasten to explain to you in a less vague manner. Here are your words:

Not content with the vast field of innocent disputes, the very truth of which leaves the people free to undertake them, though forbidden to overstep the limits of truth, he wishes to insert his own opinions into dogma and to accuse us, unjustly, of overstepping the boundaries which have been defined by the infallible authority of the Church.

Here, I must admit, I find very great difficulty in drawing some clear ideas from a phrase so singularly confusing. Do you mean to say that the discussions on which I have entered are not "innocent" in the sense that they are "guilty?" But then this crime is common to me, to the popes and all the theologians, Bossuet the first, who, like me, have "overstepped the limits of truth." This accusation goes a little further. Does the blame apply to the sentiment which I believe I should embrace? If this is the case, it will fall even more directly on the Roman pontiffs, whose acts I have reported. Nevertheless, these two senses excluded, the language shows only one thing, according to which it would be understood that in reproaching me, and also always the sovereign pontiff and the theologians, of overstepping the limits of this vast area, which you have called of innocent disputes, my wrong and theirs would be not to have felt, as you have, my lord, the obligation which the truth imposes on us to be "innocent." You appear to be so penetrated with the importance of this duty that I fear to offend you in explaining the doubt which you have of "the authority of Scripture and that of tradition."

I come now to the second reproach which you have addressed to me, "of wishing to insert my own opinions into dogma." On this I have the honor to make clear to you, from the very first, that in matters of doctrine I have no personal opinions. I believe simply that which is taught by the successor to whom Jesus Christ has said: "Feed my sheep, feed my lambs; I have prayed for you that your faith fail not."

In the second place, I have given formal notice that the doctrine established in my work, which is the doctrine of the Holy See and almost all the Churches united to the Holy See, though certainly a matter of faith, is not, nevertheless, a dogma of faith, since the contrary doctrine has not yet been attacked by any express censure. This replies sufficiently to that which you add: "accusing us, unjustly, of ourselves overstepping the bounds of that which has been defined by the infallible authority of the Church." For you intended to say, I believe: Accusing us of keeping within the bounds of that which has been defined by the infallible authority of the Church. And, to conclude on this point, permit me to reproduce here an observation which, if I am not mistaken, will serve to justify me completely [Letter to *La Quotidienne,* 4 March 1829]:

I defy anyone to show in my work a single word which can be applied to his lordship, the archbishop, personally. If he clothes himself in the universality of the Gallicans, if their doctrine is, by their own statement, opposed to that of the pope; if it is true that the Church cannot hold two contrary doctrines at the same time, it must necessarily be, so the Gallicans hold, the pope who holds a doctrine which is not that of the Church on the fundamental points which are the subject of this discussion. As for me, I say with St. Ambrose: *"Ubi Petrus, ibi Ecclesia."*

On the subject of a passage extracted from *Treatise on the Rights and Liberties of the Gallican Church,* it has been objected that this book was condemned by the ecclesiastical authority when it appeared, and that I confounded the maxims of the Church with the exaggerated maxims of the political body. Truly, he who made this objection has been known for some time as the man of France closest in line with all who hold to "innocent discussions." In spite of that, to lend him some authority in this circumstance, it seemed to me useful, having as object of showing the consequences of Gallican politics, that I should above all search for them in the works praised and approved by the masters who form the political body. Besides their manner of understanding Gallican maxims was not basically the most erroneous, because it was the most logically deduced from principles admitted even by the clergy. And if this still appears doubtful, I will try once more to make it comprehensible to whomever is capable of holding two ideas.

In the last analysis, what is the royal prerogative reduced to, as defined by the author from whom I have cited such a curious and edifying fragment? On this one, unique point: "The king, absolute monarch, can do as he wills, by virtue of his divine institution." Here the clergy made a distinction: "The king," they say, "can do anything, it is true; but if he wills that which is unjust, he damns himself. For the rest of us, it is never permitted to oppose an active resistance to his will. The true Christian would rather be killed than to concur in evil, but he must never try to arrest the course of it, never raise his arm to defend order against the unjust power which tries to overthrow it." In reference to the temporal state, to the present life, what difference is there between these two doctrines?

Gallicans, Christians or not, pose equally, then, as a basis for the political society an unlimited despotism. Only those who are forced to ally themselves with Christianity are more inconsistent than the others. Because here it is that their principles oblige them to maintain implicitly:

1) That the prince, "minister of God for the good," has only the authority which God has communicated to him. Nevertheless, if he does evil, if he revolts openly against those over whom he alone has power, or they against him, he does not cease for that to be always their minister, invested radically with the same right to command, and consequently:

2) God can give, and sometimes in fact does give, a right against itself, a right against the sovereign right. Because if Henry VIII, for example, had no right whatsoever to tyrannize his subjects, to take from an entire people the means for salvation and the fruits of the redemption, this people had itself the right to resist tyranny, each of them to oppose the force of an unjust attack:

3) That God can will, with a positive will, the destruction of the faith in a country, and all that follows it. Then, on the one hand, they would be culpable in opposing themselves to it effectively. And on the other, the power to effect this destruction, power which is not simply physical force, is comprised, in whatsoever manner, in "the right" of sovereignty which comes immediately from God:

4) That the sovereign at the time is, by the same order of God, independent as sovereign, of all law, divine and human:

5) That consequently, neither he nor the state of which he is chief is held, by any duty inherent in that same sovereignty and in society, to recognize a law of justice, to profess the true religion, nor to admit of any:

6) That thus, in the political order, all religions are equally false, equally true, equally holy or equally indifferent. When it becomes too difficult, even for men of the least suspect faith, to keep themselves "in the limits that truth forbids them to overstep," to understand a bishop publicly maintaining that the theft of vessels used in the celebrations of other cults (non-Catholic cults), supposes in effect in that which makes them culpable, "the same principle of irreligion as that of our own sacred vessels," when in fact, what could be the distance which separates the one from the other, that "nothing can hinder but the law applying the same penal disposition" [Discourse of the Archbishop of Paris to the Chamber of Peers, 6 May 1824].

To justify the servile and unholy doctrine of Gallicanism, they have said that the contrary doctrine only recognizes the difficulty without resolving it; that they must always come to a final authority which, though some part of it pleases them, can also always be an abuse. Thus, having only the choice between several abuses, the wisest would be to support in peace the one which exists, the one which they know.

But in spite of all examination, it is a fact that this counsel, often given it does not matter by whom or with what motive, has never persuaded men. Never have they understood that it is their duty to accept servitude as the primary social necessity, to submit calmly, for their own greater good, to the most oppressive yoke, and to renounce the fantasy, as it is called, of a society founded on right. Are they deceived in that, and is the existence of such a society really impossible? This is the question which I have discussed. But, one does not deny, and I defy in fact anyone who could deny that in the philosophic system power reduces itself, in its final result, to bland force and law to that which arbitrarily proscribes the will. The theory of "legal order," proclaimed today with so much zest, is nothing but the union of these two maxims. Here we have man, then, on the one side constrained to obey another man because he is stronger; and on the other, this strength constituting the only sovereignty, abstracted from all right, duty, obligatory law of truth and justice.

On the contrary, the Christian religion obliges obedience only to the man who is "the minister of God," the only eternally legitimate and absolute sovereign. According to these ideas, power is only the exterior action of God in the government of human society, the means by which peculiar and disordered wills are led back to observing immutable law, the universal law of truth and justice. It follows then that outside of this law and against this law no true power exists. That order is thus essentially inseparable from liberty. Without authority by itself, strength depends always on right, and the right is incessantly recalled, promulgated by a power spiritual of its nature and distinct from force.

Christianity has never failed to recognize the difficulty, she has resolved it as completely as it is possible to conceive of resolving it. Men have had reason to believe that God has not abandoned the society of the world to the caprices of the strongest, to an irremediable despotism, or to a still worse anarchy.

But will spiritual power never abuse the authority which she exercizes? First of all, abuse in an order founded on right is one thing. The destruction of all right and all order is quite another thing. Secondly, the abuse itself, supposing that it takes place, is necessarily confined within narrow limits. Because if it went so far as to attack the right fundamentally, the spiritual power, which exists only by right, whose proper function consists in maintaining the law of justice and truth, would radically destroy itself.

Furthermore, if one would like to come down to less general conditions, less decisively out of the way but more capable of immediate application, it would seem difficult for us not to recognize the cogent justice of that which M. le Comte de Maistre has observed in this regard:

Pontifical power is in essence less subject to the caprices of politics. Those who exercise it are for the most part old, celibate, and priests, which excludes the hundred-and-one errors and passions which trouble the states. In a word, as it is outlined, her power is of another nature than that of temporal sovereigns and, as it demands nothing for itself, one could believe legitimately enough that even if all the inconveniences were removed, which is impossible, it would result at least, however little one is permitted to hope, given human nature, in that which is for all men the nearest to the point of perfection.

Finally, the spiritual power is unique in that its jurisdiction is always voluntary, in the sense that its decisions have no effect except on those who submit to it freely. One cannot justly complain of its judgments, which can only be executed, even on those who accept them, when the tribunal from which they emanate is deprived of all exterior force of coercion.

To argue against a power, however much the abuse, supposing that it could be done, is a sophistry which would tend to nothing less than the overthrow of all authority on earth. And when the power by which it acts forms part of the spiritual power which the Church has received from Jesus Christ, or rather is this same power applied to society, as it is appied individually in all details of common life to each member of society, Catholics can no more fear abuse in one than in the other, because it is of faith that the Church cannot, whatever the particular passions of its ministers, use her power against the will and designs of God. Thus she maintains the order which is her object, which is always and necessarily, by reason of the divine help, the final result.

After that, my lord, I do not know how you can say that these doctrines, the only solid basis for power and the sole guarantee of liberty, "can only give rise to persecutions of all kinds, being represented as disquieting and jealous domination, which had the crowd at its feet." Modern Protestants and most of the philosophers who, for the past twenty years, have spoken of the epoch when these doctrines prevailed, have rendered more justice to the Church. In order to refute a Catholic archbishop on this point, it will suffice to oppose to him writers, some of whom do not believe in God, others who scarcely believe in Jesus Christ.

When one recalls that, after all, these doctrines which you have never feared to qualify so severely have been constantly, through endless ages, the doctrines of the Holy See, of the ecumenical councils, of all the theologians, all the doctors and all the canon lawyers, and the public right of Christian-

ity, how can one explain that a bishop, to confirm the faith of the people and to raise their eyes again to the authority of the Church, comes to assure them that religion, during so many centuries, was "a disquieting and jealous domination which had the crowd at its feet."

Believe me, my lord, that it is not without regret that I find myself constrained to represent to you how very strange is the direction which your zeal has taken on the sad occasion which obliges me to defend against you the vicars of Jesus Christ and the entire Church. You add yet, on the subject of the same doctrines which have given place to the above observations, that "they tend to nothing less than to overthrow society from its foundations, in destroying the love of obedience in the heart of the people, and in sowing in that of the sovereigns defiance against their subjects."

That one overthrows society by saying that she rests, by divine institution, on right or on justice; that the obligatory rule of the sovereign, whose authority, coming from God, is the one true authority, by which she is governed according to the commandments of God; that these eternal maxims of Christianity and of reason overthrow society—evidently cannot be maintained, I say, at least without posing the principle that the absence of right and of justice is the "foundation" of society, which you would not admit, surely, my lord, but which, however, you are forced to admit if you persist in rejecting the doctrines censured in your mandate.

You accuse them of destroying love of obedience in the heart of the people, and of sowing in those of the sovereigns defiance towards their subjects. In other words, you judge them equally dangerous for the people and for kings. It would be desirable if you would take the trouble to explain and to justify an assertion which would appear at first glance most extraordinary, after all that has been said. And I will never hesitate to affirm that they will so appear, always, to the extent to which they are examined attentively. Let us begin with that which concerns the people.

Are you really serious, my lord, when you alarm yourself about them, when it will be remembered that the prince should reign according to justice, according to the law of God, which obliges him as well as his subjects, to the extent that, if he goes so far as to violate them fundamentally and thus to declare himself the public enemy of those of whom he is the minister, he will lose thereby even the authority which he holds of himself, and will no longer have any right to obedience? Is it seriously that you complain of them, if it ever comes to be declared that society has prescribed to the power a rule, exteriorly obligatory, opposed a barrier to abuse, and prepared a remedy against tyranny pushed to the extreme? But is this, do you say, to sow defiance in the hearts of the sovereigns? What idea have you, then, my lord, of sovereigns? How do you suppose that they do not know how to reign in security, at least that they will not establish themselves, when they can without prejudice to their rights, as tyrants, oppressors, wicked rulers? Leave, leave to royalty its indelible character, its true and solid grandeur, which consists in the notions of justice and authority, inseparately united, combined in them as they are in God.

The true interest of the people is that their chiefs do not believe themselves to be free of the laws, that they close their ears to the unworthy flatteries which Roman slavery had written even into the laws themselves. The interest of the people is that the kings know that there is no other power but that of God, which is not given them

against justice, that is to say, against himself. Sovereignty is only an extension of the paternal power, which has its limits and conditions, known even to pagans, which renders itself useless when it is abused, as we have remarked, so that it should be said, they say, always obey the father, but never obey him when he does that in which he ceases to be a father. And this doctrine, as true as it is salutary, and salutary because it is true, is no less advantageous to sovereigns than to their subjects, because it is absurd to suppose any real advantage, conceived in any sense compatible with morality, which is not founded upon the right. Perfection of the primitive right, the Christian right, is even more favorable to the sovereignties, because it legitimizes and affirms "the love of obedience in the heart of the people," very far from destroying it, as you assure us, which is rather, as you will see in an instant, the necessary effect of Gallicanism.

First of all, the Church, in showing the prince to be the delegate of God, his minister, made the duty of obedience understandable by reason, if I may explain it in this way, and gave it an infinite force—at the same time calming, in the depths of the human heart, the fear of possible abuse of justice by teaching the people that there existed a judge, outside the political society, when these abuses became intolerable, and thus a remedy against power when it degenerated into tyranny.

But Gallicanism refused to recognize the remedy and joined, under the appearance of right, to the idea of tyranny—to the idea of an evil irreparable by any ordinary and legitimate means, and even the idea of eternity, separated first of all from the notion of sovereignty—the notion of justice and by that, secondly, frightening the people into the limitless obedience which they commanded of them, in all circumstances, to the name of God. Consider also, my Lord, what this last doctrine has produced, to what gloomy theories it has given birth, what catastrophes it has prepared in the nations ruled by it and say again, in the presence of the facts, if you continue to judge it well suited to nourish "in the heart of the people the love of obedience."

The theologians who, never seeking to be wiser than the Church, had established the contrary doctrine, among whom we will cite here only Alexander of Hales, St. Thomas, St. Bonaventure, Henri de Gand, Jean Gerson (all belonged to the University of Paris), regarded the maxims, then received universally, as the most favorable to the safety of princes, for they protect them from the attacks of their subjects, whether justly irritated or not. Cardinal Richelieu, whose advice undoubtedly carried some weight in this matter, shared the same sentiment. And in fact, during the centuries when Europe recognized the authority of Christian right, not a single hereditary throne had passed, by virtue of the power of the keys, to a new family. Order, often troubled by sovereign passions, reestablished itself little by little, by the patient firmness of the pontiffs, without catastrophes, without revolutions. What have we seen since? And what have the kings gained by the changes which they are the first to introduce in the public right?

Whatever one decides in speculation, it always presents cases where there is, in fact, debate on sovereignty or on its acts. Who will resolve these grave questions. In fact, still more, how can they be resolved? The Gallicans themselves have felt it and, as if their conscience was a stranger to these discussions in which they always agitate themselves as to whether they should obey, and how far they should obey, they have refused the decision to the spiritual authority. Whom do they attribute it to—to the people, in whom they thus recognized the primitive and radical sovereignty? Who will be judge, asks Holden, between the people and the king? Because whoever is free from party spirit will avow that there are sometimes very just causes which escape his domination. And he replies: "common reason is the only judge." Bossuet himself, in spite of his absolute principles on the admissibility of power, Bossuet who fought so strongly the sovereignty of the people maintained by Jarieu, compelled to render to this same people the judgment, which he took from the Church, of the causes which interest kings directly. Who cannot see, said he apropos of the deposition of Childeric, who cannot see that any republic or any perfect and free civil society can, according to the law of the nations and the natural law, provide her salvation for herself, and that even if she should ask counsel of others, she receives from no one that power which is inherent in her.

Here we have, then, the people invested with the right to provide for its salvation when they judge it compromised. Here we have the master to dispose of sovereignty, by virtue of a power which is inherent in him, without control and without appeal: only he accuses, only he pronounces, only he executes. Draw the consequences, my lord; or rather Bossuet draws them himself.

If we come to compare the two sentiments, that which submits the temporal to the sovereignty of the popes, and that which submits it to the people, this last state, where anger, caprice, and ignorance dominate most, would be without hesitation the most to be feared. Experience has shown the truth of this sentiment, and our age alone has shown, among those who have abandoned sovereigns to the cruel fantasies of the multitude, more examples and more tragedies against the person and the power of kings than was found during six or seven hundred years among people who, on this point, had recognized the power of Rome.

It is easy to appreciate now all the wisdom in the zeal of those who fight the doctrine of the Church for the interest of sovereigns. This zeal, when one sees it thus, tends (after having constituted political atheism) to deliver the kings to the passions of the people and to legitimize, whether for them or against them, all the excesses of force. This is, by law and in fact, the result of those wise maxims which you have seen fit, my lord, to take under your protection "with all the loyalty of a French heart." And what if there are others who also repulse the doctrines of Christianity on society, with all the loyalty of an English heart, a Russian, Swedish, Prussian, or Dutch, it is suitable to examine to what extent this loyalty is clear, in that it touches the true interest of the princes in heretical and schismatic countries. Everything, in this regard, depends upon knowing what is the position of sovereignty in these countries, whether they admit Protestant or Catholic principles.

Even though the progress of reform has been singularly favored by the avarice and ambition of princes, it did not show itself, in its beginning, penetrated by a very profound respect for them.

See in what soft and gentle tones Luther commended them to the veneration of the people: "Princes are commonly the biggest fools and the proudest knaves on the earth. One can expect nothing good of them. They are only in the world as the hangmen of God, who uses them to punish us."

Nicholas spoke also in the same way: "What is a prince? It is a hammer in the hand of God to punish the evil ones."

Following these ideas (so appropriate for giving birth to and encouraging the love of the sovereigns in the hearts of their subjects), it would be necessary to define society as a permanent torture.

Besides, all Protestants who have treated of public right admit, Hobbes excepted, the following points, which do not permit any contradiction among them:

That original and absolute sovereignty belongs to the people only.

That princes are responsible to them for the use which they make of the power which has been confided to them.

That this power can be taken away from them, when they abuse it to oppress the state.

That it is permitted, and even commanded, to take arms to defend religion against them.

In all these cases, and in other similar ones, the people have the right to use force to repulse the enterprises of tyranny; and even (adds Burlingame, following Sidney), "speaking of hardship, subjects are not obliged to wait until the prince has entirely forged the irons which he has prepared for them, which he has made them powerless to resist. It suffices, for them to be in the right, to provide for their preservation, and to take measures against the sovereign, when all his plans tend manifestly to oppress them, and when he walks, so to speak, displaying signboards to the ruin of the state."

If one asks, who will judge these things, Protestantism replies: each individual. He is the only one who decides for himself the rule which ought to guide him. According to Barclay, "man, in his quality as a reasonable being, should allow himself to be guided by the precepts of a wise and impartial reason." But Doctor Beattie disapproves this rule, and wills that when he is trying to resist sovereignty, man should determine it "by interior feelings of a certain moral instinct of which he is conscious within himself, which one is wrong to confuse with hotbloodedness and high spirits."

Such are the guarantees which the Protestant doctrine offers to sovereigns. As for Catholicism, remember first that we have said in the same work which you censure, my lord:

Christianity, in the great revolutions which have overthrown states of which it has ceased to be the constitutional principle, never agitates to reverse even that which is the most opposed to her essence. She holds herself, so to speak, in the background of the movement, and God arrives at his ends by many different ways. . . . Without doubt the obedience due to power (purely political) is not the obedience which would be due him when he presented himself to the respect of the people, as the temporal vicar, the living image of Christ the King. Nevertheless, one must not cease to say that he owes a true submission, in that he maintains a partial order in society; for this order derives originally from God, who has ordered its conservation; and force, in itself deprived of right, becomes occasionally its minister.

In the ordinary course of events, a true obedience is then due, following Catholic principles, to heretical and schismatic sovereigns, and due even by virtue of a divine command. For if one supposes a case when this obligation to obey ceased, the unique difference which would exist then between the Catholic and the Protestant is that the one would relieve himself of the duty of fidelity by his own judgment, and the other, in the strict order, could not be delivered but by the judgment of the Church.

Of these two maxims, which is the most favorable to princes, concerning the tranquillity of states? And, for example, at this moment when Ireland, oppressed for centuries, reclaims so justly her political emancipation, in this moment when all the passions, prejudices, opinions fermenting in the heart and in the head of fifteen million men, agitating and troubling Great Britain, menaced by a civil war: do you not think, my lord, that the English government, free of all prevention of and of all fetters, would not like much better to treat this great question with the pope—than to leave the decision to "the interior sentiments of a certain moral instinct of which each is conscious in himself?"

These considerations should, if I am not mistaken, at least weaken very much the fears which you have conceived, my lord, on the subject of the consequences of Catholic doctrine. For the rest, it is perhaps not without interest to observe that in 1614 the Reformers boasted of being the first to combat this doctrine, held then by all the clergy of France. And, by a remarkable singularity, Protestants today conceive that human nature can—and as it can, it *should*—throw itself again into this theocracy to find there help and salvation.

And how can one not see, in fact, that human nature, wearied of despotism and anarchy, seeks anxiously the solution of a problem which sooner or later must be resolved, since it is none other than that of social existence? Order and freedom, that is what they want. There is no life but that. There is no freedom and order for Christian people but through the Church.

I have said several times, and I repeat here, that the time is not yet come when men, deceived by their false theories, can comprehend this high truth, at the foundation of which rests the peace and salvation of the world. And that is why we must recall it, explain it, develop it—in order that right order, compared unceasingly to the errors which it opposes, will germinate little by little in souls. The vain and dangerous systems which have been substituted for it, will vanish rapidly, and soon there will remain no traces of them. Look around you and see, my lord, who it is who defends Gallicanism today. It is the enemies of the Church, who conspire publicly for her ruin and that of the Christian religion; sectarians cut off from the Catholic communion; some crafty adulators of power, who pursue it to their loss, to draw from it by flattery its rewards and favors; a small group of old men, respectable enough, no doubt, but who only live by memories of their schooldays.

And for the rest, who are they, and where are the words to paint this ignorance and baseness, this disgusting melange of bestiality and death, of stupid naiveté and foolish confidence, of little passions, little intrigues, little ambitions, and absolute powerlessness of spirit? My lord, your place is not there. Never descend to this mud. Believe me, it will stain you. Take—there is still time—more lofty thoughts. Look to the future, and deserve, as would be easy for you, its recognition and its homage. This is the wish which I make with all my heart in ending this letter, where you will recognize, I hope, the sentiments of respect of your very humble and obedient servant, which I have the honor to be.

5. *Pope Gregory XVI: Encyclical Letter, "Mirari vos," 15 August 1832*

From *Acta Gregorii Papae* (Romae, 1901), I, 169-74. Trans. by the Rev. Gregory Roettger, O.S.B.

WE TAKE it for granted that you wonder why from the time the charge of the universal Church was imposed on our humility we have not yet sent a letter to you, both as a custom practiced from the earliest times and as our benevolence toward you would have demanded. It had indeed been our sincerest wish to open our heart to you immediately and to address you with that voice by which we were commanded to confirm the brethren in the person of the blessed Peter (Luke 22, 32). But you are well aware of the inundation of evils and trials which cast us on the high seas from the first moment of our pontificate. Unless God's right hand had shown its power, you would have had to mourn our disappearance as a result of the nefarious conspiracy of impious men. The mind hesitates to recall the distress that was suffered by a sad recital of so many trials. We rather bless the Father of all consolation, who, after dispersing the enemies, saved us from the present danger and, after calming the violent tempest, deigned to grant a respite from fear. We thereupon decided to consult with you as to the means to be employed to heal the wounds of Israel, but the tremendous burden of cares which occupied us in reestablishing public order brought about a delay in our resolve.

In the meantime a new reason for silence arose because of the insolence of the factions who again attempted to raise the standard of revolt. This perverseness of men, whose boundless fury apparently was not stilled by going unpunished and by continued kindness, was rather fanned. We were obliged, though with great reluctance, to put down the rod (1 Cor. 4, 21) by the authority divinely conferred upon us. As a result, as you may readily conjecture, our daily concern has increased.

Now that we have, according to custom, taken possession of the pontificate in the Lateran basilica, a step we had delayed because of the above causes, without further hesitation we hasten to you, venerable brethren, and as a witness of our good will we address this letter to you on this auspicious day when we celebrate the solemn feast of the Assumption of the most holy Virgin into heaven, so that she whom we felt as our patroness and support in the midst of the worst calamities may graciously assist us while we are writing to you and by her heavenly aid inspire us with the counsels which will be most salutary for the Christian flock.

With a sad heart we come to you. By reason of your interest pertaining to religion we are well aware how concerned you are because of the evil days upon which we have fallen. We might indeed say with all truth, that this is the hour of the power of darkness when the children of election will be sifted like wheat (Luke 22, 53). "The earth is infected by the inhabitants thereof, because they have transgressed the laws, they have changed the ordinance, they have broken the everlasting covenant" (Is. 24, 5).

We are speaking, venerable brethren, of things which you behold with your own eyes, and which we therefore bewail in common. Brazen immorality, impudent knowledge, dissolute license abound. Holy things are despised, and the majesty of divine worship, which possesses both great power and great necessity, is attacked and polluted by malevolent men, and made a matter of ridicule. Correct doctrine is perverted and errors of all kinds are insolently disseminated. Neither the Church's laws, rights, institutions, nor the holiest matters of discipline are safe from the audacity of men speaking evil. This Roman See, in which Christ placed the foundation of the Church, is vehemently tried. Day by day the bonds of unity progressively weaken and are destroyed. The divine authority of the Church is attacked, and, her rights denied, she is subjected to earthly powers. With supreme injury she is subjected to the hatred of nations and reduced to shameful slavery.

The obedience due to bishops is rejected and their rights spurned. In an abominable manner, the schools disseminate monstrous opinions, by which the Catholic faith is no longer impugned occultly and stealthily, but horrific and deadly war is waged against it openly and everywhere. Through the instruction and example of teachers, after the minds of the youth have been corrupted, immense harm to religion and unutterable immorality has resulted. Thus, because it has rejected the guidance of religion by which alone nations are established and the force and power of governments confirmed, we now perceive the destruction of the public order, the downfall of government, and perversion of all legitimate power.

This accumulation of misfortunes must be sought in the first place in the malice and bad will of those societies into which whatever is sacrilegious, opprobrious and blasphemous in the various heresies and criminal sects has flowed as if into a sewer, full of all uncleanness.

These things, venerable brethren, and many others besides, perhaps even graver, which it would take too long at this time to enumerate (and which you already know), beset us with excruciating and unceasing pain, who, placed in the chair of the prince of the apostles, must more than others be consumed with zeal for the whole house of God. But, since we have been placed in a position where it does not suffice merely to deplore these innumerable evils, but in which we are also bound to suppress them to the best of our ability, we appeal to the help of your faith. We invoke your solicitude for the welfare of the Catholic flock, venerable brethren, whose virtue, sense of religion, prudence, and zeal offer us courage, and sustain us with sweet consolation who are afflicted with such trials. It is namely our duty to lift up our voice, to make every effort, lest the beast from the wilderness destroy the vineyard, lest the Wolves slaughter the flock. It is our affair to drive the sheep to the pastures which alone are salutary for them, in which there is not the slightest fear of harm. God forbid, dearest brethren, God forbid, that when such dire evils are threatening, when great harm is impending, that the shepherds should be wanting in their task and, struck with fear, should desert the sheep, or neglecting the flock, should while away the time in idleness and sloth. Therefore let us work in unity of spirit for our common cause, or rather God's cause, and let us oppose to the common enemy our united vigilance, our united effort, for the welfare of the entire people.

This you will well do if, as your office demands, you attend to yourselves and to doctrine, assiduously considering whether "the universal Church is disturbed by any novelty" (St. Celestine, "Letter XXI to the Bishops of Gaul"), and that, according to the admonition of St. Agatho, "nothing of the truths that have been regularly defined be lessened, nothing altered, nothing added, but that they be preserved intact in word and in meaning" ("Letter to the Emperor"). Then will come the unshakable stability of that unity which resides in this chair of blessed Peter from its foundation. When the rights of sacred communion flow to all the churches, there all may find a wall, security, a tranquil harbor, and a treasury of everything desirable (St. Innocent, "Letter XI"). In order, then, that you may repress the audacity of those who attempt to destroy the rights of this Holy See or disrupt the union of the churches with it, on which union alone they rest and by which they flourish, inculcate the utmost faith in it

and a zeal for sincere veneration, emphasizing with St. Cyprian "that he falsely thinks he is in the Church who deserts the chair of Peter, on which the Church is founded" ("On the Unity of the Church").

To this end, then, you must bend your best efforts and exercise close vigilance, so that the deposit of the faith will be preserved in the face of impious men whose attempts to tear and destroy it we sorely lament. Let all remember that the judgment concerning sound doctrine, with which the people are to be imbued, and the government as well as the administration of the universal Church is in the hands of the Roman pontiff, to whom "the full power of feeding, ruling, and governing the universal Church was committed by Christ the Lord," as the fathers of the Council of Florence explicitly declared (sess. 25). It is the duty of every bishop to adhere most faithfully to the chair of Peter, to preserve the deposit [of the faith] in a holy and religious manner, and to shepherd the flock God committed to him. Let the priests be subject, as is fitting, to the bishops whom "they are to regard as the parents of their souls," in accordance with Jerome's words ("Letter II to Nepot"). Nor may they ever forget that they are already forbidden by the ancient canons to do anything in the sacred ministry or to assume the duty of teaching and preaching "without the judgment of the bishop, to whom the people are entrusted and from whom a reckoning for their souls will be demanded" ("Apostolic Canons, XXXVIII"). Finally, let it be clearly understood that all those who conspire against this established order, disturb as far as they can the Church's position.

It would certainly be criminal and entirely foreign to the spirit of respect with which the Church's laws must be received to cavil at her established discipline, which relates to the regulation of worship, the norms of morality, the rights of the Church and her ministers, to assert that it is opposed to certain principles of the natural law or to hold that it is defective and imperfect and subject to the civil authority.

But since it is clear that the Church, to quote the fathers of Trent, "was instructed by Christ Jesus and his apostles," and that she is taught the truth unceasingly by the Holy Spirit, it is obviously absurd and most injurious to her to demand some kind of "restoration and regeneration" as necessary for her existence and growth—as if it were possible for her to be subject to defect, to decay, or other such deficiencies. By these attacks the innovators would lay the foundations of a new human institution, and what Cyprian detested would come about, namely, that from being something divine "the Church would become human" (St. Cyprian, "Letter LII"). Let those who propose such views consider that to the Roman pontiff alone, as St. Leo testifies, "the regulation of the canons has been entrusted," that it belongs solely to him, not to any private individual, to legislate "concerning the rules of the sanctions that have been handed down," and, as St. Gelasius writes, thus "to weigh the decrees of the canons and to consider the precepts of those who have gone before that what the needs of the times demand in the way of relaxation for the welfare of the churches should be tempered after diligent consideration" ("Letter to the Bishops of Lucania").

At this point we desire to call upon your constancy for holy religion against the vile attack on clerical celibacy. You know that it is growing by the day, thanks to the collusion of the most depraved philosophers of our time and some of the ecclesiastical orders who, unmindful of their person and their duty, are borne away by the allurements of pleasure. They have gone so far as to dare to direct public and, in some places, repeated demands to the rulers for the abolition of that most sacred point of discipline. But we are ashamed to speak at length of these base attempts. Instead, we request you to do everything in your power to preserve, guard, and keep intact this important law against which the darts of the impure are directed from all sides.

Then, as far as honorable Christian marriage is concerned, which St. Paul called "a great sacrament . . . in Christ and in the Church," our concern is aroused, lest wrong opinions be held or propagated regarding its sanctity or its indissoluble bond. This was already inculcated by the letter to you of our predecessor, Pius VIII. But violent attacks against it continue. The people must therefore be taught sedulously that marriage, once rightly entered into, can no longer be broken, that God made marriage a union for life, that its bond can be dissolved only by death. Let them be mindful that matrimony is something sacred and therefore subject to the authority of the Church. Let them keep before their eyes the Church's laws concerning it. Let them obey these laws conscientiously and exactly, since from their execution the force and the legitimate union of marriage depend. Let them beware lest they admit in any manner anything that may be contrary to the precepts of the sacred canons or the decrees of the councils. Let them be fully persuaded that those marriages will turn out badly which are entered upon contrary to the Church's discipline or without the blessing of God sought beforehand or under the sole impetus of lust, no thought being given on the part of the spouses to the sacrament and the mysteries signified by it.

And now we must mention another fruitful cause of evil by which the

Church is afflicted at present, namely, indifferentism—or that vicious manner of thinking, which mushrooms on all sides owing to the wiles of malicious men and which holds that the soul's eternal salvation can be obtained by the profession of any faith, provided a man's morals are good and decent. In a matter so clear and evident you will without difficulty disabuse the people committed to your care. Heed the admonition of the apostle that there is "one Lord, one faith, one baptism" (Eph. 4, 5). Let them beware, who preach that the gates of heaven open to every religion. Let them consider seriously the testimony of the Savior that some are against Christ because they are not with Christ (Luke 11, 23), that they scatter who do not gather with him, and therefore "without doubt they will perish in eternity, unless they hold to the Catholic faith and observe it whole and inviolate" (Athanasian Creed). Let them listen to Jerome; he constantly cried out, at a time when the Church suffered a threefold division as a result of schism, firm in his resolution, when someone wanted to win him over: "If one is joined to the chair of Peter, he is mine" ("Letter LVII"). A person would be deceiving himself by the fact that he had been reborn of water. Augustine here gives a telling reply: "The branch that has been cut from the vine resembles any other. But what does its form avail if it does not live off the root?" ("Commentary on the Psalms against the Donatist Party").

Now from this evil-smelling spring of indifferentism flows the erroneous and absurd opinion—or rather, derangement—that freedom of conscience must be asserted and vindicated for everyone. This most pestilential error opens the door to the complete and immoderate liberty of opinions, which works such widespread harm both in Church and state. Some people

outrageously maintain that some advantage derives from it for religion. "But what more calamitous death for the soul than the liberty of error," said Augustine ("Letter MLXVI"). When all restraint by which men are kept in the path of truth is removed, since their fallen nature already draws them to evil, then we say indeed that the "bottomless pit" (Apoc. 9, 2) has been opened, from which John saw ascending the smoke that obscured the sun, and from the smoke came forth the locusts that covered the face of the earth. Thence proceeds transformation of minds, corruption of youth, a contempt among the people for the Church, for sacred things and laws. In one word, that pestilence is more threatening to the public weal than any other, since as experience shows, or as is known from antiquity, kingdoms which flourished by reason of wealth, of rule, and of glory perished because of this sole evil: the immoderate liberty of opinions, license of speech, and the penchant for novelties.

Here reference must be made to that deleterious liberty, which can never be execrated and detested sufficiently, of printing and of publishing writings of every kind, which some dare to demand and to promote with such insolence. We are struck with horror, venerable brethren, when we see with what monstrous doctrines or rather with what portentous errors we are oppressed. They are spread far and wide by a multitude of books, pamphlets, and other writings, small indeed in size but very great in malice, from which comes that curse spread across the earth that we bewail. There are even some (alas!) who go so far in their impudence as to boldly assert that this congeries of error is sufficiently compensated for by some book which in so great a sounding forth of depravity is published that it bolsters religion and truth. It is patently wrong and forbid-

den by every law to purposely perpe-
trate a certain and greater evil—because there exists a hope that some
good may spring from it.

Far different was the attitude of the
Church in destroying the pestilence of
evil books ever since the age of the
apostles, for we read that they burned
a large number of books publicly (Acts
19). It suffices to read the decrees concerning this matter made in the Fifth
Lateran Council and the constitution
subsequently published by Pope Leo
X, lest "what was haply invented for
the increase of faith and the propagation of liberal arts should be turned
into the opposite and beget harm to the
salvation of Christ's faithful" (Fifth
Lateran Council, sess. X). The fathers
of Trent likewise were greatly concerned with this matter, and as a remedy they ordered by salutary decree
that an index of books be made to restrain impure doctrine (sess. XVIII
and XXV). In his encyclical letter
concerning the prohibition of harmful
books, our predecessor, Clement XII,
said: "Strenuous efforts must be made,
in accordance with the importance of
the matter, to exterminate the deadly
harm caused by so many books. Error
will never be suppressed unless the
criminal elements of depravity be consumed in flames" ("Christianae," 25
November 1766). From this unwavering solicitude manifested through the
ages, by which this Apostolic See has
sought to condemn suspect and harmful books, and to withdraw them from
the hands of men, it becomes abundantly clear how false, rash, and injurious to this same Apostolic See, how
fruitful of errors for the Christian people is the teaching of those who not
only reject the censorship of books as
too serious and burdensome, but proceed so far in their improbity as to
maintain that it is contrary to the principles of law and dare to deny to the

Church the right of imposing and exercising it.

Since we have learned that certain
opinions, by which due faith and submission to rulers is attacked and the
flame of rebellion enkindled, are being
broadcast in print, great solicitude
must be exercised, lest the people be
thereby deceived and led from the
right path. Let all remember the apostle's admonition that "there exists no
authority except from God, and those
who exist have been appointed by God.
Therefore he who resists the authority
resists the ordinance of God; and they
that resist bring on themselves condemnation" (Rom. 13, 2). Wherefore
both divine and human law inveigh
against those who attempt by the
shameful machinations of rebellion and
sedition to turn away subjects from
fidelity to their rulers and to snatch the
government from them.

Surely for this reason the early
Christians, lest they be guilty of such a
crime, even when the persecutions
were most violent, worked to the best
of their ability for the emperors and
the welfare of the empire, not only by
faithfulness in carrying out accurately
and promptly those things which were
not contrary to their religion, but also
by their courage and by shedding their
blood in battle. St. Augustine says:
"The Christian soldiers served the pagan emperor, but when the cause of
Christ came into question, they recognized only him who is in heaven. They
distinguished between the eternal Lord
and the temporal lord, but still they
were subject to the temporal lord for
the sake of the eternal Lord" ("Commentary on Ps. 134, 7"). This, too,
St. Maurice, that invincible martyr and
leader of the Theban legion, had in
mind when, according to the testimony
of St. Eucherius, he replied thus to the
emperor: "We are your soldiers, O
emperor, but still the servants of God,
as we freely profess. . . . Even now this

extreme necessity of our lives has not driven us into rebellion. Behold, we have these arms in our hands, but we do not resist, because we consider it better to die than to kill" (Ruinart, "Acts of the Martyrs, 4"). This fidelity of the early Christians to their rulers becomes more striking if it is borne in mind, as Tertullian says, that at that time they would have possessed sufficient numbers and power had they wished to set themselves up as enemies: "We are but of yesterday, yet we have filled every place among you —cities, islands, fortresses, towns, marketplaces, camp, tribes, town councils, palace, senate, forum. . . . For what war would we not have been fit and ready, even though unequally matched in military strength, we who are so ready to be slain, were it that, according to our rule of life, it is granted us to be killed rather than to kill . . . ? If such a multitude of men as we are had broken loose from you and had gone into some remote corner of the earth, the loss of so many citizens, of whatever kind they may be, would certainly have made your power blush for shame. In fact, it would even have punished you by this very desertion. Without a doubt you would have been exceedingly frightened at your loneliness. . . . You would have had to look around for people to rule. There would have been more enemies than citizens left to you. For, now, the enemies whom you have are fewer because of the number of Christians, inasmuch as nearly all the citizens you have in nearly all the cities are Christians" ("Apology, XXXVII").

These outstanding examples of unwavering subjection to rulers, which of necessity were produced by the sacred precepts of the Christian religion, condemn the detestable insolence and impudence of those who, burning with an unbridled desire of baneful liberty, dedicate themselves entirely to the weakening and the destruction of all rights of government and will only bring to the peoples slavery under the appearance of liberty. To the same end were directed the tendencies and the nefarious derangements of the Waldensians, Beghards, Wycliffites, and other sons of Belial, who were the shame of the human race and rightly therefore condemned with an anathema more than once by this Apostolic See. For no other reason do these insurgents apply themselves so wholeheartedly except that with Luther they may rejoice that "they are free of everything," and in order to obtain this end more speedily and more rapidly, they most daringly attempt every kind of criminal undertaking.

Nor can we hope for anything better for Church and state from those who desire the Church to be separated from the state and to break off the harmony existing between them. It is plainly to be seen that this concord, which ever worked to the benefit of the ecclesiastical and civil societies, is dreaded by lovers of a most insolent liberty.

But to the rest of the bitter causes about which we are solicitous and which constricted us with sorrow because of the general threat they represent must be added certain associations and groups, which, making common cause with the promoters of every kind of false religion and worship, by their simulated piety toward religion, which, however, masks their desire to promote novelties and sedition everywhere, preach absolute liberty, promote rebellion against Church and state, and tread under foot all authority.

With profound grief, but trusting in him who commands the winds and brings about tranquillity, we write to you, venerable brethren, urging you to take up the shield of faith and to fight manfully the battles of the Lord. You especially have the duty of standing up as a wall against every power that lifts itself up against the knowledge of God. Draw the sword of the spirit, which is the word of God, and give bread to those who hunger for justice. Since you have been called to be zealous workers in the Lord's vineyard, labor for this alone and in concert that every root of bitterness be torn up in the field committed to you and that, after all seed of vice has been destroyed, the grain of virtue may flourish. In the first place, show a paternal affection for those who devote themselves to the sacred sciences and to philosophical questions. Be their support and encouragement, lest, left to their own devices, they imprudently wander off the path of truth into the way of the impious. Let them remember that God is the guide of wisdom and the director of the wise (Wisdom 7, 15), and that we cannot learn to know God without God, who through his word teaches men to know God (St. Irenaeus, XIV, 10). It is a sign of a proud, or rather foolish, man to examine the mysteries of faith which exceed all understanding, by human criteria and to test them by reason, which because of the condition of human nature is weak and defective.

Furthermore, let our beloved sons in Christ, the rulers, favor these common endeavors for the welfare of Church and state by their aid and authority, which they should consider as having been granted to them not only for the government of the world, but more especially for the defense of the Church. Let them carefully consider that whatever is done for the welfare of the Church redounds to the advantage of their rule and of peace. In fact, let them be convinced that they must be more concerned about the cause of the faith than of their government, and that it is a matter of great moment "if to their wisdom be added the crown of faith," as Pope St. Leo says. Since they have been appointed parents and guardians as it were of their peoples, they will procure their true and constant welfare and blessed tranquillity if they bend their efforts to this end, that religion be preserved incorrupt and that there be piety shown toward God, who has written on his thigh: "King of kings and Lord of lords."

Now, in order that all these things may haply come to pass, let us lift eyes and hands to the most holy Virgin Mary, who alone destroys all heresies, in whom alone is our utmost trust, in fact, the entire basis of our hope (St. Bernard, "Sermon on the Nativity of the Blessed Virgin," 7). By her intercession may she implore for our undertakings, endeavors, and actions a favorable outcome in the present necessity of the Lord's flock. This we likewise with humble prayer beg of Peter, the prince of the apostles, and Paul, his co-apostle, that you may all stand as a wall, lest another foundation be placed beside that which has already been laid. Borne up by this comforting hope we trust that the author and finisher of faith, Jesus Christ, will finally console us in the tribulations which grievously afflict us, and as an augury of heavenly assistance we lovingly impart on you, venerable brethren, and on the flocks committed to your care the apostolic blessing.

6. *The Italian Law of Guarantees, 13 May 1871*

From *Church and State Through the Centuries,* trans. and ed. by Sidney Z. Ehler and John B. Morrall (Westminster, Maryland: Newman Press, 1954), pp. 285-291.

I, 1. THE person of the sovereign pontiff is sacred and inviolable.

2. An attack on the person of the sovereign pontiff and provocation to commit it are punished with the penalties laid down for attack and provocation to commit it on the person of the king.

Offenses and public outrages, committed directly against the person of the pontiff by words, acts, or by the means indicated in art. 1 of the law on the press, are punished with the penalties laid down in art. 19 of the same law.

Such offenses fall within the scope of the public authorities and are within the competence of the law courts of assize.

Discussion on religious matters is completely free.

3. The Italian government gives to the sovereign pontiff, in the territory of the kingdom, sovereign honors and the pre-eminence in dignity which is accorded to him by Catholic sovereigns.

The sovereign pontiff has the right to preserve the accustomed number of attendants attached to his person and to the custody of his palaces without prejudice to the obligations and duties resulting for these attendants from the laws in force in the state.

4. The endowment of an annual income of 3,225,000 lire is reserved for the benefit of the Holy See.

With this sum, equal to that which figures in the Roman budget under the headings: "Apostolic Palaces, Sacred College, Ecclesiastical Congregations, Secretariat of State and Diplomatic Representation Abroad," provision shall be made for the personal income of the sovereign pontiff and the various ecclesiastical needs of the Holy See, the usual maintenance and upkeep of the apostolic palaces and their dependencies, the salaries, gratuities and pensions of the attendants mentioned in the preceding article and of those attached to the pontifical court and for accidental expenses, such as the maintenance and upkeep of the museums and libraries pertaining to the court and the salaries, wages and pensions of those employed there.

The aforesaid endowment shall be set down to the account of the national debt under the form of a perpetual and inalienable income in the name of the Holy See and, during the vacancy of the Holy See, it shall continue to be paid to provide for the necessities of the Roman Church in this interval.

It shall be exempted from every kind of tax and governmental, municipal or provincial charge, and it shall not be lessened even if the Italian government should later decide to take over the payment of expenses relating to the museums and libraries.

5. The sovereign pontiff, apart from the endowment laid down in the preceding article, shall continue to enjoy the use of the apostolic palaces of the Vatican and the Lateran, with all the buildings, gardens and landed property pertaining to them, as well as the villa of Castel Gandolfo, with all its annexes and dependencies.

The aforesaid palaces, villa and annexes, as also the museums, libraries, artistic and archaeological collections existing therein, are inalienable, exempt from every tax or charge and from expropriation for the sake of public utility.

6. During vacancies in the pontifical see, no judicial and political authority shall apply, for any cause whatever, any hindrance or restriction to the personal liberty of the cardinals.

The government will insure that the meetings of conclaves and ecumenical councils are not disturbed by any exterior violence.

7. No representative of public authority or agent of public force shall, for the accomplishment of the duties of his office, enter the palaces which are the habitual residence or temporal dwelling of the sovereign pontiff, or in which a conclave, or ecumenical council is assembled, unless with the authorization of the sovereign pontiff, the conclave or the council.

8. It is forbidden to make visits, searches or confiscations of papers, documents, books or registers in the pontifical offices or congregations invested with purely spiritual attributes.

9. The sovereign pontiff is completely free to fulfill all the functions of his spiritual ministry and to cause all the decisions deriving from the aforesaid ministry to be affixed to the doors of basilicas and churches.

10. Clerics who, by reason of their office, participate at Rome in the publication of decisions of the spiritual authority of the Holy See, are not liable, because of these decisions, to any inquiry, investigation or prosecution by public authority.

Every foreigner holding an ecclesiastical office at Rome enjoys the personal guarantees belonging to the Italian citizens by virtue of the laws of the kingdom.

11. Envoys of foreign governments, accredited to His Holiness, shall enjoy in the kingdom all the prerogatives and immunities accorded to diplomatic agents according to international law.

Offenses against them shall be punished with the penalties liable for offenses against envoys of foreign Powers accredited to the Italian government.

Envoys of His Holiness accredited to foreign governments are assured, in the territory of the kingdom, of the prerogatives and immunities customary according to the aforesaid international law to facilitate their departure to the place of their mission and their return from it.

12. The sovereign pontiff may correspond freely with the episcopate and with the whole Catholic world, without any interference by the Italian government.

For this purpose, he is to have the right of establishing, in the Vatican or in his other residences, postal and telegraph offices staffed by his own chosen employees.

The pontifical post office will be able to correspond directly under sealed mail with the exchange post offices of foreign administrations or to send its own correspondence to Italian offices. In both cases, the transport of dispatches or correspondence certified by the stamp of the pontifical office will be exempt from every tax or charge on Italian territory.

Couriers dispatched in the name of the sovereign pontiff will be placed on the same footing as couriers of foreign governments.

The pontifical telegraph office will be linked with the telegraphic system of the kingdom at the state's expense.

Telegrams transmitted by the said bureau with the certified appellation of "pontifical" shall be received and dispatched with the privileges recognized for state telegrams, and with exemption from all taxes within the kingdom.

The same advantages are assured to telegrams from the sovereign pontiff or sent by his order which, certified by the stamp of the Holy See, shall be presented at any telegraph office whatever in the kingdom.

Telegrams addressed to the sovereign pontiff shall be exempt from taxes placed to the charge of the recipients. . . .

II, 13. In the city of Rome and in the suburban sees, the seminaries, academies, colleges and other Catholic institutions founded for the purpose of ecclesiastical education shall continue to depend wholly on the Holy See without any interference on the part of the educational authorities of the kingdom.

14. Every specific restriction on the exercise of the right to assemble by the members of the Catholic clergy is abolished.

15. The government renounces the right of "apostolic legation" in Sicily, and throughout the whole kingdom it renounces the right of nomination and presentation to major benefices.

Bishops shall not be required to take an oath to the king.

Major or minor benefices cannot be conferred on those who are not citizens of the kingdom, except in the city of Rome and in its suburban sees.

There is to be no change with respect to the collation of benefices in royal patronage.

16. The *exequatur* and royal *placet* and every other form of governmental authorization for the publication and execution of the acts of ecclesiastical authorities are abolished.

However, until otherwise provided by special law spoken of in art. 18, the acts of those authorities which have as their object the disposal of ecclesiastical goods and the provision to major or minor benefices, except those of the city of Rome and the suburban sees, shall remain subject to the *exequatur* and the royal *placet*.

Nothing is altered in the provisions of the laws relative to the creation and methods of functioning of ecclesiastical corporations and the alienation of their goods.

17. In spiritual and disciplinary matters, no objection or appeal against the acts of ecclesiastical authorities is allowed, and no implementation by public authority is granted, or recognized, to them.

The cognizance of juridical effects of the aforesaid or any other acts of these authorities, pertains to civil courts of law.

However, these acts are deprived of force, if they are contrary to the laws of the state or to public order, or if they injure the rights of individuals, and they are subject to legal penalties if criminal offenses are committed as a result of them.

18. Arrangements shall be made by a subsequent law for the reorganization, presentation, and administration of ecclesiastical property in the kingdom.

19. In all the matters which come within the scope of the present law, all arrangements which are contrary to its provisions are and shall remain abrogated.

7. *Prussian Law on the Appointment of the Clergy, 21 May 1874*

From *Church and State Through the Centuries,* trans. and ed. by Sidney Z. Ehler and John B. Morrall (Westminster, Maryland: Newman Press, 1954), pp. 295-297.

WE, WILLIAM, by the grace of God, King of Prussia, etc., in order to amend and complete the law of 11 May 1873, concerning the required education of ministers and their appointments, ordain, with the consent of both houses of the *Landtag* of our monarchy, the following:

1) The law of 11 May 1873, is hereby amended to the effect that any conferring of an ecclesiastical office, as well as the acceptance thereof, is also contrary to the provisions of arts. 1-3 of that law in the case where it has been effected without previously announcing the name of the candidate [to the *ober-praesident*, i.e., governor of the Province in question] as prescribed in art. 15 of that law, or before such announcement, or before the expiration of the period fixed in the same article for lodging appeals.

2) The penalty mentioned in art. 23 of the law of 11 May 1873, is applicable to any minister who performs acts of ministry without being able to prove that he has been appointed, in accordance with arts. 1-3 of the said law, to hold the office in question or to serve as a substitute or assistant therein.

3) If a ministry is vacant, the *ober-praesident* is entitled to order the confiscation of its property, if:

1. the vacant office has been filled up in disregard of the provisions of arts. 1-3 of the law of 11 May 1873; or if,
2. circumstances exist, which justify the assumption that the appointment to the office will not be effected in accordance with the said provisions.

The confiscations may apply to all property which belongs to the office, including the right of using goods, collecting the fruits thereof and obtaining services. The *ober-praesident* shall nominate a commissioner to seize and administer the property on behalf of the office until the same be filled up in accordance with law, or until an acting deputy be named. The commissioner may exercise, with full legal force, all property rights pertaining to a legal holder of the office. The expenses of management shall be defrayed from the revenues of the office.

4) If a vacancy has occurred in a Church office and an ecclesiastic has been subsequently condemned to a penalty according to art. 23, par. 1, of the law of 11 May 1873, or according to art. 2 of the present law, because of acts of unlawful ministering in that office, then the person enjoying the right of presentation (or of nomination, or proposition), derived from patronage or any other legal title, may fill up the vacancy and provide with a deputy to administer the office.

5) The person entitled to present may also name a deputy to the vacant office if an ecclesiastic is prohibited from living in the district, where the vacant office is situated, in virtue of art. 5 of the law of the empire of 4 May 1874, relative to the prevention of unlawful exercise of Church offices.

6) The person entitled to present is to be officially informed of the penal sentence imposed (art. 4) or of the decision limiting the right of sojourn (art. 5). As regards such sentences or decisions which have been pronounced before the promulgation of the present law, they are to be communicated to the persons entitled to present immediately after the coming into force of this law.

7) If the person entitled to present makes use of his rights (arts. 4-5), the provisions of the law of 11 May 1873, shall be applied. The penalty mentioned in art. 22, par. 1, thereof as applicable to the ecclesiastical superiors in the case of an unlawful appointment, shall be equally applicable to the said person entitled to present.

8) If the person entitled to present does not name an acting deputy to the office within two months from the date of reception of the prescribed communication (art. 6), or if the said person does not fill up the vacancy within one year from the same date,

his right shall pass over to the parish community or the community of an affiliated church or chapel. The community enjoys the rights mentioned in arts. 4 and 5 in all such cases where there exist no persons entitled to present. The provisions of art. 6 shall be applied to the community accordingly. In particular the community shall be informed of the fact that the person entitled to present did not make use of his right within the period provided by law.

9) If the conditions set forth in art. 8 are fulfilled, the *Landrat* [i.e., state official in charge of the administration of a district] or, in towns, the burgomaster, shall convoke, on the request of at least ten male members of the community—who are of age, enjoy civil rights, and do not depend upon the head of the family if he also be an elector in the same community—all the members who satisfy the said requirements, for the purpose of selecting a deputy (to the ecclesiastical office in question) or of filling up the vacancy. The decision shall be valid if more than half of those present approve. More detailed regulation as to the procedure shall be issued by the *ober-praesidents*.

10) After a valid election of the minister has taken place, a representative is to be elected according to the provisions of art. 9, who shall effect the handing over of the office to the elected minister. The provisions of art. 7 will regulate the conduct and the responsibility of this representative.

11) If, in cases falling within the scope of arts. 4-10, the competent *ober-praesident* does not raise any objection, or if his objections are rejected by the court of law, the minister is to be considered as lawfully appointed.

8. *Law of the French Republic on the Separation of Church and State, 9 December 1905*

From *Church and State Through the Centuries*, trans. and ed. by Sidney Z. Ehler and John B. Morrall (Westminster, Maryland: Newman Press, 1954), pp. 358-371.

I, 1) THE Republic assures liberty of conscience. It guarantees the free exercise of religious worship, but with the restrictions enacted below in the interest of public order.

2) The republic does not recognize any salary or subsidy to any religious body. As a result, starting from 1 January following the promulgation of the present law, all expenses relating to the practice of religious worship shall be struck off the budgets of the state, the *départements* and the communes. There can, however, be included in the said budgets expenses relative to charitable organizations and those for the purpose of assuring the free exercise of religious worship in public establishments, such as high schools, colleges, schools, hospitals, asylums and prisons.

Public establishments for religious worship are suppressed, with modifying conditions laid down in art. 3. . . .

II, 3) Establishments whose suppression is decreed by art. 2 shall continue provisionally to function in conformity with the arrangements now governing them, until the allocation of their goods to the associations, provided for by section IV and at latest until the expiration of the periods fixed below. After the promulgation of the present law, the agents of the administration of property shall proceed to the descriptive and assessory inventory of:

1. movable and immovable goods of the said foundations.

2. goods of the state, the *départements* and the communes of which the same foundations have the use.

This double inventory shall be drawn up in collaboration with the legal representatives of the ecclesiastical establishment; who, in any case, shall be duly summoned by a notification made in administrative form.

The agents entrusted with the inventory shall have the right of procuring the communication of all legal instruments and documents necessary for the proceedings.

4) During the period of a year dating from the promulgation of the present law, the movable and immovable goods of clergy—houses, buildings, meeting places, assembly rooms and other public religious establishments— shall be transferred, with all the duties and obligations which rest on them and with due respect for the special purposes for which they are destined, by the legal representatives of these establishments to associations which, in conformity with the rules of the general organization of the religion of which they intend to insure the practice, shall be legally formed, according to the requirements of art. 19, for the practice of this religion in the old delimitations of the said establishments.

5) Those goods within the scope of the preceding article, which have come from the state and which are not linked to a pious foundation created subsequently to the law of Germinal 18 of the year X, shall be returned to the state.

No disposal of goods shall be made by ecclesiastical establishments until a month after the promulgation of the ruling of the public administration provided for in art. 43. Failing this, the nullity of such disposal can be claimed before the civil law courts by every interested party or by the public ministry.

In case of alienation by the religious association of movable or immovable property forming part of the endowment of such a public establishment, the amount resulting from the sale should be invested in registered shares under the conditions provided for in paragraph 2 or art. 22.

The acquirer of the alienated goods shall be personally responsible for the regularity of this process.

Goods claimed by the state, the *départements* or the communes shall not be alienated, transformed or modified until a decision on the claim has been reached by the competent legal authorities.

6) The associations disposing of the goods of suppressed ecclesiastical establishments shall be provisionally responsible for the assets as well as the debts of these establishments, according to the arrangements of the 3rd paragraph of the present article; so long as they are not freed from this responsibility, they shall have the right to the enjoyment of the goods productive of revenues which should be returned to the state by virtue of art. 5.

The total revenue of the said goods remains subject to the payment of the balance of the customary and legal debts of the suppressed public establishment, when no religious association competent to receive the resources of this establishment shall be formed.

Annual payments from sums borrowed for expenses, relating to religious buildings shall be borne by the associations in proportion to the time during which they shall have the use of these buildings by application of the arrangements of section III.

In the case where the state, the *départements,* or the communes shall resume possession of the buildings of which they are proprietors, they shall be responsible for debts regularly contracted and relating to the said buildings.

7) The movable or immovable goods assigned to a charitable purpose or to any purpose other than the practice of religious worship shall be transferred, by the legal representatives of ecclesiastical establishments, to public services or foundations or for a public use whose purpose is in conformity with that of the said goods. This transfer should be approved by the prefect of the *département* in which the ecclesiastical foundation is situated. In case of nonapproval, the case shall be decided by a decree issued by the council of state [the supreme court of administration].

Any legal proceedings for restoration or repossession should be instituted within a period of six months, dating from the day when the prefectorial order or decree approving the transfer shall have been published in the *Journal Officiel*. Legal proceedings may only be instituted in the case of gifts or bequests and only by the donors and their heirs in their direct line.

8) If an ecclesiastical establishment fails, within the period fixed by art. 4, to effect the transfers prescribed above, the matter shall be dealt with by decree.

On the expiration of the said period, the goods to be transferred shall be placed in sequestration pending their transfer.

In the case where the goods transferred, by virtue of art. 4 and of par. 1 of the present article, shall be either immediately or later claimed by several associations formed for the practice of the same religion, the transfer which shall have been made by the representatives of the establishment or by decree may be contested by litigation before the council of state, by litigation, which shall give sentence after taking into account all the circumstances of the case.

The appeal should be brought before the council of state within the space of one year from the date of the decree or from the notification made to the prefectorial authority, by the legal representatives of the public establishment of the religious body about the transfer effected by them. This notification should be made within the period of one month.

The transfer can, subsequently, be contested in case of a schism in the association in possession of the property or of the creation of a new association as a consequence of a modification in the territory of the ecclesiastical delimitation, or in the case where the association which has received the transfer is no longer capable of fulfilling its object.

9) If there be no association to receive the goods of a public establishment of religious worship, these goods shall be transferred by decree to communal establishments for relief or charity, situated in the territorial limits of the ecclesiastical delimitation concerned.

In case of the dissolution of an association, the goods which shall have been assigned to it in virtue of arts. 4 and 8 shall be transferred, by a decree made in the council of state, either to similar associations in the same district or neighborhood or, if such do not exist, in the nearby district, or to the establishments mentioned in par. 1 of the present article.

All proceedings for restoration or recovery of possession should be commenced within a period of six months dating from the day when the decree shall have been published in the *Journal Officiel*. The proceedings may only be instituted in the case of gifts or bequests and only by the donors and their heirs in the direct line.

10) The allocations of property en-

visaged in the preceding articles shall not permit of any appropriation for the profit of the treasury.

11) The ministers of religion who, after the promulgation of the present law, shall be more than sixty years of age and who shall have, during at least thirty years, carried out ecclesiastical duties remunerated by the state, shall receive an annual pension and allowance equivalent to three-quarters of their salary.

Those who shall be more than forty-five years of age and who shall have, during at least twenty years, carried out ecclesiastical duties remunerated by the state, shall receive an annual pension and allowance equal to one-half of their salary.

The pensions allowed by the two preceding paragraphs may not exceed 1,500 francs.

In case of the decease of the holders, these pensions shall be payable to the value of half of their amount to the benefit of the widow and orphans, who are minors, left by the deceased, and to the value of one-quarter to the benefit of his widow without children who are minors. When the orphans attain their majority, the pension shall completely cease.

The ministers of religious bodies at present paid by the state, who shall not be included in the above provisions, shall receive, during four years beginning from the abolition of the budget for religious bodies, an allowance equal to the whole of their salary for the first year, to two-thirds of it for the second, to half for the third and to a third for the fourth.

In communes of less than 1,000 inhabitants and for ministers of religious bodies who shall continue to carry out their duties there, the duration of each of the four periods indicated above shall be doubled.

Départements and communes shall be able, under the same conditions as the state, to grant to ministers of religious bodies at present paid by them, pensions or allowances awarded on the same basis and for an equal period of time.

Exception is made of rights acquired in the matter of pensions by application of previous legislation, as well as of assistance granted to former ministers of different religious bodies or to their families.

The pensions mentioned in the two first paragraphs of the present article cannot be held simultaneously with any other pension or any other allowance awarded, for whatever reason, by the state, the *départements* or the communes.

The law of 27 June 1885, regarding the personnel of the suppressed faculties of Catholic theology, is applicable to the professors in charge of courses, lecturers and students of faculties of Protestant theology.

The pensions and allowances mentioned above shall be forfeited, paid, or not paid, in the same conditions as civil pensions. They shall cease fully in case of condemnation for one of the offences mentioned in arts. 34 and 35 of the present law.

The right to obtain or to enjoy a pension or allowance shall be suspended by circumstances leading to the loss of French citizenship; such suspension will last as long as the lack of citizenship persists.

Claims for a pension should, under penalty of disallowance, be submitted within the period of one year from the promulgation of the present law.

III, 12) Buildings which have been placed at the disposal of the nation and which, by virtue of the law of Germinal 18 of the year X, are used for the public worship of religious bodies or for the accommodation of their ministers (cathedrals, churches, chapels, temples, synagogues, archiepiscopal and episcopal residences, presbyteries and seminaries), as well as the immovable and movable property annexed thereto which was attached to them at the time when the said buildings were handed over to the religious bodies, are and remain properties of the state, the *départments* and the communes.

With regard to these buildings, as also with regard to those erected subsequently to the law Germinal 18 of the year X, of which the state, the *départements* and the communes shall be proprietors, including the faculties of Protestant theology, proceedings shall be taken in accordance with the provisions of the following articles.

13) Buildings used for the public worship of a religious body, as well as the movable objects attached to them, shall be left gratis at the disposal of the public establishments of the religious body, and afterwards of the associations called into being to replace them, to which the goods of these establishments shall have been assigned by application of the arrangements of section II.

The cessation of this privilege and, if necessary, its transfer, shall be pronounced by decree, provision being made for appeal to the council of state by litigation:

1. if the beneficiary association is dissolved;

2. if, apart from the case of *force majeure*, the public worship of the religious body ceases to be celebrated during more than six consecutive months;

3. if the preservation of the buildings, or that of the movable objects classified by virtue of the law of 1887 and of art. 16 of the present law, is compromised by insufficiency of attention, after warning duly notified by the municipal council or, failing it, the Prefect;

4. if the association ceases to fulfill its purpose or if the buildings are diverted from their rightful purpose;

5. if it does not satisfy the requirements of art. 6 or of the last paragraph of the present article, or the provisions relative to historical monuments.

Decisions concerning deprivation of these immovable goods can be pronounced, in the cases mentioned above, by decree made by the council of state. Apart from these cases, it cannot be pronounced, except by a law.

The immovable property sometimes attached to religious bodies, in which the ceremonies of the religious body have not been celebrated during the period of one year previously to the present law, as well as those which shall not be claimed by a religious association within the period of two years after the present law's promulgation, can be confiscated by decree.

The same applies to buildings whose confiscation shall have been requested before 1 June 1905.

The public establishments of the religious body, and afterwards the beneficiary associations, shall be responsible for repairs of any kind, as well as for costs of insurance and other charges relating to the buildings and the movable goods they contain.

14) Archiepiscopal and episcopal residences, presbyteries and their annexes, grand seminaries and faculties of Protestant theology, shall be left freely at the disposal of the public establishments of the religious body and afterwards of the associations mentioned in art. 13, according to the following arrangement: archiepiscopal and episcopal residences during a period of two years; presbyteries in communes where the minister of the religious body shall reside, grand seminaries and faculties of Protestant theology during five years, starting from the promulgation of the present law.

The establishments and associations

are subject, in matters pertaining to their buildings, to the obligations mentioned in the last paragraph of art. 13. However, they shall not be responsible for large works of repairing.

The cessation of occupancy of establishments and associations shall be pronounced in the conditions and modes determined by art. 13. The provisions of the third and fifth paragraphs of the same article are applicable to buildings mentioned in par. 1 of the present article.

The detachment of unnecessary portions of presbyteries left to the disposal of religious associations can, during the period mentioned in par. 1, be pronounced in favor of a public utility service by decree made in the Council of State.

On the expiring of periods of occupancy free of charge, the free disposal of buildings shall pass to the state, the *départements* or the communes, failing a presbytery, by application of art. 136 of the law of 5 April 1884, shall remain chargeable to them during the period of five years. These shall cease fully in the event of dissolution of the association.

15) In the *départements* of Savoy, Upper Savoy and the Maritime Alps, the occupancy of buildings erected previously to the law of Germinal 18 of the year X, for use in the public worship of religious bodies or for the accommodation of their ministers, shall be allocated by the communes of the territory in which the buildings exist, to religious associations, in the conditions indicated by art. 12 and the following articles of the present law. Apart from this obligation, the communes shall be able to dispose freely of the property of buildings.

In these same *départements,* the cemeteries shall remain the property of the communes.

16) A detailed catalogue shall be made of buildings used for the public worship of a religious body (cathedrals, churches, chapels, temples, synagogues, archiepiscopal and episcopal residences, presbyteries, seminaries), in which catalogue should be included everything in these buildings, which possesses, in whole or in part, an artistic or historical value.

Objects, movable or immovable in purpose, mentioned in art. 13, which shall not have been placed on the list of the catalogue drawn up according to the law of 30 March 1887, are as a result of the present law added to the said list. The ministry of public instruction and of fine arts shall proceed, within the period of three years, to the definite cataloguing of those of such objects whose preservation shall appear to be of sufficient importance, from the point of view of history or of art. At the expiration of this period, the other objects shall be removed finally from the catalogue *ex officio.*

In other cases, immovable and movable objects, allocated by virtue of the present law to associations, can be classified in the same conditions as if they belonged to public establishments.

There is no change otherwise in the arrangements of the law of 30 March 1887.

Ecclesiastical archives and libraries situated in archiepiscopal and episcopal residences, grand seminaries, parish churches, chapels of ease and their attached buildings shall be catalogued, and those which shall be recognized to be State property shall be restored to the State.

17) Goods immovable in their purpose and catalogued by virtue of the law of 30 March 1887, or of the present law, are inalienable and imprescriptable.

In the event where the sale or exchange of a catalogued object should be authorized by the ministry of public instruction and of fine arts, a right of pre-emption is granted (1) to religious associations; (2) to communes; (3) to *départements;* (4) to museums and societies of art and archaeology; (5) to the state. The price shall be decided by three experts to be designated by the seller, the buyer and the president of the civil tribunal.

If none of the buyers mentioned above makes use of the right of preemption, the sale shall be free; but the purchaser of a catalogued object is forbidden to take it out of France.

No work of repair, restoration, or upkeep, to be done to catalogued monuments or movable objects can be commenced without the authorization of the minister of fine arts, nor carried out except under the supervision of his officials, under penalty against the proprietors, occupants or tenants who shall have ordered these works, of a fine of 1,000-1,500 francs.

Every infringement of the above arrangements, as well as of those of art. 16 of the present law and of arts. 4, 10, 11, 12 and 13 of the law of 30 March 1887, shall be punished with a fine of 100-10,000 francs and by an imprisonment from six days to three months, or by one of these penalties only.

Entrance to buildings and the exhibition of movable objects catalogued shall be free for the public without any liability to fiscal charges.

18) Associations formed to attend to expenses and upkeep of public worship of a religious body must be constituted in conformity with arts. 5 and the following of section I of the law of 1 July 1901. They shall, in addition, be subject to the requirements of the present law.

19) The associations shall have as their exclusive object the worship of a religious body and shall be composed of at least:

In communes of less than 1,000 inhabitants—7 persons;

In communes of 1,000-20,000 inhabitants —15 persons;

In communes where the number of inhabitants is more than 20,000—25 persons, who are adult and domiciled or residing in the religious district in question.

Each of their members shall be free to withdraw at any time, after the payment of past rates and of those of the current year, notwithstanding any contrary clause.

Notwithstanding any contrary clause of the statutes, the acts of financial transactions and legal administration of goods carried out by the directors or administrators shall be presented at least every year to the scrutiny of the general assembly of members of the association and submitted to its approbation.

The associations can receive, in addition to the assessed amounts mentioned in art. 6 of the law of 1 July 1901, the proceeds of collections and contributions for expenses of religious worship; the fees for religious ceremonies and services, even by endowment; those for occupation of benches and chairs; and for the supplying of objects destined for use at funerals in religious buildings and for the decoration of these buildings.

They shall be free to transfer the surplus of their assets, free of tax to other associations constituted for the same purpose.

They shall not receive subsidies, in any form whatever from the state, the *départements* or communes. Sums allocated for repairs to catalogued monuments are not considered as subsidies.

20) These associations can, in the forms laid down by art. 7 of the decree of 16 August 1901, establish unions having a central administration or direction; these unions shall be regulated by art. 18 and by the five last paragraphs of art. 19 of the present law.

21) Associations and unions shall

keep a record of their receipts and expenses; they shall present each year the financial statement for the past year and the recorded inventory of their goods, movable and immovable.

Financial control is exercised over the associations and unions by the *administration de l'enregistrement* [i.e., a public service in France for registering private legal documents; as fees are collected for this registering, the service is a part of the financial administration] and the *inspection générale des finances* [a section of the ministry of finance].

22) Associations and unions can use their disposable resources to set up a reserve fund sufficient to provide for the costs and upkeep of the religious body and not being allowed in any event to be directed to another purpose; the amount of this reserve shall never be allowed to exceed a sum equal to three times the annual average (in the case of unions and associations having a revenue of more than 5,000 francs) and six times the annual average (in the case of other associations) of sums spent by each of them for the expenses of the religious body during the five last financial years.

Independently of this reserve, which must be placed in registered investments, they shall be able to establish a special reserve, the funds of which should be deposited, in cash or in registered securities in deposit banks and in investments to be devoted exclusively, together with the interests thereof, to the purchase, building, decoration or repair of immovable or movable property destined for the needs of the association or union.

23) The directors or administrators of an association or union which shall have contravened arts. 18, 19, 20, 21 and 22 shall be punished by a fine of 16-200 francs and, in the event of repetition, by a double fine.

The tribunals can, in the event of infringement of paragraph 1 of art. 22, condemn the association or union to transfer excess of the sum to communal establishments of assistance or of charity.

They can, furthermore, in all cases mentioned in paragraph 1 of the present article, pronounce the dissolution of the association or of the union.

24) The buildings which are intended for the worship of the religious body and which belong to the state, the *départements* or the communes shall continue to be exempt from ground rent and from the tax on doors and windows.

Buildings serving as the living quarters of ministers of religious bodies, as seminaries or as faculties of Protestant theology which belong to the state, the *départements* or the communes, and goods which are the property of associations and unions, are subject to the same taxes as those of individual persons.

Associations and unions are in no case subject to the subscription tax or to that imposed on clubs by art. 33 of the law of 8 August 1890, or to the tax of 4 per cent of the revenue, enacted by the laws of 28 December 1880 and of 29 December 1884.

V, 25) Meetings for the celebration of public worship held in the property belonging to, or put at the disposal of, a religious association are public. They are dispensed from the formalities of art. 8 of the law of 30 June 1881, but remain placed under the supervision of the authorities in the interest of public order. They cannot take place except after a declaration made in the forms of art. 2 of the same law and indicating the place in which they will be held.

A single declaration is sufficient for the total number of permanent meetings, periodical or occasional, which shall take place during the year.

26) It is forbidden to hold political

meetings in the places regularly used for the public worship of a religious body.

27) The ceremonies, processions and other external demonstrations of a religious body shall continue to be regulated in conformity with arts. 95 and 97 of the law of 5 April 1884, relating to municipalities.

The ringing of bells shall be regulated by municipal order and, in event of disagreement between the mayor and president or director of the religious association, by prefectorial /decree. The ordinance of the public administration provided for by art. 43 of the present law shall determine the conditions and cases in which bellringings for civil purposes shall take place.

28) It is forbidden in future to raise or place any religious sign or emblem on public edifices or in any public place whatsoever, with the exception of buildings used by a religious body, burial-grounds in cemeteries, funeral monuments and museums or exhibitions.

29) Contraventions of the preceding articles are punished by the ordinary legal penalties.

There are liable to these penalties, in the cases of arts. 25, 26 and 27, those who have organized the meeting or demonstration, those who have participated in it in the capacity of ministers of the religious body, and in the case of arts. 25 and 26, those who have provided the meeting place.

30) In conformity with the provisions of art. 2 of the law of 28 March 1882, religious instruction cannot be given to children between the ages of six and thirteen years, enrolled in the public schools, except outside school hours.

The stipulations of art. 14 of the present law shall be applied to ministers of religion who infringe these provisions.

31) Those who, whether by force, acts of violence or threats against an individual, by causing him to fear the loss of his employment or by exposing to injury his person, family or fortune, shall have coerced him into practicing a form of religion, becoming a member or ceasing to be a member of a religious association, to contribute or to refrain from contributing to the expenses of a religious body, are to be punished by a fine of from sixteen to 200 francs and by an imprisonment of from six days to two months, or by one of these two penalties only.

32) Those who shall have hindered, delayed or interrupted the public worship of a religious body by disturbances or disorder caused in the place used for this public worship, shall be punished with the same penalties.

33) The arrangements of the two preceding articles are not applicable except to disturbances, outrages or acts of force, the nature or circumstances of which shall not demand more severe penalties according to the provisions of the penal code.

34) Every minister of a religious body who, in the places where this religious body worships, shall have by spoken discourse, readings, writings distributed or notices exposed, publicly vilified or defamed a citizen entrusted with a public office, shall be punished with a fine of 500-3000 francs and by an imprisonment of one month–one year, or by one of these two penalties only.

The truth of the defamatory act, but only if it is relevant to the functions of the individual concerned, will have to be proved before the police court in the manner prescribed by art. 52 of the law of 29 July 1881. The requirements laid down by art. 65 of the same law, apply to offences against the present article and the article which follows it.

35) If a sermon delivered or a writ-

ing exposed or distributed publicly in places where a religious body worships contains a direct incitement to resist the execution of the laws or the legal acts of public authority, or if it tries to raise or arm one faction among the citizens against the others, the minister of the religious body who shall have been found guilty shall be punished by an imprisonment of three months–two years, without prejudice to the penalties for complicity in the case where the incitement shall have been followed by a sedition, revolt or civil war.

36) In the event of condemnation by the ordinary tribunals or police courts in pursuance of arts. 25, 26, 34 and 35, the association formed for the worship of the religious body in the immovable property where the infringement has been committed shall be legally responsible.

VI, 37) Art. 463 of the penal code and the law of 26 March 1891, are applicable to all cases in which the present law decrees penalties.

38) Religious congregations remain subject to the laws of 1 July 1901, 4 December 1902 and 7 July 1904.

39) Boys who have obtained, on the ground of being ecclesiastical pupils, the exemption mentioned in art. 23 of the law of 15 July 1889, shall continue to do so according to art. 99 of the law of 21 March 1905, on condition that at the age of twenty-six they shall be provided with employment as ministers of a religious body, financed by a religious association and with reservation of requirements which shall be fixed by the ordinances of the public administration.

40) During eight years, beginning from the promulgation of the present law, the ministers of a religious body shall be ineligible for the municipal council in the communes where they shall exercise their ecclesiastical ministry.

41) The sums made available each year by the suppression of the budget for religious bodies shall be divided among the communes in proportion to the share of the land tax on unbuilt property which has been assigned to them during the financial year which shall precede the promulgation of the present law.

42) The legal arrangements relating to present holidays are preserved.

43) An ordinance of the public administration made within three months following the promulgation of the present law shall determine the measures necessary to ensure its application.

Ordinances of the public administration shall determine the conditions in which the present law shall be applicable to Algeria and the colonies.

44) All arrangements relative to the public organization of religious bodies previously recognized by the State, as well as all arrangements contrary to the present law, are and remain abrogated, particularly:

(1) The law of Germinal 18 of the year X, enacting that the convention concluded on the Messidor 26 of the year IX between the pope and the French government together with the organic articles of the said convention and those covering the Protestant religious bodies, should be put into effect as laws of the republic; (2) The decree of 26 March 1852, and the law of 1 August 1897, on Protestant religious bodies; (3) The decrees of 17 March 1808, the law of 8 February 1831, and the ordinance of 25 March 1844, on Judaism; (4) The decrees of 22 December 1812, and 19 March 1859; (5) Articles 201-208, 260-264 and 294 of the penal code; (6) Articles 100 and 101, paragraphs 11 and 12 of art. 136, and art. 167 of the law of 5 April 1884; (7) The decree of 30 December 1809, and art. 78 of the law of 26 January 1892.

9. *Peter Paul Cahensly: Petition to President Ulysses S. Grant for International Legislation on Immigration, January 1873*

From Colman J. Barry, O.S.B., *The Catholic Church and German Americans* (Milwaukee: The Bruce Publishing Company, 1953), pp. 278-285.

THE physical and moral condition of the European emigrant has been for many decades a very sad one. The poorer classes especially, forced by reason of their limited means to travel in the lower deck, are, upon embarking and during the voyages as well as at their debarkation in the new world, exposed to a very deplorable lot. The shipping agents, the owners of the European seaports, the persons who deal with the emigrants at the landing-places, are almost all, without exception, bent upon procuring advantages for themselves, upon enriching themselves at the expense of the emigrant.

The legislation of the various European countries, moreover, is chiefly to the material advantage of the owners, etc., in the seaports. The laws have been adapted to the ships and their cargo rather than to the well-being of the emigrant. There have arisen, accordingly, for the emigrant, physical and moral conditions that are indescribably evil.

New laws, it is true, have recently been enacted in France and Germany, most especially in England, which contribute very much toward removing the most vexing inconveniences. Despite this, however, almost everything still depends on the good will and caprice of the owners and captains of the ships, so that the emigrant's lot is still one worthy of the utmost compassion. Yet, let it be said here, the international legislation we have in mind will effect no essential improvement unless the government of the United States intercedes resolutely for the well-being of the emigrant.

It is, of course, quite natural that the European governments, even with the best intentions, would be unfavorable to emigrants. Through emigration many thousands of laborers will be taken away from the countries of Europe and much capital lost to them. It is, therefore, not inconceivable that the European nations should take advantage of the fact that many of these, upon considering the great hardships of the voyage, etc., are deterred from emigrating.

As to the United States of America the situation is different. The greatest advantages of emigration are hers; she ought, then, to have the greatest interest in good legislation that will take into consideration the welfare of the emigrant. The United States can intercede in an effective and successful way. A strict law coupled with careful execution will remedy most of the inconveniences. The European shipowners must and will adapt themselves. They will arrange their ships and conduct the same according to American laws, if only for their own material advantage. Nor is it to be feared that such a stringent law geared to the welfare of the emigrant would in any way hinder emigration to the United States. Your message to Congress last year on May 14, Mr. President, puts such legislation in proximate view and has, accordingly, filled all true friends of mankind with great joy. It clearly shows that the Union which courageously broke the chains of slavery from many millions is also determined to enter the lists for the welfare of the emigrants who will be its future citizens. The undersigned committee for the protection of the German emigrant thanks you, Mr. President, most warmly for the message and for the assurances made therein. At the same time, the committee presumes to present to you some suggestions for proposed legislation, confident not only that they are worthy of your attention, but also that they will be accepted with benevolence.

I. CARE FOR THE WELFARE OF THE EMIGRANT IN GENERAL

The legislation should first of all bring about that sufficient room be assured to each emigrant, not only in the cabins, but in the lower decks as well. There are, of course, legal prescriptions in favor of this in the various countries. And yet, on this side of the ocean as well as on the other, complaints about overcrowding continually come in. During the year that has just expired, one of the New York newspapers censured the serious overcrowding of steamships as emigration increases. Universally accepted definitions in the legislation should, therefore, establish that the highest permissible number of passengers for each emigration ship be fixed by appointed officials; also the maximum number for each compartment in the lower deck. This should, as in the railroad cars, be declared in large ciphers over the entrance to each compartment, e. g., *Compartment for Ladies and Girls—150 Persons*. For each passenger exceeding this maximum number, the captain should be fined a definite sum. Obviously, overcrowding destroys the physical and moral well-being of the emigrant.

II. CARE FOR THE PHYSICAL WELFARE OF THE EMIGRANT

Special laws must be laid down for the physical health of the emigrant.

1) Persons afflicted with contagious diseases should not be permitted to make the voyage. Every emigrant must, therefore, be provided with a medical certificate or present himself before boarding the ship to a doctor in the particular seaport appointed for examination of emigrants. The examinations of women by the doctor should take place only in the presence of persons of their sex.

2) Provisions are necessary and ought not to be perfunctorily controlled by the officials appointed for this purpose. Quality should be considered as well as quantity. Drinking water must especially be pure and wholesome. To facilitate this control before the voyage the owners must be obliged to submit to the authorities a list of provisions signed by them, the accuracy of which is to be attested to only after investigation by inspectors.

3) It is important for health that the lower deck be kept clean. The captain must see to it that it is frequently cleaned and carefully ventilated. At least once a day he himself should visit the lower deck, and, of course, not only as has been customary to date when the lower deck has just been cleaned and most all of the passengers are staying on the upper deck.

4) Ships which carry a large number of emigrants, e. g., over four hundred on board, ought always to be attended by a capable doctor, who should present his report to the proper authorities at the landing dock. It is a deplorable fact that ships carrying eight hundred to one thousand emigrants, on the ocean where sickness so easily strikes, frequently carry no more medical assistance than an incomplete drug dispensary, from which according to the persuasions of thoroughly ignorant persons things are taken or handed out.

5) For every one hundred lower-deck passengers a hospital with four beds should be prepared.

III. CARE FOR THE MORAL WELFARE OF THE EMIGRANT

The most important matter in this international legislation is the maintenance of morality and decency among the emigrants. With regard to this, present arrangements are everywhere very bad. The owners and captains of emigrant ships, of course, flatly deny that numerous outrages against morality occur. They appeal to the fact that Germans are very infrequently led before American courts for this complaint. But this proves absolutely nothing as far as the moral behavior of the emigrants is concerned, since:

1) Emigrants lack, for the most part, the means to pay the expenses for a lawsuit in American seaports. They cannot delay there a long time, but must hurry on to their destinations.

2) Further, a spirit of sacrifice is most often wanting. Complaint will not undo what has already happened, so that nothing useful is accomplished for oneself. The advantage would chiefly accrue to later emigrants, and who among the lower-deck passengers wants to give up time and money for that?

3) Many emigrants do not want to bother about morality. They like the immoral excesses and desire unbridled freedom for that purpose.

4) Finally, the German emigrant, unlike the ones who come from Great Britain, is thoroughly unfamiliar with the sea, the arrangement of a ship and its voyage. It does not occur to him, therefore, to bring complaints before authorities whose language he does not understand.

In short, the excuse of the owners and captains that complaints are seldom brought forward by Germans in America concerning immoral attacks on the sea is a purely negative argument that actually proves nothing.

In point of fact, the outlook on emigrant ships, despite the new laws that have been issued in the seaports in France, etc., is very sad. It would be impossible for an ethical pen to describe all that goes on. We shall refer to one thing only, verifying it with witnesses.

There is absolutely no separation of the sexes in the lower deck. Frequently, the lower deck is nothing other than a single large room in which men and women, young people of both sexes, lie promiscuously near each other. Even when there is a special compartment for married and for single women in the lower deck, even then the separation of the sexes is not at all assured. Men and boys are to be found in the women's compartment and vice versa. Not infrequently are men and unmarried women to be found in the same bed, and in the sight of all. Quite naturally, things that are the shame of our century of culture take place there every day. Some eyewitnesses can attest to this:

On the steamer *Deutschland* Reverend Father Albrinck, of Reading (Archdiocese of Cincinnati), journeyed from Bremen to New York. He writes on March 12, 1868, after his arrival in America: "The sexes were not separated. Old and young, married and single, boys and girls—all lay about in disorder."

Gottloeb Koehl, following his voyage from Le Havre to New York, writes on March 24, 1868, about the steamer *Cordova:* "Very close to me were groups of wicked men who reveled in the most atrocious unchastity."

Concerning the *Germania,* passengers gave similar reports to the Swiss consul in Le Havre when the ship was forced to return there because of damage.

How very much immorality there is to be found on ships leaving Antwerp can be learned from the reports made before the Swiss consul in Le Havre by those few passengers who were rescued from the emigrant ship *Nelson* which burned on the open sea.

Clement Gross (with residence at 552 S. 3rd Avenue in Philadelphia) sailed on May 25, 1878, on the *Main,* Bremen steamer, from New York to Bremen. After his arrival in Germany he presented to the authorities a certified statement wherein he points out, that during the entire journey married and single persons of both sexes were placed without distinction beside and among each other and that the whole lower deck was one large room without compartments.

On the Hamburg steamer *Saxonia* an author, Mr. Kist, journeyed in August 1868, to New York. In his book, *Amerkanisches* (Mainz, Kirchheim, 1871), he relates on pages 102-111 that there was no separation of the sexes in the lower deck, but that all were placed in disorder among each other without distinction. The most horrible obscenities resulted. And yet, a separation could very easily have been arranged, since an iron wall with iron doors separated the room of the lower deck.

Mr. Cahensly, a merchant from Limburg on the Lahn and a member of the undersigned committee, found, in June, 1872, in Bremerhaven on the steamer *Deutschland,* no trace of separation of the sexes in the lower deck. Alongside unmarried young men lay single women and families as well. Women had to climb without ladders to the upper deck, under or opposite which men had their beds. Often young people of both sexes lay in the same bed. The same was true of the room set apart by boards and over which the title read, *For women traveling alone.* This scandal was not considered at all.

The same gentleman found something similar in Hamburg on the steamer *Cimbria* in June, 1872. Here, too, separation of the sexes was not enforced. Everyone was placed anywhere, young

girls had their beds placed beside young men.

Together with the witnesses we have just brought forward, to which we could add many more, numerous brochures prove us right—particularly that work which appeared under the Protectorate of the Austrian government, *Voyage of the Austrian Frigate "Novara" Around the World.* In the second volume of the popular edition, page 247 ff., it tells of the dreadful inconveniences that prevailed on emigrant ships bound for Australia. On page 250, we read: "There was not the slightest precaution taken toward separating the sexes. Male and female, old and young, single as well as married, all lived and slept together in the same room."

It is, therefore, well established that until recently very little was done on emigrant ships for the preservation of decency. That the most scandalous indecencies took place is an established fact. Only a stringent law, which leaves nothing to the discretion of the captain or shipowner, can put an end to this disgrace of our century.

The following points should be kept in mind:

1) In the lodging houses in which emigrants are sheltered often for two or three days before the voyage, a strict control should be introduced with respect to the separation of the sexes in the dormitories. Concessions should be taken away from housekeepers who formerly housed men, women, and unmarried persons of both sexes in the same dormitories.

2) On the emigrant ships, on steamers and frigates (these really ought to be forbidden to transport emigrants) *separation of the sexes* must be *enforced* with inexorable strictness. Every emigrant ship—at least those to be constructed—ought to have *three* compartments in the lower deck separated from each other by solid walls and

closed doors. Each of these compartments should have its own stairway to the upper deck.

a) *The men's compartment* should be in the prow, for men traveling alone and for unmarried persons of the male sex over fourteen years of age.

b) *The women's compartment* should be in the stern for women traveling alone and for all unmarried persons of the female sex over twelve years of age.

c) The compartment for families should be in the middle part of the ship for husbands and wives (who travel together or with their children) for their sons under fourteen years as well as for their daughters under twelve. Those children who have advanced beyond these ages should have their beds in one of the other two compartments.

No lower-deck passenger should be permitted to have his bed in any compartment other than the one to which he belongs. Only during the day and on the deck should free communication be allowed. This strict separation of the sexes among the many uneducated, even coarse and downright immoral lower-deck passengers, can only be maintained when no exceptions whatever are granted and nothing is left to the caprice of the ship's officers. The law must define the hour in the evening after which no one may tarry in any compartment other than his own. On English ships separation of the sexes is enforced by a law of August 14, 1855, Article XXII. As far as this committee knows it is strictly carried out.

This definition of the law must be expressly stated in contracts and handed by the agents to every emigrant at the conclusion of the contract. He should also remind them of it.

3) The ship's personnel should be forbidden under penalty to enter the women's compartment unless the services are necessary. The abduction of any women by an officer or sailor for unchaste actions should be punished with a severe fine or imprisonment.

4) The ship's captain should be responsible for the proper lighting of the lower deck.

5) The sale of books on the ships should be forbidden, since only immoral literature is sold, a fact established by this committee during the year just passed. Immoral books in the ship's library should be strictly forbidden.

IV. NECESSARY REGULATIONS FOR THE CARRYING OUT OF THE LAWS IN QUESTION

All these and similar legal definitions will only attain their beneficent effects when their exact execution is observed. To this end, the following regulations are desirable:

1) When a contract is arranged which takes place for the most part in the homeland, strict separation of the sexes must be kept in view. Every contract must keep persons of the same category in the same compartment of the lower deck. Accordingly, for the men's compartment, men traveling by themselves and boys over fourteen; for the women's compartment, women traveling alone and girls over twelve years; finally, for the family compartment, men traveling with their wives or men and their wives with children under fourteen years. If the contracts are issued according to these three categories, it will be easy to draw up lists of the ports of embarkation and to assign each one to his compartment upon boarding ship.

2) Before the ship goes to sea, special officials—in default of others, those who are to revise the provisions —must assure themselves that proper separation of the sexes in the three compartments of the lower deck has been taken care of. The officials must accept no fights from the owners.

3) During the voyage, the govern-

ment of the United States should have two American officials accompany every emigration boat bound for America, that is, a man for the men's compartment and an excellent woman for the woman's compartment. These should write down in a journal everything that takes place contrary to good morals or whatever is damaging to health. The first Austrian Union for the Protection of Emigrant also, and rightly, requests this in its address of August, 1872. Immigration is, after all, a national affair for the Union.

4) At the place of landing and before debarking, North American officials should board the ship and ascertain whether the passengers or persons of the ship's crew have any crimes against the emigration laws to report. Offenders should immediately be led before an international court set up for this purpose in all seaports.

5) The owners and captains of the ships are responsible for keeping order in all moral and sanitary respects. Should separation of the sexes not be observed or coarse immoralities go unchecked, or health be impaired, through fault of the captain, then the captain's right to conduct an emigration ship should be taken from him.

These, Mr. President are the suggestions which we, out of love for the well-being of the countless thousands of men who every year leave Europe to seek a better home in America, desire to submit for your kind consideration. May your Excellency cause these same to be considered in the drawing up of international legislation for emigration. It is surely of the greatest importance to the United States to put an end to the shameless outrages to which many, many thousands fall prey every year. Because immigration every year leads a tremendous number of new citizens to the Union, then, manifestly, this immigration is itself a conspicuous element to the future of the great republic what sort of elements settle every year upon its soil.

To be sure, the costs entailed in paying officials in the seaports as also those who are to accompany the emigrant ships, are not insignificant. But these will be more than counterbalanced by the material advantages which emigration will bring to the nation through the introduction of capital and labor power. Yet these costs must not even be considered when we consider the social advantages which these sound and humane institutions will bring to the United States. It is clear that the increase of honest, upright people alone can further the development of the gloriously flourishing and great union of states. On the other hand, an accumulation of morally depraved men can serve only to undermine the foundations of the nation's welfare. The great mass of those who yearly abandon Europe in order to establish a new home in the new world are certainly honest, upright people. How exceedingly useful, therefore, for the Union, nay how necessary to protect them against the wickedness and temptations of unchaste traveling companions or ship's crewmen. Any such protection rendered certain by severe legislation must win in advance the hearts of all good emigrants for the Union and fill the same with love for their new fatherland. Such protection by strict law and solicitude for the observance of these laws will secure for the Union the gratitude of all those who love and cherish true virtue and morality. And while the government of the United States prevents the unspeakable crimes and vicious excesses, of which the sea has thus far been the incessant witness, it will undoubtedly call down upon the republic the blessing of almighty God.

II. *The Voice of the Popes*

IN HER long history the Catholic Church has had to make numerous adjustments to many changing political, social, and intellectual conditions. The revolutions of the nineteenth century, however, coming with such force and rapidity, challenged the experience of the Church in adjusting to a changed society and creating an institutional framework that would enable religious influences to operate in the new order. The problem was accentuated by theories of doctrinaire nineteenth-century liberalism incompatible with sound political and ecclesiastical authority; by glorified aims of secularists who placed man's destiny in worldly affairs; by absolutist doctrines of state supremacy advocated by new nationalists who would soon lead their so-called modern and progressive world into the most destructive wars in human history.

It was impossible for the Church in the nineteenth century to endorse such ideals or to revise her policies to meet these radical aims. During his long pontificate from 1846 to 1878, Pope Pius IX, the first of these popes, found it necessary, despite his early liberal leanings, to speak out against the errors inherent in nineteenth-century liberalism. This he did in a series of masterful definitions which pointed up the philosophical and theological limitations of the new age, and re-affirmed the supremacy of the spiritual. Time has more than justified this decisive action of the Holy See which at the time so deeply affronted both skeptical and scientific secularists. Plus IX, after consulting the bishops of the world, asserted the *ex cathedra* infallibility of the pope by defining the traditional doctrine in 1854 that the Blessed Virgin Mary was miraculously exempted from original sin from the moment of her conception. This definition did not cause the uproar, however, that the publication of the SYLLABUS OF ERRORS (*No. 10*) aroused ten years later. Here eighty propositions, which had previously been commented on by the pope, are listed in index fashion as a reference to the original documents where they are fully discussed. The statements are, accordingly, intended to be taken in context. When the pope calls "progress, liberalism and modern civilization" irreconcilable with the Church, he means, in terms of the original documents, the heritage of the Enlightenment and the errors of liberalism as applied in the nineteenth century through attacks on religion, the Church, clergy, and religious schools. Pope Pius IX was simply, as Bishop Félix Dupanloup succinctly com-

mented, opposing the new secularist civilization and re-affirming unconditionally the traditional Catholic aim of a Christian civilization. The *Syllabus* was, accordingly, neither an outright confirmation of conservative
views nor a rejection of true progress and the good aspects of modern civilization. At the same time the pope spoke out against indifferentism and refused to adjust to a modern culture divorced from the supernatural. The
Church again took her stand against "the sacred word *nature*" as deified by
descendants of the Enlightenment.

If naturalistic liberals felt that the Church had shackled modern culture with the *Syllabus,* the convoking of the Vatican Council and the definition of the personal infallibility of the pope in matters of faith and morals
at this twentieth ecumenical council convinced them that Catholicism was
completely out of tune with the age. There were also voices raised within
the Church against defining papal infallibility both from a doctrinal and
prudential viewpoint. The events and discussions leading up to the council
and during its sessions are among the most fascinating in Church history.
When the large majority voted affirmatively to the FIRST DOGMATIC CON-
STITUTION OF THE CHURCH OF GOD (*No. 11*) in solemn session on 18 July
1870, only ten German professors, however, left the Church in protest and
established the Old Catholic Church. The Vatican definition of papal
powers—plenitude of jurisdiction and infallibility—was the culmination of
a long development based on the primacy of St. Peter. Gallicanism and
Church nationalism were no longer possible. Anti-papal and conciliar
theories, Protestantism, episcopalism, and contemporary unbelief were rejected as incompatible with the authentic tradition of the spiritual sovereignty and infallibility of Peter's successor, the bishop of Rome. The reality of the supernatural Church as the objective continuation of the life of
Christ in the world emerged after the Vatican definition as a challenge to
a new age of faith. It was unfortunate that the forced and abrupt ending of
Vatican Council I prevented the council fathers from continuing their discussion of the constitution of the Church. The role of the bishops, their relation to the pope, and the character of all baptized members of Christ's
Church had, accordingly, to await treatment in II Vatican Council, convoked by Pope John XXIII ninety-two years later.

Pius IX was succeeded in the papal chair in 1878 by one of the great
popes of history, and perhaps, in many ways, the most significant pontiff
of modern times. Pius had declared shortly before his death that his successor would have to alter the direction of papal policy. When Gioacchino
Cardinal Pecci was elected and took the name of Leo XIII (1903), this

frail old man brought new life to the Church with a ready-made program that he had personally developed by study and experience.

Leo XIII's grand program was simple and direct: the Church and modern culture must have a successful confrontation. His was a positive program in the tradition of the Church. An altering of the liberal society would not mean an automatic return to Catholicism as so many conservatives wishfully thought. The Church's first duty was to live in the world. Through its life and principles the Church must help to solve social problems, reconcile faith and science, and create a spirit of co-operation between Church and state. This was, in short, a design whose breadth of vision embraced accommodation to the modern world, without sacrifice of the faith, and farseeing applications of revealed truth to modern problems. As a scholar, diplomat, and patron, Pope Leo XIII determined to create anew a Catholic culture.

Three examples from his voluminous writings indicate the scope of the pope's purpose. Leo XIII had been throughout his life an ardent admirer and independent interpreter of the scholastic teaching of Thomas Aquinas. He felt that the great synthesis of the supernatural and natural perfected by St. Thomas could be fruitfully applied to modern times as the basis for the beginning of a Christian cultural revival. Accordingly, on 4 August 1879 in his ENCYCLICAL "AETERNI PATRIS" ON THE STUDY OF SCHOLASTIC PHILOSOPHY (*No. 12, A*) he restored Thomism to a prime place in Catholic philosophical and theological studies. He desired by this program that Catholic thought should once again come in contact with all reality, and that Thomas' principles should be applied to the times. It was not the pope's purpose that the angelic doctor's writings should be passively studied, or presented as a narrow, doctrinaire scholasticism that merely parroted a thirteenth-century synthesis.

The second progressive move, indicating the pope's complete confidence in the innate force of truth, was the opening of the Vatican Archives to all students, together with an enunciation of the fundamental obligations of an historian in his LETTER ON HISTORICAL STUDIES (*No. 12, B*) of 18 August 1883: not to dare to utter falsehood, not to fear to speak the truth, not to leave a suspicion of partiality or prejudice. The eminent German Protestant historian, Johann Frederick Boehmer, had strikingly requested just such a move as early as 1850 when he wrote: "Would to God that the next pope, who has been predicted as a *lumen de coelo,* would look upon the truth-loving, serious science of history as a 'light from heaven' in the darkness and errors of the want of principle of the present day."

The third example of Leo's thought, which serves as a type of his many writings on political, social, and economic matters, is his ENCYLICAL "IMMORTALE DEI" ON THE CHRISTIAN CONSTITUTION OF THE STATE (*No. 12, C*) of 1 November 1885. The pope wrote this encyclical as a summary of his attempted *rapprochément* with the Third French Republic, one of the chief aims of his pontificate (which did not materialize). The principles which he enumerated survived, however, to change the attitude of Catholics on participation in nineteenth-century political life. Leo emphasizes the positive Christian view on the origin and nature of the state; insists that religion be publicly acknowledged; questions the theories of the secular state and indicates how they will lead to decay of morals and social stability, while encouraging atheism and violent revolution. He states that Catholics can accept less than the ideal and may tolerate religious error for the sake of a greater good or to hinder great evil. He encourages Catholics to take an active part in civic and national affairs in order to improve public and private life, set an example of charity among themselves, and strive to withstand rationalism and naturalism.

The next pope emphasized a spiritual program as the continuation of the Catholic revival begun by Leo XIII. The saintly pastor of souls, Pope Pius X (1914), inaugurated a revival of the inner life of Catholicism, based in the theology of the Mystical Body of Christ, which opened the possibilities of Christians actively participating once again in the living mystery of the life of the Church. St. Pius X wanted Catholics to perceive that the liturgy of the Church is the basic catechesis of doctrine, the wellspring of spiritual vitality, the framework of living for the whole Christian people. The Church that had been centralized anew in the vicar of Christ at the Vatican Council, that had entered the political, social, and intellectual world again under Leo XIII, was now to be re-invigorated in the essentials of Christian life. The possibility of creating a Christian culture in the modern world could only materialize if at the heart of the revival was a rediscovery of spiritual essentials. Indispensable to a Christian culture was a rediscovery of the liturgy, understood and practiced by the entire Christian community as its collective and personal life of prayer and worship in Christ and the Church. Pius X's MOTU PROPRIO ON CHURCH MUSIC (*No. 13, A*) of 22 November 1903, and DECREE ON THE NECESSARY DISPOSITION FOR FREQUENT AND DAILY RECEPTION OF HOLY COMMUNION (*No. 13, B*) of 20 December 1905, explain the aims of the spiritual program. As the pope said:

"Our deepest wish is that the true Christian spirit should once again flourish in every way and establish itself among the faithful; and to that end it is necessary first of all to provide for the sanctity and dignity of the temple where the faithful meet together precisely in order to find that spirit at its primary and indispensible source, that is . . . the active participation in the most holy and sacred mysteries and in the solemn and common prayer of the Church."

In order to prevent corruption of the faith of the clergy and laity, and especially the compromising of philosophy, theology, and spirituality, Pius X spoke out against Modernism in the ENCYCLICAL "PASCENDI DOMINICI GREGIS" CONDEMNING THE DOCTRINES OF MODERNISM (*No. 13, C*) on 8 September 1907. According to this heretical mode of thought, a continuation of the controversy between certain scientific approaches and the ancient doctrine of the Church, the mind is incapable of comprehending the supernatural, and religion is only a subconscious experience. Since all things are in evolutionary flux, dogmas must be subject to change. By the pope's firm action, the small group of Catholic adherents of this "modernist" attitude were prohibited from corroding the spiritual renaissance so dear to the pope's heart.

The advent of World War I hastened the death of the broken-hearted Pius X. His successor, Pope Benedict XV (1922), exerted diplomatic efforts to end the struggle and preserve the neutrality of the Holy See, while practicing notable works of charity to victims of war on both sides of the conflict between national powers. The coming of World War I was a shattering blow to the liberal dreams of the nineteenth century, and yet it was a natural outgrowth of liberal economic doctrines and absolute theories of national state sovereignty. Pope Benedict XV, in the diplomatic tradition of Leo XIII, strove to recommend a truce and the re-establishment of peace, to both sides as his PEACE PROPOSALS OF 1 AUGUST 1917 (*No. 14*) show. The diplomatic efforts of the Holy See went unheard by leaders in both camps. But the pope's proposals attracted much popular attention at the time, and subsequently historians have evaluated them as both a constructive and practical solution that went unheeded. The fact that the pope had suggested them to the warring states was an indication, however, of the growing influence of the Holy See, renewed in modern times—but as a respected spiritual and moral power.

10. *Pope Pius IX: Syllabus of Errors, 8 December 1864*

From *The Dublin Review* LVI (1865), 513-529.

I
Pantheism, Naturalism, and Absolute Rationalism

1) THERE exists no supreme all-wise and most provident being distinct from this universe, and God is the same as the nature of things, and therefore liable to change; and God is really made both in man and in the world, and all things are God and have the self-same substance of God; and God is one and the same thing with the world, and therefore spirit is the same thing with matter, necessity with liberty, truth with falsehood, good with evil, and just with unjust.

2) All action of God on mankind and on the world is to be denied.

3) Human reason, without any regard whatever being had to God, is the one judge of truth and falsehood, of good and evil; it is a law to itself, and suffices by its natural strength for providing the good of men and peoples.

4) All the truths of religion flow from the natural force of human reason; hence reason is the chief rule whereby man can and should obtain the knowledge of all truths of every kind.

5) Divine revelation is imperfect, and therefore subject to a continuous and indefinite progress corresponding to the advance of human reason.

6) The faith of Christ is opposed to human reason; and divine revelation not only nothing profits, but is even injurious to man's perfection.

7) The prophecies and miracles recorded and narrated in Scripture are poetical fictions, and the mysteries of Christian faith a result of philosophical investigations; and in the books of both Testaments are contained mythical inventions; and Jesus Christ himself is a mythical fiction.

II
Moderate Rationalism

8) Since human reason is on a level with religion itself, therefore theological studies are to be handled in the same manner as philosophical.

9) All the dogmas of the Christian religion are without distinction the object of natural science or philosophy; and human reason, with no other than an historical cultivation, is able from its own natural strength and principles to arrive at true knowledge of even the more abstruse dogmas, so only these dogmas have been proposed to the reason itself as its object.

10) Since the philosopher is one thing, philosophy another, the former has the right and duty of submitting himself to that authority which he may have approved as true; but philosophy neither can nor should submit itself to any authority.

11) The Church not only ought never to animadvert on philosophy, but ought to tolerate the errors of philosophy, and leave it in her hands to correct herself.

12) The decrees of the Apostolic See and of Roman congregations interfere with the free progress of science.

13) The method and principles whereby the ancient scholastic doctors cultivated theology, are not suited to the necessities of our time and to the progress of the sciences.

14) Philosophy should be treated without regard to supernatural revelation.

(To the system of rationalism belong mostly the errors of Anthony Günther, which are condemned in the epistle to the cardinal-archbishop of

Cologne: *Eximiam tuam,* 15 June 1857, and in that to the bishop of Breslau, *Dolore haud mediocri,* 30 April 1860.)

III
Indifferentism, Latitudinarianism

15) Every man is free to embrace and profess that religion which, led by the light of reason, he may have thought true.

16) Men may in the practice of any religion whatever find the path of eternal salvation, and attain eternal salvation.

17) At least good hopes should be entertained concerning the salvation of all those who in no respect live in the true Church of Christ.

18) Protestantism is nothing else than a different form of the same Christian religion, in which it is permitted to please God equally as in the true Catholic Church.

IV
Socialism, Communism, Secret Societies, Bible Societies, Clerico-Liberal Societies

Pests of this kind are often reprobated, and in the most severe terms in the encyclical *Qui pluribus,* 9 November 1846; the allocution *Quibus Quantisque,* 20 April 1849; the encyclical *Noscitis et Nobiscum,* 8 December 1849; the allocution *Singulari quadam,* 9 December 1854; the encyclical *Quante conficiamur,* 10 August 1863.

V
Errors Concerning the Church and Her Rights

19) The Church is not a true and perfect society fully free, nor does she enjoy her own proper and permanent rights given to her by her divine Founder, but it is the civil power's business to define what are the Church's rights, and the limits within which she may be enabled to exercise them.

20) The ecclesiastical power should not exercise its authority without permission and assent of the civil government.

21) The Church has not the power of dogmatically defining that the religion of the Catholic Church is the only true religion.

22) The obligation by which Catholic teachers and writers are absolutely bound, is confined to those things alone which are propounded by the Church's infallible judgment, as dogmas of faith to be believed by all.

23) Roman pontiffs and ecumenical councils have exceeded the limits of their power, usurped the rights of princes, and erred even in defining matters of faith and morals.

24) The Church has no power of employing force, nor has she any temporal power direct or indirect.

25) Besides the inherent power of the episcopate, another temporal power has been granted expressly or tacitly by the civil government, which may therefore be abrogated by the civil government at its pleasure.

26) The Church has no native and legitimate right of acquiring and possessing.

27) The Church's sacred ministers and the Roman pontiff should be entirely excluded from all charge and dominion of temporal things.

28) Bishops ought not, without the permission of the government, to publish even apostolic letters.

29) Graces granted by the Roman pontiff should be accounted as void, unless they have been sought through the government.

30) The immunity of the Church and of ecclesiastical persons had its origin from the civil law.

31) The ecclesiastical forum for the temporal causes of clerics, whether civil causes or criminal, should be altogether abolished, even without con-

sulting, and against the protest of, the Apostolic See.

32) Without any violation of natural right and equity, that personal immunity may be abrogated, whereby clerics are exempted from the burden of undertaking and performing military services; and such abrogation is required by civil progress, especially in a society constituted on the model of a free rule.

33) It does not appertain exclusively to ecclesiastical jurisdiction by its own proper and native right to direct the teaching of theology.

34) The doctrine of those who compare the Roman pontiff to a prince, free and acting in the universal Church, is the doctrine which prevailed in the middle age.

35) Nothing forbids that by the judgment of some general council, or by the act of all peoples, the supreme pontificate should be transferred from the Roman bishop and city to another bishop and another state.

36) The definition of a national council admits no further dispute, and the civil administration may fix the matter on this footing.

37) National churches separated and totally disjoined from the Roman pontiff's authority may be instituted.

38) The too arbitrary conduct of Roman pontiffs contributed to the Church's division into East and West.

VI

Errors Concerning Civil Society, Considered Both in Itself and in Its Relations to the Church

39) The state, as being the origin and fountain of all rights, possesses a certain right of its own, circumscribed by no limits.

40) The doctrine of the Catholic Church is opposed to the good and benefit of human society.

41) The civil power, even when exercised by a non-Catholic ruler, has an indirect negative power over things sacred; it has consequently not only the right which they call *exequatur* but that right also which they call *appel comme d'abus*.

42) In the case of a conflict between laws of the two powers, civil law prevails.

43) The lay power has the authority of rescinding, of declaring null, and of voiding solemn conventions [concordats], concerning the exercise of rights appertaining to ecclesiastical immunity, which have been entered into with the Apostolic See—without this See's consent, and even against its protest.

44) The civil authority may mix itself up in matters which appertain to religion, morals, and spiritual rule. Hence it can exercise judgment concerning those instructions which the Church's pastors issue according to their office for the guidance of consciences; nay, it may even decree concerning the administration of the holy sacraments, and concerning the dispositions necessary for their reception.

45) The whole governance of public schools wherein the youth of any Christian state is educated, episcopal seminaries only being in some degree excepted, may and should be given to the civil power; and in such sense be given, that no right be recognized in any other authority of mixing itself up in the management of the schools, the direction of studies, the conferring of degrees, the choice or approbation of teachers.

46) Nay, in the very ecclesiastical seminaries, the method of study to be adopted is subject to the civil authority.

47) The best constitution of civil society requires that popular schools which are open to children of every class, and that public institutions generally which are devoted to teaching literature and science and providing for the education of youth, be exempted from all authority of the

Church, from all her moderating interference, and subjected to the absolute will of the civil and political authority so as to be conducted in accordance with the tenets of civil rulers, and the standard of the common opinions of the age.

48) That method of instructing youth can be approved by Catholic men, which is disjoined from the Catholic faith and the Church's power, and which regards exclusively, or at least principally, knowledge of the natural order alone, and the ends of social life on earth.

49) The civil authority may prevent the bishops and faithful from free and mutual communication with the Roman pontiff.

50) The lay authority has of itself the right of presenting bishops, and may require of them that they enter on the management of their dioceses before they receive from the Holy See canonical institution and apostolical letters.

51) Nay, the lay government has the right of deposing bishops from exercise of their pastoral ministry; nor is it bound to obey the Roman pontiff in those things which regard the establishment of bishoprics and the appointment of bishops.

52) The government may, in its own right, change the age prescribed by the Church for the religious profession of men and women, and they may require religious orders to admit no one to solemn vows without its permission.

53) Those laws should be abrogated which relate to protecting the condition of religious orders and their rights and duties, nay, the civil government may give assistance to all those who may wish to quit the religious life which they have undertaken and to break their solemn vows; and in like manner it may altogether abolish the said religious orders, and also collegiate churches and simple benefices, even those under the right of a patron, and subject and assign their goods and revenues to the administration and free disposal of the civil power.

54) Kings and princes are not only exempted from the Church's jurisdiction, but also are superior to the Church in deciding questions of jurisdiction.

55) The Church should be separated from the state, and the state from the Church.

VII

Errors Concerning Natural and Christian Ethics

56) The laws of morality need no divine sanction, and there is no necessity that human laws be conformed to the law of nature or receive from God their obligatory force.

57) The science of philosophy and morals and also the laws of a state, may and should withdraw themselves from the jurisdiction of divine and ecclesiastical authority. . . .

70) The canons of Trent, which inflict the censure of anathema on those who dare to deny the Church's power of enacting diriment impediments, are either not dogmatical, or are to be understood of this borrowed power.

71) The form ordained by the Council of Trent does not bind on pain of nullity wherever the civil law may prescribe another form, and may will that, by this new form, matrimony shall be made valid.

72) Boniface VIII was the first who asserted that the vow of chastity made at ordination annuls marriage.

73) By virtue of a purely civil contract there may exist among Christians marriage, truly so called; and it is false that either the contract of marriage among Christians is always a sacrament, or that there is no contract if the sacrament be excluded.

74) Matrimonial causes and es-

pousals belong by their own nature to the civil forum.

(To this head may be referred two other errors: on abolishing clerical celibacy, and on preferring the state of marriage to that of virginity. They are condemned, the former in the encyclical *Qui pluribus*, 9 November 1846; the latter in the apostolic letters, *Multiplices inter*, 10 June 1851.)

IX
Errors Concerning the Roman Pontiff's Civil Princedom

75) Children of the Christian and Catholic Church dispute with each other on the compatibility of the temporal rule with the spiritual.

76) The abrogation of that civil power, which the Apostolic See possesses, would conduce in the highest degree to the Church's liberty and felicity.

(Besides these errors explicitly branded, many others are reprobated in the exposition and assertion of that doctrine which all Catholics ought most firmly to hold concerning the Roman pontiff's civil princedom. This doctrine is clearly delivered in the allocution, *Quibus quantisque*, 20 April 1849; in the allocution, *Si semper*

antea, 20 May 1850; in the apostolic letters, *Cum Catholica Ecclesia*, 26 March 1860; in the allocution, *Novos*, 28 September 1861; in the allocution, *Jamdudum*, 18 March 1861; in the allocution, *Maxima quidem*, 9 June 1862.)

X
Errors Which Have Reference to the Liberalism of the Day

77) In this our age it is no longer expedient that the Catholic religion should be treated as the only religion of the state, all other worships whatsoever being excluded.

78) Hence it has been laudably provided by law in some Catholic countries, that men thither immigrating should be permitted the public exercise of their own several worships.

79) For truly it is false that the civil liberty of all worships and the full power granted to all of openly and publicly declaring any opinions or thoughts whatever, conduces to more easily corrupting the morals and minds of peoples and propagating the plague of indifferentism.

80) The Roman pontiff can and ought to reconcile and harmonize himself with progress, with liberalism, and with modern civilization.

11. *Vatican Council I: First Dogmatic Constitution of the Church of God, 18 July 1870*

From the *Dublin Review* LVII (1870), 497-507.

THE eternal shepherd and bishop of our souls, in order to make perpetual the salutary work of redemption, resolved to build up holy Church, that in her, as in the house of the living God, all the faithful might be contained in the bond of one faith and charity. Wherefore, before he was glorified, he asked his Father, not only

for the apostles, but also for those who were to believe in him through their word, that they might all be one as the Son himself and the Father are one.

And even as he sent the apostles, whom he had chosen for himself out of the world, as he himself had been sent by his Father; even so he willed that there should be pastors and doctors in his church until the consummation of the world. But in order that the episcopacy itself should be one and undivided, and that the universal multitude of believers should be preserved in unity of faith and of communion by priests mutually cohering among themselves, he placed blessed Peter above the other apostles, and instituted in him the perpetual principle and visible foundation of this twofold unity, that on his fortitude the eternal temple should be built, and that on the firmness of his faith the sublimity of the church should rise and reach to heaven.

And since the gates of hell, in order to destroy, were that possible, the Church, rise everywhere with daily increasing hate against her divinely established foundation, we, *sacro approbante Concilio,* judge it necessary for the custody, safety, and increase of the Catholic flock, to set forth, according to the ancient and constant belief of the universal Church, the doctrine to be believed and held by all the faithful, concerning the institution, perpetuity, and nature of the sacred apostolic primacy, in which consists the force and solidity of the whole Church, and to proscribe and to condemn contrary errors so pernicious to the Lord's flock.

I

We teach, therefore, and declare, in accordance with the testimony of the Gospel, that the primacy of jurisdiction over the universal Church of God was, by Christ our Lord, immediately and directly promised to, and conferred upon, blessed Peter the apostle. For to Simon alone, to whom He had said: "You shall be called *Cephas,*" after the other had uttered his confession: "You are Christ, Son of the living God," did our Lord say: "Blessed are you, Simon Bar-Jona, because flesh and blood have not revealed it to you,

but my father who is in heaven. And I say to you that you are Peter, and upon this rock I will build my Church, and the gates of hell shall not prevail against it. And I will give to you the keys of the kingdom of heaven, and whatsoever you shall bind upon earth shall be bound also in heaven, and whatsoever you shall loose on earth shall be loosed also in heaven."

And upon Simon Peter only, did Jesus after his resurrection, confer the jurisdiction of chief pastor and ruler over His whole flock, saying: "Feed my lambs. Feed my sheep."

To this so manifest teaching of holy Writ, as it has been always understood by the Catholic Church, are openly opposed the wrongful opinions of those who, perverting the form of government constituted by Christ in his Church, deny that Peter alone, in preference to the other apostles, whether to teach separately or to all collectively, was endowed by Christ with a true and proper primacy of jurisdiction, or who affirm that this primacy was transmitted not immediately and directly to blessed Peter, but to the Church, and through it to him as minister of that Church.

If, then, any shall say that blessed Peter the apostle, was not constituted by Christ our Lord, prince of all the apostles, and visible head of the whole Church militant; or that he received, directly and immediately from our Lord Jesus Christ, a primacy of honor only, and not of true and proper jurisdiction, let him be anathema.

II

That which the prince of pastors, and the great pastor of the sheep, our Lord Jesus Christ, established in the person of blessed Peter, the apostle, for the perpetual safety and perennial good of the Church, must of necessity, by his agony, constantly continue in the Church, which, being founded on the rock, will stand firm until the end of time. It is doubtful to none, it is notorious in every age, that the holy and blessed Peter, prince and chief of the apostles, the pillar of the faith, and the foundation of the Catholic Church, who received the keys of the kingdom from our Lord Jesus Christ, the savior and redeemer of the human race, lives, presides, and judges till now, and always in his successors, the bishops of the holy Roman See, which was founded by him, and consecrated by his blood.

Hence, whoever succeeds to Peter in this chair, he, by the institution of Christ himself, obtains the primacy of Peter over the universal Church. There endures, therefore, still the institution of the truth, and blessed Peter persevering in the strength of the rock imparted to him, has not abandoned the government of the Church undertaken by him. For this reason it was always necessary that every Church, that is to say, the faithful everywhere, should be in union with the Roman Church on account of its more excellent principality, in order that in this See, whence the rights of venerable communion are diffused to all, they may coalesce in one frame of body, like limbs whose fellowship is in the head.

If any, therefore, shall say that it is not of the institution of Christ our Lord, himself, or of divine right, that blessed Peter has perpetual successors in the primacy over the universal Church; or that the Roman pontiff is not the successor of blessed Peter in that primacy, let him be anathema.

III

Wherefore, relying on the clear testimony of holy Writ, and adhering to the formal and clear decrees both of our predecessors, the Roman pontiffs, and of general councils, we renew the definition of the ecumenical council of Florence, by which all the faithful of Christ are bound to believe that the holy apostolic See and the Roman pontiff have the primacy over the whole world; and that the Roman pontiff is the successor of blessed Peter the apostle, and the true vicar of Christ, and the head of the whole Church, and the father and teacher of all Christians; and that to him, in blessed Peter, full power was given by our Lord Jesus Christ to feed, rule, and govern the universal Church, as is contained also in the acts of ecumenical councils, and in the sacred canons.

Next, we teach and declare that the Roman Church, by the design of God, has the supremacy of ordinary power over all others, and that this power of jurisdiction of the Roman pontiff, which is truly episcopal, is immediate; and that pastors and faithful of every rite and rank, whether singly and separately, or collectively, are bound to it by the duty of hierarchical subordination and true obedience, not only in things which pertain to faith and morals, but also in things which pertain to the discipline and rule of the Church spread over the whole world, so that by preserving unity of communion, and of the profession of the same faith with the Roman pontiff, the Church of Christ is one flock under one chief pastor. This is the teaching of Catholic truth, from which no one can deviate without injury to faith and to salvation.

But that ordinary and immediate power of episcopal jurisdiction, with which the bishops, who placed by the Holy Ghost have succeeded the apostles, rule and govern like true pastors each the particular flock assigned to them, is so far from being hindered by this power of the supreme pontiff, that it is asserted, strengthened, and vindicated by the supreme and universal pastor, according to the words of St. Gregory of Great: "My honor is the honor of the universal Church. My honor is the solid strength of my brothers. I am truly honored when the honor due to each is not denied."

Further, from this supreme power of the Roman pontiff of governing the universal Church, it follows that he has the right of communicating freely with the pastors and flocks of the whole Church in the exercise of this his office, that so they may be taught and ruled by him in the way of salvation. Wherefore, we condemn and reprobate the opinions of those who say that this communication of the supreme head with the pastors and flocks may be lawfully impeded, or who make it dependent on the secular power, so as to contend that things appointed for the government of the Church by the apostolic See, or by its authority, have no force or value, unless they be confirmed by the *Placet* of the secular power.

And since, by the divine right of the apostolic primacy, the Roman pontiff presides over the universal Church, we also teach and declare that he is the supreme judge of the faithful, and that in all causes which are of ecclesiastical cognizance, recourse may be had to his judgment; that the judgment of the apostolic See, whose authority has no superior, can be reviewed by none; and that no one is allowed to judge its judgments. Those, therefore, stray from the straight way of truth who affirm that it is lawful to appeal from the judgments of the Roman pontiffs to an ecumenical council—as to an authority superior to the Roman pontiff.

If, then, any shall say that the Roman pontiff has only an office of inspection or direction, and not full and supreme power of jurisdiction over the universal Church, not only in things which relate to faith and morals, but also in things which relate to the discipline and government of the Church spread over the whole world, or that he has only the principal part and not the whole plenitude of this supreme power; or that this, his power, is not ordinary and immediate, both over all and singular the churches, and over all and singular the pastors and faithful, let him be anathema.

IV

That the supreme power of the *magisterium* is also contained in the apostolic primacy, which the Roman pontiff, as successor of Peter the prince of apostles, possesses over the universal Church, has always been held by this holy See, is proved by the perpetual use of the Church, and has been declared by ecumenical councils themselves, and by those especially in which the East agreed with the West in the union of faith and charity. So the fathers of the Fourth Council of Constantinople, followed the footsteps of their predecessors, put forth the solemn profession: "The first condition of safety is to keep the rule of right faith, and because it is impossible that the sentence of our Lord Jesus Christ should be set aside, who said: You are Peter, and upon this rock I will build my church; these words are verified by facts, for in the apostolic See the Catholic religion has always been preserved immaculate, and holy doctrine has always been proclaimed. Desiring, therefore, never to be separated from its faith and doctrine, we hope that we may deserve to be in the one communion which the apostolic See proclaims, in which is the whole and true solidity of the Christian religion."

And the Greeks professed with the approbation of the Second Council of Lyons: that the holy Roman Church possesses the supreme and full primacy and sovereignty over the universal Catholic Church, which it truly and humbly acknowledges itself to have received with plenitude of power from our Lord himself in blessed Peter, the prince or chief of the apostles, of whom the Roman pontiff is the successor; and as he, beyond all others, is bound to defend the truth of the faith, so also, if any questions concerning the faith shall arise, they ought to be defined by his judgment. Lastly, the Council of Florence defined: that the Roman pontiff is the true vicar of Christ and the head of the whole Church, and the father and teacher of all Christians; and that to him, in blessed Peter, was given by our Lord Jesus Christ full power to feed, rule, and govern the universal Church.

To fulfill this pastoral duty, our predecessors have labored unweariedly that the salutary teaching of Christ should be propagated among all the nations of the earth, and have watched with like care that when it had been received it should be preserved pure and uncorrupted. Wherefore the bishops of the whole world, now singly and now assembled in synod, following a long custom of the Church, and the form of the ancient rule, have reported to the apostolic See such dangers as emerged especially in matters of faith, that the injuries done to the faith might be repaired in that quarter where the faith can experience no failure. And the Roman pontiffs, as time and circumstance required, either by convening ecumenical councils, or by consulting the Church spread over the world, or by local synods, or by other helps supplied by divine providence, have defined that those things that should be held which they knew, by the help of God, to be in accordance with holy Writ and apostolic tradition. For the Holy Spirit did not promise the successors of Peter to reveal to them new doctrine for them to publish, but to assist them to keep holily and expound faithfully the revelation handed down through the apostles, i.e., the deposit of faith. Their apostolic doctrine has been embraced by all the venerable Fathers, and has been revered and followed by all the holy orthodox doctors, knowing well that this See of St. Peter remains always exempt from all error, according to the divine promise of our Lord and savior to the chief of his disciples: "I have prayed for you, that your faith fail not, and you, being once converted, confirm your brethren."

This gift of unfailing truth and faith was divinely bestowed on Peter and on his successors in this chair, that they might discharge the duties of their exalted office for the salvation of all; that the universal flock of Christ, turned by them from the poisonous food of error, might be nourished by heavenly teaching, that the occasion of schism being removed, the whole Church might be preserved in unity, and, supported by its foundation, might stand firm against the gates of hell.

But since in this our age, in which the salutary efficacy of the apostolic office is more than ever required, not a few are found who oppose its authority, we judge it to be necessary solemnly to assert the prerogative which the only begotten Son of God deigned to join to the supreme pastoral office.

Therefore, faithfully adhering to the tradition derived from the commencement of the Christian faith, to the glory of God our savior, to the exaltation of the Catholic religion, and to the salvation of Christian nations, *Sacro approbante Concilio,* we teach and define that it is a divinely revealed dogma: that the Roman pontiff, when he speaks *Ex Cathedra,* that is, when in discharge of his office of pastor and doctor of all Christians, he defines, in virtue of his supreme apostolic authority, a doctrine of faith or morals to be held by the universal Church, is endowed by the divine assistance promised to him in blessed Peter, with that infallibility with which our divine redeemer willed that the Church should be furnished in defining doctrine of faith or morals; and, therefore, that such definitions of the Roman pontiff are irreformable of themselves and not in virtue of the consent of the Church.

But if any, which may God avert, shall presume to contradict this our definition, let him be anathema.

12. *Pope Leo XIII: Three Encyclical Letters*

Selection A from *The Great Encyclical Letters of Pope Leo XIII* (New York: Benziger Brothers, 1903), pp. 34-35, 38-40, 41-43, 44, 46-50, 52-57; selection B from "Encyclical of His Holiness Pope Leo XIII," *Ave Maria*, XIX (22 September 1883), 741-43 and XIX (29 September 1883), 761-63); selection C from *The Encyclical "Immortale Dei"* (London: The Catholic Truth Society, 1886), *passim*.

A. ENCYCLICAL, "AETERNI PATRIS," ON THE STUDY OF SCHOLASTIC PHILOS-OPHY, 4 AUGUST 1879

THE only-begotten Son of the eternal Father, who came on earth to bring salvation and the light of divine wisdom to men, conferred a great and wonderful blessing on the world when, about to ascend again into heaven, he commanded the apostles to go and teach all nations, and left the Church which he had founded to be the common and supreme teacher of the peoples. For men, whom the truth had set free, were to be preserved by the truth; nor would the fruits of heavenly doctrines, by which salvation comes to men, have long remained had not the Lord Christ appointed an unfailing authority for the instruction of the faithful. And the Church built upon the promises of its own divine author, whose charity it imitated, so faithfully followed out his commands that its constant aim and chief wish was this: to teach true religion and contend forever against errors. To this end assuredly have tended the incessant labors of individual bishops; to this end also the published laws and decrees of councils, and especially the constant watchfulness of the Roman pontiffs, to whom, as successors of the blessed Peter in the primacy of the apostles, belongs the right and office of teaching and confirming their brethren in the faith.

Since, then, according to the warning of the apostle, the minds of Christ's faithful are apt to be deceived and the integrity of the faith to be corrupted among men by philosophy and vain deceit, the supreme pastors of the Church have always thought it their duty to advance, by every means in their power, science truly so called; and at the same time to provide with special care that all studies should accord with the Catholic faith, especially philosophy, on which a right apprehension of the other sciences in great part depends. Indeed, venerable brethren, on this very subject among others, we briefly admonished you in our first encyclical letter. But now, both by reason of the gravity of the subject and the condition of the time, we are again compelled to speak to you on the mode of taking up the study of philosophy which shall respond most fitly to the true faith, and at the same time be most consonant with the dignity of human knowledge. . . .

In the first place, then, this great and noble fruit is gathered from human reason, that it demonstrates that God is; for by the greatness of the beauty and of the creature the creator of them may be seen so as to be known thereby. Again, it shows God to excel in the height of all perfections, in infinite wisdom before which nothing lies hidden, and in absolute justice which no depraved affection could possibly shake; and that God, therefore, is not only true but truth itself, which can neither deceive nor be deceived. Whence it clearly follows that human reason finds the fullest faith and authority united in the word of God. In like manner reason declares that the doctrine of the Gospel has even from its very beginning been made manifest by certain wonderful signs, the established proofs, as it were, of unshaken truth; and that all, therefore, who set faith in the Gospel do not believe rashly as though following cunningly devised fables, but by a most reasonable consent they subject their intelligence and judgment to an authority which is divine. And of no less importance is it that reason most clearly sets forth that the Church instituted by Christ, as laid down in the Vatican synod, on account of its wonderful spread, its marvelous sanctity, and its inexhaustible fecundity in all places, as well as of its catholic unity and unshaken stability, is in itself a great and perpetual motive of belief and an irrefragable testimony of its own divine mission.

Its solid foundations thus laid, a perpetual and varied service is further required of philosophy, in order that sacred theology may receive and assume the nature, form, and genius of a true science. For in this, the most noble of studies, it is of the greatest necessity to bind together, as it were, in one body the many and various parts of the heavenly doctrines, so that—each being allotted to its own proper place and derived from its own proper principles—the whole may join together in a complete union; in order, in fine, that all and each part may be strengthened by its own and the others' invincible arguments. Nor is that more accurate or fuller knowledge of the things that are believed, and somewhat more lucid understanding, as far as it can go, of the very mysteries of faith which Augustine and the other Fathers commended and strove to reach, and which the Vatican synod itself declared to be most fruitful, to be passed over in silence or be belittled. They will certainly more fully and more easily attain that knowledge and understanding, who to integrity of life and love of faith join a mind rounded and finished by philosophic studies—as the same Vatican Synod teaches that the knowledge of such sacred dogmas ought to be sought as well from analogy of the things that are naturally known as from the connection of those mysteries one with another and with the final end of man.

Lastly, the duty of religiously defending the truths divinely delivered, and of resisting those who dare oppose them, pertains to philosophic pursuits. Wherefore it is the glory of philosophy to be esteemed as the bulwark of faith and the strong defense of religion. . . .

But in order that philosophy may be found equal to the gathering of those precious fruits which we have indicated, it behooves it above all things never to turn aside from that path which the fathers have entered upon from a venerable antiquity, and which the Vatican council solemnly and authoritatively approved. As it is evident that very many truths of the supernatural order which are far beyond the reach of the keenest intellect must be accepted, conscious of its own infirmity human reason dares not affect to itself too great powers, nor deny those truths, nor measure them by its own standard, nor interpret them at will; reason, rather, receives them with a full and humble faith, and esteems it the highest honor to be allowed to wait upon heavenly doctrines like a handmaid and attendant, and by God's goodness attain to them in any way whatsoever. But in the case of such doctrines as the human intelligence may perceive, it is equally just that philosophy should make use of its own method, principles, and arguments— not indeed in such fashion as to seem rashly to withdraw from the divine authority. But since it is established that those things which become known by revelation have the force of certain truth, and that those things which war against faith war equally against right reason, the Catholic philosopher will know that he violates at once faith and the laws of reason if he accepts any conclusion which he understands to be opposed to revealed doctrine.

We know that there are some who, in their overestimate of the human faculties, maintain that as soon as man's intellect becomes subject to divine authority it falls from its native dignity, and, hampered by the yoke of this species of slavery, is much retarded and hindered in its progress towards the supreme truth and excellence. Such an idea is most false and deceptive, and its sole tendency is to induce foolish and ungrateful men willfully to repudiate the most sublime truths and reject the divine gift of faith, from which the mountains of all good things flow out upon civil society. For the human mind, being confined within certain limits, and those narrow enough, is exposed to many errors and is ignorant of many things; whereas the Christian faith, reposing on the authority of God, is the unfailing mistress of truth; he who follows her will be neither immeshed in the snares of error, nor tossed back and forth on the waves of fluctuating opinion. Those, therefore, who to the study of philosophy unite obedience to the Christian faith are

philosophers indeed; for the splendor of the divine truths received into the mind helps the understanding, and not only detracts in nowise from its dignity, but adds greatly to its nobility, keenness, and stability. For surely that is a worthy and most useful exercise of reason when men give their minds to disproving those things which are repugnant to faith and proving the things which conform to faith. In the first case they make themselves masters of weighty reasons for the sound demonstration of truth and the satisfactory instruction of any reasonable person. Whoever denies that such study and practice tend to add to the resources and expand the faculties of the mind must necessarily and absurdly hold that the mind gains nothing from discriminating between the true and the false. Justly, therefore, does the Vatican council commemorate in these words the great benefits which faith has conferred upon reason: "Faith frees and saves reason from error, and endows it with manifold knowledge." A wise man, therefore, would not accuse faith and look upon it as opposed to reason and natural truths, but would rather offer heartfelt thanks to God, and sincerely rejoice that, in the density of ignorance and in the flood-tide of error, holy faith, like a friendly star, shines down upon his path and points out to him the fair gate of truth beyond all danger of wandering. . . .

But Augustine would seem to have wrested the palm from all. Of a most powerful genius and thoroughly saturated with sacred and profane learning, with the loftiest faith and with equal knowledge, he combated most vigorously all the errors of his age. What height of philosophy did he not reach? What region of it did he not diligently explore, either in expounding the loftiest mysteries of the faith to the faithful, or defending them against the sharp onslaughts of adversaries, or again when, in demolishing the fables of the academicians or the Manichaeans, he laid the safe foundations and sure structure of human science, or followed up the reason, origin, and causes of the evils that afflict man? How subtly he reasoned on the angels, the soul, the human mind, the will and free choice, on religion and the life of the blessed, on time and eternity, and even on the very nature of changeable bodies. Afterwards, in the East John Damascene treading in the footsteps of Basil and of Gregory Nazianzen, and in the West Boëthius and Anselm following the doctrines of Augustine, added largely to the patrimony of philosophy.

Later on the doctors of the middle ages, who are called scholastics, addressed themselves to a great work— that of diligently collecting, and sifting, and storing up, as it were, in one place, for the use and convenience of posterity the rich and fertile harvests of Christian learning scattered abroad in the voluminous works of the holy fathers. And with regard, venerable brethren, to the origin, drift, and excellence of this scholastic learning, it may be well here to speak more fully in the words of one of the wisest of our predecessors, Sixtus V: "By the divine favor of him who alone gives the spirit of science, and wisdom, and understanding, and who through all ages, as there may be need, enriches his Church with new blessings and strengthens it with new safeguards, there was founded by our fathers, men of eminent wisdom, the scholastic theology, which two glorious doctors in particular, the angelic St. Thomas and the seraphic St. Bonaventure, illustrious teachers of this faculty . . . with surpassing genius, by unwearied diligence, and at the cost of long labors and vigils, set in order and beautified, and, when skillfully arranged and clearly explained in a variety of ways, handed down to posterity.

"And, indeed, the knowledge and use of so salutary a science, which flows from the fertilizing founts of the sacred writings, the sovereign pontiffs, the holy fathers and the councils, must always be of the greatest assistance to the Church, whether with the view of really and soundly understanding and interpreting the Scriptures, or more safely and to better purpose reading and explaining the fathers, or for exposing and refuting the various errors and heresies; and in these late days, when those dangerous times described by the apostle are already upon us, when the blasphemers, the proud, and the seducers go from bad to worse, erring themselves and causing others to err, there is surely a very great need of confirming the dogmas of Catholic faith and confuting heresies."

Although these words seem to bear reference solely to scholastic theology, nevertheless they may plainly be accepted as equally true of philosophy and its praises. For the noble endowments which make the scholastic theology so formidable to the enemies of truth—to wit, as the same pontiff adds, "that ready and close coherence of cause and effect, that order and array as of a disciplined army in battle, those clear definitions and distinctions, that strength of argument and those keen discussions, by which light is distinguished from darkness, the true from the false, expose and strip naked, as it were, the falsehoods of heretics wrapped around by a cloud of subterfuges and fallacies"—those noble and admirable endowments, we say, are only to be found in a right use of that philosophy which the scholastic teachers have been accustomed carefully and prudently to make use of even in theological disputations. Moreover, since it is the proper and special office of the scholastic theologians to bind together by the fastest chain human and divine science, surely the theology in which they excelled would not have gained such honor and commendation among men if they had made use of a lame and imperfect or vain philosophy.

Among the scholastic doctors, the chief and master of all, towers Thomas Aquinas, who, as Cajetan observes, because "he most venerated the ancient doctors of the Church, in a certain way seems to have inherited the intellect of all." The doctrines of those illustrious men, like the scattered members of a body, Thomas collected together and cemented, distributed in wonderful order, and so increased with important additions that he is rightly and deservedly esteemed the special bulwark and glory of the Catholic faith. With his spirit at once humble and swift, his memory ready and tenacious, his life spotless throughout, a lover of truth for its own sake, richly endowed with human and divine science, like the sun he heated the world with the ardor of his virtues and filled it with the splendor of his teaching. Philosophy has no part which he did not touch finely at once and thoroughly; on the laws of reasoning, on God and incorporeal substances, on man and other sensible things, on human actions and their principles, he reasoned in such a manner that in him there is wanting neither a full array of questions, nor an apt disposal of the various parts, nor the best method of proceeding, nor soundness of principles or strength of argument, nor clearness and elegance of style, nor a facility for explaining what is abstruse.

Moreover, the angelic doctor pushed his philosophic conclusions into the reasons and principles of the things which are most comprehensive and contain in their bosom, so to say, the seeds of almost infinite truths, to be unfolded in good time by later masters and with a goodly yield. And as

he also used this philosophic method in the refutation of error, he won this title to distinction for himself: that single-handed he victoriously combated the errors of former times, and supplied invincible arms to put those to rout which might in aftertimes spring up. Again, clearly distinguishing, as is fitting, reason from faith, while happily associating the one with the other, he both preserved the rights and had regard for the dignity of each; so much so, indeed, that reason, borne on the wings of Thomas to its human height, can scarcely rise higher, while faith could scarcely expect more or stronger aids from reason than those which she has already obtained through Thomas.

For these reasons learned men, in former ages especially, of the highest repute in theology and philosophy, after mastering with infinite pains the immortal works of Thomas, gave themselves up not so much to be instructed in his angelic wisdom, as to be nourished upon it. It is known that nearly all the founders and framers of laws of the religious orders commanded their associates to study and religiously adhere to the teachings of St. Thomas, fearful lest any of them should swerve even in the slightest degree from the footsteps of so great a man. To say nothing of the family of St. Dominic, which rightly claims this great teacher for its own glory, the statutes of the Benedictines, the Carmelites, the Augustinians, the Society of Jesus, and many others, all testify that they are bound by this law. . . .

Therefore, venerable brethren, as often as we contemplate the good, the force, and the singular advantages to be derived from this system of philosophy which our fathers so dearly loved, we think it hazardous that its special honor should not always and everywhere remain, especially when it is established that daily experience, and the judgment of the greatest men, and, to crown all, the voice of the Church, have favored scholastic philosophy. Moreover, to the old teaching a novel system of philosophy has succeeded here and there, in which we fail to perceive those desirable and wholesome fruits which the Church and civil society itself would prefer. For it pleased the struggling innovators of the sixteenth century to philosophize without any respect for faith, the power of inventing in accordance with his own pleasure and bent being asked and given in turn by each one.

Hence it was natural that systems of philosophy multiplied beyond measure, and conclusions differing and clashing one with another arose about those matters even which are the most important in human knowledge. From a mass of conclusions men often come to wavering and doubt; and who knows not how easily the mind slips from doubt to error? But as men are apt to follow the lead given them, this new pursuit seems to have caught the souls of certain Catholic philosophers, who, throwing aside the patrimony of ancient wisdom, chose rather to build up a new edifice than to strengthen and complete the old by aid of the new—ill-advisedly, and not without detriment to the sciences. For a multiform system of this kind, which depends on the authority and choice of any professor, has a foundation open to change, and consequently gives us a philosophy not firm, and stable, and robust like that of old, but tottering and feeble. And if perchance it sometimes finds itself scarcely equal to sustain the shock of its foes, it should recognize that the cause and the blame lie in itself. In saying this we have no intention of discountenancing the learned and able men who bring their industry and erudition, and what is more, the wealth of new discoveries, to the service of philosophy; for, of course, we understand that this tends to the development of learning. But one should be very careful lest all or his chief labor be exhausted in these pursuits and in mere erudition. And the same thing is true of sacred theology, which, indeed, may be assisted and illustrated by all kinds of erudition, though it is absolutely necessary to approach it in the grave manner of the scholastics, in order that, the forces of revelation and reason being united in it, it may continue to be "the invincible bulwark of the faith."

With wise forethought, therefore, not a few of the advocates of philosophic studies, when turning their minds recently to the practical reform of philosophy, aimed and aim at restoring the renowned teaching of Thomas Aquinas and winning it back to its ancient beauty. . . .

We have learned with great joy that many members of your order, venerable brethren, have taken this plan to heart; and while we earnestly commend their efforts, we exhort them to hold fast to their purpose, and remind each and all of you that our first and most cherished idea is that you should all furnish a generous and copious supply to studious youth of those crystal rills of wisdom flowing in a never-ending and fertilizing stream from the fountain-head of the angelic doctor.

Many are the reasons why we are so desirous of this. In the first place, then, since in the tempest that is on us the Christian faith is being constantly assailed by the machinations and craft of a certain false wisdom, all youths, but especially those who are the growing hope of the Church, should be nourished on the strong and robust food of doctrine, that so, mighty in strength and armed at all points, they may become habituated to advance the cause of religion with force and judgment, "being ready always, according to the apostolic counsel, to satisfy every one that asks you a reason of that hope which is in you," and that they may be able to exhort in sound doctrine and to convince the gainsayers. Many of those who, with minds alienated from the faith, hate Catholic institutions, claim reason as their sole mistress and guide. Now, we think that, apart from the supernatural help of God, nothing is better calculated to heal those minds and to bring them into favor with the Catholic faith than the solid doctrine of the fathers and the scholastics, who so clearly and forcibly demonstrate the firm foundations of the faith, its divine origin, its certain truth, the arguments that sustain it, the benefits it has conferred on the human race, and its perfect accord with reason, in a manner to satisfy completely minds open to persuasion, however unwilling and repugnant.

Domestic and civil society even, which, as all see, is exposed to great danger from this plague of perverse opinions, would certainly enjoy a far more peaceful and secure existence if a more wholesome doctrine were taught in the academies and schools— one more in conformity with the teaching of the Church, such as is contained in the works of Thomas Aquinas.

For the teachings of Thomas—on the true meaning of liberty, which at this time is running into license, on the divine origin of all authority, on laws and their force, on the paternal and just rule of princes, on obedience to the higher powers, on mutual charity one towards another—on all of these and kindred subjects, have very great and invincible force to overturn those principles of the new order which are well known to be dangerous to the peaceful order of things and to public safety. In short, all studies ought to find hope of advancement and promise of assistance in this restoration of philosophic discipline which we have proposed. The arts were wont to draw from philosophy, as from a wise mistress, sound judgment and right method, and from it also their spirit as from the common fount of life. When philosophy stood stainless in honor and wise in judgment, then, as facts and constant experience showed, the liberal arts flourished as never before or since; but, neglected and almost blotted out, they lay prone since philosophy began to lean to error and join hands with folly. Nor will the physical sciences, which are now in such great repute, and by the renown of so many inventions draw such universal admiration to themselves, suffer detriment but find very great assistance in the re-establishment of the ancient philosophy. For the investigation of facts and the contemplation of nature is not alone sufficient for their profitable exercise and advance; but when facts have been established it is necessary to rise and apply ourselves to the study of the nature of corporal things, to inquire into the laws which govern them and the principles whence their order and varied unity and mutual attraction in diversity arise. To such investigations it is wonderful what force and light and aid scholastic philosophy, if judiciously taught, would bring.

And here it is well to note that our philosophy can only by the grossest injustice be accused of being opposed to the advance and development of natural science. For when the scholastics, following the opinion of the holy fathers, always held in anthropology that the human intelligence is only led to the knowledge of things without body and matter by things sensible, they well understood that nothing was of greater use to the philosopher than diligently to search into the mysteries of nature and to be earnest and constant in the study of physical things. And this they confirmed by their own example; for St. Thomas, Albertus Magnus, and other leaders of the scholastics were never so wholly rapt in the study of philosophy as not to give large attention to the knowledge of natural things; and, indeed, the number of their sayings and writings on these subjects, which recent professors approve of and admit to harmonize with truth, is by no means small. Moreover, in this very age many illustrious professors of the physical sciences openly testify that between certain and accepted conclusions of modern physics and philosophic principles of the schools there is no conflict worthy of the name.

While, therefore, we hold that every word of wisdom, every useful thing by whomever discovered or planned, ought to be received with a willing and grateful mind, we exhort you, venerable brethren, in all earnestness to restore the golden wisdom of St. Thomas, and to spread it far and wide for the defense and beauty of the Catholic faith, for the good of society, and for the advantage of all the sciences. The wisdom of St. Thomas, we say; for if anything is taken up with too great subtlety by the scholastic doctors, or too carelessly stated—if there be anything that ill agrees with the discoveries of a later age, or, in a word, improbable in whatever way, it does not enter our mind to propose that for imitation to our age. Let carefully selected teachers endeavor to implant the doctrine of Thomas Aquinas in the minds of students, and set forth clearly his solidity and excellence over others. Let the academies already founded or to be founded by you illustrate and defend this doctrine, and use it for the refutation of prevailing errors. But, lest the false for the true or the corrupt for the pure be drunk in, be watchful that the doctrine of Thomas is drawn from his own fountains, or at least from those rivulets which derived from the very fount, have thus far flowed, according to the estab-lished agreement of learned men, pure and clear; be careful to guard the minds of youth from those which are said to flow thence, but in reality are gathered from strange and unwholesome streams.

But well do we know that vain will be our efforts unless, venerable brethren, he helps our common cause who, in the words of divine Scripture, is called the God of all knowledge; by which we are also admonished that "every best gift and every perfect gift is from above, coming down from the Father of lights"; and again: "If any of you want wisdom, let him ask of God, who gives to all men abundantly, and upbraids not; and it shall be given him."

Therefore in this also let us follow the example of the angelic doctor, who never gave himself to reading or writing without first begging the blessing of God, who modestly confessed that whatever he knew he had acquired not so much by his own study and labor as by the divine gift; and therefore let us all, in humble and united prayer, beseech God to send forth the spirit of knowledge and of understanding to the children of the Church, and open their senses for the understanding of wisdom. And that we may receive fuller fruits of the divine goodness, offer up to God the most efficacious patronage of the Blessed Virgin Mary, who is called the seat of wisdom; having at the same time as advocates St. Joseph, the most chaste spouse of the virgin, and Peter and Paul, the chiefs of the apostles, whose truth renewed the earth, which had fallen under the impure blight of error, filling it with the light of heavenly wisdom. . . .

B. LETTER ON HISTORICAL STUDIES, 18 AUGUST 1883

Often reflecting on the arts on which those men principally rely who endeavor to bring the Church and the

Roman pontificate into suspicion and odium, it has become quite plain to us that their efforts are directed with great force and cunning to the history of the Christian name, and especially to that portion of it that embraces the relations of the Roman pontiffs to the Italian people. The same thing being observed by some of the bishops of this country, they have declared that they are not less alarmed at the thought of the evils that have resulted herefrom, than of the dangers of future evils. For it is not only unjust, but dangerous, for men to let themselves be guided more by hatred of the Roman pontificate than by the love of truth, as is evidently the case with those that make the monuments of the past, which they distort, turn in favor of the new state of things in Italy. Since it is our duty, therefore, not only to vindicate the other rights of the Church, but also to defend the honor and dignity of the apostolic See against unjust attacks, and desiring as we do that truth should finally be victorious, and that the people of Italy should acknowledge the source whence they derived such abundant blessings in the past, and from which they may expect so many in the future, we have determined to impart to you, beloved sons, our views in regard to a matter of so much importance, and to entrust to your wisdom the execution of them.

The incorruptible monuments of the past, to one that looks upon them calmly and with unprejudiced mind, afford a spontaneous and most magnificent defense of the Church and the pontificate. In them we can see the genuine nature and the grandeur of the Christian institutions. Through terrible struggles and glorious victories the divine energy of the Church is manifested; and by the evident testimony of facts is revealed the great benefits conferred by the sovereign pontiffs on all peoples, but especially on those in whose midst the providence of God placed the apostolic See. Therefore, it was not to be expected that those that endeavor by all manner of means to injure the pontificate itself, should let the testimony of history escape them. And, in fact, they have endeavored to destroy its integrity, and with such art and perversity that they turned those very arms against it that were best calculated to repel attacks.

This manner of assault was adopted three centuries ago by the Centuriators of Magdeburg; for, as they could not supply the authors and patrons of the new opinions with weapons to overturn the defenses of Catholic doctrine, by a new species of warfare they forced the Church into historical discussions. Nearly all the sects that abandoned the ancient doctrines followed the example of the centuriators; and, which is far more disgraceful, some that were Catholics in name and Italians by birth have done the same. With the view that we have mentioned, therefore, they have examined the most insignificant vestiges of antiquity; they have tried the secret recesses of archives; they have brought to the light of day ridiculous fables; they have repeated a hundred times fictions a hundred times refuted. Often mutilating or obscuring the prominent features of historical events, they chose to pass over in silence what was glorious and memorable, while at the same time they redoubled their attention to discover and exaggerate whatever had been done rashly, whatever had been done amiss; though to avoid everything of this kind is beyond the powers of human nature. They have even gone so far as to scrutinize with perverse sagacity the doubtful secrets of private life, thus seizing and putting before the multitude, ever eager for scandal, whatever was most likely to afford them a spectacle and give them occasion to scoff. Among the very greatest of the pontiffs, even those whose virtue was supereminent, some have been accused and defamed as covetous, proud, imperious men. When the glory of their deeds could not be contested, their motives were called in question; and thousands of times that senseless cry was raised, that the Church was an enemy to human progress, to the civilization of the nations. But in particular the most envenomed darts of malevolence and calumny have been hurled against the civil principality of the Roman pontiffs, founded by divine Providence to protect their independence and their majesty, which was most legitimate in its origin, and most beneficial in its exercise.

These same machinations are employed at the present day in such a manner that it may be said that now, if ever, the art of the historian has become a conspiracy against truth. Those accusations made in former times are renewed and scattered among the public, and we see falsehood impudently taking its place in voluminous treatises as well as in insignificant pamphlets, in ephemeral journals, and in the attractions of the theater. Too many seek to make the records of olden times countenance the outrages of the present day. There was a recent specimen of this in Sicily, when, taking occasion of a certain sanguinary anniversary, bitter invectives were hurled against our predecessors, and durable monuments were erected to blast their name. The same spirit was manifested soon afterwards when public honors were bestowed on a native of Brescia, whose seditious spirit and opposition to the Holy See were his claims to be considered glorious by posterity. On this occasion the effort was made to excite popular passions, and to enkindle the torches of calumny against the greatest pontiffs. But if it became necessary at any time to record anything entirely favorable to the Church,

anything wherein the light of truth blunted the points of calumny, care was taken, by extenuation and dissimulation, to give the very smallest proportion of merit and praise to the pontiffs.

But the most serious thing in all this is that this method of treating history has made its way even into schools. Very often, manuals with falsehood scattered through them are placed in the hands of children to be studied. Becoming accustomed to this sort of mental food, especially if their teachers be perverse or thoughtless, they easily imbibe a disgust for venerable antiquity and an overweening contempt for the most holy personages. When they have gone beyond the elements of education, they run a still greater danger; for in the higher courses of studies the recital of facts leads to the inquiry into causes; from the examination of causes, theories which very often are in direct opposition to the doctrines revealed by God are built in conformity to preconceived judgments; and the only motive for all this is to dissemble and conceal what and how much of benefit the Christian institutions exerted in the course of human things and in the succession of events. This is done by many who regard not how much they may be wanting in consistency, how repugnant to each other may be their assertions, and in how great darkness they involve what is called the philosophy of history. In short, not to enter into further details, they turn the entire method of treating history into a means of throwing suspicion on the Church, making the pontiffs odious, and especially of persuading the multitudes that the temporal dominion of the Roman pontiffs is opposed to the safety and greatness of Italy. But no assertion more opposed to truth can be made; and it seems really strange that accusations of this kind, which are refuted by so many testimonies, and so clearly, could be accepted by many as probable; for to the eternal memory of posterity history commends the merits of the Roman pontificate towards Europe, and especially towards Italy, which above all other countries, as was natural, derived from the Holy See the greatest advantages and favors. Among these must be mentioned in the first place the fact that Italy was able to enjoy impunity from discord in matters of religion, certainly for any people a very great blessing, which is a pledge of public and private prosperity to those that enjoy it. And, to come to one particular fact: no one is ignorant that, after the power of the Romans was broken by the incursions of the barbarians, the Roman pontiffs were the strongest in resisting; and by their prudence and constancy the fury of the enemy was repressed, the Italian soil was saved from sword and flame, and the city of Rome itself from destruction. And at the time when the emperors of the East turned all their thoughts and cares elsewhere, Italy, in its abandonment and poverty, found no protectors of its interests but the Roman pontiffs. In those calamities their tried charity, combined with other causes, had much to do with establishing their temporal power. And the great glory of this power was that it was always united to the greatest public good; and if the apostolic See was enabled to promote all the interests of justice and civilization, if it could employ its power efficaciously in favor of civil order, and could embrace the most important matters of government conjointly, surely no trifling meed of gratitude is due the temporal power which furnishes liberty and the opportunities necessary to effect such things. Moreover, when the consciousness of their offices impelled our predecessors to defend the rights of their government from the cupidity of enemies, in so doing they many times prevented the domination of foreign powers from being set up over a great part of Italy. This has been proved even in late times, when the apostolic See would not yield to the victorious arms of a great emperor, and obtained from the congress of kings the restitution of all the rights of his sovereignty. Nor was it less beneficial to Italy that very many times the Roman pontiffs resisted the unjust will of princes; and that by their heroism they, uniting the powers of Europe in a confederacy, sustained the terrible and repeated shocks of the Turks. Two great battles, in which the enemies of Italy and of the Christian name were destroyed—the one on the plains of Milan, the other at the Echinades islands—were undertaken and fought by the help and under the auspices of the apostolic See. The expeditions into Palestine, undertaken by the impulse of the pontiffs, produced the naval glory and power of the Italians; in like manner, the popular governments derived their laws, life, and durability from the wisdom of the popes.

To the glory of the pontiffs belongs the greater part of the renown acquired by the Italian name in the higher studies and in the arts. The literature of the Romans and of the Greeks was on the verge of destruction, had not the pontiffs and the clergy collected the remains of so many works, as it were, from shipwreck. What was done and perfected in the city speaks even more loudly: the ancient monuments preserved at immense cost; the new masterpieces created and perfected by the talent of the princes of art; the museums and the libraries established; the schools opened for the instruction of youth; the glorious foundation of great lyceums—all of which contributed to bestow on Rome the glory of being, in the common estimation of men, the mother of the fine arts.

From these and other facts it is unquestionably evident that to represent either the pontificate itself or the temporal power of the popes as hostile to the Italian name, is nothing more nor less than willful mendacity about things that are clear and evident. It is a wicked thing knowingly to deceive, and to turn history into a deadly poison: and this is far more severely to be condemned in Catholics, born in Italy, whom more than others a sense of gratitude and the honor of their religion and their love of country ought to induce not only to love, but also to patronize the truth. But since even among Protestants quite a number, of a penetrating mind and impartial judgment, have thrown aside those false opinions, and from the very force of truth do not hesitate to give due credit to the Roman pontificate as the patron of civilization and the source of very great good to society, it is certainly a disgrace to see many of our own nation doing just the contrary. In the study of history, these men love strange theories; they give the preference to foreign writers, holding them in higher esteem the more they insult Catholic institutions, treating with contempt our greatest men, who when they wrote history did not think it necessary to sacrifice to their love of country their obedience and attachment to the apostolic See.

And yet, beloved sons, it is hardly to be realized what a capital evil it is to make history subservient to the interest of parties and to the passions of men. For it will, in this case, be no longer what the ancients called it, "the teacher of life and the light of truth," but the approver of vice and the slave of corruption. More especially will this be the case in regard to young men, whose minds it will fill with nonsensical opinions, and whose morals it will divert from candor and modesty. For history offers great charms to the hasty and fervid nature of youth: the representation of antiquity and the pictures of men, which are, as it were, made visible to the eyes in history, are eagerly seized upon by the young, and are retained forever deeply engraven in their minds. Therefore, if the poison is once swallowed in youth, it will be difficult, if at all possible, to find a remedy. For there is no well-founded hope that later in life they will know better, and unlearn what they had first been taught. There are few who give themselves to the serious and profound study of history, and as they advance in years they are likely to meet in the daily course of their lives more to confirm than to correct their errors.

Therefore, it is of very great importance to provide against such imminent danger, and to see that the art of history, which is so noble, be no longer made the instrument of great harm both public and private. Upright men, well versed in this branch of knowledge, are required to undertake the writing of history with this view, and for this purpose, of showing what is true and genuine, and that the insulting accusations too long accumulating against the pontiffs may be learnedly and becomingly refuted. To meager narrations let there be opposed a laborious and mature investigation; to rash assertions, a prudent judgment; to opinions lightly hazarded, a learned selection of facts. No effort should be spared to refute inventions and falsehoods; and the writers must always bear this rule in mind: *the first law of history is not to dare to utter falsehood; the second, not to fear to speak the truth; and moreover, no room must be left for suspicion of partiality or prejudice.* But for the use of schools there is need of a summary, which, preserving the truth, and removing all danger from the young, will illustrate and extend the study of history. In order to succeed in this, after the larger works are compiled from such documents as are indisputable, it will be only necessary to extract from these works the principal headings, and to re-write them briefly and with clearness. This is a point by no means difficult, but which will be of the greatest utility, and worthy of the labors of the greatest intellects.

Nor is this a new and untrodden path; on the contrary, the greatest men have left their impressions on it. For history, which in the opinion of the ancients was more closely allied to sacred than to profane things, was studiously cultivated by the Church from the beginning. In the midst of those sanguinary persecutions through which Christianity passed in the early ages, numbers of acts and monuments were preserved entire. Hence, when more peaceful times came, the study of history began to flourish, and the East and the West beheld the learned labors of Eusebius Pamphilus, Theodoret, Socrates Sozomen, and others. And after the fall of the Roman empire, the same fate was shared by history as by the other liberal arts. Its sole refuge was in the monasteries, and its only cultivators were the clergy. Thus if the members of religious communities had neglected to write annals, there would be long periods of time of which we should have no record, not even of civil affairs. Among moderns, let it suffice to name two who have never been surpassed, Baronius and Muratori. The former, who to a mighty genius and an accurate judgment added incredible erudition; the latter, although "many things deserving of censure are found in his writings," yet has collected in illustration of the history of Italy a larger mass of documents than any other man has done. To these names it would be easy to add many others both famous and great, among whom it is pleasant to mention Angelo Mai, an honor and glory of your illustrious order.

The great doctor of the Church, Augustine, was the first to conceive and carry out the plan of the philosophy of history. Among later writers, such as did anything worthy of remembrance in this art followed Augustine as their leader and guide, and drew their inspiration from his commentaries and writings; but, on the contrary, those that forsook the guidance of so great a man, were led from the truth into a multitude of errors, because when they turned their attention to the progress and changes of states, they found themselves destitute of the real knowledge of the causes by which human events are directed.

If, therefore, the Church has at all times deserved well of history, let her continue also to merit at the present time, and especially as she is impelled to this by the very nature of the times. For since hostile weapons are drawn principally from history, as we have already said, it is proper for the Church to meet those attacks with equal arms, and where the attack is most violent she should be better prepared to resist.

With this view we have elsewhere decreed that our archives shall be accessible, so as to promote as much as possible religion and serious studies. Now in like manner we decree that for the completion of the works of which we have spoken, our Vatican library shall furnish the suitable materials. We have no doubt, beloved sons, that the authority of your office and the renown of your merits will readily induce learned men, who have already some practice in writing history, to co-operate with you, and you can assign to each one of them his special part of the work according to his individual ability, under certain conditions, however, which shall be sanctioned by our authority. We bid all those to be of good courage that shall join with you in this work, and to count on our special good will. The matter is certainly worthy of our favor and encouragement, and we feel confident that it will be of very great utility. For the opinions of men cannot but yield to solid arguments; and truth herself will vanquish the attacks on truth that have been made so persistently, and which, though they may have obscured her for a while, could not entirely extinguish her.

Would that many be excited by the desire of investigating the truth, and that, thus, documents worthy of preservation may be produced. For all history cries out in a certain way that it is God who by his all-wise providence directs the various and constant mutations of sublunary things, and turns them, even in spite of men, to the glory of his Church. History likewise shows that the Roman pontificate has always been victorious in the struggles and violences with which it had to cope; and that its opponents, frustrated in their hopes, have only brought on their own destruction. History shows with no less evidence what was the fate prepared by God for the city of Rome even from its origin; namely, that it was forever to be the dwelling place and the throne of the successors of the blessed Peter, who from this city, as from a center, should govern the entire Christian society, independent of all other powers. No one has dared to oppose this plan of divine providence without sooner or later seeing his vain efforts fail. These are facts which the testimony of twelve centuries has, as it were, engraved on a glorious monument. We have no reason to think that future ages will tell a different story. At the present day, indeed, prominent sects of men have risen up who are enemies of God and of his Church, who dare every species of hostility against the Roman pontiff, carrying the war even to his very throne. By this they strive to diminish the energy and lessen the power of the Roman pontiffs; nay, even to abolish the pontificate itself, if that were possible. The things that have been done here since the taking of the city, and which are done even today, show what is in the minds of those men who have come forward as the architects and leaders of the new order of things. There were many that took part with these men, not perhaps with the same views, but who were captivated by the wish to constitute and increase the power of their country. Thus the number of assailants of the apostolic See increased, and the Roman pontiff was reduced to that pitiful state which all Catholic people lament. But those last assailants will be no more successful than their predecessors, who entertained the same designs and with equal audacity. As far as the Italians are concerned, this fierce war against the Holy See, which was begun with equal injustice and rashness, is the source of great evils at home and abroad. To alienate the affections of the multitude, the pontificate was declared to be the enemy of the Italian interests; but that this accusation is wicked and absurd is clearly shown by what we have said above. The pontificate, on the contrary, as it was at all times in the past, so will it be in the future, a pledge of prosperity and safety to the people of Italy; because this is its constant and invariable nature, to scatter blessings and to be useful everywhere. Wherefore it is not for men who are really anxious for the public good to try to cut off from Italy this great fountain of blessings; nor is it becoming in Italians to make common cause with those that have no other desire than the destruction of the Church.

In like manner it is neither expedient nor prudent to make war on that power whose guarantee of perpetuity is God himself, as history testifies; and which, as it is religiously venerated by Catholics all the world over, so it is their interest to defend it by all means; and which the rulers set over the various governments are forced to acknowledge and to set great value on, especially in such unsettled times, when the very foundations on which civil society rests are shaken. All, therefore, who are animated by a genuine love of their country, if they are only wise, and can see things as they are, should turn all their zeal and endeavors to remove the cause of this fatal conflict, and to secure due satisfaction to the Catholic Church, which asks what is so perfectly just, and is solicitous about her rights.

But, finally, we desire nothing more earnestly than to see these facts, which are recorded in the monuments of literature, sink equally deep into the minds of men. To effect this, it will be for you, beloved sons, to bring your greatest skill and industry to bear. . . .

C. ENCYCLICAL, "IMMORTALE DEI," ON THE CHRISTIAN CONSTITUTION OF THE STATE, 1 NOVEMBER 1885

The Catholic Church, that imperishable handiwork of our all-merciful God, has for her immediate and natural purpose the saving of souls and securing our happiness in heaven. Yet in regard to things temporal she is the source of benefits as manifold and great as if the chief end of her existence were to insure the prospering of our earthly life. In truth, wherever the Church has set her foot, she has straightway changed the face of things, and has tempered the moral tone of the people with a new civilization, and with virtues before unknown. All nations which have yielded to her sway have become eminent for their culture, their sense of justice, and the glory of their high deeds.

And yet a hackneyed reproach of old date is levelled against her, that the church is opposed to the rightful aims of the civil government, and is wholly unable to afford help in spreading that welfare and progress which justly and naturally are sought after by every well-regulated State. From the very beginning Christians were harassed by slanderous accusations of this nature, and on that account were held up to hatred and execration, for being, so they were called, 'enemies' of the empire. The Christian religion was moreover commonly charged with being the cause of the calamities that so frequently befell the state, whereas in very truth, just punishment was being awarded to guilty nations by an avenging God. This odious calumny, with most valid reason, nerved the genius and sharpened the pen of St. Augustine who, notably in his treatise *On the City of God,* set forth in so bright a light the worth of Christian wisdom in its relation to the common weal, that he seems not merely to have pleaded the cause of the Christians of his day, but to have refuted for all future times impeachments so grossly contrary to truth. The wicked proneness, however, to levy the like charges and accusations has not been lulled to rest.

Many, indeed, are they who have tried to work out a plan of civil society based on doctrines other than those approved by the Catholic Church. In fact, in these latter days a novel theory of law has begun in many places to be held and to have influence—the outcome, as is maintained, of an age arrived at full stature, and the result of progressive liberty. But though endeavors of various kinds have been ventured on, it is clear that no better mode has been devised for building up and ruling the state than that which is the necessary growth of the teachings of the Gospel. We deem it, therefore, of the highest moment, and a strict duty of our apostolic office, to contrast with the lessons taught by Christ the novel theories now advanced touching the state. By this means we cherish hope that the bright shining of the truth may scatter the mists of error and doubt, so that one and all may see clearly the imperious law of life which they are bound to follow and obey.

It is not difficult to determine what would be the form and character of the state were it governed according to the principles of Christian philosophy. Man's natural instinct moves him to live in civil society, for he cannot, if dwelling apart, provide himself with the necessary requirements of life, nor procure the means of developing his mental and moral faculties. Hence it is divinely ordained that he should lead his life—be it family, social, or civil—with his fellowmen, among whom alone his several wants can be adequately supplied. But as no society can hold together unless someone be over all, directing all to strive earnestly for the common good, every civilized community must have a ruling authority, and this authority no less than society itself, has its source in nature, and has, consequently, God for its author. Hence it follows that all public power must proceed from God: for God alone is the true and supreme Lord of the world. Everything, without exception, must be subject to him, and must serve him, so that whoever holds the right to govern, holds it from one sole and single source, namely God, the sovereign ruler of all. There is no power but from God.

The right to rule is not necessarily, however, bound up with any special mode of government. It may take this or that form, provided only that it be of a nature to insure the general welfare. But whatever be the nature of the government, rulers must ever bear in mind that God is the paramount ruler of the world, and must set him before themselves as their exemplar and law in the administration of the state. For,

in things visible, God has fashioned secondary causes, in which his divine action can in some wise be discerned, leading up to the end to which the course of the world is ever tending. In like manner in civil society, God has always willed that there should be a ruling authority, and that they who are invested with it should reflect the divine power and providence in some measure over the human race.

They, therefore, who rule should rule with even-handed justice, not as masters, but rather as fathers, for the rule of God over man is most just, and is tempered always with a father's kindness. Government should moreover be administered for the well-being of the citizens, because they who govern others possess authority solely for the welfare of the state. Furthermore, the civil power must not be subservient to the advantage of any one individual, or of some few persons, inasmuch as it was established for the common good of all. But if those who are in authority rule unjustly, if they govern overbearingly or arrogantly, and if their measures prove hurtful to the people, they must remember that the Almighty will one day bring them to account, the more strictly in proportion to the sacredness of their office and pre-eminence of their dignity. "The mighty shall be mightily tormented." Then truly will the majesty of the law meet with the dutiful and willing homage of the people, when they are convinced that their rulers hold authority from God, and feel that it is a matter of justice and duty to obey them, and to show them reverence and fealty, united to a love not unlike that which children show their parents. "Let every soul be subject to higher powers." To despise legitimate authority, in whomever vested, is unlawful, as a rebellion against the divine will; and whoever resists that, rushes willfully to destruction. "He that resists the power resists the ordinance of God, and they that resist, purchase to themselves damnation." To cast aside obedience and by popular violence to incite to revolt, is therefore treason, not against man only, but against God.

As a consequence, the state, constituted as it is, is clearly bound to act up to the manifold and weighty duties linking it to God, by the public profession of religion. Nature and reason, which command every individual devoutly to worship God in holiness, because we belong to him and must return to him since from him we came, bind also the civil community by a like law. For men living together in society are under the power of God no less than individuals are; and society, not less than individuals, owes gratitude to God, who gave it being and maintains it, and whose ever-bounteous goodness enriches it with countless blessings. Since, then, no one is allowed to be remiss in the service due to God, and since the chief duty of all men is to cling to religion in both its teaching and practice—not such religion as they may have a preference for, but the religion which God enjoins, and which certain and most clear marks show to be the only one true religion—it is a public crime to act as though there were no God. So too is it a sin in the state not to have a care for religion, as a something beyond its scope, or as of no practical benefit; or out of many forms of religion to adopt that one which chimes in with the fancy. For we are bound absolutely to worship God in that way which he has shown to be his will. All who rule, therefore, should hold in honor the holy name of God, and one of their chief duties must be to favor religion, to protect it, to shield it under the credit and sanction of the laws, and neither to organize nor enact any measure that may compromise its safety. This is the bounden duty of rulers to the people over whom they rule: for one and all we are destined, by our birth and adoption, to enjoy, when this frail and fleeting life is ended, a supreme and final good in heaven, and to the attainment of this every endeavor should be directed. Since then upon this depends the full and perfect happiness of mankind, the securing of this end should be of all imaginable interests the most urgent. Hence civil society, established for the common welfare, should not only safeguard the well-being of the community, but have also at heart the interests of its individual members, in such mode as not in any way to hinder, but in every manner to render as easy as may be, the possession of that highest and unchangeable good for which all should seek. Wherefore, for this purpose, care must especially be taken to preserve unharmed and unimpeded the religion whereof the practice is the link connecting man with his God.

Now it cannot be difficult to find out which is the true religion, if only it be sought with an earnest and unbiased mind; for proofs are abundant and striking. We have, for example, the fullfillment of prophecies, miracles in great number; the rapid spread of the faith in the midst of enemies and in face of overwhelming obstacles; the witness of the martyrs, and the like. From all these it is evident that the only true religion is the one established by Jesus Christ himself, which he committed to his Church to protect and to propagate.

For the only-begotten Son of God established on earth a society which is called the Church, and to it he handed over the exalted and divine office which he had received from his Father, to be continued through the ages to come: "as the Father has sent me, I also send you. Behold I am with you all days, even to the consummation of the world." Consequently, as Jesus

Christ came into the world that men might have life and have it more abundantly, so also has the Church for its aim and end the eternal salvation of souls, and hence it is so constituted as to open wide its arms to all mankind, unhampered by any limit of either time or place: "preach the Gospel to every creature."

Over this mighty multitude God has himself set rulers with power to govern; and he has willed that one should be the head of all, and the chief and unerring teacher of truth, to whom he has given the keys of the kingdom of heaven: "Feed my lambs, feed my sheep. I have prayed for you that your faith fail not."

This society is made up of men, just as civil society is, and yet is supernatural and spiritual, on account of the end for which it was founded, and of the means by which it aims at attaining that end. Hence it is distinguished and differs from civil society; and, what is of the highest moment, it is a society chartered as of divine right, perfect in its nature and in its title, to possess in itself and by itself, through the will and loving kindness of its founder, all needful provision for its maintenance and action. And just as the end at which the Church aims is by far the noblest of ends, so is its authority the most exalted of all authorities, nor can it be looked upon as inferior to the civil power, or in any manner dependent upon it.

In very truth Jesus Christ gave to his apostles unrestrained authority in regard to things sacred, together with the genuine and most true power of making laws, as also with the two-fold right of judging and of punishing, which flow from that power: "All power is given to me in heaven and in earth. Going therefore teach all nations . . . teaching them to observe all things whatsoever I have commanded you." And in another place: "If he

will not hear them, tell the Church." And again: "In readiness to revenge all disobedience." And once more: "That . . . I may not deal more severely according to the power which the Lord has given me, unto edification and not unto destruction." Hence it is the Church, and not the state, that is to be man's guide to heaven. It is to the Church that God has assigned the charge of seeing to, and legislating for, all that concerns religion; of teaching all nations; of spreading the Christian faith as widely as possible; in short, of administering freely and without hindrance, in accordance with her own judgment, all matters that fall within her competence.

Now this authority, perfect in itself, and plainly meant to be unfettered, so long assailed by a philosophy that truckles to the State, the Church has never ceased to claim for herself, and openly to exercise. The apostles themselves were the first to uphold it when, being forbidden by the rulers of the synagogue to preach the Gospel, they courageously answered, "we ought to obey God rather than men." This same authority the holy fathers of the Church were always careful to maintain by weighty arguments, according as occasion arose, and the Roman pontiffs have never shrunk from defending it with unbending constancy. Nay more, princes and all invested with power to rule have themselves approved it, in theory alike and in practice. It cannot be called in question that in the making of treaties, in the transaction of business matters, in the sending and receiving ambassadors, and in the interchange of other kinds of official dealings, they have been wont to treat the Church as with a supreme and legitimate power. And assuredly all ought to hold that it was not without a singular disposition of God's providence, that this power of the Church was provided with a civil sovereignty as the surest safeguard of her independence.

The Almighty, therefore, has appointed the charge of the human race between two powers, the ecclesiastical and the civil, the one being set over divine, and the other over human, things. Each in its kind is supreme, each has fixed limits within which it is contained, limits which are defined by the nature and special object of the providence of each, so that there is, we may say, an orbit traced out within which the action of each is brought into play by its own native right. But inasmuch as each of these two powers has authority over the same subjects, and as it might come to pass that one and the same thing—related differently, but still remaining one and the same thing—might belong to the jurisdiction and determination of both, therefore God, who foresees all things and who is the author of these two powers, has marked out the course of each in right correlation to the other. For the powers that are, are ordained of God. Were this not so, deplorable contentions and conflicts would often arise, and not infrequently men, like travelers at the meeting of two roads, would hesitate in anxiety and doubt, not knowing what course to follow. Two powers would be commanding contrary things, and it would be a dereliction of duty to disobey either of the two.

But it would be most repugnant to them to deem thus of the wisdom and goodness of God. Even in physical things, albeit of a lower order, the Almighty has so combined the forces and springs of nature with tempered action and wondrous harmony, that no one of them clashes with any other, and all of them most fitly and aptly work together for the great purpose of the universe. There must accordingly exist between these two powers a certain orderly connection which may be compared to the union of the soul and body in man. The nature and scope of that connection can be determined only, as we have laid down, by having regard to the nature of each power, and by taking account of the relative excellence and nobleness of their purpose. One of the two has for its proximate and chief object the well-being of this mortal life; the other the everlasting joys of heaven. Whatever, therefore, in things human is of a sacred character, whatever belongs either of its own nature or by reason of the end to which it is referred, to the salvation of souls or to the worship of God, is subject to the power and judgment of the Church. Whatever is to be ranged under the civil and political order is rightly subject to the civil authority. Jesus Christ has himself given command that what is Caesar's is to be rendered to Caesar, and that what belongs to God is to be rendered to God.

There are, nevertheless, occasions when another method of concord is available, for the sake of peace and liberty: we mean when rulers of the state and the Roman pontiff come to an understanding touching some special matter. At such times the Church gives signal proof of her motherly love by showing the greatest possible kindliness and indulgence.

Such then, as we have briefly pointed out, is the Christian organization of civil society: not rashly or fancifully shaped out, but educed from the highest and truest principles, confirmed by natural reason itself.

In such an organization of the state there is nothing that can be thought to infringe upon the dignity of rulers, and nothing unbecoming them; nay, so far from degrading the sovereign power in its due rights, it adds to its permanence and luster. Indeed, when more fully pondered, this mutual coordination has a perfection in which all other forms of government are lacking, and from which excellent results would flow were the several component parts to keep their place, and duly discharge the office and work appointed respectively for each. And, without a doubt, in the constitution of the state such as we have described, divine and human things are equitably shared; the rights of citizens assured to them, and fenced round by divine, by natural, and by human law; the duties incumbent on each one being wisely marked out, and their fulfillment fittingly insured. In their uncertain and toilsome journey towards the city made without hands, all see that they have safe guides and helpers on their way, and are conscious that others have charge to protect their persons alike and their possessions, and to obtain or preserve for them everything essential for their present life. Furthermore, domestic society acquires that firmness and solidity so needful to it, from the holiness of marriage, one and indissoluble. . . .

In political affairs, and in all matters civil, the laws aim at securing the common good, and are not framed according to the delusive caprices and opinions of the mass of the people, but by truth and by justice; the ruling powers are invested with a sacredness more than human, and are withheld from deviating from the path of duty, and from over-stepping the bounds of rightful authority; and the obedience of citizens is rendered with a feeling of honor and dignity, since obedience is not the servitude of man to man, but submission to the will of God, exercising his sovereignty through the medium of men. Now, once this is recognized as undeniable, it is felt that the high office of rulers should be held in respect; that public authority should be constantly and faithfully obeyed; that no act of sedition should be committed; and that the civic order of the commonwealth should be maintained as sacred.

So also, as to the duties of each one towards his fellowmen, mutual forbearance, kindliness, generosity are placed in the ascendant; the man who is at once a citizen and a Christian is not drawn aside by conflicting obligations; and, lastly, the abundant benefits with which the Christian religion, of its very nature, endows even the mortal life of man, are acquired for the community and civil society. And this to such an extent that it may be said in sober truth: "The condition of the commonwealth depends on religion with which God is worshiped: and between one and the other there exists an intimate and abiding connection. . . ."

There was once a time when states were governed by the principles of Gospel teaching. Then it was that the power and divine virtue of Christianity had diffused itself throughout the laws, institutions and morals of the people, permeating all ranks and relations of civil society. Then, too, the religion instituted by Jesus Christ, established firmly in befitting dignity, flourished everywhere by the favor of princes and the legitimate protection of magistrates; and Church and state were happily united in concord and friendly interchange of good offices.

The state, constituted in this wise, bore fruits important beyond all expectation, whose remembrance is still, and always will be, in renown, witnessed to as they are by countless proofs which can never be blotted out or even obscured by any craft of any enemies. Christian Europe has subdued barbarous nations, and changed them from a savage to a civilized condition, from superstition to true worship. It victoriously rolled back the tide of Mohammedan conquest; retained the headship of civilization; stood forth in the front rank as the leader and teacher of all, in every branch of national culture; bestowed on the world the gift of true and many-sided liberty; and most wisely founded very numerous institutions for the solace of human suffering. And if we inquire how it was able to bring about so altered a condition of things, the answer is: beyond all question, in large measure, through religion; under whose auspices so many great undertakings were set on foot, through whose aid they were brought to completion.

A similar state of things would certainly have continued had the agreement of the two powers been lasting. More important results even might have been justly looked for, had obedience waited upon the authority, teaching, and counsels of the Church, and had this submission been specially marked by greater and more unswerving loyalty. For that should be regarded in the light of an ever-changeless law which Ivo of Chartres wrote to Pope Paschal II: "When kingdom and priesthood are at one, in complete accord, the world is well ruled, and the Church flourishes, and brings forth abundant fruit. But when they are at variance, not only smaller interests prosper not, but even things of greatest moment fall into deplorable decay."

Sad it is to call to mind how the harmful and lamentable rage for innovation, which rose to a climax in the sixteenth century, threw first of all into confusion the Christian religion, and next, by natural sequence, invaded the precincts of philosophy, whence it spread among all classes of society. From this source, as from a fountain head, burst forth all those later tenets of unbridled license which, in the midst of the terrible upheavals of the last century, were wildly conceived and boldly proclaimed as the principles and foundation of that new jurisprudence which was not merely previously unknown, but was at variance on many

points with not only the Christian but even the natural law.

Among these principles the main one lays down that as all men are alike by race and nature, so in like manner all are equal in the control of their life; that each one is so far his own master as to be in no sense under the rule of any other individual; that each is free to think on every subject just as he may choose, and to do whatever he may like to do; that no man has any right to rule over other men. In a society grounded upon such maxims, all government is nothing more nor less than the will of the people, and the people, being under the power of itself alone, is alone its ruler. It does choose nevertheless some to whose charge it may commit itself, but in such wise that it makes over to them not the right so much as the business of governing, to be exercised, however, in its name. The authority of God is passed over in silence, just as if there were no God, or as if he cared nothing for human society; or as if men, whether in their individual capacity or bound together in social relations, owed nothing to God; or as if there could be a government of which the whole origin and power and authority did not reside in God himself. Thus, as is evident, a state becomes nothing but a multitude which is its own master and ruler. And since the populace is declared to contain within itself the spring-head of all rights and of all power, it follows that the state does not consider itself bound by any kind of duty towards God. Moreover, it believes that it is not obliged to make public profession of any religion; or to inquire which of the very many religions is the only true one; or to prefer one religion to all the rest; or to show to any form of religion special favor; but, on the contrary, is bound to grant equal rights to every creed, so that public order may not be disturbed by any particular form of religious belief.

And it is a part of this theory that all questions that concern religion are to be referred to private judgment; that every one is to be free to follow whatever religion he prefers, or none at all if he disapprove of all. From this the following consequences logically flow: that the most unrestrained opinions may be openly expressed as to the practice or omission of divine worship and that every one has unbounded license to think whatever he chooses and to publish abroad whatever he thinks.

Now when the state rests on foundations like those just named—and for the time being they are greatly in favor—it readily appears into what and how unrightful a position the Church is driven. For when the management of public business is in harmony with doctrines of such a kind, the Catholic religion is allowed a standing in civil society equal only, or inferior, to societies alien from it; no regard is paid to the laws of the Church, and she who, by the order and commission of Jesus Christ, has the duty of teaching all nations, finds herself forbidden to take any part in the instruction of the people. With reference to matters that are of twofold jurisdiction, they who administer the civil power lay down the law at their own will, and in matters that appertain to religion they defiantly put aside the most sacred decrees of the Church. They claim jurisdiction over the marriages of Catholics, even over the bond as well as the unity and the indissolubility of matrimony. They lay hands on the goods of the clergy, contending that the Church cannot possess property. Lastly, they treat the Church with such arrogance that, rejecting entirely her title to the nature and rights of a perfect society, they hold that she differs in no respect from other socie-

ties in the state, and for this reason possesses no right nor any legal power of action, save that which she holds by the concession and favor of the government. If in any state the Church retains her own right—and this with the approval of the civil law, owing to an agreement publicly entered into by the two powers—men forthwith begin to cry out that matters affecting the Church must be separated from those of the state.

Their object in uttering this cry is to be able to violate unpunished their plighted faith, and in all things to have unchecked control. And as the Church, unable to abandon her chiefest and most sacred duties, cannot patiently put up with this, and asks that the pledge given to her be fully and scrupulously acted up to, contentions frequently arise between the ecclesiastical and the civil power, of which the issue commonly is that the weaker power is beaten by the one which is stronger in human resources.

Accordingly, it has become the practice and determination under this condition of public policy, now so much admired by many, either to forbid the action of the Church altogether, or to keep her in check and bondage to the state. Public enactments are in great measure framed with this design. The drawing up of laws, the administration of state affairs, the godless education of youth, the spoliation and suppression of religious orders, the overthrow of the temporal power of the Roman pontiff, all alike aim at this one end—to paralyze the action of Christian institutions, to cramp to the utmost the freedom of the Catholic Church, and to curtail her every single prerogative.

Now, natural reason itself proves convincingly that such concepts of the government of a state are wholly at variance with the truth. Nature itself bears witness that all power, of every kind, has its origin from God, who is its chief and most august source.

The sovereignty of the people, however, and this without any reference to God, is held to reside in the multitude, which is doubtless a doctrine exceedingly well calculated to flatter and to inflame many passions, but which lacks all reasonable proof, and all power of insuring public safety and preserving order. Indeed, from the prevalence of this teaching, things have come to such a pass that many hold as an axiom of civil jurisprudence that seditions may be rightfully fostered. For the opinion prevails that princes are nothing more than delegates chosen to carry out the will of the people; whence it necessarily follows that all things are as changeable as the will of the people, so that risk of public disturbance is ever hanging over our heads.

To hold, therefore, that there is no difference in matters of religion between forms that are unlike each other, and even contrary to each other, most clearly leads in the end to the rejection of all religion in both theory and practice. And this is the same thing as atheism, however it may differ from it in name. Men who really believe in the existence of God must, in order to be consistent with themselves and to avoid absurd conclusions, understand that differing modes of divine worship, involving dissimilarity and conflict even on most important points, cannot all be equally probable, equally good and equally acceptable to God.

So, too, the liberty of thinking and of publishing whatsoever each one likes without any hindrance is not in itself an advantage over which society can wisely rejoice. On the contrary, it is the fountain-head and origin of many evils. Liberty is a power perfecting man, and hence should have truth and goodness for its object. But the character of goodness and truth, can-

not be changed at option. These remain ever one and the same, and are no less unchangeable than nature herself. If the mind assents to false opinions, and the will chooses and follows after what is wrong, neither can attain its native fullness, but both must fall from their native dignity into an abyss of corruption. Whatever, therefore, is opposed to virtue and truth, may not rightly be brought temptingly before the eye of man, much less sanctioned by the favor and protection of the law. A well-spent life is the only passport to heaven, whither all are bound, and on this account the state is acting against the laws and dictates of nature whenever it permits the license of opinion and of action to lead minds astray from the truth, and souls away from the practice of virtue. To exclude the Church, founded by God himself, from the business of life, from the power of making laws, from the training of youth, from domestic society, is a grave and fatal error. A state from which religion is banished can never be well regulated; and already perhaps more than is desirable is known of the nature and tendency of the so-called civil philosophy of life and morals. The Church of Christ is the true and sole teacher of virtue and guardian of morals. She it is who preserves in their purity the principles from which duties flow, and by setting forth most urgent reasons for virtuous life, bids us not only to turn away from wicked deeds, but even to curb all movements of the mind that are opposed to reason; even though they be not carried out in action.

To wish the Church to be subject to the civil power in the exercise of her duty is a great folly and a sheer injustice. Whenever this is the case, order is disturbed, for things natural are put above things supernatural; the many benefits which the Church, if free to act, would confer on society are either prevented or at least lessened in number; and a way is prepared for enmities and contentions between the two powers; with how evil a result to both, the issue of events has taught us only too frequently. . . .

The origin of public power is to be sought for in God himself, and not in the multitude, and this it is repugnant to reason to allow free scope for sedition. Again, that it is not lawful for the state, any more than for individuals, either to disregard all religious duties, or to hold in equal favor different kinds of religion; that the unrestrained freedom of thinking and of openly making known one's thoughts is not inherent in the rights of citizens, and is by no means to be reckoned worthy of favor and support [is clear]. In like manner it is to be understood that the Church no less than the state itself is a society perfect in its own nature and its own right, and that those who exercise sovereignty ought not so to act as to compel the Church to become subservient or subject to them, or to hamper her liberty in the management of her own affairs, or to despoil her in any way of the other privileges conferred upon her by Jesus Christ. In matters, however, of mixed jurisdiction, it is in the highest degree consonant to nature, as also to the designs of God, that so far from one of the powers separating itself from the other, or still less coming to conflict with it, complete harmony, such as is suited to the end for which each power exists, should be preserved between them.

This, then, is the teaching of the Catholic Church concerning the constitution and government of the state. By the words and decrees just cited, if judged dispassionately, no one of the several forms of government is in itself condemned, inasmuch as none of them contains anything contrary to Catholic doctrine, and all of them are capable, if wisely and justly managed, of insuring the welfare of the state. Neither is it blameworthy in itself, in any manner, for the people to have a share, greater or less, in the government: for at certain times, and under certain laws, such participation may not only be of benefit to the citizens, but may even be of obligation. Nor is there any reason why any one should accuse the Church of being wanting in gentleness of action or largeness of view, or of being opposed to real and lawful liberty. The Church, indeed, deems it unlawful to place various forms of divine worship on the same footing as true religion, but does not, on that account, condemn those rulers who for the sake of securing some great good, or of hindering some great evil, tolerate in practice that these various forms of religion have a place in the state. And in fact the Church is wont to take earnest heed that no one shall be forced to embrace the Catholic faith against his will, for, as St. Augustine wisely reminds us: "Man cannot believe otherwise than of his own free will."

In the same way the Church cannot approve of that liberty which begets a contempt of the most sacred laws of God, and casts off the obedience due to lawful authority, for this is not liberty so much as license, and is most correctly styled to St. Augustine the "liberty of self-ruin," and by the apostle St. Peter the cloak for malice. Indeed, since it is opposed to reason, it is a true slavery, for whoever commits sin is the servant of sin. On the other hand, that liberty is truly genuine, and to be sought after, which in regard to the individual does not allow men to be the slaves of error and of passion, the worst of all masters; which, too, in public administration guides the citizens in wisdom and provides for them increased means of well-being, and which, further, protects the state from foreign interference.

This honorable liberty, alone worthy of human beings, the Church approves most highly and has never slackened her endeavor to preserve, strong and unchanged, among nations. And in truth whatever in the state is of chief avail for the common welfare; whatever has been usefully established to curb the license of rulers who are opposed to the true interests of the people, or to prevent governments from unwarrantably interfering in municipal or family affairs; whatever tends to uphold the honor, manhood, and equal rights of individual citizens —of all these things, as the monuments of past ages bear witness, the Catholic Church has always been the originator, the promoter, or the guardian. Ever therefore consistent with herself, while on the one hand she rejects that exorbitant liberty which in individuals and in nation sends in license or in thraldom, on the other hand, she willingly and most gladly welcomes whatever improvements the age brings forth, if these really secure the prosperity of life here below, which is as it were a stage in the journey to the life that will know no ending.

Therefore, when it is said that the Church is jealous of modern political systems, and that she repudiates the discoveries of modern research, the charge is a ridiculous and groundless calumny. Wild opinions she does repudiate, wicked and seditious projects she does condemn—and especially that habit of mind in which are seen the beginnings of a willful departure from God. But as all truth must necessarily proceed from God, the Church recognizes in all truth that is reached by research, a trace of the divine intelligence. And as all truth in the natural order is powerless to destroy belief in the teachings of revelation, but can do much to confirm it, and as every newly

discovered truth may serve to further the knowledge or the praise of God, it follows that whatever spreads the range of knowledge will always be willingly and ever joyfully welcomed by the Church. She will always encourage and promote, as she does in other branches of knowledge, all study occupied with the investigation of nature. In these pursuits, should the human intellect discover anything not known before, the Church makes no opposition. She never objects to search being made for things that minister to the refinements and comforts of life. So far indeed from opposing these she is now, as she ever has been, hostile alone to indolence and sloth, and earnestly wishes that the talents of men may bear more and more abundant fruit by cultivation and exercise. Moreover she gives encouragement to every kind of art and handicraft, and through her influence, directing all strivings after progress towards virtue and salvation, she labors to prevent man's intellect and industry from turning him away from God and from heavenly things.

All this, though so reasonable and full of counsel, finds little favor nowadays, when states not only refuse to conform to the rules of Christian wisdom, but seem even anxious to recede from them further on each successive day. Nevertheless, since truth when brought to light is wont of its own nature to spread itself far and wide and gradually take possession of the minds of men, moved by the great and holy duty of our apostolic mission to all nations we speak as we are bound to do, with freedom. Our eyes are not closed to the spirit of the times. We repudiate not the assured and useful improvements of our age, but devoutly wish affairs of state to take a safer course than they are now taking, and to rest on a more firm foundation without injury to the true freedom of the people. For the best parent and guardian of liberty among men is truth. The truth shall make you free.

If in the difficult time in which our lot is cast, Catholics will give ear to us, as it behooves them to do, they will readily see what are the duties of each one in matters of opinion as well as action. As regards opinion, whatever the Roman pontiffs have hitherto taught, or shall hereafter teach, must be held with a firm grasp of mind, and so often as occasion requires, must be openly professed.

Especially with reference to the so-called "liberties" which are so greatly coveted in these days, all must stand by the judgment of the Apostolic See, and have the same mind. Let no man be deceived by the outward appearance of these liberties, but let each one reflect whence these have had their origin, and by what efforts they are everywhere upheld and promoted. Experience has made us well acquainted with their results to the state, since everywhere they have borne fruits which the good and wise bitterly deplore. If there really exists anywhere, or if we in imagination conceive, a state, waging wanton and tyrannical war against Christianity, and if we compare with it the modern form of government just described, this latter may seem the more endurable of the two. Yet, undoubtedly, the principles on which such a government is grounded are, as we have said, of a nature which no one can approve.

Secondly, action may relate to private and domestic matters, or to matters public. As to private affairs, the first duty is to conform life and conduct to the Gospel precepts, and to refuse to shrink from this duty when Christian virtue demands some sacrifice difficult to make. All, moreover, are bound to love the Church as their common mother, to obey her laws, promote her honor, defend her rights, and to endeavor to make her respected and loved by those over whom they have authority. It is also of great moment to the public welfare to take a prudent part in the business of municipal administration, and to endeavor above all to introduce effectual measures: so that, as becomes a Christian people, public provision may be made for the instruction of youth in religion and true morality. Upon these things the well-being of every state greatly depends.

Furthermore, it is in general fitting and salutary that Catholics should extend their efforts beyond this restricted sphere, and give their attention to national politics. We say in general, because these our precepts are addressed to all nations. However, it may in some places be true that, for most urgent and just reasons, it is by no means expedient for Catholics to engage in public affairs or to take an active part in politics. Nevertheless, as we have laid down, to take no share in public matters would be equally as wrong (we speak in general) as not to have concern for, or not to bestow labor upon, the common good. And this all the more because Catholics are admonished by the very doctrines which they profess to be upright and faithful in the discharge of duty; while if they hold aloof, men whose principles offer but small guarantee for the welfare of the state will the more readily seize the reins of government. This would tend also to the injury of the Christian religion, forasmuch as those would come into power who are badly disposed towards the Church, and those who are willing to befriend her would be deprived of all influence.

It follows therefore clearly that Catholics have just reasons for taking part in the conduct of public affairs. For in so doing they assume not the responsibility of approving what is blameworthy in the actual methods of government, but seek to turn these very methods, so far as is possible, to the genuine and true public good, and to use their best endeavors at the same time to infuse as it were into all the veins of the state the healthy sap and blood of Christian wisdom and virtue. The morals and ambitions of the heathens differed widely from those of the Gospel, yet Christians were to be seen living undefiled everywhere in the midst of pagan superstition and, while always true to themselves, coming to the front boldly wherever an opening was presented. Models of loyalty to their rulers, submissive, so far as was permitted, to the sovereign power, they shed around them on every side a halo of sanctity; they strove to be helpful to their brethren, and to attract others to the wisdom of Jesus Christ, yet were bravely ready to withdraw from public life, nay even to lay down their life, if they could not without loss of virtue retain honors, dignities, and offices. For this reason Christian ways and manners speedily found their way not only into private houses but into the camp, the Senate, and even into the imperial palaces. "We are but of yesterday," wrote Tertullian, "yet we swarm in all your institutions, we crowd your cities, islands, village, town, assemblies, the army itself, your wards and corporations, the palace, the senate, and the law courts." So that the Christian faith, when once it became lawful to make public profession of the Gospel, appeared in most of the cities of Europe, not like an infant crying in its cradle, but already grown up and full of vigor.

In these our days it is well to revive these examples of our forefathers. First and foremost it is the duty of all Catholics worthy of the name and wishful to be known as most loving children of the Church, to reject without swerving whatever is inconsistent with so fair a title; to make use of

popular institutions, so far as can honestly be done, for the advancement of truth and righteousness; to strive that liberty of action shall not transgress the bounds marked out by nature and the law of God; to endeavor to bring back all civil society to the pattern and form of Christianity which we have described. It is barely possible to lay down any fixed method by which such purposes are to be attained, because the means adopted must suit places and times widely differing from one another. Nevertheless, above all things, unity of aim must be preserved, and similarity must be sought after in all plans of action. Both these objects will be carried into effect without fail, if all will follow the guidance of the Apostolic See as their rule of life, and obey the bishops whom the Holy Ghost has placed to rule the Church of God. The defense of Catholicism, indeed, necessarily demands that in the profession of doctrines taught by the Church all shall be of one mind and all steadfast in believing; and care must be taken never to connive, in any way, at false opinions, never to withstand them less strenuously than truth allows. In mere matters of opinion it is permissible to discuss things with moderation, with a desire to searching into the truth, without unjust suspicion or angry recriminations.

Hence, lest concord be broken by rash charges, let this be understood by all; that the integrity of Catholic faith cannot be reconciled with opinions verging on naturalism, or rationalism, the essence of which is utterly to sterilize Christianity, and to install in society the supremacy of man to the exclusion of God. Further, it is unlawful to follow one line of conduct in private and another in public, respecting privately the authority of the Church, but publicly rejecting it. For this would amount to joining together good and evil, and to putting man in conflict with himself; whereas he ought always to be consistent, and never in the least point nor in any condition of life to swerve from Christian virtue.

But in matters merely political, as for instance the best form of government, and this or that system of administration, a difference of opinion is lawful. Those, therefore, whose piety is in other respects known, and whose minds are ready to accept in all obedience the decrees of the Apostolic See, cannot in justice be accounted as bad men because they disagree as to the subjects we have mentioned; and still graver wrong will be done them if—as we have more than once perceived with regret—they are accused of violating, or of wavering in the Catholic faith.

Let this be well borne in mind by all who are in the habit of publishing their opinions, and above all by journalists. In the endeavor to secure interests of the highest order there is no room for internal strife or party

rivalries, since all should aim with one mind and purpose to make safe that which is the common object of all—the maintenance of religion and of the state.

If therefore, there have hitherto been dissensions, let them henceforth be gladly buried in oblivion. If rash or injurious acts have been committed, whoever may have been at fault, let mutual charity make amends and let the past be redeemed by a special submission of all to the Apostolic See.

In this way Catholics will attain two most excellent results: they will become helpers to the Church in preserving and propagating Christian wisdom; and they will confer the greatest benefit on civil society, the safety of which is exceedingly imperilled by evil teachings and bad passions.

This, venerable brethren, is what we have thought it our duty to expound to all nations of the Catholic world touching the Christian constitution of states and the duties of individual citizens.

13. *Pope St. Pius X: The True Christian Spirit*

From the *Motu Proprio of Church Music* (Toledo: Gregorian Institute of America, 1950), by permission of the Gregorian Institute of America, Inc., Copyright owners; Vinvent A. Yzermans, ed., *All Things in Christ* (Westminster, Maryland: Newman Press, 1954), pp. 93-96, 89, 101-109.

A. MOTU PROPRIO ON CHURCH MUSIC, 22 NOVEMBER 1903

AMONG the pastoral cares not only of this supreme chair, which we though unworthy hold by the inscrutable disposition of Providence, but of every individual church, doubtless the foremost is that of upholding and advancing the decorum of God's house, where the august mysteries of religion are celebrated and where the Christian people gather to receive the grace of the sacraments, to assist at the holy sacrifice of the altar, to adore the most

sublime sacrament of the Lord's body, and to join in the common prayer of the Church in public and solemn liturgical services. Nothing, therefore, must take place in the temple which may disturb or even lessen the piety and devotion of the faithful, nothing that might give reasonable cause of distaste or scandal, nothing especially that might directly offend the decorum and holiness of the sacred functions and would thus be unworthy of the house of prayer and of God's majesty. . . .

If we refer to our own personal experience and consider the very numerous complaints that come to us from all sides, in the short time since it pleased the Lord to raise our lowly person to the highest summit of the Roman pontificate, we believe it our first duty to raise our voice at once in reproof and condemnation of whatever is found out of order in the functions of worship and ecclesiastical offices. It being our most eager wish that the true Christian spirit may flower again in every way and be upheld by all the faithful, before anything else it is necessary to see to the holiness and dignity of the temple, where the faithful gather to gain that spirit from its first and indispensable source: the active participation in the sacred mysteries and the public and solemn prayer of the Church. And it is vain to hope that the blessing of heaven will come down on us in abundance, when our homage to the most high, instead of rising in the odor of sweetness, places in the hand of the Lord the scourge with which the divine redeemer once drove the unworthy profaners from the temple.

Therefore, in order that henceforth no one may be able to plead in excuse that he did not clearly know his duty, and in order that every ambiguity may be excluded in the understanding of what has already been ordered, we have judged it expedient to add briefly these principles that regulate sacred music in the functions of worship and to gather together in a single table the principal prescriptions of the Church against the commoner abuses in this matter. Therefore, and with certain knowledge, we do publish this our instruction [*Motu Proprio*] to which, as to a juridical code of sacred music, we will with the fullness of our apostolic authority that the force of law be given, imposing on all by our present handwriting the most scrupulous observance.

Sacred music as an integral part of the solemn liturgy shares in its general purpose, which is the glory of God and the sanctification and edification of the faithful. It contributes to the increase of decorum and splendor of the ecclesiastical ceremonies, and since its principal function is to adorn with suitable melody the liturgical text proposed to the understanding of the faithful, its proper purpose is to add greater efficacy to the text itself, so that by this means the faithful may be more easily moved to devotion and better disposed to receive in themselves the fruits of grace proper to the celebration of the sacred mysteries.

Consequently, sacred music must possess, in the highest degree, the qualities proper to the liturgy, namely holiness and goodness of form, from which spontaneously there springs its other mark, universality.

It must be holy, and hence exclude all profanity, not only in itself but also in the manner in which it is presented by the performers.

It must be true art, for otherwise it is not possible for it to have that effect on listeners which the Church intends to achieve in admitting the art of music into her liturgy.

But, at the same time, it must be universal, in the sense that though every nation is allowed to admit into its ecclesiastical compositions those particular forms that constitute, so to speak, the specific character of its own music, still these must be subordinated in such a way to the general character of sacred music that no one of another nation may receive a bad impression on hearing them.

These qualities are found, in the highest degree, in Gregorian chant, which consequently is the chant proper to the Roman Church, the only chant that she has inherited from the ancient fathers, which she has jealously guarded throughout the centuries in her liturgical codices, which she directly proposed to the faithful as her own, which she prescribes exclusively for some parts of the liturgy, and which very recent studies have so faithfully restored to its integrity and purity.

For these reasons Gregorian chant has always been considered the supreme model of sacred music, so that the following rule may rightly be set down: The more closely a composition for church approaches the Gregorian melody in movement, inspiration, and flavor, the more sacred and liturgical it is; and the more it departs from that supreme model, the less worthy it is of the temple.

The ancient traditional Gregorian chant must therefore be widely restored in the functions of worship, and it must be held by all as certain that an ecclesiastical function loses none of its solemnity when accompanied by no other music than this alone.

In particular let care be taken to restore Gregorian chant to the use of the people, so that the faithful may again take more active part in ecclesiastical offices, as it did in ancient times.

The Church has always recognized and favored the progress of the arts, admitting to the service of worship everything good and beautiful that genius has been able to discover throughout the centuries, always however with due regard for liturgical laws. Consequently, modern music is also admitted in church, as it also offers compositions of such goodness, seriousness, and gravity that they are not at all unworthy of liturgical functions. Nevertheless, since modern music has risen principally for profane uses, greater care must be taken so that musical compositions in modern style which are admitted in church may contain nothing profane, nothing reminiscent of theatrical motifs, and may not be fashioned even in their external patterns on the movement of profane pieces.

Among the several kinds of modern music, what appears less suitable for accompanying the functions of worship is the theatrical style that was in greatest vogue during the last century, especially in Italy. By its very nature this offers the greatest opposition to Gregorian chant and to classical polyphony, and therefore to the most important of all good sacred music. Besides the intrinsic structure, the rhythm and so called conventionalism of this style correspond badly to the requirements of true liturgical music.

For the exact carrying out of what has here been laid down, the bishops, if they have not already done so, are to set up in their dioceses a special commission of persons truly competent in matters of sacred music, to which commission the duty of watching over the music performed in their churches should be entrusted, in the way that they may judge most opportune. Nor should they only take care that the music be good, but that it correspond to the abilities of the singers and be always well performed.

In seminaries of clerics and in ecclesiastical institutes, according to the Tridentine prescriptions, let the traditional Gregorian chant be cultivated by all with diligence and love, and let superiors be generous in encouragement and praise toward their young charges. In the same way, where it is possible let the founding of a *schola cantorum* be furthered among clerics for the performance of sacred polyphony and good liturgical music.

In the ordinary classes of liturgy, moral, and canon law given to students of theology, let care be taken not to omit treating those points which refer more directly to the principles and laws of sacred music, and let an attempt be made to complete the teaching with some special instruction on the aesthetics of sacred art, in order that the clerics may not leave the seminary ignorant of all these ideas, so necessary for full ecclesiastical culture.

Let care be taken to restore, at least in the principal churches, the ancient *scholae cantorum*, as is already done most fruitfully in a great many places. It is not difficult for zealous clergy to instruct such *scholae,* even in smaller, rural churches; indeed in them is found a very easy means of uniting boys and adults around the clergy, for their profit and the edification of the people.

Let care be taken to support and promote in every best way higher schools of sacred music where they already exist, and to help in founding them where they do not yet exist. It is of very great importance that the Church herself provide for the instruction of her choirmasters, organists, and singers, according to the true principles of sacred art.

Finally, it is recommended to choirmasters, to singers, to members of the clergy, to superiors of seminaries, of ecclesiastical institutions and of religious communities, to parish priests and rectors of churches, to canons of collegiate churches and cathedrals, and especially to diocesan ordinaries to favor with all zeal these wise reforms, long desired and called for by all, in order that the very authority of the Church, which has repeatedly proposed them and now calls for them anew, may not fall into contempt.

B. DECREE ON THE NECESSARY DISPOSITION FOR FREQUENT AND DAILY RECEPTION OF HOLY COMMUNION, 20 DECEMBER 1905

The holy Council of Trent, having in view the ineffable riches of grace which are offered to the faithful who receive the most holy Eucharist, makes the following declaration: "The holy council wishes indeed that at each Mass the faithful who are present should communicate, not only in spiritual desire, but sacramentally, by the actual reception of the Eucharist." These words declare plainly enough the wish of the Church that all Christians should be daily nourished by this heavenly banquet and should derive therefrom more abundant fruit for their sanctification.

The wish of the council fully conforms to that desire wherewith Christ our Lord was inflamed when he instituted this divine sacrament. For he himself, more than once, and in clarity of word, pointed out the necessity of frequently eating his flesh and drinking his blood, especially in these words: "This is the bread that has come down from heaven; not as your fathers ate the manna, and died. He who eats this bread shall live forever." From this comparison of the food of angels with bread and with manna, it was easily to be understood by his disciples that, as the body is daily nourished with bread, and as the Hebrews were daily fed with manna in the desert, so the Christian soul might daily partake of this heavenly bread and be refreshed thereby. Moreover, we are bidden in the Lord's Prayer to ask for "our daily bread" by which words, the holy fathers of the Church all but unanimously teach, must be understood not so much that material bread which is the support of the body as the Eucharistic bread which ought to be our daily food.

Moreover, the desire of Jesus Christ and of the Church that all the faithful should daily approach the sacred banquet is directed chiefly to this end, that the faithful, being united to God by means of the sacrament, may thence derive strength to resist their sensual passions, to cleanse themselves from the stains of daily faults, and to avoid these graver sins to which human frailty is liable; so that its primary purpose is not that the honor and reverence due to our Lord may be safe-guarded, or that it may serve as a reward or recompense of virtue bestowed on the recipients. Hence the holy council calls the Eucharist "the antidote whereby we may be freed from daily faults and be preserved from mortal sin."

The will of God in this respect was well understood by the first Christians; and they daily hastened to this table of life and strength. "They continued steadfastly in the teaching of the apostles and in the communion of the breaking of the bread." The holy fathers and writers of the Church testify that this practice was continued into later ages and not without great increase of holiness and perfection.

Piety, however, grew cold, and especially afterward because of the widespread plague of Jansenism, disputes began to arise concerning the dispositions with which one ought to receive frequent and daily communion; and writers vied with one another in demanding more and more stringent conditions as necessary to be fulfilled. The result of such disputes was that very few were considered worthy to receive the holy Eucharist daily, and to derive from this most health-giving sacrament its most abundant fruits; the others were content to partake of it once a year, or once a month, or at most once a week. To such a degree, indeed, was rigorism carried that whole classes of persons were excluded from a frequent approach to the holy table, for instance, merchants or those who were married.

Some, however, went over to the opposite view. They held that daily communion was prescribed by divine law and that no day should pass without communicating, and besides other practices not in accord with the approved usage of the Church, they determined that the Eucharist must be received even on Good Friday and in fact so administered it.

Toward these conditions, the Holy See did not fail in its duty. A decree of this sacred congregation, which begins with the words *Cum ad aures,* issued on 12 February 1679, with the approbation of Pope Innocent XI, condemned these errors, and put a stop to such abuses. At the same time it declared that all the faithful of whatsoever class, merchants or married persons not at all excepted, could be admitted to frequent communion according to the devotion of each one and the judgment of his confessor. Then on 7 December 1690, by the decree of Pope Alexander VIII, *Sanctissimus Dominus noster,* the proposition of Baius was condemned, requiring most pure love of God, without any admixture of defect, on the part of those who wish to approach the holy table.

The poison of Jansenism, however, which under the pretext of showing due honor and reverence to the Eucharist had infected the minds even of good men, was by no means a thing of the past. The question as to the dispositions for the proper and licit reception of holy communion survived the declarations of the Holy See, and it was a fact that certain theologians of good repute were of the opinion that daily communion could be permitted to the faithful only rarely and subject to many conditions.

On the other hand, there were not wanting men endowed with learning and piety who offered an easier approach to this practice, so salutary and so pleasing to God. They taught, with the authority of the fathers, that there is no precept of the Church which prescribed more perfect dispositions in the case of daily than of weekly or monthly communion; while the fruits of daily communion will be far more abundant than those of communions received weekly or monthly.

In our own day the controversy has been continued with increased warmth, and not without bitterness, so that the minds of confessors and the consciences of the faithful have been disturbed, to the no small detriment of Christian piety and fervor. Certain distinguished men, themselves pastors of souls, have as a result of this urgently begged Pope Pius X, to deign to settle, by his supreme authority, the question concerning the dispositions required to receive the Eucharist daily; so that this practice, so salutary and so pleasing to God, not only might suffer no decrease among the faithful, but rather that it increase and everywhere be promoted, especially in these days when religion and the Catholic faith are attacked on all sides, and the true love of God and piety are so frequently lacking. His Holiness, being most earnestly desirous, out of his solicitude and zeal, that the faithful should be invited to the sacred banquet as often as possible, even daily, and should benefit by its most abundant fruits, committed the aforesaid question to this sacred congregation, to be studied and decided definitely.

1) Frequent and daily communion, as a practice most earnestly desired by Christ our Lord and by the Catholic Church, should be open to all the faithful, of whatever rank and condition of life; so that no one who is in the state of grace, and who approaches the holy table with a right and devout intention can be prohibited therefrom.

2) A right intention consists in this: that he who approaches the holy table should do so, not out of routine, or vain-glory, or human respect, but that he wish to please God, to be more closely united with him by charity, and to have recourse to this divine remedy for his weakness and defects.

3) Although it is especially fitting that those who receive Communion frequently or daily should be free from venial sins, at least from such as are fully deliberate, and from any affection thereto, nevertheless, it is sufficient that they be free from mortal sin, with the purpose of never sinning in the future; and if they have this sincere purpose, it is possible by that daily communicants should gradually free themselves even from venial sins, and from all affection thereto.

4) Since, however, the sacraments of the new law, though they produce their effect *ex opere operato,* nevertheless produce a great effect in proportion as the dispositions of the recipient are better, therefore, one should take care that holy communion be preceded by careful preparation, and followed by an appropriate thanksgiving, according to each one's strength, circumstances and duties.

5) That the practice of frequent and daily communion may be carried out with greater prudence and more fruitful merit, the confessor's advice should be asked. Confessors, however, must take care not to dissuade anyone from frequent or daily communion, provided he is found to be in a state of grace and approaches with a right intention.

6) But since it is plain that by the frequent or daily reception of the holy Eucharist union with Christ is strengthened, the spiritual life more abundantly sustained, the soul more richly endowed with virtues, and the pledge of everlasting happiness more securely bestowed on the recipient, therefore, parish priests, confessors and preachers, according to the approved teaching of the *Roman Catechism,* should exhort the faithful frequently and with great zeal to this devout and salutary practice.

7) Frequent and daily communion is to be promoted especially in religious institutes of all kinds; with regards to which, however, the decree

Quemadmodum issued on 17 December 1890, by the Sacred Congregation of Bishops and Regulars, is to remain in force. It is to be promoted especially in ecclesiastical seminaries, where students are preparing for the service of the altar; as also in all Christian establishments which in any way provide for the care of the young.

8) In the case of religious institutes, whether of solemn or simple vows, in whose rules, or constitutions, or calendars, communion is assigned to certain fixed days, such regulations are to be considered as *directive* and not preceptive. The prescribed number of communions should be regarded as a minimum but not a limit to the devotion of the religious. Therefore, access to the Eucharistic table, whether it be rather frequently or daily, must always be freely open to them according to the norms above laid down in this decree. Furthermore, in order that all religious of both sexes may clearly understand the prescriptions of this decree, the superior of each house will provide that it be read in community, in the vernacular, every year within the octave of the Feast of Corpus Christi.

9) Finally, after the publication of this decree, all ecclesiastical writers are to cease from contentious controversy concerning the dispositions requisite for frequent and daily Communion. . . .

C. ENCYCLICAL, "PASCENDI DOMINICI GREGIS," CONDEMNING THE DOCTRINES OF MODERNISM, 8 SEPTEMBER 1907

One of the primary obligations assigned by Christ to the office divinely committed to us of feeding the Lord's flock is that of guarding with the greatest vigilance the deposit of the faith delivered to the saints, rejecting the profane novelties of words and the gainsaying of knowledge, falsely so-

called. There has never been a time when this watchfulness of the supreme pastor was not necessary to the Catholic body, for owing to the efforts of the enemy of the human race, there have never been lacking "men speaking perverse things," "vain talkers and seducers," "erring and driving into error." It must, however, be confessed that these latter days have witnessed a notable increase in the number of the enemies of the cross of Christ, who, by arts entirely new and full of deceit, are striving to destroy the vital energy of the Church, and, as far as in them lies, utterly to subvert the very kingdom of Christ. Wherefore we may no longer keep silence, lest we should seem to fail in our most sacred duty, and lest the kindness that, in hope of wiser counsels, we have hitherto shown them, should be set down to lack of diligence in the discharge of our office.

That we should act without delay in this matter is made imperative especially by the fact that the partisans of error are to be sought not only among the Church's open enemies; but, what is to be most dreaded and deplored, in her very bosom, and are the more mischievous the less they keep in the open. We allude, venerable brethren, to many who belong to the Catholic laity, and, what is much more sad, to the ranks of the priesthood itself, who, animated by a false zeal for the Church, lacking the solid safeguards of philosophy and theology, nay more, thoroughly imbued with the poisonous doctrines taught by the enemies of the Church, and lost to all sense of modesty, put themselves forward as reformers of the Church; and, forming more boldly into line of attack, assail all that is most sacred in the work of Christ, not sparing even the person of the divine redeemer, whom with sacrilegious audacity, they degrade to the condition of a simple and ordinary man.

Although they express their astonishment that we should number them among the enemies of the Church, no one will be reasonably surprised that we should do so, if, leaving out of the account the internal disposition of the soul, of which God alone is the judge, he considers their tenets, their manner of speech, and their action. Nor indeed would he be wrong in regarding them as the most pernicious of all the adversaries of the Church. For, as we have said, they put into operation their designs for her undoing, not from without but from within. Hence, the danger is present almost in the very veins and heart of the Church, whose injury is the more certain from the very fact that their knowledge of her is more intimate. Moreover, they lay the axe not to the branches and shoots, but to the very root, that is, to the faith and its deepest fibres. And once having struck at this root of immortality, they proceed to diffuse poison through the whole tree, so that there is no part of Catholic truth which they leave untouched, none that they do not strive to corrupt. Further, none is more skillful, none more astute than they, in the employment of a thousand noxious devices; for they play the double part of rationalist and Catholic, and this so craftily that they easily lead the unwary into error; and as audacity is their chief characteristic, there is no conclusion of any kind from which they shrink or which they do not thrust forward with pertinacity and assurance. To this must be added the fact, which indeed is well calculated to deceive souls, that they lead a life of the greatest activity, of assiduous and ardent application to every branch of learning, and that they possess, as a rule, a reputation for irreproachable morality. Finally, there is the fact which is all but fatal to the hope of cure that their very doctrines have given such a bent to their minds, that they disdain all authority and brook no restraint; and relying upon a false conscience, they attempt to ascribe to a love of truth that which is in reality the result of pride and obstinacy.

Once indeed we had hopes of recalling them to a better mind, and to this end we first of all treated them with kindness as our children, then with severity; and at last we have had recourse, though with great reluctance, to public reproof. It is known to you, venerable brethren, how unavailing have been our efforts. For a moment they have bowed their head, only to lift it more arrogantly than before. If it were a matter which concerned them alone, we might perhaps have overlooked it; but the security of the Catholic name is at stake. Wherefore we must interrupt a silence which it would be criminal to prolong, that we may point out to the whole Church, as they really are, men who are badly disguised.

It is one of the cleverest devices of the Modernists, as they are commonly and rightly called, to present their doctrines without order and systematic arrangement, in a scattered and disjointed manner, so as to make it appear as if their minds were in doubt or hesitation, whereas in reality they are quite fixed and steadfast. For this reason it will be of advantage, venerable brethren, to bring their teachings together here into one group, and to point out their interconnection, and thus to pass to an examination of the sources of the errors, and to prescribe remedies for averting the evil results. . . .

At this point, venerable brethren, the way is opened for us to consider the Modernists in the theological arena —a difficult task, yet one that may be disposed of briefly. It is a question of effecting the conciliation of faith with science, but always by making the one subject to the other. In this matter the

Modernist theologian takes exactly the same principles which we have seen employed by the Modernist philosopher—the principles if immanence and symbolism—and applies them to the believer. The process is an extremely simple one. The philosopher has declared: The principle of faith is immanent. The believer has added: This principle is God. And the theologian draws the conclusion: God is immanent in man. Thus we have theological immanence.

So, too, the philosopher regards it as certain that the representations of the object of faith are merely symbolical. The believer has likewise affirmed that the object of faith is God in himself. And the theologian proceeds to affirm that: The representations of the divine reality are symbolical. And thus we have theological symbolism.

These errors are truly of the gravest kind and the pernicious character of both will be seen clearly from an examination of their consequences. For, to begin with symbolism, since symbols are but symbols in regard to their objects and only instruments in regard to the believer, it is necessary first of all, according to the teachings of the Modernists, that the believer does not lay too much stress on the formula, as formula, but avail himself of it only for the purpose of uniting himself to the absolute truth which the formula at once reveals and conceals—that is to say, which it endeavors to express but without ever succeeding in doing so. They would also have the believer make use of the formulas only in as far as they are helpful to him, for they are given to be a help and not a hindrance; with proper regard, however, for the social respect due to formulas which the public magisterium has deemed suitable for expressing the common consciousness until such time

as the same magisterium shall provide otherwise.

Concerning immanence it is not easy to determine what Modernists precisely mean by it, for their own opinions of the subject vary. Some understand it in the sense that God working in man is more intimately present in him than man is even in himself; and this conception, if properly understood, is irreproachable. Others hold that the divine action is one with the action of nature, as the action of the first cause is one with the action of the secondary cause; and this would destroy the supernatural order. Others, finally, explain it in a way which savors of pantheism, and this, in truth, is the sense which best fits in with the rest of their doctrines.

With this principle of immanence is connected another which may be called the principle of divine permanence. It differs from the first in much the same way as the private experience differs from the experience transmitted by tradition. An example illustrating what is meant will be found in the Church and the sacraments. The Church and the sacraments, according to the Modernists, are not to be regarded as having been instituted by Christ himself. This is barred by agnosticism, which recognizes in Christ nothing more than a man whose religious consciousness has been, like that of all men, formed by degrees; it is also barred by the law of immanence, which rejects what they call external application; it is further barred by the law of evolution, which requires, for the development of the germs, time and a certain series of circumstances; it is finally barred by history, which shows that such in fact has been the course of things. Still it is to be held that both Church and sacraments have been founded mediately by Christ. But how? In this way: all Christian consciences were, they affirm, in a manner virtually included in the conscience of Christ as the plant is included in the seed. But as the branches live the life of the seed, so, too, all Christians are to be said to live the life of Christ. But the life of Christ, according to faith, is divine, and so, too, is the life of Christians. And if this life produced, in the course of ages, both the Church and the sacraments, it is quite right to say that their origin is from Christ and is divine. In the same way they make out that the holy Scriptures and the dogmas are divine. And in this, the Modernist theology may be said to reach its completion. A slender provision, in truth, but more than enough for the theologian who professes that the conclusions of science, whatever they may be, must always be accepted! No one will have any difficulty in making the application of these theories to the other points with which we propose to deal.

Thus far we have touched upon the origin and nature of faith. But as faith has many branches, and chief among them the Church, dogma, worship, devotions, the Books which we call "sacred," it concerns us to know what the Modernists teach concerning them.

To begin with dogma, we have already indicated its origin and nature. Dogma is born of the sort of impulse or necessity by virtue of which the believer elaborates his thought so as to render it clearer to his own conscience and that of others. This elaboration consists entirely in the process of investigating and refining the primitive mental formula, not indeed in itself and according to any logical explanation, but according to circumstances, or vitally as the Modernists somewhat less intelligibly describe it. Hence it happens that around this primitive formula secondary formulas, as we have already indicated, gradually continue to be formed, and these subsequently grouped into one body, or one doc-trinal construction, and further sanctioned by the public magisterium as responding to the common consciousness, are called dogma. Dogma is to be carefully distinguished from the speculations of theologians which, although not alive with the life of dogma, are not without their utility as serving both to harmonize religion with science and to remove opposition between them, and to illumine and defend religion from without, and it may be even to prepare the matter for future dogma.

Concerning worship there would not be much to be said, were it not that under this head are comprised the sacraments, concerning which the Modernist errors are of the most serious character. For them the sacraments are the resultant of a double impulse or need—for, as we have seen, everything in their system is explained by inner impulses or necessities. The first need is that of giving some sensible manifestation to religion; the second is that of expressing it, which could not be done without some sensible form and consecrating acts, and these are called sacraments. But for the Modernists, sacraments are bare symbols or signs, though not devoid of a certain efficacy—an efficacy, they tell us, like that of certain phrases vulgarly described as having caught the popular ear, inasmuch as they have the power of putting certain leading ideas into circulation, and of making a marked impression upon the mind. What the phrases are to the ideas, that the sacraments are to the religious sense, that and nothing more. The Modernists would express their mind more clearly were they to affirm that the sacraments are instituted solely to foster the faith—but this is condemned by the Council of Trent: "If anyone say that these sacraments are instituted solely to foster the faith, let him be anathema."

We have already touched upon the nature and origin of the Sacred Books. According to the principles of the Modernists they may be rightly described as a summary of experiences, not indeed of the kind that may now and again come to anybody, but those extraordinary and striking experiences which are the possession of every religion. And this is precisely what they teach about our books of the Old and New Testament. But to suit their own theories they note with remarkable ingenuity that, although experience is something belonging to the present, still it may draw its material in like manner from the past and the future inasmuch as the believer by memory lives the past over again after the manner of the present, and lives the future already by anticipation. This explains how it is that the historical and apocalyptic books are included among the Sacred Writings. God does indeed speak in these books through the medium of the believer, but according to Modernist theology, only by immanence and vital permanence. We may ask, what then becomes of inspiration? Inspiration, they reply, is in nowise distinguished from that impulse which stimulates the believer to reveal the faith that is in him by words or writing, except perhaps by its vehemence. It is something like that which happens in poetical inspiration, of which it has been said: there is a God in us, and when he stirs he sets us afire. It is in this sense that God is said to be the origin of the inspiration of the Sacred Books. The Modernists moreover affirm concerning this inspiration, that there is nothing in the Sacred Books which is devoid of it. In this respect some might be disposed to consider them as more orthodox than certain writers in recent times who somewhat restrict inspiration, as, for instance, in what have been put forward as so-called tacit citations. But in all this

we have mere verbal conjuring. For if we take the Bible, according to the standards of agnosticism, namely, as a human work, made by men for men, albeit the theologian is allowed to proclaim that it is divine by immanence, what room is there left in it for inspiration? The Modernists assert a general inspiration of the Sacred Books, but they admit no inspiration in the Catholic sense.

A wider field for comment is opened when we come to what the Modernist school has imagined to be the nature of the Church. They begin with the supposition that the Church has its birth in a double need; first, the need of the individual believer to communicate his faith to others, especially if he has had some original and special experience, and secondly, when the faith has become common to many, the need of the collectivity to form itself into a society and to guard, promote, and propagate the common good. What, then, is the Church? It is the product of the collective conscience, that is to say, of the association of individual consciences which, by virtue of the principle of vital permanence, depend all on one first believer, who for Catholics is Christ. Now every society needs a directing authority to guide its members towards the common end, to foster prudently the elements of cohesion, which in a religious society are doctrine and worship. Hence the triple authority in the Catholic Church, disciplinary, dogmatic, liturgical. The nature of this authority is to be gathered from its origin, and its rights and duties from its nature. In past times it was a common error that authority came to the Church from without, that is to say directly from God; and it was then rightly held to be autocratic. But this conception has now grown obsolete. For in the same way as the Church is a vital emanation of the collectivity of consciences, so too authority emanates vitally from the Church itself. Authority, therefore, like the Church, has its origin in the religious conscience, and, that being so, is subject to it. Should it disown this dependence it becomes a tyranny. For we are living in an age when the sense of liberty has reached its highest development. In the civil order the public conscience has introduced popular government. Now there is in man only one conscience, just as there is only one life. It is for the ecclesiastical authority, therefore, to adopt a democratic form, unless it wishes to provoke and foment an intestine conflict in the consciences of mankind. The penalty of refusal is disaster. For it is madness to think that the sentiment of liberty, as it now obtains, can recede. Were it forcibly pent up and held in bonds, the more terrible would be its outburst, sweeping away at once both Church and religion. Such is the situation in the minds of the Modernists. Their one great anxiety is, in consequence, to find a way of conciliation between the authority of the Church and the liberty of the believers.

But it is not only within her own household that the Church must come to terms. Besides her relations with those within, she has others with those who are outside. The church does not occupy the world all by herself; there are other societies in the world, with which she must necessarily have dealings and contact. The rights and duties of the Church towards civil societies must, therefore, be determined, and determined, of course, by her own nature, that, to wit, which the Modernists have already described to us. The rules to be applied in this matter are clearly those which have been laid down for science and faith, though in the latter case the question turned upon the object, while in the present case we have one of ends. In the same way, then, as faith and science are alien to each other by reason of the diversity of their objects, Church and state are strangers by reason of the diversity of their ends, that of the Church being spiritual while that of the state is temporal. Formerly it was possible to subordinate the temporal to the spiritual and to speak of some questions as mixed, conceding to the Church the position of queen and mistress in all such, because the Church was then regarded as having been instituted immediately by God as the author of the supernatural order. But this doctrine is today repudiated alike by philosophers and historians. The state must, therefore, be separated from the Church, and the Catholic from the citizen. Every Catholic, from the fact that he is also a citizen, has the right and the duty to work for the common good in the way he thinks best, without troubling himself about the authority of the Church, without paying any heed to its wishes, its counsels, its orders—nay, even in spite of its rebukes. For the Church to trace out and prescribe for the citizen any line of action, on any pretext whatsoever, is to be guilty of an abuse of authority, against which one is bound to protest with all one's might. Venerable brethren, the principles from which these doctrines spring have been solemnly condemned by our predecessor, Pius VI, in his apostolic constitution *Auctorem fidei*.

But it is not enough for the Modernist school that the state should be separated from the Church. For as faith is to be subordinated to science as far as phenomenal elements are concerned, so too in temporal matters the Church must be subject to the state. This, indeed, Modernists may not yet say openly, but they are forced by the logic of their position to admit it. For granted the principle that in temporal matters the state possesses the sole power, it will follow that when the believer, not satisfied with merely internal acts of religion, proceeds to external acts—such for instance as the reception or administration of the sacraments—these will fall under the control of the state. What will then become of ecclesiastical authority, which can only be exercised by external acts? Obviously it will be completely under the dominion of the state. It is this inevitable consequence which urges many among liberal Protestants to reject all external worship—nay, all external religious fellowship, and leads them to advocate what they call individual religion. If the Modernists have not yet openly proceeded so far, they ask the Church in the meanwhile to follow of her own accord in the direction in which they urge her and to adapt herself to the forms of the state. Such are their ideas about disciplinary authority. But much more evil and pernicious are their opinions on doctrinal and dogmatic authority. The following is their conception of the magisterium of the Church: no religious society, they say, can be a real unit unless the religious conscience of its members be one, and also the formula which they adopt. But this double unity requires a kind of common mind whose office is to find and determine the formula that corresponds best with the common conscience; and it must have, moreover, an authority sufficient to enable it to impose on the community the formula which has been decided upon. From the combination and, as it were, fusion of these two elements, the common mind which draws up the formula and the authority which imposes it, arises, according to the Modernists, the notion of the ecclesiastical magisterium. And, as this magisterium springs, in its last analysis, from the individual consciences and possesses its mandate of public utility for their benefit, it necessarily follows that the ecclesiastical

magisterium must be dependent upon them, and should therefore be made to bow to popular ideals. To prevent individual consciences from expressing freely and openly the impulses they feel, to hinder criticism from urging forward dogma in the path of its necessary evolution, is not a legitimate use but an abuse of a power given for the public weal. So too a due method and measure must be observed in the exercise of authority. To condemn and proscribe a work without the knowledge of the author, without hearing his explanations, without discussion, is something approaching to tyranny. And here again it is a question of finding a way of reconciling the full rights of authority on the one hand and those of liberty on the other. In the meantime the proper course for the Catholic will be to proclaim publicly his profound respect for authority, while never ceasing to follow his own judgment. Their general direction for the Church is as follows: that the ecclesiastical authority, since its end is entirely spiritual, should strip itself of that external pomp which adorns it in the eyes of the public. In this, they forget that while religion is for the soul, it is not exclusively for the soul, and that the honor paid to authority is reflected back on Christ who instituted it.

To conclude this whole question of faith and its various branches, we have still to consider, venerable brethren, what the Modernists have to say about the development of the one and the other. First of all they lay down the general principle that in a living religion everything is subject to change, and must in fact be changed. In this way they pass to what is practically their principal doctrine, namely, evolution. To the laws of evolution everything is subject under the penalty of death—dogma, Church, worship, the Books we revere as sacred, even faith itself. The enunciation of this principle will not be a matter or surprise to anyone who bears in mind what the Modernists have had to say about each of these subjects. Having laid down this law of evolution, the Modernists themselves teach us how it operates.

And first, with regard to faith: The primitive form of faith, they tell us, was rudimentary and common to all men alike, for it had its origin in human nature and human life. Vital evolution brought with it progress, not by the accretion of new and purely adventitious forms from without, but by an increasing perfusion of the religious sense into the conscience. The progress was of two kinds: negative, by the elimination of all extraneous elements, such, for example, as those derived from the family or nationality; and positive, by that intellectual and moral refining of man, by means of which the idea of the divine became fuller and clearer, while the religious sense became more acute. For the progress of faith the same causes are to be assigned as those which are adduced above to explain its origin.

But to them must be added those extraordinary men whom we call prophets—of whom Christ was the greatest—both because in their lives and their words there was something mysterious which faith attributed to the divinity, and because it fell to their lot to have new and original experiences fully in harmony with the religious needs of their time. The progress of dogma is due chiefly to the fact that obstacles to the faith have to be surmounted, enemies have to be vanquished, and objections have to be refuted. Add to this a perpetual striving to penetrate ever more profoundly into those things which are contained in the mysteries of faith. Thus, putting aside other examples, it is found to have happened in the case of Christ; in him that divine something which faith recognized in him was slowly

and gradually expanded in such a way that he was at last held to be God.

The chief stimulus of the evolution of worship consists in the need of accommodation to the manners and customs of peoples, as well as the need of availing itself of the value which certain acts have acquired by usage. Finally, evolution in the Church itself is fed by the need of adapting itself to historical conditions and of harmonizing itself with existing forms of society. Such is their view with regard to each.

And here, before proceeding further, we wish to draw attention to this whole theory of necessities or needs, for beyond all that we have seen, it is, as it were, the base and foundation of that famous method which they describe as historical.

Although evolution is urged on by needs or necessities, yet, if controlled by these alone, it would easily overstep the boundaries of tradition, and thus, separated from its primitive vital principle, would make for ruin instead of progress. Hence, by those who study more closely the ideas of the Modernists, evolution is described as a resultant from the conflict of two forces, one of them tending towards progress, the other towards conservation. The conserving force exists in the Church and is found in tradition; tradition is represented by religious authority, and this both by right and in fact. By right, for it is in the very nature of authority to protect tradition: and in fact, since authority, raised as it is above the contingencies of life, feels hardly, or not at all, the spurs of progress. The progressive force, on the contrary, which responds to the inner needs, lies in the individual consciences and works in them—especially in such of them as are in more close and intimate contact with life. Already we observe, venerable brethren, the introduction of that most pernicious doctrine which would make of the laity the factor of progress in the Church. Now it is by a species of covenant and compromise between these two forces of conservation and progress, that is to say between authority and individual consciences, that changes and advances take place. The individual consciences, or some of them, act on the collective conscience, which brings pressure to bear on the depositories of authority to make terms and to keep to them.

With all this in mind, one understands how it is that the Modernists express astonishment when they are reprimanded or punished. What is imputed to them as a fault they regard as a sacred duty. They understand the needs of consciences better than anyone else, since they come into closer touch with them than does the ecclesiastical authority. Nay, they embody them, so to speak, in themselves. Hence, for them to speak and to write publicly is a bounden duty. Let authority rebuke them if it pleases— they have their own conscience on their side and an intimate experience which tells them with certainty that what they deserve is not blame but praise. Then they reflect that, after all, there is no progress without a battle and no battle without its victims; and victims they are willing to be like the prophets and Christ himself. They have no bitterness in their hearts against the authority which uses them roughly, for after all they readily admit that it is only doing its duty as authority. Their sole grief is that it remains deaf to their warnings, for in this way it impedes the progress of souls, but the hour will most surely come when further delay will be impossible, for if the laws of evolution may be checked for a while they cannot be finally evaded. And thus they go their way, reprimands and condemnations notwithstanding, masking an incredible audacity under a mock semblance of humility. While they make a pretense of bowing their heads, their minds and hands are more boldly intent than ever on carrying out their purposes. And this policy they follow willingly and wittingly, both because it is part of their system that authority is to be stimulated but not dethroned, and because it is necessary for them to remain within the ranks of the Church in order that they may gradually transform the collective conscience. And in saying this, they fail to perceive that they are avowing that the collective conscience is not with them, and that they have no right to claim to be its interpreters.

14. *Pope Benedict XV: Peace Proposals of 1 August 1917*

From *Church and State Through the Centuries*, trans. and ed. by Sidney Z. Ehler and John B. Morrall (Westminster, Maryland: Newman Press, 1954), pp. 374-377.

To THE heads of the belligerent peoples.

From the beginning of our pontificate, amid the horrors of the terrible war unleashed upon Europe, we have kept before our attention three things above all: to preserve complete impartiality in relation to all the belligerents, as is appropriate to him who is the common father and who loves all his children with an equal affection; to endeavor constantly to do to all the most possible good, without personal exceptions and without national or religious distinctions, a duty which the universal law of charity, as well as the supreme spiritual charge entrusted to us by Christ, dictates to us; finally, as our peace-making mission equally demands, to leave nothing undone within our power, which could assist in hastening the end of this calamity, by trying to lead the peoples and their heads to more moderate frames of mind and to the calm deliberations of peace, of a "just and lasting" peace.

Whoever has followed our work during the three unhappy years which have just elapsed, has been able to recognize with ease that if we have always remained faithful to our resolution of absolute impartiality and to our practical policy of welldoing, we have never ceased to urge the belligerent peoples and governments to become brothers once more, even although publicity has not been given to all which we have done to attain the most noble end.

Towards the end of the first year of war, we addressed to the conflicting nations the most lively exhortations, and in addition we indicated the way to follow in order to arrive at a lasting and honorable peace for all. Unhappily, our appeal was not heeded; and the war continued bitterly for two more years, with all its horrors; it even became more cruel and spread over land and sea, even in the air; desolation and death were seen to fall upon defenseless cities, peaceful villages and their innocent populations. And at the present moment no one can imagine how the sufferings of all may increase and become more intense, if further months, or still worse, further years are added to these bloodstained three years. Will the civilized world then become nothing but a field of death? And will Europe, so glorious and so flourishing before, rush, as if driven on by a universal folly, to the abyss and be the agent of her own suicide?

In so agonizing a situation, in face of so great a danger, we who have no special aim, who pay no attention to the suggestions of the interests of either of the belligerent groups, but are moved only by the feeling of our lofty duty as common father of the faithful and by the solicitations of our children who beg for our intervention and our peace-making word, we raise anew a cry for peace and we renew an urgent appeal to those who hold in their hands the destinies of nations. But so as not to confine ourselves any longer to general terms, as circumstances have advised us in the past, we now wish to descend to more concrete and practical propositions, and to invite the governments of the belligerent peoples to reach agreement on the following points, which seem to be the basis of a just and lasting peace, leaving to them the task of making them more precise and of completing them.

First of all, the fundamental point should be that for the material force of arms should be substituted the moral force of law; hence a just agreement by all for the simultaneous and reciprocal reduction of armaments, according to rules and guarantees to be established to the degree necessary and sufficient for the maintenance of public order in each state; then, instead of armies, the institution of arbitration, with its lofty peace-making function according to the standards to be agreed upon and with sanctions to be decided against the state which might refuse to submit international questions to arbitration or to accept its decisions.

Once the supremacy of law has been established, let every obstacle to the ways of communication between the peoples be removed, by insuring through rules to be fixed in similar fashion, the true freedom and common use of the seas. This would, on the one hand, remove many reasons for conflict and, on the other, would open new sources of prosperity and progress to all.

With regard to reparations for damage and to the expenses of the war, we see no way of settling the question other than by laying down as a general principle, a complete and reciprocal condonation, justified by the immense benefits to be drawn from disarmament, and all the more because one could not understand the continuation of slaughter solely for reasons of an economic nature. If, however, in certain cases there exist special reasons, let them be pondered with justice and equity.

But pacifying agreements, with the advantages flowing from them, are not possible without the reciprocal restitution of territories actually occupied. In consequence, on the part of Germany, there should be total evacuation of Belgium, with a guarantee of its full political, military and economic independence *vis-a-vis* any power whatsoever; similarly the evacuation of French territory. On the side of the other belligerent parties, there should be a corresponding restitution of the German colonies.

With regard to territorial questions, such as those disputed between Italy and Austria, and between Germany and France, there is ground for hope that in consideration of the immense advantages of a lasting peace with disarmament, the conflicting parties will examine them in a conciliatory frame of mind, taking into account, so far as it is just and practicable, as we have said previously, the aspirations of the peoples and co-ordinating, according to circumstances, particular interests with the general good of the great human society.

The same spirit of equity and justice should direct the examination of other territorial and political questions, notably those relating to Armenia, the Balkan States and the territories composing the ancient kingdom of Poland, for which especially its noble historical traditions and the sufferings which it has undergone, particularly during the present war, ought rightly to enlist the sympathies of the nations.

Such are the principal foundations upon which we believe the future reorganization of peoples should rest. They are of a kind which would make impossible the recurrence of such conflicts and would pave the way for a solution of the economic question, so important for the future and the material welfare of all the belligerent states. Thus, in presenting them all to you who preside at this tragic hour over the destinies of the belligerent nations, we are animated by a sweet hope, that of seeing them accepted and thus of seeing the earliest possible end to the fearful struggle which has the ever-increasing appearance of a useless massacre. Everybody recognizes, furthermore, that on both sides the honor of arms has been satisfied. Give attention, then, to our entreaty, accept the paternal invitation which we address to you in the name of the divine redeemer, Prince of Peace. Reflect on your very grave responsibility before God and before men; on your decisions depend the rest and joy of countless families, the life of thousands of young people, in short, the happiness of the peoples, whose well-being it is your overriding duty to procure. May the Lord inspire you with decisions agreeable to his most holy will. May heaven bring it about that, by earning the applause of your contemporaries, you will also gain for yourselves the beautiful name of peacemakers among future generations.

As for us, closely united in prayer and penitence to all faithful souls who sigh for peace, we implore for you from the Divine Spirit light and counsel.

III. *The Catholic Intellectual Revival*

THERE were many intelligent and well-informed figures who were convinced that the movements of the eighteenth and nineteenth centuries had sounded the death knell for the faith, and that Christianity would not survive into the twentieth century. Voltaire, for instance, had said that he hoped all monks would not disappear so there would be something left to laugh at. But these predictions could not have been more wrong, for Christianity, in the midst of the apparent triumph of secular forces, displayed a striking vitality as new life broke forth on all fronts. The Church emerged resilient from persecutions and set-backs, more potent as a revived factor in the affairs of mankind than at any time since the renaissance of the eleventh century.

One of the main characteristics of this nineteenth-century vitality of the Church was a notable burst of intellectual and literary creativity. The forerunner of the Catholic revival was the royalist François Auguste Viscount de Chateaubriand (1848), most celebrated French author of his day. In his GENIUS OF CHRISTIANITY (*No. 15*), written in 1802, he elaborated a popular, naïvely romantic outline of the beauties of Catholicism which made the faith aesthetically and emotionally respectable. All higher feelings, humanity, true liberty, and beauty are nurtured in Catholicism, he declared, and in the spirit of romanticism he appealed to the personal and vital movements of the heart. Although his substituting of sentiment for reason led to an overemphasis on subjectivism, his approach was an effective defense of the breadth and beauty of tradition in a revolutionary age.

Another voice raised in France to reconcile the Church with society was that of Jean Baptiste de Lacordaire (1861), liberal priest who became a Dominican and helped in the rehabilitation of the Order of Preachers. This "son of the age," as he called himself, drew crowds of up to 6,000 persons to hear his famed series of sermons in the cathedral of Notre Dame. Here, despite an official outcry, he appeared in the traditional white Dominican habit that Paris had known so well in former ages. In the presence of Archbishop Hyacinth Louis de Quelen, who was little prepared by temperament or training to enjoy the flavor of the modern, he presented a brilliant new style of apologetic homily, of which SERMON XVI ON THE ZEAL OF STATESMEN AND MEN OF GENIUS AGAINST CATHOLIC DOCTRINE (*No. 16*), delivered on the First Sunday of Advent, 1843, is a stirring example.

He described the Church as a living, necessary, and powerful influence; he explained dogmas, Scripture, tradition, and the means of acquiring faith. This daring republican orator, whose early associations with *L'Avenir* had not weakened his orthodoxy, won a number of the young intellectuals of the period to a re-appreciation of the Church as part of their hopes for the future, as well as of the valid tradition of their native France.

Documentary sources of the Church in the United States have been passed by in this collection because they are available in an excellent and thorough book of readings (John Tracy Ellis, *Documents of American Catholic History* [Milwaukee, 1956]). An exception is made here in order to include two examples of American Catholics, one lay and the other cleric, whose mark on the age had particular international significance. The first one, the versatile philosopher, publicist, and convert, Orestes A. Brownson (1876), had a certain influence on the intellectual heritage of Western society. He firmly advanced the thesis that democracy to survive must have moral fiber, and that Catholicism can offer that essential stability, as he explains in CATHOLICITY NECESSARY TO SUSTAIN POPULAR LIBERTY (*No. 17*). Another American who was a confirmed and vigorous advocate of the Church responding fully to the challenge of the age was the dynamic John Ireland (1918), Archbishop of St. Paul. His early training in France had convinced him that the civil religion and atheism introduced by doctrinaire liberal democrats was not the crown of the age. It was rather religious authority and ascertained truth, presented in clear language, that would repair the ruin of revolutions and insure the advances of modern society. He advanced these ideas in his typical forthright manner throughout his lifetime. One of his most famed addresses, AMERICA IN FRANCE (*No. 18*), was delivered at the suggestion of Pope Leo XIII on 18 June 1892 in Paris. Here he strove to reconcile French Catholics to their republican government and advocated, as he did in several controversies during his lifetime, that the Church must adjust herself to the age as Catholics had done in the United States.

A nineteenth-century Catholic pioneer, a voice raised not only in negative criticism but offering a positive, constructive program rooted in a thorough understanding of the situation, was Wilhelm Emmanuel von Ketteler (1887), Bishop of Mainz. This German aristocrat turned from conservativism to become the first Catholic champion of the working class of his age, and a forerunner who paved the way for the social encyclicals of Pope Leo XIII. Ketteler advocated organizing works of charity to alleviate workers' misery, and constructive Catholic activity in the realm of social theory. His well-known sermon at Offenbach, THE LABOR MOVEMENT AND ITS EF-

FECTS IN RELATION TO RELIGION AND MORALS *(No. 19)*, on 25 July 1869, was a noble cry for the removal of all injustice and indignity toward labor, the need of a just wage, and protection of spiritual values. Man's life in modern society had been changed by mechanization, a materialistic urban culture, the struggle for existence in a capitalist society, and unjust exploitation of labor for industrial gain. The offenses of liberal capitalists against fundamental human rights of freedom and justice in the nineteenth century gave rise to the classic socialist reaction. Socialists advocated a materialistic culture rooted in an economic interpretation of life. Labor, the source of all social value, must revolt and through organized effort overthrow the individualistic, liberal, national forces that held it in bondage. In place of a bourgeois society with its decadent religion, socialists promised a new international and classless society. Those social Catholics who saw the injustices of liberal capitalism, and the resultant socialistic dangers it was breeding, were few and far between in the nineteenth century. Ketteler's contribution emerges consequently as all the more significant in terms of the unresolved social problem that the "progressive" nineteenth century bequeathed to contemporary society.

The intellectual giant and most appealing figure of the century's Catholic revival was England's John Henry Cardinal Newman (1890). His contribution with the years challenges analysis. This convert from Anglicanism after the emancipation of Catholics was, significantly, the first cardinal appointed by Pope Leo XIII. Newman, more than anyone else, fulfilled Leo's aim of creating a Catholic synthesis to meet the forces and problems of the age. He did this with such literary genius, logical force, and moderation amid the tragic cross-currents of suspicion and misunderstanding from his fellow Catholics, that he stands forth as, perhaps, the major religious personality of the century. His voluminous writings cover the major fields at issue with classic simplicity and depth. A typical example of Newman's thought, if any one selection can be termed typical, are the TWO ESSAYS ON THE DEVELOPMENT OF CHRISTIAN DOCTRINE *(No. 20)*, of 6 October 1845 and 15 February 1868, the theory that turned him toward Catholicism. Recently there was discovered an illuminating essay of Newman's which he had written on the same idea of doctrinal development some twenty years later and after the definition of papal infallibility. It is attached here to the original document as further elucidation of his doctrinal development thesis, which in the judgment of some is the most original and significant theological clarification of that age. Newman had conceived the essay as an explanation of Anglican difficulties, which Nicholas Cardinal Wiseman had described succinctly:

They imagined that, whatever Christianity had acquired in outward form, since its foundation, must be an interpolation of its creed; that whatever development in outward or inward life it has exhibited, was an addition to what God revealed. If they could not find in his written word the practices observed, to their full extent, and the very terms applied to them, as they admitted of no power of development, they rejected all these its results, and generally with them the principles from which they gradually evolved.

Another erudite English Catholic of the period was Lord John Acton (1902), architect of the *Cambridge Modern History,* and first Catholic in modern times to hold the Regius Chair of Modern History in the University of Cambridge. Acton led a group of liberal Catholics in England in opposition to the antiquarian methods of the embattled Catholic minority. He questioned the expediency of defining papal infallibility, although he did not break with the Church after the Vatican Council, as did his close friend and mentor Professor Ignatius Doellinger in Germany. Acton was a strong defender of the liberal society but also of the necessity of a moral structure to sustain it, as his lecture at the Agricultural Hall to the Bridgenorth Institute on the HISTORY OF FREEDOM IN CHRISTIANITY *(No. 21)*, of 28 May 1877, reveals. He unequivocally stated to the English people that "the cause of religion, even under the unregenerate influence of worldly passion, had as much to do as any clear notions of policy in making this country the foremost of the free."

The Oxford convert, Henry Edward Cardinal Manning (1892), succeeded Wiseman as archbishop of Westminster in 1865. During his long life he was the symbol of the English Catholics' slow return to national life and the re-establishment of the Church as almost a missionary faith in a foreign land. Manning distinguished himself as a champion of labor and social justice, as well as for public achievements. He could not, however, appreciate the liberal Catholic position in other areas. His temperamental and psychological inability to see the worth of Newman's approach was a major limitation of Catholic potential during their lives. Manning two years before his death wrote a penetrating analysis of HINDRANCES TO THE SPREAD OF THE CATHOLIC CHURCH IN ENGLAND *(No. 22)* which explains better than any other contemporary document the character and nature of the return of the Church in England, and by extension in many ways throughout the English-speaking world.

The Austrian diplomat at the Vatican, Dr. Ludwig von Pastor (1928), began in 1883 a monumental series on *The History of the Popes.* This pathfinding effort presented, according to the mandate of Leo XIII, an honest and unbiased account of the popes so maligned by the Magdeburg

Centuriators and their copiers since the Reformation period. His success and prodigious research established his work as the primary account of the popes since the fifteenth century. An example of Pastor's technique is his essay on THE LITERARY RENAISSANCE IN ITALY AND THE CHURCH (*No. 23*), which presented a revisionist and soundly balanced evaluation. His work was also a felicitous refutation of the "scientific" bias of the nineteenth-century German historical school idealized by Leopold von Ranke.

The large majority of sincere Christians in communion with the Orthodox Church during the nineteenth century believed firmly that pure Christianity had been handed down exclusively by that branch of the Church. A brilliant, mystic Russian Orthodox, Vladimir S. Soloviev (1900), who wrote on theology, morality, and philosophy, challenged this thesis that the Slavs had been divinely directed to preserve the purity of the faith under the guardianship of holy Russia and the Russian Orthodox Church. Soloviev spoke out against the ironclad control of religion by the Russian state, and showed how Orthodoxy had been used for the ends of the Tsar's autocratic, nationalistic policies. With erudition and ardent religious fervor he looked for the union of all Christians, as his RUSSIA AND THE UNIVERSAL CHURCH (*No. 24*) evidences. Soloviev was a unique ecumenical voice in his century speaking for the dimmed vision of a united Christendom (he became a Catholic near the end of his life). His Christian understanding of history and marked ability to synthesize the aspirations of the human mind and heart set him apart from his contemporaries. His prophetic stature endured into the twentieth century to be an inspiration to such writers as Nicholas A. Berdyaev, and that stature continues to grow with time.

15. *François Auguste Chateaubriand: The Genius of Christianity, 1802*

From Viscount de Chateaubriand, *Genius of Christianity* (Baltimore: John Murphy and Co., 1856), pp. 43-51, 619-20, 664-68, 673-85.

EVER since Christianity was first published to the world, it has been continually assailed by three kinds of enemies: heretics, sophists, and those apparently frivolous characters who destroy everything with the shafts of ridicule. Numerous apologists have given victorious answers to subtleties and falsehoods, but they have not been so successful against derision. St. Ignatius of Antioch, St. Irenaeus of Lyons, and Tertullian, in his *Prescriptions,* which Bossuet calls "divine," combated the innovators of their time, whose extravagant expositions corrupted the simplicity of the faith.

Calumny was first repulsed by Quadratus and Aristides, philosophers of Athens. We know, however, nothing of their apologies for Christianity, except a fragment of the former, which Eusebius has preserved. Both he and St. Jerome speak of the work of Aristides as a masterpiece of eloquence.

The pagans accused the first Christians of atheism, incest and certain abominable feasts, at which they were said to partake of the flesh of a newborn infant. After Quadratus and Aristides, St. Justin pleaded the cause of the Christians. His style is unadorned, and the circumstances attending his martyrdom prove that he shed his blood for religion with the same sincerity with which he had written in its defense. Athenagoras has shown more address in his apology, but he has neither the originality of Justin nor the impetuosity of the author of the *Apologetic.* Tertullian is the unrefined Bossuet of Africa. St. Theophilus, in his three books addressed to his friend Autolychus, displays imagination and learning; and the *Octavius* of Minucius Felix exhibits the pleasing picture of a Christian and two idolaters conversing on religion and the nature of God during a walk along the seashore.

Arnobius, the rhetorician, Lactantius, Eusebius, and St. Cyprian, also defended Christianity; but their efforts were not so much directed to the display of its beauty, as to the exposure of the absurdities of idolatry.

Origen combated the sophists, and seems to have had the advantage over Celsus, his antagonist, in learning, argument and style. The Greek of Origen is remarkably smooth; it is, however, interspersed with Hebrew and other foreign idioms, which is frequently the case with writers who are masters of various languages.

During the reign of the emperor Julian commenced a persecution, perhaps more dangerous than violence itself, which consisted in loading the Christians with disgrace and contempt. Julian began his hostility by plundering the churches; he then forbade the faithful to teach or to study the liberal arts and sciences. Sensitive, however, to the important advantages of the institutions of Christianity, the emperor determined to establish hospitals and monasteries and, after the example of the gospel system, to combine morality with religion; he ordered a kind of sermon to be delivered in the pagan temples.

The sophists, by whom Julian was surrounded, assailed the Christian religion with the utmost violence. The emperor himself did not disdain to combat those whom he styled contemptible "Galileans." The work which he wrote has not reached us; but St. Cyril, patriarch of Alexandria, quotes several passages of it in his refutation, which has been preserved. When Julian is serious, St. Cyril proves too strong for him; but when the emperor has recourse to irony, the patriarch loses his advantage. Julian's style is witty and animated; Cyril is sometimes passionate, obscure, and confused. From the time of Julian to that of Luther, the Church, flourishing in full vigor, had no occasion for apologists; but when the western schism took place, with new enemies arose new defenders. It cannot be denied that at first the Protestants had the superiority, at least in regard to forms, as Montesquieu has remarked. Erasmus himself was weak when opposed to Luther, and Theodore Beza had a captivating manner of writing, in which his opponents were too often deficient.

When Bossuet at length entered the lists, the victory remained not long undecided; the hydra of heresy was once more overthrown. His *Exposition de la Doctrine Catholique* and *Histoire des Variations,* are two masterpieces which will descend to posterity.

It is natural for schism to lead to

infidelity, and for heresy to engender atheism. Bayle and Spinoza arose after Calvin, and they found in Clarke and Leibniz men of sufficient talents to refute their sophistry. Abbadie wrote an apology for religion, remarkable for method and sound argument. Unfortunately his style is feeble, though his ideas are not destitute of brilliance. "If the ancient philosophers," observes Abbadie, "adored the virtues, their worship was only a beautiful species of idolatry."

While the Church was yet enjoying her triumph, Voltaire renewed the persecution of Julian. He possessed the baneful art of making infidelity fashionable among a capricious but amiable people. Every species of self-love was pressed into this insensate league. Religion was attacked with every kind of weapon, from the pamphlet to the folio, from the epigram to the sophism. No sooner did a religious book appear than the author was overwhelmed with ridicule, while works which Voltaire was the first to laugh at among his friends were extolled to the skies. Such was his superiority over his disciples, that sometimes he could not forbear diverting himself with their irreligious enthusiasm. Meanwhile the destructive system continued to spread throughout France. It was first adopted in those provincial academies, each of which was a focus of bad taste and faction. Women of fashion and grave philosophers alike read lectures on infidelity. It was at length concluded that Christianity was no better than a barbarous system, and that its fall could not happen too soon for the liberty of mankind, the promotion of knowledge, the improvement of the arts, and the general comfort of life.

To say nothing of the abyss into which we were plunged by this aversion to the religion of the gospel, its immediate consequence was a return, more affected than sincere, to that mythology of Greece and Rome to which all the wonders of antiquity were ascribed. People were not ashamed to regret that worship which had transformed mankind into a herd of madmen, monsters of indecency, or ferocious beasts. This could not fail to inspire contempt for the writers of the age of Louis XIV who, however, had reached the high perfection which distinguished them only by being religious. If no one ventured to oppose them face to face, on account of their firmly established reputation, they were nevertheless attacked in a thousand indirect ways. It was asserted that they were unbelievers "in their hearts," or, at least, that they would have been much greater characters had they lived "in our times." Every author blessed his good fortune for having been born in the glorious age of the Diderots and d'Alemberts, in that age when all attainments of the human mind were ranged in alphabetical order in the *Encyclopedie,* that Babel of the sciences and of reason.

Men distinguished for their intelligence and learning endeavored to check this torrent; but their resistance was vain. Their voice was lost in the clamors of the crowd, and their victory was unknown to the frivolous people who directed public opinion in France, and upon whom, for that reason, it was highly necessary to make an impression.

Thus, the fatality which had given a triumph to the sophists during the reign of Julian, made them victorious in our times. The defenders of the Christians fell into an error which had before undone them: They did not perceive that the question was no longer to discuss this or that particular tenet since the very foundation on which these tenets were built was rejected by their opponents. By starting from the mission of Jesus Christ, and descending from one consequence to another, they established the truths of faith on a solid basis; but this mode of reasoning, which might have suited the seventeenth century extremely well, when the groundwork was not contested, proved of no use in our days. It was necessary to pursue a contrary method, and to ascend from the effect to the cause; not to prove that the "Christian religion is excellent because it comes from God," but that "it comes from God because it is excellent."

They likewise committed another error in attaching importance to the serious refutations of the sophists, a class of men whom it is utterly impossible to convince because they are always in the wrong. They overlooked the fact that these people are never in earnest in their pretended search after truth; that they esteem none but themselves; that they are not even attached to their own system, except for the sake of the noise which it makes, and are ever ready to forsake it on the first change of public opinion.

For not having made this remark, much time and trouble were thrown away by those who undertook the vindication of Christianity. Their object should have been to reconcile to religion, not the sophists, but those whom they were leading astray. They had been seduced by being told that Christianity was the offspring of barbarism, an enemy of the arts and sciences, of reason and refinement; a religion whose only tendency was to encourage bloodshed, to enslave mankind, to diminish their happiness, and to retard the progress of the human understanding.

It was, therefore, necessary to prove that, on the contrary, the Christian religion, of all the religions that ever existed, is the most humane, the most favorable to liberty and to the arts and sciences; that the modern world is indebted to it for every improvement, from agriculture to the abstract sciences, from the hospitals for the reception of the unfortunate to the tem-

ples reared by the Michelangelos and embellished by the Raphaels. It was necessary to prove that nothing is more divine than its morality, nothing more lovely and more sublime than its tenets, its doctrine, and its worship; that it encourages genius, corrects the taste, develops the virtuous passions, imparts energy to the ideas, presents noble images to the writer, and perfect models to the artist; that there is no disgrace in being believers with Newton and Bossuet, with Pascal and Racine. In a word, it was necessary to summon all the charms of the imagination, and all the interests of the heart, to the assistance of that religion against which they had been set in array.

The reader may now have a clear view of the object of our work. All other kinds of apologies are exhausted, and perhaps they would be useless at the present day. Who would now sit down to read a work professedly theological? Possibly a few sincere Christians who are already convinced. But, it may be asked, may there not be some danger in considering religion in a merely human point of view? Why so? Does our religion shrink from the light? Surely one great proof of its divine origin is that it will bear the test of the fullest and severest scrutiny of reason. Would you have us always open to the reproach of enveloping our tenets in sacred obscurity, lest their falsehood should be detected? Will Christianity be the less true for appearing the more beautiful? Let us banish our weak apprehensions; let us not, by an excess of religion, leave religion to perish. We no longer live in those times when you might say, "Believe without inquiring." People "will" inquire in spite of us; and our timid silence, in heightening the triumph of the infidel, will diminish the number of believers.

It is time that the world should know to what all those charges of absurdity, vulgarity, and meanness, that are daily alleged against Christianity, may be reduced. It is time to demonstrate, that, instead of debasing the ideas, it encourages the soul to take the most daring flights, and is capable of enchanting the imagination as divinely as the deities of Homer and Virgil. Our arguments will at least have this advantage, that they will be intelligible to the world at large, and will require nothing but common sense to determine their weight and strength. In works of this kind authors neglect, perhaps rather too much, to speak the language of their readers. It is necessary to be a scholar with a scholar, and a poet with a poet. The Almighty does not forbid us to tread the flowery path, if it serves to lead the wanderer once more to him; nor is it always by the steep and rugged mountain that the lost sheep finds its way back to the fold.

We think that this mode of considering Christianity displays associations of ideas which are but imperfectly known. Sublime in the antiquity of its recollections, which go back to the creation of the world, ineffable in its mysteries, adorable in its sacraments, interesting in its history, celestial in its morality, rich and attractive in its ceremonial, it is fraught with every species of beauty. Would you follow it in poetry? Tasso, Milton, Corneille, Racine, Voltaire, will depict to you its miraculous effects. In the *belles-lettres,* in eloquence, history, and philosophy, what have not Bossuet, Fénelon, Massillon, Bourdaloue, Bacon, Pascal, Euler, Newton, Leibnitz, produced by its divine inspiration! In the arts, what masterpieces! If you examine it in its worship, what ideas are suggested by its antique Gothic churches, its admirable prayer, its impressive ceremonies! Among its clergy, behold all those scholars who handed down to you the languages and the works of Greece

and Rome; all those anchorites of Thebais; all those asylums for the unfortunate; all those missionaries to China, to Canada, to Paraguay; not forgetting the military orders whence chivalry derived its origin. Every thing has been engaged in our cause—the manners of our ancestors, the pictures of days of yore, poetry, even romances themselves. We have called smiles from the cradle, and tears from the tomb. Sometimes, with the Maronite monk, we dwell on the summits of Carmel and Lebanon; at others we watch with the Daughter of Charity at the bedside of the sick. Here two American lovers summon us into the recesses of their deserts; there we listen to the sighs of the virgin in the solitude of the cloister. Homer takes his place by Milton, and Virgil beside Tasso; the ruins of Athens and of Memphis form contrasts with the ruins of Christian monuments, and the tombs of Ossian with our rural churchyards. At St. Denis we visit the ashes of kings; and when our subject requires us to treat of the existence of God, we seek our proofs in the wonders of nature alone.

In short, we endeavor to strike the heart of the infidel in every possible way; but we dare not flatter ourselves that we possess the miraculous rod of religion which caused living streams to burst from the flinty rock. . . .

VI, 1. To have only a superficial acquaintance with the benefits conferred by Christianity would be, in fact, to know nothing of the subject. If we would understand the extent of her beneficence, we must enter into its details. We must consider the ingenuity with which she has varied her gifts, dispensed her succors, distributed her treasures, her remedies, and her intelligence. In soothing all the sorrows of humanity she has paid a due regard to its imperfection, consulting with a wise condescension even our delicacy of feeling, our self-love, and our frailties. During the few years that we have devoted to these researches, so many acts of charity, so many admirable institutions, so many inconceivable sacrifices, have passed in review before us that we firmly believe that this merit alone of the Christian religion would be sufficient to atone for all the sins of mankind. Heavenly religion, that compels us to love those wretched beings by whom it is calumniated!

The facts which we are about to state form but a very small portion of the mass which we might have adduced, and many volumes could be filled with what has been omitted. Neither are we sure of having selected the most striking illustrations of Christian charity. Impossible as it is to describe everything, and to judge which of so great a number of charitable works are superior in virtue to the others, we select, almost at random, the subjects of the following pages.

In order to form a just idea of the immensity of these benefits, we should look upon Christendom as a vast republic, where all that we relate concerning one portion is passing at the same time in another. Thus, when we treat of the hospitals, the missions, the colleges, of all France, the reader should also picture to himself the hospitals, the missions, and the colleges, of Italy, Spain, Germany, Russia, England, America, Africa, and Asia. He should take into his view two hundred millions of men at least, among whom the like virtues are practiced, the like sacrifices are made. He should recollect that for eighteen hundred years these virtues have existed and these same acts of charity have been repeated. Now calculate, if your mind is not lost in the effort, the number of individuals cheered and enlightened by Christianity among so many nations and during such a long series of ages. . . .

VI, 12. It is difficult to discover how far it is pleasing to the Almighty that men should presume to take into their feeble hands the vindication of his eternity, should make themselves advocates of the Creator at the tribunal of the creature, and attempt to defend by human arguments those counsels which gave birth to the universe. Not without extreme difference, therefore, convinced as we are of the incompetency of our talents, do we here present the general recapitulation of this work.

Every religion has its mysteries. All nature is a secret. The Christian mysteries are the most sublime that can be; they are the archetypes of the system of man and of the world.

The sacraments are moral laws, and present pictures of a highly poetical character.

Faith is a force, charity a love, hope complete happiness, or, as religion expresses it, a complete virtue.

The laws of God constitute the most perfect code of natural justice.

The fall of our first parents is a universal tradition.

A new proof of it may be found in the constitution of the moral man, which is contrary to the general constitution of beings.

The prohibition to touch the fruit of knowledge was a sublime command, and the only one worthy of the Almighty.

All the arguments which pretend to demonstrate the antiquity of the earth may be contested.

The doctrine of the existence of a God is demonstrated by the wonders of the universe. A design of Providence is evident in the instincts of animals and in the beauty of nature.

Morality of itself proves the immortality of the soul. Man feels a desire of happiness, and is the only creature who cannot attain it; there is consequently a felicity beyond the present life; for we cannot wish for what does not exist.

The system of atheism is founded solely on exceptions. It is not the body that acts upon the soul, but the soul that acts upon the body. Man is not subject to the general laws of matter; he diminishes where the animal increases.

Atheism can benefit no class of people—neither the unfortunate, whom it bereaves of hope, nor the prosperous, whose joys it renders insipid, nor the soldier, of whom it makes a coward, nor the woman, whose beauty and sensibility it mars, nor the mother who has a son to lose, nor the rulers of men, who have no surer pledge of the fidelity of their subjects than religion.

The punishments and rewards which Christianity holds out in another life are consistent with reason and the nature of the soul.

In literature, characters appear more interesting and the passions more energetic under the Christian dispensation than they were under polytheism. The latter exhibited no dramatic feature, no struggles between natural desire and virtue.

Mythology contracted nature, and for this reason the ancients had no descriptive poetry. Christianity restores to the wilderness both its pictures and its solitudes.

The Christian marvellous may sustain a comparison with the marvels of fable. The ancients founded their poetry on Homer, while the Christians found theirs on the Bible: and the beauties of the Bible surpass the beauties of Homer.

To Christianity the fine arts owe their revival and their perfection; in philosophy it is not hostile to any natural truth. If it has sometimes opposed the sciences, it followed the spirit of the age and the opinions of the greatest legislators of antiquity.

In history we should have been in-

ferior to the ancients but for the new character of images, reflections and thoughts, to which Christianity has given birth. Modern eloquence furnishes the same observation.

The relics of the fine arts, the solitude of monasteries, the charms of ruins, the pleasing superstitions of the common people, the harmonies of the heart, religion, and the desert, lead to the examination of the Christian worship.

This worship everywhere exhibits a union of pomp and majesty with a moral design and with a prayer either affecting or sublime. Religion gives life and animation to the sepulchre. From the laborer who reposes in a rural cemetery to the king who is interred at St. Denis, the grave of the Christian is full of poetry. Job and David, reclining upon the Christian tomb, sing in their turn the sleep of death by which man awakes to eternity.

We have seen how much the world is indebted to the clergy and to the institutions and spirit of Christianity. If Schoonbeck, Bonnani, Giustiniani, and Helyot, had followed a better order in their laborious researches, we might have presented here a complete catalogue of the services rendered by religion to humanity. We would have commenced with a list of all the calamities incident to the soul or the body of man, and mentioned under each affliction the Christian order devoted to its relief. It is no exaggeration to assert that, whatever distress or suffering we may think of, religion has, in all probability, anticipated us and provided a remedy for it. From as accurate a calculation as we were able to make, we have obtained the following results:

There are computed to be on the surface of Christian Europe about four thousand three hundred towns and villages. Of these four thousand three hundred towns and villages, three thousand two hundred and ninety-four are of the first, second, third, and fourth rank. Allowing one hospital to each of these three thousand two hundred and ninety-four places (which is far below the truth), you will have three thousand two hundred and ninety-four hospitals, almost all founded by the spirit of Christianity, endowed by the Church, and attended by religious orders. Supposing that, upon an average, each of these hospitals contains one hundred beds, or, if you please, fifty beds for two patients each, you will find that religion, exclusively of the immense number of poor which she supports, has afforded daily relief and subsistence for more than a thousand years to about three hundred and twenty-nine thousand four hundred persons.

On summing up the colleges and universities, we find nearly the same results; and we may safely assert that they afford instruction to at least three hundred thousand youths in the different states of Europe.

In this statement we have not included either the Christian hospitals and colleges in the other three quarters of the globe, or the female youth educated by nuns.

To these results must be added the catalogue of the celebrated men produced by the Church, who form nearly two-thirds of the distinguished characters of modern times. We must repeat, as we have shown, that to the Church we owe the revival of the arts and sciences and of letters; that to her are due most of the great modern discoveries, as gunpowder, clocks, the mariners' compass, and, in government, the representative system; that agriculture and commerce, the laws and political science, are under innumerable obligations to her; that her missions introduced the arts and sciences among civilized nations and laws among savage tribes; that her institution of chivalry powerfully contributed to save Europe from an invasion of new barbarians; that to her mankind is indebted for:

"The worship of one only God;

"The more firm establishment of the belief in the existence of that Supreme Being;

"A clearer idea of the immortality of the soul, and also of a future state of rewards and punishments;

"A more enlarged and active humanity;

"A perfect virtue, which alone is equivalent to all the others—charity.

"A political law and the law of nations, unknown to the ancients, and, above all, the abolition of slavery."

Who is there but must be convinced of the beauty and the grandeur of Christianity? Who but must be overwhelmed with this stupendous mass of benefits? . . .

VI, 13. . . . Jesus Christ may therefore, with strict truth be denominated, in the material sense, that Savior of the world which he is in a spiritual sense. His career on earth was, even humanly speaking, the most important event that ever occurred among men, since the regeneration of society commenced only with the proclamation of the gospel. The precise time of his advent is truly remarkable. A little earlier, his morality would not have been absolutely necessary, for the nations were still upheld by their ancient laws; a little later, that divine Messiah would have appeared after the general wreck of society. We boast of our philosophy at the present day; but, most assuredly, the levity with which we treat the institutions of Christianity is anything but philosophical. The gospel has changed mankind in every respect and enabled it to take an immense step toward perfection. . . .

Christianity has unquestionably shed a new light upon mankind. . . . The truths of Christianity, so far from requiring the submission of reason, command, on the contrary, the most sublime exercise of that faculty.

This remark is so just, and Christianity, which has been characterized as the religion of barbarians, is so truly the religion of philosophers, that Plato may be said to have almost anticipated it. . . .

With respect to the "morality" of the gospel; its beauty is universally admitted: the more it is known and practiced, the more will the eyes of men be opened to their real happiness and their true interest. . . .

Destroy the influence of the gospel, and you must give to every village its police, its prisons, its executioners. If, by an impossibility, the impure altars of paganism were ever re-established among modern nations—if, in a society where slavery is abolished, the worship of "Mercury the robber" and "Venus the prostitute" were to be introduced—there would soon be a total extinction of the human race. . . .

It is high time to be alarmed at the state in which we have been living for some past years. Think of the generation now springing up in our towns and provinces; of all those children who, born during the revolution, have never heard anything of God, nor of the immortality of their souls, nor of the punishments or rewards that await them in a future life: think what may one day become of such a generation if a remedy be not speedily applied to the evil. The most alarming symptoms already manifest themselves: we see the age of innocence sullied with many crimes. Let philosophy, which after all cannot penetrate among the poor, be content to dwell in the mansions of the rich, and leave the people in general to the care of religion; or, rather, let philosophy, with a more enlightened zeal and with a spirit more worthy of her name, remove those barriers which she proposed to place between man and his creator. . . .

As for us, we are convinced that Christianity will rise triumphant from the dreadful trial by which it has just been purified. What gives us this assurance is that it stands the test of reason perfectly, and the more we examine it the more we discover its profound truth. Its mysteries explain man and nature; its works corroborate its precepts; its charity in a thousand forms has replaced the cruelty of the ancients. Without losing anything of the pomp of antiquity, its ceremonies give greater satisfaction to the heart and the imagination. We are indebted to it for everything—letters, sciences, agriculture, and the fine arts. It connects morality with religion, and man with God; Jesus Christ, the savior of moral man, is also the savior of physical man. His coming may be considered as a most important and most felicitous advent designed to counterbalance the deluge of barbarism and the total corruption of manners. Were we even to reject the supernatural evidences of Christianity, there would still remain in its sublime morality, in the immensity of its benefits, and in the beauty of its worship, sufficient proof of its being the most divine and the purest religion ever practiced by men.

"With those who have an aversion for religion," says Pascal, "you must begin with demonstrating that it is not contradictory to reason; next show that it is venerable, and inspire them with respect for it; afterward exhibit it in an amiable light, and excite a wish that it were true; then let it appear by incontestable proofs that it is true; and, lastly, prove its antiquity and holiness by its grandeur and sublimity."

Such is the plan which that great man marked out, and which we have endeavored to pursue. Though we have not employed the arguments usually advanced by the apologists of Christianity, we have arrived by a different chain of reasoning at the same conclusion, which we present as the result of this work.

Christianity is perfect; men are imperfect.

Now, a perfect consequence cannot spring from an imperfect principle.

Christianity, therefore, is not the work of men.

If Christianity is not the work of men, it can have come from none but God.

If it came from God men cannot have acquired a knowledge of it but by revelation.

Therefore, Christianity is a revealed religion.

16. *Jean Baptiste de Lacordaire, O.P.: Sermon XVI on the Zeal of Statesmen and Men of Genius Against Catholic Doctrine, First Sunday of Advent, 1843*

From *Conferences of the Reverend Père Lacordaire Delivered in the Cathedral of Nôtre Dame in Paris* (New York: O'Shea Publishing Co., 1870), pp. 237-250.

IT APPEARS to me that I ought to pass on, and no longer occupy my attention with the question which I treated before you last, since I have drawn from it, in favor of Catholic doctrine, all the conclusions which were contained in it. I desire, however, to halt here a little longer for it is not an insignificant phenomenon—to have excited, with regard to a doctrine, in the passions of men that repulsion which we see in the world with regard to Catholic doctrine. I can easily conceive that each man, taken singly, wounded in his pride and in his passions, might revolt against Christianity. But what will result from it? Partial revolts, protestations lost in the general respect of mankind. Vice will hide itself; it will even deck itself with the mask of truth, and will leave the mass of society like an army ranged in battle-array, to pursue its course without troubling itself with the obscure treasons which become lost in the general fidelity. As an army is not retarded in its march or in its designs by the cowardly hearts which beat under the arms of warfare, so also (if it were only a question of isolated repulsions), society would pass by, bearing along all that mire in its billows, as a great stream bears along impure sands in its course, carrying us all towards the infinite in that ocean of life, of which Catholic doctrine is here below only the course and the motion.

But there is something more, gentlemen. The war against Catholic doctrine is not a war carried on by isolated attacks. It is a civil war, a social war, and as that war is all the history of the last eighteen centuries, as it includes your destiny and that of your posterity, we must still halt here and consider more profoundly that public zeal of statesmen and men of genius against Catholic doctrine. The question is grave, gentlemen. It is delicate. But comfort yourselves: I will treat you as Massillon treated Louis XIV, in the chapel of Versailles. Whatever may be your exigencies and my good will, I cannot do better for you than to treat you as the great age treated its great king.

One of the strongest passions of men is the passion for power. Man not only wants to be free, he wants also to be master. Not only does he desire to be master of himself and of that which belongs to him, but he wants also to be master of others and of that which belongs to them. "The rage for dominion," said the illustrious Comte de Maistre, "is innate in the heart of man." I blame him for that expression: for the craving for power in man is not a "rage," it is a generous passion. A man is loaded with all the gifts of birth and fortune; he can live in the enjoyments of his family, of friendship, of luxury, of honors, of tranquillity; he will not. He shuts himself up in a cabinet, and there he heaps up, designedly, toils and difficulties. He grows hoary under the weight of affairs which are not his own, having only for recompense the ingratitude of those whom he serves, the rivalry of ambitions equal to his own, and the blame of the indifferent. The first child leaving the swaddling clothes of the school takes a pen in his hand, and *he* who has but a shadow of talent at its dawn, who has no ancestors, has performed no services, to whom society owes nothing but the forgiveness of his temerity— attacks the statesman; who, instead of enjoying his fortune and his name, reserves to himself hardly time enough between the disquiet of the morning and that of the evening to drink a glass of water to quench his feverish thirst. The statesman does not heed these things. He passes from his cabinet to fields of battle; he watches by the side of the sword of Alexander to give his counsel; he signs treaties of which the passions of men will require him to give an account before posterity. And at last he dies, his course shortened by his labors, by anxieties, and by calumny; he dies, and his contemporaries engrave an epigram upon his tomb in anticipation of the time when the future might rise up in his favor.

Gentlemen, ambition may be a passion, I will not deny it, but at least it is a passion which demands energy. And, after the disinterested service of God, I know of nothing more heroic than the public service of the statesman. The Comte de Maistre ought to have said that "the want of power is innate in the heart of man." And why not? Do you know the first words which were addressed to you when you left the hands of God? Do you know what was the first benediction of mankind? Hearken to it, son of Adam, and learn your greatness: "Increase and multiply," it was said to the human race when God spoke to it for the first time. "Increase and multiply, and fill the earth and subdue it, and rule over the fishes of the sea, and the fowls of the air, and all living creatures that move upon the earth." If such is your vocation, gentlemen, if you have been called to govern the earth, as the celestial spirits have been called to govern the higher spheres— why should you not have the ambition of your nature? That ambition has, without doubt, got into disorder; but, in the last analysis, in its source it was the will of God. And if it did not exist mankind would perish. Therefore Christianity has never attacked human sovereignty.

From the beginning, the sons of Adam, divided into families, dispersed themselves upon the earth and, in whatever way it might have been accomplished, they confided the sovereignty either to an assembly, or to a man, or to a race; and, by the constitution of sovereignty, families became elevated to the rank of nations or of states. The state! Man in his highest power. The state! That moral force which sits upon the frontiers of nations, which guards their territory, by forcing respect from foreigners. The state! The protection of all rights and of all duties, the living justice which at each moment watches over millions of men, and does not permit a hair of their heads to fall with impunity. The state! The blood which has been shed during centuries by a people—it is its ancestry, its history, its victories, and its defeats; it is its banner without stain (for even if it might have had them, we would never avow it because it is our duty that the national banner should be judged only by God). The state! The unity and solidity of a great human family!

Ah yes! the state is a sublime and sacred thing, and Christianity has never touched it. It could have touched the heart of nations, justice, peace, glory, unity . . . but do not believe it. When Christianity came it found human sovereignty dishonored by excesses, prostrate in the midst of crimes—and it has lifted it up again and purified it. It has anointed sovereignty in its temples by the hands of its pontiffs. It has held up Clovis upon the shield, by giving him lessons which awoke in the minds of nations, confidence, respect, and love. It has created Christian loyalty, and with it fidelity, that sentiment which makes a child of royal blood to be sacred in the eyes of a whole nation, and as devotion to God does not withdraw men from their devotion of the state, it has caused an ejaculation to rise from all hearts, which the poet has thus expressed:

If it be great to die for one's king,
What would it be to die for one's God!

Christianity has, then, labored for the state; it has worked for human sovereignty, in the sight of God and the country; it has elevated the statesman higher than any doctrine had lifted him. And I feel sure that, but just now when I commenced to speak, you understood, even by my inflection, whether or not I thought lightly of a great statesman.

And yet, gentlemen, the representatives and the organs of human sovereignty have often counted, and a large number still count among the adversaries of Catholic doctrine. What is the cause of this? By what error or by what ingratitude have they thus rewarded it? It is, gentlemen, because in recognizing, serving, and honoring human sovereignty, Catholic doctrine declares that it has limits, and that, at least, it is not more extended than the sovereignty of God. Now, God has in himself a law, which is the limit, if we may so speak, of his omnipotence: that is to say, his justice, his goodness, his wisdom, which are himself, do not permit that in the exercise of his omnipotence he can ever overleap the boundaries of that which is true, holy, and just. God is not only the living sovereignty, but he is also the living law, the eternal law, and he has given us an emanation of that law in the natural law and in the divine law. And these two laws, the unchangeable expression of the relations of all intelligent beings, to whom have they been confided from the beginning? Is it to human sovereignty, to the state? No, never! The state has never been the depository of the divine law and of the natural law. And who, then, from the commencement has held them in charge? Who? A great power, gentlemen, a power which is not subdivided like nations, a power which is spread from one end of the world to the other, a power which, like electricity, or like the loadstone, runs without interruption from one pole of humanity to the other—conscience.

It is conscience which from the beginning was the depository of the natural law and of the divine law, and which has always produced in the world the counterpoise to human sovereignty. And, before Christianity—or rather before Jesus Christ, for Christianity ascends to the cradle of all things—before Jesus Christ, the human conscience was weak; it had betrayed the trust which was confided to it; and what has Jesus Christ done? He has raised up the human conscience. He said to it one day, breathing upon it: "Receive the Holy Spirit; whose sins you shall forgive, they are forgiven them; and whose sins you shall retain, they are retained. Whatsoever you shall bind on earth shall be bound in heaven, and whatsoever you shall loose on earth shall be loosed in heaven." He also said to it: Fear not those who kill the body, but cannot kill the soul; they shall bring you before deified human consciences, before kings, before presidents, they shall ask you questions; take no heed as to what you shall say, for I will put words into your mouths, which no one shall be able to resist. Jesus Christ has renewed conscience; he has given to it a power which it did not possess before; he has commanded it to obey God rather than men; he has armed it with martyrdom against human sovereignty degenerated into tyranny. "My soul belongs to God, my heart to my king, my body is in the hands of the wicked; let them do with me as they please." This is the conscience placed in the world by Jesus Christ, the Catholic conscience. It was not a priest who said this, but Achille d'Harlay, the first president in the parliament of Paris. And neither was it to the profit of the priesthood that the spiritual power of conscience was raised up and reconstituted.

What have we gained by it? Before Jesus Christ, the priesthood, although dishonored by error, was honored, loved, borne in the arms of the empire. The pontifical colleges were composed of the most illustrious families of Egypt, of Greece, and of Rome; and if in those times a man had been found, who had dared to say of the heathen priesthood what is now said of the Catholic priesthood, the *fasces* of the republic would have opened of their own accord to overwhelm the profaner of the rights and of the guardians of the human conscience. But for us, Catholic priests, our lot is very different. We have been given that which they had not—strength and grace to resist you. We have been given

the sovereignty of conscience, with the command to shed even the last drop of our blood to defend it; and we have done so, we do so daily. We do more: martyrdom is a small matter. More difficult is it to resist the powers which do not persecute, the desires of statesmen often worthy of the highest esteem, to struggle foot by foot, day by day, with them. Ah, when a priest would be quiet and enjoy this world, his course is very clear. Let him yield. Let him retreat before human sovereignty. Let him act on each exigency like a heathen priest, instead of acting like a Christian priest: distinctions, public piety, the renown of toleration, the favor of opinion will surround him, vying with each other to do him honor. It would not require much skill even for him to hide his weakness, and keep up the appearance of pontifical and Catholic dignity. But let a poor priest preserve his conscience rather than his life, let him defend the entry into it against the efforts of human sovereignty — then commences the grievous martyrdom of combating those whom we esteem, and whom we love, and of drinking the bitter cup of hatred so much the more unmerited because we labor and suffer for those even who pursue us.

For, for whose benefit then has the power of conscience been instituted? For whose benefit? For yours, gentlemen. For the benefit of mankind. That natural and divine law, of which we are the guardians, and not the usufructuaries; the victims, and not the beneficiaries: that law contains your rights, your liberties, your eternal charter, even the essence of God, inasmuch as it is wisdom, justice, goodness; inasmuch as it protects you against your passions, and the passions of the whole universe. Look, then, once in your lives, to the body of the Church. From that large wound which you see there, that cicatrice never dry, flows continually the most pure and persevering blood which has ever been shed for mankind.

Great God, you know these things, you who have accomplished them. You know why you have established the power of conscience at the same time as the power of human sovereignty. I pray you, then, in the presence of this great assembly, deign to extend your hand upon us; enlighten minds; teach them to understand where are the true defenders of their rights and of their most sure interests. Protect that work which you have formed in the heart of nations; maintain the sovereignty of conscience with regard to human sovereignty; maintain the distinction between the temporal power and the spiritual power, from whence has come the civilization of the world. O God, protect Christianity! O God, save Christianity!

I pass on without transition to the zeal of men of genius against Catholic doctrine.

Genius is the greatest power which has been created by God, humanly speaking, for grasping at and receiving truth. It is a sudden and vast intuition of the connections which bind beings together; a limpid lake, in which God and the universe are reflected with as much of coloring as of clearness. It is also the faculty of rendering ideas visible to those who would not have discovered them by themselves, of incarnating them in striking images, and of casting them into the soul, with a sentiment which touches it by enlightening it; which subjugates it; which causes it to humble itself under the action of genius, and give itself up to it by something analogous to that which happens when love seizes upon us and commands us.

Thus, gentlemen, men of genius naturally hold the scepter of ideas, as statesmen hold the scepter of things. And, in reality, before the coming of

Christ they exercised that empire almost fully; they created fables, and those fables became gods. One day, a man of genius left his cabinet, and went to walk in his garden; there he opened his mouth of gold; young men like yourselves eager to know, came to hear him, to surround him, to hang about his neck; behold the Platonists, the Peripatetics, the Stoics. Every man of genius had the pleasure of collecting around him intelligent men—of forming a school from them, of governing them, in order to satisfy that spiritual ambition, which flatters more even than the ambition of kings. Men are born on a throne; but although one may be born poet, philosopher, or orator, nature does not by these gifts at all exclude the necessity of advancing towards renown, and the honor of calling oneself the son of her works, and the father of her sovereignty. Nothing, without doubt, draws man nearer to the image of God, who has no cause, but who exists by himself. Nothing, I say, renders man more like God, with regard to origin, than existing of himself, than forming himself, than having gained his name, than being able to say, "I owe myself only to myself." And that want of glory, that self-love, so much flattered by the position of the leader of a school, those effusions of pride, form the propensity of genius; like the horse of the Scriptures, which neighs at the sound of the trumpet, when the man of genius hears the rumor of ideas, his heart beats, his eye becomes bright, he rouses himself into action, and he creates: he pronounces a fiat! And as God takes pleasure in those armies of suns which he has ranged round his throne, genius takes delight in the systems which it evokes around itself; so that humanity may adore them, as formerly it adored the stars of the firmament. This is, doubtless, great pride; but let us not say too much against it; even when the man of genius wanders into error, let us pity him; let us remember that, when Plato condemned the poets to leave his city, he ordered that they should be crowned with flowers and conducted to the gates of the city, with the sounds of the lyre, in order to do honor to the ray of the divinity which was within them, while at the same time he would not accept their domination.

Now, gentlemen, we have broken this scepter of ideas. Yes, let us confess it; for why should we hide it? Yes, we have broken this scepter of ideas in the hands of men of genius. Since Christ, there are no more philosophical schools. Socrates, Plato, Zeno, and so many others and their disciples who, even centuries after their death, swore by their names, and did not venture to swerve from a single page which they had written—all that is no more. Philosophy is become powerless to form schools, and to cause itself to be obeyed. Men ask themselves in Europe, where there exists a system of philosophy, a constituted school. They ask this, and obtain no answer. And yet you have great men. I do not say this ironically; yes, you have great men. Yet they are unable to found, I do not say a school existing for a thousand years, but a school which might last as long as their lives; they are like dethroned sovereigns, wanting a place where their sheathed sword might believe itself at home. See, in addition, to whom the scepter of ideas has been given, instead of to the men of genius. One day, Christ gathered together the fishermen who were casting their nets on the borders of a lake; and another day he said to them: "Go and teach all nations!" And again on another day those fishermen being together in a chamber, a breeze of wind passed over them; they went out into the public squares, they spoke, they collected thousands of men together to hear their words, they shattered the edifice of pagan science and religion. It is to those humble men, to the successors of those humble men, that the scepter of ideas, the most elevated which can be held upon earth, has been given. A herdsman, a workman, who has, during his whole life, only handled wood or iron, watching his child at play in his workshop, exclaims, "I will make a prophet, an apostle of him." He goes to the temple, he presents that child to the pontiff, the pontiff receives him in his arms, rears him, gives to him the milk of the Gospel, and when he has grown, he one day prostrates him upon the floor in his temple; he pronounces over him some mysterious words, he anoints his forehead and his hands with oil, and then he says to him: "Son of the herdsman, stand up; mount upon the throne of truth, speak to men, to kings, to nations; fear nothing, for every authority bends before your words; bring down every high thing which lifts itself up against the knowledge of God; nothing shall resist you, if you bear in your bosom the faith and charity which your master had."

Behold, gentlemen, a strange spectacle; and do you not easily conceive that at sight of it these men of genius become indignant and say to us: You priests of Catholic doctrine, you think yourselves the sovereign lords of truth and ideas; but see, you have no learned among you; you have no authors; you have no orators. Where are your books? Here is the bulletin of bibliography—where is your name; if we meet it by hazard, and ask the world who you are, the world passes by whistling like the wind, which only answers those who question it by laughing them to scorn.

It is true, gentlemen, it is just so. We have not much worldly wisdom; and when we have it, it is not the best thing which reaches us. We have not much of your wisdom; and why should we have it? Hear, then, St. Paul: "It is written: I will destroy the wisdom of the wise; and the prudence of the prudent, I will reject. Where is the wise? Where is the scribe? Where is the disputer of this world? Has not God made foolish the wisdom of this world?" And St. Paul, triumphant in the idea of our personal foolishness, exclaims again: "See your vocation, brethren, that not many among you are wise according to the flesh, not many mighty, not many noble; but the foolish things of the world God has chosen that he may confound the wise; and the weak things of the world God has chosen, that he may confound the strong: and the mean things of the world, and the things that are contemptible, God has chosen, and the things that are not, that he might destroy the things that are."

Where, indeed, would be the divinity of our mission, if we had knowledge other than the rest of the world, and by exception? If our books were, on each page, signed by the hand of genius, we should be nothing more than a human power. We must be men of no consideration, fools for Jesus Christ, because nations which possess good sense, and men of genius, who have enough of it when they wish, will then exclaim: "It is, however, very extraordinary, that these lowly men, after eighteen centuries, should be masters of everything, and that we should be obliged to convoke the powers of the world to struggle against them!" I do not laugh at you, gentlemen, nor do I humble myself; but I am armed with the power which God has given to us in our weakness; and I rejoice in it. We alone are able to triumph without self-love, because our triumph does not come from ourselves.

But, in fine, to whose profit has the scepter of ideas been transmitted from the strong to the weak, from the hands of genius to the hands of the Church?

To the profit of whom, if not to the profit of mankind? The most precious treasure of man is truth; for truth is God made known; it is God diffusing himself into our minds, as light diffuses itself into our eys. Now, powerful and creating genius adores itself much more than it adores truth. It is by no means a sure guardian of truth; it tends constantly to put even it own ideas in the place of the divine idea. God, considering then that the world had not willed, by wisdom, as St. Paul said, to preserve truth—God has confided truth to the foolishness of faith; he has preferred faith, which is the worship of truth, the humble adoration of truth, to knowledge and genius, without excluding them, however, when they themselves desire to adore and to serve. He has preferred to descend into a vessel of wood, respectful and pure, rather than to remain in a vessel of gold, too often impure and rebellious. Yet, God has preferred the holy democracy of faith and charity to the proud oligarchy of genius. I thank him for it from the bottom of my heart. I pray to him earnestly that it may continue to be so, and that virtue may always here below be something greater and more powerful than genius.

Gentlemen, we celebrate tonight the anniversary of the Son of God, come in the simplicity and humility of infancy, and recognized by shepherds before being recognized by kings. I invite you to this solemnity, which is a festival of the whole human family. That child, born among vile animals, represents all mankind; it is the announcement that glory was taken away from man to be given to God, that we may receive, in exchange for it, peace. I desire for you, then, in the name of that birth, heart-felt peace; I anticipate it for you; I will pray, that this affecting anniversary may touch your souls, and that you may repeat with the child Jesus those words, which sum up all that we have just said: "I give thanks to you O Father, Lord of heaven and earth, because you have hid these things from the wise and prudent, and have revealed them to little ones." Begin, gentlemen, to be little ones, humble and childlike, in order to become true men of genius, the preservers, the vessels of truth, and consequently, in order to cooperate in the establishment upon earth of duties, right, liberties, and salvation; all founded upon the power given by Jesus Christ to conscience and to faith.

Enter, gentlemen, into that army of truth. God calls you from the midst of the world to eternal thoughts by many warnings. May this assembly, this spectacle, that attention which you accord to me, awaken you. Finally, may this night, which draws near to speak to you of God, be to you a good night!

17. *Orestes A. Brownson: Catholicity Necessary to Sustain Popular Liberty, October 1845*

From *Brownson's Quarterly Review*, II (October, 1845), pp. 1-16.

BY POPULAR liberty, we mean democracy; by democracy, we mean the democratic form of government; by the democratic form of government, we mean that form of government which vests the sovereignty in the people as population, and which is administered by the people, either in person or by their delegates. By sustaining popular liberty, we mean not the introduction of institutions of democracy, but preserving it when and where it is already introduced, and securing its free, orderly, and wholesome action. By Catholicity, we mean the Roman Catholic Church, faith, morals, and worship. The thesis we propose to maintain is, therefore, that without the Roman Catholic religion it is impossible to preserve a democratic government, and secure its free, orderly, and wholesome action. Infidelity, Protestantism, heathenism may institute a democracy, but only Catholicity can sustain it.

Our own government, in its origin and constitutional form, is not a democracy, but, if we may use the expression, a limited elective aristocracy. In its theory, the representative, within the limits prescribed by the constitution, when once elected, and during the time for which he is elected, is, in his official action, independent of his constituents, and not responsible to them for his acts. For this reason, we call the government an elective aristocracy. But, practically, the government framed by our fathers no longer exists, save in name. Its original character has disappeared, or is rapidly disappearing. The constitution is a dead letter, except so far as it serves to prescribe the modes of election, the rule of the majority, the distribution and tenure of offices, and the union and separation of the functions of government. Since 1828, it has been becoming in practice, and is now, substantially, a pure democracy, with no effective constitution but the will of the majority for the time being. Whether the change has been for the better or the worse, we need not stop to inquire. The change was inevitable, because men are more willing to advance themselves by flattering the people and perverting the constitution, than they are by self-denial to serve their country. The change has been effected, and there is no return to the original theory of the government.

Any man who should plant himself on the constitution, and attempt to arrest the democratic tendency—no matter what his character, ability, virtues, services—would be crushed and ground to powder. Your Calhouns must give way for your Polks and Van Burens, your Websters, for your Harrisons and Tylers. No man, who is not prepared to play the demagogue, to stoop to flatter the people, and, in one direction or another, to exaggerate the democratic tendency, can receive the nomination for an important office, or have influence in public affairs. The reign of great men, of distinguished statesmen and firm patriots, is over, and that of the demagogues has begun. Your most important offices are hereafter to be filled by third and fourth-rate men, men too insignificant to excite strong opposition, and too flexible in their principles not to be willing to take any direction the caprices of the mob—or the interests of the wire-pullers of the mob—may demand. Evil or no evil, such is the fact, and we must conform to it.

Such being the fact, the question comes up, How are we to sustain popular liberty, to secure the free, orderly, and wholesome action of our practical democracy? The question is an important one, and cannot be blinked with impunity.

The theory of democracy is, Construct your government and commit it to the people to be taken care of. Democracy is not properly a government; but what is called the government is a huge machine contrived to be wielded by the people as they shall think proper. In relation to it the people are assumed to be what almighty God is to the universe, the first cause, the medial cause, the final cause. It emanates from them; it is administered by them, and for them; and, moreover, they are to keep watch and provide for its right administration.

It is a beautiful theory, and would work admirably, if it were not for one little difficulty, namely, the people are fallible, both individually and collectively, and governed by their passions and interests which not unfrequently lead them far astray and produce much mischief. The government must necessarily follow their will; and whenever that will happens to be blinded by passion, or misled by ignorance or interest, the government must inevitably go wrong; and government can never go wrong without doing injustice. The government may be provided for, the people may take care of that; but who or what is to take care of the people, and assure us that they will always wield the government so as to promote justice and equality, or maintain order, and the equal rights of all, of all classes and interests?

Do not answer by referring us to the virtue and intelligence of the people. We are writing seriously, and have no leisure to enjoy a joke, even if it be a good one. We have too much principle, we hope, to seek to humbug, and have had too much experience to be humbugged. We are Americans, American born, American bred, and we love our country, and will, when called upon, defend it, against any and every enemy, to the best of our feeble ability; but, though we by no means rate American virtue and intelligence so low as do those who will abuse us for not rating it higher, we cannot consent to hoodwink ourselves, or to claim for our countrymen a degree of virtue and intelligence they do not possess. We are acquainted with no salutary errors, and are forbidden to seek even a good end by any but honest means. The virtue and intelligence of the American people are not sufficient to secure the free, orderly, and wholesome action of the government; for they do not secure it. The government commits, every now and then, a sad blunder, and the general policy it adopts must prove, in the long run, suicidal. It has adopted a most iniquitous policy, and its most unjust measures are its most popular measures, such as it would be fatal to any man's political success directly and openly to oppose; and we think we hazard nothing in saying, our free institutions cannot be sustained without an augmentation of popular virtue and intelligence. We do not say the people are not capable of a sufficient degree of virtue and intelligence to sustain a democracy; all we say is, they cannot do it without virtue and intelligence, nor without a higher degree of virtue and intelligence than they have as yet attained to. We do not apprehend that many of our countrymen, and we are sure no one whose own virtue and intelligence entitle his opinion to any weight, will dispute this. Then the question of the means of sustaining our democracy resolves itself into the question of augmenting the virtue and intelligence of the people.

The press makes readers, but does little to make virtuous and intelligent readers. The newspaper press is, for the most part, under the control of men of very ordinary abilities, lax principles, and limited acquirements. It echoes and exaggerates popular errors, and does little or nothing to create a sound public opinion. Your popular literature caters to popular tastes, passions, prejudices, ignorance, and errors; it is by no means above the average degree of virtue and intelligence which already obtains, and can do nothing to create a higher standard of virtue or tone of thought. On what, then, are we to rely?

"On education," answers Frances Wright, Abner Kneeland, Horace Mann, and the educationists generally.

But we must remember that we must have virtue and intelligence. Virtue without intelligence will only fit the mass to be duped by the artful and designing; and intelligence without virtue only makes one the abler and more successful villain. Education must be of the right sort, if it is to answer our purpose; for a bad education is worse than none. The Mohammedans are great sticklers for education, and, if we recollect aright, it is laid down in the Koran, that every believer must at least be taught to read; but we do not find their education does much to advance them in virtue and intelligence. Education, moreover, demands educators, and educators of the right sort. Where are these to be obtained? Who is to select them, judge of their qualifications, sustain or dismiss them? The people? Then you place education in the same category with democracy. You make the people through their representatives the educators. The people will select and sustain only such educators as represent their own virtues, vices, intelligence, prejudices, and errors. Whether they educate mediately or immediately, they can impart only what they have and are. Consequently, with them for educators, we can, by means even of universal education, get no increase of virtue and intelligence to bear on the government. The people may educate, but where is that which takes care that they educate in a proper manner? Here is the very difficulty we began by pointing out. The people take care of the government and education; but who or what is to take care of the people, who need taking care of quite as much as either education or government?—for, rightly considered, neither government nor education has any other legitimate end than to take care of the people.

We know of but one solution of the difficulty, and that is in religion. There is no foundation for virtue but in religion, and it is only religion that can command the degree of popular virtue and intelligence requisite to insure to popular government the right direction and a wise and just adminstration. A people without religion, however successful they may be in throwing off old institutions, or in introducing new ones, have no power to secure the free, orderly, and wholesome working of any institutions. For the people can bring to the support of institutions only the degree of virtue and intelligence they have; and we need not stop to prove that an infidel people can have very little either of virtue or intelligence, since, in this professedly Christian country, this will and must be conceded us. We shall, therefore, assume, without stopping to defend our assumption, that religion is the power or influence we need to take care of the people, and secure the degree of virtue and intelligence necessary to sustain popular liberty. We say, then, if democracy commits the government to the people to be taken care of, religion is to take care that they take proper care of the government, rightly direct and wisely administer it.

But what religion? It must be a religion which is above the people and controls them, or it will not answer the purpose. If it depends on the people, if the people are to take care of it, to say what it shall be, what it should teach, what it shall command, what worship or discipline it shall insist on being observed, we are back in our old difficulty. The people take care of religion; but who or what is to take care of the people? We repeat, then, what religion? It cannot be Protestantism, in all or any of its forms; for Protestantism assumes as its point of departure that almighty God has indeed given us a religion, but has given it to us not to take care of us,

but to be taken care of by us. It makes religion the ward of the people; assumes it to be sent on earth a lone and helpless orphan, to be taken in by the people, who are to serve as its nurse.

We do not pretend that Protestants say this in just so many words; but this, under the present point of view, is their distinguishing characteristic. What was the assumption of the reformers? Was it not that almighty God had failed to take care of his church, that he had suffered it to become exceedingly corrupt and corrupting, so much so as to have become a very Babylon, and to have ceased to be his church? Was it not for this reason that they turned reformers, separated themselves from what had been the church, and attempted, with such materials as they could command, to reconstruct the church on its primitive foundation, and after the primitive model? Is not this what they tell us? But if they had believed the Son of Man came to minister and not to be ministered unto, that almighty God had instituted his religion for the spiritual government of men, and charged himself with the care and maintenance of it, would they ever have dared to take upon themselves the work of reforming it? Would they ever have fancied that either religion or the church could ever need reforming, or, if so, that it could ever be done by human agency? of course not. They would have taken religion as presented by the church as the standard, submitted to it as the law, and confined themselves to the duty of obedience. It is evident, therefore, from the fact of their assuming to be reformers, that they, consciously or unconsciously, regarded religion as committed to their care, or abandoned to their protection. They were, at least, its guardians, and were to govern it, instead of being governed by it.

The first stage of Protestantism was

to place religion under the charge of the civil government. The Church was condemned, among other reasons, for the control it exercised over princes and nobles, that is, over the temporal power: and the first effect of Protestantism was to emancipate the government from this control, or, in other words, to free the government from the restraints of religion, and to bring religion in subjection to the temporal authority. The prince, by rejecting the authority of the church, won for himself the power to determine the faith of his subjects, to appoint its teachers, and to remove them whenever they should teach what he disapproved, or whenever they should cross his ambition, defeat his oppressive policy, or interfere with his pleasures. Thus was it and still is it with the Protestant princes in Germany, with the temporal authority in Denmark, Sweden, England, Russia—in this respect also Protestant—and originally was it the same in this country. The supreme civil magistrate makes himself sovereign pontiff, and religion and the church, if disobedient to his will, are to be turned out of house and home, or dragooned into submission. Now, if we adopt this view, and subject religion to the civil government, it will not answer our purpose. We want religion, as we have seen, to control the people, and through its spiritual governance to cause them to give the temporal government always a wise and just direction. But, if the government control the religion, it can exercise no control over the sovereign people, for they control the government. Through the government the people take care of religion, but who or what takes care of the people? This would leave the people ultimate, and we have no security unless we have something more ultimate than they, something which they cannot control, but which they must obey.

The second stage in Protestantism is to reject, in matters of religion, the authority of the temporal government, and to subject religion to the control of the faithful. This is the full recognition in matters of religion of the democratic principle. The people determine their faith and worship, select, sustain, or dismiss their own religious teachers. They who are to be taught judge him who is to teach, and say whether he teaches them truth or falsehood, wholesome doctrine or unwholesome. The patient directs the physician what to prescribe. This is the theory adopted by Protestants generally in this country. The congregation select their own teacher, unless it be among the Methodists, and to them the pastor is responsible. If he teaches to suit them, well and good; if he crosses none of their wishes, enlarges their numbers, and thus lightens their taxes and gratifies their pride of sect, also well and good; if not, he must seek a flock to feed somewhere else.

But this view will no more answer our purpose than the former; for it places religion under the control of the people, and therefore in the same category with the government itself. The people take care of religion, but who takes care of the people?

The third and last stage of Protestantism is individualism. This leaves religion entirely to the control of the individual, who selects his own creed, or makes a creed to suit himself, devises his own worship and discipline, and submits to no restraints but such as are self-imposed. This makes a man's religion the effect of his virtue and intelligence, and denies it all power to augment or to direct them. So this will not answer. The individual takes care of his religion, but who or what takes care of the individual? The state? But who takes care of the state? The people? But who takes care of the people? Our old difficulty again.

It is evident from these considerations that Protestantism is not and cannot be the religion to sustain democracy; because take it in which stage you will, it, like democracy itself, is subject to the control of the people, and must command and teach what they say, and of course must follow, instead of controlling, their passions, interests, and caprices.

Nor do we obtain this conclusion merely by reasoning. It is sustained by facts. The Protestant religion is everywhere either an expression of the government or of the people, and must obey either the government or public opinion. The grand reform, if reform it was, effected by the Protestant chiefs consisted in bringing religious questions before the public, and subjecting faith and worship to the decision of public opinion—public on a larger or smaller scale, that is, of the nation, the province, or the sect. Protestant faith and worship tremble as readily before the slightest breath of public sentiment, as the aspen leaf before the gentle zephyr. The faith and discipline of a sect take any and every direction the public opinion of that sect demands. All is loose, floating, is here today, is there to-morrow; and, next day, may be nowhere. The holding of slaves is compatible with Christian character south of a geographical line, and incompatible north; and Christian morals change according to the prejudices, interests, or habits, of the people (as evinced by the recent divisions in our own country among the Baptists and Methodists). The Unitarians of Savannah refuse to hear a preacher accredited by Unitarians of Boston.

The great danger in our country is from the predominance of material interests. Democracy has a direct tendency to favor inequality and injustice. The government must obey the people; that is, it must follow the passions and interests of the people, and of course the stronger passions and interests. These with us are material, such as pertain solely to this life and this world. What our people demand of government is that it adopt and sustain such measures as tend most directly to facilitate the acquisition of wealth. It must, then, follow the passion for wealth, and labor especially to promote worldly interests.

But among these worldly interests, some are stronger than others, and can command the government. These will take possession of the government, and wield it for their own especial advantage. They will make it the instrument of taxing all the other interests of the country for the special advancement of themselves. This leads to inequality and injustice, which are incompatible with the free, orderly, and wholesome working of the government.

Now, what is wanted is some power to prevent this, to moderate the passion for wealth, and to inspire the people with such a true and firm sense of justice, as will prevent any one interest from struggling to advance itself at the expense of another. Without this, the stronger material interests predominate, make the government the means of securing their predominance, and of extending it by the burdens which, through the government, they are able to impose on the weaker interests of the country.

The framers of our government foresaw this evil, and thought to guard against it by a written constitution. But they entrusted the preservation of the constitution to the care of the people, which was as wise as to lock up your culprit in prison and trust him with the key. The constitution, as a restraint on the will of the people or the governing majority, is already a dead letter. It answers to talk about, to declaim about, in electioneering speeches, and even as a theme of newspaper leaders, and political essays in reviews; but its effective power is a morning vapor after the sun is well up.

Even Mr. Calhoun's theory of the constitution, which regards it not simply as the written instrument, but as the disposition or the constitution of the people into sovereign states united in a federal league or compact, for certain purposes which concern all the states alike, and from which it follows that any measure unequal in its bearing, or oppressive upon any portion of the confederacy, is *ipso facto* null and void, and may be vetoed by the aggrieved state—this theory, if true, is yet insufficient; because, 1) it has no application within the state governments themselves; and because, 2) it does not, as a matter of fact, arrest what are regarded as the unequal, unjust, and oppressive measures of the federal government. South Carolina, in 1833, forced a compromise, but in 1842, the obnoxious policy was revived, is pursued now successfully, and there is no state to attempt again the virtue of state interposition. Not even South Carolina can be brought to do so again. The meshes of trade and commerce are so spread over the whole land, the controlling influences of all sections have become so united and interwoven, by means of banks, other moneyed corporations, and the credit system, that henceforth state interposition becomes practically impossible. The constitution is practically abolished, and our government is virtually, to all intents and purposes, as we have said, a pure democracy, with nothing to prevent it from obeying the interest or interests which for the time being can succeed in commanding it. This, as Mr. Caleb Cushing would say, is a "fixed fact." There is no restraint of predominating passions and interests but in religion. This is another "fixed fact."

Protestantism is insufficient to restrain these, for it does not do it, and is itself carried away by them. The Protestant sect governs its religion, instead of being governed by it. If one sect pursues, by the influence of its chiefs, a policy in opposition to the passions and interests of its members, or any portion of them, the disaffected, if a majority, change its policy; if too few or too weak to do that, they leave it and join some other sect, or form a new sect. If the minister attempts to do his duty, reproves a practice by which his parishioners "get gain," or insists on their practicing some real self-denial not compensated by some self-indulgence, a few leading members will tell him very gravely that they hired him to preach and pray for them, not to interfere with their business concerns and relations; and if he does not mind his own business, they will no longer need his services. The minister feels, perhaps, the insult; he would be faithful; but he looks at his lovely wife, at his little ones. These to be reduced to poverty, perhaps to beggary—no, it must not be; one struggle, one pang, and it is over. He will do the bidding of his masters. A zealous minister in Boston ventured, one Sunday, to denounce the modern spirit of trade. The next day, he was waited on by a committee of wealthy merchants belonging to his parish, who told him he was wrong. The Sunday following, the meek and humble minister publicly retracted, and made the *amende honorable*.

Here, then, is the reason why Protestantism, though it may institute, cannot sustain popular liberty. It is itself subject to popular control, and must follow in all things the popular will, passion, interest, ignorance, prejudice, or caprice. This, in reality, is its boasted virtue, and we find it commended because under it the people have a voice in its management. Nay, we ourselves shall be denounced, not for saying

Protestantism subjects religion to popular control, but for intimating that religion ought not to be so subjected. A terrible cry will be raised against us. "See, here is Mr. Brownson," it will be said, "he would bring the people under the control of the pope of Rome. Just as we told you. These papists have no respect for the people. They sneer at the people, mock at their wisdom and virtue. Here is this unfledged *papistling,* not yet a year old, boldly contending that the control of their religious faith and worship should be taken from the people, and that they must believe and do just what the emissaries of Rome are pleased to command; and all in the name of liberty too." If we only had room, we would write out and publish what the anti-Catholic press will say against us, and save the candid, the learned, intellectual, and patriotic editors the trouble of doing it themselves (and we would do it with the proper quantity of *italics,* small capitals, CAPITALS, and exclamation points)! Verily, we think we could do the thing up nearly as well as the best of them. But we have no room. Yet it is easy to foresee what they will say. The burden of their accusation will be that we labor to withdraw religion from the control of the people, and to free it from the necessity of following their will; that we seek to make it the master, and not the slave, of the people. And this is good proof of our position, that Protestantism cannot govern the people—for they govern it—and therefore that Protestantism is not the religion wanted; for it is precisely a religion that can and will govern the people, be their master, that we need.

If Protestantism will not answer the purpose, what religion will? The Roman Catholic or none. The Roman Catholic religion assumes, as its point of departure, that it is instituted not to be taken care of by the people, but to take care of the people; not to be governed by them, but to govern them. The word is harsh in democratic ears, we admit; but it is not the office of religion to say soft or pleasing words. It must speak the truth even in unwilling ears, and it has few truths that are not harsh and grating to the worldly mind or the depraved heart. The people need governing, and must be governed, or nothing but anarchy and destruction await them. They must have a master. The word must be spoken. But it is not our word. We have demonstrated its necessity in showing that we have no security for popular government, unless we have some security that the people will administer it wisely and justly; and we have no security that they will do this, unless we have some security that their passions will be restrained, and their attachments to worldly interests so moderated that they will never seek, through the government, to support them at the expense of justice; and this security we can have only in a religion that is above the people, exempt from their control, which they cannot command, but must, on peril of condemnation, obey. Declaim as you will; quote our expression—the people must have a master—as you doubtless will; hold it up in glaring capitals, to excite the unthinking and unreasoning multitude, and doubly to fortify their prejudices against Catholicity; be mortally scandalized at the assertion that religion ought to govern the people, and then go to work and seek to bring the people into subjection to your banks or moneyed corporations through their passions, ignorance, and worldly interests, and in doing so, prove what candid men, what lovers of truth, what noble defenders of liberty, and what ardent patriots you are. We care not. You see we understand you, and, understanding you, we repeat: the religion which is to answer our purpose must be above the people, and able to command them. We know the force of the word, and we mean it. The first lesson to the child is, obey; the first and last lesson to the people, individually or collectively, is obey; and there is no obedience where there is no authority to enjoin it.

The Roman Catholic religion, then, is necessary to sustain popular liberty, because popular liberty can be sustained only by a religion free from popular control, above the people, speaking from above and able to command them—and such a religion is the Roman Catholic. It acknowledges no master but God, and depends only on the divine will in respect to what it shall teach, what it shall ordain, what it shall insist upon as truth, piety, moral and social virtue. It was made not by the people, but for them; is administered not by the people, but for them; is accountable not to the people, but to God. Not dependent on the people, it will not follow their passions; not subject to their control, it will not be their accomplice in iniquity; and speaking from God, it will teach them the truth, and command them to practice justice. To this end the very constitution of the church contributes. It is catholic, universal; it teaches all nations, and has its center in no one. If it were a mere national church, like the Anglican, the Russian, the Greek or, as Louis XIV in his pride sought to make, the Gallican, it would follow the caprice or interest of that nation, and become but a tool of its government or of its predominating passion. The government, if antipopular, would use it to oppress the people, to favor its ambitious projects, or its unjust and ruinous policy. Under a popular government, it would become the slave of the people, and could place no restraint on the ruling interest or on the majority; but would be made to sanction and consolidate

its power. But having its center in no one nation, extending over all, it becomes independent of all, and in all can speak with the same voice and in the same tone of authority. This the church has always understood, and hence the noble struggles of the many calumniated popes to sustain the unity, catholicity, and independence of the ecclesiastical power. This, too, the temporal powers have always seen and felt, and hence their readiness, even while professing the Catholic faith, to break the unity of Catholic authority, for, in so doing, they could subject the church in their own dominions, as did Henry VIII, and as does the Emperor of Russia, to themselves.

But we pray our readers to understand us well. We unquestionably assert the adequacy of Catholicity to sustain popular liberty, on the ground of its being exempted from the popular control and able to govern the people; and its necessity, on the ground that it is the only religion, which, in a popular government, is or can be exempted from popular control, and able to govern the people. We say distinctly that this is the ground on which, reasoning as the statesman and not as the theologian, we assert the adequacy and necessity of Catholicity; and we object to Protestantism, in our present argument, solely on the ground that it has no authority over the people, is subject to them, must follow the direction they give it, and therefore cannot restrain their passions, or so control them as to prevent them from abusing their government. This we assert, distinctly and intentionally, and so plainly, that what we say cannot be mistaken.

But in what sense do we assert Catholicity to be the master of the people? Here we demand justice. The authority of Catholicity is spiritual, and the only sense in which we have here urged or do urge its necessity is as the means of augmenting the virtue and intelligence of the people. We demand it as a religious, not as a political power. We began by defining democracy to be that form of government which vests the sovereignty in the people. If, then, we recognize the sovereignty of the people in matters of government, we must recognize their political right to do what they will. The only restriction on their will we contend for is a moral restriction; and the master we contend for is not a master that prevents them from doing politically what they will, but who, by his moral and spiritual influence, prevents them from willing what they ought not to will. The only influence on the political or governmental action of the people which we ask from Catholicity, is that which it exerts on the mind, the heart, and the conscience—an influence which it exerts by enlightening the mind to see the true end of man, the relative value of all worldly pursuits, by moderating the passions, by weaning the affections from the world, inflaming the heart with true charity, and by making each act in all things seriously, honestly, conscientiously. The people will thus come to see and to will what is equitable and right, and will give to the government a wise and just direction, and never use it to effect any unwise or unjust measures. This is the kind of master we demand for the people, and this is the bugbear of "Romanism" with which miserable panders to prejudice seek to frighten old women and children. Is there any thing alarming in this? In this sense, we wish this country to come under the pope of Rome. As the visible head of the church, the spiritual authority which almighty God has instituted to teach and govern the nations, we assert his supremacy, and tell our countrymen that we would have them submit to him. They may flare up at this as much as they please, and write as many alarming and abusive editorials as they choose or can find time or space to do —they will not move us, or relieve themselves of the obligation almighty God has placed them under of obeying the authority of the Catholic Church, pope and all.

If we were discussing the question before us as a theologian, we should assign many other reasons why Catholicity is necessary to sustain popular liberty. Where the passions are unrestrained, there is license, but not liberty; the passions are not restrained without divine grace; and divine grace comes ordinarily only through the sacraments of the church. But from the point of view we are discussing the question, we are not at liberty to press this argument, which, in itself, would be conclusive. The Protestants have foolishly raised the question of the influence of Catholicity on democracy, and have sought to frighten our countrymen from embracing it by appealing to their democratic prejudices, or, if you will, convictions. We have chosen to meet them on this question, and to prove that democracy without Catholicity cannot be sustained. Yet in our own minds the question is really unimportant. We have proved the insufficiency of Protestantism to sustain democracy. What then? Have we in so doing proved that Protestantism is not the true religion? Not at all; for we have no infallible evidence that democracy is the true or even the best form of government. It may be so, and the great majority of the American people believe it is so; but they may be mistaken, and Protestanism be true, notwithstanding its incompatibility with republican institutions. So we have proved that Catholicity is necessary to sustain such institutions. But what then? Have we proved it to be the true religion? Not at all. For such institutions may themselves be false and mischievous. Nothing in this way is settled in favor of one religion or another, because no system of politics can ever constitute a standard by which to try a religious system. Religion is more ultimate than politics, and you must conform your politics to your religion, and not your religion to your politics. You must be the veriest infidels to deny this.

This conceded, the question the Protestants raise is exceedingly insignificant. The real question is, Which religion is from God? If it be Protestantism, they should refuse to subject it to any human test, and should blush to think of compelling it to conform to any thing human; for when God speaks, man has nothing to do but to listen and obey. So, having decided that Catholicity is from God, save in condescension to the weakness of our Protestant brethren, we must refuse to consider it in its political bearings. It speaks from God, and its speech overrides every other speech, its authority every other authority. It is the sovereign of sovereigns. He who could question this, admitting it to be from God, has yet to obtain his first religious conception, and to take his first lesson in religious liberty; for we are to hear God, rather than hearken unto men. But we have met the Protestants on their own ground, because, though in doing so we surrendered the vantage-ground we might occupy, we know the strength of Catholicity and the weakness of Protestantism. We know what Protestantism has done for liberty, and what it can do. It can take off restraints, and introduce license, but it can do nothing to sustain true liberty. Catholicity depends on no form of government; it leaves the people to adopt such forms of government as they please, because under any or all forms of government it can fulfill its mission of training up souls for heaven; and the eternal salvation of one single soul is worth more than, is

a good far outweighing, the most perfect civil liberty, nay, all the worldly prosperity and enjoyment ever obtained or to be obtained by the whole human race.

It is, after all, in this fact, which Catholicity constantly brings to our minds, and impresses upon our hearts, that consists its chief power, aside from the grace of the sacraments, to sustain popular liberty. The danger to that liberty comes from love of the world—the ambition for power or place, the greediness of gain or distinction. It comes from lawless passions, from inordinate love of the goods of time and sense. Catholicity, by showing us the vanity of all these, by pointing us to the eternal reward that awaits the just, moderates this inordinate love, these lawless passions, and checks the rivalries and struggles in which popular liberty receives her death blow. Once learn that all these things are vanity, that even civil liberty itself is no great good, that even bodily slavery is no great evil, that the one thing needful is a mind and heart conformed to the will of God, and you have a disposition which will sustain a democracy wherever introduced, though doubtless a disposition that would not lead you to introduce it where it is not.

But this last is no objection, for the revolutionary spirit is as fatal to democracy as to any other form of government. It is the spirit of insubordination and of disorder. It is opposed to all fixed rule, to all permanent order. It loosens every thing, and sets all afloat. Where all is floating, where nothing is fixed, where nothing can be counted on to be tomorrow what it is today there is no liberty, no solid good. The universal restlessness of Protestant nations, the universal disposition to change, the constant movements of the populations, so much admired by shortsighted philosophers, are a sad spectacle to the sober-minded Christian, who would, as far as possible, find in all things a type of that eternal fixedness and repose he looks forward to as the blessed reward of his trials and labors here. Catholicity comes here to our relief. All else may change, but it changes not. All else may pass away, but it remains where and what it was, a type of the immobility and immutability of the eternal God.

18. *Archbishop John Ireland: America in France,* *18 June 1892*

From *The Church and Modern Society* (New York: D. H. McBride and Company, 1903), I, 365-395.

YOU do me a great honor this evening in giving me your attention. I will take back to my distant American home a sweet and lasting memory of this scene. It is for me a privilege which I deeply appreciate to make a public address before so distinguished an audience in the capital of France. I am well aware that the gentlemen who invited me to speak, who are now seated on this platform, are men whose names are the glory of France; I am well aware that my audience is the intellectual elite of the city of Paris.

I must, however, confess that I dread the responsibility of the occasion. How can I do justice to my theme? How can I worthily respond to your expectations? In the midst of the distractions of a hurried passage through your city I could not even attempt to gather thoughts that might be of interest to my distinguished hearers, or to clothe those thoughts in words that would not be wholly unworthy of the occasion. I speak tonight in a language to which I am long unaccustomed. There was, indeed, a time when your language was familiar to my ears, when I spoke it by day and dreamed in it by night; that time is long gone by, and now my tongue no longer knows the music of your accents.

All that I promise this evening is a plain and simple talk on the United States of America. I will tell of things as they occur to my mind; I will give expression, as best I can, to the feelings that stir my heart; and I shall be amply rewarded if, when I have done, I may believe that I have not taxed your patience too severely.

Of the United States, and of the United States only, will I speak.

Monsieur de Vogüé has been so good as to say that I am in some measure a child of France. I thank Monsieur de Vogüé for this compliment. Yes; please take me to be in some measure a child of France. I rejoice to believe that I am her child in not a few fibers of my being. In her schools the years of my youth were passed. France is largely the mother of my ideas, and much of my heart has always belonged to her. Whenever during the years of mature life I step again upon the soil of France, my soul grows young. I am back to the land of my youth.

For myself, I love France, because I have known her anear. But who could not love France, the country of exalted ideas and of generous sacrifices? In peace and in war France has during ages done battle for honor, for religion, for all that lifts up and ennobles the soul. At no epoch of history could France be spared from the moral, the intellectual or the religious world.

A citizen of the United States speaking of America will never be a stranger in France. To France America owes her freedom; to France this evening I pay homage; I offer her the tribute of my gratitude. Over a century ago the English colonies in North America were fighting for independence. The soldiers of the American Revolution were brave and devoted, but victory did not light upon their banners; America was becoming fearful of the result of the war. Suddenly soldiers of France, commanded by Rochambeau and Lafayette, landed on the shores of America, and the soldiers of France and of America, united, were invincible in battle.

Long before the days of the American Revolution, a great part of our country had been the domain of France. Indeed, you might have founded a mighty empire beyond the Atlantic! In the seventeenth century, the French, who had established extensive colonies on the banks of the St. Lawrence, sent explorers and missionaries even as far as the waters of the Ohio and the Northern Mississippi. The French colony of Louisiana covered the whole southwest of the valley of the Mississippi. The colonies of England hugged the eastern seaboard. The Far West, the Southwest, the Northwest, were French possessions, and north of all that is now the territory of the United states was again the vast region of Canada, then, also, an appanage of France.

The state of Minnesota was the northwestern frontier of the possessions of France. It was in 1680 that the northern Mississippi was first seen by a white man. This man was Father Louis Hennepin, who in the name of Church and of France, pushed his frail canoe as far north as the present site of the city of St. Paul, where he

was captured by the savages of the Sioux tribe. During his captivity he baptized some infants, and blessed by prayer and invocation those new regions; and thus it was that the first ministrations of Christianity in Minnesota were dispensed by a messenger of France. It was Father Hennepin who gave to the Falls of the Mississippi the name of St. Anthony—a name which has never since been effaced from the map of the American continent. It was about the same time that a French explorer, Le Sieur Du Luth, first navigated the extreme western waters of Lake Superior, and at the point where those waters receive the tribute of the St. Louis River, on the northeastern limit of the territory of the present state of Minnesota, a city of great promise is called by his name—Duluth.

Seven years before Louis Hennepin had sped his frail canoe over the waters of the Mississippi northward from the mouth of the Illinois to the Falls of St. Anthony, the saintly missionary Jacques Marquette had, in 1673, navigated the great river from the mouth of the Wisconsin to that of the Arkansas; and later, in 1682, another Frenchman, the dauntless voyager, the Chevalier de La Salle floated down its waters from the mouth of the Illinois to the Gulf of Mexico. Thus, before the end of the year 1682, the whole of the mighty river upon whose banks today flourish imperial commonwealths, had been, with the exception of its extreme northern waters, explored by Frenchmen and by them made known to the civilized world. The earlier discovery of the Mississippi by the Spaniard, Ferdinand de Soto, had revealed to Europeans only a small part of the river, and had not resulted in further Spanish discoveries nor in Spanish occupancy of the neighboring lands.

In 1727, Le Sieur de la Perriere built upon the western shore of Lake Pepin, in what is now Minnesota, Fort

Beauharnois—so named in honor of Charles de Beauharnois, at that time governor of Canada. This was the last post in the upper Mississippi Valley over which floated the *drapeau Fleur-de-Lis*. Jesuit missionaries accompanied de la Pierriere and his soldiers, and they dedicated to the service of God, under the patronage of the Archangel St. Michael, the first Christian church ever erected in Minnesota, and indeed in the whole upper Mississippi Valley. A few hundred yards from the spot where this church stood, a convent has lately been erected and a year ago I had the pleasure of dedicating the convent chapel, and of calling it— as of yore the chapel of Beauharnois had been called—St. Michael's. Thus the memory of France lives in my far-distant western home.

Within the present century, French religious ardor has been at work preaching Christ's Gospel amid our forests and over our prairies. The city of St. Paul was founded when, in the year 1842, a French priest, a native of Puy, Father Lucien Galtier, dedicated on the banks of the Mississippi, a humble log chapel, calling it in honor of the apostle of nations, St. Paul. A few families made up the spiritual flock of Father Galtier—they were children of Canada, grandchildren of France. The first bishop of Dubuque, in the state of Iowa, was Mathias Loras, a native of Lyons, and the first bishop of St. Paul was Joseph Cretin, a son of Montluel, in your *département* of Ain. Where Father Galtier erected his modest chapel fifty years ago, there now stands the great city of St. Paul with 160,000 inhabitants, adjoining which, and embracing within its borders the falls discovered by Louis Hennepin, is the city of Minneapolis, with 200,000 inhabitants. The little chapel of St. Paul, sixteen feet in length and twelve feet in width, built by Father Galtier, has yielded its name and traditions to the cathedral of St. Paul, around which, in the two cities of St. Paul and Minneapolis, thirty-six other Catholic temples open their doors to more than a hundred thousand children of the Church.

Your explorers made known to the civilized world the territory of the United States. Your missionaries were among the first to preach the Catholic faith to the aborigines and the settlers in America; your armies created the republic of the United States. France stood sponsor for the republic of the west when America was born into the galaxy of the nations of the world. Well, let me say to you, France has reason to be proud of the infant of a century ago—the giant of today. The census of 1890 gives to the United States sixty-five millions of people; the census of 1900, God meanwhile blessing us, will tell of a population nearing the hundredth million. May I not be allowed to say, that the great and historic nations of Europe cannot afford to ignore the United States? The size alone of the republic commands the attention of the world.

Our population increases, of course, largely by immigration from European countries. A flood of immigrants has been pouring in upon us during the latter half of this century. In the early days of the republic the population counted only three millions. There have been many causes at work to attract to our shores millions of European immigrants; many causes at work to give to all the people of America, native and adopted, the extraordinary material prosperity and social happiness that have fallen to their lot. Among these causes is the beauty, the fertility, the natural richness of our country. Heaven has been generous in gifts to America. From the Atlantic to the Pacific, from the Mexican Gulf to the British boundary, are lakes, vast inland seas, navigable rivers majestic in their flow, soil most fertile, mines most opulent, climate most varied and salubrious. The people, too, merit no small meed of praise; they are energetic and enterprising; they delight in labor; they are quick to put to profit all the natural advantages of the continent. The great and wondrous inventions of this nineteenth century have marvelously contributed to the development of America. America is the favored child of the age. Without the discoveries and inventions of the age, without steamboats and railroads, without telegraph lines and electricity, the United States of to-day could not exist. It is not surprising that America loves material progress, loves the magnificent inventions of the century, the fruit of the genius of man, the gift of the Creator to his children of earth. Finally, the development of our country is to be attributed to our free institutions, which encourage in the highest degree private initiative and private enterprise. Our population would not today touch the Mississippi—certainly five great railroads would not span the continent—if the men of America had not of their own individual courage said to themselves: we must do great things; and if the spirit of their civil and political institutions did not invite them as individuals to mighty undertakings.

To this day immigrants are thronging to our shores. On this account the United States affords social science a most interesting field of study. We have in our population representatives of all the nations of the earth—Englishmen, Irishmen, Frenchmen, Germans, Bohemians, Poles, Scandinavians, Italians, Arabs, Syrians, and Chinamen. Well, the number of immigrants is so great that we are beginning to be somewhat fastidious as to the quality. So far, however, the only country whose immigrants we have determined to exclude totally, is China.

We are sometimes blamed for our exclusion of the Chinese; our action in this matter, it is said, is at variance with our professions of freedom for ourselves and for others. But the social question, as it exists in America, has determined us to exclude Chinese immigrants; our working men cannot, with due respect for our standard of civilization and of the comfort of life due to all our people, enter into competition with Oriental labor. Moreover, Orientals show no readiness or disposition to assimilate with our American population, and one of the conditions upon which we invite immigrants to our shores, is that they loyally adopt our institutions and become with us one and the same people.

As to immigrants from Europe, they, with a few exceptions, will be welcome in the future as in the past. Let them come; we have a great country within which to offer them homes, we have great civil and political freedom with which to bless them; and, in turn, we need the aid of bright minds and strong arms to increase our own prosperity. I have said: with a few exceptions. It is not unknown to us that in some countries in Europe—though not in your beloved France—when a city or village finds an individual too burdensome, the patriotic authorities say to him: Go to America. Here we cry halt. Our congress has been asked to pass a law, according to which immigrants from Europe or elsewhere must be able to show certificates of good conduct and good health, signed by our own consuls in foreign lands—otherwise those people will be generously restored by us to their mother country.

But how, you may ask me, is this possible, that the heterogeneous elements brought by immigration to your shores become fused into one people, and constitute one undivided nation? How the vast masses of immigrants are assimilated into one people, I cannot clearly explain; but it is done. There is something in the air, something in the soil, something in the sweet freedom of our institutions; almost as soon as immigrants set foot upon our shores they love America; they rejoice in the freedom they receive from her; they live of her life; they acquire the spirit of the country. The transformation is particularly noticeable in the children of immigrants; they form a type of men, different from their ancestors—they are Americans. The first English colonists in the New England or northeastern states, have, more than any other element of our population, contributed to the formation of our present American type; they have, beyond doubt, given to our whole population an impress which is ineffaceable, communicated to it a spirit which remains unchanged in the American, despite our varied aggregations of types from other countries. But these aggregations have, in turn, influenced in no small degree our original elements; influenced them, we are glad to say, for the better. We shall offer to the world in our growth a new type of humanity; this new type will be more perceptibly differentiated as years go by. As a population, we are of the eclectic school. We take from each country its best elements of manhood, and of these elements we build up a new people—the American people. This new people will have the spirit of individual enterprise of the Saxon, the steadfast perseverance of the Teuton, the high-born sentiments, the poetry, the love of the ideal, that characterize the Frenchman. Will not such a people be worthy of your esteem?

Americans are not always understood by foreigners. They have their defects; but, I take pleasure in proclaiming it, they have also their virtues, many and grand virtues. European papers will blazon abroad some one abnormal occurrence which has happened beyond the ocean, and this will be accepted as a sample of what is daily taking place in America. Beware, I pray you, of judging us by the sophistic maxim—*Ab uno disce omnes*. Europe has the habit of locating in distant countries, and preferably in America, whatever things it dreams of as exaggerated and terrible, whatever things it wishes to have removed from its own territories.

To no people is law so sacred and inviolable as the American people; but because in rare and extraordinary circumstances, under strong provocation, or in some remote and semi-civilized region of our vast country, the forms of law are for a moment set aside, and lynch law holds sway, the American people are rated as lawless. And yet, in the eyes of the American citizen law is most sacred. Law appeals to his conscience, and has the support of his conscience. Sometimes he may not like certain provisions of the law; but then, he says to himself: It is the law; I must obey it—in two or four years I will change it. This is a great privilege of the American people, a privilege which they value, and in which they find comfort for all temporary dissatisfaction—they change their laws, they change their lawmakers, without, however, ever thinking for a moment of setting aside the republic.

We are sometimes spoken of as a people of materialistic tendencies, worshiping money and bending all our energies to amass riches. Americans, it is true, do love money; they are by nature energetic and aggressive; money represents to them the result of their labor, and as they love their labor, they love its reward. They strive to accumulate wealth; they glory in thousands and in millions. But, at the same time, their hands are open to give—

and give in princely fashion. They spend money as freely as they make it. The beneficences of rich Americans are on a scale of surprising munificence; all classes of the people are generous within the limits of their fortunes.

The reproach is made that we build cities, and railroads and factories, but do nothing for art and science and the culture of life. It is true that we build cities and railroads and factories, because they are needed for the development of our country. Europeans built their cities long ago, and their narrow territories and limited resources may not call for many new enterprises; the rich among them have had their fortunes made for them; they have more leisure than we for poetry, painting and music. We too, shall have leisure for those things. We are growing up to them very fast. Only give us time, and you will not have to complain of us.

> *Petit poisson deviendra grand,*
> *Pourvu que Dieu lui prete la vie.*

With time we shall have all that is best in the highest forms of civilization, all that you are so justly proud of in your own France. Already, even, our libraries, museums and art institutes are assuming large proportions; and our universities are becoming world-known centers of thought and research. Mind is prized in America. Among the American people, apparently so devoted to money-getting, the man of brilliant intellect is esteemed far above the man who is possessed of dollars by the million but is devoid of the accomplishments of intellect.

We have, it is said, no monuments, so that our country is uninteresting and uninstructive. Here, again, we need time. The monuments of God abound—ours is a grand, unequaled continent. Nowhere are rivers so mighty, lakes so ocean-like, mountains so sublime; nowhere does nature show

herself so majestic and yet so entrancing. The monuments of man also are rapidly coming into existence—the palaces of our national government, the stately homes of many of our citizens, tell that Americans are ambitious to adorn their land with noble monuments of architecture; and within our museums and private residences richest treasures of art are being steadily amassed. I know that it is said that we value things only so far as they pay good dividends, and that art, to be admitted into America, must prove her ability to fill the purse as well as to minister to cultivated taste. You have heard the story of a countryman of mine, on a visit to the city of popes and Ceasars, standing admiringly before the Coliseum. "Nothing like this in America," remarked his Italian friend. The tourist looked for a few moments longer at the massive walls of travertine, that have defied two thousand years, and then calmly remarked: "The cost would be considerable; a coliseum in America would not pay. That is why we have none." The story proves, not that Americans are devoid of artistic refinement, but that they are undaunted by seeming impossibilities.

The woman of America is reported to be forward and frivolous; in reality she is only independent, and conscious of her power of self-control. You are surprised to hear of women in America combining to enlarge the sphere of women's rights and influence, and even to obtain for woman the use of the ballot. All our women are not in the category of agitators. All of them, however, are possessed of an energy and an independent of spirit that do them honor. They are, moreover, usually practical and endowed with good sense. The system of education under which they are brought up is such, that if, in later years, fortune fails to smile on them, they are fitted to work for their living.

I am not ready to decide for or against woman suffrage. It is tried in some states of the Union, and those states have no reason to complain of it. A short time ago a woman was elected to the mayoralty of a town in one of the Western states; the day following her installation in office all the saloons were closed. This is but one of many indications that the interests of the commonwealth need not be despaired of even if women do secure the right of suffrage.

America is the country of democracy —the democracy of the nineteenth century. Americans are democratic in their ideas and in their manner of living. This you will easily remark if you travel in our railroad cars, sojourn in our hotels, mingle freely with our people: But, you will ask, are not Americans fond of titles? Yes, but of military titles. Numbers of them are captains, colonels and generals. Where did they obtain those titles? The Lord only knows. Americans esteem and enjoy work. The millionaire of to-day freely tells that twenty or thirty years ago he worked for a dollar a day; he considers it an honor to have been able by toil and talent to rise from a humble station to his present condition.

Americans are, of course, democratic in their institutions. We even imagine, whether in this we are right or wrong, that we are the apostles of political democracy to the world, and we are not loathe to take to ourselves the honor of winning over to political democracy the love of old conservative Europe.

Have we reason to regret that democracy is enthroned in America? Most assuredly not. What is political democracy? Abraham Lincoln has well defined it: "A government of the people, for the people, and by the people." It is a government by the people. If the

people—the multitude, the masses— have risen to such a degree of enlightenment and self-control that they can be entrusted with the right to govern themselves, who would not rejoice to see them in the exercise of that right? What was Christianity in its earliest manifestations, if not a true democracy? When Christ appeared on earth it could be said: "The human race lives for the benefit of the few—*humanum genus paucis vivit.*" Christ preached that all men are brothers, having above them one common Father. An apostle of Christ, when sending back a fugitive slave to his master, admonished the master to receive the slave as a brother. In the Roman catacombs, amid hundreds of thousands of inscriptions, we find only three or four times the word: "slave—*servus, ancilla.*" The inscriptions always read: "brother, sister— *frater, soror.*" The slave maid of the proud Roman matron was buried by the side of her mistress; in the eyes of the Church all were equal. Age after age the Church of Christ struck off the fetters of the slave, until the day came when a Roman pontiff was able to say: "There are no slaves in Europe." In feudalistic times serfdom existed, but change after change was introduced and the condition of the masses was steadily ameliorated. The people were constantly gaining in rights and power until, at last, in America they believed they had risen so high that they could take their destinies in their own hands and be their own political masters.

American democracy understands the value of personal liberty. Decentralization is carried out as far as possible. Each state of the union enjoys autonomy. Within the state each county has its liberties; within the county each city, village, has its liberties; and everywhere we leave to the individual citizen all possible freedom—all freedom consistent with the safety of the commonwealth.

We are not all of one mind upon religious and social questions; indeed, upon many matters, we are at variance. But we know one another, and we love liberty—and we take as our rule to grant to others what we wish to have for ourselves. We never use the law to enforce our own personal ideas. We respect others because we wish ourselves to be respected.

You are well acquainted with the form of government of the United States. It is the organized expression of democracy. We have, as you have, our president and our national legislature. Our senators represent the sovereignty of the several states. Each state, through its own legislature, chooses two senators, and thus the smallest state in the Union has an equal representation with the largest. The members of the House represent the population. They are chosen in each state by the entire body of voters, and their number is in proportion to the population of the state. Each state in the union has its own senate and its own representatives, all chosen directly by the popular vote. The governor of the state has within his own territory much the same powers of the president has for the entire country.

This year, we are to choose a president. A week ago, the Republican party, assembled in convention in Minneapolis, named Mr. Benjamin Harrison as its candidate. Next week, the Democratic party will assemble in Chicago to nominate its candidate. You may ask: What is the difference between these two great political parties of the country? The difference is chiefly one of tendencies. The Republican party endeavors, more or less, to strengthen the central government in Washington, while the Democratic party would prefer to extend the prerogatives of the several states. When both parties have chosen their candidates, the turmoil begins, and until

next November we shall have almost daily in every village political discourses, in which one party will invariably declare that with the victory of the opposite party, the country is lost, and with the country, the entire world. A stranger, traveling through America during the four months to come, would declare civil war to be inevitable. Well, in the first week of November, the elections are over and the vanquished will simply say: "Our candidate has not been elected, but we have a president."

It is sometimes asked whether in America there is not shameful political corruption? I am not an optimist. Wherever there are men, they have their shortcomings. There can be found among us instances of political corruption, but the impression which is sometimes had of political corruption in America is entirely exaggerated, and, I must say, exaggerated through the fault of the Americans themselves. The vanquished party will always say on the morrow of the battle: "We were defeated despite our merits; we were beaten by bribery." Meanwhile those who speak in this strain do not believe what they say; it is a manner we have of consoling ourselves. Much money, no doubt, is disbursed on our elections, but it is for necessary expenses. Speakers and organizers are sent by the thousand to every part of the country. Large sums are disbursed, but not to purchase votes. Besides, the Australian system of balloting is now generally adopted throughout the country, and on this account temptation to purchase votes is minimized, as it cannot be known how the voter will use his ballot.

You wish me to say something about the condition of the Church in the United States. In America we have a free Church in a free country, and the church is happy in her freedom. Many Americans, unfortunately, have no positive creed; they have, however, deep religious instincts. Religion—respect and love of religion—permeates all the institutions of the country. We have, indeed, our apostles of unbelief; but their sophistries do not find favorable soil in the American mind. Americans have no love for the materialist who tells them there is no hope beyond this life, and who mocks the physical and moral miseries of man with his accents of despair.

America has its national and religious festivals. Each year the President of the United States issues a proclamation appointing a day of thanksgiving to God for all the blessings received during the preceding year by the country, and the day is religiously observed by all—Catholics not being the least conspicuous in readiness to respond to the invitation of the chief magistrate. Congress and state legislatures have their chaplains; their sessions invariably open with prayer to the deity. At public banquets a minister of religion invokes the blessings of heaven upon those present. All this is truly admirable. The Sunday is observed with a solemnity that surprises those who come among us the first time. The religious instincts and customs of the American people give reason to entertain great hope for the future of the country.

In America there is no established church. All religious confessions, Catholic, Protestant, Israelite, are absolutely equal before the law; all have common rights; none enjoy particular privileges. Each Catholic parish may form a civil corporation with unrestricted right to buy and sell. The law facilitates the organization of such church corporations. Furthermore, churches, religious houses of education, hospitals, orphan asylums, are free from taxation; for, say Americans, such institutions are a great moral power in the land; they diminish the general rate of taxation; it is to the welfare of the country to promote the interests of religion. Our churches, Catholic and Protestant, are supported by the voluntary contributions of their members. While we adhere very firmly to our own faith, we live in peace with those of other beliefs. We have our rights, and we freely concede the rights of others.

Catholics in America number to-day about ten millions. Exact statistics are difficult to be had. At the beginning of this century there were in the United States twenty-five thousand Catholics, one bishop and thirty priests. To-day the Church in America counts ten million Catholics, ninety bishops and nine thousand priests. It is no longer a missionary Church; it is duly established with all canonical rights. In choosing candidates for bishoprics the principal priests of a diocese speak first, then the bishops of the ecclesiastical province, then Rome. When it is a question of filling an archiepiscopal see, all the archbishops of the country are consulted. If in America the Catholic Church does not make progress, it is not the fault of the republic. The republic allows the Church the fullest liberty; and the Church, conscious of her divine mission, feels within herself all the vital forces necessary to grow and conquer without alliance with, or aid from, the state.

It has been asked whether the Church in America has not lost in membership. At a congress recently held at Liege, some one ventured to assert that in America the Church has lost ten million members. He who made this statement knew not whereof he was speaking, or knew that he was not stating the truth. I estimate at a million, or, perhaps a million and a half, the Catholic emigrants and their descendants who are lost to-day to the Church. The cause of this loss was chiefly the lack of priests and the isolation of Catholics in the first half of this century. Since the Church has been thoroughly organized, losses have ceased, or if here and there losses are still sustained, they are far more than counterbalanced by the number of conversions from non-Catholic bodies. These conversions are not so notable in number as we might wish them to be, but they are counted by hundreds annually in every diocese in the country. We have each year new accessions by immigration. The natural increase in the number of Catholics must also be taken into account. The future of the Catholic Church in America is bright and encouraging. To people of other countries, American Catholicism presents features which seem unusual; these features are the result of the freedom which our civil and political institutions give us; but in devotion to Catholic principles, and in loyalty to the successor of Peter, American Catholics yield to none.

The Church in America is the church of the people. Priests and bishops live among the people, and are recognized as the protectors and friends of the people. We give, of course, due time to sacristy and sanctuary; but we give time also to the public life of the country. It is not, for example, unusual for me to make addresses on industry, agriculture, railroads, social questions. Last year, I addressed one evening, a convention of presidents of the city railroads of the country. In speaking to the employees I strove to be a friend and defender of their rights. The following morning a newspaper remarked that on that account I would have a difficult task to face in addressing the presidents of city railroads; I think I got over the difficulty. To the presidents I said: "Gentlemen, when, last evening, I spoke to workingmen of their rights, and bade them defend their rights, I also defended your rights—for employers of labor will enjoy their rights only so far as they concede the rights of labor."

To the praise of the American people, Catholic and Protestant, I must say that they are pleased to see clergymen taking part in the social and political affairs of the country. They desire to enlist in behalf of the public interests all the intellectual and moral forces of the land. They know that the clergy are a great social power. They who differ from Catholics in religious belief, and even have but little sympathy for the Catholic faith, realize today that the country must reckon with ten million Catholics. Besides, those who differ from us in faith, have no distrust of Catholic bishops and priests. Why should they? By word and act we prove that we are patriots of patriots. Our hearts always beat with love for the republic. Our tongues are always eloquent in celebrating her praises. Our hands are always uplifted to bless her banners and her soldiers.

A Protestant minister lately remarked that the growth of Catholics in social and political influence is greater even than their growth in numbers. This is true. Fifty years ago, Catholics were for the most part newly arrived immigrants. They were poor. They could aspire to fill but few public offices. Today they are wealthy; they are well represented among the officials of city and state; they are found in the higher as well as in the lower ranks of society; anti-Catholic prejudices have almost disappeared.

Formerly, Americans thought the Catholics aimed at importing ideas of monarchy and imperialism into the United States, and that the Catholic Church could not be reconciled with the principles of the republic; not so now. The Church has breathed the air of the republic, and has prospered. No one to-day doubts the patriotism of Catholics. Some time ago, in one of our cities, a lecturer announced as his subject "The Roman Catholic Church, the Enemy of Republican Institutions."

He was at once told that his subject was wholly out of place and would not be listened to, "for the most ardent adherents of republican institutions in this city are the Roman Catholic bishop and priests."

Recently, as your papers have informed you, a memorial was addressed by some Catholics in Germany to the Holy See, asking that, in the nomination of bishops in the United States, the question of nationality be taken into account, and that German, Italian, French, Polish, and Bohemian priests be appointed bishops in proportion to the number of Catholics of their respective nationalities. The American Episcopate at once forwarded to Rome a formal protest against this memorial, and their protest was heeded. Had the memorial been listened to by the Holy See, the episcopate of America would now be an object of suspicion to the government, and Catholics would be looked upon as foreigners encamped upon the soil of the republic. We choose our bishops, and we will always choose them, from among priests worthy of the episcopate, irrespective of their origin or nationality; we will never allow foreigners to impose bishops upon us.

In civil matters we have, as you are aware, our Monroe Doctrine. Let Europeans, we say, arrange their own affairs as they think best. Americans will arrange theirs as they think best. In religious matters we recognize willingly and loyally the supreme authority of Christ's vicar, the pontiff at Rome; but let no one imagine that our country is a Congo to be partitioned at the good pleasure of foreigners. We have, under Peter's successor, our autonomy, and for the sake of the American Church and of the American republic, we will maintain that autonomy.

As a citizen of a republic, I recognize this evening a special obligation to the country through which the approbation and the benediction of the head of the Church have come to the republican form of government—I must give expression to the gratitude which wells up in my heart tonight for the great country which gave to Leo XIII the occasion "to canonize the republic." Heretofore when I came to Europe, I heard it whispered about that I was a dangerous man, that I believed in democracy, that I loved republics. Indeed, it was darkly hinted that I was almost a heretic. All that even friends would say to me was: "Your ideas may pass current in far away America where people are not yet fully civilized." To all this I had but little to reply. Certainly, I had not at the service of my mind and heart the strong, proud words which are to-day upon my lips. Arriving in Rome, a few months ago, I heard from the summit of the Vatican hill: "Of all the forms of civil government which the Church has recognized, and of which she has made trial, she cannot say from which she has received more harm or more good." Just now she is resolved to make trial in France of the republic; and I, as a citizen of a republic, say to the Church: "In this experiment you shall succeed."

I have been asked to say a word on the social question in the United States. America, as well as Europe, has its social difficulties; and these difficulties, although to-day much less grave in America than in Europe, may possibly grow more serious with time in our country. As things are in the United States, the social question is easier of solution there than elsewhere. Our democracy helps us. With us the working man knows that he is the civil and political equal of his richer neighbor, and the rich man freely recognizes the civil and political rights of his poorer brother. The fundamental principle of the republic is the dignity of man—the self-same principle which underlies Christian sociology. Once the dignity of man is recognized, even though social inequalities do necessarily exist, still no man is to be regarded as a piece of machinery or a mere beast of burden; no man is to be deprived of the sublime right which God bestowed upon him in creating him—the right to live in accordance with human dignity and to gain a decent competency for himself and wife and children. In the light of this principle, the social question is one of justice not of charity. A true democracy helps considerably to solve the social question. Another fact which contributes to the same result is to be noticed in our country. We have no hereditary classes, and few hereditary fortunes. We have no rigid social strata, which force men to remain where they begin life. The workingman of to-day is the employer of tomorrow. A fellow-feeling is thus begotten, and is easily maintained between employer and employee; they are more likely to understand each other, to eliminate harshness and distrust from their dealings with each other, and to respect each other's rights.

Our workingmen are usually educated. They read, study, think. Generally speaking, each trade has its own union or association. The well-known society of the Knights of Labor draws its membership from all trades. These unions discuss in their meetings the interests of workingmen, and devise methods for their advancement. One who has not been present at their meetings can hardly realize what calmness and practical good sense they bring to their deliberations. Many of our laws enacted in favor of labor were suggested by our labor unions, and adopted through their influence by our legislatures.

We have in America some excellent labor laws, such as those regulating the work of women and children, preventing an excess of working hours, ordering the regular inspection of factories, and securing life and health from defective machinery or bad ventilation. We do not fear the intervention of the state in labor matters, we demand that the law should protect the natural rights which the poorest and the weakest have to life and health and legitimate means of amelioration. We trust much to the mutual sense of justice of employer and employee and to the power of a sound public opinion; but those failing, we invoke the intervention of the state. The state is organized society, whose duty it is to protect the rights of all its members, rich or poor. In America there is a different conception of the state from that which is common among other peoples. In a free country like ours, the state is truly the expression of the will of the people. For us, the state is no specter hanging over us in mid-air, with intent we know not whither directed. The state is ourselves. The government at Washington or in the capital of any of our sovereign states, is the will of the people. This is why we love the state and the state's law; state and law are begotten of the people.

We have had strikes, and we are not sure that we shall not again have them. Public opinion, however, is turning strongly against such methods of social warfare. The more intelligent leaders of labor unions strongly deprecate them. The results of strikes have usually been detrimental to the interests of workingmen, and toilers are not slow to perceive the fact. The spread of true principles as to the relations of labor and capital, the growth of intelligence, of respect for social order and the rights of others, of the recognition of human dignity, and of brotherly love for all men, the growth of religion and of virtue in rich and poor, in employer and employee, will in America, as elsewhere, be the antidote to social warfare, and will provide the solution of all social questions.

Ladies and gentlemen, I thank you for the patience with which you have listened to me. All my life will I sacredly preserve the memory of this evening. It is an honor for me that you have come to hear me; it is an honor for the republic of the West that such distinguished citizens of France have been pleased to take so much kindly interest in its institutions and to show so much warm sympathy with its people.

Above me the *tricolor* of France, and the star-spangled flag of the United States intertwine their folds— the symbol of the union of love and respect which exists between the two great republics of the world. May the union last. May each one of these two sister republics enjoy within its own borders peace and prosperity. May both together be to the entire world the inspiration of liberty and of happiness.

Flag of the United States, flag of my country! I offer to thee the tribute of most sincere allegiance and most warm affection. My heart, my life are thine. I am proud of thee for the glories that thou dost represent; I cherish thee for the liberty that thou dost insure. As a bishop of the Catholic Church I praise and thank thee for the freedom which is granted to her wherever thou reignest. I pray the God of nations to bless and guard America.

And, while I am most loyal to my country, ladies and gentlemen, permit me to say that whenever I see the *tricolor* of France, my soul will go out to it in esteem and gratitude, and whenever the music of the name of France echoes in my ear, the deep fullness of my heart will vibrate in love, and my lips will invoke upon your country the blessings of heaven.

19. *Wilhelm Emmanuel von Ketteler, Bishop of Mainz: The Labor Movement and Its Effects in Relation to Religion and Morals, 25 July 1869*

From William Edward Hogan, *The Development of Bishop Emmanuel von Ketteler's Interpretation of the Social Problem* (Washington: The Catholic University of America Press, 1946), pp. 268-283.

. . . There are many reasons for my calling you workers here. You make up the largest part of the population of this area. Your villages are either built up into factory areas or you are migrating in large numbers into the industrial cities which surround you. I sympathize deeply with all that concerns your well being.

The sincere love which I bear for all of you has only increased with the years since I have been your bishop and have learned to know and to visit you. I am moved to love you especially by the thought that I represent among you one who was himself a laborer and

wanted to be the son of a carpenter so that he might have pity on men in their needs. The mother of this divine child of a carpenter whose picture we honor here, this mother who with all her maternal love stands so close to every man and woman worker in all their trials, would surely approve were I in this house to discuss what is called the labor question in its relation to religion.

The general outline of the thoughts I wish to offer presents itself quite naturally. The laboring class in our times, that is, the factory workers, have been affected by a labor movement which gains strength daily. You find yourselves at the very heart of this labor movement. At the same time you are true children of the Catholic Church.

I have again, as so often in the past, been witness with the sincerest gratitude and joy to this fact as I have visited you in your communities. Neither harvest time, nor the wages you had to pass up in the factory prevented you from participating in all Church festivities. On the other hand, you were unable to remain unaffected by these movements. To each of you, to each Catholic worker, the question presented itself: What is there in all these movements which now are passing through the ranks of the workers in Europe which is justified, what is not justified, what is dangerous? How far can I as a Christian and a Catholic participate in these movements without offending my religion and my conscience? Against which dangers must I defend myself? Every conscientious Catholic worker must be able to answer these questions clearly. I will endeavor to answer each of these questions as briefly as possible but with perfect frankness, with that openness which is without reservation and which promotes the truth and which alone becomes my position as representative to you of him who is truth itself. You will understand in my explanation that whatever is worthwhile in the labor movement of our times can only be realized in the most intimate connection with religion and morals. Without religion and without morals all the efforts to improve the lot of the workers will be without success.

An appreciation of this truth is of the utmost importance. Let us pass over to the individual considerations. First let us consider the chief goal of the workers and the demands which they seek to impress upon us, then we can point out the relationship of workers to religion and morals and we can then call attention to some of the dangers. The general policy which gives the labor movement its signification and distinguishes it is built upon the association idea, the association of workers by means of which the workers once united will be able to push their own interests.

This development among workers is merely a result of the economic principles which since the French Revolution have come to the surface and have gradually won for themselves unconditional superiority and have taken upon themselves the quality of natural necessity. Religion has nothing to oppose to such natural striving but can only bless these efforts and wish them success in the interests of the workers and religion should support them. Unlimited freedom in every field of economic life—no one can deny, not even he who considers it necessary and is convinced that in its final stage it will be wholesome unlimited freedom—has reduced the laboring class to a most desperate condition. Through the dissolution of all the earlier associations the laboring class has become isolated and thrown upon its own resources. Each worker was left alone with his individual ability to work, and this was his only protection. Opposed to him was capitalism, which is dangerous to the individual worker because the capitalist is without conscience and religion. Capitalism increases in danger in the degree that the capitalist uses his wealth for the satisfaction of his own ego.

The principles of modern economics had opposite effects in its relation to human energy in the case of the worker and in its relation to money power in the case of the capitalist. The worker and his energy, as we have already said, were isolated while the money power was centralized. The labor class was divided into mere individual workers until each was left powerless; the monied interests did not divide themselves up into even quantities but on the contrary united forces into even greater and unequal bodies. A Rothschild who leaves his children 1,700 million francs is a good example of a product of this economic school. The human bond was destroyed and replaced by the shackles of wealth on a frightful scale. As a consequence, everywhere that these conditions were allowed to advance without check the most terrifying results have followed for the workers. About forty years ago a great part of the English laboring class had fallen into the deepest abyss of moral and physical misery.

To oppose any further isolation of the laborers and the stamping out of human energy through the power of wealth, this same England that gave birth to such destruction has been a mighty leader in the movement toward associations and the general organization of workers.

From England the movement has affected workers everywhere including the workers of Germany. This movement which seeks to organize the workers, to take advantage of the common striving to realize the rights and interests of the workers is justified and wholesome, even necessary, if the workers are not to be destroyed by the might of centralized wealth.

But already there are indications of how these efforts to unite the workers must remain without any lasting success as long as they are without religion. Workers need many aids in carrying out these strivings for unity. It is impossible for them to realize all their chances for unity without outside assistance. They need leaders who will strive for the common good of the working class.

Who will guarantee the laboring class that these leaders will not become blind or deceitful leaders? It is precisely these leaders who continue to declare that the great capitalists for their own egoism mercilessly exploit the laborers.

But these labor leaders are themselves human with the very same human nature with which capitalists are clothed. If a person who has at his disposal the power of capital takes advantage of his workers without even slight regard for their rights, in the measure that such a person is without regard for God, who can give these workers any certainty that the so-called friend of the people will not exploit them in his own interest if he is a man without conscience, without God, without religion? Just as the monied interests exploited the workers, so will these leaders, as long as they are enemies of Christianity and are filled with hatred of it.

You can see for yourself how among such men who place themselves at the head of labor movements violent quarrels always break out periodically (at this very moment that is again the case), how these men accuse one another of the very self-seeking of which they have just accused the capitalists. It could not be otherwise. Without religion we all become victims of our own self love, whether we be rich or poor, capitalists or workers; we exploit our neighbor as long as we are in possession of the power to do so.

As justified as is the movement among German workers to organize, they will be successful only when their leaders renounce their hatred of Christianity and take up at least a respectful, benevolent position toward religion and the Church. There are evidences of this truth in the great differences between results of the English labor movement and that of Germany. Just as the English workers outdid us in their development of the most disastrous consequences of modern economics, so too is England superior to us in her great program to organize labor. That is because above all else the English understand the importance of religion for all social questions, while in Germany the very leaders of the labor movement parade their hatred of religion.

Let us consider the single demands of the labor class which are to be attained through the processes of association. We shall see step by step how closely religion is connected with the labor question and with every single demand of the workers and how Godlessness is the greater enemy of the laboring class.

The first demand of the laborers is an increase in salary commensurate with their labor. This demand is in general most proper; religion demands that human work be not handled as a commodity and that it not be evaluated merely on the basis of supply and demand.

The above-mentioned economic principles abstracted from all morals and religion have brought matters to this low level.

Labor was not only treated as a commodity. Man himself and his ability to work was looked upon as a machine. Just as men buy machines as cheaply as possible and use them day and night until they can no longer run, so too, according to this system, is a man and his labor to be treated. This development had already attained a frightful growth in England. In opposition to this evil there appeared the English trade unions which soon won for themselves wide popularity. The chief means the trade unions employed against capital and against the large scale employers were the strikes. It has frequently been said that these strikes in so far as they disturbed business and meant that workers had to sacrifice wages for the duration of the strike, were more harmful to the workers than they were useful. In general that statement is not true. The strike, as the Englishman Thornton has just shown beyond all doubt, played an important role in raising wages. Wages in the last forty years since trade unions have been at

work have in some trades increased 50%, in many others from 25 to 30%, and in all trades the increase has been at least 15%. Thornton calls our attention to the fact that in the strikes the general rule has been that the worker apparently was the loser, but as a result, soon after the close of the strike an increase in the wages of workers has been granted so that the defeat was only apparent. After the pattern of these trade unions the associations in Germany have been fashioned, and many of you are members of such unions. This striving to obtain a just increase of wages is indeed worthy of defense. That a fair wage be paid for human labor is a demand of justice and Christianity.

If this effort to seek for human labor a wage different from that paid for the work of machines is justified, which is another way of asserting that human dignity must be returned to human labor (something liberal economic principles have stolen from the workers), then we already see, my dear workers, that this effort will only bring true benefits and be of lasting success if it remains in close contact with religion and morals. This is evident from a twofold consideration:

First of all, do not deceive yourselves, beloved workers. The increase of wages has its limitations, and even the highest possible increase will only yield a very modest income. The natural limit of a worker's salary lies in the salability of the business in which he works. Both the intellectual and material capital which has taken an interest in a given business would withdraw from it and turn to another industry as soon as the wage demands became so high that no worthwhile profit remained for its capital investment. But that would mean a shutdown for labor. Wages therefore have a limit in spite of all the associations laborers might form. It would be disastrous for you if you did not clearly understand this and were to believe, as a result of the unbounded promises made to you, that unlimited increases were possible.

Even the highest possible wage will guarantee you sufficient standards of living only if great temperance and economy become the foundation of your lives. These valuable goods—temperance and frugality—will be the qualities the laboring class possesses only when the entire life of the worker is truly and inwardly a religious life. The fact has been thoroughly demonstrated that the well-being of the worker does not only depend upon the income he receives. In fact, there are regions where trades are engaged which offer very high wages while the need among workers is acute, and yet there are other regions in which, in spite of very poor wages, workers have attained a much higher standard of living.

One of the greatest dangers in this regard is overindulgence in intoxicating liquors which is encouraged by the numerous taverns which spring up everywhere to entertain large numbers of laborers. Such things are tolerated by governments in such proportion as they have lost their own sense of morals and religion. I once heard an official state that the increase in taverns was to the interest of the state, because taxes were thus increased. These taverns are not only blood suckers upon the workers; they also suck out his gold, his wages; they are planned precisely to take the hard earned money from the pockets of the worker. Only a brief period need be dedicated to intemperance to go through even the highest salary. Of what use is the highest salary to the worker who is a slave to intemperance?

On the other hand, great moral strength is required if the worker is to protect himself against all wasteful spending and intemperance. Perhaps

never before has there been such trying, uninterrupted, restless work as factory labor. The many workers who day for day put in the same number of hours at this labor act as a check on one another. Each minute that their hands are idle is noticed immediately. How easily it happens that those who toil within the same room on the same workers' bench for the same hours each day and at the same mechanical work, when freed from their dismal task, seek in intemperance and carousing a certain amount of recuperation. In such a way of life great moral strength is required to remain temperate and frugal. If the increase in wages is truly to benefit you, beloved workers, then you must live as true Christians.

And secondly, you have need of religion and morals in your efforts to secure an increase in wages, if you are not to exceed the proper limits in your demands. We have already seen that wage increases have limits. In these our days when the movement toward bettering the material position of workers grows stronger and more widespread, it is of the greatest importance that the demands made do not exceed reasonable measures, and that the workers do not permit themselves to be used as means toward entirely different purposes.

A conflict between employers and employees should not be the goal, but a sensible peace between these two.

The godlessness of capital which exploits the worker as mere energy and as a machine until he is destroyed must be done away with. Such treatment is a crime against the laboring class and a dishonor. Such conflict belongs with the theory that maintains men descended from the ape. But the godlessness of the working class must be avoided, too. If this movement for increased wages exceeds its proper bounds, a catastrophe will result whose evil results will descend with their entire weight upon the workers. Capital can always discover new ways to save itself when the business in which it once had an interest is ruined. The deplorable credit system of our modern states has arranged that every speculator in our money exchanges can find within its toils a limitless field for his activities.

The worker, on the contrary, cannot so easily find another paying job when business fails. It is not only the large capitalists who suffer from unjust demands for wage increases, but the many smaller businesses as well, which are in the hands of the middle class and these masters and craftsmen also suffer. If the working class in its striving maintains a just position and avoids the danger of becoming a means for the purposes some selfish men have and if it is to avoid the reefs of the unordered egoism which it is attempting to combat in the capitalists, then the laboring class must be imbued with a noble moral outlook; it must be an upright, Christian, and religious laboring class. The power of wealth without religion is an evil thing. So, too, is the strength of the worker without religion. Both can lead to destruction.

The second demand of the workers is for a shorter work day. I cannot judge how much ground you have to complain about regarding your working hours. But it is certain that as the matter of working hours has proceeded, so has the matter of wages. The principles of present day economics which entirely disregard all the moral and religious sides of human existence and entirely neglect the true dignity of men, have brought it about that wherever capital served their purpose, they have not only lowered wages to the minimum, but likewise given hours drawn-out to the farthest possible point. Day and night work, as is done by machines, they could not demand, but human energy which in this system is looked upon merely as human machinery was taxed as far as possible. Wherever, therefore, hours of work are drawn out beyond the point nature and considerations of health permit, the workers have a well established right to resist the misuse of money power through a united organized program.

But here, too, dear workers, the real value of such a movement, if it is to succeed, depends upon morals and a religious outlook. If the workers use the leisure hours gained in order to fulfill their duties in the family as a father, in order to take care of the needs of the house or in order to improve the land he has bought himself, then these hours are worthwhile both for himself and for his family. If, on the other hand, he uses this time merely to roam the streets evenings in bad company or to remain just that much longer in taverns, then this time will profit neither his health nor his general wellbeing. It will serve only the sooner to ruin him physically and spiritually and to more surely waste his wages.

The third demand of the working class is the observance of a day of rest. This demand, too, is justified. Religion not only supports you in this demand, it long before you demanded this observance. God demanded such observance in his command, "Remember that you keep holy the Sabbath."

In this regard, too, the principles of modern economics and the party which serves such principles have committed a crime against the human race which cries to heaven for vengeance and they continue to this day to repeat such crimes. Not only do the great industrialists participate in such crime who force their employees to work on Sundays but likewise those craftsmen of all types, the landowners and the keepers of servants who insist upon their service on Sundays. All those officials also participate in such crime who out of cowardice in the face of the rich leave the unprotected workers without any protection and dare not extend the laws. The hypocrisy which men practice with the help of liberal principles has been exposed in recent times by some leaders of the labor movement. The monied interests in this exploitation have always sought to clothe themselves with the robes of the noblest humanness, and have sought to present the demands of the Church for days of rest as an inhuman treatment of the poor working class. How often have the capitalists with studied exactness counted the Sundays and the holidays and calculated how much money in wages these days would represent if work were permitted?

It would then appear that in the ranks of the money men there grew apace a lively interest in the welfare of the workers for such men sought to turn over to workers these considerable sums as wages, while the role of the Church was made to appear one of hardheartedness for it sought to deprive workers of this money. In answer to this approach the organs of workers' parties have answered that there remains another means of crediting the workers with these sums without killing them with work. This means involves granting workers as high a wage for six days of labor as they formerly received for seven days. The advantage in money for the worker would be the same and together with this financial gain the worker would retain an existence worthy of a human being. Who can fail to understand the truth of this view and the deceit and treachery of the view of the capitalists who in recent years in Baden and Bavaria have so frequently made these charges? If they were correct then it would have been inhuman to allow the workers to continue to sleep. It would be a simple thing to demonstrate to you without emotion what kind of salary night work would net you. Just as certainly as a

man needs a number of hours of rest every twenty-four hours, so too, every seven days he needs a day of rest. Not only his soul demands this, so that on this day he may have an opportunity to acknowledge himself as a child of God, his body, too, makes this demand so that it might remain healthy and strong. And just as the employer who works an employee all day is under obligation to grant him the necessary night of rest and must still pay him his wage, so must the industrialist who makes use of the strength of the workers all week, grant a day of rest and yet pay his workers for it. Even rest time must be reckoned with work time, in as far as rest time is necessary as a result of work expended and in as far as rest is a necessary condition of any future labor.

It is not enough, beloved workers, that political parties demand a day of rest. You yourselves must support this movement that hours of work may not encroach upon the day of rest. Even while the workers' party demands a day of rest there are unfortunately still many workers who, not under pressure but on their own initiative, work on Sundays whenever and wherever they can earn money. Such workers not only sin against God and his commandment; they sin, too, against the working class of which they are members, in as far as out of selfish motives they contribute to a condition which renders it easier for employers to rob their employees of the day of rest. Let all workers, girl servants included, who are exploited by an unsympathetic ruling class, as well as the last of the railroad workers who are exploited by an over-wealthy organization, demand with one voice their day of rest as a human right. Of what avail are the so-called human rights (embodied in the constitution) which benefit the workers very little as long as the capitalists stamp upon these social human rights?

As certainly as religion supports you, beloved workers, in demanding a day of rest and as all the efforts of the workers in this regard would be in vain if the forces of religion and the command of God, "Remember that thou keep holy the Sabbath" did not support these demands—so it is certain too, that this day of rest is necessary for your health, for your recreation and for the recuperation of your working power, for your souls, and for the true uplifting of your spiritual life and finally for your families from whom you are withdrawn so long throughout the week and for the cementing of a family spirit. If you are to remain real Christian workers you must remain closely joined to religion and the Church; without religion, a day of rest would only be used to ruin both the worker and the family of the worker both as to their health and their prosperity. "Blue Monday" is nothing but a day following a day of rest spent without religion. In many a territory such a day of "rest" has cut the deepest wounds into the moral and material welfare of the working class.

What a vast difference between the workingman's family in which the day of rest is spent in conformity with the principles of religion, and the family which spends the holiday without the aid of religion. I shall not develop this picture here. You yourselves can find examples of such a family. A day of rest spent in a tavern, in bad company, in drunkenness, in impurity, will ruin one's health, one's inheritance and family and the laborer himself—and will lead him to perdition just as surely as a day of rest spent in a Christian fashion will lead another to special blessings.

A fourth demand of the workers is the prohibition of work in factories for children who are of school age. I cannot unfortunately refer to this demand as a universal striving of the workers, for there are workers who because of the chance to obtain money send their children into factories. I must therefore speak of this demand as a demand of the articulate leaders of the workers. Fritzsche, who is head of the cigar makers union of Germany and is well known to you all, lately demanded in the parliament of the Nordbund in Berlin that the work of school children be prohibited. In defending his plea he spoke touchingly on the experiences of his own life for he had himself as a youth worked in the factories.

In the first place he pointed out that the morals of the children are seriously endangered through factory labor. It is true that factory work for children has been limited, but it has not been prohibited. I have complained bitterly about this situation and have seen in this situation a victory of materialistic viewpoints over great moral principles. All the experience of my own life completely vindicates the declaration of labor leader Fritzsche regarding the effect of factory work upon school children. I am acquainted with the reasons offered to excuse the employment of children; and I am aware that certain men who are sincerely in favor of the working class condone factory work for children with certain qualifications. Among the various excuses offered for such child labor there is one that the child is under obligation to assist the parent at work, at home and on the farm. The vast difference between the family work of the child and factory labor is quite obvious. Factory work involving children destroys in the child the family spirit which, as we shall see, is the chief danger for the laboring class. Factory work furthermore robs the child of all free time for *play*—a thing so essential to children. As a consequence, the health of the child is ruined, his moral life seriously jeopardized. I consider child labor in factories a gruesome act of cruelty in our times, which both the spirit of our times and the selfishness of parents make light of. I consider such work slow murder of young bodies and souls. At the cost of the sacrifice of the joys of childhood, at the sacrifice of their health and morals, these children are forced to increase the profits of a business. And often they must feed parents who because of their own irresponsibility are unable to earn bread for their children.

I rejoice because this defense of working children has been made. Religion with its great love of children can only support this demand: that child labor be abolished. I urge you, beloved workers, to join this movement of workers—and warn you, never allow your children to work in a factory.

The fifth demand of the workers is that women and mothers be excluded from factory work. A Frenchman, Julius Simon, says in his book, *The Woman Worker,* which gives so much evidence of his warm feeling for the laborer, "Our entire economic structure suffers under a deplorable error which is responsible for the misery of the working class and must be overcome, cost what it may, if we are not to destroy ourselves and this error is the destruction of family life." He introduces the statement of Michelet: "Woman worker—frightful word, which was unknown to earlier languages, which no age before this iron era understood, and which of itself is capable of wiping out our vaunted progress." This is the danger we face when a mother no longer is a mother but a working woman. A woman who has become a factory hand is no longer a woman; she no longer lives the hidden, protected chaste life, surrounded by the loving, holy impressions of family life which are so beneficial to the happiness of the woman and the happiness of the family. Such a factory hand no longer lives subject to her husband but to a foreman and she

works with women of questionable morals, in continuous contact with men; she is separated from husband and from children. In a working family of this kind, father and mother are apart fourteen hours a day. There is consequently no longer any family life. The mother can no longer care for her own children. A frightening morality results. Children of three and four years of age loiter on the streets tortured by hunger and the cold. When finally at seven o'clock in the evening, father, mother and children meet in the single room they possess, mother and father are exhausted from their work, the children are hungry and weary and there is nothing prepared. The room has been empty all day. No one was there to pick up and clean up. There is no fire in the stove. The mother wants only to rest, she lacks energy even to prepare a meal; her own clothes and those of her husband and children are untidy. This is the tragic picture of a family such as our factory system produces. No one is surprised when the father, tired from his day's work, finds it an effort to return to this narrow, dirty, unaired hole in the wall where half-naked children await him and a wife he almost no longer recognizes, for she no longer lives in his home—no one is surprised that he prefers a tavern to this room and in the tavern wastes his pay and destroys his health. The end result of these conditions is great poverty among many workers in the midst of flourishing industry.

I will quote you the words of Simon after he spent long years visiting the factory districts of France where women work in factories, and as a result families are ruined. He comes to the conclusion that all pay increases will be of no advantage to the workers without a better moral life, and that all improvement of the morals of the working class depends upon the elevation of family life wherever it has suffered through modern industrial and factory life.

"It is a disgrace," he cries out, "that bread is often wanting to the family of the worker rather through the fault of the father, than through the fault of industry itself. Blue Monday swallows up a quarter or perhaps half the entire wages of the week; the best paid workers who might well care for their family are almost everywhere those generally addicted to drink. Prosperity depends more upon moral circumstances than it does upon wages. The evil, therefore, is rather a moral condition and the problem which must be solved is this—how can the worker through his own efforts be saved? We can do the worker a greater service than merely giving him work and money, and this greater service is to teach him love of thrift and morality. The day that our places of work are filled and our taverns are empty the evil will be defeated."

All the evil conditions of French factory life which Julius Simon here describes and which are still more applicable to England have not entered Germany, at least in these factory areas on such a wide scale. For here, as far as I am aware, there are hardly any women and mothers at work in factories. The knowledge which makes itself felt more and more among our workers, namely, how important for the success of the working class the family is, shows us how closely religion is bound up with so many goals of the working class and how these goals can be attained only in and through religion. Religion demands, too, that the mother spend her day at home in pursuit of her high and holy duties to husband and to children. Everything that Julius Simon has said in the quotation introduced above, and everything that any friend of labor has said about the importance of the family would be far surpassed by the things all of you from your early youth have heard the Church say of the holiness of family life. It is absolutely true that the labor question is in the first place a moral question and is closely bound up with family life. It is just as true that only in and through religion can it be solved. The closer you identify yourselves with the Church, the better will be the wives you will have, the better will the mothers of your children be, the more genuine will your family life become, the more certainly will this family circle be protected against all the dangers threatening the labor class, the dangers of the tavern, the dangers of wastefulness.

The sixth demand frequently made by workers, the one which is closely bound up with their earlier demands, is that girls no longer be employed in factories.

Several reasons are given for such a demand. Sometimes it is said girls can work for less wages because their needs are fewer and consequently any large scale employment of girls would considerably lower the wage scale for men. In England things have reached such an unnatural state (as a result of the purely materialistic economic principles in vogue there), that men no longer work but care for children; and instead of caring for children, women work in factories. The second and principal reason used to argue against the employment of girls in factories is the deplorable influence upon the morals of working girls and indirectly upon future families. Workers and their spokesmen in recent years have frequently spoken in startling terms of these results. In their conferences they have declared: We demand good and happy families for the laboring class. But to insure good and happy families we must have virtuous, honest women and mothers; we shall never have such women while we continue to lock our girls up in factories and there inject into them the germ of immorality and boldness.

I cannot tell you, beloved workers, how these voices heard among the ranks of the workers have moved and gladdened me. This was a language which ten years ago when the labor movement was not widely distributed in Germany was heard almost exclusively from Christian pulpits. The liberal party understood none of the moral dangers for working girls, and when the girls were thoroughly perverted in the factories, the liberals with their wonted hypocrisy maintained they were actually benefactors of the working class, in that they afforded girls an opportunity to earn money.

This knowledge of the dangers inherent in factory work for the morals of the working girl, and consequently for the working man's family, is now becoming widespread even among industrial leaders. This is a wholesome phenomenon and shows that as in many other fields so, too, in the development of the labor movement all important questions revert to religion and morality. "The care of the purity of young girls" is, according to the *Official Report of the Commission on Prizes at the World Exposition* in Paris in 1867, one topic which was awarded a prize. Among means named to this end were: separation of places of occupation for girls; strict supervision of work of young girls; institutions for young girls without family ties; special dining rooms; direction of young girls through a female supervisor, rather than through male foremen.

God has protected you, my dear factory workers, from most of the harm which can come upon girls who earn their livelihood within the factory system. Factory life among us is comparatively new and for the most part we have preserved a genuine Christian family life which has strongly resisted such immorality. I can assure you with keen joy that very many of our young factory girls are morally pure. On the other hand, we cannot fail to reveal to you the great dangers which threaten the morals of your daughters. These dangers are in these very neighborhoods far greater than in other areas because in many factories almost nothing is done to protect the morals of girl workers. All these important considerations which I have presented to you regarding the separation of working places, the supervision of girls by responsible women and the like, are in these areas almost entirely neglected. I can only recommend to you, beloved working people, that you join your full energy to this phase of the labor movement for the protection of the morals of your daughters. This is a matter which concerns all workers, it is a sacred responsibility of the laboring class, it is, finally a duty of religion.

The honor of your daughters is your honor, you who are fathers and brothers. The shame of your daughters is your shame; the morals of your daughters condition the morals and the happiness of your families. He who contaminates this source contaminates not only your honor—he destroys the future of your families. These are your daughters. Cursed be the father who can look on and be patient with the things which demoralize his daughter. You must cooperate, you brothers, for these are your sisters. Shame upon the brother who can look quietly upon whatever dishonors his sister. All of you who belong to this community must cooperate in this matter, for these are children of your community whose happiness or unhappiness is your concern. You, too, must cooperate, you older virgins; you must with human and Christian love protect your younger sisters from so many dangers which would rob them of the most costly thing the virgin possesses, her good name, her moral reputation. Consequently, in the factories which employ you, do not tolerate a foreman who uses his position to fulfill the devil's work, to spoil his workers and above all, avoid becoming the tools of such evil doing of foremen out of fear of losing your work. Often some of the factory workers are aware of the evil practices of foremen, yet there is none who has the courage to oppose them and such evil, despicable persons can continue to betray innocence over a long period without interference.

Here, beloved workers, you can again appreciate the most intimate relationship of religion with the welfare or the misery of the people and the demands of the working class. All that religion has said to your children from the most tender years of childhood to this very day, all it has said to your daughters has this constant purpose: to preserve them pure and undefiled and to protect them against all dangers, to so educate them that they may one day become good wives of the workers, good mothers to the children of workers, that they may become the foundations of a genuine family life within the working class.

I have, beloved workers, considered some of the chief demands of workers which are directly practical and whose connection with religion I could most easily indicate. I am aware I have not exhausted the subject. There are many other demands which affect you. I could have spoken of the various associations which are partly dedicated to the saving of workers' funds, partly to the procurement at a reasonable price of the necessities of life for working men, and I could have explained in detail their content. I could have spoken to you of those associations such as the trade unions which have as their goal the increase of wages, while they likewise strive to divert to the workers a portion of the profits of business and strive to make possible for workers to become part owners. I would have enjoyed speaking of these so-called partnerships, for I am convinced that they can nowhere be more easily introduced than among the cigar workers since this business does not demand any great investment.

We have seen that these demands of the workers in the measure that they are justified have their true support in religion and morals. I have had to warn you against trespassing the right boundaries and becoming self-seekers as are the capitalists, and again I have warned you not to break out into confused and fantastic socialistic tendencies which do not contribute to the salvation of workers, but rather to the satisfaction of their vanity and selfishness. By following such a selfish course the workers would become the means for political ends which would finally destroy them. I cannot at this time enter into a discussion of all these matters, but will rather conclude by calling to our attention some special dangers which arise out of the matters I have already discussed.

First of all, guard yourself against those who ridicule religion and seek to confuse you and deter you from fulfilling your religious duties. These are your greatest enemies, for, as we have seen, the peculiar situation in which the laborers find themselves is such that every possible improvement of their condition implies the support of religion and morals. He who claims to come to your assistance and at the same time attacks your religion you may conclude is either ignorant of the labor question or is a deceiver.

There are in our midst men who give the impression that their ridicule of religion could be transformed into bread and gold to aid the workers. That is not true. On the contrary, their criticism, their entire manner of thinking, speaking and acting has no other purpose than to inconvenience us Catholics.

Your striving for freedom, for progress, your patriotism, your love of the people, your solicitude for the welfare of the people—all these things, these men consider blasphemy; all is a ridiculing of religion, and all is against us Catholics. Beware of these men, they are not leaders of our workers, they are deceivers of the workers.

Protect yourselves secondly against bad, impure thoughts and never freely consent to them. The freely admitted unclean thought is the start of foulness within us. You are more exposed to such thoughts for you are in those years which are most dangerous, the years in which the passions are most alert the entire day long; you stand in closest contact with one another. You children who today are still in school and in a family where you have perhaps never heard a dishonorable word and never have entertained an unlawful thought, will tomorrow be in the midst of all these dangers. There you will have countless stimuli to unclean thoughts. If you freely consent to these, the purity of your soul is lost. Interior decay steadily increases, the passions grow constantly stronger and you fall victim finally to hidden and then to open sins which first destroy your health, then your morals, and toss you from one abyss into another, until finally you reach the last deep abyss. There are many reasons why death takes such a toll in many working classes. One of the chief reasons is because of the immorality among workers.

Guard yourselves against bad conversations, suggestive songs, shameless pictures and books. What I said of thoughts applies as well to these things. Guard yourselves, you young workers, boys and girls, for the same reason against new acquaintances. You have perhaps often believed that religion demands too much from you in this regard, and that in these matters which lead to immorality there is not as much

evil existing as you have often been told from the pulpit. Immorality takes the appearance of being nothing but a rationalization on the weaknesses of youth and it creates the impression that the teachers of morality within the Church are hard-hearted and pessimistic. When you think of what I have said, even when you consider what the workers themselves demand of the family of the laborer, then you must acknowledge the contrary, you must admit that the demands of religion upon your moral sense is the truly friendly attitude toward humanity and all that harms morality is an indescribably hostile attitude toward mankind.

You want pure brides, morally good wives, you want honest mothers for your children. Such women are angels for the family. Fortunate the man who has such a wife and the child who has such a mother. Yet how can you expect such women for your families when you make light of early companionship? Such companionships destroy everything in the young girl which could have made her a model workingman's wife. Consider the contrast between the girl who soon after her school days accustomed herself to suggestive conversation and joking and has filled her heart with sordid thoughts and images, who has gone from boldness to boldness and established all kinds of acquaintances, who has passed her time in questionable company, in taverns, on the street and in dance halls. In a life such as this she has lost respect, never learned to save, whatever she has earned she has wasted. Then comes one more misfortune and in her twentieth year or twenty-first year, in order to deliver herself from her misery she marries the first person who appears. Out of this background we do not derive our happy workingmen's families, but those families which are loaded down with misery and worry such as we have already considered. On the other hand, consider the girl who up to her twenty-fourth year has preserved her virtue without stain, who through proper care of her money has managed to save something, how entirely different is this picture! Such a girl may freely choose her marriage partner. The best characters will seek a girl of this type and such a girl can offer all that a workingman might expect from a wife. If you hope to become worthy brides, flee from early acquaintances for these bring to the working class families only spoiled and useless girls. Beware, finally, dear workers, of intemperance and drunkenness, beware of those houses in which workers are robbed of their wages. Frequent visits to the taverns, the habit of finding joy only in taverns, where one seeks compensation for the wear and tear of one's work, is according to the conviction of all who are occupied with the improvement of the

lot of workers in various countries one of the greatest dangers to their work. *The Committee on Prizes of the Paris World's Exposition* places under the heading "Institutions for the overcoming of delinquency," in the first place the overcoming of alcoholism and recommends societies for this purpose: the isolating, or the suspension, of taverns.

These are the words, beloved workers, I would leave with your good community at the end of my stay here. Let them be an expression of my deep feeling toward you and my warmest sympathy for your interest. In these words you realize that you may, as Catholics, support the goals and the labor program without violating your religion in its great fundamental principles. And you understand now that all these efforts will be vain unless they build upon religion and moral principles.

20. *John Henry Newman: Two Essays on the Development of Christian Doctrine*

Selection A from *An Essay on the Development of Christian Doctrine* (London: Longmans, Green and Co., 1897), pp. 2-9, 55-75. Selection B from "An Unpublished Paper by Cardinal Newman on the Development of Doctrine," *Gregorianum*, XXXIX (1958), 585-75; Gregorian University Press, Rome.

A. FIRST ESSAY, 6 OCTOBER 1845

CHRISTIANITY has been long enough in the world to justify us in dealing with it as a fact in the world's history. Its genius and character, its doctrines, precepts, and objects cannot be treated as matters of private opinion or deduction, unless we may reasonably so regard the Spartan institutions or the religion of Mohammed. It may indeed legitimately be made the subject-matter of theories; what is its moral and political excellence, what its due location in the range of ideas or of facts which we possess, whether it be divine or human, whether original or

eclectic, or both at once, how far favorable to civilization or to literature, whether a religion for all ages or for a particular state of society, these are questions upon the fact, or professed solutions of the fact, and belong to the province of opinion; but to a fact do they relate, on an admitted fact do they turn, which must be ascertained as other facts, and surely has on the whole been so ascertained, unless the testimony of so many centuries is to go for nothing. Christianity is no theory of the study or the cloister. It has long since passed beyond the letter of documents and the reasonings of individual minds, and has become public property. Its "sound has gone out into all lands," and its "words unto the ends of the world." It has from the first had an objective existence, and has thrown itself upon the great concourse of men. Its home is in the world; and to know what it is, we must seek it in the world, and hear the world's witness of it.

The hypothesis, indeed, has met with wide reception in these latter times, that Christianity does not fall within the province of history—that it is to each man what each man thinks it to be, and nothing else; and thus in fact is a mere name for a cluster or family of rival religions all together, religions at variance one with another, and claiming the same appellation, not because there can be assigned any one and the same doctrine as the common foundation of all, but because certain points of agreement may be found here and there of some sort or other, by which each in its turn is connected with one or other of the rest. Or again, it has been maintained, or implied, that all existing denominations of Christianity are wrong, none representing it as taught by Christ and his apostles; that the original religion has gradually decayed or become hopelessly corrupt; nay that it died out of the world at its birth, and was forthwith succeeded by a counterfeit or counterfeits which assumed its name, though they inherited at best but some fragments of its teaching; or rather that it cannot even be said either to have decayed or to have died, because historically it has no substance of its own, but from the first and onwards it has, on the stage of the world, been nothing more than a mere assemblage of doctrines and practices derived from without, from Oriental, Platonic, Polytheistic sources, from Buddhism, Essenism, Manichaeism; or that, allowing true Christianity still to exist, it has but a hidden and isolated life, in the hearts of the elect, or again as a literature or philosophy, not certified in any way, much less guaranteed, to come from above, but out of the various separate informations about the supreme being and human duty, with which an unknown providence has furnished us, whether in nature or in the world.

All such views of Christianity imply that there is no sufficient body of historical proof to interfere with, or at least to prevail against, any number whatever of free and independent hypotheses concerning it. But this surely is not self-evident, and has itself to be proved. Till positive reasons grounded on facts are adduced to the contrary, the most natural hypothesis, the most agreeable to our mode of proceeding in parallel cases, and that which takes precedence of all others, is to consider that the society of Christians, which the apostles left on earth, were of that religion to which the apostles had converted them; that the external continuity of name, profession, and communion, argues a real continuity of doctrine; that, as Christianity began by manifesting itself as of a certain shape and bearing to all mankind, therefore it went on so to manifest itself; and that the more, considering that prophecy had already determined that it was to be a power visible in the world and sovereign over it, characters which are accurately fulfilled in that historical Christianity to which we commonly give the name. It is not a violent assumption, then, but rather mere abstinence from the wanton admission of a principle which would necessarily lead to the most vexatious and preposterous scepticism, to take it for granted, before proof to the contrary, that the Christianity of the second, fourth, seventh, twelfth, sixteenth, and intermediate centuries is in its substance the very religion which Christ and his apostles taught in the first, whatever may be the modifications for good or for evil which lapse of years, or the vicissitudes of human affairs, have impressed upon it.

Of course I do not deny the abstract possibility of extreme changes. The substitution is certainly, in idea, supposable of a counterfeit Christianity—superseding the original, by means of the adroit innovations of seasons, places and persons, till, according to the familiar illustration, the "blade" and the "handle" are alternately renewed, and identity is lost without the loss of continuity. It is possible; but it must not be assumed. The *onus probandi* is with those who assert what it is unnatural to expect; to be just able to doubt is no warrant for disbelieving.

Accordingly, some writers have gone on to give reasons from history for their refusing to appeal to history. They aver that, when they come to look into the documents and literature of Christianity in times past, they find its doctrines so variously presented, and so inconsistently maintained by its professors, that, however natural it be *a priori,* it is useless, in fact, to seek in history the matter of that revelation which has been vouchsafed to mankind; that they cannot be historical Christians if they would. They say, in the words of Chillingworth, "There are popes against popes, councils against councils, some fathers against others, the same fathers against themselves, a consent of fathers of one age against a consent of fathers of another age, the Church of one age against the Church of another age." Hence they are forced, whether they will or not, to fall back upon the Bible as the sole source of revelation, and upon their own personal private judgment as the sole expounder of its doctrine. This is a fair argument, if it can be maintained, and it brings me at once to the subject of this essay. Not that it enters into my purpose to convict of misstatement, as might be done, each separate clause of this sweeping accusation of a smart but superficial writer; but neither on the other hand do I mean to deny everything that he says to the disadvantage of historical Christianity. On the contrary, I shall admit that there are in fact certain apparent variations in its teaching which have to be explained; thus I shall begin, but then I shall attempt to explain them to the exculpation of that teaching in point of unity, directness, and consistency.

Meanwhile, before setting about this work, I will address one remark to Chillingworth and his friends: Let them consider, that if they can criticize history, the facts of history certainly can retort upon them. It might, I grant, be clearer on this great subject than it is. This is no great concession. History is not a creed or a catechism, it gives lessons rather than rules; still no one can mistake its general teaching in this matter, whether he accept it or stumble at it. Bold outlines and broad masses of color rise out of the records of the past. They may be dim, they may be incomplete; but they are definite. And this one thing at least is certain; whatever history teaches, whaever it omits, whatever it exaggerates or extenuates, whatever it says and unsays, at least the Christianity of history is not Protestantism. If ever there were a safe truth, it is this.

And Protestantism has ever felt it so. I do not mean that every writer on the Protestant side has felt it; for it was the fashion at first, at least as a rhetorical argument against Rome, to appeal to past ages, or to some of them; but Protestantism, as a whole, feels it, and has felt it. This is shown in the determination already referred to of dispensing with historical Christianity altogether, and of forming a Christianity from the Bible alone: men never would have put it aside, unless they had despaired of it. It is shown by the long neglect of ecclesiastical history in England, which prevails even in the English Church. Our popular religion scarcely recognizes the fact of the twelve long ages which lie between the Councils of Nicea and Trent, except as affording one or two passages to illustrate its wild interpretations of certain prophesies of St. Paul and St. John. It is melancholy to say it, but the chief, perhaps the only English writer who has any claim to be considered an ecclesiastical historian, is the unbeliever Gibbon. To be deep in history is to cease to be a Protestant.

And this utter incongruity between Protestantism and historical Christianity is a plain fact, whether the latter be regarded in its earlier or in its later centuries. Protestants can as little bear its Ante-nicene as its Post-tridentine period. I have elsewhere observed on this circumstance:

"So much must the Protestant grant that, if such a system of doctrine as he would now introduce ever existed in early times, it has been clean swept away as if by a deluge, suddenly, silently, and without memorial; by a deluge coming in a night, and utterly soaking, rotting, heaving up, and hurrying off every vestige of what it found in the Church, before cock-crowing: so that 'when they rose in the morning' her true seed 'were all dead corpses'— nay, dead buried—and without gravestone. 'The waters went over them; there was not one of them left; they sunk like lead in the mighty waters.' Strange antitype, indeed, to the early fortunes of Israel!—then the enemy was drowned, and 'Israel saw them dead upon the sea-shore.'

"But now, it would seem, water proceeded as a flood 'out of the serpent's mouth,' and covered all the witnesses, so that not even their dead bodies lay in the streets of the great city.' Let him take which of his doctrines he will, his peculiar view of self-righteousness, of formality, of superstition; his notion of faith, or of spirituality in religious worship; his denial of the virtue of the sacraments, or of the ministerial commission, or of the visible Church; or his doctrine of the divine efficacy of the Scriptures as the one appointed instrument of religious teaching; and let him consider how far antiquity, as it has come down to us, will countenance him in it. No; he must allow that the alleged deluge has done its work; yes, and has in turn disappeared itself; it has been swallowed up by the earth, mercilessly as itself was merciless."

That Protestantism, then, is not the Christianity of history, it is easy to determine, but to retort is a poor reply in controversy to a question of fact, and whatever be the violence or the exaggeration of writers like Chillingworth, if they have rasied a real difficulty, it may claim a real answer, and we must determine whether on the one hand Christianity is still to represent to us a definite teaching from above, or whether on the other its utterances have been from time to time so strangely at variance, that we are necessarily thrown back on our own judgment individually to determine, what the revelation of God is, or rather if in fact there is, or has been, any revelation at all. . . .

If Christianity is a fact, and impresses an idea of itself on our minds and is a subject-matter of exercises of the reason, that idea will in course of time expand into a multitude of ideas, and aspects of ideas, connected and harmonious with one another, and in themselves determinate and immutable, as is the objective fact itself which is thus represented. It is a characteristic of our minds, that they cannot take an object in, which is submitted to them simply and integrally. We conceive by means of definition or description: whole objects do not create in the intellect whole ideas, but are, to use a mathematical phrase, thrown into series into a number of statements, strengthening, interpreting, correcting each other, and with more or less exactness approximating, as they accumulate, to a perfect image. There is no other way of learning or of teaching. We cannot teach except by aspects or views, which are not identical with the thing itself which we are teaching. Two persons may each convey the same truth to a third, yet by methods and through representations altogther different. The same person will treat the same argument differently in an essay or speech, according to the accident of the day of writing, or of the audience, yet it will be substantially the same.

And the more claim an idea has to be considered living, the more various will be its aspects; and the more social and political is its nature, the more complicated and subtle will be its issues, and the longer and more eventful will be its course. And in the number of these special ideas, which from their very depth and richness cannot be fully understood at once, but are more and more clearly expressed and taught the longer they last—having aspects many and bearings many, mutually connected and growing one out of another, and all parts of a whole, with a sympathy and correspondence keeping pace with the ever-changing necessities of the world, multiform, prolific, and ever resourceful—among these great doctrines surely we Christians shall not refuse a foremost place to Christianity. Such previously to the determination of the fact, must be our anticipation concerning it from a contemplation of its initial achievements.

It may be objected that its inspired documents at once determine the limits of its mission without further trouble; but ideas are in the writer and reader of the revelation, not the inspired text itself: and the question is whether those ideas which the letter conveys from writer to reader, reach the reader at once in their completeness and accuracy on his first perception of them, or whether they open out in his intellect and grow to perfection in the course of time. Nor could it surely be main-

tained without extravagance that the letter of the New Testament, or of any assignable number of books, comprises a delineation of all possible forms which a divine message will assume when submitted to a multitude of minds.

Nor is the case altered by supposing that inspiration provided in behalf of the first recipients of the revelation, what the divine fiat effected for herbs and plants in the beginning, which were created in maturity. Still, the time at length came, when its recipients ceased to be inspired; and on these recipients the revealed truths would fall, as in other cases, at first vaguely and generally, though in spirit and in truth, and would afterwards be completed by developments.

Nor can it fairly be made a difficulty that thus to treat of Christianity is to level it in sum to sects and doctrines of the world, and to impute to it the imperfections which characterize the productions of man. Certainly it is a sort of degradation of a divine work to consider it under an earthly form; but it is no irreverence, since our Lord himself, its author and guardian, bore one also. Christianity differs from other religions and philosophies, in what is superadded to earth from heaven; not in kind, but in origin; not in its nature, but in its personal characteristics; being informed and quickened by what is more than intellect, by a divine spirit. It is externally what the apostle calls an "earthen vessel," being the religion of men. And, considered as such, it grows "in wisdom and stature"; but the powers which it wields, and the words which proceed out of its mouth, attest its miraculous nativity.

Unless then some special ground of exception can be assigned, it is as evident that Christianity, as a doctrine and worship, will develop in the minds of recipients, as that it conforms in other respects, in its external propagation or its political framework, to the general methods by which the course of things is carried forward.

Again, if Christianity be a universal religion, suited not simply to one locality or period, but to all times and places, it cannot but vary in its relations and dealings towards the world around it, that is, it will develop. Principles require a very various application according as persons and circumstances vary, and must be thrown into new shapes according to the form of society which they are to influence. Hence all bodies of Christians, orthodox or not, develop the doctrines of Scripture. Few but will grant that Luther's view of justification had never been stated in words before his time: that his phraseology and his positions were novel, whether called for by circumstances or not. It is equally certain that the doctrine of justification defined at Trent was, in some sense, new also. The refutation and remedy of errors cannot precede their rise; and thus the fact of false developments or corruptions involves the correspondent manifestation of true ones. Moreover, all parties appeal to Scripture, that is, argue from the Scripture; but argument implies deduction, that is, development. Here there is no differences between early times and late, between a pope *ex cathedra* and an individual Protestant, except that their authority is not on a par. On either side the claim of authority is the same, and the process of development.

Accordingly, the common complaint of Protestants against the Church of Rome is, not simply that she has added to the primitive or the Scriptural doctrine (for this they do themselves), but that she contradicts it, and moreover imposes her additions as fundamental truths under sanction of an *anathema*. For themselves they deduce by quite as subtle a method, and act upon doctrines as implicit and on reasons as little analyzed in time past, as Catholic schoolmen. What prominence has the royal supremacy in the New Testament, or the lawfulness of bearing arms, or the duty of public worship, or the substitution of the first day of the week for the seventh, or infant baptism, to say nothing of the fundamental principle that the Bible and the Bible only is the religion of Protestants? These doctrines and usages, true or not, which is not the question here, are surely not gained by the direct use and immediate application of Scripture, nor by a mere exercise of argument upon words and sentences placed before the eyes, but by the unconscious growth of ideas suggested by the letter and habitual to the mind.

And, indeed, when we turn to the consideration of particular doctrines on which Scripture lays the greatest stress, we shall see that is is absolutely impossible for them to remain in the mere letter of Scripture, if they are to be more than mere words, and to convey a definite idea to the recipient. When it is declared that "the Word became flesh," three wide questions open upon us on the very announcement. What is meant by "the Word," what by "flesh," what by "became"? The answers to these involve a process of investigation, and are developments. Moreover, when they have been made, they will suggest a series of secondary questions; and thus at length a multitude of propositions is the result, which gather round the inspired sentence of which they come, giving it externally the form of a doctrine, and creating or deepening the idea of it in the mind.

It is true that, so far as such statements of Scripture are mysteries, they are relatively to us but words, and cannot be developed. But as a mystery implies in part what is incomprehensible or at least unknown, so does it in part imply what is not so; it implies a partial manifestation, or a representation by economy. Because then it is in a measure understood, it can so far be developed, though each result in the process will partake of the dimness and confusion of the original impression.

This moreover should be considered —that great questions exist in the subject-matter of which Scripture treats, which Scripture does not solve; questions too so real, so practical, that they must be answered, and, unless we suppose a new revelation, answered by means of the revelation which we have, that is, by development. Such is the question of the canon of Scripture and its inspiration: that is, whether Christianity depends upon a written document as Judaism;—if so, on what writings and how many;—whether that document is self-interpreting, or requires a comment, and whether any authoritative comment or commentator is provided—whether the revelation and the document are commensurate, or the one outruns the other;— all these questions surely find no solution on the surface of Scripture, nor indeed under the surface in the case of most men, however long and diligent might be their study of it. Nor were these difficulties settled by authority, as far as we know, at the commencement of the religion; yet surely it is quite conceivable that an apostle might have dissipated them all in a few words, had Divine Wisdom thought fit. But in matter of fact the decision has been left to time, to the slow process of thought, to the influence of mind upon mind, the issues of controversy, and the growth of opinion.

To take another instance just now referred to: if there was a point on which a rule was desirable from the first, it was concerning the religious duties under which Christian parents lay as regards their children. It would be natural indeed in any Christian father, in the absence of a rule, to bring his children for baptism; such in this instance would be the practical development of his faith in Christ and love for his offspring; still a development it is—necessarily required, yet, as far as we know, not provided for his need by direct precept in the revelation as originally given.

Another very large field of thought, full of practical considerations, yet, as far as our knowledge goes, but only partially occupied by any apostolical judgment, is that which the question of the effects of baptism opens upon us. That they who came in repentance and faith to that holy sacrament received remission of sins, is undoubtedly the doctrine of the apostles; but is there any means of a second remission for sins committed after it? St. Paul's Epistles, where we might expect an answer to our inquiry, contain no explicit statement on the subject; what they do plainly say does not diminish the difficulty: namely, first, that baptism is intended for the pardon of sins before it, not in prospect; next, that those who have received the gift of Baptism in fact live in a state of holiness, not of sin. How do statements such as these meet the actual state of the Church as we see it at this day?

Considering that it was expressly predicted that the kingdom of heaven, like the fisher's net, should gather of every kind, and that the 'tares' should grow with the wheat until the harvest, a graver and more practical question cannot be imagined than that which it has pleased the divine author of the Revelation to leave undecided, unless indeed there be means given in that Revelation of its own growth or development. As far as the letter goes of the inspired message, every one who holds that Scripture is the rule of faith, as all Protestants do, must allow that "there is not one of us but has exceeded by transgression its revealed ritual, and finds himself in consequence thrown upon those infinite resources of divine love which are stored in Christ, but have not been drawn out into form in the appointments of the Gospel." Since then Scripture needs completion, the question is brought to this issue:

whether defect or inchoateness in its doctrines be, or be not, an antecedent probability in favor of a development of them.

There is another subject, though not so immediately practical, on which Scripture does not, strictly speaking, keep silence, but says so little as to require, and so much as to suggest, information beyond its letter—the intermediate state between death and the resurrection. Considering the long interval which separates Christ's first and second coming, the millions of faithful souls who are waiting it out, and the intimate concern which every Christian has in the determination of its character, it might have been expected that Scripture would have spoken explicitly concerning it, whereas in fact its notices are but brief and obscure. We might indeed have argued that this silence of Scripture was intentional, with a view of discouraging speculations upon the subject, except for the circumstance that, as in the question of our post-baptismal state, its teaching seems to proceed upon a hypothesis inapplicable to the state of the Church after the time when it was delivered. As Scripture contemplates Christians, not as backsliders, but as saints, so does it apparently represent the day of judgment as immediate, and the interval of expectation as evanescent. It leaves on our minds the general impression that Christ was returning on earth at once, "the time short," worldly engagements superseded by "the present distress," persecutors urgent, Christians, as a body, sinless and expectant, without home, without plan for the future, looking up to heaven. But outward circumstances have changed, and with the change, a different application of the revealed word has of necessity been demanded, that is, a development. When the nations were converted and offenses abounded, then the Church came out to view, on the one hand as a temporal establishment, on the other as a remedial system, and passages of Scripture aided and directed the development which before were of inferior account. Hence the doctrine of penance as the complement of baptism, and of purgatory as the explanation of the intermediate state. So reasonable is this expansion of the original creed, that, when some ten years since the true doctrine of baptism was expounded among us without any mention of penance, our teacher was accused by many of us of Novatianism; while, on the other hand, heterodox divines have before now advocated the doctrine of the sleep of the soul because they said it was the only successful preventive of belief in purgatory.

Thus developments of Christianity are proved to have been in the contemplation of its divine author, by an argument parallel to that by which we infer intelligence in the system of the physical world. In whatever sense the need and its supply are a proof of design in the visible creation, in the same do the gaps, if the word may be used, which occur in the structure of the original creed of the Church, make it probable that those developments, which grow out of the truths which lie around it, were intended to fill them up.

Nor can it be fairly objected that in thus arguing we are contradicting the great philosopher, who tells us, that "upon supposition of God affording us light and instruction by revelation, additional to what he has afforded us by reason and experience, we are in no sort judges by what methods, and in what proportion, it were to be expected that this supernatural light and instruction would be afforded us," because he is speaking of our judging before a revelation is given. He observes that "we have no principles of reason upon which to judge *beforehand,* how it were to be expected revelation should have been left, or what was most suitable to the divine plan of government," in various respects; but the case is altogether altered when a revelation is vouchsafed, for then a new precedent, or what he calls "principle of reason," is introduced, and from what is actually put into our hands we can form a judgment whether more is to be expected. Butler, indeed, as a well-known passage of his work shows, is far from denying the principle of progressive development.

The method of revelation observed in Scripture abundantly confirms this anticipation. For instance, prophecy, if it had so happened, need not have afforded a specimen of development; separate predictions might have been made to accumulate as time went on, prospects might have opened, definite knowledge might have been given, by communications independent of each other, as St. John's Gospel or the Epistles of St. Paul are unconnected with the first three Gospels' though the doctrine of each apostle is a development of their matter. But the prophetic revelation is, in matter of fact, not of this nature, but a process of development: the earlier prophecies are pregnant texts out of which the succeeding announcements grow; they are types. It is not that first one truth is told, then another; but the whole truth or large portions of it are told at once, yet only in their rudiments, or in miniature, and they are expanded and finished in their parts, as the course of revelation proceeds. The seed of the woman was to bruise the serpent's head; the scepter was not to depart from Judah till Shiloh came, to whom was to be the gathering of the people. He was to be 'wonderful,' 'counselor,' the 'prince of peace.' The question of the Ethiopian rises in the reader's mind, "Of whom does the prophet speak this?" Every word requires a comment. Accordingly, it is no uncommon theory with unbelievers, that the messianic idea, as they call it,

was gradually developed in the minds of the Jews by a continuous and traditional habit of contemplating it, and grew into its full proportions by a mere human process; and so far seems certain, without trenching on the doctrine of inspiration, that the books of Wisdom and Ecclesiasticus are developments of the writings of the prophets, expressed or elicited by means of current ideas in the Greek philosophy, and ultimately adopted and ratified by the apostle in his epistle to the Hebrews.

But the whole Bible, not its prophetical portions only, is written on the principle of development. As the revelation proceeds, it is ever new, yet ever old. St. John, who completes it, declares that he writes no "new commandment unto his brethren," but an old commandment which they "had from the beginning." And then he adds, "A new commandment I write unto you." The same test of development is suggested in our Lord's words on the Mount, as has already been noticed, "Think not that I am come to destroy the law and the prophets; I am not come to destroy, but to fulfill." He does not reverse, but perfect, what has gone before. Thus with respect to the evangelical view of the rite of sacrifice, first the rite is enjoined by Moses; next Samuel says, "to obey is better than sacrifice"; then Osee, "I will have mercy and not sacrifice"; Isaias, "Incense is an abomination unto me"; then Malachia, describing the times of the Gospel, speaks of the "pure offering" of wheatflour; and our Lord completes the development, when he speaks of worshiping "in spirit and in truth." If there is anything here left to explain, it will be found in the usage of the Christian Church immediately afterwards, which shows that sacrifice was not removed, but truth and spirit added.

Nay, the *effata* of our Lord and his apostles are of a typical structure, parallel to the prophetic announcements above mentioned, and predictions as well as injunctions of doctrine. If then the prophetic sentences have had that development which has really been given them, first by succeeding revelations, and then by the event, it is probable antecedently that those doctrinal, political, ritual, and ethical sentences, which have the same structure, should admit the same expansion. Such are, "This is my body," or "you are Peter, and upon this rock I will build my church," or "The meek shall inherit the earth," or "Suffer little children to come unto me," or "The pure in heart shall see God."

On this character of our Lord's teaching, the following passage may suitably be quoted from a writer already used. "His recorded words and works when on earth . . . come to us as the declarations of a Lawgiver. In the Old Covenant, almighty God first of all spoke the Ten Commandments from Mount Sinai, and afterwards wrote them. So our Lord first spoke his own Gospel, both of promise and of precept, on the Mount, and his evangelists have recorded it. Further, when he delivered it, he spoke by way of parallel to the Ten Commandments. And his style, moreover, corresponds to the authority which he assumes. It is of that solemn, measured, and severe character, which bears on the face of it tokens of its belonging to one who spoke as none other man could speak. The Beatitudes, with which his sermon opens, are an instance of this incommunicable style, which befitted, as far as human words could befit, God incarnate.

"Nor is this style peculiar to the Sermon on the Mount. All through the Gospels it is discernible, distinct from any other part of Scripture, showing itself in solemn declarations, canons, sentences, or sayings, such as legislators propound, and scribes and lawyers comment on. Surely everything our Savior did and said is characterized by mingled simplicity and mystery. His emblematical actions, his typical miracles, his parables, his replies, his censures, all are evidences of a legislature in germ, afterwards to be developed, a code of divine truth which was ever to be before men's eyes, to be the subject of investigation and interpretation, and the guide in controversy. 'Verily, verily, I say unto you,'—'But, I say unto you,'—are the tokens of a supreme teacher and prophet.

"And thus the fathers speak of his teaching. 'His sayings,' observes St. Justin, 'were short and concise; for he was no rhetorician, but his word was the power of God.' And St. Basil, in like manner, 'Every deed and every word of our Savior Jesus Christ is a canon of piety and virtue.' When then you hear word or deed of his, do not hear it as by the way, or after a simple and carnal manner, but enter into the depth of his contemplations, become a communicant in truths mystically delivered to you."

Moreover, while it is certain that developments of revelation proceeded all through the Old Dispensation down to the very end of our Lord's ministry, on the other hand, if we turn our attention to the beginnings of apostolical teaching after his ascension, we shall find ourselves unable to fix a historical point at which the growth of doctrine ceased, and the rule of faith was once for all settled. Not on the day of Pentecost, for St. Peter had still to learn at Joppa that he was to baptize Cornelius; not at Joppa and Cæsarea, for St. Paul had to write his epistles; not on the death of the last apostle, for St. Ignatius had to establish the doctrine of Episcopacy; not then, nor for centuries after, for the canon of the New Testament was still undetermined. Not in the creed, which is no collection of definitions, but a summary of certain *credenda,* an incomplete summary, and, like the Lord's Prayer or the Decalogue, a mere sample of divine truths, especially of the more elementary. No one doctrine can be named which starts complete at first, and gains nothing afterwards from the investigations of faith and the attacks of heresy. The Church went forth from the old world in haste, as the Israelites from Egypt "with their dough before it was leavened, their kneading troughs being bound up in their clothes upon their shoulders."

Further, the political developments contained in the historical parts of Scripture are as striking as the prophetical and the doctrinal. Can any history wear a more human appearance than that of the rise and growth of the chosen people to whom I have just referred? What had been determined in the counsels of the Lord of heaven and earth from the beginning, what was immutable, what was announced to Moses in the burning bush, is afterwards represented as the growth of an idea under successive emergencies. The divine voice in the bush had announced the exodus of the children of Israel from Egypt and their entrance into Canaan; and added, as a token of the certainty of his purpose, "When you have brought forth the people out of Egypt, you shall serve God upon this mountain." Now this sacrifice or festival, which was but incidental and secondary in the great deliverance, is for a while the ultimate scope of the demands which Moses makes upon Pharaoh. "You shall come, you and the elders of Israel, unto the king of Egypt, and you shall say to him, The Lord God of the Hebrews has met with us, and now let us go, we beseech thee, three days' journey into the wilderness, that we may sacrifice to the Lord our God." It had been added that Pharaoh would first refuse their request, but that after miracles he would let them go al-

together, nay with "jewels of silver and gold, and raiment."

Accordingly the first request of Moses was, "Let us go, we pray you, three days' journey into the desert, and sacrifice unto the Lord our God." Before the plague of frogs the warning is repeated, "Let my people go that they may serve me"; and after it Pharaoh says, "I will let the people go, that they may do sacrifice unto the Lord." It occurs again before the plague of flies; and after it Pharaoh offers to let the Israelites sacrifice in Egypt, which Moses refuses on the ground that they will have to "sacrifice the abomination of the Egyptians before their eyes." "We will go three days' journey into the wilderness," he proceeds, "and sacrifice to the Lord our God"; and Pharaoh then concedes their sacrificing in the wilderness, "only," he says, "you shall not go very far away." The demand is repeated separately before the plagues of murrain, hail, and locusts, no mention being yet made of anything beyond a service or sacrifice in the wilderness. On the last of these interviews, Pharaoh asks an explanation, and Moses extends his claim: "We will go with our young and with our old, with our sons and with our daughters, with our flocks and with our herds will we go, for we must hold a feast unto the Lord." That it was an extension seems plain from Pharaoh's reply: "Go now ye that are men, and serve the Lord, for that ye did desire." Upon the plague of darkness Pharaoh concedes the extended demand, excepting the flocks and herds; but Moses reminds him that they were implied, though not expressed in the original wording: "You must give us also sacrifices and burnt offerings, that we may sacrifice unto the Lord our God." Even to the last, there was no intimation of their leaving Egypt for good; the issue was left to be wrought out by the Egyptians. "All these your servants," says

Moses, "shall come down unto me, and bow down themselves unto me, saying, Go out and all the people that follow you, and after that I will go out"; and, accordingly, after the judgment on the first-born, they were thrust out at midnight, with their flocks and herds, their kneading troughs and their dough, laden, too, with the spoils of Egypt, as had been fore-ordained, yet apparently by a combination of circumstances, or the complication of a crisis. Yet Moses knew that their departure from Egypt was final, for he took the bones of Joseph with him; and that conviction broke on Pharaoh soon, when he and his asked themselves, "Why have we done this, that we have let Israel go from serving us?" But this progress of events, vague and uncertain as it seemed to be, notwithstanding the miracles which attended it, had been directed by him who works out gradually what he has determined absolutely; and it ended in the parting of the Red Sea, and the destruction of Pharaoh's host, on his pursuing them.

Moreover, from what occurred forty years afterwards, when they were advancing upon the promised land, it would seem that the original grant of territory did not include the country east of Jordan, held in the event by Reuben, Gad, and half the tribe of Manasses; at least they undertook at first to leave Sihon in undisturbed possession of his country, if he would let them pass through it, and only on his refusing his permission did they invade and appropriate it.

It is in point to notice also the structure and style of Scripture, a structure so unsystematic and various, and a style so figurative and indirect, that no one would presume at first sight to say what is in it and what is not. It cannot, as it were, be mapped, or its contents catalogued; but after all our diligence, to the end of our lives and to the end of the Church, it must be an unexplored and unsubdued land, with heights and valleys, forests and streams, on the right and left of our path and close about us, full of concealed wonders and choice treasures. Of no doctrine whatever, which does not actually contradict what has been delivered, can it be peremptorily asserted that it is not in Scripture; of no reader, whatever be his study of it, can it be said that he has mastered every doctrine which it contains. Butler's remarks on this subject were just now referred to. "The more distinct and particular knowledge," he says, "of those *things,* the study of which the apostle calls 'going on unto perfection,'" that is, of the more recondite doctrines of the Gospel, "and of the prophetic parts of revelation, like many parts of natural and even civil knowledge, may require very exact thought and careful consideration. The hindrances too of natural and of supernatural light and knowledge have been of the same kind. And as it is owned the whole scheme of Scripture is not yet understood, so, if it ever comes to be understood, before the 'restitution of all things,' and without miraculous interpositions, it must be in the same way as natural knowledge is come at, by the continuance and progress of learning and liberty, and by particular persons attending to, comparing, and pursuing intimations scattered up and down it, which are overlooked and disregarded by the generality of the world. For this is the way in which all improvements are made, by thoughtful men tracing on obscure hints, as it were, dropped us by nature accidentally, or which seem to come into our minds by chance. Nor is it at all incredible that a book, which has been so long in the possession of mankind, should contain many truths as yet undiscovered. For all the same phenomena, and the same faculties of investigation, from which such great discoveries in natural knowledge have been made in the present and last age, were equally in the possession of mankind several thousand years before. And possibly it might be intended that events, as they come to pass, should open and ascertain the meaning of several parts of Scripture." Butler of course was not contemplating the case of new articles of faith, or developments imperative on our acceptance, but he surely bears witness to the probability of developments taking place in Christian doctrine considered in themselves, which is the point at present in question.

It may be added that, in matter of fact, all the definitions or received judgments of the early and medieval Church rest upon definite, even though sometimes obscure sentences of Scripture. Thus purgatory may appeal to the "saving by fire," and "entering through much tribulation into the kingdom of God"; the communication of the merits of the saints to our "receiving a prophet's reward" for "receiving a prophet in the name of a prophet," and "a righteous man's reward" for "receiving a righteous man in the name of a righteous man"; the real presence to "This is my body"; absolution to "Whose sins you shall forgive, they are forgiven"; extreme unction to "Anointing him with oil in the name of the Lord"; voluntary poverty to "Sell all that you own"; obedience to "He was in subjection to his parents"; the honor paid to creatures, animate or inanimate, to *Laudate Dominum in sanctis ejus,* and *Adorate scabellum pedum ejus;* and so of the rest.

Lastly, while Scripture nowhere recognizes itself or asserts the inspiration of those passages which are most essential, it distinctly anticipates the development of Christianity both as a polity and as a doctrine. In one of our Lord's parables "the Kingdom of Heaven" is even compared to "a grain of mustardseed, which a man took and hid in his field; which indeed is the least of all seeds, but when it is grown it is the greatest among herbs, and becomes a tree," and, as St. Mark words it, "shoots out great branches, so that the birds of the air come and lodge in the branches thereof." And again, in the same chapter of St. Mark, "So is the kingdom of God, as if a man should cast seed into the ground, and should sleep, and rise night and day, and the seed should spring and grow up, he knows not how; for the earth brings forth fruit of herself." Here an internal element of life, whether principle or doctrine, is spoken of rather than any mere external manifestation; and it is observable that the spontaneous, as well as the gradual, character of the growth is intimated. This description of the process corresponds to what has been above observed respecting development, viz., that it is not an effect of wishing and resolving, or of forced enthusiasm, or of any mechanism of reasoning, or of any mere subtlety of intellect; but comes of its own innate power of expansion within the mind in its season, though with the use of reflection and argument and original thought, more or less as it may happen, with a dependence on the ethical growth of the mind itself, and with a reflex influence upon it. Again, the parable of the leaven describes the development of doctrine in another respect, in its active, engrossing, and interpenetrating power.

From the necessity, then, of the case, from the history of all sects and parties in religion, and from the analogy and example of Scripture, we may fairly conclude that Christian doctrine admits of formal, legitimate, and true developments, that is, of developments contemplated by its divine author.

The general analogy of the world, physical and moral, confirms this conclusion, as we are reminded by the great authority who has already been quoted in the course of this section. "The whole natural world and government of it," says Butler, "is a scheme or system; not a fixed, but a progressive one; a scheme in which the operation of various means takes up a great length of time before the ends they tend to can be attained. The change of seasons, the ripening of the fruits of the earth, the very history of a flower is an instance of this; and so is human life. Thus vegetable bodies, and those of animals, though possibly formed at once, yet grow up by degrees to a mature state. And thus rational agents, who animate these latter bodies, are naturally directed to form each his own manners and character by the gradual gaining of knowledge and experience, and by a long course of action. Our existence is not only successive, as it must be of necessity, but one state of our life and being is appointed by God to be a preparation for another; and that to be the means of attaining to another succeeding one: infancy to childhood, childhood to youth, youth to mature age. Men are impatient, and for precipitating things; but the author of nature appears deliberate throughout his operations, accomplishing his natural ends by slow successive steps. And there is a plan of things beforehand laid out, which, from the nature of it, requires various systems of means, as well as length of time, in order to the carrying of its several parts into execution. Thus, in the daily course of natural providence, God operates in the very same manner as in the dispensation of Christianity, making one thing subservient to another; this, to somewhat farther; and so on, through a progressive series of means which extend, both backward and forward, beyond our utmost view. Of this manner of operation, everything we see in the course of nature is as much an instance as any part of the Christian dispensation."

B. AN UNPUBLISHED PAPER ON THE DEVELOPMENT OF DOCTRINE, 15 FEBRUARY 1868

I dare say I have not been consistent or logically exact in what from time to time I have said about the extent and subject matter of the Church's infallibility, for it is a very large question and I have never set myself formally to answer it.

Certainly I have ever thought that the logical deductions of truths in the *depositum* were capable of definition and made portions of the dogma of faith. For those deductions come under the head of developments; and it is now going on for twenty years since Stanislas wanted me to say (saying it was what was received in France) that developments generally, though notoriously existing, continually coming to light, and indefinitely and without limit numerous, were necessarily external to the dogma, and incapable of definition. This admission, I understood him to say, would reconcile him to the *Essay* I wrote on the subject; but I recollect I would not make it.

I have no reason to suppose that since that time I have been reconciled to a view of the subject, which I would not admit then.

As to the *Apologia,* it must be recollected that it was not a didactic work —nor did it contain a statement of my own personal views about infallibility, but was addressed to Protestants *in order to show* them what it was that a Catholic fairly undertook in the way of theological profession, when he became a Catholic. I myself, for instance, have ever held as a matter of theological opinion the infallibility of the pope; but I carefully abstain from asserting it in the general view which I give of Catholic doctrine. I felt I should be as obviously wrong in setting down theological opinions, when I was declaring the Church's doctrine as such, as I have thought Archbishop Manning obviously wrong in introducing into his pastorals the pope's infallibility; and I think I bore in mind, as I wrote, because I have ever remembered, our bishop's remark that what made Fr. Faber's book on the Holy Eucharist so unsettling to nuns was that he mixed up dogma with theological opinion, and that in a popular work theological opinions ought to be kept under. It was for this reason that I introduced into my statement two or three sentences from Chrismann, which professed less about the province of infallibility than I held myself. It was for this reason that I spoke so vaguely about the *Pomoeria.* I myself hold that the doctrines which may be considered as belonging to it are in some cases of obligation and in others not; but which are such which not, is decided by theological opinion and it varies. Such, for instance, would be the infallibility of canonization—to him who thinks it infallible, it is such. And there are two motives, short of *fides divina,* which occasion silence and acquiescence on such points, or at least very cautious and restrained avowals in opposition to them; the *pietas fidei* (which I think I did not refer to) and the duty of obedience. It was for the same reason, that, in speaking of condemned propositions, I did not expressly say, whether the condemnation was infallible or not, because a distinct assertion could not be made without turning a statement of twenty pages into a volume. All I did, was to say that such condemnations from their general character constituted no great burden for our faith to bear.

In the second edition I withdrew the two sentences from Chrismann, because they seemed too strong an *assertion,* and to be taking a side—whereas I wished to be vague. No two theologians perhaps can exactly agree where *fides divina* ends, and *pietas* and submission begin. No two thinkers can say how far the habit of the day extends, and where it stops. For instance, if I were to say that the inspiration of the text of Scripture was not a point *de fide,* I should be saying what I believe to be true—but to say so would not correctly exhibit and represent the current opinion; it is a consideration of comfort to individuals who are perplexed, but, if forwarded prominently, might perplex and unsettle those who have no difficulties. I cannot bear tyrant majorities, and I am tender about minorities, but I have no wish that minorities should kick up their heels, and throw the majority into confusion.

So much on what I have said in my *Essay on Development* and in the *Apologia.* I don't recollect having said any thing on the subject elsewhere. What I have said in conversation, I cannot of course recollect; but one conversation I recollect having with Father Knox, either at Littlemore or after he had seen Brownson, which remains on my memory, because I have ever repeated it to myself; and perhaps I have got the substance of it somewhere in writing, though not printed. The immediate subject was how St. Hilary and St. Irenaeus could use expressions or make statements about the Holy Trinity or the Incarnation, which the great subsequent Catholic development or doctrine afterwards discarded, without his failing in a real apprehension of the doctrine itself. And, as what I maintained in the case of the apostles as regards all doctrines whatever, I have ever meant the explanation which I gave of the state of mind of St. Hilary as regards the Incarnation to apply (*mutatis mutandis*) to the state of mind of St. Paul as regards, say, the Immaculate Conception. (I say "*mutatis mutandis,*" because the apostles were inspired, and the fathers were not.)

Now as to the apostles: What do we mean by a man's being *master* of any subject, say science? What is meant by *knowing* the Aristotelian philosophy? Does it mean that he has before his mind always every doctrinal statement, every sentiment, opinion, intellectual and moral tendency of Aristotle? This is impossible. Not Aristotle himself, no human mind, can have a host of thoughts present to it at once. The philosophy, as a system, is stored in the *memory,* deeply rooted there if you will, but still in the memory, and is brought out according to the occasion. A learned Aristotelian is one who can answer any whatever philosophical questions in the way that Aristotle would have answered them. If they are questions which could not occur in Aristotle's age, he still answers them; and by two means, by the instinct which a thorough Aristotelian intellect, the habit set up in his mind, possesses; next, by never-swerving processes of ratiocination. And as a thoroughly grounded anatomist knows whether the smallest bone or bit of bone shown him is human or not, so the perfect Aristotelian will know whether this or that opinion, sentiment, conjecture, generalization, negation, is Aristotelian or not. In one respect he knows more than Aristotle; because, in new emergencies after the time of Aristotle, he *can* and *does* answer what Aristotle would have answered, but for the want of the opportunity did not. There is another point of view in which he seems to have the advantage of Aristotle, though it is no real superiority, viz., that from the necessities of the interval between Aristotle and himself there has been the growth of technology, a scientific vocabulary, which makes the philosophy easier to remember, easier to communicate and to defend—nay, which enables him to view it as a whole, *per modum unius,* with a grasp of mind which would be superior to the view taken of it by any equal intellect, or in other words, *caeteris paribus,* and, if not more vigorous than Aristotle's grasp, because of the superiority of Aristotle's vigorous creative intellect. Such a technology with its explanations bears up his intellect, as corks a swimmer, as a pole a rope dancer, as a belt a runner, and keeps him from accidental mistakes, momentary slips, from which Aristotle's more vigorous perspicacious intellect was the safeguard. It keeps his learning well about him, and at command at any moment, as being a sort of *memoria technica,* both as embodying elementary principles, and as condensing the tradition of a thousand questions and answers, of controversies and resolutions of them, which have taken place between Aristotle's time and his.

Such a scientific apparatus has its evils; for common minds, instead of throwing themselves into the *genius* and *animus* of the philosophy, will make the technology the beginning and end of their study; and will be formalists, pedants, bigots, and will be as little made philosophers by their verbal knowledge, as boys can swim, because they have corks, or run, because they have belts. I am not concerned with an inconvenience which is accidental and indirect, and no fault of technology itself—its advantage is obvious. Take, for instance, an instance in theology—nay, I had better pass on at once to theology, for the sake of which these remarks, already sufficient for their purpose, have been made—let then the words be taken *"Spiritus Sanctus superveniet in te, et Virtus Altissimi & C"*— what Person of the Blessed Trinity is meant by *"Spiritus Sanctus"*? I conceive that an apostle would have answered promptly, emphatically, "The Third"—so has answered the Church, but some of the earlier fathers, I think, answered "The Second." Why do they say "The Second?" because they were not individually perfect theologians— the difference between them being that the apostle answers promptly, the Church uncertainly, at intervals, for what the apostle is in his own person, that the Church is in her whole evolution of ages, *per modum unius,* a living, present treasury of the mind of the Spirit of Christ.

Now to continue the contrast between the apostles and the Church. The apostles did not merely know the Apostles Creed; what knowledge could be more jejune, unless the meaning of each separate word of it was known in fullness? They must know all and more than all about the word "Son of God," which the Church has enunciated since their time. And so of every article, and portion of an article. What then is meant by the *depositum?* is it a list of articles that can be numbered? no, it is a large philosophy; all parts of which are connected together, and in a certain sense correlative together, so that he who really knows one part, may be said to know all, as *ex pede Herculem.* Thus the apostles had the *fullness* of revealed knowledge, a fullness which they could as little realize to themselves, as the human mind, as such, can have all its thoughts present before it at once. They are elicited according to the occasion. A man of genius cannot go about with his genius in his hand; in an apostle's mind a great part of his knowledge is from the nature of the case latent or implicit; and taking two apostles, St. Peter and St. John, according to their respective circumstances, they either may teach the same thing in common, or again what is explicit in St. Paul might be latent in St. John and what is explicit in St. John may be latent in St. Paul.

But how could such a knowledge, partly explicit partly implicit, and varying day by day as to what was the one and what the other, be transmitted to the Church after them? Thus: I believe the creed (i.e., the deposit, I say creed as more intelligible, since it consists of articles) was delivered to the *Church with the gift of knowing its true and full meaning.* A divine philosophy is committed to her keeping: not a number of formulas such as a modern pedantic theologian may make theology to consist in, but a system of thought, *sui generis* in such sense that a mind that was possessed of it, that is, the Church's mind, could definitely and unequivocally say whether this part of it, as traditionally expressed, meant this or that, and whether this or that was agreeable to, or inconsistent with it in whole or in part. I wish to hold that there is nothing which the Church has defined or shall define but what an apostle, if asked, would have been fully able to answer and would have answered, as the Church has answered, the one answering by inspiration, the other from its gift of infallibility; and that the Church never will be able to answer, or has been able to answer, what the apostles could not answer, e.g., whether the earth is stationary or not, or whether a republic is or is not better than a monarchy. The differences between them being that an apostle could answer questions at once, but the Church answers them intermittently, in times and seasons, often delaying and postponing, according as she is guided by her Divine Instructor; and secondly and on the other hand, that the Church does in fact make answers which the apostles did not make, and in one sense did not know, though they would have known them, i.e., made present to their consciousness, and made those answers, had the questions been asked.

I have taken notice of this particular superiority (so to call it) of later times over apostolic, when speaking of Aristotle in illustration, and how I must notice that other point of superiority, which lies in the existence and knowledge of scientific phraseology. Had St. Paul been asked whether our Lady's conception was immaculate, or whether she was born in original sin, is it wrong to say that he would have been puzzled by the words "conception," "immaculate," and "original sin?" Is it detracting from his perfect knowledge of all that which the Church in after times has developed and shall develop to the end, if I allow he would have kept in silence and have left the question unanswered? Is it more than saying, that scientific phraseology was not among the languages which were comprised in the Pentecostal gift? But if he had been asked whether or not our Lady had the grace of the Spirit anticipating all sin whatever, including Adam's imputed sin, I think he would have answered in the affirmative. If he never was asked the question, I should say he had in his mind the decision of the Church in 1854 *in confuso* or *implicite*. I speak under correction.

One other question I must notice. What is meant by the *mind* of the Church? or of the apostles committing their philosophy to the Church, yet not to each individual father and doctor? for the Church is not a person, as an apostle is, but is merely *made up* of fathers and theologians, and how can they altogether have one mind, which is not the mind of each? It is no answer to this question to say that the mind to which the *depositum* is committed, is the infallible mind of the pope, unless indeed we considered him infallible as an apostle at all times, whereas we only say that he is infallible *ex cathedra*. However, the theory of his infallibility will illustrate the question, and serve to answer it. We all know how different

a boy's or a man's state of mind is, when he is in an idle, relaxed, careless mood, and when he is put on his mettle. A boy in a class will make gross mistakes, because his mind is not roused; threaten him with some punishment, and he, as it were, wakes up, and to your surprise knows a great deal about the matter on which he is questioned. In like manner we never could take a friend's conversational sayings even in his own province of thought for his deliberate enunciations. I conceive then that the *depositum* is in such sense committed to the Church or to the pope, that when the pope sits in St. Peter's chair, or when a council of fathers and doctors is collected around him, it is capable of being presented to their minds with that fullness and exactness, under the operation of supernatural grace (so far forth and in such portion of it as the occasion requires), with which it habitually, not occasionally, resided in the minds of the apostles—a vision of it, not logical, and therefore consistent with errors of reasoning and of fact in the enunciation, after the manner of an intuition or an instinct. Nor do those enunciations become logical, because theologians afterwards can reduce them to their relations to other doctrines, or give them a position in the general system of theology. To such theologians they appear deductions from the creed or formularized deposit, but in truth they are original parts of it, communicated *per modum unius* to the apostles' minds, and brought to light to the minds of the fathers of the council, under the temporary illumination of Divine Grace.

I put all this on paper with great diffidence, though it is the view I have entertained for so many years.

21. *Lord John Emerich Dalberg-Acton: Lecture on the History of Freedom in Christianity, 28 May 1877*

From Lord Acton, *The History of Freedom and Other Essays* (London: The Macmillan Company, 1907), pp. 30-60.

WHEN Constantine the Great carried the seat of empire from Rome to Constantinople he set up in the market-place of the new capital a porphyry pillar which had come from Egypt, and of which a strange tale is told. In a vault beneath he secretly buried the seven sacred emblems of the Roman state, which were guarded by the virgins in the temple of Vesta, with the fire that might never be quenched. On the summit he raised a statue of Apollo, representing himself, and enclosing a fragment of the cross; and he crowned it with a diadem of rays consisting of the nails employed at the crucifixion, which his mother was believed to have found at Jerusalem.

The pillar still stands, the most significant monument that exists of the converted empire; for the notion that the nails which had pierced the body of Christ became a fit ornament for a heathen idol as soon as it was called by the name of a living emperor indicated the position designed for Christianity in the imperial structure of Constantine. Diocletian's attempt to transform the Roman government into a despotism of the Eastern type had brought on the last and most serious persecution of the Christians; and Constantine, in adopting their faith, intended neither to abandon his predecessor's scheme of policy nor to renounce the fascinations of arbitrary authority, but to strengthen his throne with the support of a religion which had astonished the world by its power of resistance, and to obtain that support absolutely and without a drawback he fixed the seat of his government in the East, with a patriarch of his own creation.

Nobody warned him that by promoting the Christian religion he was tying one of his hands, and surrendering the prerogative of the Caesars. As the acknowledged author of the liberty and superiority of the Church, he was appealed to as the guardian of her unity. He admitted the obligation; he accepted the trust; and the divisions that prevailed among the Christians supplied his successors with many opportunities of extending that protectorate, and preventing any reduction of the claims or of the resources of imperialism.

Constantine declared his own will equivalent to a canon of the Church. According to Justinian, the Roman people had formally transferred to the emperors the entire plenitude of its authority, and, therefore, the emperor's pleasure, expressed by edict or by letter, had force of law. Even in the fervent age of its conversion the empire employed its refined civilization, the accumulated wisdom of ancient sages, the reasonableness and subtlety of Roman law, and the entire inheritance of the Jewish, the pagan, and the Christian world, to make the Church serve as a gilded crutch of absolutism. Neither an enlightened philosophy, nor all the political wisdom of Rome, nor even the faith and virtue of the Christians availed against the incorrigible tradition of antiquity. Something was wanted beyond all the gifts of reflection and experience—a faculty of self-government and self-control, developed like its language in the fiber of a nation, and growing with its growth. This vital element, which many centuries of warfare, of anarchy, of oppression had extinguished in the countries that were still draped in the pomp of ancient civilization, was deposited on the soil of Christendom by the fertilizing stream of migration that overthrew the empire of the West.

In the height of their power the Romans became aware of a race of men that had not abdicated freedom in the hands of a monarch; and the ablest writer of the empire pointed to them with a vague and bitter feeling, that to the institutions of these barbarians, not yet crushed by despotism, the future of the world belonged. Their kings, when they had kings, did not preside at their councils; they were sometimes elective; they were sometimes deposed; and they were bound by oath to act in obedience with the general wish. They enjoyed real authority only in war. This primitive republicanism, which admits monarchy as an occasional incident, but holds fast to the collective supremacy of all free men, of the constituent authority over all constituted authorities, is the remote germ of parliamentary government. The action of the state was confined to narrow limits; but, besides his position as head of the state, the king was surrounded by a body of followers attached to him by personal or political ties. In these, his immediate dependents, disobedience or resistance to orders was no more tolerated than in a wife, a child, or a soldier; and a man was expected to murder his own father if his chieftain required it. Thus these Teutonic communities admitted an independence of government that threatened to dissolve society; and a dependence on persons that was dangerous to freedom. It was a system very favorable to corporations, but offering no security to individuals. The state was not likely to oppress its subjects; and was not able to protect them.

The first effect of the great Teutonic migration into the regions civilized by Rome was to throw Europe back many centuries to a condition scarcely more advanced than that from which the institutions of Solon had rescued Athens. Although the Greeks had preserved the literature, the arts, and the science of antiquity and all the sacred monuments of early Christianity with a completeness of which the rended fragments that have come down to us give no commensurate idea, and even the peasants of Bulgaria knew the New Testament by heart, Western Europe lay under the grasp of masters the ablest of whom could not write their names. The faculty of exact reasoning, of accurate observation, became extinct for five hundred years, and even the sciences most needful to society, medicine and geometry, fell into decay, until the teachers of the West went to school at the feet of Arabian masters. To bring order out of chaotic ruin, to rear a new civilization and blend hostile and unequal races into a nation, the thing wanted was not liberty but force. And for centuries all progress is attached to the action of men like Clovis, Charlemagne, and William the Norman, who were resolute and peremptory, and prompt to be obeyed.

The spirit of immemorial paganism which had saturated ancient society could not be exorcised except by the combined influence of Church and state; and the universal sense that their union was necessary created the Byzantine despotism. The divines of the empire who could not fancy Christianity flourishing beyond its borders, insisted that the state is not in the Church, but the Church in the state. This doctrine had scarcely been uttered when the rapid collapse of the Western Empire opened a wider horizon; and Salvianus, a priest at Marseilles, proclaimed that the social virtues, which were decaying amid the civilized Romans, existed in greater purity and promise among the pagan invaders. They were converted with ease and rapidity; and their conversion was generally brought about by their kings.

Christianity, which in earlier times had addressed itself to the masses, and relied on the principle of liberty, now made its appeal to the rulers, and threw its mighty influence into the scale of authority. The barbarians, who possessed no books, no secular knowledge, no education, except in the schools of the clergy, and who had scarcely acquired the rudiments of religious instruction, turned with childlike attachment to men whose minds were stored with the knowledge of Scripture, of Cicero, of St. Augustine; and in the scanty world of their ideas, the Church was felt to be something infinitely vaster, stronger, holier than their newly founded states. The clergy supplied the means of conducting the new governments, and were made exempt from taxation, from the jurisdiction of the civil magistrate, and of the political administrator. They taught that power ought to be conferred by election; and the councils of Toledo furnished the framework of the parliamentary system of Spain, which is, by a long interval, the oldest in the world. But the monarchy of the Goths in Spain, as well as that of the Saxons in England, in both of which the nobles and the prelates surrounded the throne with the semblance of free institutions, passed away; and the people that prospered and overshadowed the rest were the Franks, who had no native nobility, whose law of succession to the crown became for one thousand years the fixed object of an unchanging superstition, and under whom the feudal system was developed to excess.

Feudalism made land the measure and the master of all things. Having no other source of wealth than the produce of the soil, men depended on the landlord for the means of escaping starvation; and thus his power became paramount over the liberty of the subject and the authority of the state. Every baron, said the French maxim, is sovereign in his own domain. The nations of the West lay between the competing tyrannies of local magnates and of absolute monarchs, when a force was brought upon the scene which proved for a time superior alike to the vassal and his lord.

In the days of the conquest, when the Normans destroyed the liberties of England, the rude institutions which had come with the Saxons, the Goths, and the Franks from the forests of Germany were suffering decay, and the new element of popular government afterwards supplied by the rise of towns and the formation of a middle class was not yet active. The only influence capable of resisting the feudal hierarchy was the ecclesiastical hierarchy; and they came into collision, when the process of feudalism threatened the independence of the Church by subjecting the prelates severally to that form of personal dependence on the kings which was peculiar to the Teutonic state.

To that conflict of four hundred years we owe the rise of civil liberty. If the Church had continued to buttress the thrones of the kings whom it anointed, or if the struggle had terminated speedily in an undivided victory, all Europe would have sunk down under a Byzantine or Muscovite despotism. For the aim of both contending parties was absolute authority. But although liberty was not the end for which they strove, it was the means by which the temporal and the spiritual power called the nations to their aid. The towns of Italy and Germany won their franchises, France got her states-general, and England her parliament out of the alternate phases of the contest; and as long as it lasted it prevented the rise of divine right. A disposition existed to regard the crown as an estate descending under the law of real property in the family that possessed it. But the authority of religion, and especially of the papacy, was thrown on the side that denied the indefeasible title of kings. In France what was afterwards called the Gallican theory maintained that the reigning house was above the law, and that the sceptre was not to pass away from it as long as there should be princes of the royal blood of St. Louis. But in other countries the oath of fidelity itself attested that it was conditional, and should be kept only during good behavior; and it was in conformity with the public law to which all monarchs were held subject, that King John was declared a rebel against the barons, and that the men who raised Edward III to the throne from which they had deposed his father invoked the maxim: *vox populi, vox dei.*

And this doctrine of the divine right of the people to raise up and pull down princes, after obtaining the sanctions of religion, was made to stand on broader grounds, and was strong enough to resist both Church and king. In the struggle between the house of Bruce and the house of Plantagenet for the possession of Scotland and Ireland, the English claim was backed by the censures of Rome. But the Irish and the Scots refused it, and the address in which the Scottish Parliament informed the pope of their resolution shows how firmly the popular doctrine had taken root. Speaking of Robert Bruce, they say: "Divine Providence, the laws and customs of the country, which we will defend till death, and the choice of the people, have made him our king. If he should ever betray his principles, and consent that we should be subjects of the English king, then we shall treat him as an enemy, as the subverter of our rights and his own, and shall elect another

in his place. We care not for glory or for wealth, but for that liberty which no true man will give up but with his life." This estimate of royalty was natural among men accustomed to see those whom they most respected in constant strife with their rulers. Gregory VII had begun the disparagement of civil authorities by saying that they are the work of the devil; and already in his time both parties were driven to acknowledge the sovereignty of the people, and appealed to it as the immediate source of power.

Two centuries later this political theory had gained both in definiteness and in force among the Guelphs, who were the Church party, and among the Ghibellines, or imperialists. Here are the sentiments of the most celebrated of all the Guelphic writers: "A king who is unfaithful to his duty forfeits his claim to obedience. It is not rebellion to depose him, for he is himself a rebel whom the nation has a right to put down. But it is better to abridge his power, that he may be unable to abuse it. For this purpose, the whole nation ought to have a share in governing itself; the constitution ought to combine a limited and elective monarchy, with an aristocracy of merit, and such an admixture of democracy as shall admit all classes to office, by popular election. No government has a right to levy taxes beyond the limit determined by the people. All political authority is derived from popular suffrage, and all laws must be made by the people or their representatives. There is no security for us as long as we depend on the will of another man." This language, which contains the earliest exposition of the Whig theory of the revolution, is taken from the works of St. Thomas Aquinas, of whom Lord Bacon says that he had the largest heart of the school divines. And it is worthwhile to observe that he wrote at the very moment when Simon de Montfort summoned the Commons; and that the politics of the Neapolitan friar are centuries in advance of the English statesman's.

The ablest writer of the Ghibelline party was Marsilius of Padua. "Laws," he said, "derive their authority from the nation, and are invalid without its assent. As the whole is greater than any part, it is wrong that any part should legislate for the whole; and as men are equal, it is wrong that one should be bound by laws made by another. But in obeying laws to which all men have agreed, all men, in reality, govern themselves. The monarch, who is instituted by the legislature to execute its will, ought to be armed with a force sufficient to coerce individuals, but not sufficient to control the majority of the people. He is responsible to the nation, and subject to the law; and the nation that appoints him, and assigns him his duties, has to see that he obeys the constitution, and has to dismiss him if he breaks it. The rights of citizens are independent of the faith they profess; and no man may be punished for his religion." This writer, who saw in some respects farther than Locke or Montesquieu, who, in regard to the sovereignty of the nation, representative government, the superiority of the legislature over the executive, and the liberty of conscience, had so firm a grasp of the principles that were to sway the modern world, lived in the reign of Edward II, five hundred and fifty years ago.

It is significant that these two writers should agree on so many of the fundamental points which have been, ever since, the topic of controversy; for they belonged to hostile schools, and one of them would have thought the other worthy of death. St. Thomas would have made the papacy control all Christian governments. Marsilius would have had the clergy submit to the law of the land; and would have

put them under restrictions both as to property and numbers. As the great debate went on, many things gradually made themselves clear, and grew into settled convictions. For these were not only the thoughts of prophetic minds that surpassed the level of contemporaries; there was some prospect that they would master the practical world. The ancient reign of the barons was seriously threatened. The opening of the East by the Crusades had imparted a great stimulus to industry. A stream set in from the country to the towns, and there was no room for the government of towns in the feudal machinery. When men found a way of earning a livelihood without depending for it on the good will of the class that owned the land, the landowner lost much of his importance, and it began to pass to the possessors of moveable wealth. The townspeople not only made themselves free from the control of prelates and barons, but endeavored to obtain for their own class and interest the command of the state.

The fourteenth century was filled with the tumult of this struggle between democracy and chivalry. The Italian towns foremost in intelligence and civilization, led the way with democratic constitutions of an ideal and generally an impracticable type. The Swiss cast off the yoke of Austria. Two long chains of free cities arose, along the valley of the Rhine, and across the heart of Germany. The citizens of Paris got possession of the king, reformed the state, and began their tremendous career of experiments to govern France. But the most healthy and vigorous growth of municipal liberties was in Belgium, of all countries on the continent, that which has been from immemorial ages the most stubborn in its fidelity to the principle of self-government. So vast were the resources concentrated in the Flemish towns, so widespread was the movement of democracy, that it was long doubtful whether the new interest would not prevail, and whether the ascendancy of the military aristocracy would not pass over to the wealth and intelligence of the men that lived by trade. But Rienzi, Marcel, Artevelde, and the other champions of the unripe democracy of those days, lived and died in vain. The upheaval of the middle class had disclosed the need, the passions, the aspirations of the suffering poor below; ferocious insurrections in France and England caused a reaction that retarded for centuries the readjustment of power, and the red specter of social revolution arose in the track of democracy. The armed citizens of Ghent were crushed by the French chivalry; and monarchy alone reaped the fruit of the change that was going on in the position of classes, and stirred the minds of men.

Looking back over the space of a thousand years, which we call the Middle Ages, to get an estimate of the work they had done, if not towards perfection in their institutions, at least towards attaining the knowledge of political truth, this is what we find: representative government, which was unknown to the ancients, was almost universal. The methods of election were crude; but the principle that no tax was lawful that was not granted by the class that paid it—that is, that taxation was inseparable from representation—was recognized, not as the privilege of certain countries, but as the right of all. Not a prince in the world, said Philip de Commines, can levy a penny without the consent of the people. Slavery was almost everywhere extinct; and absolute power was deemed more intolerable and more criminal than slavery. The right of insurrection was not only admitted but defined, as a duty sanctioned by religion. Even the principles of the Habeas Corpus Act, and the method of the income tax, was already known. The issue of ancient politics was an absolute state planted on slavery. The political produce of the Middle Ages was a system of states in which authority was restricted by the representation of powerful classes, by privileged associations, and by the acknowledgment of duties superior to those which are imposed by man.

As regards the realization in practice of what was seen to be good, there was almost everything to do. But the great problems of principle had been solved, and we come to the question—how *did* the sixteenth century husband the treasure which the Middle Ages had stored up? The most visible sign of the times was the decline of the religious influence that had reigned so long. Sixty years passed after the invention of printing, and thirty thousand books had issued from European presses, before anybody undertook to print the Greek Testament. In the days when every state made the unity of faith its first care, it came to be thought that the rights of men, and the duties of neighbors and of rulers towards them, varied according to their religion; and society did not acknowledge the same obligations to a Turk or a Jew, a pagan or a heretic, or a devil worshiper, as to an orthodox Christian. As the ascendancy of religion grew weaker, this privilege of treating its enemies on exceptional principles was claimed by the state for its own benefit; and the idea that the ends of government justify the means employed was worked into system by Machiavelli. He was an acute politician, sincerely anxious that the obstacles to the intelligent government of Italy should be swept away. It appeared to him that the most vexatious obstacle to intellect is conscience, and that the vigorous use of statecraft necessary for the success of difficult schemes would never be made if governments allowed themselves to be hampered by the precepts of the copy-book.

His audacious doctrine was avowed in the succeeding age by men whose personal character stood high. They saw that in critical times good men have seldom strength for their goodness, and yield to those who have grasped the meaning of the maxim that you cannot make an omelette if you are afraid to break the eggs. They saw that public morality differs from private, because no government can turn the other cheek or can admit that mercy is better than justice. And they could not define the difference or draw the limits of exception; or tell what other standard for a nation's acts there is than the judgment which heaven pronounces in this world by success.

Machiavelli's teaching would hardly have stood the test of parliamentary government, for public discussion demands at least the profession of good faith. But it gave an immense impulse to absolutism by silencing the consciences of very religious kings, and made the good and the bad very much alike. Charles V offered 5,000 crowns for the murder of an enemy. Ferdinand I and Ferdinand II, Henry III and Louis XIII each caused his most powerful subject to be treacherously dispatched. Elizabeth and Mary Stuart tried to do the same to each other. The way was paved for absolute monarchy to triumph over the spirit and institutions of a better age, not by isolated acts of wickedness, but by a studied philosophy of crime and so thorough a perversion of the moral sense that the like of it had not been seen since the Stoics reformed the morality of paganism.

The clergy, who had in so many ways served the cause of freedom during the prolonged strife against feudalism and slavery, were associated now with the interest of royalty. Attempts had been made to reform the Church on the constitutional model; they had failed, but they had united the hierarchy and the crown against the system of divided power as against a common enemy. Strong kings were able to bring the spirituality under subjection in France and Spain, in Sicily and in England. The absolute monarchy of France was built up in the two following centuries by twelve political cardinals. The kings of Spain obtained the same effect almost at a single stroke by reviving and appropriating to their own use the tribunal of the Inquisition, which had been growing obsolete but now served to arm them with terrors which effectually made them despotic. One generation beheld the change all over Europe, from the anarchy of the days of the Roses to the passionate submission, the gratified acquiescence in tyranny that marks the reign of Henry VIII and the kings of his time.

The tide was running fast when the Reformation began at Wittenberg, and it was to be expected that Luther's influence would stem the flood of absolutism. For he was confronted everywhere by the compact alliance of the Church with the state; and a great part of his country was governed by hostile potentates who were prelates of the court of Rome. He had, indeed, more to fear from temporal than from spiritual foes. The leading German bishops wished that the Protestant demands should be conceded; and the Pope himself vainly urged on the Emperor a conciliatory policy. But Charles V had outlawed Luther, and attempted to waylay him; and the dukes of Bavaria were active in beheading and burning his disciples, although the democracy of the towns generally took his side. But the dread of revolution was the deepest of his political sentiments; and the gloss by which the Guelphic divines had got over the passive obedience of the apostolic age was characteristic of that medieval method of interpretation which he rejected. He swerved for a moment in his later years; but the substance of his political teaching was eminently conservative, the Lutheran states became the stronghold of rigid immobility, and Lutheran writers constantly condemned the democratic literature that arose in the second age of the Reformation. For the Swiss reformers were bolder than the Germans in mixing up their cause with politics. Zurich and Geneva were republics, and the spirit of their governments influenced both Zwingli and Calvin.

Zwingli indeed did not shrink from the medieval doctrine that evil magistrates must be cashiered; but he was killed too early to act either deeply or permanently on the political character of Protestantism. Calvin, although a republican, judged that the people are unfit to govern themselves, and declared the popular assembly an abuse that ought to be abolished. He desired an aristocracy of the elect, armed with the means of punishing not only crime but vice and error. For he thought that the severity of the medieval laws was insufficient for the need of the times; and he favored the most irresistible weapon which the inquisitorial procedure put into the hand of the government, the right of subjecting prisoners to intolerable torture, not because they were guilty, but because their guilt could not be proved. His teaching, though not calculated to promote popular institutions, was so adverse to the authority of the surrounding monarchs, that he softened down the expression of his political views in the French edition of his *Institutes*.

The direct political influence of the Reformation effected less than has been supposed. Most states were strong enough to control it. Some, by intense exertion shut out the pouring flood. Others, with consummate skill, diverted it to their own uses. The Polish government alone at that time left it to its course. Scotland was the only kingdom in which the Reformation triumphed over the resistance of the state; and Ireland was the only instance where it failed, in spite of government support. But in almost every other case, both the princes that spread their canvas to the gale and those that faced it, employed the zeal, the alarm, the passions it aroused as instruments for the increase of power. Nations eagerly invested their rulers with every prerogative needed to preserve their faith, and all the care to keep Church and state asunder, and to prevent the confusion of their powers, which had been the work of ages, was renounced in the intensity of the crisis. Atrocious deeds were done, in which religious passion was often the instrument, but policy was the motive.

Fanaticism displays itself in the masses, but the masses were rarely fanaticized, and the crimes ascribed to it were commonly due to the calculations of dispassionate politicians. When the king of France undertook to kill all the Protestants, he was obliged to do it by his own agents. It was nowhere the spontaneous act of the population, and in many towns and in entire provinces the magistrates refused to obey. The motive of the court was so far from mere fanaticism that the queen immediately challenged Elizabeth to do the like to the English Catholics. Francis I and Henry II sent nearly a hundred Huguenots to the stake, but they were cordial and assiduous promoters of the Protestant religion in Germany. Sir Nicholas Bacon was one of the ministers who suppressed the Mass in England. Yet when the Huguenot refugees came over he liked them so little that he reminded Parliament of the summary way in which Henry V at Agincourt dealt with the Frenchmen who fell into his hands. John Knox thought that every Catholic in Scotland ought to be put to death, and no man ever had disciples of a sterner or more relentless temper. But his counsel was not followed.

All through the religious conflict policy kept the upper hand. When the last of the Reformers died, religion, instead of emancipating the nations, had become an excuse for the criminal art of despots. Calvin preached and Bellarmine lectured, but Machiavelli reigned. Before the close of the century three events occurred which mark the beginning of a momentous change. The massacre of St. Bartholomew convinced the bulk of Calvinists of the lawfulness of rebellion against tyrants, and they became advocates of that doctrine in which the bishop of Winchester had led the way, and which Knox and Buchanan had received, through their master at Paris, straight from the medieval schools. Adopted out of aversion to the king of France, it was soon put in practice against the king of Spain. The revolted Netherlands, by a solemn act, deposed Philip II, and made themselves independent under the prince of Orange, who had been, and continued to be, styled his lieutenant. Their example was important, not only because subjects of one religion deposed a monarch of another, for that had been seen in Scotland, but because, moreover, it put a republic in the place of a monarchy, and forced the public law of Europe to recognize the accomplished revolution. At the same time, the French Catholics, rising against Henry III, who was the most contemptible of tyrants, and against his heir, Henry of Navarre, who, as a Protestant, repelled the majority of the nation, fought for the same principles with sword and pen.

Many shelves might be filled with the books which came out in their defense during half a century, and they include the most comprehensive treatises on laws ever written. Nearly all are vitiated by the defect which disfigured political literature in the Middle Ages. That literature, as I have tried to show, is extremely remarkable, and its services in aiding human progress are very great. But from the death of St. Bernard until the appearance of Sir Thomas More's *Utopia,* there was hardly a writer who did not make his politics subservient to the interest of either pope or king. And those who came after the Reformation were always thinking of laws as they might affect Catholics or Protestants. Knox thundered against what he called the 'monstrous regiment of women,' because the queen went to Mass, and Mariana praised the assassin of Henry III because the king was in league with Huguenots. For the belief that it is right to murder tyrants, first taught among Christians, I believe, by John of Salisbury, the most distinguished English writer of the twelfth century, and confirmed by Roger Bacon, the most celebrated Englishman of the thirteenth, had acquired this time a fatal significance. Nobody sincerely thought of politics as a law for the just and the unjust, or tried to find out a sct of principles that should hold good alike under all changes of religion. Hooker's *Ecclesiastical Polity* stands almost alone among the works I am speaking of, and is still read with admiration by every thoughtful man as the earliest and one of the finest prose classics in our language. But though few of the others have survived, they continued to hand down masculine notions of limited authority and conditional obedience from the epoch of theory to generations of free men. Even the coarse violence of Buchanan and Boucher was a link in the chain of tradition that connects the Hildebrandine controversy with the Long Parliament, and St. Thomas with Edmund Burke.

That men should understand that governments do not exist by divine right, and that arbitrary government is the violation of divine right, was no doubt the medicine suited to the malady under which Europe languished. But although the knowledge of this truth might become an element of salutary destruction, it could give little aid to progress and reform. Resistance to tyranny implied no faculty of constructing a legal government in its place. Tyburn tree may be a useful thing, but it is better still that the offender should live for repentance and reformation. The principles which discriminate in politics between good and evil, and make states worthy to last, were not yet found.

The French philosopher Charron was one of the men least demoralized by party spirit, and least blinded by zeal for a cause. In a passage almost literally taken from St. Thomas, he describes our subordination under a law of nature, to which all legislation must conform; and he ascertains it not by the light of revealed religion, but by the voice of universal reason, through which God enlightens the consciences of men. Upon this foundation Grotius drew the lines of real political science. In gathering the materials of international law, he had to go beyond national treaties and denominational interests for a principle embracing all mankind. The principles of law must stand, he said, even if we suppose that there is no God. By these inaccurate terms he meant that they must be found independently of revelation. From that time it became possible to make politics a matter of principle and of conscience, so that men and nations differing in all other things could live in peace together, under the sanctions of a common law. Grotius himself used his discovery to little purpose, as he deprived it of immediate effect of admitting that the right to reign may be enjoyed as a freehold, subject to no conditions.

When Cumberland and Pufendorf unfolded the true significance of his doctrine, every settled authority, every triumphant interest recoiled aghast. None were willing to surrender advantages won by force or skill, because they might be in contradiction, not with the Ten Commandments but with the unknown code, which Grotius himself had not attempted to draw up, and touching which no two philosophers agreed. It was manifest that all persons who had learned that political science is an affair of conscience rather than of might or expediency, must regard their adversaries as men without principle, that the controversy between them would perpetually involve morality, and could not be governed by the plea of good intentions, which softens down the asperities of religious strife. Nearly all the greatest men of the seventeenth century repudiated the innovation. In the eighteenth, the two ideas of Grotius, that there are certain political truths, by which every state and every interest must stand or fall, and that society is knit together by a series of real and hypothetical contracts, became, in other hands, the lever that displaced the world. When, by what seemed the operation of an irresistible and constant law, royalty had prevailed over all enemies and all competitors, it became a religion. Its ancient rivals, the baron and the prelate, figured as supporters by its side. Year after year, the assemblies that represented the self-government of provinces and of privileged classes, all over the continent, met for the last time and passed away, to the satisfaction of the people, who had learned to venerate the throne as the constructor of their unity, the promoter of prosperity and power, the defender of orthodoxy, and the employer of talent.

The Bourbons, who had snatched the crown from a rebellious democracy, the Stuarts, who had come in as usurpers, set up the doctrine that states are formed by the valor, the policy, and the appropriate marriages of the royal family; that the king is consequently anterior to the people, that he is its maker rather than its handiwork, and reigns independently of consent. Theology followed up divine right with passive obedience. In the golden age of religious science, Archbishop Ussher, the most learned of Anglican prelates, and Bossuet, the ablest of the French, declared that resistance to kings is a crime and that they may lawfully employ compulsion against the faith of their subjects. The philosophers heartily supported the divines. Bacon fixed his hope of all human progress on the strong hand of kings. Descartes advised them to crush all those who might be able to resist their power. Hobbes taught that authority is always in the right. Pascal considered it absurd to reform laws, or to set up an ideal justice against actual force. Even Spinoza, who was a republican and a Jew, assigned to the state the absolute control of religion.

Monarchy exerted a charm over the imagination, so unlike the unceremonious spirit of the Middle Ages, that, on learning the execution of Charles I, men died of the shock; and the same thing occurred at the death of Louis XVI and of the duke of Enghein. The classic land of absolute monarchy was France. Richelieu held that it would be impossible to keep the people down if they were suffered to be well off. The chancellor. affirmed that France could not be governed without the right of arbitrary arrest and exile; and that in case of danger to the state it may be well that a hundred innocent men should perish. The minister of finance called it sedition to demand that the crown should keep faith. One who lived on intimate terms with Louis XIV says that even the slightest disobedience to the royal will is a crime

to be punished with death. Louis employed these precepts to their fullest extent. He candidly avows that kings are no more bound by the terms of a treaty than by the words of a compliment; and that there is nothing in the possession of their subjects which they may not lawfully take from them. In obedience to this principle, when Marshal Vauban, appalled by the misery of the people, proposed that all existing imposts should be repealed for a single tax that would be less onerous, the king took his advice, but retained all the old taxes while he imposed the new. With half the present population, he maintained an army of 450,000 men (nearly twice as large as that which the late Emperor Napoleon assembled to attack Germany). Meanwhile the people starved on grass. France, said Fénelon, is 'one enormous hospital.' French historians believe that in a single generation six millions of people died of want. It would be easy to find tyrants more violent, more malignant, more odious than Louis XIV, but there was not one who ever used his power to inflict greater suffering or greater wrong; and the admiration with which he inspired the most illustrious men of his time denotes the lowest depth to which the turpitude of absolutism has ever degraded the conscience of Europe.

The republics of that day were, for the most part, so governed as to reconcile men with the less opprobrious vices of monarchy. Poland was a state made up of centrifugal forces. What the nobles called liberty was the right of each of them to veto the acts of the diet, and to persecute the peasants on his estates—rights which they refused to surrender up to the time of the partition, and thus verified the warning of a preacher spoken long ago: "You will perish, not by invasion or war, but by your infernal liberties." Venice suffered from the opposite evil of excessive concentration. It was the most sagacious of governments, and would rarely have made mistakes if it had not imputed to others motives as wise as its own, and had taken account of passions and follies of which it had little cognizance. But the supreme power of the nobility had passed to a committee, from the committee to a council of ten, from the ten to three inquisitors of state; and in this intensely centralized form it became, about the year 1600, a frightful despotism. I have shown you how Machiavelli supplied the immoral theory needful for the consummation of royal absolutism; the absolute oligarchy of Venice required the same assurance against the revolt of conscience. It was provided by a writer as able as Machiavelli, who analyzed the wants and resources of aristocracy, and made known that its best security is poison. As late as a century ago, Venetian senators of honorable and even religious lives employed assassins for the public good with no more compunction than Philip II or Charles IX.

The Swiss cantons, especially Geneva, profoundly influenced opinion in the days preceding the French Revolution, but they had had no part in the earlier movement to inaugurate the reign of law. That honor belongs to the Netherlands, alone among the Commonwealths. They earned it, not by their form of government, which was defective and precarious, for the Orange party perpetually plotted against it, and slew the two most eminent of the republican statesmen, and William III himself intrigued for English aid to set the crown upon his head; but by the freedom of the press, which made Holland the vantage-ground from which, in the darkest hour of oppression, the victims of the oppressors obtained the ear of Europe. The ordinance of Louis XIV, that every French Protestant should imme-

diately renounce his religion, went out in the year in which James II became king. The Protestant refugees did what their ancestors had done a century before. They asserted the deposing power of subjects over rulers who had broken the original contract between them, and all the powers, excepting France, countenanced their argument, and sent forth William of Orange on that expedition which was the faint dawn of a brighter day.

It is to this unexampled combination of things on the continent, more than to her own energy, that England owes her deliverance. The efforts made by the Scots, by the Irish, and at last by the Long Parliament to get rid of the misrule of the Stuarts had been foiled, not by the resistance of monarchy, but by the helplessness of the republic. State and Church were swept away; new institutions were raised up under the ablest ruler that had ever sprung from a revolution; and England, seething with the toil of political thought, had produced at least two writers who in many directions saw as far and as clearly as we do now. But Cromwell's constitution was rolled up like a scroll; Harrington and Lilburne were laughed at for a time and forgotten; the country confessed the failure of its striving, disavowed its aims, and flung itself with enthusiasm, and without any effective stipulations, at the feet of a worthless king.

If the people of England had accomplished no more than this to relieve mankind from the pervading pressure of unlimited monarchy, they would have done more harm than good. By the fanatical treachery with which, violating the parliament and the law, they contrived the death of King Charles, by the ribaldry of the Latin pamphlet with which Milton justified the act before the world, by persuading the world that the republicans were hostile alike to liberty and to authority, and did not believe in themselves, they gave strength and reason to the current of royalism, which, at the Restoration, overwhelmed their work. If there had been nothing to make up for this defect of certainty and of constancy in politics England would have gone the way of other nations.

At that time there was some truth in the old joke which describes the English dislike of speculation by saying that all our philosophy consists of a short catechism in two questions: "What is mind? No matter. What is matter? Never mind." The only accepted appeal was to tradition. Patriots were in the habit of saying that they took their stand upon the ancient ways, and would not have the laws of England changed. To enforce their argument they invented a story that the constitution had come from Troy, and that the Romans had allowed it to subsist untouched. Such fables did not avail against Strafford; and the oracle of precedent sometimes gave responses adverse to the popular cause. In the sovereign question of religion, this was decisive, for the practice of the sixteenth century, as well as of the fifteenth, testified in favor of intolerance. By royal command, the nation had passed four times in one generation from one faith to another, with a facility that made a fatal impression on Laud. In a country that had proscribed every religion in turn, and had submitted to such a variety of penal measures against Lollard and Arian, against Augsburg and Rome, it seemed there could be no danger in cropping the ears of a Puritan.

But an age of stronger conviction had arrived; and men resolved to abandon the ancient ways that led to the scaffold and the rack, and to make the wisdom of their ancestors and the statutes of the land bow before an unwritten law. Religious liberty had been the dream of great Christian writers in the age of Constantine and Valentinian, a dream never wholly realized in the empire, and rudely dispelled when the barbarians found that it exceeded the resources of their art to govern civilized populations of another religion, and unity of worship was imposed by laws of blood and by theories more cruel than the laws. But from St. Athanasius and St. Ambrose down to Erasmus and More, each age heard the protest of earnest men in behalf of the liberty of conscience, and the peaceful days before the Reformation were full of promise that it would prevail.

In the commotion that followed, men were glad to get tolerated themselves by way of privilege and compromise, and willingly renounced the wider application of the principle. Socinus was the first who, on the ground that Church and state ought to be separated, required universal toleration. But Socinus disarmed his own theory, for he was a strict advocate of passive obedience.

The idea that religious liberty is the generating principle of civil, and that civil liberty is the necessary condition of religious, was a discovery reserved for the seventeenth century. Many years before the names of Milton and Taylor, of Baxter and Locke were made illustrious by their partial condemnation of intolerance, there were men among the Independent congregations who grasped with vigor and sincerity the principle that it is only by abridging the authority of states that the liberty of churches can be assured. The great political idea, sanctifying freedom and consecrating it to God, teaching men to treasure the liberties of others as their own, and to defend them for the love of justice and charity more than as a claim of right, has been the soul of what is great and good in the progress of the last two hundred years. The cause of religion, even under the unregenerate influence of worldly passion, had as much to do as any clear notions of policy in making this country the foremost of the free. It had been the deepest current in the movement of 1641, and it remained the strongest motive that survived the reaction of 1660.

The greatest writers of the Whig party, Burke and Macaulay, constantly represented the statesmen of the revolution as the legitimate ancestors of modern liberty. It is humiliating to trace a political lineage to Algernon Sidney, who was the paid agent of the French king; to Lord Russell, who opposed religious toleration at least as much as absolute monarchy; to Shaftesbury, who dipped his hands in the innocent blood shed by the perjury of Titus Oates; to Halifax, who insisted that the plot must be supported even if untrue; to Marlborough, who sent his comrades to perish on an expedition which he had betrayed to the French; to Locke, whose notion of liberty involves nothing more spiritual than the security of property, and is consistent with slavery and persecution; or even to Addison, who conceived that the right of voting taxes belonged to no country but his own. Defoe affirms that from the time of Charles II to that of George I he never knew a politician who truly held the faith of either party; and the perversity of the statesmen who led the assault against the later Stuarts threw back the cause of progress for a century.

When the purport of the secret treaty became suspected by which Louis XIV pledged himself to support Charles II with an army for the destruction of parliament, if Charles would overthrow the Anglican Church, it was found necessary to make concession to the popular alarm. It was proposed that whenever James should succeed, great part of the royal prerogative and patronage should be transferred to parliament. At the same time, the disabilities of Nonconformists and Catholics would have been removed. If the Limitation Bill, which Halifax supported with signal ability, had passed, the monarchical constitution would have advanced, in the seventeenth century, farther than it was destined to do until the second quarter of the nineteenth. But the enemies of James, guided by the prince of Orange, preferred a Protestant king who should be nearly absolute, to a constitutional king who should be Catholic. The scheme failed. James succeeded to a power which, in more cautious hands, would have been practically uncontrolled, and the storm that cast him down gathered beyond the sea.

By arresting the preponderance of France, the revolution of 1688 struck the first real blow at continental despotism. At home it relieved dissent, purified justice, developed the national energies and resources, and ultimately, by the Act of Settlement, placed the crown in the gift of the people. But it neither introduced nor determined any important principle, and, that both parties might be able to work together, it left untouched the fundamental question between Whig and Tory. For the divine right of kings is established, in the words of Defoe, the divine right of freeholders; and their domination extended for seventy years, under the authority of John Locke, the philosopher of government by the gentry. Even Hume did not enlarge the bounds of his ideas; and his narrow materialistic belief in the connection between liberty and property captivated even the bolder mind of Fox.

By this idea that the powers of government ought to be divided according to their nature, and not according to the division of classes, which Montesquieu took up and developed with consummate talent, Locke is the originator of the long reign of English institutions in foreign lands. And his doctrine of resistance, or, as he finally termed it, the appeal to heaven, ruled the judgment of Chatham at a moment of solemn transition in the history of the world. Our parliamentary system, managed by the great revolution families, was a contrivance by which electors were compelled, and legislators were induced to vote against their convictions; and the intimidation of the constituencies was rewarded by the corruption of their representatives. About the year 1770 things had been brought back, by indirect ways, nearly to the condition which the revolution had been designed to remedy for ever. Europe seemed incapable of becoming the home of free states. It was from America that the plain ideas that men ought to mind their own business, and that the nation is responsible to heaven for the acts of the state—ideas long locked in the breast of solitary thinkers, and hidden among Latin folios—burst forth like a conqueror upon the world they were destined to transform, under the title of the 'rights of man.' Whether the British legislature had a constitutional right to tax a subject colony was hard to say, by the letter of the law. The general presumption was immense on the side of authority; and the world believed that the will of the constituted ruler ought to be supreme, and not the will of the subject people. Very few bold writers went so far as to say that lawful power may be resisted in cases of extreme necessity. But the colonizers of America, who had gone forth not in search of gain, but to escape from laws under which other Englishmen were content to live, were so sensitive even to appearances that the blue laws of Connecticut forbade men to walk to church within ten feet of their wives. And the proposed tax, of only £12,000 a year, might have been easily borne. But the reasons why Edward I and his council were not allowed to tax England were reasons why George III and his parliament should not tax America. The dispute involved a principle, namely, the right of controlling government. Furthermore, it involved the conclusion that the parliament brought together by a derisive election had no just right over the unrepresented nation, and it called on the people of England to take back its power. Our best statesmen saw that whatever might be the law, the rights of the nation were at stake. Chatham, in speeches better remembered than any that have been delivered in parliament, exhorted America to be firm. Lord Camden, the late chancellor, said: "Taxation and representation are inseparably united. God hath joined them. No British parliament can separate them."

From the elements of that crisis Burke built up the noblest political philosophy in the world. "I do not know the method," said he, "of drawing up an indictment against a whole people. The natural rights of mankind are indeed sacred things, and if any public measure is proved mischievously to affect them, the objection ought to be fatal to that measure, even if no charter at all could be set up against it. Only a sovereign reason, paramount to all forms of legislation and administration, should dictate." In this way, just a hundred years ago, the opportune reticence, the politic hesitancy of European statesmanship, was at last broken down; and the principle gained ground, that a nation can never abandon its fate to an authority it cannot control. The Americans placed it at the foundation of their new government. They did more; for having subjected all civil authorities to the popular will, they surrounded the popular will with restrictions that the British legislature would not endure.

During the revolution in France the

example of England, which had been held up so long, could not for a moment compete with the influence of a country whose institutions were so wisely framed to protect freedom even against the perils of democracy. When Louis Philippe became king, he assured the old republican, Lafayette, that what he had seen in the United States had convinced him that no government can be so good as a republic. There was a time in the presidency of Monroe, about fifty-five years ago, which men still speak of as "the era of good feeling," when most of the incongruities that had come down from the Stuarts had been reformed, and the motives of later divisions were yet inactive. The causes of old-world trouble —popular ignorance, pauperism, the glaring contrast between rich and poor, religious strife, public debts, standing armies and war—were almost unknown. No other age or country had solved so successfully the problems that attend the growth of free societies, and time was to bring no further progress.

But I have reached the end of my time, and have hardly come to the beginning of my task. In the ages of which I have spoken, the history of freedom was the history of the thing that was not. But since the Declaration of Independence, or, to speak more justly, since the Spaniards, deprived of their king, made a new government for themselves, the only known forms of liberty, republics and constitutional monarchy, have made their way over the world. It would have been interesting to trace the reaction of America on the monarchies that achieved its independence; to see how the sudden rise of political economy suggested the idea of applying the methods of science to the art of government; how Louis XVI, after confessing that despotism was useless, even to make men happy by compulsion, appealed to the nation to do what was beyond his skill, and thereby resigned his sceptre to the middle class, and the intelligent men of France, shuddering at the awful recollections of their own experience, struggled to shut out the past, that they might deliver their children from the prince of the world and rescue the living from the clutch of the dead, until the finest opportunity ever given to the world was thrown away, because the passion for equality made vain the hope of freedom.

And I should have wished to show you that the same deliberate rejection of the moral code which smoothed the paths of absolute monarchy and of oligarchy, signalized the advent of the democratic claim to unlimited power— that one of its leading champions avowed the design of corrupting the moral sense of men in order to destroy the influence of religion, and a famous apostle of enlightenment and toleration wished that the last king might be strangled with the entrails of the last priest. I would have tried to explain the connection between the doctrine of Adam Smith, that labor is the original source of all wealth, and the conclusion that the producers of wealth virtually compose the nation, by which Sieyes subverted historic France; and to show that Rousseau's definition of the social compact as a voluntary association of equal partners conducted Marat, by short and unavoidable stages, to declare that the poorer classes were absolved, by the law of self-preservation, from the conditions of a contract which awarded to them misery and death; that they were at war with society, and had a right to all they could get by exterminating the rich, and that their inflexible theory of equality, the chief legacy of the revolution, together with the avowed inadequacy of economic science to grapple with problems of the poor, revived the idea of renovating society on the principle of self-sacrifice, which had been the generous aspiration of the Essenes and the early Christians, of fathers and canonists and friars, of Erasmus, the most celebrated precursor of the reformation, of Sir Thomas More, its most illustrious victim, and of Fénelon, the most popular of bishops, but which, during the forty years of its revival, has been associated with envy and hatred and bloodshed and is now the most dangerous enemy lurking in our path.

Last, and most of all, having told so much of the unwisdom of our ancestors, having exposed the sterility of the convulsion that burned what they adored, and made the sins of the republic mount up as high as those of the monarchy, having shown that legitimacy, which repudiated the revolution, and imperialism, which crowned it, were but disguises of the same element of violence and wrong, I should have wished, in order that my address might not break off without a meaning or a moral to relate by whom, and in what connection, the true law of the formation of free states was recognized, and how that discovery, closely akin to those which, under the names of development, evolution, and continuity, have given a new and deeper method to other sciences, solved the ancient problem between stability and change, and determined the authority of tradition on the progress of thought; how that theory, which Sir James Mackintosh expressed by saying that constitutions are not made, but grow; the theory that custom and the national qualities of the governed, and not the will of the government, are the makers of the law; and therefore that the nation, which is the source of its own organic institution, should be charged with the perpetual custody of their integrity, and with the duty of bringing the form into harmony with the spirit, was made, by the singular co-operation of the purest conservative intellect with

red-handed revolution, of Niebuhr with Mazzini, to yield the idea of nationality, which, far more than the idea of liberty, has governed the movement of the present age.

I do not like to conclude without inviting attention to the impressive fact that so much of the hard fighting, the thinking, the enduring that has contributed to the deliverance of man from the power of man, has been the work of our countrymen, and of their descendants in other lands. We have had to contend, as much as any people, against monarchs of strong will and of resources secured by their foreign possession, against men of rare capacity, against whole dynasties of born tyrants. And yet that proud prerogative stands out on the background of our history. Within a generation of the conquest, the Normans were compelled to recognize, in some grudging measure, the claims of the English people. When the struggle between Church and state extended to England, our churchmen learned to associate themselves with the popular cause; and, with few exceptions, neither the hierarchical spirit of the foreign divines, nor the monarchical bias peculiar to the French, characterized the writers of the English school. The civil law, transmitted from the degenerate empire to be the common prop of absolute power, was excluded from England. Canon law was restrained, and this country never admitted the Inquisition, nor fully accepted the use of torture which invested continental royalty with so many terrors. At the end of the Middle Ages foreign writers acknowledged our superiority, and pointed to these causes. After that, our gentry maintained the means of local self-government such as no other country possessed. Divisions in religion forced toleration. The confusion of the common law taught the people that their best safeguard was the independence and the integrity of the judges.

All these explanations lie on the surface, and are as visible as the protecting ocean; but they can only be successive effects of a constant cause which must lie in the same native qualities of perseverance, moderation, individuality, and the manly sense of duty, which give to the English race its supremacy in the stern art of labor, which has enabled it to thrive as no other can on inhospitable shores, and which (although no great people has less of the bloodthirsty craving for glory and an army of 50,000 English soldiers has never been seen in battle) caused Napoleon to exclaim, as he rode away from Waterloo, "It has always been the same since Crécy."

Therefore, if there is reason for pride in the past, there is more for hope in the time to come. Our advantages increase, while other nations fear their neighbors or covet their neighbors' goods. Anomalies and defects there are, fewer and less intolerable, if not less flagrant than of old.

But I have fixed my eyes on the spaces that heaven's light illuminates, that I may not lay too heavy a strain on the indulgence with which you have accompanied me over the dreary and heart-breaking course by which men have passed to freedom; and because the light that has guided us is still unquenched, and the causes that have carried us so far in the van of free nations have not spent their power; because the story of the future is written in the past, and that which hath been is the same thing that shall be.

22. *Henry Edward Cardinal Manning: Hindrances to the Spread of the Catholic Church in England, 17 July - 30 August 1890*

From Edmund S. Purcell, *Life of Cardinal Manning* (London: Macmillan and Co., 1896), pp. 773-96.

THE Catholic religion has existed in England from the foundation of the hierarchy of St. Gregory the Great. I set aside the remnants of British Christianity wrecked by the Saxons, which were either absorbed in the Church of St. Augustine or died out in Wales.

But the Catholic Church was extinguished when Elizabeth destroyed the hierarchy. The religion survived, and a number of priests, but the Church was gone. It was long without a bishop. Then it had a vicar-apostolic for England and Scotland; then for long years no bishop at all. Then a vicar-apostolic or two, then four and in this century eight; then at last the hierarchy of Pius IX. From that Michaelmas Day 1850, dates the Catholic Church in England, after three hundred years of ruin.

The effect of this interval of desolation has been the loss of the English people. The people of Ireland have been sustained in their faith because the succession of their bishops and pastors has never been interrupted. But for this unbroken and watchful pastoral care millions would have fallen away as in England.

If it be answered that the persecution of the civil power fell more heavily on England than on Ireland, the answer is at once easy. The persecution fell first on England, but it fell more heavily and for a longer time on Ireland. In England it had ceased by the reign of James I, or at least of Charles I. In Ireland it continued down to the atrocities of Cromwell, and even into the time of Charles II, in whose reign Archbishop Plunket was martyred at Tyburn. No, this is no answer. The Catholic faith lived on in England secretly all over the land in great multitudes of individuals and of families, even to the time of William III. In every county of England many of the chief families remained Catholic. They had their chaplains to keep their faith alive. But the multitude of the poor had no pastor. Their faith died out. At the end of the last century, Burke put the number of Catholics in England at 30,000 or 36,000. No doubt they were chiefly of English blood. The great Irish immigration had not yet begun.

Neither is it true that it was impossible to restore Catholic bishops in England, because of the persecution of Government. In Tierney's edition of Dod's *History* there is evidence to show that under the two first Stuarts the government would not have prevented the consecration of bishops, provided that they did not assume the titles of the Anglican sees. At one time a consent was on the point of being granted, when some Catholic false brother told the government that the plan was to assume the title of York.

Moreover, if priests could come into England, why not bishops? If they were to be hung, drawn, and quartered, why not a bishop as well as a priest? The power of confirming and ordaining was not more terrible to the civil power than the power of saying Mass. The extinction of the episcopate destroyed the priesthood.

I. In 1848 I was in Rome and read Gioberti's *Primato degli Italiani.* In describing England and its religion he says that the Anglican clergy are "un clero colto e civile."

As to culture they certainly have a literary and scientific culture, more general and more advanced than the body of our priests; sacred science and theology hardly exist among them. Here and there only such men as Lightfoot and Westcott are to be found. Nevertheless they are literary: history, constitutional law, and experience in politics they have very generally. Moreover, they have an interest in public affairs, in the politics and welfare of the country. They are therefore *civiles.* They share and promote the civil life of the people. It is here that we are wanting and mischievously wanting.

The long persecution of the Catholic Church by the laws of England has alienated the hearts of Catholics from the public and political life of England. Till fifty years ago they were legally *ex-lex.* The law is changed, but not the habit of mind formed by it. *Ecclesia patria nostra.* Catholics have not only been alienated from public life, but have been tempted to think that patriotism is hardly reconcilable with Catholic fidelity. Penal laws are gone, but social ostracism still exists. It is dying, but to this day hardly a Catholic can get to parliament. No doubt it will die out, but not until we have a priesthood *colto e civile,* for as the priest so is the people. *Sicut sacerdos, sic populus.* The 200,000 English Catholics have much of John Bull in them, but the million of our people are born into an animosity against Queen Elizabeth, Cromwell, and William III. It is with difficulty that our people will petition parliament for anything. Once it was my fate to ask the people at St. Mary's to sign a petition to parliament. The petition lay for signature in the school next to my house. I found that a young Irishman had emptied the ink-bottle over it as a protest against parliament.

By the law of nature a people grows up into social and civil life on the soil where they are born. By the sin and persecution of England this has never been true of the people of Ireland. They are the most Christian people on the face of the earth. But not the most civilized in Gioberti's sense. Christianity is their civilization, and before God it is the highest, but for this world it is not so. We have a million of people, priests and faithful of Irish blood, faith, and civilization in England, and they are not only alienated from our laws and legislature, but would upset the ink-bottle over the statute book. So long as this habit of mind lasts we shall never have a civil priesthood; and so long as our priesthood is not civil it will be confined to the sacristy as in France, not by a hostile public opinion, but by our own incapacity to mix in the civil life of the country; and this incapacity hitherto has sprung from hostility, suspicion, and fear. A capacity for civil and public action needs, of course, a training and education, but it springs from a love of our country. The Irish have this intensely for Ireland, but can hardly have it as yet for England. Many English Catholics, also, from religious prejudice are quite as incapable and useless.

In truth, the whole civil and political life of England is open to us if we know how to enter and how to bear ourselves. Our faith must go with us and govern us everywhere, but except on the rarest occasions it need not be proclaimed. If such occasion arise let it be done in an open and manly way, and not only no offense is given or taken, but confidence and respect are notably increased. In my forty years in London I have had all manner of proof of what I write.

The dictum of Terence: "Homo sum et humani nihil a me alienum puto" is not repealed by "Thou shalt love thy neighbor as thyself." It is quickened, enforced, extended, and elevated. Everything, therefore, that affects the human sufferings and state of the people, it is the duty of every civilized man to note

and tend, much more of every Christian man, and above all of every Catholic man and woman, and emphatically of every priest and bishop. We cannot multiply loaves or heal lepers as our Lord did, by which the people were won to follow and learn of him, but we can be prompt and foremost in working with all who are laboring to relieve every form of human suffering, sorrow, and misery. If we come forward gladly and usefully the people of this country are visibly glad to receive us among them.

July 17

II. A still greater obstacle to the spread of the faith is the shallowness of our preaching. This appears to me to come, first, from a want of wise choice of the subjects we preach upon; and secondly, from a shallow mode of treatment.

As to the choice of subjects: compare the Epistles of St. Paul with a volume of modern sermons. The chief and prominent topics of St. Paul are—God, the Incarnation, the Holy Ghost, that is the eternal truths from which all other truths descend. These are always present. Whatever details follow, they are as consequence from the theology, which is always present as the sun at noonday. St. Paul tells the Corinthians that he knew nothing among them but "Jesus Christ, and him crucified." This truth contains and justifies the whole faith and piety of the Gospel. But how often do we hear it preached upon? If the great truths are not perpetually held up, all consequent truths seem to be arbitrary and mere assertion; e.g., the title "Mother of God" is incomprehensible without the explicit knowledge of the Incarnation, and the Incarnation itself without the explicit knowledge of the holy Trinity. A French priest of Pontigny published a book on "The Deified *Soul*" of our Lord, because he had found the Appolinarian heresy so widely held by pious Catholics. The articles of the Apostolic Creed ought to be so continually held up before the intelligence of the faithful that all other subjects, such as the dignity and sanctification of the Blessed Virgin, the real and substantial presence of our Lord in the Blessed Sacrament, may be seen to be direct and evident consequences. There is also a majesty and greatness in these divine and eternal realities that subdue and attract the intellect and conscience. It would seem inevitable that our preachers should preach the Gospel in all its length and truth and depth and height.

The confraternities of the Sacred Heart and the Most Precious Blood, the devotion of the Five Sacred Wounds, the mysteries of the Rosary and the Crucifix, all are the Gospel in its fullness. So also the work of the Holy Ghost, the Sanctifier and the Absolver, with the Sacrament of Penance, enable us to preach and to out-preach all Evangelists, Methodists, and Salvationists that were ever made. Why then do we not draw men as Spurgeon and "General" Booth or Hugh Price Hughes? I am afraid that there are two obvious reasons. We choose our topics unwisely, and we are not on fire with the love of God and of souls.

Nevertheless, when we give retreats or missions our priests can preach the eternal truths and the gospel as fully and as powerfully as anybody. But why reserve these vital and sovereign truths to once a year? Surely they ought to be proclaimed "upon the housetops." If they were, the English people would feel that we are more scriptural and more evangelical than their own preachers. When we preach pieties and controversies it does not touch their souls. They are neither won nor moved by us. But surely we ought to win and move, and draw and soften the souls of men as our Lord did, and by the same truths. His preaching of the eter-nal truth was "as fire, and as the hammer that breaketh the rocks in pieces." So also was the preaching of the apostles, when they preached in the name of Jesus. This preaching converted the world, and no other will convert England. The English people as a whole, still believe in our Lord, his love, his passion, his absolution, his most precious blood—and also in repentance, grace and conversion. Why do not we meet these truths in their minds and the needs of their souls, by offering to them all these things in greater freshness and beauty? They come to hear us hoping for these things, and they go empty away, saying that our preaching does not come home to them, and is not what they need. When we have got them to confession we can teach the rosaries and the use of holy water.

July 19

Another cause of our shallowness is our shallow treatment of the subject we have chosen.

No doubt overwork is the reason with some. But a priest who is overworked in the saving of souls can never be much at a loss to preach the Gospel. He is always habitually speaking of God, his will, his kingdom and he has only to think aloud. Our difficulty is in ourselves. It is what we are that preaches, and we are not only what we know but what we feel, what we realize, what by experience has become a part of ourselves. Every man speaks readily of that which chiefly fills his mind. If we lived more for God, with God, and in God, we should have little difficulty of speaking about him. But is this true of us? Even good priests preach daily: and choose dogmatic or moral subjects rather than mystical or ascetic. By mystical I do not mean in the sense of St. Teresa's visions—but on such texts as *"Quam magna multitudo,"* etc., or *"Gustate et videte quo-*

niam suavis est Dominus." Is not this because our wells are shallow, or dry?

Another cause is hurry and haste. I have known men who have not even chosen their subject or their text till they are on their way to the Church. Surely this is tempting God, if not doing his work deceitfully. Others again take the first subject that comes to their mind, or that comes most easily to them because they have so often talked about it. But surely we ought first to think what our people most need.

III. A third hindrance to the spread of the faith is the reaction against the popular use of the holy Scriptures—I say reaction because it has followed and been caused by the profane and heretical abuse of the holy Scriptures by the so-called Protestants. St. Teresa said that one of the chief causes of evil in her day was the ignorance of holy Scripture. It is certainly so among us. It lowers the standard of Christian life and aspiration. The Scriptures are the voice of the Divine Spirit, and they that know them aspire after a higher life. The standard of society, and even of good people is the human spirit at best, and its standard is immensely below the standard of the divine.

This lowers the standard of our preachers and confessors. The law of liberty is the most constraining we have to aim at perfection. It is used to sanction everything which is not intrinsically sinful. All things are lawful to me, but not all things are expedient or edifying, but we must not limit human liberty, and therefore what is expedient and edifying is not of obligation. This gospel of narrowness and illiberality is in the ascendant. Some have been found to say that to keep souls out of mortal sin is all that secular priests can do. Many of us, I fear, have earned this rebuke.

IV. A fourth hindrance is the unconsciousness of the hereditary Catholic of the spiritual state of the English people.

They and their forefathers have until 1829 been so shut out of the society and life of the English people, and so thrown in upon themselves, and so wounded by the pride, suspicion, and religious prejudice of Englishmen, that they have been always in an antagonistic attitude of mind, bitter and hardly charitable.

They have, therefore, held with all rigor the axiom *extra ecclesiam nulla salus*. They have believed Protestants as a whole to be without faith or baptism; or even if baptized, to be none the better. This has so possessed even priests, that I have known instances of priests refusing to receive a convert into the Church; and also of a priest who said, "Thank God, I never received a convert into the Church." They supposed us (Anglicans) to be impostors, or to have worldly motives, as we did when Jews came to be received. This temper is now happily passing away.

It is a strange state of mind, for they could not help knowing that the great majority of the English people are baptized, and are therefore elevated to the supernatural order. If they live in charity with God and man, their baptism would save them; if they have forfeited their union with God by charity, nevertheless, they are still in the supernatural order by faith and hope. And who can limit the grace of God? Nineveh repented and was spared. Therefore, not only the time, but the grace of repentance was given to Nineveh. If Tyre and Sidon had repented they might have been saved, therefore repentance was possible to them, but repentance is impossible without the grace of repentance.

I have found among hereditary Catholics a belief that the English people are without faith, without Christian doctrine, without means of contrition, and that, therefore, the hope of their salvation is most uncertain. This error paralyzes their hopefulness, and without hope men do little. How men that have read the treatise of grace can believe such things I cannot tell. But I see that as soon as they come to know the singular goodness and piety of non-Catholics, they swing round into the other extreme, and believe that all religions are the same. This seems to me to be Scylla and Charybdis of no hope and false hope: both very mischievous, hindering zeal and breeding laxity.

1) I have found not only laymen, but priests ignore absolutely the fact that the greater part of the English people are baptized, and therefore are in the supernatural state of grace.
2) They take for granted that they have lost their baptismal grace by mortal sin.
3) And that therefore, as they have not the sacrament of Penance they have no means of rising again to the grace of Baptism.
4) That for this reason their life is without merit.
5) And their salvation most uncertain.

I do not believe one of these propositions to be true, and I am convinced that no one ever believes them without being checked in his action, and chilled in his charity towards the non-Catholic people of England. What I believe in this matter may be seen in a sermon in my old Anglican fourth volume, called "Christ preached every way a cause of joy," which has been read without censure by two Catholic theologians; and also in a letter to Dr. Pusey on "The Workings of the Spirit in the Church of England," in "England and Christendom."

Both these arguments are founded on Catholic theology; and especially on the *systema morale* of St. Alphonsus, and on moral theologians as Pichler and others.

Our Lord said, "I am come that they might have life, and that they may have it more abundantly," by which I understand that the fullness of grace in his precious blood does not revoke or take away, or diminish in a jot or tittle, the grace of salvation under the old Law of Israel, or of nature.

And what was this? Suarez calls it *gratia naturalis,* i.e., the grace of the Holy Ghost in the state of nature.

1) That every man born of Adam is born into a world redeemed in the blood of the Lamb slain from the beginning of the world.
2) That to all men, i.e., to all mankind, *etiam infidelibus et haereticis* is given grace sufficient *ad evitandum mortem eternam.*
3) That the *virtus penitentiae* is universal, from the fall of man.
4) That to those to whom the sacrament of Penance is physically or morally impossible the virtue of penance is sufficient. And to us the sacrament, without virtues, is not sufficient.
5) That to those who use the grace they have received an *augmentum atque proportionatum* is given.
6) That God would have all men to be saved, and to come to the knowledge of the truth.
7) That to all who seek the truth is given so much as will bring them to the soul of the Church, if not to its visible body.
8) That no member of the soul dying in union with God can be lost. "No penitent soul can perish, and no soul that loves God can be lost."
9) Will any one affirm that souls born again of water and the Holy Ghost cannot be penitent or cannot love God?

10) Now a life of forty years out of the Church has taught me what I have written.

11) And the experience of a priest's life of nearly forty years has confirmed all I have written.

August 1

My experience among those who are out of the Church confirms all I have written of the doctrines of grace. I have intimately known souls living by faith, hope and charity, and the sanctifying grace with the seven gifts of the Holy Ghost, in humility, absolute purity of life and heart, in constant meditation on holy Scripture, unceasing prayer, complete self-denial, personal work among the poor; in a word, living lives of visible sanctification, as undoubtedly the work of the Holy Ghost as I have ever seen. I have seen this in whole families, rich and poor, and in all conditions of life.

Moreover, I have received into the Church I do not know how many souls in whom I can find no mortal sin. They are evidently in the grace of their Baptism. This same is the testimony of priests whom I have consulted; and it was the unanimous testimony of the Jesuits in Stonyhurst, in 1848, as Fr. Cardella, I think if I remember right, told me. How with these facts can men go on speaking of those who are out of the Church in England as in the state of nature and in bad faith, and to be avoided as immoral? There are no doubt such persons among them. But what is the state of France, Italy, Spain, South America? All the light and grace of the Catholic Church is in vain for multitudes in those Catholic nations.

And further, all the great works of charity in England have had their beginning out of the Church, for instance the abolition of the slave trade and of slavery; and the persevering protest of the Anti-Slavery Society. Not a Catholic name so far as I know shared in this. France, Portugal, and Brazil have been secretly or openly slave trading or, till now even, slave holding. The whole temperance movement. It was a Quaker that made Fr. Mathew a total abstainer. Catholic Ireland and the Catholics of England, until now, have done little for temperance. The Anglican and Dissenting ministers are far more numerously total abstainers than our priests. The act of parliament to protect animals from cruelty was carried by a non-Catholic Irishman. The Anti-Vivisection Act also. Both are derided to my knowledge among Catholics. The acts to protect children from cruelty were the work of Dissenters. On these three societies there is hardly a Catholic name. On the last, mine was for long the only one. So again in the uprising against the horrible depravity which destroys young girls—multitudes of ours—I was literally denounced by Catholics, not one came forward. If it was ill done why did nobody try to mend it? I might go on. There are endless works for the protection of shop assistants, overworked railway and tram men, women and children ground down by sweaters, and driven by starvation wage upon the streets. Not one of the works in their behalf were started by us, hardly a Catholic name is to be found on their reports. Surely we are in the sacristy. It is not that our Catholics deliberately refuse, but partly they do not take pains to know, partly they are prejudiced. "Can any good thing come out of Nazareth?" and finally they live on easily, unconscious that Lazarus lies at their gate full of sores.

I pray God that when a better man comes into my place he will go and see with his own eyes that my place may not remain empty.

If he will do this the English people will know him and trust him; and seek his presence and help in their own works with a sensible confidence and good will. Surely we are bound to work with them in everything that is not contrary to faith or morals. The millions outside the Established Church draw away from them from social jealousy. They draw to us because we have nothing to do with the state of the world. Because in fact we are Dissenters and the chief of Nonconformists.

August 3

V. A fifth hindrance is what I, for want of a better name, must call sacramentalism. Priests have a danger of becoming Mass-priests, or sacrament-mongers. They possess, by Divine commission, the power of administering sacraments which confer grace *ex opere operato,* to which they can add nothing, nor can their own unworthiness hinder its effect. It is easily possible for a priest, *citra peccatum mortale commissum,* to neglect his meditation, examination of conscience, and spiritual exercises, and therefore to become unspiritual and dry. Still he administers sacraments exactly and mechanically. He has committed no mortal sin. And a thousand venial sins are venial still; but the man is dry, and everybody feels it when he preaches or is in the confessional, or by a deathbed, or in a house of sorrow. Now, under the old law the subjective piety was everything. Both priest and people in this were alike. But there was great discipline to train the priests to higher subjective piety, and a still higher subjective fitness was required for a priest ministering in his course in the temple. Surely this subjective fitness is raised to a higher degree and standard under the new law of grace. The objective efficacy of sacraments was not intended to dispense with the subjective fitness either in the minister or in the receiver. All that was required for the *sacramentalia* is *a fortiori* required for sacraments. A Christian priest is bound

to be all that a Jewish priest was bound to be, and much more as the substance exceeds the shadow. When a priest went in to minister in his course he was forbidden to drink wine or strong drink. But a Christian priest goes in to minister every morning in the holy Mass. I do not say that he is by this type forbidden to drink wine. But the precept becomes a strong counsel.

August 5

VI. A sixth hindrance is what I may call officialism, that is a dependence for our work not on our subjective fitness, but upon official powers. It is curious that in the Anglican body, High Churchmen are dry, and Low Churchmen exalt their own persons. In the Catholic Church all priests are High Churchmen. And there is a danger of official assumption. But for this we should not have had the hatred and contempt or sacerdotalism. I am sorry to say that even good priests sometimes swagger; they think to magnify their office, but they belittle themselves. This has been the cause of endless troubles in hospitals and workhouses. Unfortunately even good priests are not always refined, and they resent any hindrance in the way of their sacred office with want of self-control which gains nothing, and often loses everything. The main contention is lost in a personal dispute. I have often said that our priests are always booted and spurred like cavalry officers in time of war. But they will not fight worse for being chivalrous and courteous.

I may now say that has been the one chief aim of my whole life since I became a priest, and in a special fixedness since I became what I am, five and twenty years ago. It has been the perfection of the priesthood first in ourselves as Oblates, and then in the priesthood of the Diocese of Westminster.

Humanly speaking this idea came to me from St. Charles. Some years before I was in the Church I read his life, and I bought the *Acta*. This filled me with the idea of the pastoral office, I had already written on the Good Shepherd, and I was full of the image of the pastoral care. But St. Charles made it concrete and practical. After my weak way I tried to live by it.

When I came into the Church I remember being attacked by a zealous Sacramentarian convert for saying "Our work is what we are." Taken *ut sonat* this dictum would indeed exclude not only sacraments, but the holy Trinity. And, if I had been talking to a Scotsman, I should have guarded myself by theology, *"Paulus baptizat, Christus baptizat."* But Paul was also inwardly conformed to his divine Master, and outside of all sacraments he won souls by what he was in himself. Indeed he said "Christ sent me not to baptize, but to preach the Gospel." The old law with its *sacramentalia* demanded a subjective fitness of a very high degree. The new law with its sacraments demands not only the same subjective sanctification in the priest, but a perfection as complete as he can attain. This was my idea of St. Charles's Congregation of Oblates. What I had in my mind in 1856 and 1857 was this and nothing else. What I intended and did I have written in my *ms.* books which are at Bayswater, and I need not say more.

My chief subject then is what I have tried to do in the last twenty-five years, and my reasons.

First I must say that I found myself set over a body of clergy better than myself. For goodness, conscientiousness even to scruple in the life of priestly duty, they were exemplary and highly meritorius.

They were chiefly formed at St. Edmund's in a system of humble and unworldly goodness. But St. Edmund's had not all the advantages of sacred and spiritual science which it might have acquired by longer life and greater maturity. It was only fifty odd years old, and it was the offspring of the culture and quality of the old vicariate. Good as it was it had much to learn, to master and to complete both intellectually and spiritually.

The clergy in 1865 were 214. The diocesans were 160, the regulars 54. There were 9 religious orders of men, and of women 31.

The regulars were Jesuits, Augustinians, Passionists, Carmelites, Pallotini, Rosminians, Servites, Marists, Oblates of Mary.

My first thought was that no provincial or father-general had any obligation to multiply and perfect his order greater or more absolute than I had to multiply and to perfect the priesthood of the diocese of Westminster. Now I have borne my testimony to what they were, and to what they themselves, or the more thoughtful of them, desired to see growing and ripening among them.

But I must add, what was the esteem in which the laity held them?

They, with exceptions, were held to be a disadvantage as compared to the regulars: as preachers, confessors, directors, judges of vocations, advisers in spiritual, and even in worldly, things they were held to be of less esteem. Many of them no doubt were so. But the whole as such was higher in parts. On the other hand many of the regulars, with longer training and greater advantages, were better qualified than the priests of the diocese, but many were not so. And yet the laity took for granted that the clergy were "seculars," and spoke of them as such. "He is only a secular priest" was often heard, and it revealed a whole world of prejudice, depreciation, and mistrust. This was bad enough, but there was worse to come. The priesthood accepted the depreciation which depresses and paralyzes the will. A conquered people lose the sense of power, and what is worse take their state as a standard; so that priests have come to plead against invitations and exhortations to higher things, "I am only a secular priest." What can be greater than a priest? For itself does it not contain all perfection? What can black or white or brown cloth add to it? This seemed to me to be the first thing wanting. The world is governed by ideas; and the idea of our Lord's priesthood, truly and fully conceived, has a motive power to raise men to anything.

The first thing needed, as it seemed to me, was to bring out into the clearest light what the priesthood is.

It seemed to me to be obscured by the traditional prejudice that to be a regular is to be everything, and to be a priest is to be functionary for sacraments and ceremonies. Even the priesthood of the regular was lost sight of in his order, habit, and privileges.

This conviction was the motive of all that I did and wrote at Bayswater.

And more explicitly since 1865 in St. Thomas's Seminary and in two books, the *Pastoral Office* and the *Eternal Priesthood*.

The next aim I had was to make the priests of the diocese conscious of their own power as priests.

For this cause I have held the diocesan synod every year. At first some murmured at the trouble; but they have come to see that it is good for them to be conscious of their number, and their corporate existence, relations, and power. It is the one only day and place in which they meet together.

It is also the only day and place where the bishop can speak to them all at once.

I have tried to make use of this opportunity.

Our first synod had a representation

of a hundred and sixty priests. Our last of 353.

But it forced itself upon me that dormant powers diminish, faculties in activity are enlarged, energies exerted continually grow in strength.

Why then, I asked, should our priests always ask others to preach for them, to give missions and retreats?

Is it because they know themselves to be incapable? Or because they have come to believe themselves to be incapable because the laity so regard them?

Is it true? If so *in nomine Domini* let us wipe away this reproach as speedily as ever we can.

Is it that our priests are discouraged and believe themselves to be what is said of them?

At all events the way to cure this incapacity is to do the things of which they are told that they are incapable. Let them preach, give missions and retreats, "use legs and have legs."

I have therefore encouraged them to give parochial missions, which have greatly prospered; chiefly to the priests themselves. Many have told me that they had no knowledge they possessed such power over their people; that in giving the missions a new light and strength came to them, and a new piety came to their people. They had never before made full trial of the priesthood and of the powers dormant in it.

They also saw that the apparent success of triennial missions comes from two causes—the one that the accumulation of three years has to be worked off, the other that the number of confessions heard is explained by the fact that the central mission gains what the neighboring missions lose. The aggregate within an hour feel the same.

If the pontifical law had not ordered that the ordinary confessors of convents should be secular priests, and forbidden the appointment of regulars except under stress of necessity, we should perhaps be told that no secular priest is capable of hearing the confessions of nuns and of directing them.

Of the eighty convents of this diocese I have labored to provide confessors of my own clergy, and to call in regulars only in case of need.

I believe the hearing and direction of nuns is one of the surest means to illuminate, and to sanctify the priests of the diocese.

August 28

Surely this phrase *in auxilium saecularium* shows that the priests ought to be ahead of any and every work, and only helped, not superseded or supplanted, when they fail numerically, intellectually, or spiritually. This does not justify voluntary or deliberate failure in capacity *data opera*. But the abdication of the highest functions of the priesthood is a culpable self-depression, an ὑστέρησις, like folding the talent in a napkin. Against this I have labored by making everyone do his own work to the best of his power, and I hope I have not spared myself. The result I see in the visible and palpable increase of efficiency in a large number as preachers, confessors and pastors.

It will be said that the *auxilium saecularium* is not only from the *penuria sacerdotum,* the fewness of priests in number, but emphatically the help of higher intellectual culture, and riper spiritual perfection, which regulars attain by their life in community, their learned leisure, their spiritual asceticism.

Now, this is precisely the evil I am contending against. Priests as such are *perfectores aliorum,* and before ordination, as St. Alphonsus affirms, according to the doctrine of fathers and theologians, *uno ore,* they ought to have attained "interior spiritual perfection" as a pre-requisite to ordination.

Moreover it is an axiom that the priesthood is a sign *perfectionis jam adeptae.* The imperfect enter religious orders *ad perfectionem adquirendam.* The secular priesthood therefore is supposed to be already in moral, intellectual, and spiritual maturity, and the auxilium they need is not to supply what they have not already, but to support them in the spiritual qualities and acquirements they have already attained by the same qualities and acquirements.

To this it will be answered: "Look at the secular clergy, where is their spiritual perfection?" I answer look at the regulars, are they all perfect? The secular priests are hundreds of thousands, the regulars not twenty thousand. There may be less mud in a canal than in the river St. Lawrence; but the one is God's creation, the other is of man. Moreover, if the secular clergy are on a lower spiritual level than regulars, which I am granting, but not conceding, I ascribe it to three brief causes:

1) First, to the low and depressed notion of the priesthood which has become tradition. The higher the mark the higher the aim. A low standard breeds a low desire, and paralyzes the affections and energies of the soul.

When are our seminarists told that they must aim at perfection: and that, without this, no treatise of philosophy or theology will be enough.

2) Secondly, the inefficient state of our seminaries. We have boys from twenty-one to twenty-four. If they are ordained without "interior spiritual perfection," who is to blame? Who is responsible? Where is the remedy? With a postulance of eight years and a novitiate of four we ought to bring them up to spiritual perfection. And so we should if we ourselves were spiritually perfect. They are what we are; and they will be what we make them.

Is it not the want of a higher aspiration in ourselves that depresses the standard of our seminarists?

One consequence of this is that when they grow up and become prefects and professors they have no unity of mind, no union of will for the college, no zeal *in solidum,* so as to take to heart not only their own class, but the studies and discipline of the whole house. How can men work together if they have no community of heart or spirit?

3) Lastly the clergy of a diocese will be what the bishop is: if he is lax they will be lax, if he is strict they will be strict also. If he keeps up the aim and standard, not all, indeed, will do the same, but those who have a good will and the same aspiration will surround him, and even the lax and the lower will not preach laxity even if they practice it.

But further, a bishop must not be a dependant on the upper ten thousand, nor a diner-out, nor a waster of time, nor a joker of jokes, nor a reader of newspapers, nor a center of favorites, but open to all his priests, at any day and at any hour, sharing their burdens and troubles, and unselfish in word and deed. He ought to live for his priests, and among them; in the habits of his life as like to their habits as possible. God knows how imperfect we are, but if we aim at perfection, and say "Come," our priests will follow us. If we aim at anything lower and say "Go," they will fall back. If the diocesan priesthood is lower in life and attainments than the regulars, the chief cause is to be found in the bishop, first in the seminary, and next in his life, spirit, and discipline.

Now some bishops having a clergy of a lower culture are disappointed and discouraged, and tempted to turn away from their own priests, and to call in regulars to do what they need to be done. The effect of this is to chill and depress the clergy still more, and even to confirm them in their lower state. The duty of the bishop is to elevate, and to encourage them to make efforts for their own advancement. If they are passed over or set aside they will sink lower, and losing heart and hope they will become less efficient and productive even in their spiritual life.

No bishop thoroughly penetrated by the belief that the priesthood demands perfection, and gives the grace to attain, and to maintain what it demands, could act in the way I have written.

His way of treating his priests is the *experimentum crucis* to detect and to measure his convictions. If even bishops have not the *zelus sacerdotii* to believe the priesthood to demand perfection I do not wonder at the depression and decline of the so-called "secular clergy."

So far as I can find they were never called "secular" till about the thirteenth century, and I suspect that many deserved the name. The multiplication of regulars, and of regular pontiffs led to the distinction; at first no doubt without an adverse intention, or slighting animus. But though the word may mean living and laboring in the world, striving and suffering for the sanctification and salvation of the world, its worse sense has prevailed over its true meaning; and it is understood to mean a lower life and a lower mind.

For this cause I have for long years never used it, and have excluded it from the heading of pastorals.

Believing the priesthood to be the first religious and regular order instituted by our Lord himself, and the highest state of perfection in the world, for the episcopate is only the *sacerdotium supremum et absolutum,* and contains the priesthood with all its obligations and graces. With this belief I look upon all religious orders as of ecclesiastical institution *ad auxilium*. They are reforms not of the priesthood but of the laxities of priests in all ages and lands, *in auxilium non in supplantationem*. I have felt it to be my duty to leave nothing undone to make the clergy of the diocese able to do all its own work, and "to edify itself in charity."

August 30

VII. A seventh and grave hindrance to the spread of the Catholic religion has been the controversial spirit both in matter and in manner of preaching and writing. There is no doubt that this was forced upon the Church in England by the so-called Reformation, which denied Catholic truth and affirmed doctrinal errors. But controversy is at best polemical theology, and polemical theology is simply if not wholly destructive. But destruction builds up nothing. At best it only clears the rubbish off the site so as to make building up possible. And yet positive theology will clear away rubbish, without seeming to do so. For clearness of statement is evidence in itself. *Evidentia* is truth looking out of the cloud and making itself visible like light. The great majority of men are convinced, not so much by reasoning, as by a clear conception of truth. There are two ways of proving a problem. The one to show that every other conception is impossible; this is polemical and destructive. The other to show that the true conception is evident. This is positive and expository. The advantage of this method is that you refute an adversary without naming him or his assertions. This is therefore peaceful and conciliatory. There is no doubt, as the founder of the Quakers said, "when I am in argument I take care not to provoke my antagonist, for so long as he is calm, all the grace of God there is in him is on my side." Thus far I have spoken of

the natural power of clearness in convincing by pervading the intelligence by coherent and intelligible conceptions. Clearness is light and light is self-evident. It manifests itself.

But there is in truth when held up in its evident clearness a supernatural, and sacramental power. The grace of baptism needs the *magisterium* of the Church to elicit and to inform it. But it is in the soul not only by the affinity of charity to the truth revealed by the Spirit of truth, but by the infused virtue of faith which responds to the truth as its proper object. Moreover it is certain that an actual grace goes with every truth, enabling the hearer to believe if he will.

VIII. And this leads on to another hindrance in our way. We do not sufficiently ascertain before we begin to teach what those who hear us already believe. In truth, teaching is like a game of dominoes. If the hearers put down three we must meet it with a three, but for this we must know their intellectual holdings.

Now the people of England believe:

1) That Christianity is revealed by God.

2) That the Baptism of children is a duty.

3) That education ought to be Christian.

4) That the baptismal creed is true.

5) That our Lord is a Divine Person.

6) That he died for our salvation.

7) That if we sin we shall be lost.

8) That if we repent God will forgive our sins.

9) That the Bible is the Word of God.

I might add a long list of Christian truths which may be taken for granted.

But my object is to show that so long as we appeal to these truths as they exist in the minds of the English people they will respond to us, and we shall thereby gain their ear and their confidence. And if we preach these things better than their own preachers, we shall thereby establish a superiority of fire.

Having once laid this foundation, all other truths which flow from these "Waters that are above the firmament" will be seen to be consequences, inevitable, true, and safe, as, for instance, the Incarnation once believed, two things follow, or radiate like two beams of light: (1) the real and substantial presence and (2) the dignity and the glory of our Blessed Mother. St. Paul and the "Unknown God at Athens" precisely shows what I mean. Our work is to build up, and to build upon the foundation. But the foundation consists of the eternal and sovereign truths which are still taken for granted.

We have lost the people of England. They have lost the faith, and, as a dead body generates all manner of corruption, the loss of faith has brought on all manner of immoralities. Half of the population nearly is gathered into towns and cities. London alone has in its streets four millions, of whom half are without God in the world. From Wesley to "General" Booth the non-Catholics are working among them. Is the Catholic Church to do nothing? Certainly our first work is *ad intra* on our own people, and grievously we need it. But are we to do nothing *ad extra?* What can we do, a million and a half among twenty-six millions? I believe we could do much. But it must be by a simpler and more self-sacrificing way of work. The Catholic Church has adequate means to its internal ends. The priesthood and the nuns can deal with the needs of the Church *ad intra*. Its missionaries, priests, and nuns are adequate in quality not in quantity to its work *ad extra*. But London is a mission; and we need both priests and nuns for the English people out of unity. I have said before

that we ought to play at dominoes with the English people. Where is the good of preaching on the Immaculate Conception to people who do not believe in the Incarnation? Or in the Church to those who do not believe in Christianity? Surely a procession through the streets would do better to sing or say the litany of the Holy Name than the litany of Loretto. Give the English people what they can understand, and they will listen, and listen gravely. Is it not better, as St. Paul says, "to speak five words with my understanding, that I may instruct others also, than ten thousand words in a tongue." So again to sing English hymns through the streets—rather than to say the rosary. Hymns are intelligible to all. The rosary is to non-Catholics not only unintelligible, but by its perpetual repetition a stumbling block. We need open-air preaching, and instructions given anywhere and everywhere in secular places—not in our churches. The Little Servants of the Mother of God, and the Little Auxiliatrices, the Sisters of St. Francis of Sales, have as their work the helping of the poor in their homes, doing all domestic and menial works of the lowest kind, spending the whole day with them, but returning to their convent at night. This is the most direct agency to teach the domestic life, and where it is possible to restore it. But we need also the help of women who are not nuns. They may be tertiaries, and under strict direction but without the habit, and free as to hours, going two and two. We ought to be able to do this in London as well as in China.

The work of the Salvation Army, with all its faults, is too real to be any longer disregarded and ascribed to the devil. We are bound not to be outdone in self-sacrifice and in love of souls.

At a meeting in the United States it is said "that the mention of Jesus

Christ was received with applause, and the mention of the Church with hisses." This is a terrible sentence. A doom of death to the human element of the Christian Church, but it showed a belief and love for Christ himself. So long as this survives we can appeal to it.

I have long thought with fear that the visible Church is now as Jerusalem was in the time of Isaias, and when Titus was round the walls. The Divine Spirit reigns over the *Ecclesia docens et regens,* but the human spirit reigns over the Christian society. If this were not so London could never be as it is at this day. And how to deal with it? Certainly not with the pieties of our Upper Ten Thousand, nor with the devotion of the *Faubourg St. Germain.* They are good in their place, and the Church must keep its garden in all the order, beauty, and perfume of flower and fruit. The fervor of its heart and head keeps the central light and fire by which the whole body is quickened and sustained in its energies. Therefore we must have our pieties and fashions in devotion. But the world is dying *positus in maligno,* and we must go into it through fire.

I fully see that we cannot relax the parish work of our priests and nuns. Therefore we must have missionary priests and nuns separate from all parish work, as if they had no faculties *ad intra.*

Our chief difficulty would be want of money, at least at first. Our Lord would not forsake us, nor the poor, nor those who would be roused and moved to help.

Moreover the nuns at least ought to give alms in all forms of temporal help. If priests give there is the danger of interested motives. It would be less with nuns; but hypocrisy must always exist till the regeneration of all things, and we must not cease from what is lawful and good, because it is abused by hypocrites.

There can be no doubt that the "Tudor settlement in religion" is gone. It has departed from its intellectual type, and is now without outline or theology. It has no hold on the intellect of the people. It is unintelligible to them and in perpetual flux. Not so the Catholic faith. But I do not believe that the English people will be won back through the intellect. Their will has been lost by the sins and miseries of the past. But their will is already changing and may be won by finding sympathy and care in the bishops and priests of the Church, that is to say by the law and power of the Incarnation, human love, care, and brotherhood drawing the human will to the divine presence. There is no other way to open the ear, the intellect, and the soul of man. And we are happily as independent and detached from the world, from its titles, wealth, classes, and privileges as the Church of the apostles. Woe to the man that entangles the Church with governments and politics. And woe to the bishop who is of any party or prejudice within the Church. He ought to be above them all. Being in the state of perfection, he ought to be both human and Christian: human in all sympathy with the creatures of God, from the sorrows of man to the sufferings of the lower animal world; Christian in the charity of God and man, to friends and to enemies, in tenderness of heart, self-sacrifice, humility, and patience.

Sin, sorrow, and suffering, not only in the unity of the Church but out of it, ought to command his sympathy and service.

The charities of London are manifold, and without number, and any man holding the office ought, subject only to faith, to sympathize with all, and so far as possible to share in them, if not by alms at least by encouragement. Till now what have we done? We have left them all to those who are out of unity.

The conclusion of all I have written, I believe to be this—"that whosoever represents the Catholic Church in England is bound to aim at the highest standard in all things." "All things are lawful to me, but all things are not expedient," nor are they "edifying." And though he is not bound by commandment, or precept, yet he is bound by counsel to the highest life of prudence, charity, and self-denial; to set up the highest standard and example of priestly and pastoral perfection. St. Gregory says "summa dicere et ima facere" is the ruin of a pastor. He certainly means all that "summa dicere et mediocria facere" is a miserable and dangerous and downward path. A pastor is "alter Christus, imago Jesu, forma Gregis, vicarius Spiritus Sancti." How can he aim at anything lower than the highest? Every priest is bound to charity, poverty, and obedience in the measure and spirit of the apostles. Bishops are in the state of perfection already, and need no admonition beyond their own conscience. Surely for a bishop to aim at anything lower than the *vita apostolica* is not without the sin of sloth at least. It is interpreting the Divine Spirit by the human.

Why should a bishop be a diner-out?

Because it is lawful? expedient? edifying?

Why should he be a drinker of wine?

Who will be the better for his examples of "temperance"? moderation?

Why should he encourage theatricals in schools, convents, and colleges?

Why is he forbidden to go to theaters?

Why should he encourage, even by his silence, the doing works of charity on worldly and mixed motives?

What would he lose by taking the highest line in all these things?

What would he not gain of spiritual fervor? both in his own soul and in his flock?

Why should he encourage a lower or laxer way of sanctifying the Lord's Day?

Is he not surrounded by those who are relaxing and declining in spiritual life and practice?

Why should he go down with them because it is not unlawful?

Would not a raising hand and a cheering voice lead them upward?

What is the meaning of "With Christ I am nailed to the cross?"

Who can say this? And if we cannot, are we aiming as St. Paul aimed? Do we not feel ourselves to be unreal when we say these words? What reparation or expiation are we making for the sins of men or for our own?

If there were no center of gravity would not all things go to pieces? If there were not somewhere a will that inflexibly tends upward, and a voice that is always calling "Come up hither," would not the spirit and standard, the mind and the life of the Christian and the Catholic be always settling down through all the levels of things lawful to the border line where liberty passes into license? And what a world of occasions, and what a thicket of temptations are upon that border line. The laity are lifted by the life of their bishop. His self-denial, if it silently reproves them, does not provoke or anger them. They are secretly encouraged by it, and they commend it even if they do not imitate it. But a multitude sooner or later follows the example, and does likewise. But not if he comes down to their level. This disappoints them.

No man having care of souls can

fail, when anything of evil comes, to accuse himself of being positively or by omission directly or incidentally the cause, or the occasion. He will ask our Lord whether it be not for his rebuke and chastisement, and he will redouble his watchfulness over himself, and will go even to the contrary extreme of distance from the evil, and from the brink. He will desire to make reparation and expiation for his people. What was the whole life of our Lord but a continuous expiation? How can we be like him if we have not this motive?

Under the old law of commandments the people are bound to pay tithes. Under the new law of liberty people are free to give as they will, and the measure of their gift is the measure of their will. The will is regenerated in Baptism, and the law of God is written on the heart, and the heart is united by love to the love of God, and the will is conformed by love to the will of God, *pondus voluntatis amor;* and the will in all its liberty becomes a law to itself. What limit ought a bishop to put upon the use of his liberty in the service of his divine Master? No limit short of the use that our Lord made of his liberty for us. He gave himself for us, and we ought to give ourselves to him. And if a priest is called to this use of his liberty: how much more a bishop as the head and leader of his priests?

Therefore "summa dicere" means: *summa semper velle, et summa facere.*

I should not have written what is in this journal if I had not been bid to do so. What I have written will perhaps seem to some to be extreme, but it seems to me that some one ought to be extreme, that is, to pursue truth to the utmost, and to hold up in everything the highest standard. There will always be many, too many, and those good men, who will refine and palliate and enlarge the ways of liberty. Let one then, at least, bear witness for the higher and the best, the happiest and the safest way.

I have been led to this by the study of the New Testament, and by devotion to the Holy Ghost, to whom almost palpably I owe all things.

About the year 1841 or 1842, I published a volume of sermons. A simple soul asked me why I had so seldom spoken of the Holy Ghost. I went over the book and found the question to be well founded. From that day I have never passed a day without acts of reparation to the Holy Ghost. I bought every book I could find on the work of the Holy Ghost and studied them. After five or six years I reached the last step to which reason alone could lead me, namely that the unanimous witness of the universal Church is the maximum of historical evidence for the revelation of Christianity. But historical evidence is only human, and human evidence is fallible after all. Then and not before, I saw that the perpetual presence and office of the Holy Ghost, etc., raises the witness of the Church from a human to a divine certainty. And to him I submitted in the unity of the one faith and fold.

Since then the Holy Ghost has been the chief thought and devotion of my whole soul.

And I have found that in him there is no relaxation, or diminution of commandments, precepts, or counsels. As he speaks in the New Testament, so I believe we ought to speak. We are debtors to the believing and to the unbelieving, to lift up before them the way of perfect sanctification. We are bound to speak in his own words. The world is the world still. The way of salvation is narrow and straight. The preaching of the apostles is our rule, and their standard of the Christian life is our measure. As they taught we must teach, as they directed souls, so, if we desire to save souls, even our own, we ought also to direct them without fear. I would rather by counsel and free choice make all men 'tutiorists,' rather than have on my conscience the laxity of one soul. We have no right to constrain men, except in the sacraments, to be 'tutiorists,' but they have absolute freedom to become 'tutiorists,' and we have perfect liberty to advise them so to use their liberty. . . .

23. *Dr. Ludwig von Pastor: The Literary Renaissance in Italy and the Church, 15 August 1885*

From *History of the Popes* (London: John Hodges, 1891), pp. 1, 6-13, 47-56.

WITH the exception of the period which witnessed the transformation of the pagan into the Christian world, the history of mankind hardly offers one more striking than that of the transition from the Middle Ages to modern times. One of the most powerful elements in this epoch of marked contrasts was the exhaustive appreciation and extension of the study of the ancient world, commonly known as the Renaissance, or the new birth of classical antiquity. This movement naturally began in Italy, where the memory of the classic past had never been wholly effaced, and with it opens a new epoch.

The object of this work is not to demonstrate the origin and development of this revolution, effected in science, poetry, art, and life. The historian of the popes is only concerned with the Renaissance in so far as it comes in contact with the Church and the Holy See. . . .

It is, therefore, not correct to look on the movement, known as the Renaissance, the literary manifestation of which is humanism, as, in its origin and its whole scope, directed against the Church. On the contrary, the true Renaissance, the study of the past in a thoroughly Christian spirit, was in itself a legitimate intellectual movement, fruitful in fresh results, alike for secular and spiritual science.

The many-sided and methodical study of the intellectual works of former days, with its tendency to deliver men's minds from the formalism of the degenerate scholastic philosophy, and to make them capable of a fresher and more direct culture of all sciences, especially of philosophy and theology, could not but be approved from a strictly ecclesiastical point of view. In the eyes of the Church, everything depended on the method and the aim of the humanistic studies; for the movement could only be hostile to her, if the old ecclesiastical methods were forsaken, if classical studies, instead of being used as means of culture, became their own end, and were employed not to develop Christian knowledge, but rather to obscure and destroy it.

So long, then, as the absolute truth of Christianity was the standing ground from which heathen antiquity was apprehended, the Renaissance of classical literature could only be of service to the Church. For just as the ancient world in all its bearings could only be fully manifested to the spiritual eye when viewed from the heights of Christianity, so Christian faith, worship, and life could not fail to be more amply comprehended, esteemed, and admired from a clear perception of the analogies and contrasts furnished by classic heathenism. The conditions imposed by the popes and other ecclesiastical dignitaries upon the revived study of antiquity could but serve, as long as this study was pursued in a right spirit, to promote the interests of the Church, and these conditions corresponded with the old ecclesiastical traditions.

Proceeding from the principle that knowledge is in itself a great good, and that its abuse can never justify its suppression, the Church, ever holding the just mean, from the first resisted heathen superstition and heathen immorality, but not the Graeco-Roman intellectual culture. Following the great Apostle of the Gentiles, who had read the Greek poets and philosophers, most of the men who carried on his work esteemed and commended classical studies. When the Emperor Julian endeavored to deprive Christians of this important means of culture, the most sagacious representatives of the Church perceived the measure to be inimical and most dangerous to Christendom. Under the pressure of necessity, books on science were hastily composed for teaching purposes by Christian authors, but after the death of Julian the old classics resumed their place.

The danger of a one-sided and exaggerated interest in heathen literature, regardless of its dark side, was never ignored by Christians. "For many," writes even Origen, "it is an evil thing, after they have professed obedience to the law of God, to hold converse with the Egyptians, that is to say, with heathen knowledge." And those very fathers of the Church, who judged the ancient writers most favorably, were careful from time to time to point out the errors into which the young may fall in the study of the ancients, and the perils which may prove their destruction. Efforts were made by a strict adherence to the approved principles of Christian teaching, and by a careful choice of teachers, to meet the danger which lurked in classical teachers, to meet the danger which lurked in classical literature. Thus, history tells us, did the Church succeed in obviating the perils to moral and religious life attendant on its perusal. Zealots, indeed, often enough arose declaring, "In Christ we have the truth, we need no other learning," and there were not wanting Christians who abhorred classical learning, as dangerous and obnoxious to Christian doctrine. But the severity with which St. Gregory Nazianzen blames these men, proves this party to have been neither enlightened nor wholly disinterested. In espousing the cause of ignorance, they were mainly seeking their own advancement, regardless of the great interests of science and intellectual culture in Christian society, which they would have left to perish, if they had got the upper hand. The most clearsighted of those who watched over the destinies of the Church, were always intent on the protection of these interests, as were also the great majority of the eastern and western fathers.

"The heathen philosophy," writes Clement of Alexandria, "is not deleterious to Christian life, and those who represent it as a school of error and immorality, calumniate it, for it is light, the image of truth, and a gift which God has bestowed upon the Greeks; far from harming the truth by empty delusions, it but gives us another bulwark for the truth, and, as a sister science, helps to establish faith. Philosophy educated the Greeks, as the law educated the Jews, in order that both might be led to Christ." "He, therefore, who neglects the heathen philosophy," says Clement in another passage, "is like the fool who would gather grapes without cultivating the vineyard. But as the heathens mingle truth with falsehood we must borrow wisdom from their philosophers as we pluck roses from thorns."

In like manner spoke St. Basil, St. Gregory Nazianzen, St. Augustine, St. Jerome, and other celebrities of the early Church. They all manifested a clear perception of, and a warm susceptibility for, the beauties of classical literature. Without closing their eyes to the disadvantages and dark shadows of heathenism, they also saw the sunshine, the rays of the eternal light, which beamed forth from these glorious achievements of the human intellect; they heard the prophetic voices which rose from their midst, and sought to bring them into unison with the language of Christendom. They discriminated between the common human element contained in classical literature, and the heathen element which enfolds it; the latter was to be rejected, and the former to take its place within the circle of Christian ideas. They constantly repeated that everything depends on the manner in which the heathen classics are read and employed in education. These expressions of disapprobation are not directed against the classics in themselves, but against a wrong spirit and a perverted method in their use; they agree in this respect with St. Amphilochius, who gave the following advice with regard to the perusal of these works: "Be circumspect in dealing with them, collect the good that is in them, shun whatever is dangerous; imitate the wise bee, which rests upon all flowers and sucks only sweet juices from them." In the same sense, and with true Attic elegance, St. Basil the Great wrote his celebrated *Discourse to Christian Youths, on the Right Use of the Heathen Authors.* In opposition to the unjust attacks which treated heathen books without exception as vain lies of the devil, this great doctor of the Church, whose fame is still fresh in the Basilian Order, dwells with mani-

fest affection on the value and excellence of the classic studies as a preparation for Christian science. The writings of St. Gregory Nazianzen furnish proof of even greater esteem, love, and enthusiasm for the literature of the ancients. "It has cost me little," he says in one of his discourses, "to give up all the rest: riches, high position, influence, in short all earthly glory, all the false joys of the world. I cleave to but one thing, eloquence, and I do not regret having undergone such toils by land and sea to acquire it."

The necessity of combining classical culture with Christian education, henceforth became a tradition in the Church, especially as the scientific development of the period to which most of the above-mentioned fathers belong, has had an enduring influence on the ages which have followed.

Amid the storms of later times, the Church preserved these glorious blossoms of ancient culture, and endeavored to turn them to account in the interest of Christendom. Monasteries, founded and protected by the popes, while the genuine spirit of the Church yet lived within them, rendered valuable service in guarding the intellectual treasures of antiquity. With all their enthusiasm for classical literature, the true representatives of the Church were, nevertheless, firmly convinced that the greatest and most beautiful things antiquity could show came far short of the glory, the loftiness and the purity of Christianity. No exaggerated deification of the heathen writers, but their prudent use in a Christian spirit; no infatuated idolatry of their form, but the employment of their substance in the interest of morality and religion, the combination, in short, of classical learning with Christian life—this was the aim of the Church.

This utilization for Christian ends of the ancient writers was eminently fruitful. "The direct use which the fathers made of these writings in their warfare against idolatry and vain philosophy, is obvious." "But," Stolberg adds, "who can estimate all that Origen, the Sts. Gregory, St. Basil, St. Chrysostom and others gained indirectly in the way of culture and grace, and—more important still—in intellectual energy from the ancients?"

The discourses and treatises of those fathers of the Church who had studied the classics, furnish ample proof that the simplicity of the faith is far from being impaired by the ornaments of rhetoric. Their poems, as among others, St. Gregory Nazianzen's tragedy, "The Suffering Savior," render the conceptions of patrology as clearly as Dante's immortal poem does those of scholastic theology. The efforts of Julian the Apostate to dissolve this alliance between Christian faith and Graeco-Roman culture are a clear indication of the increase of strength which Christianity was then deriving from this source.

In regard to the reaction towards antiquity, which was the almost necessary consequence of a period of decay of classical learning, the attitude to be adopted by the representatives of the Church was clearly defined. Their promotion of the newly-revived studies certainly in some sense denoted a breach with the later Middle Ages, which had unduly repressed the ancient literature, and, in consequence, fallen into a most complete and deplorable indifference as to elegancies of form, but it involved no breach with the Middle Ages as a whole, far less with Christian antiquity in general.

But this reaction in the Renaissance took a special coloring and shape from the circumstances of the time in which it occurred. It was a melancholy period of almost universal corruption and torpor in the life of the Church, which from the beginning of the fourteenth century had been manifesting itself in the weakening of the authority of the pope, the worldliness of the clergy, the decline of scholastic philosophy and theology, and the terrible disorders in political and civil life. The dangerous elements which no doubt the ancient literature contained were presented to a generation intellectually and physically over-wrought, and in many ways unhealthy. It is no wonder, therefore, that some of the votaries of the new tendency turned aside into perilous paths. The beginnings of these defections can already be traced in Petrarch and Boccaccio, the founders of the Renaissance literature, though they never themselves forsook the Church.

The contrasts here apparent became more and more marked as time went on.

On the one side the banner of pure heathenism was raised by the fanatics of the classical ideal. Its followers wished to bring about a radical return to paganism both in thought and manners. The other side strove to bring the new element of culture into harmony with the Christian ideal, and the political and social civilization of the day. These two parties represented the false and the true, the heathen and the Christian Renaissance.

The latter party, whose judgment was sufficiently free from fanatical bias to perceive that a reconciliation between existing tendencies would be more profitable than a breach with the approved principles of Christianity and the development of more than a thousand years, could alone produce real intellectual progress. To its adherents the world owes it, that the Renaissance was saved from bringing about its own destruction.

Not a few humanists wavered between the two streams. Some sought to find a happy mean, while others were in youth carried away by the one cur-

rent, and in mature age by the other.
. . .

The position occupied by the representatives of the Christian Renaissance in relation to the ancient world was the only true one, and they have in some degree solved the problem how justly to appreciate antiquity. Their enthusiasm for the intellectual treasures of the past never went so far as to endanger their devotion to the Christian religion. Unlike the extreme humanists, they held fast the principle, that the works of the heathens are to be judged by a Christian standard. They saw the danger of so idealizing the moral and religious teaching of heathenism, as to make it appear that by its means alone the highest end of life could be attained, thus ignoring the necessity of Christian doctrines and morality, of remission of sin and grace from on high.

In the light of Christianity alone can the ancient world be fully and justly estimated, for the pagan ideal of humanity, as exhibited in its heroes and divinities, is not, as a modern philosopher justly observes, a full or complete one. It is but a shadowy outline, wanting the color and life which something higher must supply—a fragmentary form, which has yet to find its complement in a more perfect whole. This higher image of human perfection is the incarnate Son of God, the prototype of all creatures; no creation of fancy or product of human reason, but the truth and the life itself. The ideals of Greece grow pale before this form, and only vanity and folly could ever turn from it to them. This folly was perpetrated by the adherents of the false Renaissance, by those humanists who instead of ascending from the Greek poets and philosophers to Christ, turned their backs on the glory of Christianity to borrow their ideal from the genius of Greece.

The twofold character of the Italian Renaissance renders it extremely difficult justly to weigh its good and evil in relation to the Church and to religion. A sweeping judgment in such cases would generally be a rash one, even were the notices of the individuals concerned less scanty than those which are before us; here, as elsewhere, human penetration is baffled in the endeavor to appreciate all its bearing.

A modern historian has forcibly remarked that every genuine advance of knowledge must in itself be of advantage to religion and to the Church, inasmuch as truth, science, and art are alike daughters of heaven. From this point of view we must contemplate the encouragement given by ecclesiastics to the revival of classical literature. A distinction should evidently here be drawn between the two schools of the Renaissance, and judgment pronounced accordingly. Those members of the Church who promoted the heathen view acted wrongly, and were, if we look at their conduct with a view to the interests of the Church, blameworthy. Impartial inquiry will, however, lead us to temper this blame by a consideration of all the attendant circumstances, and to bear in mind the difficulty of avoiding the abuse, to which the ancient literature, like all other goods things of the intellect, is liable.

The common impression that the dangerous tendencies of the Renaissance were not recognized by the Church is very erroneous. On the contrary, from the beginning men were never wanting who raised their voices against the deadly poison of the false humanism. One of the first in Italy to indicate its pernicious influence on education was the Dominican Giovanni Dominici. This preacher, who labored ardently for the reformation of his order, enjoyed the favor of Pope Innocent VII, and was raised to the purple by Gregory XII. In his celebrated *Treatise on the Order and Discipline of Family Life*, written very early in the fifteenth century, he denounces, with all the energy of his ardent nature, the system "which lets youth and even childhood become heathen rather than Christian; which teaches the names of Jupiter and Saturn, of Venus and Cybele rather than those of God the Father, the Son, and the Holy Ghost; which poisons minds that are still tender and powerless by sacrifice to the false gods, and brings up wayward nature in the lap of unbelief."

In yet stronger terms does Dominici express himself in a writing which has but recently been brought to light, and which is dedicated in courteous language to the celebrated chancellor of Florence, Coluccio Salutato. Its primary object was to warn him against being seduced by the charms of the false Renaissance; but at the same time, it aimed at protecting youth in general from the questionable elements contained in the classic literature, and at counteracting its perversion and misuse. The Dominican condemns those who give themselves up with blind and deluded zeal to heathen learning and are thus led to depreciate the Christian religion. Looking at the subject from an esthetic point of view, he is at times blind to the ancient literature. In his horror at the new heathenism, which was rising before his eyes, he is even betrayed into the utterance of such paradoxes as, that it is more useful to a Christian to plough the ground than to study the heathen authors! Exaggerations of this kind provoked exaggerations from the opposite party, and in this way it became more and more difficult, if not absolutely impossible, to arrive at a clear understanding in regard to the proper use of the ancient classics.

The Franciscans, as well as the Dominicans, distinguished themselves by their opposition to the humanists, or poets, to use the name by which they were commonly called. It cannot be denied that most of these men were full of holy zeal for the interests of Christianity, and that their courageous efforts were of real advantage to the Church, at a time when many other dignitaries, from a spirit of worldliness, favored the false humanist tendencies. Still, it is much to be regretted that the majority of the opponents of the poets went a great deal too far. Correctly to understand the position, we must bear in mind the furious attacks on the religious orders and their scholastic teaching by Poggio, Filelfo, and other elegant and well-known humanist authors. The new movement had gained strength so fast that the monks were left almost defenseless against the ribaldry of these men. Further, the alarming errors and excesses of the extreme admirers of antiquity justified the worst apprehensions for the future. Consequently, most of those who withstood the false Renaissance, lost sight of the fact that these errors had their origin, not in the revival of classical studies, but in their abuse, and in the deplorable social, political, and ecclesiastical conditions of the times. Corrupt intellectual elements, struggling for complete emancipation, had gathered round the banner of the Renaissance, and they often led the great humanist movement into crooked paths. Thus it came to pass, that the larger number of the monks, in their zeal, overlooked the distinction between the true and the false Renaissance, and made humanism in general responsible for the excesses of the most extreme of its votaries. Against such attacks the humanists could most justly appeal to the works of St. Jerome, St. Augustine, St. Ambrose, St. Cyprian, and other fathers of the Church, which are full of quotations from the poets and of classical reminiscences. The monks often waged war in a very unskillful manner, as, for instance, when they treated Valla's attacks on Priscianus and the medieval grammarians as heretical.

The partial and short-sighted view, which condemned the whole Renaissance movement as dangerous to faith and morals, cannot be considered as that of the Church. At this time, as throughout the whole of the Middle Ages, she showed herself to be the patroness of all wholesome intellectual progress, the protectress of all true culture and civilization. She accorded the greatest possible liberty to the adherents of the Renaissance, a liberty which can hardly be comprehended by an age which has lost the unity of the faith. Once only in the period of which we are about to treat, did the head of the Church directly attack the false Renaissance, and this censure was called forth by a shameless eulogy of heathen vices, which the pope, as the chief guardian of morals, could not pass over in silence.

Otherwise the Church gave liberal encouragement to humanist studies, fully endorsing the beautiful words of Clement of Alexandria, that the learning of the heathens, as far as it contains good, is not to be considered heathen, but a gift of God. And, indeed, the speedy degeneracy of the Renaissance in Italy was not the fault of the ancient literature, but rather of its abuse. That the many irreconcilable enemies of the Renaissance, who are to be found in the religious orders, are not the true representatives of the Church, is evident from the fact that the greater number of the popes adopted a very different attitude towards the new movement.

The friendly relations which existed between the popes and the two founders of the Renaissance literature, Petrarch and Boccaccio, have already been mentioned; these relations were not impaired by the passionate language used by these two great writers in denouncing the corruptions which had made their way into ecclesiastical affairs during the Avignon period. No less than five times was Petrarch invited to fill the office of apostolic secretary, but the poet could not make up his mind to undertake the charge, fearing that it would compel him to give up literature, his special vocation. But he gladly employed himself, at the desire of the learned Pope Clement VI, in the collection of early manuscripts of Cicero's works for the papal library. When the tidings of the death of Petrarch, whom he had once invited to Avignon by an autograph letter, reached Pope Gregory XI, he commissioned Guillaume de Noellet, cardinal vicar of the Church in Italy, to make diligent inquiries after his writings and to have good copies made for him, especially of the *Africa, Eclogues, Epistles, Invectives,* and the beautiful work, *On the Solitary Life.*

Gregory XI, whom a modern writer has justly characterized as the best of the Avignon popes, showed a notable interest in the half-forgotten heritage from the ancient world. When he heard that a copy of *Pompeius Trogus* had been discovered at Vercelli, he at once sent a letter to the bishop of that city, desiring him immediately to look after this book and to have it conveyed to the papal court by a trusty messenger. A few days later the same pope charged a canon of Paris to make researches in the Sorbonne library regarding several works of Cicero's, to have them transcribed as soon as possible by competent persons and to send the copies to him at Avignon. It might, at first sight, have seemed likely that the storms which burst over the papacy after the death of Gregory XI would have deterred the popes from showing favor to the Renaissance, which was now asserting its power in the realm of literature, and yet it was actually at this very period that a great number of the humanists found admission into the Roman court.

A closer study of this time, in connection with which the previous years of the residence of the popes at Avignon must also be considered, will bring to light the causes of the gradual and, in some respects, hazardous influx of humanism into the papal court. A review of the history of the popes from the beginning of the exile to Avignon until the end of the Great Schism seems all the more necessary, as without an intimate acquaintance with this period of peril to the papacy, the latter course of events cannot be understood.

In the progress of the following work we shall show that the Renaissance gradually took root in Rome under Martin V, and Eugenius IV; that Albergati, Cesarini, and Capranica, the most distinguished among the wearers of the purple in the fifteenth century, encouraged humanism in its best tendencies; that the sojourn of Eugenius IV in Florence, and the general council held there, produced marked effects in the same direction; until at last, in the person of Nicholas V, a man mounted the throne of St. Peter, who, full of confidence in the power of Christian science, ventured to put himself at the head of this great intellectual movement. This circumstance was the beginning of a new epoch in the history of the papacy, as well as in that of science and art—an epoch which reached its climax in the reigns of Julius II and Leo X.

It has often been said that the Renaissance itself ascended the papal throne with Nicholas V, yet it must not be forgotten that this great pontiff was throughout on the side of the genuine and Christian Renaissance. The founder of the Vatican library, like Fra Angelico whom he employed to paint his study in that palace, knew how to reconcile his admiration for the intellectual treasures of the past with the claims of the Christian religion: he could honor both Cicero and St. Augustine, and could appreciate the grandeur and beauty of heathen antiquity without being thereby led to forget Christianity.

The leading idea of Nicholas V was to make the capital of Christendom the capital also of classical literature and the center of science and art. The realization of this noble project was, however, attended with many difficulties and great dangers. If Nicholas V overlooked or underestimated the perils which threatened ecclesiastical interests from the side of the heathen and revolutionary Renaissance, this is the only error that can be laid to his charge. His aim was essentially lofty and noble and worthy of the papacy. The fearlessness of this large-hearted man, in face of the dangers of the movement— "a fearlessness which has in it something imposing"—strikes us all the more forcibly, when we consider the power and influence which the Renaissance had at this time attained in Italy. The attempt to assume its guidance was a great deed, and one worthy of the successor of the Gregories and Innocents.

To make the promotion of the Renaissance by the Holy See a matter of indiscriminate reproach betrays total ignorance of the subject. For, deep and widespread as was the intellectual movement, excited by the resuscitation of the antique, it involved no serious danger to Christian civilization, but rather was an occasion of new activity and energy, as long as the unity and purity of the Christian faith were maintained unimpaired under the authority of the Church and her head. If in later days, in consequence of the undue influence obtained by the heathen Renaissance, a very different development ensued; if the intellectual wealth, won by the revived study of the past, was turned to evil purposes, Nicholas V, whose motives were of the highest and purest, cannot be held responsible. On the contrary, it is to the glory of the papacy that, even in regard to the great Renaissance movement, it manifested that magnanimous and all-embracing comprehensiveness which is a portion of its inheritance. As long as dogma was untouched, Nicholas V and his like-minded successors allowed the movement the most ample scope; the

founder of the Vatican library had no foreboding of the mischief which the satire of the humanists was preparing. The whole tenor of his pure life testifies that his words proceeded from an upright heart, when he earnestly exhorted the cardinals assembled around his death-bed to follow the path he had chosen in laboring for the welfare of the Church—the Bark of Peter, which, by the wonderful guidance of God, has ever been delivered out of all storms. . . .

24. *Vladimir S. Soloviev: Russia and the Universal Church, 1889*

From Vladimir S. Soloviev, *Russia and the Universal Church* (London: Geoffrey Bles Ltd., 1958), pp. 8-15, 30-31, 34-35, 43-55.

MEN have imagined that the acknowledgment of the divinity of Christ relieves them of the obligation of taking his words seriously. They have twisted certain texts of the Gospel so as to get out of them the meaning they want, while they have conspired to pass over in silence other texts which do not lend themselves to such treatment. The precept "Render to Caesar the things that are Caesar's, and to God the things that are God's" is constantly quoted to sanction an order of things which gives Caesar all and God nothing. The saying "My kingdom is not of this world" is always being used to justify and confirm the paganism of our social and political life, as though Christian society were destined to belong to this world and not to the kingdom of Christ. On the other hand the saying "All power is given me in heaven and earth" is never quoted. Men are ready to accept Christ as sacrificing priest and atoning victim; but they do not want Christ the King. His royal dignity has been ousted by every kind of pagan

despotism, and Christian peoples have taken up the cry of the Jewish rabble: "We have no king but Caesar!" Thus history has witnessed, and we are still witnessing, the curious phenomenon of a society which professes Christianity as its religion but remains pagan not merely in its life but in the very basis of that life.

This dichotomy is not so much a logical *non sequitur* as a moral failure. That is obvious from the hypocrisy and sophism which are characteristic of the arguments commonly used to justify this state of affairs. "Slavery and severe hardship," said a bishop renowned in Russia thirty years ago, "are not contrary to the spirit of Christianity; for physical suffering is not a hindrance to the salvation of the soul, which is the one and only end of our religion." As though the infliction of physical suffering by a man on his fellow-men did not imply in him a moral depravity and an act of injustice and cruelty which were certainly imperilling the salvation of his soul! Granted even—though the supposition is absurd—that a Christian society can be insensible to the sufferings of the oppressed, the question remains whether it can be indifferent to the sin of the oppressors.

Economic slavery, even more than slavery properly so called, has found its champions in the Christian world. Society and the state, they maintain, are in no way bound to take general and regular measures against pauperism; voluntary almsgiving is enough; did not Christ say that there would always be the poor on earth? Yes, there will always be the poor; there will also always be the sick, but does that prove the uselessness of health services? Poverty in itself is no more an evil than sickness; the evil consists in remaining indifferent to the sufferings of one's neighbor. And it is not a question only of the poor; the rich also have a claim on our compassion. These poor rich! We do everything to develop their bump of acquisitiveness, and then we expect them to enter the kingdom of God through the imperceptible opening of individual charity. Besides, it is well known that authoritative scholars see in the phrase "the eye of a needle" simply a literal translation of the Hebrew name given to one of the gates of Jerusalem which it was difficult for camels to pass through. Surely then it is not the infinitesimal contribution of personal philanthrophy which the Gospel enjoins upon the rich, but rather the narrow and difficult, but nevertheless practicable, way of social reform.

This desire to limit the social action of Christianity to individual charity, this attempt to deprive the Christian moral code of its binding character and its positive legal sanction is a modern version of that ancient Gnostic antithesis (the system of Marcion in particular) so often anathematized by the Church. That all human relationships should be governed by charity and brotherly love is undoubtedly the ex-press will of God and the end of his creation; but in historic reality, as in the Lord's Prayer, the fulfillment of the divine will on earth is only realized after the hallowing of God's name and the coming of his kingdom. The name of God is truth; his kingdom is justice. It follows that the knowledge of the truth and the practice of justice are necessary conditions for the triumph of evangelical charity in human society.

In truth all are one: and God, the absolute unity, is all in all. But this divine unity is hidden from our view by the world of evil and illusion, the result of universal human sin. The basic condition of this world is the division and isolation of the parts of the Great Whole; and even man, who should have been the unifying rationale of the material universe, finds himself split up and scattered over the earth, and has been unable by his own efforts to achieve more than a partial and unstable unity, the universal monarchy of paganism. This monarchy, first represented by Tiberius and Nero, received its true unifying principle when "grace and truth" were manifested in Jesus Christ. Once united to God, the human race recovered its own unity. But this unity had to be threefold to be complete; it had to realize its ideal perfection on the basis of a divine fact and in the midst of the life of mankind. Since mankind is objectively separated from the divine unity, this unity must in the first place be given to us as an objective reality independent of ourselves—the kingdom of God coming among us, the external, objective Church. But once reunited to this external unity, men must translate it into action, they must assimilate it by their own efforts—the kingdom of God is to be taken by force, and the men of violence possess it. At first manifested for us and then by us, the kingdom of God must finally be revealed in us in all its intrinsic, absolute perfection as love, peace and joy in the Holy Spirit.

Thus the Church Universal (in the broad sense of the word) develops as a threefold union of the divine and the human: there is the priestly union, in which the divine element, absolute and unchangeable, predominates and forms the Church properly so called (the Temple of God); there is the kingly union, in which the human element predominates and which forms the Christian state (the Church as the living Body of God); and there is lastly the prophetic union, in which the divine and the human must penetrate one another in free mutual interaction and so form the perfect Christian society (the Church as the spouse of God).

The moral basis of the priestly union, or of the Church in the strict sense of the word, is faith and religious devotion; the kingly union of the Christian state is based on law and justice; while the element proper to the prophetic union or the perfect society is freedom and love.

The Church, in the narrower sense, represented by the hierarchy, reunites mankind to God by the profession of the true faith and the grace of the sacraments. But if the faith communicated by the Church to Christian humanity is a living faith, and if the grace of the sacraments is an effectual grace, the resultant union of the divine and the human cannot be limited to the special domain of religion, but must extend to all man's common relationships and must regenerate and transform his social and political life. Here opens up a field of action which is man's own proper sphere. The divine-human action is no longer an accomplished fact as in the priestly Church, but a task awaiting fulfillment, the task of making the divine truth a reality in human society, of putting truth into practice; and truth, expressed in practice, is called justice.

Truth is the absolute existence of all in unity; it is the universal solidarity which exists eternally in God, but which has been lost by the natural man and recovered in principle by Christ, the spiritual man. It remains for human activity to continue the unifying work of the God-Man by contesting the world with the contrary principle of egoism and division. Each single being, whether nation, class, or individual, in so far as it asserts its own individuality in isolation from the divine-human sum of things, is acting against truth; and truth, if it is alive in us, must react and manifest itself as Justice. Thus having recognized the universal solidarity, the All-in-One, as truth, and having put it into practice as justice, regenerate man will be able to perceive it as his inmost essence and to enjoy it fully in the spirit of freedom and love.

All are one in the Church through the unity of hierarchy, faith, and sacraments; all are made one in the Christian state through justice and law; all must be one in natural charity and free co-operation. These three modes or rather degrees of unity are inseparably connected. In order to impose that universal solidarity which is the kingdom of God on nations and classes and individuals, the Christian state must believe in it as absolute truth revealed by God himself. But the divine revelation cannot be made directly to the state as such, that is to say to a natural humanity outside the sphere of the divine operation: God has revealed himself, he has entrusted his truth and his grace to an elect humanity, that is to the Church, sanctified and organized by himself. If the state, itself the product of human agencies and historic circumstances, is to bring mankind under the sway of absolute justice, it must justify itself by submission to the

Church which provides the moral and religious sanction and the actual basis for its work. It is equally clear that the perfect Christian society or the prophetic union, the reign of love and spiritual freedom, presupposes the priestly and kingly union. For the divine truth and grace cannot fully control the moral being of mankind nor effect its inner transformation unless they first have an objective force in the world, unless they are incarnate in a religious fact and upheld by law, unless, that is, they exist as Church and state.

Since the priestly institution is a fact, and the brotherhood of perfect freedom is an ideal, it is the middle term especially—the state in its relation to Christianity—which determines the historic destiny of mankind. The state exists in order to protect human society against evil in its external and public form—that is, against manifest evil. The true social good being the solidarity of the whole, universal justice and peace, social evil is simply the violation of this solidarity. The actual life of mankind shows forth a threefold violation of that universal solidarity which is justice; justice is violated, firstly, when one nation attacks the existence or freedom of another, secondly, when one social class oppresses another, and thirdly, when an individual by committing a crime openly revolts against the social order.

As long as there existed in the history of mankind several separate states, absolutely independent of one another, the immediate task of each in the sphere of foreign policy was confined to maintaining this independence. But the ideal or rather the instinct of international solidarity persisted throughout human history, and found its expression either in that tendency to universal monarchy which culminated in the ideal and the historic reality of the *pax Romana,* or (among the Jews) in the religious principle which affirmed the natural unity and common origin of the whole human race, of all the sons of Adam (*bene-Adam*)—a conception afterwards completed by the Christian religion which added to this natural unity the spiritual fellowship of all those who are regenerate and made sons of the second Adam, the Christ (*bene-Mashiah*).

This new ideal was realized, however incompletely, in medieval Christendom, which despite its turbulent condition did as a rule regard any war between Christian peoples as a civil war and therefore as a sin and a crime. The modern nations, having shattered the papal monarchy which was the foundation of this imperfect but genuine unity, have had to substitute for the ideal of Catholic Christendom the fiction of the European balance of power. On all hands it is recognized, whether sincerely or not, that the true objective of international politics must be universal peace.

Two equally obvious facts, then, are to be noted: first, that there exists a general consciousness of the solidarity of mankind and a desire for international unity, for the *pax Christiana* or, if you will, the *pax humana;* secondly, that this unity does not exist in fact, and that the first of the three problems of society is as far from being solved at the present day as it was in the ancient world. The same is true of the other two problems.

Universal solidarity implies that each element of the sum total—each nation, society or individual—not only has the right to exist but possesses in addition a peculiar and intrinsic worth which forbids its being treated as a mere means to the general well-being. The true positive conception of justice can be expressed in the following formula: each particular being, whether collective or individual, has always a place to itself in the universal organism of the race. This positive justice was unknown to the ancient state; the state protected itself and maintained the social order by exterminating its enemies in war, reducing its laboring class to a condition of slavery, and torturing or killing its criminals. Christianity, regarding every human being as of infinite worth, was bound to bring about a complete change in the character and action of the state. The ills of society remained the same, in their threefold form: international, civil, and criminal; the state as before had to fight evil in these three spheres, but the specific objective and the methods of the struggle could not remain the same. It was no longer a matter of defending a particular social group; this negative aim was replaced by a positive task; universal solidarity had to be established in the face of national differences; there had to be a reaction against class-antagonism and individual egoism in the name of true social justice. The pagan state had to deal with the enemy, the slave and the criminal; the enemy, the slave and the criminal had no rights. But the Christian state has only to deal with the members of Christ, whether suffering, sick or corrupt; it must pacify national hatreds, mend the iniquities of society, and correct the vices of individuals. In it the foreigner has a right to citizenship, the slave a right to freedom, and the criminal a right to moral regeneration. In the city of God there is no enemy or foreigner, no slave or proletarian, no criminal or convict. The foreigner is simply a brother from a far country; the proletarian is an unfortunate brother who needs succor; the criminal is a fallen brother who must be helped up.

It follows that in the Christian state three things are absolutely ruled out: first, wars inspired by national selfishness, or conquests which build up one nation upon the ruins of another (for the prime objective of the Christian state is universal solidarity or the *pax Christiana*); next, civil and economic slavery which makes one class the passive instrument of another; and lastly, vindictive punishment, especially capital punishment, inflicted by society upon the guilty individual in order to make him a buttress of public safety. By committing a crime the individual shows that he regards society simply as a means to, and his neighbors as the instrument of, his own selfishness. But this injustice must not be countered with the further injustice of belittling the criminal's own human dignity and of reducing him to the level of passive instrumentality by a punishment which leaves no room for his amendment or regeneration.

In the purely human order, the sphere of temporal relations, it was the duty of the state to give expression to that absolute solidarity of each individual with the whole universe which the Church represents in the spiritual order by the unity of her priesthood, her faith and her sacraments. Belief in this unity had to precede its realization in practice; before becoming Christian in fact, the state had to accept the Christian faith. This first step was taken at Constantinople; it sums up the whole Christian achievement of the second empire.

The Byzantine transformation of the Roman empire, begun by Constantine the Great, continued by Theodosius and finally achieved by Justinian, produced no more than a nominally Christian state. Its laws, its institutions, and a good deal of its public morality, all retained unmistakable characteristics of the old paganism. Slavery continued to be legal; and crimes, especially political misdemeanors, were punished by law with an exquisite cruelty. This contrast between professed Christianity and practical savagery is aptly personified in the founder of the second empire; Constantine believed sincerely in the Christian God, paid honor to the bishops and discussed the Trinity with them; yet he had no scruple about exercising the right of a pagan husband and father, and putting Fausta and Crispus to death.

So glaring a contradiction between faith and life, however, could not last long without some attempt to reconciliation. Rather than sacrifice its actual paganism, the Byzantine empire attempted in self-justification to pervert the purity of the Christian idea. This compromise between truth and error lies at the heart of all those heresies (often devised by the imperial power and always except in certain individual instances, favored by it) which distracted Christendom from the fourth century to the ninth.

The fundamental truth and distinctive idea of Christianity is the perfect union of the divine and the human individually achieved in Christ, and finding its social realization in Christian humanity, in which the divine is represented by the Church, centered in the supreme pontiff, and the human by the state. This intimate relation between Church and state implies the primacy of the former, since the divine is previous in time and superior in being to the human. Heresy attacked the perfect unity of the divine and the human in Jesus Christ precisely in order to undermine the living bond between Church and state, and to confer upon the latter an absolute independence. Hence it is clear why the emperors of the second Rome, intent on maintaining within Christendom the absolutism of the pagan state, were so partial to all the heresies, which were but manifold variations on a single theme:

Jesus Christ is not the true Son of God, consubstantial with the Father; God has not become incarnate; nature and mankind remain cut off from divinity, and are not united to it; and

consequently the human state may rightly keep its independence and supremacy intact. Constantius and Valens had indeed good reason to support Arianism. . . .

For lack of an imperial power genuinely Christian and Catholic, the Church has not succeeded in establishing social and political justice in Europe. The nations and states of modern times, freed since the Reformation from ecclesiastical surveillance, have attempted to improve upon the work of the Church. The results of the experiment are plain to see. The idea of Christendom as a real though admittedly inadequate unity embracing all the nations of Europe has vanished; the philosophy of the revolutionaries has made praiseworthy attempts to substitute for this unity the unity of the human race—with what success is well known. A universal militarism transforming whole nations into hostile armies and itself inspired by a national hatred such as the Middle Ages never knew; a deep and irreconcilable social conflict; a class struggle which threatens to entomb everything in fire and blood; and a continuous lessening of moral power in individuals, witnessed to by the constant increase in mental collapse, suicide and crime—such is the sum total of the progress which secularized Europe has made in the last three or four centuries.

The two great historic experiments, that of the Middle Ages and that of modern times, seem to demonstrate conclusively that neither the Church lacking the assistance of a secular power which is distinct from but responsible to her, nor the secular state relying upon its own resources, can succeed in establishing Christian justice and peace on the earth. The close alliance and organic union of the two powers without confusion and without division is the indispensable condition of true social progress. It remains to inquire whether there is in the Christian world a power capable of taking up the work of Constantine and Charlemagne with better hope of success.

The profoundly religious and monarchic instinct of the Russian people, certain prophetic events in its past history, the enormous and compact bulk of its empire, the great latent strength of the national spirit in contrast to the poverty and emptiness of its actual existence—all this seems to indicate that it is the historic destiny of Russia to provide the universal Church with the political power which it requires for the salvation and regeneration of Europe and of the world.

Great tasks cannot be accomplished with small means. It is not a matter of religious compromise between two hierarchies, nor of diplomatic negotiations between two governments. It is primarily a moral and intellectual bond that must be forged between the religious conscience of Russia and the truth of the universal Church; and in order to commend to our reason the truth of a principle of which the historical realization is foreign and even repugnant to us, we must seek the ultimate ground of this truth in the fundamental idea of Christianity. . . .

As a member of the true and venerable Eastern or Greco-Russian Orthodox Church which does not speak through an anti-canonical synod nor through the employees of the secular power, but through the utterance of her great fathers and doctors, I recognize as supreme judge in matters of religion him who has been recognized as such by St. Irenaeus, St. Dionysius the Great, St. Athanasius the Great, St. John Chrysostom, St. Cyril, St. Flavian, the Blessed Theodoret, St. Maximus the Confessor, St. Theodore of the Studium, St. Ignatius, etc., etc. —namely, the Apostle Peter, who lives in his successors and who has not heard in vain our Lord's words: "You are Peter and upon this rock I will build my Church"; "Strengthen your brethren"; "Feed my sheep, feed my lambs."

O deathless spirit of the blessed apostle, invisible minister of the Lord in the government of his visible Church, you know that she has need of an earthly body for her manifestation. Twice already you have embodied her in human society: in the Greco-Roman world, and again in the Romano-German world; you have made both the empire of Constantine and the empire of Charlemagne to serve her. After these two provisional incarnations she awaits her third and last incarnation. A whole world full of energies and of yearnings but with no clear consciousness of its destiny knocks at the door of universal history. What is your word, you peoples of the world? The multitude knows it not yet, but powerful voices issuing from your midst have already disclosed it. Two centuries ago a Croatian priest announced it with prophetic tongue, and in our own days a bishop of the same nation has more than once proclaimed it with superb eloquence. The utterance of the spokesmen of the western Slavs, the great Krishanitch and the great Strossmayer, needs only a simple *Amen* from the eastern Slavs. It is this *Amen* that I come to speak in the name of a hundred million Russian Christians, in full and firm confidence that they will not repudiate me.

Your word, O peoples of the world, is free and universal theocracy, the true solidarity of all nations and classes, the application of Christianity to public life, the Christianizing of politics; freedom for all the oppressed, protection for all the weak; social justice and good Christian peace. Open to them therefore, you key-bearer of Christ, and may the gate of history be for them and for the whole world the gate of the kingdom of God! . . .

But at this point I am interrupted by the familiar cry of my countrymen: "Let no one speak to us of our needs, of our shortcomings, least of all of our duties towards the decadent West! It has had its day! We have no need of it and no obligation towards it. We have in the East everything that we need. *In Oriente lux*. The true representative and crowning achievement of Christianity is holy Russia. What have we to do with old Rome in her decay, when we are ourselves the Rome of the future, the third and last Rome? The eastern Church has fulfilled her great historic task in Christianizing the Russian people, that people which has identified itself with Christianity and to which belongs the whole future of mankind."

This view would reduce the ultimate historical objective of Christianity and the *raison d' être* of the human race to the existence of a single nation. But to accept such an assertion would involve the formal denial of the very notion of a universal Church. It implies a reversion to ancient Judaism, with the difference that the unique part played by the Jewish people in the designs of providence is attested by the word of God, whereas the exclusive importance of Russia can only be maintained on the word of certain Russian propagandists whose inspiration is far from infallible.

Moreover since the ideas of our inspired patriots on the subject of the grounds of religious faith are by no means settled or clear, we must get on to more general ground and examine their claims from a purely natural and human point of view.

For the last forty or fifty years the patriots of Russia have been engaged in the fanatical repetition, with variations in every key, of one invariable phrase: Russia is great and has a sublime mission to fulfill in the world. In what exactly this mission consists and what Russia must do, what we ourselves must do, to fulfill it is always left undefined. Neither the old Slavophils nor their present-day descendants nor M. Katkov himself have said anything definite on that subject. They have talked of "light from the East," but it does not appear that this light has as yet enlightened their understanding or clarified their outlook. We may perhaps be allowed therefore, while acknowledging the patriotic sentiments of these worthy gentlemen, to put to them plainly the question which they attempt to evade, the great question for our national conscience: How is Russia to justify her existence in the world?

For centuries the history of our country was moving towards a single objective, the formation of a great national monarchy. The union of the Ukraine and of a part of White Russia with Muscovite Russia under the Czar Alexis was a decisive moment in this historic work; for that union put an end to the dispute for primacy between the Russia of the north and that of the south, between Moscow and Kiev, and gave a real meaning to the title of "Czar of all the Russias." From that moment there was no longer any doubt of the success of the arduous task which the archbishops and princes of Moscow had undertaken since the fourteenth century. And by the logic of providence it was the son of this very Czar Alexis who went beyond the word of his predecessors and boldly put the further question: What must Russia do now that she is united and has become a powerful state? To this question the great emperor gave the provisional reply that Russia must go to school with the civilized peoples of the West and assimilate their science and culture. That was indeed all that we needed for the moment. But this solution, simple and clear as it was, became more and more inadequate as the young society of Russia made progress in the school of Europe. The question then arose: What was she to do after her years of apprenticeship? The reformation of Peter the Great introduced Russia to the workshop of Europe in order to teach her how to handle all the tools of civilization, but it ignored those higher principles and ideals which guided the use of these tools. Consequently, though that reformation gave us the means of asserting ourselves, it did not reveal the ultimate aim of our existence as a nation. If it was justifiable to ask, What must barbarian Russia do? and if Peter was right in replying, She must be reformed and civilized; it is no less justifiable to ask, What must Russia do now that she has been reformed by Peter the Great and his successors? What is the aim of Russia to-day?

The Slavophils must be given credit for having realized the extent of the problem; but they have done nothing to solve it. Reacting against the nebulous and barren idealism of Pan-Slavism, harder-headed patriots have in our time declared that it is not necessary that a nation should entertain a definite ideal or pursue any higher aim for mankind, but that it is quite enough that it should be independent and should enjoy institutions suited to its national genius and sufficient power and prestige to defend its material interests in the affairs of this world; for a good patriot it is enough to desire this much for his country and to labor to make her rich and powerful. All of which amounts to saying that nations live by their daily bread alone; and this is neither true nor desirable. The peoples of history have lived not merely for themselves but for the whole of mankind; by imperishable achievements they have purchased the right to affirm their nationhood. That is the distinctive mark of a great people, and the patriotism which does not realize the price it must pay is a poor patriotism indeed.

No one asks what is the historic mission of the Ashanti or of the Eskimos. But when a Christian nation as vast and populous as ours, which has existed for a thousand years and is materially equipped to play a part in world history, asserts its rank as a great power and claims an hegemony over other nations of the same race and a decisive influence in international politics, then it may well be asked what its real claims are to such a part in history, what principles or ideals it is contributing to the world, and what it has done or has still to do for the good of mankind as a whole.

But to answer these questions, we are told, is to anticipate the future. True, if we were concerned with a nation still in its infancy, the Russia of Kiev in the days of St. Vladimir, or the Muscovite Russia of Ivan Kalita. But modern Russia, which for the past two hundred years has played a continuous part on the stage of world history and which at the beginning of this century measured its strength against the greater part of Europe—this Russia ought to have some clear consciousness of its present tendencies and its future aims. Granted that the fulfillment of our historic mission belongs to the future, yet we must at least have some conception of that future; there must be in the Russia of to-day the living seed of its future destinies.

Little is achieved by those who are at a loss what to do next. Our ancestors of the fifteenth century saw clearly the future for which they were striving— the empire of all the Russias. It surely cannot be that we, for whom that supreme goal of their endeavors is already an accomplished fact, have a less clear conception of our own future than they had of theirs. Nor can we imagine that that future will be realized without our co-operation in thought and action.

The distinctively religious character of the Russian people as well as the mystical tendency exhibited in our philosophy, our literature and our arts seem to indicate for Russia a great religious mission. Moreover, when our patriots are pressed to state what it is that constitutes the supreme vocation of our country, or the Russian "idea," as it is called nowadays, they have no choice but to appeal to religion. According to them Orthodoxy, or the religion of the Greco-Russian Church, in contrast to the religious bodies of the West, constitutes the true basis of our national being. Here, to begin with, is an obvious vicious circle. If we ask how the separated Eastern Church justifies its existence we are told: by having formed the Russian people and provided its spiritual nurture. And when we inquire how that people justifies its existence the answer is: by belonging to the separated Eastern Church. We are brought to this impasse by the difficulty of really deciding what we mean by this "orthodoxy" of which we would claim the monopoly. This difficulty does not exist for those folk who are really orthodox in all good conscience and in the simplicity of their heart. When questioned intelligently about their religion, they will tell you that to be orthodox is to be baptized a Christian, to wear a cross or some holy image on your breast, to worship Christ, to pray to the Blessed Virgin most immaculate and to all the saints represented by images and relics, to rest from work on all festivals and to fast in accordance with traditional custom, to venerate the sacred office of bishops and priests, and to participate in the holy sacraments and in the divine worship. That is the true "orthodoxy" of the Russian people, and it is ours also. But it is not that of our militant patriots.

It is obvious that true Orthodoxy contains nothing particularist and can in no way form a national or local attribute separating us in any sense from the Western peoples; for the greater part of these peoples, the Catholic part, has precisely the same religious basis that we have. Whatever is holy and sacred for us is also holy and sacred for them. To indicate only one essential point: not only is devotion to the Blessed Virgin—one of the characteristic features of Catholicism—generally practiced by Russian Orthodoxy, but there are even special miraculous images venerated in common by Roman Catholics and Russian Orthodox (for example, the holy Virgin of Czestochowa in Poland). If "piety" is indeed the distinctive characteristic of our national genius, the fact that the chief emblems of that piety are common to us and the Westerns compels us to recognize our oneness with them in what we regard as the most essential thing of all. As regards the profound contrast between the contemplative piety of the East and the active religion of the West, this contrast being purely human and subjective has nothing to do with the divine objects of our faith and worship; so far from being a good reason for schism it should rather bring the two great parts of the Christian world into a closer and mutually complementary union.

But under the influence of that evil principle which is constantly at work on earth, this difference has been abused and twisted into a division. At the moment when Russia was receiving baptism from Constantinople, the Greeks, though still in formal communion with Rome after the temporary schism of Photius, were already strongly imbued with national particularism which was fostered by the contentious spirit of the clergy, the political ambitions of the emperors and the disputes of the theologians. The result was that the pearl of the Gospel purchased by the Russian people in the person of St. Vladimir was all covered with the dust of Byzantium. The bulk of the nation was uninterested in the ambitions and hatreds of the clergy and understood nothing of the theological quibbles which were their fruit; the bulk of the nation received and preserved the essence of orthodox Christianity pure and simple, that is to say, faith and the life of religion formed by divine grace and expressed in works of piety and charity. But the clergy, recruited in the early days from the Greeks, and the theologians accepted the disastrous inheritance of Photius and Cerularius as an integral part of the true religion.

This pseudo-Orthodoxy of our theological schools, which has nothing in common with the faith of the universal Church or the piety of the Russian people, contains no positive element; it consists merely of arbitrary negations produced and maintained by controversial prejudice:

"God the Son does not contribute in the divine order to the procession of the Holy Spirit."

"The Blessed Virgin was not immaculate from the first moment of her existence."

"Primacy of jurisdiction does not belong to the see of Rome and the pope has not the dogmatic authority of a pastor and doctor of the universal Church."

Such are the principal negations which we shall have to examine in due course. For our present purpose it is enough to observe in the first place that these negations have received no sort of religious sanction, and do not rest on any ecclesiastical authority accepted by all the Orthodox as binding and infallible. No ecumenical council has condemned or even passed judgment on the Catholic doctrines anathematized by our controversialists; when we are offered this new kind of negative theology as the true doctrine of the universal Church, we can see in it only an extravagant imposture originating either in ignorance or in bad faith. In the second place, it is obvious that this false Orthodoxy is no more adequate than true Orthodoxy as a positive basis for the "Russian idea." Let us try to substitute real values for this unknown quantity called "Orthodoxy" over which a pseudo-patriotic press is always working up an artificial enthusiasm. According to you the ideal essence of Russia is Orthodoxy, and this Orthodoxy which you especially contrast with Catholicism amounts in your view simply to the divergences between the two professions of faith. The real religious basis which is common to us and the Westerns seems to have no more than a secondary interest for you; it is the differences between us to which you are really attached. Very well then, substitute these specific differences for the vague term "orthodoxy" and declare openly that the religious ideal of Russia consists in denying the *Filioque,* the Immaculate Conception, and the authority of the pope. It is the last point that you are chiefly concerned with. The others, you know well, are only pretexts; the sovereign pontiff is your real bugbear. All your "orthodoxy," all your "Russian idea" is at bottom, then, simply a national protest against the universal power of the pope. But in the name of what?

Here begins the real difficulty of your position. This bitter protest against the monarchy of the Church, if it is to win men's minds and hearts should be justified by some great positive principle. You should confront the form of theocratic government of which you disapprove with another and better form. And that is exactly what you cannot do. What kind of ecclesiastical constitution would you confer upon the Western peoples? Are you going to extol conciliar government and talk to them of ecumenical councils? *Medice, cura teipsum.* Why has not the East set up a true ecumenical council in opposition to those of Trent or the Vatican? How are we to explain this helpless silence on the part of truth when faced with the solemn self-assertion of error? Since when have the guardians of Orthodoxy become mean-spirited curs that can only bark from behind a wall? In point of fact, while the great assemblies of the Church continue to fill a prominent place in the teaching and life of Catholicism, it is the Christian East which has for a thousand years been deprived of this important feature of the universal Church, and our best theologians, such as Philaret of Moscow, themselves admit that an ecumenical council is impossible for the Eastern Church as long as she remains separated from the West. But it is the easiest thing in the world for our self-styled Orthodox to confront the actual councils of the Catholic Church with a council that can never take place and to maintain their cause with weapons that they have lost and under the flag of which they have been robbed.

The papacy is a positive principle, an actual institution, and if Eastern Christians believe this principle to be false and this institution to be evil, it is for them to create the organization which they desire to see in the Church. Instead of doing so, they refer us to antiquarian traditions, though they admit that they can have no relevance to the present situation. Our anti-Catholics have indeed good reason for going so far afield in search of support for their thesis; the fact is that they dare not expose themselves to the ridicule of the whole world by declaring the synod of St. Petersburg or the patriarchate of Constantinople to be the real representative of the universal Church. But how can they talk of appealing after all this time to ecumenical councils when they are obliged to admit that they are no longer feasible? Such beating of the air is only a complete revelation of the weakness of this anti-Catholic Orthodoxy. If the normal

organization and proper constitution of the universal Church requires ecumenical councils, it is obvious that the Orthodox East, fatally deprived of this essential organ of Church life, possesses no longer a true Church constitution or a regular Church government. During the first three centuries of Christianity the Church, cemented by the blood of the martyrs, convoked no world-wide councils because she had no need for them; the Eastern Church of to-day, paralyzed and dismembered, is unable to convoke them though she feels her need of them. Thus we are placed in a dilemma: either we must admit, with our extreme sectarians, that since a certain date the Church has lost her divine character and no longer actually exists upon earth; or else, to avoid so dangerous a conclusion, we must recognize that the universal Church, having no organs of government or representation in the East, possesses them in her Western half. This will involve the recognition of a historical truth now admitted even by the Protestants, namely that the present-day papacy is not an arbitrary usurpation but a legitimate development of principles which were in full force before the division of the Church and against which that Church never protested. But if the papacy is recognized as a legitimate institution, what becomes of the "Russian idea" and the privilege of national Orthodoxy? If we cannot base our religious future on the official Church, perhaps we can find deeper foundations for it in the Russian people.

If we wish to state Orthodoxy in terms of the Russian national ideal, logic compels us to seek the true expression of that ideal among our native sects and not within the domain of the official Church, whose origin is Greek and whose organization, given her by Peter the Great, is Teutonic. Deprived of any specific principle or practical independence, this "Ministry of the Spiritual Affairs of the Orthodox Communion" can only reproduce the imperial clericalism of Byzantium modified by the easy-going good nature of our own people and the Teutonic bureaucracy of our administration. Apart from the particular causes which produced the Raskol, and which have only a historical importance, it may be confidently asserted that the reason for the persistence of this schism within the nation is the obvious inadequacy of Russian Church government coupled with its exaggerated pretentions. This Church "established" by the Czar, though totally subservient to the secular power and destitute of all inner vitality, none the less makes use of the hierarchical idea to assume over the people an absolute authority which by right belongs only to the independent universal Church founded by Christ. The emptiness of these claims, sensed rather than consciously recognized, has driven one section of our dissenters to fruitless attempts at constituting a Russian Orthodox Church independent of the state, while another and larger section has quite frankly declared that the true Church has completely disappeared from the world since the year 1666, and that we are living under the spiritual rule of antichrist resident at St. Petersburg. It is plain why the advocates of the "Russian idea" take good care not to look too closely into the Raskol nor to seek this elusive "idea" in that quarter. A doctrine which affirms that the Russian Church and monarchy are subject to the absolute rule or antichrist and which postpones all hope of a better state of affairs to the end of the world, obviously does not harmonize very well with an extravagant patriotism which represents Russia in her present condition as the second Israel and the chosen people of the future. Nevertheless it is of interest to note that it is precisely

those who would have Russia undertake a religious mission all her own, namely the Slavophils, who are compelled to ignore or to depreciate the one historical phenomenon in which the religious genius of the Russian people has shown a certain originality. On the other hand, in some of our liberal and radical "Westernizing" circles our national Protestantism, in spite of the barbarous forms it assumes, finds ready champions who imagine that they discern in it the promise of a better future for the Russian people. We ourselves, having no reason either to belittle or to over-estimate this typical phenomenon of our religious history, are able to view it more objectively. We do not underrate the great part played in the rise of the Raskol by the profoundest ignorance, ultra-democratic tendencies, and the spirit of revolt. We shall not therefore look to it for any higher truth or any positive religious ideal. Nevertheless we are bound to note that there has always been a spark of the divine fire in this crude and even senseless incitement of the passions of the mob. There is in it a burning thirst for religious truth, a compelling need for a true and living Church. Our national Protestantism aims its shafts at a partial and imperfect manifestation of ecclesiastical government and not at the principle of the visible Church. Even the most advanced section of our "old believers" regard an actual organized Church as so necessary that, because they are robbed of it, they believe themselves to be already under the rule of antichrist. Allowing for the ignorance which leads them to mistake Russia for the whole world, there is to be found at the bottom of all these queer errors the idea or the axiom of a Church independent of the state and closely bound up with the whole intimate social life of the people—a free, powerful and living Church. And if our dissenters see the official Church, whether Russian or Greek, without independence or vitality, and declare that therefore she is not the true Church of Christ, they are at least consistent in their error.

The negative truth implied in the Raskol remains unassailable. Neither the bloody persecutions of the past generations nor the oppression of a modern bureaucracy nor the official hostility of our clergy has done anything to meet the unanswerable contention that there exists no truly spiritual government in the Greco-Russian Church. But this is as far as the truth of our national Protestantism goes. As soon as the "old believers" abandon this simple denial and claim to have discovered some outlet for their religious instincts or to have realized their ideal of the Church, they fall into obvious contradictions and absurdities which make them an easy target for their opponents. It is not difficult for the latter to meet the "Popovtsy" by proving that a religious society which has been for generations deprived of the episcopate and which has only partially recovered this fundamental institution by entirely uncanonical proceedings cannot be the genuine continuation of the ancient Church and the sole guardian of the Orthodox tradition. It is no less easy to establish in answer to the "Bespopovtsy" the proposition that the reign of antichrist cannot be of indefinite length, and that logically these dissenters should repudiate not only the Church of the present day but also that of former times which in their opinion was destroyed in the year of grace 1666; for a Church against which the gates of hell have prevailed cannot have been the true Church of Christ.

The great historical importance of the Raskol with its thousands of martyrs is the witness which it bears to the depth of religious sentiment among the Russian people and to the lively interest aroused in them by the theocratic conception of the Church. If it is on the one hand a matter for great joy that the majority of the populace has remained faithful to the official Church which, despite the absence of any lawful Church government, has at least preserved the apostolic succession and the validity of the sacraments, it would on the other hand have been deplorable had the entire Russian people been content with this official Church such as it is; that would be a convincing proof that there was no religious future to be hoped for. The vehement and persistent protest of these millions of peasants gives us an earnest of the future regeneration of our Church life. But the essentially negative character of this religious movement is a sufficient proof that the Russian people, just like every other human power left to its own resources, is incapable of realizing its highest ideal. All these aspirations and tentative movements towards a true Church indicate no more than a passive capacity for religion which needs an act of moral regeneration coming from a higher source than the purely national and popular element if it is to be effectively realized in a concrete organic form.

We may grant that the official Church ruled by a civil servant is nothing but a state institution, a minor branch of the bureaucratic administration; but the Church conceived by our dissenters would at the most be a merely national and democratic Church. It is the idea of the universal Church which is lacking on both sides. The article of the Creed concerning the one, holy, catholic and apostolic Church, though sung at every Mass and recited at every Baptism, remains as much a dead letter for the "old Orthodox" as for the "ruling Church." For the former the Church is the Russian nation—in its entirety up to the time of Patriarch Nikon, and since his time in that section of it which has remained faithful to the old national rite. As for the theologians of the official Church, their ideas on the subject are as vague as they are inconsistent. But the feature which is constant among all their variations and common to them all in spite of their differences is the absence of a positive faith in the universal Church. Here, to confine ourselves to a single writer who is worth a host of others is the theory of the Church expounded by Archbishop Philaret, the able metropolitan of Moscow, in one of his most important works:

"The true Christian Church includes all the particular Churches which confess Jesus Christ 'come in the flesh.' The doctrine of all these religious societies is fundamentally the same divine truth; but it may be mingled with the opinions and errors of men. Hence there is in the teaching of these individual Churches a distinction of greater and less purity. The doctrine of the Eastern Church is purer than the rest; indeeed it may be recognized as completely pure, since it does not link the divine truth to any human opinion. However as each religious communion makes exactly the same claim to perfect purity of faith and doctrine, it does not behoove us to judge others but rather to leave the final judgment to the Spirit of God who guides the churches."

Such is the opinion of Msgr. Philaret and the majority of the Russian clergy agree with him. The breadth and conciliatory nature of this view cannot conceal its essential defects. The principle of unity and universality in the Church only extends, it would seem, to the common ground of Christian faith, namely the dogma of the Incarnation. This truly fundamental faith in Jesus Christ, the God-Man, is not regarded as the living and fruitful seed of a further development; the theologian of Moscow would rather see in it the final

unity of the Christian world and the only unity which he considers necessary. He is content to ignore the divergences that exist in the Christian religion and declares himself satisfied with the purely theoretical unity thus obtained. It is a unity based on a broad but hollow indifference, implying no organic bond and requiring no effective fellowship between particular Churches. The universal Church is reduced to a logical concept. Its parts are real, but the whole is nothing but a subjective abstraction. Even if it has not always been thus, if the Church in her entirety was once a living body, yet that body is today a prey to death and dissolution; it is only the existence of the separate parts that is actually manifest before our eyes, while their substantial unity has vanished into the realm of the unseen world.

This idea of a "dead Church" is not merely the logical conclusion which we believe to be implicit in the propositions advanced by our renowned theologian; he has labored to describe to us the universal Church as he conceived it under the form of a lifeless body made up of heterogeneous and distinct elements. He has even been inspired to apply to the Church of Christ and to the states of its historical existence the vision of the great idol recorded in the book of Daniel. The golden head of the idol is the early Christian Church; the chest and arms of silver signify "the Church growing in strength and extent" (the age of the martyrs); the brazen stomach is "the Church in prosperity" (the triumph of Christianity and the age of the great doctors). Finally the Church of the present, "the Church in its divided and fragmentary condition," is represented by the two feet with their toes, in which clay is mingled with iron by the hands of men. To accept this ill-omened symbol seriously would mean the denial of the one, infallible and impregnable Church of God founded to last for all generations. The author perceived as much, and in subsequent editions of his work he erased the whole of this allegory; but he found nothing to put in its place. It must, however, be confessed that in limiting the application of this symbol to the official Greco-Russian Church the distinguished representative of that institution displayed both acumen and impartiality. Iron and clay mixed by the hand of man—violence and impotence. And an artificial unity which needs only a shock to reduce it to powder. No simile could better depict the actual condition of our established Church. . . .

IV. *The Spiritual Mission of the Century*

THE baneful two-hundred-year influence of Jansenism on Catholic piety was ended in the mid-nineteenth century, and the subjectively oriented formulas of prayers which had been introduced in direct opposition to the Council of Trent were laid to rest. The diocesan priest who restored the ancient Abbey of Solesmes in France, Dom Prosper Gueranger (1875), was responsible more than anyone else in bringing the liturgy back to life as the "untiring affirmation of the works of God, the solemn acknowledgement of those divine facts, which, though done but once, are imperishable in man's remembrance, and are every year renewed by the commemoration he makes of them." Gueranger urged a return to authentic forms of Catholic worship and liturgical piety which can bring out so strikingly the homogeneous character of the Church. His writings on the history of the Roman liturgy and on THE LITURGICAL YEAR (*No. 25*) spiritually stirred Christians to live the life of the Church as a living mystery as they had not been moved since early medieval if not early Christian times. The revival of other Benedictine houses in the nineteenth century advanced by example and publications the traditional ideal of the Christian community glorifying God. The freedom of modern society, which enabled the Church to have again her religious communities as centers of public worship, opened the possibilities in the spiritual realm in the same way as the restoration of Catholic universities did in the intellectual realm, of creating a Christian culture. The research and developments of Gueranger's successors in France, Belgium, and Germany prepared the way for the official action which Pope Pius X took for the universal Church at the beginning of the next century. The works of the early liturgists, however, reveal excesses of romanticism, and a lack of critical understanding of actual liturgical developments. The liturgy was carried out in a more practical way on the parish level in the next century, when sound historical scholarship had made more headway among liturgists.

Popular piety continued to exercise a deep influence on Catholic people through the century. Places of pilgrimages, devotion to the rosary, confraternities, scapular devotions, devotions to the Sacred Heart of Jesus and

255

to the Blessed Virgin Mary, Catholic and Eucharistic Days, the Way of the Cross, Benediction of the Blessed Sacrament—all had a deep and valid effect on the broad currents of piety among the people. The Church, however, more closely directed individual and subjective forms of piety after authority had been centralized in the papacy. At the same time she placed at the disposal of all Christians, in this age as in every age, the means to actualize Christ in their lives. Under the leadership of Pope Pius X and his successors the pious practices which had developed, which were fruitful and had been employed by saints, were slowly drawn back into the spirit of the liturgy—as auxiliaries of this main-stream of official spiritual life, instead of substitutes for it.

In England a former Anglican, Father William Frederick Faber (1863), followed Newman into the Church in 1845, and into the Congregation of the Oratory of St. Philip Neri three years later. As superior of the London Oratory, Faber introduced schools for the poor, nightly services with sermons, and processions of the Blessed Sacrament, unknown in England until then. He exhibited in his large body of writings just such an ability to combine a profound knowledge of the Scriptures, the Fathers, and liturgy with a keen insight into the psychological needs of the individual soul. He strove to harmonize the ancient and modern spirituality of the Church for the English Catholics in their own native language, thought, and feeling. His writings were among the most popular spiritual books in the English-speaking world during the nineteenth century. Faber's THE BLESSED SACRAMENT, THE DEVOTION OF CATHOLICS (*No. 26*) typifies his characteristic approach of combining mysticism and asceticism with liturgical piety in a practical and effective manner.

A remarkable aspect of nineteenth century piety was the almost instant popular response to the example and spirit of a young French Carmelite at Lisieux which spread across the world. This was Térèse Martin, who became St. Thérèse of the Child Jesus (1897). At the early age of fifteen she became a Carmelite and lived only nine years as a religious. Yet in that period she advanced to union with God and has left the secrets of her "little way" to sanctity in her AUTOBIOGRAPHY (*No. 27*). She has been made a patroness of the missions of the Church as an indication of her own deep love of souls while never leaving the cloister, and as an indication, too, of the primary place of spiritual perfection as the basis of all missionary activity.

Another unique French spiritual personality of this period combined a contemplative, mystical life with a missionary apostolate; he was Charles de Foucauld (1916), a former army officer and Trappist priest. Foucauld had a deep vision of the necessity of coming in poverty to the Muslims of Africa as a modern St. Anthony of the desert. He lived a hidden, eremetical life among the Tuareg tribes at Beni-Abbes. There he practiced, in solitary, humble toil, the example of charity, continual prayer, and generosity to the 100,000 souls of the Sahara whose chaplain he said he must be. "Poor Charles of Jesus" left a record of his ideals, mortifications, work, and desire for martyrdom, which he finally achieved, in his remarkable DIARY AND LETTERS (*No. 28*) written from 1902 until his death in 1916. Charles de Foucauld understood, as so few Christians have, the long tragic history of relations with the followers of Mohammed. The prophet's disciples, who embrace more than one-seventh of the world's population, have come in contact with a Christianity torn by schism and open heresy. The Christianity they see is involved with irreligious aims of Western nations dating from the questionable ideals and procedures of the Crusades through to the colonial nations of modern times. Père Charles attempted in his life to give an example of the true unity and faith of Catholicism. By example and education, and despite his own excessive French patriotism, he made a small beginning in this challenging Christian apostolate to the Islamic world.

In the mission fields of the Pacific Oceania slow progress was made by intrepid Catholic missionaries who worked against major obstacles in the vast expanses of the Philippines, South Seas, New Zealand, and Australia. Archbishop William Ullathorne, O.S.B. (1806-89), recorded his early Australian experiences along with those of Bishop John Bede Polding, O.S.B., after religious freedom had been granted in England and her colonies. Their ministrations to Catholics among the convicts who had been expelled to Australia, as well as their first efforts to plant the Church among the "down under" pioneers, is graphically told in his autobiographical MISSION TO AUSTRALIA (*No. 29*).

25. *Abbot Prosper Gueranger, O.S.B.: The Liturgical Year* *16 November 1841*

From Prosper Gueranger, O.S.B., *The Liturgical Year* (Westminster, Maryland: The Newman Press, 1948), I, 1-19.

Prayer is man's richest boon. It is his light, his nourishment, and his very life, for it brings him into communication with God, who is light, nourishment, and life. But of ourselves we know not what we should pray for as we ought; we must, therefore, address ourselves to Jesus Christ, and say to him as the apostles did: "Lord, teach us how to pray." He alone can make the dumb speak, and give eloquence to the mouths of children; and this prodigy he effects by sending his Spirit of grace and of prayers, who delights in helping our infirmity, asking for us with unspeakable groanings.

Now it is in the holy Church that this divine Spirit dwells. He came down to her as an impetuous wind, and manifested himself to her under the expressive symbol of tongues of fire. Ever since that day of Pentecost, he has dwelt in this his favored bride. He is the principle of everything that is in her. He it is that prompts her prayers, her desires, her canticles of praise, her enthusiasm, and even her mourning. Hence her prayer is as uninterrupted as her existence. Day and night is her voice sounding sweetly in the ear of her divine spouse, and her words are ever finding a welcome in his heart.

At one time, under the impulse of that Spirit, who animated the wonderful psalmist and the prophets, she takes the subject of her canticles from the books of the Old Testament; at another, showing herself to be the daughter and sister of the holy apostles, she intones the canticles written in the books of the New Covenant; and finally, remembering that she, too, has had given to her the trumpet and harp, she at times gives way to the Spirit who animates her, and sings her own new canticle. From these three sources comes the divine element which we call the *liturgy*.

The prayer of the Church is, therefore, the most pleasing to the ear and heart of God; and therefore the most efficacious of all prayers. Happy, then, is he who prays with the Church, and unites his own petitions with those of this bride, who is so dear to her Lord that he gives her all she asks. It is for this reason that our blessed Savior taught us to say "our Father," and not "my" Father; give us, forgive us, deliver us, and not give me, forgive me, deliver me. Hence we find that, for upwards of a thousand years, the Church,

who prays in her temples seven times in the day and once again during the night, did not pray alone. The people kept her company, and fed themselves with delight on the manna which is hidden under the words and mysteries of the divine liturgy. Thus initiated into the sacred cycle of the mysteries of the Christian year, the faithful, attentive to the teachings of the Spirit, came to know the secrets of eternal life; and, without any further preparation, a Christian was not unfrequently chosen by the bishops to be a priest, or even a bishop, that he might go and pour out on the people the treasures of wisdom and love, which he had drunk in at the very fountain-head.

For while prayer said in union with the Church is the light of the understanding, it is the fire of divine love for the heart. The Christian soul neither needs nor wishes to avoid the company of the Church when she would converse with God, and praise his greatness and his mercy. She knows that the company of the bride of Christ could not be a distraction to her. Is not the soul herself a part of this Church, which is the bride? Has not Jesus Christ said. "Father, may they be one, as we also are one"? And, when many are gathered in his name, does not this same Savior assure us that he is in the midst of them? The soul, therefore, may converse freely with her God, who tells her that he is so near her. She may sing praise, as David did, in the sight of the angels, whose eternal prayer blends with the prayer which the Church utters in time.

But now for many ages past, Christians have grown too solicitous about earthly things to frequent the holy vigils, and the mystical hours of the day. Long before the rationalism of the sixteenth century had become the auxiliary of the heresies of that period by curtailing the solemnity of the divine service, the people had ceased to unite themselves exteriorly with the prayer of the Church, except on Sundays and festivals. During the rest of the year, the solemn and imposing grandeur of the liturgy was gone through. The people took no share in it. Each new generation increased in indifference for that which their forefathers in the faith had loved as their best and strongest food. Social prayer was made to give way to individual devotion. Chanting, which is the natural expression of the prayers and even of the sorrows of the Church, became limited to the solemn feasts. That was the first sad revolution in the Christian world.

But even then Christendom was still rich in churches and monasteries; and there, day and night, was still heard the sound of the same venerable prayers which the Church had used through all the past ages. So many hands lifted up to God drew down upon the earth the dew of heaven, averted storms, and won victory for those who were in battle. These servants of God, who thus kept up an untiring choir that sang the divine praises, were considered as solemnly deputed by the people, which was still Catholic, to pay the full tribute of homage and thanksgiving due to God, his blessed Mother, and the saints. These prayers formed a treasury which belonged to all. The faithful gladly united themselves in spirit to what was done. When any affliction, or the desire to obtain a special favor, led them to the house of God, they were sure to hear, no matter at what hour they went, that untiring voice of prayer which was forever ascending to heaven for the salvation of mankind. At times they would give up their worldly business and cares, and take part in the office of the Church. All still understood, at least in a general way, the mysteries of the liturgy.

Then came the so-called Reformation, and at the outset it attacked the very life of Christianity: it would put an end to man's sacrifice of praise to God. It strewed many countries with the ruins of churches: the clergy, the monks, and virgins consecrated to God were banished or put to death; and in the churches which were spared the divine offices were not permitted. In other countries, where the persecution was not so violent, many sanctuaries were devastated and irremediably ruined, so that the life and voice of prayer grew faint. Faith, too, was weakened; rationalism became fearfully developed; and now our own age seems threatened with what is the result of these evils— the subversion of all social order.

For, when the Reformation had abated the violence of its persecution, it had other weapons wherewith to attack the Church. By these several countries which continued to be Catholic were infected with that spirit of pride which is the enemy of prayer. The modern spirit would have it that prayer is not action: as though every good action done by man were not a gift of God: a gift which implies two prayers, one of petition that it may be granted, and another of thanksgiving because it is granted. There were found men who said: "Let us abolish all the festival days of God from the earth." Then came upon us that calamity which brings all others with it, and which the good Mardochai besought God to avert from his nation, when he said: "Shut not, O Lord, the mouths of them that sing to you!"

But by the mercy of God we have not been consumed; there have been left remnants of Israel; and the number of believers in the Lord has increased. What is it that has moved the heart of our God to bring about this merciful conversion? Prayer, which had been interrupted, has been resumed. Numerous choirs of virgins consecrated to God, and, though far less in number, of men who have left the world to spend themselves in the divine praises, make the voice of the turtle-dove heard in our land. This voice is every day gaining more power: may it find acceptance from our Lord, and move him to show the sign of his covenant with us, the rainbow of rec-onciliation! May our venerable cathe-drals again re-echo those solemn for-mulae of prayer, which heresy has so long suppressed! May the faith and munificence of the faithful reproduce the prodigies of those past ages, which owed their greatness to the acknowl-edgment paid by all, even the very civic authorities, to the all-powerfulness of prayer.

But this liturgical prayer would soon become powerless were the faithful not to take a real share in it, or at least not to associate themselves to it in heart. It can heal and save the world, but only on the condition that it be un-derstood. Be wise, then, ye children of the Catholic Church, and obtain that largeness of heart which will make you pray the prayer of your mother. Come, and by your share in it fill up that har-mony which is so sweet to the ear of God. Where would you obtain the spirit of prayer if not at its natural source? Let us remind you of the exhortation of the apostle to the first Christians: "Let the peace of Christ rejoice in your hearts; let the word of Christ dwell in you abundantly, in all wisdom; teach-ing and admonishing one another, in psalms, hymns, and spiritual canticles, singing in grace in your hearts to God."

For a long time, a remedy has been devised for an evil which was only vaguely felt. The spirit of prayer, and even prayer itself, has been sought for in methods and prayer-books, which contain, it is true, laudable, yes, pious thoughts. But, after all, only human thoughts. Such nourishment cannot sat-isfy the soul, for it does not initiate her into the prayer of the Church. In-stead of uniting her with the prayer of the Church, it isolates her. Of this kind

are so many of those collections of prayers and reflections, which have been published under different titles during the last two hundred years, and by which it was intended to edify the faithful, and suggest to them, either for hearing Mass, or going to the sac-raments, or keeping the feasts of the Church, certain more or less common-place considerations and acts, always drawn up according to the manner of thought and sentiment peculiar to the author of each book. Each manual had consequently its own way of treating these important subjects. To Chris-tians already formed to piety, such books as these would, indeed, serve a purpose, especially as nothing better was offered to them; but they had not influence sufficient to inspire with the spirit of prayer such as had not other-wise received it.

It may perhaps be objected that, were all practical books of Christian piety to be reduced to mere explana-tions of the liturgy, we should run the risk of impoverishing, and even de-stroying, by excessive formalities, the spirit of prayer and contemplation, which is such a precious gift of the Holy Ghost to the Church of God. To this we answer, firstly, that by assert-ing the immense superiority of liturgi-cal over individual prayer, we do not say that individual methods should be suppressed; we would only wish them to be kept in their proper place. Then secondly, we answer that in the divine psalmody there are several degrees: the lowest are near enough to the earth to be reached by souls that are still plodding in the fatigues of the purga-tive way; but in proportion as a soul ascends this mystic ladder, she feels herself illuminated by a heavenly ray; and still higher, she finds union and rest in the sovereign Good. Whence, for instance, did the holy doctors of the early ages, and the venerable patri-archs of the desert, acquire their spiritual knowledge and tender devotion, of which they have left us such treasures in their writings and their works? It was from those long hours of psalmody, during which truth, simple yet manifold, unceasingly passed before the eyes of their soul, filling it with streams of light and love. What was it that gave to the seraphic Bernard that wonderful unction, which runs in streams of honey through all his writings? To the author of the *Imitation of Christ* that sweetness, that hidden manna, which seems ever fresh? To Louis Blosius, that inexpressible charm and tenderness which move the heart of every reader? It was the daily use of the liturgy, in the midst of which they spent their days, intermingling their songs of joy with those of their sorrow.

Let not then the soul, the bride of Christ, that is possessed with a love of prayer, be afraid that her thirst cannot be quenched by these rich streams of the liturgy, which now flow calmly as the streamlet, now roll with the loud impetuosity of a torrent, and now swell with mighty heavings of the sea. Let her come and drink this clear water which springs up unto life everlasting; for this water flows from the very fountains of her Savior; and the Spirit of God animates it by his virtue, rendering it sweet and refreshing to the panting stag. Neither let a soul that is in love with the charms of contemplation be afraid of the pomp and harmony of the chants of liturgical prayer, as though they could distract her; for what is this soul herself but an instrument of harmony responding to the touch of that divine Spirit who possesses her? Would she, when she wishes to enjoy the heavenly interview, comport herself differently from the royal psalmist himself, that model of all true prayer, recognized as such by God and the Church? Yet he, when he would enkindle the sacred flame within his breast, has recourse to his harp: "My heart is ready," he says; "O God, my heart is ready; I will sing, I will give forth a psalm. Arise, my glory! arise, psaltery and harp! I will arise in the morning early. I will praise you, O Lord, among the people; and I will sing unto you among the nations. For your mercy is great above the heavens, and your truth even unto the clouds." At other times, if, in the interior recollection of the senses, he has entered into the powers of the Lord, then, in his meditation, a fire flames out, a fire of holy excitement; and, to assuage the heat which is burning within him, he bursts out into another canticle, saying: "My heart has uttered a good word; I speak my works to the king"; and publishes again and again the beauty and victories of the bridegroom, and the graces of the bride. So true is it, that for contemplative souls liturgical prayer is both the principle and the consequence of the visits they receive from God.

But in nothing is the excellency of the liturgy so apparent, as in its being milk for children, and solid food for the strong; thus resembling the miraculous bread of the desert, and taking every kind of taste according to the different dispositions of those who eat. It is, indeed, a divine property, which has not unfrequently been noticed even by those who are not of the true fold, and has forced them to acknowledge that the Catholic Church alone knows the secret of prayer. Nay, might it not be said that the reason that the Protestants have no ascetic writers, is that they have no real liturgical prayer? It is true that a sufficient explanation of the absolute want of unction, which characterizes all that the reformation has produced, is to be found in its denying the holy sacrament of the Eucharist, which is the center of all religion: but this is virtually the same as saying that Protestants have no liturgical prayer, inasmuch as the liturgy is so essentially and intimately connected with the Eucharist. So true is this, that wheresoever the dogma of the real presence has ceased to be believed, there also have the canonical hours ceased, and could not but cease.

It is therefore Jesus Christ himself who is the source as well as the object of the liturgy; and hence the ecclesiastical year, which we have undertaken to explain in this work, is neither more nor less than the manifestation of Jesus Christ and his mysteries, in the Church and in the faithful soul. It is the divine cycle, in which appear all the works of God, each in its turn: the seven days of the creation; the Pasch and Pentecost of the Jewish people; the ineffable visit of the Incarnate Word; his sacrifice and his victory; the descent of the Holy Ghost; the holy Eucharist; the surpassing glories of the Mother of God, ever a virgin; the magnificence of the angels; the merits and triumphs of the saints. Thus the cycle of the Church may be said to have its beginning under the patriarchal law, its progress under the written law, and its completion under the law of love, in which, at length, having attained its last perfection, it will disappear in eternity, as the written law gave way the day on which the invincible power of the Blood of the Lamb rent asunder the veil of the temple.

Would that we might worthily describe the sacred wonders of this mystical calendar, of which all others are but images and humble auxiliaries! Happy indeed should we deem ourselves, if we could make the faithful understand the grand glory which is given to the blessed Trinity, to our Savior, to Mary, to the angels, and to the saints, by this annual commemoration of the wondrous works of our God! If, every year, the Church renews her youth as that of the eagle, she does so because, by means of the cycle of the liturgy, she is visited by her divine spouse, who supplies all her wants. Each year she again sees him an Infant in the manger, fasting in the desert, offering himself on the cross, rising from the grave, founding his Church, instituting the sacraments, ascending to the right hand of his Father, and sending the Holy Ghost upon men. The graces of all these divine mysteries are renewed in her; so that, being made fruitful in every good thing, the mystic garden yields to the spouse, in every season, under the influence of the Spirit he breathes into her, the sweet perfume of aromatic spices. Each year the Spirit of God retakes possession of his well-beloved and gives her light and love; each year she derives an increase of life from the maternal influence which the blessed Virgin exercises over her, on the feasts of her joys, her sorrows, and her glories; and lastly, the brilliant constellation formed by the successive appearance of the nine choirs of the angels, and of the saints in their varied orders of apostles, martyrs, confessors, and virgins, sheds on her, each year, powerful help and abundant consolation.

Now, what the liturgical year does for the Chuch at large, it does also for the soul of each one of the faithful that is careful to receive the gift of God. This succession of mystic seasons imparts to the Christian the elements of that supernatural life, without which every other life is but a sort of death, more or less disguised. Nay, there are some souls, so far acted upon by the divine succession of the Catholic cycle, that they experience even a physical effect from each evolution: the supernatural life has gained ascendancy over the natural, and the calendar of the Church makes them forget that of astronomers.

Let the Catholic who reads this work be on his guard against that coldness of faith, and that want of love, which have well-nigh turned into an object of indifference that admirable cycle of the Church, which heretofore was, and always ought to be, the joy of the people, the source of light to the learned, and the book of the humblest of the faithful.

The reader will rightly infer, from what we have said, that the object we have in view is not, in any way, to publish some favorite or clever method of our own with regard to the mysteries of the ecclesiastical year, nor to make them subjects for eloquence, philosophy, or intellectual fancy. We have but one aim, and we humbly ask of God that we may attain it; it is to serve as interpreter to the Church, in order thus to enable the faithful to follow her in her prayer of each mystic season, nay, of each day and hour. God forbid that we should ever presume to put our human thoughts side by side with those which our Lord Jesus Christ, who is the wisdom of God, dictates by the Holy Ghost to his well-beloved bride the Church. All that we would do is to show what is the spirit which the Holy Ghost has put into each of the several periods of the liturgical year; and for this purpose, to study attentively the most ancient and venerable liturgies, and embody in our explanation the sentiments of the holy fathers and the oldest and most approved liturgists. With these helps, we hope to give to the faithful the flowers of ecclesiastical prayer, and thus unite, as far as possible, practical usefulness with the charm of variety.

In this work we shall lay great stress on the cult of the saints, inasmuch as it is always needed, but now more than ever. Devotion to the adorable person of our Savior has revived among us with a vigorous development; devotion to our blessed Lady has wonderfully spread and increased; let the saints also receive our honor and our confidence, and then the last traces of the unhappy spirit introduced by Jansenism will disappear. But, since we cannot introduce all the saints into our calendar, we shall limit ourselves, almost exclusively, to those inserted in that of Rome.

Nevertheless, the Roman liturgy is not the only one we intend to give; though of course it will be the most prominent, as being the very basis of our *Liturgical Year*. The Ambrosian, the Gallican, the Gothic or Mozarabic, the Greek, the Armenian, the Syriac liturgies will, each in its turn, give us of their riches and form our treasury of prayers; and thus, never will the voice of the Church have been fuller and more impressive. The western Churches, during the middle ages, have inserted into the liturgy of some of the feasts Sequences so admirable for their unction and doctrine, that we shall consider it a duty to give them to the faithful as often as occasion serves.

The plan we shall follow in the several volumes of this *Liturgical Year* will depend upon the subjects which must be treated of in each. Everything that relates to the merely scientific bearing of the liturgy, will be reserved for our *Liturgical Institutions*. The present work will be limited to those details, which the faithful must necessarily understand in order to enter into the spirit of the Church during the several mystic seasons of the year. The sacred formulae will be explained and adapted to the use of the laity by means of a commentary, in which we shall endeavor to avoid both the imprudence of a literal translation, and the dullness of a tedious and insipid paraphrase.

Since, as we have already said, our aim is to present to the faithful the most solid and useful portions of the liturgies, we have excluded from our selection all such as seemed to us not to answer our purpose. This observation refers mainly to the portions selected from the offices of the Greek Church. Nothing is finer and more impressive than this liturgy, when read in chosen extracts; but nothing is so disappointing when taken as a whole. The monotony of phrases is insupportable, and the endless repetitions of the same idea spoil the real unction contained in it. We have therefore selected only the richest flowers of this over-stocked garden: more than these would have been a burden. These remarks apply especially to the *Menoea* and *Anthologia* of the Greek Church. The liturgical books of the other Eastern churches are generally drawn up with better taste and more discretion.

In order to conform with the wishes of the Holy See, we do not give, in any of the volumes of our *Liturgical Year,* the literal translation of the ordinary and canon of the Mass; we have in its place endeavored to give, to such of the laity as do not understand Latin, the means of uniting in the closest possible manner with everything that the priest says and does at the altar.

The first part of the *Liturgical Year* is devoted to Advent. The second contains the explanation of the divine service from Christmas to the Purification. The third takes us from the Purification as far as Lent, and is called *Septuagesima.* The fourth comprises the four first weeks of Lent. The fifth consists of Passion-week and Holy Week. The sixth includes the time of Easter. The seventh will explain the office of the Church from the feast of the most holy Trinity to the end of the time after Pentecost.

The year thus planned for us by the Church herself produces a drama the sublimest that has ever been offered to the admiration of man. God intervening for the salvation and sanctification of men; the reconciliation of justice with mercy; the humiliations, the sufferings, and the glories of the God-Man; the coming of the Holy Ghost, and his workings in humanity and in the faithful soul; the mission and the action of the Church—all are there portrayed in the most telling and impressive way. Each mystery has its time and place by means of the sublime succession of the respective anniversaries. A divine fact happened nineteen hundred years ago. Its anniversary is kept in the liturgy, and its impression is thus reiterated every year in the minds of the faithful, with a freshness, as though God were then doing for the first time what he did so many ages past. Human ingenuity could never have devised a system of such power as this. And those writers who are bold and frivolous enough to assert that Christianity has no longer an influence in the world, and is now but the ruin of an ancient thing—what would they say at seeing these undying realities, this vigor, this endlessness of the liturgical year? For what is the liturgy, but an untiring affirmation of the works of God? a solemn acknowledgment of those divine facts, which, though done but once, are imperishable in man's remembrance, and are every year renewed by the commemoration he makes of them? Have we not our writings of the apostolic age, our acts of the martyrs, our decrees of ancient councils, our writings of the fathers, our monuments, taking us to the very origin of Christianity, and testifying to the most explicit tradition regarding our feasts? It is true that the liturgical cycle has its integrity and its development nowhere but in the Catholic Church; but the sects which are separated from her, whether by schism or by heresy, all pay the homage of their testimony to the divine origin of the liturgy by the pertinacity with which they cling to the remnants they have preserved—remnants, by the way, to which they owe whatever vitality they still retain.

But though the liturgy so deeply impresses us by annually bringing before us the dramatic solemnization of those mysteries which have been accomplished for the salvation of man and for his union with his God, it is nevertheless wonderful how the succession of year after year diminishes not one atom of the freshness and vehemence of those impressions, and each new beginning of the cycle of mystic seasons seems to be our first year. Advent is ever impregnated with the spirit of a sweet and mysterious expectation. Christmas ever charms us with the incomparable joy of the birth of the divine child. We enter, with the well-known feeling, into the gloom of Septuagesima. Lent comes, and we prostrate ourselves before God's justice, and our heart is filled with a salutary fear and compunction, which seems so much keener than they were the year before. The passion of our Redeemer, followed in every minutest detail—does it not seem as though we never knew it till this year? The pageant of Easter makes us so glad that our former Easters appear to have been only half kept. The triumphant Ascension discloses to us, upon the whole economy of the Incarnation, secrets which we never knew before this year. When the Holy Ghost comes down at Pentecost, is it not the case that we so thrill with the renewal of the great presence that our emotions of last Whitsunday seem too tame for this? However habituated we get to the ineffable gift which Jesus made us on the eve of his Passion, the bright feast of Corpus Christi brings a strange increase of love to our heart; and the blessed sacrament seems more our own than ever. The feasts of our blessed Lady come round, each time revealing something more of her greatness; and the saints—with whom we fancied we had become so thoroughly acquainted —each year as they visit us seem so much grander, we understand them better, we feel more sensibly the link there is between them and ourselves.

The renovative power of the liturgical year, to which we wish to draw the attention of our readers, is a mystery of the Holy Ghost, who unceasingly animates the work which he has inspired the Church to establish among men; that thus they might sanctify that time which has been given to them for the worship of their creator. The renovation works also a twofold growth in the mind of man: the increase of knowledge of the truths of faith, and the development of the supernatural life. There is not a single point of Christian doctrine which, in the course of the liturgical year, is not brought forward, nay, is not inculcated with that authority and unction wherewith our holy mother the Church has so deeply impregnated her words and her eloquent rites. The faith of the believer is thus enlightened more and more each year; the theological *sensus* is formed in him; prayer leads him to science. Mysteries continue to be mysteries; but their brightness becomes so vivid, that the mind and heart are enchanted, and we begin to imagine what a joy the eternal sight of these divine beauties will produce in us, when the glimpse of them through the clouds is such a charm to us.

Yes, there must needs be a great progress in a Christian soul, when the object of her faith is ever gaining greater light; when the hope of her salvation is almost forced upon her by the sight of all those wonders which God's goodness has wrought for his creatures; and when charity is enkindled within her under the breath of the Holy Ghost, who has made the liturgy to be the center of his working in men's souls. Is not the formation of Christ within us the result of our uniting in his various mysteries, the joyful, sorrowful, and the glorious? These mysteries of Jesus come into us, are incorporated into us each year, by the power of the special grace which the liturgy produces by communicating them to us: the new man gradually grows up, even on the ruins of the old. Then again, in order that the divine type may the more easily be stamped upon us, we need examples; we want to see how our fellow-men have realized that type in themselves: and the liturgy fulfills this need for us, by offering us the practical teaching and the encouragement of our dear saints, who shine like stars in the firmament of the ecclesiastical year. By looking upon them we come to learn the way which leads to Jesus, just as Jesus is our way which leads to the Father. But above all the saints, and brighter than them all, we have Mary, showing us, in her single person, the 'mirror of justice,' in which is reflected all the sanctity possible in a pure creature.

Finally, the *Liturgical Year,* the plan of which we have been explaining, will bring continually before us the sublimest poetry that the human mind has conceived. Not only will it enable us to understand the divine songs of David and the prophets, on which mainly the liturgy has formed her own; but the cycle will elicit from the Church, according as the different seasons and feasts come round, canticles and hymns the finest, the sublimest, and the worthiest of the subject. We shall hear the several countries, united as they are in one common faith, pouring forth their admiration and love in accents, wherein are blended the most perfect harmony of thought and sentiment with the most marked diversity of genius and expression. We exclude from our collection, as duty requires we should, certain modern compositions which had too close a resemblance to pagan literature, and which, as they had not received the sanction of the Church's acceptance, were likely to be short-lived: but the productions of liturgical genius, no matter of what age in the Church, are profusely admitted; from Sedulius and Prudentius, down to Adam and St. Victor and his contemporaries, for the Latin Church; and from St. Ephrem, down to the latest Catholic Byzantine hymnologists for the Greek Church. A rich vein of poetry will be found as well in the prayers which have been composed in simple prose, as in those which are presented to us in the garb of measure and rhythm. Poetry, being the only language adequate to the sublime thought which is to be expressed, is to be found everywhere in the liturgy, as it is in the inspired writings; and a complete collection of the formulae of public prayer would be, at the same time, the richest selection of Christian poetry, of that poetry which sings on earth the mysteries of heaven and prepares us for the canticles of eternity.

In concluding this general preface, we beg to remind our readers, that in a work like the present, the success of the writer is absolutely dependent upon the Holy Spirit, who breathes where he will, and that the most which man can do is to plant and water. We venture therefore to ask the children of the Church, who desire to see her prayer loved and used above all others, to aid us by recommending our work to God, that so our unworthiness may not be an obstacle to what we have undertaken, and which we feel to be so much above our strength.

We have only to add that we submit our work, both in its substance and its form, to the sovereign and infallible judgment of the holy Roman Church, which alone is the guardian both of the words of eternal life, and of the secret prayer. . . .

26. Frederick William Faber: The Blessed Sacrament, The Devotion of Catholics, 29 December 1854

From Frederick W. Faber, *The Blessed Sacrament* (Baltimore: John Murphy Company, 1885), pp. 129-58.

I. IT MAY seem at first sight strange, and not altogether respectful, to the real presence of our Blessed Lord in his great Sacrament to number it among the subjects of a special devotion. For a special devotion, in the sense in which spiritual writers use the words, means that, from a natural turn of mind, or from certain associations with the secret history of our souls, or from the peculiar mysteries of our Lord's life, or particular attributes of God, or particular angels and saints, rather than to others. It is intelligible that an active professional man should experience greater sweetness in meditating on our Lord's public ministry than on his hidden life in the holy house of Nazareth. The examples come more home to him and are more readily applied to his own trials and difficulties in the discharge of public duties. While the nun, the seminarist, or one who from any cause is leading a retired life, goes to the house of Nazareth as, to such persons at least, a fresher and a fuller fountain of consolation, encouragement and strength, some for the moment, like Peter, seem to prefer Thabor to Calvary, which is an instance of an indiscreet special devotion. Some prefer Bethlehem to Calvary, and as the cross is equally in both, this is an example of a legitimate and safe special devotion. A virgin saint is more to some minds than a martyr; and there are those who prefer a doctor of the Church to both. All this is intelligible, even when it concerns the choice and preference of certain mysteries of the Incarnation over others. But how is it at all rightly applicable to the Blessed Sacrament, which is nothing else than Jesus himself in the veils which he has chosen?

This surely we may say is rather a part of the direct universal worship of God, than the lawful subject of a special devotion. We do not directly worship the Visitation, or the Finding in the Temple, or the Agony in the Garden; but we do directly worship the Blessed Sacrament, as the living God himself in mystic veils. How then can we speak of persons having a special devotion to the Blessed Sacrament; by which we do not simply mean that they are distinguished themselves by an unusual amount of devotion to the Blessed Sacrament; but that it is their special devotion?

A very little consideration will suffice to explain the difficulty. The adoration of the Blessed Sacrament is truly part of the direct universal worship of God which is paid to him by the faithful. In the daily sacrifice of the Mass, in the receiving of holy Communion, and in the proper observant homage of his sacramental Presence in churches, this worship is bound by the Church on the consciences of her children; and Benediction has now become to the people almost what choir is to religious, or the divine office to the clergy. And this worship and homage is of course not included under the idea of a special devotion. It is something which every one must have, which every one must do, else is he a rebel, a renegade, or a heretic. It belongs to Catholic dutifulness. It is a necessary part of the profession of Christian faith, and of the homage which the instructed reason of the creature owes to the majesty and presence of his Creator, wheresoever they are revealed to him.

But as it is a kindred mystery to the

Incarnation and almost a part of it, or rather its very complement, there is another view which may be taken of devotion to the Blessed Sacrament; according to which view it may be truly and reverently regarded as the subject of what we call a special devotion. For example, some persons can keep themselves in the presence of God anywhere, in their own rooms or in the crowded streets, as well as in Church and before the tabernacle. The Blessed Sacrament does not seem to be necessary to their devout recollections or to the fervor of their prayers. At the time, the fact of their being in Church does not seem to exercise any discernible influence on their devotion. Others again find the utmost difficulty in praying well anywhere except before the Blessed Sacrament. Prayer is quite another thing to them when they are in church. However much outward duties and distractions, or internal conflicts and struggles, may have caused them to lose the sensible presence of God, they are no sooner before our Lord then they are calmed almost without their own co-operation; all disquietude is allayed, and the spirit of prayer triumphantly resumes its happy empire over their minds. The Blessed Sacrament is to the latter class of people something which it is not to the former, and yet the former may be in a far higher spiritual condition. Again, some persons will by preference say Mass at an altar where the Blessed Sacrament is reserved, because they find themselves so much more fervent and recollected there. Others will by preference say Mass where it is not reserved, because they realize our Lord's sacramental presence with such an absorbing intensity of faith that it disturbs them, makes it difficult for them to observe with the proper calm attention the minute ceremonies and rubrics of the Mass, and hinders for the moment their realizing the sacrifice. Others,

again, experience a distinct loss of sensible devotion at high Mass or in great functions, because the lights, incense, vestments, and actions of the sacred ministers, combined with the tumult of the music, seem to disturb and disarrange the quiet supremacy of the tabernacle, while multitudes of excellent persons experience none of these three things.

Obviously these are three modes in which a special devotion to the Blessed Sacrament variously discloses itself. Again, there are some, with a really tender and intense devotion to the passion, who actually do not know what to do with themselves on Good Friday, because there is no Blessed Sacrament, and whose minds are occupied less with the mystery of our Lord's death, of the expectation of his resurrection, than by the thought of the many sacristies in which the Blessed Sacrament is lying hid, to be ready as viaticum for those in their agony. Their thoughts are haunting these hiding-places, with a feeling of almost perverse devotion, seeing that the Church so studiously withdraws them from our homage and our gaze. Sometimes members of a community, from which the Blessed Sacrament is temporarily withdrawn for some unavoidable reason, feel so unhinged that the observances of their rule, or the practices of penance, or even acts of obedience which do not appear to have so much as a remote connection with the Blessed Sacrament, are almost impossible, or require an absurdly disproportioned effort, just as a family goes wrong in slight things when its master is away. While in the same community others are merely deploring one means of grace suspended, one spiritual exercise intermitted. . . .

The spirit of the Blessed Sacrament is plainly two-fold, according as we look at the sacrifice or the sacrament. The spirit of the sacrifice is without doubt the spirit of Calvary, for it is a renewal of the mysteries of the passion, and it is itself the very same sacrifice. But this is hardly the subject with which we are concerned. It is true that in one sense of the words persons may have a special devotion, meaning thereby a peculiarly great one, to the adorable sacrifice of the Mass; but it is scarcely true that, in the other sense of the words, the Mass can be the subject of a separate special devotion to Catholics. It enters too much into our duties, obligations, and the essence of the whole system of the Christian religion, which is eminently a religion of sacrifice. It is the spirit of sacrifice which creates the church, maintains it, multiplies it, holds it together, and circulates through its veins as its life's blood. Sacrifice is the key to the difficulties of its dogmas; it is the soul of its mysteries, the cause of its asceticism, the pattern of its mystical unions with God. Ritual is the action of sacrifice, prayer is the language of sacrifice, contemplation is the thought of sacrifice, and interior mortification is sacrifice itself. Sacrifice is to the Church what soul is to the body; it is whole in the whole body, and whole in every part of the body and whatever part of the body has ceased to be informed by it, has thereby ceased to be a living part of the body at all. Where there is no Mass, there is also no Christianity. Wherever we turn there is sacrifice. The outward life of the Church is nothing but a glorious and unmistakable preaching of sacrifice: the papacy is itself only an incessant, continuous, unflinching martyrdom. To the discerning eye, the Church has never left the catacombs, or if it has, it has been only to seek for new ways of suffering, as St. Mary Magdalen of Pazzi says that our Lord finding all delights in heaven, save the jewelled stole of suffering, left heaven and the bosom of the Father and came on earth to seek it. If we penetrate into the inner life of the Church, her solitudes of divine union, her peopled deserts of silent love, her cloisters of vowed and supernatural loveliness, the further in we penetrate the more do we discover that it is nothing but a concentration, a transformation, a spiritualizing, of sacrifice.

All this lies in the vital force and omnipotent energy of the Mass. That far reaching sacrifice is everywhere, and does everything for every one. It belongs therefore too much to the existence of the Church to be the subject of what we call a special devotion, one of many, something which can be compared with other things, a shining mystery with other mysteries shining round about it. The wants of souls are almost infinitely various; some have the grace to feel the want of much, and to be ever wanting more; others unhappily want little, and can be contented with almost less; but just as the running stream fills the vessels, great or small, which are dipped into its abundance, and just as the sun gives full light to the various powers of vision of different men and animals, so it is with the Mass. It is coextensive with the wants of all, embraces all, satisfies all, stimulates all. Our all is there, our bread for the day, our viaticum for the journey to eternity.

It is enough if the daily Sacrifice of the Mass cease, for the Church at once to fall on those unutterable latter days when antichrist shall persecute and reign. Laws against Mass, insults to it, inabilities to bequeath foundations for it, all these are of the essence of persecution. In the same way that all souls are equal, so Mass is equal to all; and in the same way that every degree of mental power and glorious giftedness, from the sublimest intelligence of the theologian to the limited understanding of the peasant, is secured and sustained, as much as it wants and no more, by the immortal soul, so the broad edifice of the saint's sanctity and the small beginnings of the sinner's efforts have all they want, and no more, in the sacrifice of the Mass. The adorable sacrifice fills all spiritual depths and shallows; it is its gift that it should fill wherever it is; fullness is its prerogative. Hence its character does not admit of its being precisely the subject of a special devotion.

When we speak, therefore, of the Blessed Sacrament being the subject of a special devotion we mean, not the sacrifice, nor the communion, but the sacramental life of our Lord, the residence of Jesus among us under the mystic veils of the species. The presence of God is as it were the atmosphere of the spiritual life, and the practice of his presence includes and combines all the practices of devotion; and just as God's putting on a visible nature in the Incarnation enabled men to picture him to themselves and to avoid idolatry, so to many souls the practical though not absolute omnipresence of the sacred humanity in the Blessed Sacrament supplies them with a practice of the divine presence, which in their case far surpasses what they could attain by endeavoring to realize the spiritual presence of God. The Blessed Sacrament does for the immensity of God what the Incarnation does for his invisibility. It is this life of Jesus in the Blessed Sacrament which is the subject of a special devotion.

Jesus lives many lives in the Blessed Sacrament. In one sense he may be said to lead many exterior lives. For in each tabernacle where he is reserved, he meets with different treatment, performs different miracles of grace, receives different petitions of want and sorrow, abides a different length of time, and is the object of different degrees of love. There is in this sense what may be called an outward biography to every consecrated host. But this is not what is meant by saying that Jesus lives many lives in the Blessed

Sacrament. What is meant is interior, mystical, and of a spiritual character. His life in the Blessed Sacrament is different from the life he leads in heaven; it is under different conditions, and follows peculiar laws, according as he has willed it. His life is a state of mystical death. It is a life in which he foregoes the use of his human senses. In the adorable host he does not see with his man's eyes, nor hear with his man's ears. He restrains all these things, and hushes himself into a mystical death in order that we may be the more fearless, though not the less humble, in approaching his mysterious presence. But besides this, there are senses in which he leads in the Blessed Sacrament an active life and a contemplative life, a life of poverty and a life of divine riches, a life of suffering yet also a life of glory. As many states as there are in the spiritual life of the faithful, so many lives are there which he leads in the Blessed Sacrament. The apostolic missionary, the cloistered nun, the lonely hermit, the busy merchant, the prelate and the child, the fresh penitent and the experienced contemplative, behold him in the manifold depths of his sweet sacrament leading their lives, and winning them to himself by a sympathy of state and occupations, so marked and decided as seemingly to exclude any others. While he is the pattern of all states, he seems to be the exclusive representative of none, just as his whole passion was all for each one of us, while it was also all the while for the whole world. But we shall have occasion to return another time to these various lives in the Blessed Sacrament. We have now to examine the peculiar spirit which devotion to these lives of Jesus gives out and impresses upon our souls.

The Blessed Sacrament was markedly instituted in commemoration of our Lord's passion. The time and the circumstances of its first institution leave no doubt whatever upon the subject, even independently of the positive precept of commemorating the passion thereby. The Mass is itself externally a sort of drama of the passion, and internally it is the identical sacrifice perpetually and bloodlessly renewed. Yet, on the most superficial consideration of the matter, we cannot avoid being struck by the obvious analogies between the Blessed Sacrament and the sacred infancy; and when we come to examine it fully, we arrive at the conclusion, that while the spirit of the sacrifice is the spirit of Calvary, the spirit of the sacrament is the spirit of Bethlehem; and the whole character of the devotion resembles, as closely as two devotions can resemble each other, the devotion to the sacred infancy. Let us now proceed first to establish the fact, next to discover reasons for it, and then to draw out the analogy at length.

We naturally look first to the language and practice of the Church. In the hymns and office for the octave of Corpus Christi we are continually being reminded of the childhood of Jesus, in such a way as to show that the two mysteries were united in the mind of the composer. There is no proper Preface allotted to the Masses of the Blessed Sacrament, but the Preface of the Nativity is borrowed, as if it were equally applicable to both. Passing from the conduct of the Church to the interior life of her children, we find the two devotions to the Blessed Sacrament and the holy infancy constantly united, and connected as it were naturally together. With certain differences the one seems to produce the same spiritual fruits as the other, to suggest corresponding devout exercises, and to lead to the same ascetical practices. Sister Margaret of the Blessed Sacrament, a Carmelite of Beaune, whom God raised up to give such an impulse and fresh extension to the devotion to

the sacred infancy, is a case in point. Her whole life illustrates the connection which we are now considering. Indeed our Lord himself seems to point to it by the manner in which he vouchsafes to appear to his saints and servants in the Blessed Sacrament. No one can be conversant with the lives of the saints without being struck, not only by the similarity of nearly all these apparitions one with another, but also by their being almost uniformly apparitions of him as an infant, with or without his mother, and most commonly without her. There are instances of his appearing in the host as he was after the scourging, another time as crowned with thorns, another as carrying his cross, and another as risen. But these are quite the exceptions, and very rare ones. In almost every instance, when he vouchsafes to cheer or to instruct his saints by these visions, he appears as the babe of Bethlehem, sometimes struggling as if in pain, and reluctant to be given to some one in Holy Communion, and sometimes imparting benediction to the assembled people. In that vast and various system of private revelations which our Lord condescends to make of himself, his ways, and wishes, in the hidden wonders, the visions, dreams, locutions and ecstasies of the saints, there is no fact more undeniable than this, nor more striking, from the frequency of its occurrence and the uniformity of its manifestations; and it clearly shows that the connection between the Blessed Sacrament and the sacred infancy is real and divine.

But if this remarkable phenomenon arrests our attention we may venture also to search for the reasons of it. The very facts of the two mysteries present themselves to our minds at the outset. The one seems to foreshow the other. The Blessed Sacrament appears to reflect in its own peculiar way every detail, however minute, of the sacred infancy. The babe is born in Bethlehem, the "house of bread," and born in a manger, as if to be the food of men, who through sin have become, in the psalmist's words, as it were beasts in the sight of God. The altar and the manger are too full of parallels for any one to need to have them drawn out. The swaddling clothes of Bethlehem are the accidents of the host. The consecration in the Mass answers to the mystery of his birth; and the various offices and familiarities of his priests with his body are but so many renewals of the manifold ministrations, which he submitted to receive at the hands of his foster-father, St. Joseph. So that if we meditate, first on one and then on the other of these mysteries, we find the same trains of thought arising in our minds and the same aspirations forming on our lips. The method of the divine condescensions is the same in both cases. If we look at devotion to the Blessed Sacrament in a doctrinal point of view, we shall see why this is so. Although we cannot separate the sacred humanity from the person of the eternal Word, nor worship it apart from the hypostatic union, it is nevertheless true that the worship of the Blessed Sacrament is peculiarly a worship and the highest worship, of the sacred humanity; because it is the sacred humanity which is prominently present in the Blessed Sacrament by the precise power of the words of consecration, while the divinity is there, not by the force of consecration, but by concomitance, and so also is our Lord's human soul. Thus the Blessed Sacrament is in a special sense the body and blood of our dearest Lord. It is the presence of his sacred humanity, and the peculiar theatre of its wonders.

If we compare devotion to the passion with devotion to the sacred humanity, we shall see how this bears upon our subject. In the passion our thoughts are occupied, not so much with the fact that our Lord is God and that he is man also, as with the intensity of his sufferings, or the beauty of his patience, or the liberality of his love, or the dreadfulness of sin, or the terrible consequences of the Father's wrath, or the horror of the people's malice and our own. What Jesus said, did, thought, endured, how he looked and felt, and why he went through all this—these are the subjects of our contemplation in the passion; and the interest of them all is not only heightened immensely by the continued remembrance of his being God made man; but that remembrance is simply necessary to the contemplation altogether. This is the case, because it is not a romantic story which is moving our affections, but it is a mystery of Christian doctrine which is stirring the depths of our nature, overwhelming us with its majesty and heavenly pathos, and calling up all those complicated natural and supernatural feelings which form the Christian mind and sentiment.

Still the remembrance of our Lord's divinity is not the single or the overwhelming thought in the passion. Now, in the sacred infancy our Lord's character, his doings and his sufferings, and his interior dispositions are far less prominent in our meditations. Indeed many persons hardly ever think of them at all. It is the grand fact of the incarnation which is present to our minds, diversified it is true in countless ways, yet still the same one fact or mystery. Jesus sleeps, and we reflect with delighted wonder on the sleep of the uncreated and unsleeping, of the "watcher of Israel who neither slumbers nor sleeps." He sheds tears; and if our tears follow the sweet memory of his, it is because it is so touching to behold in the omnipotent God the evidences of true humanity, the most tender of our infantine weaknesses and the most graceful of our infirmities. If he deigns to seek his Mother's breast, we see in it the mystery of his asking food from his own creature, when he is himself at that very moment feeding all the beasts of the field, and the birds of the air, and the fishes of the deep, and the populous tribes of men.

In other words, every action and every suffering of the sacred infancy interests us, not so much for its own sake, as gentleness under suffering, sweetness under desertion, silence under wrong, and the like, interest us in the passion; but it interests as a new way of realizing the incarnation, as a fresh usage of the incarnation, as if we could hardly have our fill of gazing upon that most wonderful mystery, and went round it and round it to look at it in every conceivable light and from every possible point of view, and multiplied our ways of expressing it, and always found it equally new and equally delightful. The devotion to the sacred infancy is the devotion of one thought, of one idea, of one mystery, while the devotion of the passion embraces the practices of all virtues, the varieties of character and spirit, and a thousand other considerations, with the remembrance of the incarnation lying at the bottom of them all, sustaining them and making them what they are. The devotion to the Blessed Sacrament resembles that to the sacred infancy. It has the same character in unity, the same varying and diversifying of a single idea, a single mystery; and moreover, the idea and the mystery in the one are the same as in the other, namely, the Incarnation, not in its results, not in its blessings, not in its magnificent developments, but in its simple beautiful self.

Love delights to multiply the object of its affections. It varies the thought of it in every possible way, and clothes it in every conceivable form. It seems as if it thus gained fresh fuel for its fire, as if new excellences were revealed in the beloved object, and as if in its own

fervor and fidelity were manifested more feeling and more loyalty. So is it with us and our incarnate Lord. We may live a long life, and through all that life by his grace may serve him faithfully, and have no other love but him. Yet never do we seem to have fathomed that one depth of his love, the gracious mystery of the incarnation. We study it with the keenest powers we have, we meditate upon it with anxious diligence and devout application, we repose upon it in the tranquillity of prayer, we salute it with swift and fiery ejaculations. And still it is ever new. Still each day we return upon it again and again with the same blissful fascination. That one thought is enough for us. As children turn and turn their kaleidoscope, and yet never come to the end of its brilliant combinations, so is it with the incarnation and ourselves. It is one thing to us in Jesus sleeping, another thing in Jesus weeping, and again another in Jesus at the breast. This is the peculiarity of the devotion to the sacred infancy. It is the turning of the kaleidoscope; the brilliants are ever the same, yet the changes are infinite even when they are like, the beauty endless, the sweetness beyond words.

I am speaking of the devotion to the sacred infancy as it exists among the great multitude of the faithful, and as it is handed down to us in spiritual works. There are two classes of persons to whom this devotion seems wider and more various; but we shall not find on examination that its character is really changed in either of the two classes. Persons who unite with the practice of mental prayer accurate and minute theological studies, find a greater separateness and distinctness in the different mysteries of the sacred infancy, from having continually present to their minds the Catholic teaching that our Lord's soul was exempt from all imperfection of ignorance, and that he had of course the full use of reason from the very first moment of his incarnation.

Thus our Lord is not simply helpless and passive, allowing his inanimate creatures, heat and cold, wind and wet, night and day, to work their will upon him, permitting the unreasonable animals to draw nigh to his infant body and warm it with their breath, and suffering with a mere unresisting patience the passions and affections, the wants and weaknesses, the pains and incommodities, incidental to human childhood. Everything is as much intended, is accompanied by as much mental process, and directed by as much actual energy of will, as the mysteries of his three year's ministry. Thus, as each action of his blessed passion had many intentions consciously referred to several ends, and comprised several fitnesses, far more than we can ever compass or exhaust, in like manner each mystery of the sacred infancy was characterized by the same variety, seeing that while he was a child in stature he was a full-grown man in the use and empire of his consciousness and understanding.

True as all this is, there is nevertheless more fancy than reality in the change which it makes in the character of the devotion. Our Lord, both as a child and as adult, vouchsafes to perform human actions, and the proper actions of infancy and manhood according to the season. The character of the actions is determined by their own nature, circumstances, and moral signficance, and not by the amount of consciousness or intention which actuates them; for every one of our Lord's actions was of infinite value, the least as well as the greatest, and merited immensely. His grace was incapable of growth or of degrees, and therefore the supernatural character of his human actions was equal in all of them: and ordinarily speaking, devo-

tion to the mysteries of our blessed Lord is devotion to those external manifestations which he was pleased to make of his human nature and of the grace with which it was anointed.

Thus it remains true that while our Lord uttered every infantine cry with as much clear use of reason as when he uttered his awful cry of dereliction on the cross, he was still as an infant really helpless, suffering, weak and infirm, and that he condescends to exhibit to us as truly, and to endure for us as really, the peculiar ignominies and abasements of childhood, as he does the quite different ignominies and abasements of maturer life. The character of the devotion is only apparently changed by the memory of the theological doctrine; it is not really so; and while we should be far from denying the great assistance which prayer often derives from scholastic theology, it must be remembered that the processes in prayer are lofty in proportion to their simplicity. Hence it may be questioned whether we do not sometimes lose tenderness of love and intimacy of union with our dearest Lord by thus refining on the devotions to the sacred humanity.

According to God's ordinary method, prayer must be affective before it is contemplative, and discursive before it is affective. Yet it will be a serious hindrance to our progress if we value it in proportion as it is discursive, instead of seeking to simplify our reasonings as much as possible, and to get out of them and beyond them as quickly as we can. We should thus be cherishing an imperfection, and canonizing it as if it were something to be retained and cherished. The consequence would be that our prayer would at best become unprofitable and dry, and would rather bring with it the science that inflates us, than the humble sense of our own wretchedness, and the self-revengeful appetite of mortification, without which prayer is worth nothing. For the crown of prayer is the worship of God through the subjection of our passions.

The other class of persons who might be disposed to quarrel with any description of devotion to the sacred infancy as being a devotion of one idea, and by this very characteristic distinguished from devotion to the passion, are those whose attraction leads them to dwell rather on the interior disposition of Jesus than on the details and circumstances of his outward actions. Beautiful as this spirit is, to which so many saints have set their seal, it does not seem to interfere with the character of the devotion in question. For, as in the former case, the full use of reason only causes our Lord's infantine actions to differ from ours, and does not in any way destroy the reality of their helplessness and weakness, so in this case the existence of certain interior dispositions stands upon the same footing as the use of reason, distinguishing our Lord's actions from those of common men, but leaving untouched the distinction between his actions as infant and as adult.

Persons devoted to the interior dispositions of Jesus may sometimes imedge of theology nor our familiarity the spirit of oblations, or charity to men, or the love of his Mother, or the spirit of penance and abandonment, may predominate respectively in different mysteries of the infancy; his sleep may thus be distinguished from his tears; his cries from his smiles, and his hunger from his voluntary concealment of the possession of reason. Yet the value of these pious reflections depends more upon the dispositions of the soul that gives birth to them than upon anything else, unless some private revelation or some infused science give a higher character to them.

I do not mean to say that they are not most valuable, and far more pre-

cious even than the delicate refinements of theology, or that they do not give a very much more divine character to our devotion to the sacred infancy. In fact that devotion is but imperfect when separated either from the fullness and minuteness of some doctrine, or from the consideration of our Lord's interior dispositions. All I mean is, that, while the one gives greater truth and the other greater depth to this most beautiful and efficacious devotion, neither the one nor the other changes its character, or gives it the same sort of variety as devotion to the passion, or hinders its being a devotion of one idea, which love, knowledge, and spiritual discernment represent to us a thousand-fold. Neither our knowledge of theology nor our familiarity with the interior dispositions of our Lord will make our devotion to the infancy the same as our devotion to the passion, nor make ours a really different devotion from that of the multitude of the faithful; although if we are on our guard against fancifulness and subtlety both our scholastic doctrine and our interior spirit will immensely heighten our devotion. Still it is not a question of kind, but of degree.

But the connection between the devotion to the Blessed Sacrament, and to the sacred infancy, does not result only from their both being devotions of one idea; but also from the fact that the one idea is the same in both of them, namely, the Incarnation. For the great mercy designed in the Blessed Sacrament is the renewal, and not the renewal only, but the extension also, of the Incarnation. The presence of the Eternal word made man, residing in his own creation, and sharing and participating in it, was the greatest gift which God could confer upon the world; because the hypostatic union was the closest intimacy which was possible between ourselves and him. The sun shone upon the incarnate

Word, the moon lighted up the mountain steeps where he was at prayer, the wind stirred his hair, and the ground was pressed by his feet. Silence listened to his words as if it were enchanted, and they fell upon the thirsty hearts of men like dews of grace. When the day was done, and sleep stole gratefully over tired nature, it ventured to lay its hand upon the heavy eyelids of the incarnate Word, and he slept. The elements obeyed him, or he obeyed them, as he willed. He was a sight, a sound, a touch, a fragrance in the world, such as never had been before, and which was worth infinite creations, nay, far transcended all possible creations whatsoever. If the eye of the eternal Father had looked with merciful complacency over the virgin world, when it came fresh from his creative hand, and had deigned to pronounce it beautiful and good and blessed, how beautiful and good and blessed must it have been then, when he who was co-equal and co-eternal with himself was therein, having assumed a created nature, so that human actions of infinite price and of unspeakable loveliness and of divinest grace were issuing from him at all hours. From the very moment of the Incarnation, creation became quite a different thing from what it ever was before, simply from the presence of our Lord in the flesh.

Now God's gifts are "without repentance." It is not his way (blessed be his holy name!) to withdraw what he has once given. There is nothing retrograde in the course of the divine compassions. One mercy is superseded by a greater; it does not retire, and give place to a less. Such is the royal munificence and exuberance of heavenly love. Hence to withdraw from the earth the presence of the incarnate Word, once conferred upon it, would be indeed to leave the children of men orphans; our Lord himself implies this, when reading the anxious thoughts of

their hearts, he said to his disciples, I will not leave you orphans; I will come to you. Either then our Lord's visible presence upon earth was to be continued, or its place was to be supplied by a presence, every way as real and substantial, and of a higher, more befitting, and more spiritual character. Indeed human life as God has ordained it in the world would have become impossible, if the visible presence of Jesus had continued, when his resurrection had been proclaimed, his faith taught, and his Church established.

It must have given rise to an entirely new state of things, and to laws of life, of moral life, as different from the present, as life in Jupiter or Saturn would be in physical respects. The doom of the world would have been hastened and precipitated.

The presence of Jesus, conversant with men, would have been a touchstone which would have driven all mankind very speedily either into the reprobation of the Jews, or into the grace of the apostles. All wickedness would have put on the awful characteristics of the wickedness during the passion; and all the probations of life would have centered in the one trial of respecting or accepting the visible mission of Christ. Besides the whole population of the world would have been thrown in vehement and irresistible pilgrimage upon one region and such social and political consequences would have ensued as would have utterly destroyed the equilibrium of the world. Under the present dispensation of things earth is not capable of enduring a transformation into a sensible heaven.

Moreover, it was necessary for our Lord's own friends that his visible presence should have performed its transient mission, and be discontinued, and the heavens contain him until the consummation of all things. It is expedient for you that I go away, were his own words to the apostles. For, as several of the ancient fathers as well as the modern doctors of the mystical life teach, they had become attached to his visible presence with an attachment which not only impeded their own progress in spirituality, but was not so honorable to him as the profound adoration mingled with sweet familiar love, which his absence and the descent of the Holy Ghost would pour into their souls. Thus, it was not only expedient for them that he should go away, because for them and for us, all things considered, the descent of the Holy Ghost was a more fitting and so more excellent thing than the continuance of his visible presence, but also because its place would be supplied by another presence of his own dear self, more wonderful and more excellent and more spiritual than his visible presence had been.

So much was there in those few words. A little while, and you shall not see me; and again a little while, and you shall see me, because I go to the Father! It was necessary then, it was in the usual course of divine gifts, that his new presence should exceed his former one; and this is his presence in the Blessed Sacrament. It was not precisely our Lord beautiful, or our Lord gentle, or patient, or consoling, or holy, or powerful, that earth could not do without and wanted back again. It was not precisely the babe of Bethlehem, or the boy of Nazareth, or the man of Calvary, without whom heavenly love seemed as if it must faint and die away upon the earth, when the mystery of the Ascension left it all widowed, leaning its whole weight on the prayers and presence of his immaculate Mother, the queen of the apostles. It was the Word incarnate, it was Jesus himself simply, it was the human flesh and

blood which he had taken to himself and which men had touched and handled, and had been straightway healed and forgiven: this it was which we wanted, him as incarnate, him one of whose natures made him our brother, and him with that nature whereby he was our brother; and thus it is that we receive him in the Blessed Sacrament. It is his Incarnation which is our stay, our blessing, our love, our consolation, in his new sacramental residence amongst us; and as in each Mass he is ever renewing and reproducing his Incarnation, it comes to us, as in the mysteries of the sacred infancy, day after day, with all the novelty and freshness of his first coming.

Thus the ritual of the Church, and the apparitions which God vouchsafes to the saints, and the actual phenomena of the interior life, establish for us beyond a doubt the striking fact that there is a real and peculiar connection between the devotion to the Blessed Sacrament and the devotion to the sacred infancy. And when we venture to search for reasons, we seem to find them first in the fact that the various mysteries of the Blessed Sacrament are copies or repetitions, with some additional divine touches, of the mysteries of the sacred infancy; secondly, in the fact that both the devotions are devotions of one idea, variously represented, and as such are distinct on the one hand from such devotions as those to the passion, or the three years' ministry, and on the other from devotions to single mysteries, like the scourging or the crowning, or to compendiums of the Incarnation, like the precious blood of the Sacred Heart; and thirdly in the fact that the single idea of the two devotions is the same, namely, the Incarnation. . . .

27. *St. Thérèse of Lisieux: Autobiography, 3 June - 16 September 1896*

From *Autobiography of St. Thérèse of Lisieux,* trans. by Ronald Knox (New York: P. J. Kenedy and Sons, 1958), pp. 258-263, 271-279, 307-312. Copyright 1958, P. J. Kenedy & Sons.

23. MOTHER, I can hardly believe my eyes when I look at the scrawl I produced for you yesterday. My hand shook so that I had to stop, and I'm sorry now that I tried to write at all. Let's hope my writing will be more legible today, because I'm no longer tucked up in bed; I shall do better in this dear little white arm-chair.

Mother, I quite see that I'm always wandering off the point; but I did want, before going on to recall the past, to say something about my feelings at the moment, for fear I should forget about them later on. And the first thing I want to say is that I really am touched by all these motherly attentions of yours; my heart really is overflowing with gratitude, and I shall never forget what I owe you, never. The most touching thing of all is this novena which you're making to our Lady of Victories, all the Masses you're having said for my recovery. What a wealth of spiritual resources! No wonder I feel, already, that it's done a lot of good to my soul. At the beginning of the novena, I told you that the Blessed Virgin really must either cure me or carry me off to heaven; I couldn't bear the thought of you and the community being burdened with the care of a young religious who had fallen ill. But now I'm ready to be an invalid all my life if God wants to have it like that, and I don't care how long my life is; the only grace I ask for is that it shall be a wounded life, wounded by love.

No, it's not that I'm afraid of having a long life. I'm not going to shirk the field of battle; the Lord is my rock-fastness, he makes these hands strong for battle, these fingers skilled in fight; he protects me and gives me confidence. So I've never asked God for an early death, but I've always hoped that this may be his will for me. You see, when it's a question of undertaking work for his divine glory, he often allows the will to count for the deed; and you know what my ambitions have been like—enormous.

You know, too, mother that Jesus has more than once put a cup of bitterness to my lips, and then taken it away before I could drink it, but not before I had tasted how bitter it was. Dear mother, King David was quite right when he said: "Gracious the sight, and full of comfort, when brethren dwell united," it's true, and I've felt it often enough, but always, here on earth, unity like that has to be cradled in sacrifice. I didn't enter Carmel for the joy of living with the nuns here; I did it entirely in answer to the call of Jesus. And I knew well enough that it was going to be a mortification all the time, living with your fellow-religious when you were determined to restrain your natural affection for them. I don't mean it's a virtue to keep your distance from your own companions in religion; how can people think that? Nobody has ever blamed a set of brothers for fighting on the same field of battle, or sallying out in company to win the crown of martyrdom; obviously they will encourage one another, and, what is more, the martyrdom of each will be a kind of martyrdom for the rest. And there is the same kind of solidarity about the religious life—which, indeed, has been described by the theologians as a martyrdom. One's heart, in giving itself to God, does not lose a natural sensitiveness; on the contrary, it grows more sensitive as its love becomes purer and more divine. I have my full share of this sensitiveness, in the love which I bear towards you and my sisters; nothing would please me better than to go on living among my own family, to fight God's battles side by side with the rest. But at the same time I'm quite ready to hurry off at a moment's notice to some other battlefield, if my divine commander wanted me to. I shouldn't wait for express orders from him; a mere look, a mere gesture, would be enough.

Ever since I took shelter in the ark of holy religion, I've had the idea that if Jesus didn't take me away to heaven quite soon, he might make the same use of me as Noah made of that poor little dove. One day, God would let me out of the window and tell me to fly far away, far away, to some heathen shore, carrying a tiny olive branch with me. The very thought, mother, lent wings to my soul; I felt as if I were flying through the air with all creation at my feet! And I realized that there could be such a thing as separation, even in Carmel; there could be no complete or lasting union except in heaven. If only my soul could make its dwelling-place there, and see everything that happens on earth as if it were happening a long distance away! I used to resign myself to the idea of exile in an unknown country, and—what hurt much more— to the idea of my sisters in religion having to undergo that exile. I shall never forget the second of August, 1896, the date when our missionaries did actually sail, and it was an open question whether Mother Agnes of Jesus wouldn't be one of them.

Oh, I wouldn't have lifted a finger to prevent it. But there was a terrible load on my heart. Surely a soul like hers, with all that sensitiveness, that delicacy of feeling, was never made to live among people who couldn't possibly appreciate her! A thousand anxieties of this sort came surging up into my mind, and Jesus wouldn't interfere, wouldn't calm the waves. So I said: "Dear God, I'm ready to put up with anything for the love of you; I'm quite ready to die of sorrow, if that is your will for me." And with that act of resignation, Jesus was satisfied.

A few months later, there was talk of two other sisters going out: Sister Geneviève and Sister Mary of the Trinity. This, too, was a searching test; it went very deep. I used to picture to myself all the trials and disappointments they would have to undergo, till I could see no rift in the clouds; it was only at the very depths of my heart that there was any peace and calm left. Dear mother, you were wise enough to know what God wanted done about it, and in his name you told these novices of yours not to leave the nursery yet. It wasn't that you didn't understand their ambitions; you yourself, in earlier days, had asked to be sent out to Saigon. How often it happens that a mother's wish finds an echo in the hearts of her children!

In my own soul, dear mother, this apostolic ambition of yours, as you know, has found a faithful echo. Just let me tell you why it is that it has always been my wish, and still is my wish, if our Lady should restore me to health, to get out into the wilderness, and leave this delightful oasis where I live so happily under your motherly care.

You told me once that being a Carmelite in a missionary country needs a special vocation, and many people think they've got it when they haven't; you also told me that I have got it, and my health is the only obstacle which makes the idea impossible for me. Clearly, if God wanted me to serve him in distant parts, this obstacle would disappear, so I can make my mind easy about it. But supposing I had to leave you, leave this dear Carmel of mine? Don't imagine that such a parting could be painless; Jesus didn't mean me to have a heart of stone! And it's just because my heart suffers so easily that I mean it to offer Jesus all the suffering it's capable of.

Mother, look at the life I live here! Untouched by the anxieties which make the world such a miserable place —all I've got to do is carry out the work you've given me to do, such pleasant, such easy work! And then, all this motherly care you shower on me! I never feel the pinch of poverty; I've always got everything I want. But above all, here at Carmel I have your love and the love of all the sisters, and it means so much to me! So my dream, you see, is of a convent where I should be quite unknown, where I should really have to face poverty, and the want of affection. Exile of the heart. If I'm ready to give up so much that's dear to me, it's not because I imagine I could be of any use to the foreign Carmel which would take me in. Of course I'd do whatever was expected of me, but I know how incompetent I am; I should do my best, but I should do everything badly, because as I was saying just now I've no head for anything practical. No, my only aim would be to do God's will, and sacrifice myself to him in whatever way pleases him best.

A disappointing experience? Clearly it couldn't be that. When you are looking forward to pure, unadulterated suffering, the least ray of happiness comes to you as a surprise packet! And besides, mother, as you know very well, the greatest happiness of all is the suffering itself, once you've come to regard it as the only treasure worth looking for. But if I'm anxious to go off to the missions, it's not with the idea of having anything to show for my pains. If that were in my mind, I shouldn't be

enjoying this delicious sense of peace. I should be suffering from the mere fact of not being able to follow up my vocation. As it is, I've ceased to be my own mistress, this long while back; I've given myself up entirely to Jesus instead, so he is at liberty to do exactly what he likes with me. He gave me this longing for complete exile, and at the same time he made it clear to me what sufferings such a life would involve. Was I ready to drink the chalice of its dregs? Immediately, I put out my hand to take it, this cup Jesus was offering me. But he, thereupon, held it back, and let me see that all he wanted was my willingness to accept it.

Isn't it extraordinary, Mother, what a lot of nervous strain you can avoid by taking the vow of obedience? How enviable it is, the simple creed of the religious, who has only one compass to steer by—the will of her superiors! She knows for certain, all the time, that she is on the right path. There's no fear that she can go wrong, even when she feels fairly certain that her superiors are wrong. When people lose sight of this unfailing guide, refusing to follow it and claiming to follow the will of God, which has been misunderstood by his representatives, they find themselves, all at once, wandering about on desert paths where the supply of grace is bound to dry up before long.

As far as I'm concerned, dear mother, you are the compass; Jesus means you to guide me safe to the shore of eternity. And I can't tell you what a comfort it is to look at you, look hard at you, and keep on doing God's will like that. Ever since he began to let me have temptations against the virtue of faith, he has established the spirit of faith more firmly than ever in my heart; so that I see in you not merely a mother, greatly loving and greatly loved, but beyond all that Jesus himself, alive in your soul and communicating his will to me through you. Of course, you treat me like a special case, like a spoilt child, so that obedience costs me nothing.

But something deep down in my heart tells me that I should act just as I do, love you as much as I do, if you saw fit to treat me harshly. I should still know that it was the will of Jesus. You would only be doing it for the greater good of my soul. . . .

25. What is the novelty of our Lord's new commandment? He has told us himself, in the Gospel: "You have heard that it was said, You shall love your neighbor and hate your enemy. But I tell you, love your enemies, pray for those who persecute you." Of course, you don't meet enemies in Carmel. But when all is said and done you have your sympathies. One sister attracts you. Another sister —well, you'd go a good long way round to avoid meeting her; without knowing it, she is your persecutress. Good. Then Jesus tells me this is the sister I've got to love, the sister I've got to pray for. Her behavior, to be sure, suggests that she isn't any too fond of me; yes, but, "What credit is it to you, if you love those who love you? Even sinners love those who love them." And just loving her isn't enough; you've got to prove it. We find a natural satisfaction in making presents, especially if they're surprise presents, to people we are fond of; but that's not charity—sinners find the same. Another point in our Lord's teaching. He says: "Give to every man who asks, and if a man takes what is yours, do not ask him to restore it." Giving what one's asked for—how much less enjoyable than offering something of one's own accord, out of the goodness of one's heart!

Moreover, people have different ways of asking for a thing. If they do it nicely, the gift doesn't cost you much, but if they don't succeed in wording the request so tactfully, your pride is

up in arms at once—unless your soul is well grounded in charity. You hit upon a thousand reasons for refusing it altogether. First of all, you have to impress on the wretched woman a sense of her great tactlessness, and only after that do you do what she asks, as a special favor—probably some tiny service which wouldn't have taken a twentieth of the time you spent in airing your imaginary grievance!

And when it comes to letting people take away what belongs to you, without asking to have it back—that's much harder than giving things to people who ask for them. Of course, mother, when I say it's more difficult I really mean it seems more difficult. The Lord's yoke, after all, is a light and easy yoke, and once you have taken it on your shoulders you feel the charm of it—those words of the psalmist come to your lips: "Do but open my heart wide, and easy lies the path you have decreed." What is going to open my heart wide? Nothing but love. Once the heart has been melted down in this gentle flame, what a pleasure it is, dear Jesus, to run along this new path you've traced for us, your new commandment! I mean to go on running like that, till the blessed day comes when you let me join the retinue of virgins that escorts you to the marriage-feast. Then, with no narrow path, but infinite space at my feet, I shall be able to follow you with a new song; what song will it be? It can only be the song of love.

What was I saying? Oh yes, Jesus tells me not to claim the restoration of my own property. Surely I ought to find that easy and natural enough—it isn't as if there were anything I could call mine. I've taken a vow of poverty, renouncing all worldly goods; so I've no right if somebody takes away a thing which doesn't belong to me. How nice to feel really poor! Arguing like that, I used to imagine that I was completely free from all attachments; it's only since I've begun to understand what Jesus meant, that I've realized how bad I am at rising to the occasion. When I'm painting, for instance, I know perfectly well that none of the things belong to me. Then I sit down to work, and find the brushes and the colors all jumbled up anyhow. Or there's something missing, a ruler or a pen-knife. And there I am, all at once, at the end of my patience! I have to hold myself unpleasant when I ask if I can have the missing things back. Naturally, one has to ask for them sometimes, if one can't get on without them. But that's all right —it's not disobeying Jesus if you do it humbly. The thing is to behave like a beggar, holding your hand out (because you've got to make a living), but not being in the least surprised if people refuse. After all, you've no rights.

Oh, how peace comes flooding into the soul, when once it learns to rise above its natural sensitiveness! To be really poor in spirit—there's no joy like it. You ask, with complete unconcern, for something you really need, and the other person not only refuses, but wants you to hand over something you've got already. What do you do? Why, what our Lord advises us to do: "If a man is ready to go to law with you over your coat, let him have it and your cloak with it." I suppose the idea of giving up one's cloak is renouncing the last shred of dignity, treating oneself as everybody's drudge, everybody's slave. Well, now that you've taken off you coat, you're in a good position for walking—running, if you want to. So our Lord goes on: "If he compels you to attend him on a mile's journey, go two miles with him of your own accord." You see, it's not enough to give people what they ask for. We've got to go one better. When I do a service to other people, they ought to get the impression that I'm grateful and honored to have the opportunity; when they

take away something I'm wanting to use, there must be no show of reluctance; I must look as if I was glad to be rid of it. Of course, dear mother, when I tell you that I've got these ideas, I don't mean for a moment that I carry them out. But somehow I get peace merely from wanting to carry them out.

To-day, more than ever, I seem to have expressed myself very badly; I've written a sort of sermon about charity, and it must have been uphill work for you reading it. Please forgive me, dear mother. You've got to consider that the infirmarian sisters, at the moment, are treating me just in the way I've been describing—they don't hesitate to walk a mile where twenty yards would do, so I'm in a good position for watching charity in action! This devotion of theirs, which ought of course to be balm to my soul, has a rather paralyzing effect on my brain, so that my pen has lost something of its briskness. I can't put down my thoughts properly unless I'm as lonely as a sparrow on the house-top, and this isn't a common experience. The moment I take up my pen to write, one of the dear sisters comes along with a pitch-fork on her shoulder, passing close by me—a little chat, she thinks, would do me good. First it's the haymaking, then it's the ducks, then it's the chickens, then it's a visit from the doctor, one thing after another. It doesn't really last long, but there are quite a lot of the sisters who are kind to me like this. . . . Sudden appearance of another haymaker, who puts down some flowers in my lap, presumably by way of giving me some ideas for writing poetry! But I don't want to write poetry just now, and I'd rather the flowers were left to wave on their stalks. So it goes on. At last I get tired of opening and shutting the famous autobiography, and open a book instead (not that it will stay open), with the intimation that now I'm going to copy out some texts from the Psalms and the Gospels, for our Lady's feast —that's quite true, because I'm always free with my quotations.

It would make you laugh, Mother, if I told you about all my adventures in the tangled undergrowth of Carmel; I don't think I've ever managed to write ten lines without being interrupted. No laughing matter, you'd think, for me. But I'm so grateful to God, and to the dear sisters themselves for all their charity to me, that I do try to look pleased and above all to be pleased about it. . . . What's this? A haymaking nun has just taken leave of me with the words: "Poor little sister, it must be very tiring for you to be writing like that all day." "Don't worry about that," I said, "I look as if I were writing a great deal, but there's hardly anything to show for it." She seemed rather relieved at that. "A good thing too," she said, "but all the same it's just as well we're getting the hay in; a bit of a distraction for you." I should think it did distract me, quite apart from the infirmarians' visits (it was no exaggeration to say that I hardly got anything written).

Fortunately, it takes a lot to discourage me. In proof of that, mother, I'm going to go on telling you about the light Jesus has given me on the subject of charity. So far, I've only spoken of its outward manifestation; now I want to let you know my ideas about a charity which is wholly spiritual. I'm certain to get the two kinds mixed up before I know where I am; but it's you I'm talking to, and I'm perfectly certain you'll be able to see what I mean—it won't be the first time you've taken my skein out of tangle.

In Carmel, one can't always carry out the gospel precepts to the letter. Sometimes you've got work to do, and an act of kindness has to be refused. But if charity is deep rooted in the soul, it shows up for all that. If you've

got to say no, there are more ways of doing it than one; a refusal can be so gracious as to afford almost more pleasure than the gift. . . . If you are an obliging sort of person, the other sisters will have less compunction about asking you to do things for them; but don't forget that our Lord has told us we mustn't turn away from the borrower: it wouldn't do to edge away from the sister who's always wanting something, merely on the excuse that you would have to refuse this time in any case.

Another thing—you mustn't show obligingness merely so as to create an impression, perhaps in the hope that your good offices will be repaid in kind. Our Lord has said: "What credit is it to you, if you lend to those from whom you expect repayment? Even sinners lend to sinners, to receive as much in exchange. No, you must lend without any hope of return; then your reward will be a rich one." A rich one, even here on earth . . . on this path of generosity, it's only the first step that takes it out of you. To lend without expecting to see your money back—that does go against the grain. You would rather give the thing outright, and see it pass out of your possession. Someone comes up to you and says, with an air of complete assurance: "Dear sister, could you give me some help for an hour or two? It's all right, I've got Reverend Mother's leave to give you some of my own time in return; I know how busy you are." Knowing, as you do, that she won't really repay the loan of your time, you're tempted to say: "Not at all; I'll make you a gift of it." That would gratify one's self-esteem; a gift is more generous than a loan—and besides, it would show the sister exactly how much confidence you have in her offer.

Ah yes, our Lord's teaching does run counter to the instincts of nature. Without his grace, we shouldn't merely be unable to carry them out—we shouldn't even understand them. Charity, mother, has mysterious depths, and if our Lord has given a daughter of yours the grace to get to the bottom of them, it ought to sound like heavenly music in your ears when she tells you about them. But from me, unfortunately, you only get childish prattling; if his own words didn't lend me support, I would be tempted to ask if you would excuse me, and throw away my pen. Never mind. I started under obedience, and under obedience I'll go on.

Dear mother, I was saying yesterday that if somebody robs me of any worldly possession, I mustn't ask to have it back again. I ought to be able to do without it, because it doesn't really belong to me. That's true about the good things of earth. What about the good things of heaven? They don't belong to me either; they're only loans from God, and I've no right to complain if he takes them back. But . . . there are certain movements of the mind and the heart, certain deep-reaching thoughts, that go to form a treasury of your very own. Nobody else, you feel, has a right to tamper with it. For instance, I tell one of the sisters, when we have leave to talk, about some light that has been given to me in prayer, and she, quite soon afterwards, mentions it to a third party in conversation as if it were an idea of her own. Isn't that pilfering? Or again, in recreation,—I whisper some remark to the person next me, a good remark, absolutely to the point—and she repeats it aloud without mentioning where it came from. Isn't that a theft of my property? I can't say so at the time, but I'd like to, and if opportunity arises, I determine to let it be known, with all the delicacy in the world, that somebody's been misappropriating my thoughts.

If I can describe them so exactly, mother, these deplorable instincts of our nature, it is because I have felt them in my own heart. How gladly I would have nourished the illusion that I was the only person affected by them! But it was no good, because you put me in charge of these dear novices, and I had to hear all about their temptations too. I can't tell you how much I've learnt from doing this work for you; and, best of all, I've had to practice what I preach! I really think I can say, now, that our Lord's given me the grace to care as little about gifts of the mind and the heart as about worldly possessions. An idea occurs to me, and I say something which is well received by the other sisters—why shouldn't they adopt it as their own? I find it quite natural. You see, this idea doesn't belong to me, it belongs to the Holy Spirit. Doesn't St. Paul tell us that we can't even say "Father" to our Father in heaven without the aid of his loving Spirit? Surely, then, he can make use of me if he wants to convey to any soul some profitable thought? To suppose that this "thought" belongs to me would be to make the same mistake as the donkey carrying the relics, which imagined that all the reverence shown to the saints was meant for its own benefit!

Don't think that I undervalue them, these deep-reaching thoughts which help to feed the soul and unite it to God. But it has been borne in upon me, long since, that you must never make them the ground of your confidence. Perfection has nothing to do with receiving a whole lot of lights in prayer! They don't amount to anything by themselves. Action is what counts. To other people, of course, they may be very useful; people who are humble enough to thank God for letting them share in such a treat, and for enriching a soul with such dainties. But the person so enriched mustn't take credit to herself for these profitable thoughts, plume herself on them like the Pharisee in the temple. That would be like a man dying of hunger in full sight of his own well-stocked table, while his guests, helping themselves generously, looked round with envy at a man who was so well off!

How true it is that only God can see into the depths of our hearts, and all our human views are short-sighted! The moment we see a soul more highly gifted than others, we say to ourselves: "Jesus doesn't love me as he loves that soul; I can't be called to the same level of perfection as that!"

Really?

And since when has our Lord lost the right to use one of his creatures for his own purposes, to provide the souls he loves with their appropriate nourishment? He hadn't in Pharaoh's time. This is what he says to Pharaoh: "This is the very reason why I have made you what you are, so as to give proof, in you, of my power, and to let my name be known all over the earth." Since those words were spoken, century after century has gone by, and still he has not altered his way of dealing with us; he is always using this or that creature of his to produce an effect in the lives of others. . . .

40. They are possessions with which you yourself have entrusted me, and when I think of them, I am emboldened to make your words my own—those words which you addressed to your heavenly Father, on the last evening that saw you on earth, a pilgrim, a mortal still. Dear Jesus, I don't know how long it will be before my banishment comes to an end. There may be many evenings yet that will find me telling the tale of your mercies, still in exile. But for me, too, there will be a last evening, and then, my God, I would like to be able to offer to you the same prayer.

"I have exalted your glory on earth, by achieving the task which you gave me to do. I have made your name known to those whom you have entrusted to me; they belonged to you, and now they are mine by your gift. Now they have learned to recognize all the gifts you gave me as coming from you. I have given them the message which you gave me, and they, receiving it, recognized it for truth that it was you who did send me. I am praying for those whom you have entrusted to me. They belong to you. I am remaining in the world no longer, but they remain, while I am on my way to you. Holy Father, keep them true to your name, your gift to me. Now I am coming to you, and while I am still in the world I am telling them this, so that the joy which comes from you may reach its full measure in them. I am not asking that you should take them out of the world, but that you should keep them clear of what is evil. They do not belong to the world, as I, too, do not belong to the world. It is not only for them that I pray. I pray for those who are to find faith in you through their word. This, Father, is my desire, that all those whom you have entrusted to me may be with me where I am, and that the world may know that you have bestowed your love upon them, as you have bestowed it upon me."

Those are the words I would like to repeat after you, dear Lord, before I take refuge in your arms. Am I being rash? I don't think so; you've allowed me to take liberties with you this long time past. You've said to me what the father said to the prodigal son in the parable: "Everything that I have already is yours." And as these are your words, dear Jesus, they belong to me. So I'm at liberty to use them, in the hope of bringing down on the souls that are linked with mine whatever blessings our heavenly Father has to give. But of course when I ask that the people you've entrusted to my care may be "where I am," I'm not suggesting that they may not reach a much higher degree of glory than you see fit to give me. I'm merely asking that we may all meet, one day, to share with you the splendors of heaven.

My God, you know that the only thing I've ever wanted is to love you. I have no ambition for any other glory except that. In my childhood, your love was there waiting for me. As I grew up, it grew with me. And now it is like a great chasm whose depths are past sounding. Love breeds love; and mine, Jesus, for you, keeps on thrusting out towards you, as if to fill up that chasm which your love has made —but it's no good. Mine is something less than a drop of dew lost in the ocean. Love you as you love me? The only way to do that is to come to you for the loan of your own love; I couldn't content myself with less. Dear Jesus, I can have no certainty about this, but I don't see how you could squander more love on a human soul than you have on mine! That's why I venture to ask that these souls you've entrusted to me may experience your love as I have. One day, maybe, in heaven, I shall find out that you love them better than me, and I shall be glad of that, glad to think that these people earned your love better than I ever did. But, here on earth, I just don't find it possible to imagine a greater wealth of love than the love you've squandered on me without my doing anything to earn it.

Dear mother, it's time I came back to you. I can't think how I came to write what I've written above; I never meant to, but there it is, so it had better stay there. Only, before I go back to the story of my brothers, I do just want to explain two things. When I talk about handing on the message God has given to me, I'm not thinking of them, only of the novices. I don't, after all, set up to teach missionaries; it's a good thing I'm not conceited enough for that. And indeed, if I've managed to give some advice to these sisters of mine, it's to you, mother, as God's representative, that I owe the grace for it. On the other hand, when I say that I don't want them taken out of the world, or pray for those who will come to believe through their words, I'm only thinking of those others, spiritual sons of yours, spiritual brothers of mine. I can't help praying for the souls that will be saved, in those distant mission-fields, by their preaching.

And now, mother, about that passage in the Song of Songs: "Draw me after you; we hasten"—I think some further explanation is called for, because what I've tried to write about is a bit difficult to follow. Our Lord says: "Nobody can come to me without being attracted towards me by the Father who sent me." Then, by those splendid parables of his, and often by less popular ways of talking, he teaches us about the door that will be opened if we only knock, about finding what we want if we only look for it, getting what we ask for if we only stretch out our hands in humble supplication. Again, he tells us that if we ask the Father for anything in his name, it will be granted to us. All that, surely, explains why the Holy Spirit, long before our Lord came into the world, looked on ahead and prescribed to us this formula of prayer: "Draw me after you; we hasten."

When we ask to be "drawn" we mean, surely, that we want to be united as closely as possible with the object which has cast its spell over our hearts. Suppose that fire and iron were capable of reason: suppose that a piece of iron says to the fire: "Draw me to yourself." Doesn't that mean that it wants to be identified with the fire, to be penetrated with it, steeped in it, this burning force, till the two seem to be merged into one? My prayer, mother, is like that—I want our Lord to draw me into the furnace of his love, to unite me ever more closely with himself, till it is he who lives and acts in me. Still, as that flame kindles, I shall cry out to be drawn closer, closer, and its effect on those around me will be the same, although I am only a poor piece of iron filing, that outside the furnace would be inert. They will be as active as I am—like those women of the Canticles who ran, allured by his perfumes, where the royal lover went. The soul that is enfolded by divine love can't remain inactive; though it may, like Mary, sit at the feet of Jesus and listen to those words of his, so full of fire, so full of comfort; not appearing to contribute anything, but really contributing so much! More than Martha, as she hurries distractedly to and fro, and wishes her sister would do the same. (Not that our Lord has any fault to find with Martha's exertions; his own mother, mother of God though she was, put up with humble work of that kind all her life—didn't she get the meals ready for the holy family? Martha is a devoted hostess, but she won't keep calm; that's the trouble.) All the saints have seen the importance of Mary's attitude, and perhaps particularly the ones who have done most to fill the world with the light of Gospel teaching. Surely those great friends of God, people like St. Paul and St. Augustine and St. John of the Cross and St. Thomas and St. Francis and St. Dominic, all went to prayer to find the secret of their wisdom, a divine wisdom which has left the greatest minds lost in admiration.

"Give me a lever and a fulcrum," said the man of science, "and I'll shift the world." Archimedes wasn't talking to God, so his request wasn't granted; and in any case he was only thinking of the material world. But the saints

really have enjoyed the privilege he asked for. The fulcrum God told them to use was himself, nothing less than himself, and the lever was prayer. Only it must be the kind of prayer that sets the heart all on fire with love; that's how the saints shift the world in our own day, and that's how they'll do it to the end of time.

And now, dear mother, I must just tell you what I understand by these "perfumes" which tempt the soul to set out on its loving search. Our Lord has ascended into heaven, so I can only follow him by means of the traces he has left behind him. But they're so full of light, so full of fragrance! One glance at the holy Gospel, and the life of Jesus becomes a perfume that fills the very air I breathe. I know at once which way to run. Oh, I don't try to jostle into the front rank, the last is good enough for me. I won't put myself forward, like the pharisee, I'll take courage from the humble prayer of the publican. But the Magdalen, she, most of all, is the model I like to follow—that boldness of hers, which would be so amazing if it weren't the boldness of a lover, won the heart of Jesus, and how it fascinates mine! I'm certain of this—that if my conscience were burdened with all the sins it's possible to commit, I would still go and throw myself into our Lord's arms, my heart all broken up with contrition. I know what tenderness he has for any prodigal child of his that comes back to him. No, it's not just because God, in his undeserved mercy, has kept my soul clear of mortal sin, that I fly to him on the wings of confidence and of love. . . .

28. *Charles de Foucauld: Diary and Letters,*
30 September 1902 - 1 December 1916

From René Bazin, *Charles de Foucauld, Hermit and Explorer*
(New York: Benziger Brothers, 1923), pp. 158-160, 172, 189-191,
262-263, 268-269, 306-308, 323, 330, 332-333, 337-338.

SEPTEMBER 30, 1902.—. . . Get up at four (when I hear the alarm, which is not always!). *Angelus, Veni Creator,* Prime and Terce, Mass, Thanksgiving.

At six, a few dates or figs and the discipline; immediately afterwards, an hour's adoration of the most Blessed Sacrament. Then manual labor (or its equivalent: correspondence, copies of various things, extracts of authors to be kept, reading aloud, or explanation of the Catechism to anyone), until eleven. At eleven Sext and None, short mental prayers, particular examen until half-past eleven.

At half-past eleven, dinner.

Midday, *Angelus,* and *Veni Creator* (this latter is sung. You will laugh when you hear me singing! Unintentionally, I have certainly invented a new air.)

The afternoon is given entirely to God, to the Blessed Sacrament, except an hour devoted to necessary conversation, to various replies, to cooking, the sacristy, etc., necessary housework, and to alms; this hour is divided up throughout the whole day.

From noon to half-past twelve, adoration; from half-past twelve to half-past one, Stations of the Cross, some vocal prayers, the reading of a chapter of the Old and New Testaments, a chapter of the *Imitation* and a few pages of a spiritual author (St. Teresa, St. John Chrysostom, St. John of the Cross, perpetually follow one another).

From one to two, written meditation on the holy Gospel.

From two to half-past two, moral or dogmatic theology.

From half-past two to half-past three, reserved for the catechumens.

From half-past three to half-past five, adoration; after Mass and the night, this is the best moment of the day; work is over, I say to myself, I have only to look to Jesus . . . this is an hour full of sweetness.

At half-past five, Vespers.

At six, collation. . . .

At seven, explanation of the holy Gospel to some soldiers, prayers and benediction of the Blessed Sacrament with the holy ciborium, followed by the *Angelus, Veni Creator.* Then the soldiers leave after a short conversation in the open air. I say the rosary (and I say compline, if I have not been able to say it before the short explanation of the holy Gospel), and I go to sleep in my turn about half-past eight.

At midnight I get up (when I hear the alarm), and sing the *Veni Creator,* recite Matins and Lauds: this is also a very sweet moment: alone with the spouse, in the profound silence of the Sahara, under the vast sky, this hour of tête-a-tête is a supreme comfort. I go back to bed at one.

October 29, 1901.—Celebrated Mass for the first time at Beni-Abbes. *Ex voto* to our Lady of Africa.

November 5.—Erection of the first Stations of the Cross.

November 30.—Formal opening of the Chapel of the Fraternity of the Sacred Heart.

December 25.—First exposition of the Blessed Sacrament for over ten hours.

We have had the Blessed Sacrament exposed from midnight to 7 o'clock in the evening. We shall have it on New Year's Day from 7 o'clock in the morning till 7 in the evening. I was far from hoping there would be enough adorers for it to be possible. Jesus provided them.

The good-will, the unhoped-for piety of the poor soldiers round me enable me to give a reading and explanation of the holy Gospel *every evening* (I cannot get over my surprise at their willingness to come and listen to me); Benediction is followed by a very short evening prayer. . . . This Benediction and Holy Mass are both a consolation and an infinite joy.

January 9, 1902.—First slave ransomed; Joseph of the Sacred Heart. . . . This afternoon there was very little hope of freeing this child; his master refused to sell him at any price; but yesterday, Wednesday, the day of good St. Joseph, I had changed the name of the child to that of *Joseph of the Sacred Heart* and promised St. Joseph to erect an altar to him in the bay on the Gospel side, and one to the Blessed Virgin in the one on the Epistle side, if he obtained the liberation of the child for me. To this good Father everything is easy: at 5 in the evening, the master came to claim the child for the last time, and in two minutes accepted the price I offered him. I paid it on the spot, and you would have been delighted at the joy of poor "Joseph of the Sacred Heart" reiterating that "God was his only master." . . . He is a Musulman, but more in the name than in fact. I hope that, naturally and of himself (I shall avoid anything like pressure—he will be quite free) he will go to Jesus and to the Heart which willed him to be free.

I could get a small sum by taking stipends for Masses. The good Father Abbot of Notre-Dame-des-Neiges has offered me some, and if I have no means of living and paying my debts, I shall make use of it; but as long as a glimmer of hope of my being able to do without it exists, I shall do so because I believe that much more per-fect; I live on bread and water, which costs me seven francs a month. . . . As for clothes, Staueli gave me a coat and two shirts with twelve napkins, a rug, and a cloak; these are a gift of good Father Henry, or rather a loan, because he has only lent me them, so that I may not give them away; a very nice officer here, Captain d'U—— offered me so graciously a rug and two small knitted vests that I could not refuse; you see I am well set up. . . . For myself I want nothing. To help me to get the slaves, travelers, and the poor together to tell them of Jesus and induce them to love him, I want a small sum to buy barley; I asked G—— for thirty francs a month for the slaves' barley, and M—— for twenty for that of the travelers. . . . I confess I must also pay for the ground I bought, and go to some expense in planting some dates which, in three years will provide food for me and the poor, please God. My only capital on leaving France was what it still is, the word of Jesus: "Seek therefore first the kingdom of God and his justice, and all these things shall be added unto you." I was quite at ease here up to the last few days; the purchase and freeing of Joseph of the Sacred Heart made me get to the bottom of my little purse, but our heavenly Father's is still full.

I wish to accustom all the inhabitants, Christians, Musulman's, Jews and idolaters, to look upon me as their brother, the universal brother. . . . They begin to call the house the Fraternity (the *Khaua,* in Arabic), and I am delighted.

For *the slaves,* I have a little room in which I gather them and where they always find a lodging, a reception, daily bread and friendship; by degrees I teach them to pray to Jesus. Since January 15, the day on which their little room was finished, I have had some every night at the Fraternity. Sometimes I see twenty slaves a day.

The poor travelers also find a humble shelter and a poor meal at the Fraternity, with a good reception and a few words to bring them to goodness and to Jesus; but the place is so small, the virtue of the monk and his skill are still less; more virtue, intelligence and means, would allow of much more good being done. . . . Sometimes I see thirty or forty travellers a day.

The infirm and aged here find a shelter with a roof, food and attention when forsaken . . . but what inadequate care and what poor food! . . . And for want of separate places, I can only take in those who get on with the others, and women not at all; yet the women, even more than the men, need a home for old people.

For the Christian teaching of the children I do absolutely nothing; it seems to me that I can do nothing. I sometimes see as many as sixty children in a single day at the Fraternity, and with a heart full of sorrow have to send them away without doing anything for them. And the list of replies continues; the military hospital, the civil hospital for the natives, visiting the sick at their homes, "are beyond my power and vocation; nuns are required." So it is with the visits to the homes of the poor. Doubtless he daily distributes remedies to ten or fifteen people, but he is very cautious, having little confidence in his talents. There is a doctor at the Arab Office, he is very good, but women and children cannot go to him—they come to the Fraternity, and the men themselves prefer applying to the marabout. What is to be done? Nuns would do all the good that he can only look on at, estimate and plan. At the hermitage gate, in a single day, taken at hazard, he has counted seventy-five poor people. He begins to know his people; but how much help was wanted! What need there was of intelligent almoners for

such great poverty and so many outstretched hands!

If I do not ask you to send any White Sisters out here, it is because I know that you will settle them wherever you can, and never have enough to put wherever they are required. . . .

I am still alone: I am not faithful enough for Jesus to give me a companion, still less . . . I follow to the best of my abilities the little Rule you know. . . .

May, 1903.—Thirty years ago today I made my first communion and received my God for the first time. . . . This is the first time that I celebrate the holy Mass on that day. . . . What graces I have received in these thirty years! How good God has been! How many times I have received Jesus with these unworthy lips! And lo, here I hold him in my poor hands! He puts himself into my hands! And now I officiate at an oratory; night and day, I have the holy tabernacle—I possess it, so to speak, as mine alone! Now, every morning I consecrate the holy Eucharist, every morning I give Benediction with it! And here at last and above all I have the permission to make a foundation! What graces!

July 4.—There is nothing new in my life; oh yes, there is! I have had the great joy of being able to buy and free a slave; he is staying with me provisionally as a guest, and working in the garden; . . . he appears to be twenty five years of age. . . . Pray for his conversion! Pray also for that of a good Musulman Turco who is most devoted to me . . . and pray for mine!

June 28, 1902.—Saturday is the day for giving out the barley distribution. We must make our Sundays and feastdays known. It is a very inferior way, but just now the only practical method, I believe, of evangelizing.

July 12, 1902.—First baptism at Beni-Abbes: Marie-Joseph Abdjesu

Carita, a little Negro of three and a half.

July 21.—Four soldiers of the garrison have died this month of extreme heat. Not one of them refused the sacraments; two died very piously after a long illness. . . .

August 13.—I am still alone—the only religious—with Abdjesu, a Negro of twenty-five redeemed and liberated some time ago; an artilleryman who serves my Mass; some sharpshooters who are repairing the chapel, the roof of which is getting weak. The Fraternity, very silent at night and from 10 to 3 in the afternoon, is a beehive from 5 to 9 in the morning; and from 4 to 8 in the evening. I never stop talking and seeing people; slaves, poor people, invalids, soldiers, travelers, and inquirers; the latter—inquirers—I have but rarely, but the slaves, invalids, and poor increase. . . . I celebrate Mass, except on Sundays and great Festivals —I say it, on those days, when the military desire—to which nobody ever comes on weekdays, before daybreak, so as not to be too much disturbed by the noise, and to make my thanksgiving in some peace; but however early I may be, I am always called three or four times while making my thanksgiving.

September 12.—What are wonderful here are the sunsets, the evenings, and the nights. . . . The evenings are so calm, the nights so serene; the great sky and the vast horizons half lit by the stars are so peaceful, and in silence thrill the soul by hymning the eternal, the infinite, and the beyond, so that one could spend entire nights in such contemplation; however, I curtail it and return after spending a few moments before the tabernacle, for there is more in the humble tabernacle; nothing is nothing, compared to the well-beloved.

14th.—Ransomed two slaves: a father of a family and a young man of fifteen, whom Brother Charles provisionally named Paul.

November 5, 1902.—It has rained twice, so I hide the altar furniture under the altar; and the altar, as soon as the sky grows cloudy, under a waterproof covering—a little tarpaulin. At the Fraternity, as at the camp and in the village, it rains as much inside the rooms (and chapel) as outside. The roofs protect only from the sun. That, far from hindering, contributed to happiness: in making the inclemencies of the weather felt, God reminds us that Jesus had not a stone whereon to lay his head. All that makes us like the well-beloved unites us to him and is perfect happiness. . . . The very sight of my nothingness, instead of afflicting me, helps me to forget myself and to think only of Him who is all.

June 1, 1903.—Mgr. Guérin left for Taghit. Here are some of his remarks:

1) Talk a good deal to the natives, and not of things commonplace, but always bring the talk back to God; if we cannot preach Jesus to them because they would certainly not accept such teaching, prepare them little by little to receive it, by unceasingly preaching natural religion in our talks . . . Speak much and always so as to improve and uplift and bring souls nearer to God, and prepare the ground for the Gospel.

2) Arrange benches and shelters in the yards, make visitors sit down, and don't leave them standing. . . . When people are sitting conversation more easily takes a serious and intimate turn.

3) Make temporal alms help the soul by speaking of God, and give the spiritual alms of good instruction to those to whom you are giving material alms.

4) The work of evangelists in Musulman countries is not only to take children and try and inculcate Christian principles in them, but also to convert grown men as far as possible.

. . . Children will not be able to make the evangelical seed cast into their souls germinate, if they do not find the society in which they live somewhat prepared beforehand and well disposed. Besides, all men are made for the light, for Jesus; all are his heritage, and not one, *if he has good-will,* is incapable of knowing and loving him. . . . Musulmans are then by no means unfitted for conversion. . . . Let us try hard to evangelize men of riper years, first by conversations turning only to God and natural religion; then, according to circumstances, giving to each such truth as we hope to get him to accept.

5) While evangelizing the poor, do not neglect the rich. Our Lord did not neglect them; neither did St. Paul, his imitator. On account of their influence their reformation is a blessing to the poor. Their sincerity is less doubtful, there is less reason to fear that they are "soupers" listening to Christian truths only for material interests.

6) I build too much, stop, don't go on building. . . .

7) The Musulmans of the Sahara receive their false religion solely through confidence in their ancestors, in their marabouts, in those who surround them, solely through the authority which these have over them, and without a shadow of reasoning or verification. . . . We ought, then, to try more to gain their confidence, and to acquire more authority than those who surround them and indoctrinate them. For that, three things are necessary: First, to be very holy; Second, to show ourselves to the natives a great deal; and Third, to speak a good deal to them. Holiness, which is the main thing, will sooner or later give us the authority and inspire confidence. Constantly seeing us will bring them round to our cause, and, if we are holy, that will be preaching without words, and strengthening our authority.

8) To bring Musulmans to God, must we try to make them esteem us by excelling in things which they esteem; for instance, by being audacious, a good horseman, a good shot, and slightly ostentatious in liberality, etc., or by practicing the Gospel in its abjection and poverty, going about on foot and without luggage, working with our hands as Jesus in Nazareth, living poorly, like a petty workman? It is not from the Chambãa that we ought to learn to live, but from Jesus. . . . We ought not to take lessons from them, but to give them some. Jesus said to us: "Follow Me." St. Paul said to us: "Be imitators of me as I also am of Christ." . . . Jesus knew the best way of bringing souls to himself, and St. Paul was his incomparable disciple. Do we hope to do better than they? Musulmans do not make a mistake. Of a priest who is a good horseman, a good shot, etc., they say: "He is an excellent rider, none shoot better than he"; and maybe they will add, "He would be worthy of being a Chambi!" They do not say: "He is a saint." Let a missionary lead the life of St. Anthony in the desert, they will all say: "He is a saint." For natural reasons they will often give their friendship to the first, to the Chambi; if they give their confidence in matters of the soul, they will only give it to the second.

December 9, 1907.—I am happy, happy in resorting to the presence of the Blessed Sacrament at any time, happy in the great solitude of the place, happy to be and do—excepting my sins and miseries—whatever Jesus wishes; happy, above all, in the infinite happiness of God. If there were not this inexhaustible source of happiness and peace of the well-beloved, the evil that one sees around one on all sides, and also the miseries one sees in oneself, would quickly lead one to depression. If, in Christian countries, there is so much good and so much evil, think what these countries can be, in which there is, so to speak, nothing but evil, where good is almost totally absent; here all is lies, duplicity, cunning, all kinds of covetousness and violence, and how much ignorance and barbarism! The grace of God can do all things, but in face of so many moral miseries . . . one sees clearly that human means are powerless, and that God alone can effect so great a transformation. Prayer and penance! The farther I go, the more I see that these are the principal means of acting upon these poor souls. What am I doing in the midst of them? The great good that I do is that my presence procures that of the Blessed Sacrament. . . . Yes, there is at least one soul between Timbuctoo and El-Golea who adores Jesus. Lastly, my presence in the midst of the natives familiarizes them with Christians and particularly with priests. . . . Those who will follow me will find men's minds less distrustful and better disposed. It is very little; it is all that can be done at present; to wish to do more would compromise everything in the future.

June 1, 1908.—No doubt the Sahara is not one of the most inhabited countries, but after all the oases, including the Tuaregs, contain 100,000 people, who are born, live and die without any knowledge of Jesus who died for them nineteen hundred years ago. He gave his blood for each of them, and what are we doing? It seems to me that two things are necessary:

First, a sort of third order, having for one of its objects the conversion of infidel peoples—a conversion which is, at the present time, a strict duty for Christian nations, whose position in the last seventy years has totally changed with regard to the infidels. On the one hand, the infidels are nearly all subjects of Christians; on the other hand, the rapidity of communications, and the exploration of the entire world, now give comparatively easy access to all. From these two facts follows quite a strict duty—above all, for nations having colonies—the duty of Christianizing.

Second, not everywhere, but in countries where there are special difficulties, like yours, we ought to have missionaries, *à la Sainte-Priscille* of both sexes. They might be gleaned either here and there, or grouped in order to give them a common preparation before sending them. The thought of a kind of third order, having for one of its aims the conversion of infidels, came to me last September, at the time of my retreat. It has recurred to me very often since, with the consideration that it is a duty and not solely a work of zeal and counsel for Christian nations to work energetically for the conversion of infidels and, above all, of those of their colonies. There would, I think, be occasions for showing this duty to those who appear to have no suspicion of it, and for urging them to accomplish it. During Holy Week and Easter Week I put down what the association might be. I am revising this and re-copying it. . . . I shall show it you in November. If you think it contains anything good, you will make use of it. But certainly there is something to be done. . . . For twenty years France has had an immense colonial empire, which imposes evangelizing duties on French Christians. . . . It is not with ten, fifteen, twenty, or thirty priests, even if you were given them, that you will convert the vast Sahara; you must therefore find other auxiliaries.

Pardon me, my well-beloved father, getting mixed up in what is none of my business, and an old sinner and quite insignificant priest of very recent ordination, and still a poor sinner, who has never been able to attain anything, or even to get a companion, who has had nothing but desires without effect, and whose plan of life, constitutions

294   PART 1. *The Church and the Liberal Society*

and Rule are always but useless papers, daring to expose my thoughts and continuing to form plans. My excuse is the souls around me who are being lost and will perpetually remain in that state, if we do not try to find the means of acting efficaciously on them.

December 11, 1912.—We French have two essential duties to fulfill in Africa: The first thing is the administration and civilization of our North-West African Empire. Algeria, Morocco, Tunis, the Sahara, and the Sudan form an immense and magnificent empire in one lump, having this unity for the first time. . . . How are we to attach this empire to us? By civilizing it, by working to raise its inhabitants morally and intellectually as much as possible. The inhabitants of our African empire are very varied: some, the Berbers, may rapidly become like us; others, Arabs, are slower in progress; the Negroes are very different from each other; but all are capable of progress.

The second thing is the evangelization of our colonies. . . . Now, what are we doing for the evangelization of our North-West African empire? One might say, nothing. In Algeria, Tunis, and the Sahara, the only priests engaged in the evangelization of the natives are the White Fathers; they are, according to their 1910-1911 report, fifty-six in North Africa, eleven in the Sahara. A drop of water. I can well understand that the White Fathers, seeing the evangelization of the Musulmans to be slow and difficult, have turned aside their efforts and sent the great majority of their missionaries into Equatorial Africa, where they are working wonders, and affecting conversions as rapid as they are numerous, and winning heaven for a host of souls. Here they would have saved few, there they save many: so I can understand their going there. It is nevertheless true that Algeria, Tunis, and Morocco

(where there are only chaplains at the consulates) are entirely neglected. . . . This is a situation which French Christians ought to remedy. It will be a work of time, demanding self-sacrifice, character, and constancy. We want good priests in fair quantity (not to preach: they would be received as Turks coming to preach Mohammed would be received in Breton villages, or much worse with the help of barbarism), but to establish contact, to make themselves loved, to inspire esteem, trust, and friendship; then we should want good lay Christians of both sexes to fulfill the same rôle, to enter into still closer contact, to go where the priest hardly can—above all, to Musulmans' homes, to give an example of Christian virtue, to show the Christian life, family, and spirit: then we want good nuns to take care of the sick and to bring up the children, mingling much with the population, dispersed by twos or threes wherever there are priests and Christians. . . . That being done, conversions, at the end either of twenty-five, fifty, or a hundred years, will come of themselves, as fruit ripens, according to the spread of education. . . . But if these unfortunate Musulmans know no priest, see, as self-styled Christians, only unjust and tyrannical speculators giving an example of vice, how can they be converted? How can they but hate our holy religion? How are they not to become more and more hostile to us? . . .

After drawing your attention to these two very important points, let me add a word: whether it be to administer and civilize our African empire, or to evangelize it, we must first get to know its population. But we know very little of it. That is partly due to Musulman customs, but that is an obstacle which can be overcome; this deplorable fact remains, that we are alarmingly ignorant of our native African population. I have hardly quitted North Africa for the last thirty-two years (except during the ten years, from 1890 to 1900, which I spent in Turkey, in Asia, Armenia, and the Holy Land); I have seen nobody, neither officer, nor missionary, nor colonist or any other person who knows enough of the natives; as for myself, I have a fair knowledge of my little corner of Tuaregs, but a very superficial acquaintance with the rest. . . . There is a vice which must be remedied; our administrators, officers, and missionaries must have a much closer contact with the populations, long residence in the same stations (with promotion on the spot for administrators and officers), that they may know and instruct their Superiors correctly, and that the latter may get to know through them. . . .

February 21, 1915.—Like you, I find that the work (to pray for the conversion of our colonial infidels) is more indispensable than ever, now that so many of our infidel subjects give their blood for us. The loyalty and courage with which our subjects serve us show everyone that more must be done for them than we have done in the past. The first duty is the one we know—the salvation of souls. But everything is bound up together, and many things which don't properly involve the action of priests and monks are very important for the good of souls: their education, their good civil administration, their close contact with honest French people, for some their settling down and an increase of material welfare. Also I should like our "union," which ought before everything to urge each of us to unite ourselves to our Lord and to be filled with his spirit, living according to his will and grace, also to urge each one to do, according to his conditions and means, all that he can for the salvation of the infidels of our colonies.

Whit-Monday.—Every year the month of June brings in the anniversary of my ordination, and renews and increases my gratitude to you who adopted me and made me a priest of Jesus Christ. With my whole heart I pray for you. More than fifteen years ago you accepted me as a son, and I also pray for your beloved diocese of Viviers.

In body I am here, where I shall remain till peace comes, believing I am more useful here than elsewhere; but how often my spirit is in France at the front, where the struggle must be at this moment more ardent than ever, and behind the lines, where so many families are weeping for their most beloved, or are in mortal anxiety.

Around me, the native population is calm and faithful; its attitude is excellent.

I still greatly desire to see the confraternity started in France for the conversion of the French colonies, the scheme of which you were good enough to approve. During this Whitsuntide I think more than ever of the fifty millions of native infidels in our colonies. May the Holy Ghost set up his reign in their souls, and may the French, who ask for this help to defend their own temporal fatherland, help them to obtain the eternal fatherland!

July 16, 1916.—Such isolated missionaries as I am are very few. Their rôle is to prepare the way, so that the missions which replace them will find a friendly and trustful population, souls somewhat prepared for Christianity, and, if possible, a few Christians. You have partly set forth their duties in your article in the *Echo de Paris:* "The greatest service." We must get ourselves accepted by the Musulmans, become their sure friends, to whom they come when in doubt or trouble; on whose affection, wisdom, and justice they can absolutely rely. It is only when we arrive at this point that we shall come to do good to their souls.

Therefore my life consists in having the greatest possible intercourse with those who surround me, and in rendering all the services I can. As soon as intimacy is established, I speak, always or nearly always, in a tête-à-tête, of our good God, and briefly giving each man what he can bear: avoidance of sin, a perfect act of love, a perfect act of contrition, the two great commandments of the love of God and of our neighbor, examination of conscience, meditation on the last things, the creature's duty of thinking of God, etc., giving to each according to his strength, and going on slowly and prudently.

There are very few isolated missionaries fulfilling this pioneer work; I wish there were many of them: every parish priest in Algeria, Tunis, or Morocco, every military chaplain, every pious Catholic layman, could be one. The government forbids the secular clergy to carry on anti-Musulman propaganda; but it is not a question of open and more or less noisy propaganda; friendly intercourse with many natives, tending to induce Musulmans slowly, gently, and silently to come closer to Christians and become their friends. This nobody can be forbidden to do. Every parish priest in our colonies could exert himself to train his male and female parishioners to be Priscillas and Aquilas. There is quite a loving and discreet propaganda to be carried on among the infidel natives— a propaganda which requires as great kindness, love and prudence, as when we wish to bring a relation who has lost the faith back to God. . . .

Let us hope that when we have won the war our colonies will make fresh progress. What a beautiful mission for our younger sons of France, to go and colonize the African territories of the mother-country, not to get rich, but to make France beloved, to make souls French, and above all to obtain eternal salvation for them.

I think that if the Musulmans of our colonial empire of North Africa are not converted gradually and gently, a national movement like that of Turkey will come about; an intellectual élite will be formed in the large towns, educated *à la française,* but having neither the French mind nor heart, an élite which will have lost all the faith of Islam, but which will keep the label in order to be able to use it to influence the masses. On the other hand, the crowd of nomads and countrymen will remain ignorant, estranged from us, firmly Mohammedan, incited to hatred and contempt of the French by their religion, their marabouts, and by their contact with the French (representatives of authority, colonists, merchants)—contacts which too often are not apt to make them love us. National or barbarian feeling will therefore become worked up in the educated élite; when it finds an opportunity—for instance, at a time of France's difficulties at home or abroad—it will make use of Islam as a lever to rouse the ignorant mass, and seek to create an independent Musulman African Empire.

The French North-West African Empire—Algeria, Morocco, Tunis, French Western Africa, etc.—has a population of thirty millions; it will, thanks to peace, have doubled in fifty years. It will then be in full material progress, rich, intersected with railways, inhabited by people trained to the use of arms, the élite of which will have received its education in our schools. If we have not been able to make these people French, they will drive us out. The only means of making them French is for them to become Christians.

November 28, 1916 (to the Prioress of the Poor Clares of Nazareth, who had fled to Malta).—France, in spite of appearances, is still the France of Charlemagne, St. Louis, and Jeanne d'Arc; the old soul of the nation lives on in our generation: the saints of France are always praying for her; the gifts of God are without repentance, and the people of Saint-Rémi and Clovis are still the people of Christ. . . . In choosing France for the birth-place of the devotion to the Sacred Heart and the apparitions of Lourdes, our Lord has clearly shown that he keeps France's rank of the first-born for her.

I can regularly say holy Mass every day. I have another happiness: that of having the reserved sacrament in my little chapel. I am always by myself. Some Frenchmen come to see me from time to time: every thirty or forty days I see one of them on his way.

We live in days when the soul strongly feels the need of prayer. In the tempest which is blowing over Europe we feel the nothingness of the creature, and turn to the Creator. In the bark tossed about by the billows we turn to the divine master, and implore him who can give victory with a word, and restore a great and durable peace. We raise our hands to heaven as Moses did during the battle of his people, and where man is powerless we pray to him who is almighty. Before the Blessed Sacrament we feel so clearly in the presence of real being, when all that is created appears so plainly bordering upon nothingness!

Pray very much, most Reverend Mother, for the poor infidels who surround me and for their poor missionary. With you, I pray for France.

December 1, 1916.—Very Dear Brother in Jesus, I have this morning received your letters of October 3 and 9, moved by the thought of the greater dangers that you are perhaps going to meet, that you probably are already incurring. You have done quite right in asking to join the troops. We must never hesitate to ask for posts in which danger, sacrifice, and devotion are greatest: let us leave honor to any who desire it, but let us always ask for danger and toil. As Christians we should give an example of self-sacrifice and devotion. It is a principle to which we must be faithful all our life, in simplicity, without asking ourselves whether pride does not enter into our conduct: it is our duty, let us do it, and ask the well-beloved spouse of our soul that we may do it in all humility, in all love of God and our neighbor. . . .

Don't be anxious about your home. Trust yourself and it to God, and walk in peace. If God preserves your life, which with my whole heart I ask him to do, your home will be more blessed because, sacrificing yourself more, you will be more united to Jesus, and will have a more supernatural life. If you die, God will keep your wife and son without you, as he would have kept them through you. Offer your life to God through the hands of our Mother, the most blessed Virgin, in union with the sacrifice of our Lord Jesus Christ, and with all the intentions of his heart, and walk in peace. Be sure that God will give you the best lot for his own glory, the best for your soul, the best for the souls of others, since that is all you ask of him, since you will fully and without any reservation all that he wills for you.

Our corner of the Sahara is peaceful. I pray for you with my whole heart, and at the same time for your home.

This will reach you about Christmas and the 1st of January. Look for me quite near you on those two days. A happy and holy New Year to you; many holy New Years, if it be God's will; and then heaven! God guard you and protect France! May Jesus, Mary and Joseph between them guard you in all your life on earth, at the hour of death, and in eternity.

I embrace you, as I love you in the Heart of Jesus.

29. *Archbishop William Ullathorne, O.S.B.: Mission to Australia, 1868*

From *The Autobiography of Archbishop Ullathorne* (London: Burns and Oates, Limited, 1891).

RETURNING to Downside in 1831, I had scarcely settled down in my old monastery and begun to teach in the school, when Dr. Polding received briefs of appointment as visitor-apostolic to the Mauritius, where his uncle, Dr. Slater, was the bishop. But he feared lest the intense heat of that island should relax his energies, and so respectfully declined the appointment.

6. Through the recommendation of Bishop Bramston, vicar-apostolic of the London district, Dr. Morris, a member of the Downside community, who had for several years been the only member of any regular order employed on the London mission, was then appointed as apostolic visitor to the Mauritius, which appointment he accepted. He naturally wished to obtain co-operators from the house of his profession, and accordingly made application to the superiors of Downside. In reply to his application he was told that if I were asked I should probably not be unwilling to go.

This impression was, I believe, derived from an incident which took place several years before that time. I had been suffering for some two years from an acute inflammation of the liver, combined with sharp and continuous attacks of ague. I was going with other young religious, in company with Dr. Polding, in a post chaise, to Bath, to consult a physician, when Dr. Polding began to talk of the great want of missioners in Australia; he spoke of the sufferings of the convicts, and observed that there was not such a field in the wide world for missionary labor. He gave his own ideas as to the way in which such a mission should be managed, expressed his attraction for it,

and asked us which of us would be ready to join him. I at once declared myself ready to do so. This conversation had evidently been laid up in Dr. Polding's mind, and had led to the mentioning of my name to Dr. Morris. When, therefore, Dr. Morris wrote to me, I replied that I had about a hundred reasons against going to the Mauritius, and almost as many for going to Australia.

It must here be observed that the bishop of the Mauritius had at that time a most extensive jurisdiction; it reached, on the one side, to South Africa; and on the other, over Australia and the South Sea Islands, including New Zealand. Dr. Morris replied that he equally required help for Australia, and asked me to go to New South Wales. I therefore submitted the question to my superiors. The prior at that time was Father Turner, an old Douay monk, a truly meek and holy man, while Drs. Polding and Brown filled the next offices. Dr. Polding advised me to wait, thinking that the time for the Australian mission was not yet mature. But the prior and Dr. Brown advised me to write to the president-general, who gave me up to the jurisdiction of Bishop Morris for the Australian mission.

I therefore proceeded to London, where I received the kindest hospitality from my relatives; nor can I ever forget the affectionate co-operation or the prolonged hospitality of my *confrère,* the Rev. Dr. Heptonstall, who was the procurator of the English Benedictines in London, and had a small mission at Acton. At that time I had no prospect of aid from the colonial government, but was going out at my own expense. That is to say, I had a little legacy from my father, which I was allowed to use and which was doubled by my mother and two brothers. My first work was to form a library, for I knew that the books I should require could not be found in Australia. I therefore spent months in the old book shops and among their catalogues, and gathered together about a thousand volumes of theology, fathers, Canon law, and sacred literature, in every language of which I knew something. I then made a visit to Scarborough, where I bade farewell to my dear mother, brothers, and sisters, never expecting to see them again.

Meanwhile a dispatch had come from the governor of New South Wales to the secretary for the colonies, which changed my position altogether. His excellency represented to the secretary of state that there was no authorized head of the Catholic clergy in that colony, that difficulties had consequently arisen between the government and the senior priest respecting grants of land, and that it was desirable to obtain the appointment of a Catholic ecclesiastic invested with due authority. Bishop Morris was in consequence invited to an interview at the colonial office, and he informed the secretary of state that he had an ecclesiastic in view, whom he could appoint as his vicar-general for Australia, with residence in Sydney, who would have all the authority required. This was agreed to, and a stipend was assigned by the government of £200 a year, an allowance of £1 a day when traveling on duty, and for voyage and outfit £150. The title assigned to me by government, in documents, beyond that of vicar-general, was that of his majesty's Catholic chaplain in New South Wales. I also received a letter from the colonial secretary, recommending me to the governors of the Australian colonies.

Dean Kenny, in his *Progress of the Catholic Religion in Australia,* gives an anecdote about the spirit of my departure, as derived from Dr. Heptonstall, which I may as well put in its authentic form. Just before sailing, I happened to meet, in the streets of London, my old professor, Dr. Brown, and our old professor of Greek, Dr. Heptonstall. On bidding them farewell they expressed their surprise that, going out alone, to the furthest extremity of the world, and leaving country and friends behind me, I should be so calm and, apparently, so indifferent. I simply intimated that, having God with me, the authority of the Church and a great vocation before me, I felt I was in my right place and had nothing else to care for.

7. I sailed in the *Sir Thomas Munro,* on September 16th, 1832. . . .

We entered the Derwent, sailing up between its beautiful sloping shores until we turned into Sullivan's Cove, when we beheld the city, with Mount Wellington towering over it.

The one priest was absent on his annual visit to Launceston, on the opposite side of the island. I was hospitably lodged and entertained by Mr. Hackett, a native of Cork, and a distiller; a man of information, popular among the few Catholics, and influential in the town. Meeting the leading Catholics, all of Irish origin, I soon began to hear a sad account of the state of Catholic affairs, which my own subsequent knowledge but too much confirmed.

I must refer to my two pamphlets, "The Catholic Mission in Australasia," published in England in 1837, and "The Reply to Judge Burton," published in Sydney in 1839, for the history of Catholic affairs before my arrival. The first priest who arrived with authority in New South Wales was the Very Rev. Jeremiah O'Flynn, who was invested by the Holy See with the title of Archpriest, with power to administer the Sacrament of Confirmation. He arrived in Sydney, by the ship "Duke of Wellington," on August 3rd, 1817. All those Catholics who remembered him spoke with great reverence of his mild, religious character, his great charity, and his fluency in speaking the Irish language. He was of a religious order, and, if I remember rightly, a Trappist. There was no charitable institution at that time for receiving the helpless poor, and he took into his residence several aged and decrepit people, whom he lived with and maintained. But as he had come without any authority from the home government, the colonial government, influenced by a strong anti-Catholic party, illegally seized upon him, put him in prison, and sent him back to England by the first ship. This tyrannical act produced a great sensation at home: Mr. Hutchison, of the Donoughmore family, member for Cork, brought the whole case before Parliament; and under the influence of Lord Bathurst two priests were sent out, Father Connolly and Father Therry, each with a stipend of £100 a year. They arrived in Sydney in 1820, but soon afterwards they disagreed, and Father Connolly went to Hobart Town, where he landed in March, 1821, and remained there without seeing a brother priest until 1833.

A state of things grew up under his regime which gave rise to many complaints. I found the chapel in a most disgraceful state, though the house was decent. Built of boards with the Government broad arrow on them, the floor had never been laid down, but consisted of loose planks, with their edges curled by the heat, and sharp as well as loose under the knees of the people. There was a coating of rough plaster on the wall behind the altar, covered with a black glazed cotton all over filth, that had hung there ever since the death of George IV. The altar, a framework of wood, had a simi-lar black glazed cotton for the frontal, and the dirty altar-cloths were covered with stains. The space between the two ends of the altar and the side walls were refuge holes for all kinds of rubbish, such as old hats, buckets, mops, and brooms. There were no steps to the altar, but the same loose planks that formed the entire floor, and no seats for the people. The chalice and ciborium were tarnished as black as ink. I cleaned the sacred vessels, cleared out the rubbish from the sides of the altar, and laid smooth planks down across the front of it to make the footing steady. On two Sundays I preached to the people, who, unaccustomed to be spoken to sympathetically were moved to tears.

Sir George Arthur, the governor, received me with great courtesy, and invited me to meet at dinner the Protestant Archdeacon Broughton, who was on a visit with his large family from Sydney, and was afterwards the first Anglican bishop of Australia. At a later interview the governor opened up the subject of religion, and we had a long private conversation on the subject. He was himself a very earnest Anglican of the evangelical school. He put certain questions to me, not mentioning that his friend, the archdeacon, was at that very time writing a pamphlet on the subject, which I had afterwards to answer in Sydney. Yet I recall with pleasure the courtesies I received from Governor Arthur.

Father Connolly returned before I left Hobart Town; he expressed no discontent at what I had done in the chapel, as the people thought he would, but rather approval, gave me his own ideas of the state of things in Sydney, and we parted friends.

8. I made it a point of policy not to send any previous notice of my coming to Sydney, where I arrived in the month of February, 1833. I walked up straight to the priest's residence,

and there I found a grave and experienced priest in Father McEncroe, who had formerly been vicar-general to Bishop England in South Carolina. He had come from Ireland to Sydney the year previous with Mr. Attorney-General Plunkett, his wife, and sister. From him I learnt a good deal of how things stood. Father Therry had gone to Parramatta, but quickly hearing of the arrival of another priest, returned that evening. The housekeeper was the widow of the celebrated John Maguire, who kept the British troops at bay in the Wicklow Mountains after the insurrection of 1798 had been put down in the west of Ireland. At last he surrendered, on condition that he and his family should be conveyed out free to New South Wales. Father Therry had promised the gallant old man on his death-bed that he would protect his wife and family.

I looked so youthful that the first language of Father Therry, and even of his housekeeper, was naturally patronizing; but after dinner I produced the document appointing me vicar-general, with jurisdiction over the whole of New South Wales, as well as the rest of New Holland, after reading which Father Therry immediately went on his knees. This act of obedience and submission gave me great relief. I felt that he was a truly religious man, and that half the difficulty was over. At his invitation I went with him that evening to the house of a gentleman, where I found myself in company with precisely the three persons with whom it was represented to me in England that I should find my difficulty. But, in fact, they were all very good men, and we became great friends. Still I was internally amused, for they evidently took me for a raw college youth; and I humored the notion, and was told at a later time that after I had left they had talked of sending me to Bathurst, then the remotest part of the Colony.

The next morning as I came from Mass in the little chapel, Father Therry met me and said: "Sir, there are two parties among us, and I wish to put you in possession of my ideas on the subject." I replied: "No, Father Therry, if you will pardon me, there are not two parties." He warmed up, as his quick sensitive nature prompted, and replied, with his face in a glow: "What can you know about it? You have only just arrived, and have had no experience." "Father Therry," I said, with gravity, "listen to me. There were two parties yesterday; there are none to-day. They arose from the unfortunate want of some person endowed with ecclesiastical authority, which is now at an end. For the present, in New South Wales, I represent the Church, and those who gather not with me scatter. So now there is an end of parties."

That day I went by coach to Parramatta, to see the governor at his country residence. Sir Richard Bourke had recently lost his wife, to whom he was much attached, and was ill in bed. But he was anxious to have the Catholic affairs settled, and gave me an audience in his bedroom. The fine old soldier was one of the most polished men I ever met. In his younger days he had been a good deal under the influence of the celebrated Edmund Burke, and was a man of extensive information as well as experience. The statue erected to his memory in Sydney bears recorded on its base the great measures by which he gave freedom and social progress to the colony. Though not a Catholic, he had a great respect for the Catholic religion, and had many Catholic relatives and friends. He received me with great kindness, and we soon understood each other. I listened to his remarks, and then asked leave to see him again after I had inquired into the points of which he spoke. I returned to Sydney, and on the Sunday I announced my powers to the people from the altar, and stated that I suspended all affairs connected with the business of the Church for a fortnight, when, after making due inquiries, I would call a public meeting of the Catholics.

Father Therry was quite an exceptional character. He was truly religious, never omitting to say Mass daily even in difficult circumstances; and up the country, when he could find no appropriate roof for the purpose, he would have a tent erected in some field or on some mountain side. He also said the rosary in public almost every evening, gathering as many people as he could. He was of a highly sensitive temperament, and readily took offense, but was ready soon after to make reparation. He was full of zeal, but wanting in tact, so that he repeatedly got into trouble with the government, and sometimes with the successive ecclesiastical authorities. Hence the long difficulties which arose after he was superseded as vicar-general in Tasmania by its first bishop. Having passed from trade to his studies, he had sufficient knowledge of his duties, but was too actively employed to be a reader. Having been the sole priest in the colony for some eleven years, he was very popular, not only with the poor Catholics, for whose sake he did not spare himself, but with all classes of the population. Being the one representative of the Church in those times, landed property was bequeathed to him in various places by Catholics who had no relatives in the colony. This he always treated as his private property, though he never took much trouble about it. But in his will he bequeathed it all to religious purposes.

Government policy was still strongly in favor of an exclusive established church under the Crown. A royal commissioner, Mr. Briggs, was sent out to report on the condition of the colony; Mr. Thomas Hobbs Scott, formerly a wine merchant, accompanied him as secretary. On their return Mr. Scott was made the first Protestant archdeacon of the colony; and on his arrival announced his intention to organize the Protestant Church, to establish parishes and schools, and to hand over to a corporation one-seventh of the land of the colony for that purpose. This was accomplished by a deed under the sign manual of George IV. Moreover, in the orphanage established by government at Parramatta, the children left without parents were all to be taught the Protestant religion. This new state of affairs was very alarming to the Catholic population, and Father Therry addressed a letter to the *Sydney Herald* (which was at that time also the *Government Gazette*) on June 6, 1825, in which he signified his intention of forming a Catholic School Society, and also of doing his best to establish Catholic cemeteries, which would prevent may inconveniences, besides avoiding collision with the Anglican clergy. But at the close of the letter he spoke of the Protestant clergy as entertaining for them (as it appeared in print) "qualified respect." Father Therry explained that this was a misprint, and that he had written the word "unqualified." Nevertheless the letter was made an excuse for withdrawing his small salary, and of excluding him from officiating in any government establishment; thus prohibiting him from visiting the prisons, hospitals, and similar institutions.

"While still under this ban Father Therry went to visit a dying man at one of the hospitals, but was stopped by the guard when about to enter. Father Therry said: 'The salvation of this man depends on my ministration; which is your first duty?' The guard lowered his arms and permitted him to pass. On another occasion, going to the infirmary to visit a sick person, the doorkeeper bade him wait till he should have ascertained from the attendant surgeon whether he could be admitted. While he was away, Father Therry, who knew all the passages of the place, gave the sick person the consolations of religion, and on returning met the official, who told him he could not be admitted," said Dean Kenny in his *History of Catholicity in Australia* (p. 51).

All this occurred under the government of Sir Thomas Brisbane, and soon after the arrival of Archdeacon Scott with the purely Protestant scheme of an exclusive establishment. It is said that Father Therry was offered a small sum of money, £300, to leave the colony, but of that I never heard, and have no proof.

In the year 1829 Sir Roger Therry arrived as solicitor-general and commissioner of the Court of Requests. He was the first Catholic appointed by the home government after the Emancipation Act. On taking office, the Protestant oath was tendered to him. He asked for the Catholic one. The official replied: "Now that the point of honor is settled, it can make no difference." "It makes all the difference in life," replied Sir Roger. So the Catholic oath was produced. In 1832 Father McEncroe arrived, in company with Mr. Plunkett, his wife, and sister. Mr. Plunkett came with the appointment of attorney-general. These two Catholic gentlemen, both of high character, were the first men of position who were earnest in the practice and support of their religion, and their influence was of great value. Two other Catholic gentlemen had come out with office at an earlier time, but they concealed their religion until it was lost to themselves and their families. It was a saying in Sydney when I arrived that Lady Therry's was the first bonnet that had appeared in the Catholic congregation. But when I reached Sydney things had very much changed in that respect. In 1829 the

Rev. J. V. Dowling also arrived, and made his residence at Windsor. These were the only two clergymen besides Father Therry whom I found in the colony in 1833, and both of them had stipends from the government.

9. After his arrival in the colony, Sir Roger Therry opened a correspondence with Mr. Blount, then member for Steyning, on the religious wants of that distant penal settlement. Mr. Blount, in consequence, made an energetic appeal to Parliament upon the injustice and cruelty of sending away the criminals of the country to the other extremity of the world without providing them with adequate provision for their religious instruction or requirements. He dwelt with strong emphasis on the religious destitution of the Catholics. Meanwhile, Sir Richard Bourke was devising a systematic plan for meeting those wants, which ultimately took shape in his celebrated dispatch to Lord Stanley, at that time Secretary of State for the Colonies, of date September 30, 1833. About the same date I addressed a letter through the governor to his Lordship, asking for four additional Catholic chaplains. His excellency begins his dispatch by stating that he has received the order of the king in council for dissolving the Protestant Church and School Corporation; but without any information of the views of his majesty's government as to the future maintenance and regulation of churches and schools within the colony. His excellency then points out that there are large bodies of Roman Catholics and Scotch Presbyterians, and that probably one-fifth of the whole population of the colony were Catholics. "The charge on the public treasury next year would be: for the Church of England, £11,542; for the Scotch Presbyterians, £600; and for the Catholic chaplains and chapels, £1,500. The Catholics possess one large and handsome church at Sydney,

not yet completed, and to aid its completion the Government had given donations at different times amounting in all to £1,200. The sum of £400, included in the £1,500, had been appropriated in aid of private subscriptions for erecting Catholic chapels at Campbell Town at Maitland. A chapel was begun in Campbell Town and in Parramatta some years ago; but neither have been completed for want of funds. Such an unequal support cannot be acceptable to the colonists, who provide the funds from which the distribution is made.

Sir Richard then proposed the following arrangements to be applied equally to the Church of England, the Catholics, and the Scotch Presbyterians. That whenever a congregation applies for the erection of a church and clergyman's residence, on their subscribing not less than £300 and up to £1,000, the government shall give an equal subscription, the building to be invested in trustees. That where a hundred adults, including convict servants living within a reasonable distance, shall subscribe a declaration of their wish to attend that church or chapel, £100 a year shall be paid out of the treasury to the clergyman of that church. That when two hundred adults so subscribe, £150 a year shall be paid: and that when five hundred adults so subscribe, £200 a year shall be paid; beyond which no higher stipend shall be paid by the government. Thus the three great national denominations of England, Ireland, and Scotland were to be treated alike and on the same footing. Before the warrant was issued for payment by the Treasury, a certificate was required from the religious authority at the head of each denomination that the clergymen were in performance of their duty.

In the same dispatch his excellency was pleased to say a kind word of the Catholic vicar-general, preliminary to stating that "he thought £200 a year too low for the office, and that it might advantageously be raised to £400, to enable him to visit frequently the chapels in the interior." Before this dispatch was sent the governor kindly gave me an opportunity, through Sir Roger Therry, of seeing it. I could only express my gratitude for a scheme so well calculated to meet all requirements, while it left ecclesiastical authority in such perfect freedom. Sir Richard had privately expressed his opinion that the result of this scheme would be to provide the colony with all the clergy required, after which the government, supported by popular opinion, would cease to give its support to any religious denomination, and thus the several communions would support their own churches. To use his own phrase, "they would roll off state support like saturated leeches." And so it has come about.

The scheme received the complete approval of the English government, and was passed as an Act of Legislative Council on July 29, 1836. About the same time a scheme of denominational education was arranged, in which the schools were supported by the government, partly by a fixed annual sum, partly regulated by the numbers in attendance.

On making my application the year previous for four additional priests I had more than one object in view. I strongly felt that a bishop was required for Australia. I had written some time before to Bishop Morris in the Mauritius, by one of the very few ships that ever went to that island, and had explained to him the very unsatisfactory state of things in Van Diemen's Land. I had also sent to him certain cases requiring dispensations, to which my special faculties did not extend. In reply I received a letter, stating that he was sending another priest to Van Diemen's Land, and that the faculties would come by another letter. The letter never came or the priest either. New Zealand was but one thousand miles distant, and though Protestant missions had been established there for a considerable time, no priest had ever reached it. Norfolk Island was a penal settlement, quite as far off, but no priest had ever visited it. Moreton Bay (now Queensland) was another penal settlement far to the north of Sydney, which had only been once visited by Father Therry. A new colony was also beginning to be formed in the extensive region which finally took the name of Victoria.

Under the clear conviction that so large a responsibility required the immediate superintendence of a bishop, I wrote to the superiors at Downside, explained the case, mentioned the application I had made to the home government for additional priests, and urged them to move for the appointment of a bishop of Sydney. Lord Stanley had sent a copy of Sir Richard Bourke's dispatch to Mr. Blount, and stated that he should consult Bishop Bramston as to the priests to be sent out; and thus the way was opened.

In May, 1834, my old novice-master, Father Polding, was appointed first bishop of Sydney by Gregory XVI. He undertook to provide the other three priests applied for, and the four received the usual passage and outfit provided by government. Meanwhile Lord Stanley had replied to my letter, not only approving my application, but adding that, should our wants increase, he would be happy to attend to any further recommendation supported by the governor of the colony. Not long after, Sir Richard Bourke received a letter from Lord Stanley, announcing the appointment of the four priests, one of whom, Dr. Polding, was invested with the dignity of a bishop. He then expressed his regret at my being superseded, and proposed that I should go to Hobart Town with the same stipend. When Sir Richard read the letter to me, I laughed, and said: "Your excellency will understand our ways better than Lord Stanley. I should be of material use to the bishop in the beginning. Let him take the stipend of £400 a year which you recommended for the vicar-general, and let me take the ordinary stipend of a priest." "Well," he said, "there is no other man in the colony who would have made such an offer." So I remained in my old position, and the bishop received the £400 a year. My next point was to secure a proper residence for the bishop before his arrival, a residence that would suitably represent his dignity as the head of the Catholics of Australia. I succeeded in renting a large and stately house, built for the first Protestant archdeacon, and which at that time alone occupied the Vale of Woolomooloo, with an extensive domain attached to it. It joined the Sydney Park, in which stood his Cathedral. (In the preface to a volume of sermons published in 1842, Dr. Ullathorne alludes to the various places in which these sermons were delivered, contrasting their condition then with that in which they were at the above date: "They were preached," he says, "in the 'old court house' in Sydney, where there is now a large Cathedral, a magnificent parish church, two chapels, and ten thousand Catholics; the jail at Parramatta, where the only light except the candles on the altar came from the opening of a wooden shutter, which gave the priest a prospect of a busy tavern over the way, where now is a handsome church, flanked by a school and convent; an old barn at Windsor, where is now a goodly church, with a congregation of eight hundred persons, besides free schools, a boarding school, and an orphanage; an assembly room at Bathurst, beyond the Blue Mountains, placed over some livery stables, now is a church ample for one thousand persons, and served by two priests; in the police court of Maitland, which now contains two churches; in a public-house on Patrick's Plains, or a room house at Wollongong, all which places now have their churches and clergy." It is needless to say that the contrast here drawn out is indefinitely greater at the present day, when the Church in Australia has taken developments not dreamed of when the above remarks were written.)

Meanwhile, having had to remove the priest from Windsor for six months, I had unexpectedly heavy Sunday duties to perform. I went to Windsor, a distance from Sydney of forty-five miles, and put up at a Protestant tavern. The next morning at six o'clock I had to say Mass, preach and administer the sacraments, to attend the convict and military hospitals; then to ride to Parramatta, a distance of twenty miles, there to put up at the Woolpack Inn, and perform the same duties in the military guard house, a long dark room without a single window, erected over the prison of a chain-gang. The only light I had was from the opening of a wooden shutter at the back of the temporary altar. Before me I had the prospect of a busy public-house. When I turned to the people I got a Rembrandt view of the first row, while the rest of the congregation were buried in darkness. On one occasion two Catholic ladies were on a visit at the governor's country residence. On Sunday they prepared to come to Mass. The governor and his suite insisted that they could not appear in such a place. They insisted that they must go. So an aide-de-camp was sent to the barracks to secure two steady Catholic sergeants to kneel behind them for their protection. After this duty I attended the military and convict hospitals, about a mile from each other,

and then to breakfast at the inn. After while I rode to Sydney, fifteen miles further, to preach in the evening. The next morning by eleven o'clock came on the sense of fatigue, from which I recovered by lying for a couple of hours on a sofa with a light book. On one of these occasions at Windsor, I had a sick call after night came on, which was a couple of miles beyond the river Hawkesbury. When I and my man reached the river, there was no getting the ferry-boat across for a very long time. The convict ferry-men were sleeping in their hut on the other side of the river, and were unwilling to hear with all our shouting. It was a cold, sharp night in the open air, and we got back to the inn at a quarter to twelve. I was hungry with fasting till one o'clock the next day before me. Everyone else was in bed, so I searched all about the house till I found a piece of bread and a jar of pickled walnuts, of which I made a hasty supper before midnight, which I had to regret the next day.

Father McEncroe generally attended the executions at Sydney, and prepared the condemned for death. It is a fact that two-thirds of the Protestant criminals sought the aid of the Catholic priests after their condemnation to the gallows. This at last produced such an impression that the Protestant archdeacon printed and circulated a thousand copies of a pamphlet on the subject, in which, among other things, he said that this fact ought not to awaken any surprise. That these poor creatures had very little religion, and that the soothing ways of the priests, and their less guarded system of confession, acted as a fascination on criminals in their last moments. *A propos* of these and similar remarks, I remember having been summoned to a bushranger immediately after his sentence. My first words to him were: "You are not a Catholic—why have you sent for me?"

He was a finely-formed young man, with an intelligent face, and in full vigor of life. With tears he replied: "Sir I want to tell you what is on my mind; and if I tell it to a parson he will tell it again." I felt the archdeacon's pamphlet would do more good than harm, so I took no notice of it.

Two men, after their condemnation, were sent by sea to Newcastle, to be executed on the scene of their crimes. It was for beating an overseer to death in the midst of a chain-gang employed in making a breakwater. One of them, though not a Catholic, applied for a priest, and I went with them a distance of about seventy miles from Sydney. On arrival at the jail at Newcastle I was told by the governor of the jail that the Protestant chaplain particularly desired to see me. I thought it singular, because, though a stranger to me, he had recently written an attack upon me in a Wesleyan magazine. On his entrance he was embarrassed, and told me that as he had to attend one of the men, and this kind of duty was new to him, I should greatly oblige him if I would give him some guidance what to do. I gave him such hints as I thought would be useful to the poor man, and he left me with thanks. The execution was to take place early next morning on a promontory, upon which a lofty scaffold was erected, that it might be visible to a thousand men, forming a chain-gang. These men were dressed, as usual, in alternate brown and yellow clothing of frieze, were all in irons, and were guarded by a company of soldiers. The execution took place soon after sunrise, because the deputy sheriff and executioner had afterwards to proceed up the river to hang some blacks. I was therefore very early at the jail. We had to walk with the condemned about a mile to the scaffold, and it was blowing a furious gale of wind from the sea. The Anglican clergyman again wished to see me.

He asked what I should do on the way and on the scaffold? I told him that my poor man was well instructed, that on the way I should repeat a litany which he would answer, and I should occasionally address words to him suited to his state. "Very good, sir; and what will you do on the scaffold?" "The man," I replied, "is well taught to offer his life to God for his sins, which he will do with me in the words I have taught him. And when the executioner is quite ready for the drop, he will give me a sign, and I shall descend the ladder and pray for his soul." "Very good, sir, will you please to walk first with your man?" "Certainly." He followed in a nervous condition, and when we reached the scaffold each knelt at the foot of a very tall ladder. The wind blew tremendously, and sent my ladder down falling across the back of my Anglican friend; but I seized him by the coat laps, and just saved him from the descending blow. The ladders were then tied, and I mounted first. What a spectacle were those upturned faces on that desolate rocky promontory! The scaffold shook in the wind, and I had to put one foot against the framework and to hold the man from being blown off, speaking to him, or rather praying with him, while the executioners made their preparations. The young man was bent on speaking to his comrades below, but I would not let him: for such speeches at the dying moment are commonly exhibitions of vanity. He obeyed me, I pressed his hand, and he was cast off. After all was over I walked back with my Anglican friend, who said to me: "Sir, this is a painful and humiliating duty. Had I known that I should be subject to it I should never have taken orders. . . ."

11. On September 13, 1835, the Right Rev. Father Bede Polding, bishop of Hierocoesarea, vicar-apostolic of New Holland and Van Diemen's Land, arrived in Sydney, accompanied by

three priests and four ecclesiastical students. He had stayed for a time in Hobart Town, where he was received by Governor Sir George Arthur with marked courtesy and hospitality. He found things in the same state in which I had found them; but left there a Benedictine priest, the Rev. Father Cottram, and an ecclesiastical student, afterwards Dean Kenny, to open and teach a school for the people.

The bishop's house was ready for his reception. The Catholic population received him with great joy, and presented him with a handsome carriage and pair as expressive of their wish to maintain him in his dignity. He was well received by the governor and the chief officials, to most of whom he was the bearer of letters. He received a stipend of £400 a year, and I retained mine and remained to assist him in my former office.

Everything in the Church now began to assume larger proportions. The bishop took a position which gradually raised the tone and spirit of the whole Catholic body. We had pontifical functions with as much solemnity as our resources could command, which much impressed the people, to whom they were new. Then the vast body of the Catholics, who had never been confirmed, received this sacrament. As the bishop's house was large, he turned half of it into a boarding school, over which I presided for a time. Thus was begun a solicitude for raising the sons of the settlers who were acquiring property, that they might take their suitable position. As the bishop was inexperienced in official correspondence, and as the work began to increase, I continued that duty under his direction to the end. When resident, later, at Parramatta, I rode once or twice a week over to Sydney, to perform this duty under the eye of the bishop, and to call at the government offices when business required it. I had

also to look after the completion of the church begun at Maitland, and to start another at Parramatta. I had the assistance of the government architect in devising the plans. But what was my surprise, on arriving one day at Maitland, to find that without my knowledge Father Therry had been there, and had doubled the number of windows in the walls. This was one of his singularities, to put as many windows in a building as the walls would allow of, without any consideration for the intense glare of heated light. Thus in the old cathedral of Sydney he put seventy large windows, two rows in one wall. At Maitland he spoiled what would have been a well-proportioned nave in the old lancet style. His taste in architecture was for what he called "opes." If a plan was brought to him, his first question was: "How many more *opes* would it admit of?" He could not understand the principle of adapting the light of a building to the climate.

Riding at Maitland along the fertile banks of the river Hunter, it was impossible not to admire the beauty of those primitive forests and the fertile abundance produced by the deep and rich alluvial soil. Then there were the varied notes of the birds. I was riding through the wood with Mr. Walker, the chief supporter of our religion in that locality, when I heard at some distance first a whistle, then the crack of a whip, then the reverberation of the lash. I asked: "What road is that over there?" "There is no road," he replied. "But I heard a man driving, and there again," "Oh! that's the coachman." "But a coachman must have a road." "The coachman's a bird," said he. And a bird it was, exactly imitating the whistle of a coachman and the crack and lashing of his whip. Then the bell bird rang its silver bell, and another species cried like a child in trouble, while the flocks of parrots made a croaking din, and flights of black cockatoos spread over the fields of maize with a noise like the rusty hinges of an old castle all flapping together in the wind.

The bishop himself began that wonderful course of missionary labor among the convicts. This attracted so much attention, produced so great an influence, and, more than any other part of his ministry, drew so great a veneration towards him; he had not merely the heart of a father, but the heart of a mother towards them. When they came into his presence he wept over them, and they could never resist the influence of his words. The first step he took was to obtain leave from the government for all the Catholic prisoners, as they arrived by ship, to be retained in the convict barracks of Sydney for ten days before they were sent up the country. When a ship arrived from Ireland there would be as many as three hundred to look after. They were brought to the church at six in the morning and remained until eleven; again marched to the church at three and remained until six. It was a kind of retreat adapted to their circumstances. The bishop was there the whole time, assisted by the Sydney clergy. After an address by the bishop, they were classified by the clergy into those who had not performed their religious duties for one, for three, for five, or for ten years. After the clergy had examined into the amount of instruction which each possessed, they were re-classified for instruction, the ecclesiastical students acted as catechists, and some of the men were picked out as monitors. Then began the confessions, in which the bishop took his large share. He gave most of the instruction, and after the religious duties were completed by Communion, a special course of instruction and advice was given to them regarding their position as convicts, what power their master had over them, how the law af-

fected them, to what dangers they were exposed, and how they would most effectually succeed in obtaining mitigation, good treatment, and their ticket of leave; after this they proceeded to their assignment.

I need scarcely say that this system produced a most beneficial result which was widely recognized. In my evidence before the Parliamentary Committee on Transportation in the year 1838, I was able to quote a letter from the bishop, stating that, of 1,400 prisoners who had already gone through this system, only two had found their way into the Sydney jail; and that, whereas hitherto our clergy had attended not less than twenty executions yearly, during the six months since this system was adopted only one Catholic has been executed, and he for a crime of three years' standing. In short, it was a common remark among the clergy, that those whom they had in hand on their arrival very rarely found their way into jail.

This was but a part of the bishop's labors among the convicts. At regular intervals he visited the felons' jail, instructed the Catholics, heard their confessions, and said Mass for them in the press room. Shortly after he had said his first Mass there, the head jailer, a good Catholic, and a man of mild manners though of resolute will, said to me: "I will tell you something, sir, and you will tell it to no one else. You know how this place is infested with small vermin, so that even our rough men can hardly stand it. Well, when we are crowded we are obliged to put a lot of men in the press room of a night to sleep. But ever since the bishop has said Mass there, there is a rush of men to get to that end of the room, because there have been no vermin there since that time." If there were men to be executed he always prepared them, although a priest attended them on the scaffold.

Every Sunday morning, the convicts, from their barracks, were marched to the last Mass in the cathedral, where they crowded to the bishop's confessional; and when he had to officiate, the congregation had consequently to be detained a long time before the service began. Occasionally it became my duty to represent the great inconvenience to the congregation. He would then weep, and say: "Anyone else I could put off, but I cannot resist these poor creatures." After the Sunday Vespers, he would mount his horse and proceed to a large chain-gang on Goat Island, or perhaps to some other chain-gang working on the roads, but boxed up in wooden huts on Sundays. There he would have the Catholics drawn out, and after an earnest address to them would use some retired place for a confessional. After the hard labors of the Sunday were over, he delighted to have all the Sydney clergy at his house to a late dinner, and took the opportunity to invite any lay gentleman to whom he wished to show respect.

When he went up the country the convicts were always his first care, and he got as many to Mass as he could and spent much of his time with them. When they knew he was coming, the Catholic settlers met him on the confines of the district, on horseback, and conducted him to the church, if there was one, or to the temporary place where he was to officiate. He made it a point, before leaving, to ride through the district in company with the priest, calling at the house of every free Catholic or Emancipist who respected himself, and was of good conduct. But if a man was not living properly, or neglected his duty to his family, he rode past his house without taking any notice of him. He thus inspired the Emancipists to respect themselves, and with the same view he established respectable schools for their sons and founded a Catholic newspaper, which taught them their public rights and duties.

Having such an influence over the convicts they ran to him, as to a father, in their hours of distress. Let me give an example. He was walking in his large garden on a certain day, saying his office, when a man in a wretched plight came from his hiding-place among the trees and knelt before him. He then told his story. He had absconded from service 150 miles up the country, because the overseer had been down upon him, and had unjustly reported him so often to his master that he had been flogged several times. He then showed his back covered with wounds and scars, and declared he was so miserable that he could bear it no longer. He had come all that way, avoiding the roads, and had had nothing to eat for three days but a green cob of maize, for he was obliged to keep in hiding. After questioning him closely, the bishop sent him to the kitchen for food, and went straight to the principal superintendent of convicts, an officer of great authority. To him he told the whole tale, expressed his conviction of the truth, and pleaded for mercy. The superintendent replied: "The man must be sent to the barracks, and must be punished; but I promise you he shall be sent to another master, and to one who will do justice."

The bishop's servants were mostly convicts, and, of course, he was kind to them. There was an old man among them, who worked in the garden, who was very simple, and, in the main honest; but seeing the bishop's jewelled miter, wrapped it in a cloth, carried it to the principal hatter in the city, said it was a curious Indian cap, and asked the master of the shop what he would give for it. The master suspected at once that it was something belonging to the Catholic bishop. He detained the old man, and sent a messenger to the bishop's house. A priest went to the shop, took possession of the miter and the old man, and on his arrival at home he was saluted with general laughter. No more notice was taken of it. The old man worked on, but never heard the last of the miter from his fellow-servants.

Our wants of all kinds increased so much that the bishop thought it desirable that I should go to England, and thence to Ireland, and do the best I could to provide for them. . . .

PART II

The Church and the Contemporary Scene
1917——

V. Church and State Relations

THE secularization of society that had progressed at an accelerated pace from the time of the Enlightenment through the nineteenth century came to full fruit in the twentieth century. The aggrandizements of man in the nineteenth century became in the twentieth century an open drive for world domination. From the heartland of Christianity a series of nationalistic, revolutionary movements and successive wars arose to menace international peace and at times to seem to imperil the very existence of the Church.

The first half of the twentieth century was marked by distortions and perversions of Christian values. Prophets arose who expressed their conviction that the failure of Christians to carry out a life of faith in a contemporary society would reduce their influence to an insignificant role in modern affairs. The striving of all humanity to free itself from oppression and to advance its material well-being would be a movement away from the Church. The human aspiration, which Christianity had fostered as an expression of the individual's dignity, would bring forth new and more vital ideologies.

This contemporary challenge to Catholicism was, accordingly, a mixture of the heritage of the previous two hundred years and the tragic contradictions marking the spirit of the age. Under the leadership of several remarkably able popes, and sparked by a vigorous revival among Catholics, the Church's difficult mission to the modern world was carried forward. Its main aim was to achieve a positive position over and against excesses of liberal individualism and nationalism on the one hand, and to root out the errors of totalitarianism, socialism, and communism on the other. World War I wiped away the last vestiges of feudalism and monarchy, and Catholics attempted to work with moderate Socialists in establishing parliamentary democracies. But a lack of principles among secularized pragmatic democrats, the spreading fire of pagan nationalistic aspirations, and social unrest fomented by an international Communist conspiracy against the existing political order, hastened a second and more devastating world conflict.

The destruction of the pagan totalitarian systems in 1945 did not bring lasting peace as men had hoped. In the post-war years the alliances of democratic, capitalist societies stood opposed to the massive system of state power imposed by a dynamic, materialistic Communism. This titanic struggle continues today as the people of new nations strive to hasten industrialization and social betterment. In the midst of these currents it is not entirely apparent where the young neutral nations will ally themselves. The outcome of the struggle for law, freedom, and a just world order is likewise still undecided.

The experience of history, however, evidences that this contemporary struggle, in the same way as the many struggles of the Church's life throughout twenty centuries, will not dominate the providential plan of God. Thoughtful men have become more conscious of the sovereignty of God in His creation at a time when scientific advances push back previously unknown realms of outer space and make interplanetary contacts. God's gift of freedom to man is today, as in all ages, a challenge to realize good in the midst of the distortion of spiritual and natural values. No group of men can repudiate God and natural law without inviting social chaos. Nor can terrorism stop this process of moral corruption, which often occurs before a true revival takes shape. The Lord and Savior of the world has promised that his Holy Spirit will remain with the Church until the end of time. The historical developments of the Church's long history can serve as a guide for modern man in his effort to spread the kingdom of God, sanctify his soul, and achieve contemplative union with the beginning and end of all reality.

One of the first major clashes between the Church and the Communists of modern times took place in Mexico where anti-religious movements were spearheaded by advocates of Marxist doctrine and practice. Communists capitalized on strong Mexican anti-clerical and Masonic traditions, the graft-ridden and unstable democratic governments of the nineteenth century, and the alignment of a segment of the Catholic clergy and upper-class laity with conservative political and social policies. The radicals wrote a new constitution into law in 1917 which contained anti-religious clauses similar to earlier doctrines of the French Revolution. The political ascendancy (1924-1936) of the atheistic president, Plutareo E. Calles, brought further government control of religious life and practice. The embattled Mexican hierarchy called for active resistance to this penal legislation on the part of Mexico's people, who were in great majority Catholic. A temporary agreement by the bishops to lift the ban on public worship in 1929 was not reciprocated by the government and persecution raged again in the early 1930's, as the selected documents on CHURCH-STATE RELATIONS IN MEXICO (*No. 30*) demonstrate. Pope Pius XI was deeply concerned over

what policy the Church should pursue over against such a modern persecuting state. Should the Church actively resist unjust measures, or should
she suffer temporary spiritual setbacks in order to keep the sacramental life
springs available to the people? Finally with the presidency of General
Lazaro Cárdenas in 1935 Calles' power was broken, and Pius XI issued
his encyclical letter *Firmissimam constantiam* of 28 March 1937. Here he
took the stand that Catholics should be won back to God after the long
government oppression; the clergy should be rejuvenated and lay apostles
should assist them in the work of Catholic Action; the principles of the
great social encyclicals *Rerum Novarum* and *Quadragesimo Anno* should
be applied in the fields of agriculture and labor; Catholics, while defending
their rights, should not directly participate in political resistance to oppression. In this way the tragic results of the Mexican persecution were gradually mitigated, and an improved atmosphere gradually developed by the
1950's. Anti-religious laws are still on the books, however, and the Communists continue to exert influence especially in labor organizations. Mexico, as a heritage of the violent persecution, does not as yet grant full legal
status to the religion of the majority of the nation.

The events in Mexico, as well as an all-out war against Catholicism
during the civil war in Spain on the part of the Communist-controlled
Spanish government of the late 1930's, moved Pope Pius XI to issue a comprehensive ENCYCLICAL LETTER ON ATHEISTIC COMMUNISM (*No. 31*) on
19 March 1937. This remarkable document exposed the true nature and
aims of Communism at a time when confused liberals, exalting freedom
and action over thought, and viewing Communism as a movement for progressive social reform, were unable to condemn obvious evil as categorically
wrong and iniquitous. Pius XI, as his predecessor Pope Pius IX had done
at the time of the *Syllabus of Errors,* issued a clear exposé of the evils of
Communist doctrine, and of the impending political and social enslavement
that would follow its inception.

Under three headings the pope strove to awaken the world to the nature of Communism. In the first division he traced the historical and dialectical materialism of Marxism, its chaotic theory of class warfare, denial of
human freedom, degradation of the institutions of marriage and the family,
and its aim to implant a Godless society. Pius XI explained that liberal
abuses, economic crises engendered by capitalist industrialism, skillful
Communist propaganda, and the inability of free men to oppose the propaganda of Communists had encouraged the growth, unparallelled in human
history, of this calamitous error among the Russian, Mexican, and Spanish
peoples. In the second division the pope advanced traditional Christian prin-

ciples of political and social action as the best solution to Marxist errors: inalienable rights of man received from God, civil institutions of society established for the use of man, and the carrying out of the principles of the two social encyclicals, *Rerum Novarum* and *Quadragesimo Anno*. In the third division Pius XI advanced a positive remedial program: reform of Catholic public and private life; promotion of charity and social justice, especially through family wages; and a corporative society of organizations.

In Austria and Portugal, Catholics sought to establish experiments in corporative societies based on principles outlined in the social encyclicals. In Austria a short-lived corporative government was swallowed up by the *Anschluss* of the German Nazis in 1938. In Portugal, however, the experiment has extended from the POLITICAL CONSTITUTION OF THE PORTUGUESE REPUBLIC (*No. 32*) of 11 April 1933 to the present time. Portugal had been heir to extreme travesties of democracy during the nineteenth and early twentieth centuries: parliamentary chaos, doctrinaire secularism, Masonic intrigue, corrupt administration, and the worst financial situation in Europe. After the military revolt of 1926 an authoritarian regime was established with Dr. Oliveira Salazar, professor of economics in the University of Coimbra, being invited by the junta first to assume charge of finances. Salazar took control of the regime as prime minister in 1932. As a dedicated patriot and competent socio-economist, Dr. Salazar accomplished much in stabilizing the government and effecting financial recovery. He believed that the social ideas of the encyclicals could be applied to Portuguese life by developing a corporative state along vertical lines of solidarity of avocation and not by democratic free enterprise or socialist animosities and division of classes. The corporative social program of Portugal can be found in the separate articles of the constitution. The government theoretically was to build up administrative, cultural, moral, and economic corporatives, and to co-ordinate social activities. In practice, however, Salazar's ideal *estado novo* never fully developed. Social inequalities and injustices were not resolved, Catholics were not allowed to influence affairs, an unhealthy nationalism and colonialism developed, elections were limited to governmental candidates, opposition removed, and no succession provided. The strong executive and authoritarian spirit of the constitution itself, as well as the personal inclinations of Salazar, have militated against the realization of the social and moral ideals of the experiment. Several members of the Portuguese hierarchy have protested that, despite its sound theory and some substantial results, the corporative experiment has not been as organic and spontaneous as originally conceived.

Much less authoritarian and more representative of sound Catholic political theory was the CONSTITUTION OF THE REPUBLIC OF EIRE (*No. 33*) of 29 December 1937. In Ireland the tradition of a "mixed government" was successfully developed. The theory and practice of democracy in the English-speaking world, as well as the influence of Catholic political philosophy, are apparent in the phraseology of this instrument of government. An evident advance is made from earlier constitutions of the eighteenth and nineteenth centuries. The objectives of political action are brought into conformity with man's final end, true social order, and the common good. Earlier doctrinaire theories of individual freedom are balanced in the Irish constitution with moral and corporate responsibility. At the same time all political, religious, and class discrimination is outlawed, as is state monopoly of education. The family is safeguarded in the natural law; religious toleration is guaranteed; private property is secured; but all according to principles of social justice and exigencies of the common good. Nowhere in the twentieth century has a nation so completely combined Catholic principles, as derived from sound spiritual and philosophical dictates, with a practical, historical recognition of mankind's political and social experience. The accomplishment of the Republic of Ireland, and the carrying out in practice of this constitution's provisions, is a pilot project of democracy in action amid the storms and disorders of contemporary times.

The story is quite different when modern developments in Italy and Germany are studied. There the raw power of the totalitarian state reappeared in the twentieth century. Social disturbances and the collapse of parliamentary democracy after World War I brought forth in those two countries a Socialist collective system of one-party power, omnipotent state authority, and a strident emotional idealization of the national fatherland. Benito Mussolini's absolute state in Italy had to cope, however, with the reality of the papacy and the Catholic faith of the citizens. The Fascists were ready to come to an understanding on the Roman Question which they had inherited from nineteenth-century liberals, and overtures were made to the Vatican which met with a response. The result of these negotiations was the LATERAN TREATY AND CONCORDAT BETWEEN THE HOLY SEE AND ITALY (*No. 34*) of 11 February 1929. The State of the Vatican City, totalling 109 acres, was restored to the pope, Catholicism was recognized as the state religion in Italy, the pope renounced all claim to the old Papal States and agreed to recognize the Italian kingdom, while canon law was recognized by the Italian judicial system.

But mutual distrust continued between the Holy See and the Fascist government. When Mussolini's followers attacked Catholic youth centers the pope responded with a vigorous letter, published abroad, exposing the true nature of Fascism, and Pius XI made it clear that no Catholic could be a Fascist. The government did not reply to this pronouncement and a tenuous *modus vivendi* existed throughout the war years.

In Germany the accession of Adolf Hitler to power in 1933 and the establishment of the National Socialist Party in absolute control of the nation marked the culmination of the Nazis' totalitarian ambitions. Following the pattern established by Mussolini, the *Fuehrer* was willing to reach an agreement with the Holy See that would prohibit participation of the German clergy in politics and would disband the Catholic Center Party. In turn, the Church was to be guaranteed freedom of communication, religious instruction in schools, and Catholic Action activity in religious, cultural, and charitable spheres. The Holy See agreed to these apparently generous concessions in the CONCORDAT BETWEEN THE HOLY SEE AND THE GERMAN REICH (*No. 35*) of 20 July 1933. By this act Pope Pius XI continued his policy of signing concordats to preserve elementary Catholic life in hostile states as the best possible arrangement for the faithful in the given circumstances. The experience of Mexico or Spain was not to be repeated in Italy or Germany. The *de facto* disappearance of the Center Party as a political force in German politics was also a consideration in signing this concordat. However, the agreement to disband the Center Party ended the long and fruitful influence of that noble political group on German affairs, eliminated any possible Catholic influence on the new government, and seemed to indicate to the ordinary German Catholic that the Holy See had given some type of official recognition to the regime.

Nor was the possibility that the Nazis would honor the clauses of the concordat long in doubt. Like the Fascists, they soon opposed Catholic Action organizations, the Catholic press, and religious instruction of youth. With a heavy heart but courageous directness Pope Pius XI condemned the flagrant infringements of the Nazis and denounced their entire method of action as un-Christian in his ENCYCLICAL LETTER ON THE CHURCH IN GERMANY (*No. 36*) of 14 March 1837. This powerful document gave moral support to the German Catholics in their "day of anguish," as the pope called the Nazi interlude in Germany.

Liberation from totalitarianism and its aggression was not accomplished without the unparalleled destruction and suffering which modern men and nations had to undergo during the long years of occupation and conflict during World War II. Pope Pius XI died at the beginning of the momentous struggle. His Secretary of State, Eugenio Cardinal Pacelli (1958), succeeded him and continued the policies of his predecessor which he had such a major part in formulating. It is still too early to attempt an historical evaluation of this learned pontiff who became a symbol of spiritual encouragement in one of history's darkest hours. During the war years, as one indication of his efforts to further peace, Pope Pius XII delivered annual Christmas messages to all people on the subject most desired by all mankind. Two of these allocutions, in 1939 and 1945, at the beginning and end of World War II, gave a clear outline of Christian EF-FORTS FOR PEACE (*No. 37*) in a war-torn world. The pope also explained the attitude of the Church toward contemporary politics and ideologies on several occasions. On 2 October 1945 he emphasized in his address to the Roman Rota the juridical power of the Church as compared to that of the state. The state may achieve its purpose of the common good in a true democracy, as representative thinkers of the Church have taught. Totalitarian systems of government were rejected, and the distinct origin and structure of the Church, as based on divine precepts, was explained anew by Pius XII.

30. *Relations Between the Church and the United States of Mexico, 1917, 1929, 1934*

From *The Catholic Mind*, XVI (22 May 1917), 217-232; XXX (8 November 1932), 427-428; XXXII (8 December 1934), 447-448. Reprinted with permission from *America*, The National Catholic Weekly Review.

A. PROTEST OF THE MEXICAN CATHO-
LIC HIERARCHY TO THE 5 FEB-
RUARY 1917 CONSTITUTION,
24 FEBRUARY 1917

To THE extreme miseries which pestilence, famine, war and religious persecution have brought upon the faithful of our dioceses there has now come a further infliction to embitter our situation. It had been our hope that the heroic patience with which our clergy and our people have borne such formidable calamities would serve to assuage the seething passions and in response to the dictates of reason, justice and public policy would bring about at last the recognition of religious freedom, which the revolution had solemnly pledged to the Mexican nation and to foreign governments. But neither the becoming conduct of the Faithful nor our own serene and pacific attitude, nor the public calamities endured by the people of every class have sufficed to allay passion. Rather does the Constitution promulgated at Querétaro on February 5 last, give final form and sanction to religious persecution.

We are thus placed in the most trying dilemma. This instrument strikes at the most sacred rights of the Catholic Church, of the social order of Mexico, and the personal rights of every Christian; it proclaims principles opposed to the truth taught by Jesus Christ which forms the treasure of the Church and most invaluable inheritance of mankind; and destroys, root and branch, the few rights which the Constitution of 1857, accepted as the fundamental law by all Mexicans so far as its essential principles are concerned, yields to the Church as an institution and to Catholics as individuals.

Can we be silent at such spoliation, we who are by virtue of our episcopal investiture the representatives of the Catholic Church in Mexico and are so recognized by the Constitution of 1857? On the other hand, how can we raise our voice in protest when our mere words of peace may serve as a new pretext for the charge of conspiracy against established order and result in making the persecution still fiercer?

As Mexican citizens and in the exercises of our rights we might well question the validity of a constitution enacted and promulgated by a single political group without previously meeting the indispensable conditions fixed by the Constitution of 1857 for its own amendment, the disregard of which nullifies such action. Not only were the other political groups existing in the country not represented in the assembly which prepared this instrument but they were even formally excluded from it, thus ignoring the will of the nation. Finally, the constitution previously in force has been abolished; with what authority nobody knows. But since we do not claim to meddle in political questions but to defend in such manner as we may the religious freedom of the Christian element of our population against the severe onslaught made on religion, we shall confine ourselves to a protest against this onslaught, made energetically and in due form. We preface our protest with the following formal declarations:

1) Abiding by the teachings of the Roman pontiffs, especially those of the encyclical *Quod Apostolici Muneris,* and patriotically inspired, we are far from approving armed rebellion against constituted authority. But this passive acceptance of any government must not be taken to signify intellectual and voluntary approval or acceptance of any anti-religious or otherwise unjust laws emanating from that government.

Nor should it be inferred therefrom that Catholics may be denied their right as citizens peacefully and legally to seek the annulment of whatever the laws of the nation may contain hurtful to their conscience and their rights.

2) In taking this step our single motive is not the slightest desire of vengeance nor even our natural zeal to procure our own temporal welfare or that of our clergy, which might better be secured by compromise or silence, but to fulfill the duty imposed upon us to defend the rights of the Church and of religious freedom.

If after these declarations our protest should awaken a greater outburst of religious persecution, the responsibility will not rest upon those who have done their duty but rather upon those who will not hear nor permit to be heard the voice of truth and justice; and the Church which has known how to live through persecution will return to the days of endurance and of martyrdom.

The systematic outrages committed by the revolution against the Catholic religion, its temples, its clergy and its institutions, including even those of an educational or charitable character, almost from the beginning of the revolution of 1913 and down to today, indicate beyond a shadow of doubt that that movement, purely political in its inception, soon was transformed into an anti-religious movement. In order to deny its shameful character, the leaders of this movement have resorted to various explanations whose very variety reveals their falsehood. At one stage they said that the bishops and clergy had aided in overthrowing the national government established in 1911; at another, that we had been accomplices of the government established in 1913; again, they assert that we sought to seize the government of the Republic and destroy liberty forever; again, it is alleged that, united with the power which ruled for many years of peace, and leagued with the well-to-do classes of society, we tyrannize over the people. No lie was left untold to justify the sacrilege committed by the revolutionists; the clergy were accused of every kind of vice; it was rumored as certain that stores of arms had been found in the churches; it was affirmed that there were priests and even bishops who had led the reactionary ranks in battle. First they denied the outrages committed by the revolution, and then they admitted them, attributing the excesses to the rage of combatants who seized towns by force, as if it were not obvious that these outrages were ordered by the chiefs and committed by the troops even in those places which surrendered in terror and without resistance, for the majority of the towns taken belonged to this class.

The existence of this spirit, so hostile to religion, was at first indignantly denied, but soon the revolutionary press frankly declared that the purpose of the movement was to take from the clergy the excessive power they had possessed in the Republic. And since this power could not be civil, for that the Church in Mexico has never enjoyed, nor any power based upon its union with the state, for that had been discontinued more than half a century ago, the only power left to destroy was the moral power, that is to say, the natural and necessary moral influence which every religion exercises on the lives of the individuals professing it, and through that means, on the family and on society.

That such is the revolutionists' object has been completely demonstrated in the addresses delivered in the assembly of Querétaro and in the committee reports on articles 3 and 130 of the constitution; for in these documents, and especially in the report on the latter, it is frankly confessed that the object is to deprive the clergy of its moral power.

Against this tendency, destructive of religion, culture and traditions, which would disrupt peace everywhere, but particularly in Mexico, we protest in our capacity as leaders of the Catholic Church in our native land before both the Mexican people and the civilized nations of the earth.

It was inevitable that a constitution so constructed should be followed by the very worst consequences. Though it seemed to menace only the rights of the clergy, in reality it attacked the elementary and natural rights of all citizens.

A paragraph of article 130 says: "The law recognizes no juridical personality in the religious institutions known as churches." Now it cannot be denied that even if the Catholic Church were not divine and had not received from its divine Founder the personality and character of a real society, it would inherently possess, independent of any civil power, its own personality and character based upon its individual right to freedom of religious belief and practices; and since this right is anterior to the state, and hence does not depend upon the state, violation of and assault upon the group becomes violation of and assault upon the right of the individual. We protest, therefore, against this paragraph as infringing upon the rights which we Mexican Catholics inherently possess to the recognition of our Church as a juridical person, and furthermore as contravening the recognition of this right in the Constitution of 1857 and even in the Laws of Reform.

Article 3 reads as follows: "Instruction is free; that given in public institutions of learning shall be secular. Primary instruction, whether higher or lower, given in private institutions shall likewise be secular. No religious corporation nor minister of any religious creed shall establish or direct schools of primary instruction. Private primary schools may be established only subject to official supervision. . . ." Article 31 says: "It shall be the duty of every Mexican to compel the attendance at either private or public schools of their children or wards, when under fifteen years of age, in order that they may receive primary instruction and military training for such periods as the law of public instruction in each state shall determine."

On the one hand, freedom of instruction is restricted by prohibiting instruction in religion, even in private schools. On the other, the right which every man enjoys to devote himself to teaching is abridged in the case of the clergy. Lastly, the right of every father to bring up his children in accordance with his conscience and his religion is attacked, since he is compelled to have them receive secular instruction, that is to say, positively irreligious instruction, to use the words of the committee which reported this article. We cannot be silent in the face of such monstrous outrages. As Mexican citizens, and as leaders of the religion professed by the majority of our people, we are compelled in conscience to protest, and we do hereby protest, against the violation of these sacred rights.

Article 5 provides: "The state shall not permit any contract, covenant or agreement to be carried out having for its object the abridgment, loss or irrevocable sacrifice of the liberty of man, whether by reason of labor, education or religious vows. The law therefore does not permit the establishment of monastic orders, of whatever denomination or for whatever purpose contemplated."

The right to choose any state of life is the corollary of individual and religious liberty. Just as no one can be prevented from entering the bonds of matrimony, nor compelled to take this step, so an attempt to prevent anyone from devoting himself for a greater or less time to religious practices or to charitable work is an infringement upon his freedom. We accordingly protest against this article not only because it prevents the exercise of the religious life but because it abridges the liberty of association for such lawful purposes as works of charity, and restricts the right which every man has to order his life as his conscience may dictate.

Article 27, section II, reads:

The religious institutions known as churches, irrespective of creed, shall in no case have legal capacity, hold or administer real property or loans made on such real property; all such real property or loans as may be at present held by the said religious institutions, either on their own behalf or through third parties, shall vest in the nation, and anyone shall have the right to denounce property so held. Presumptive proof shall be sufficient to declare the denunciation wellfounded. Places of public worship are the property of the nation, as represented by the Federal Government, which shall determine which of them may continue to be devoted to their present purposes. Episcopal residences, rectories, seminaries, orphan asylums, and collegiate establishments of religious associations, convents, or any other buildings built or designed for the administration, propaganda, or teaching of the tenets of any religious creed, shall forthwith vest as of full right directly in the nation, to be used exclusively for the public services of the Federation or of the States within their respective jurisdictions. All places of public worship which shall later be erected shall be the property of the nation.

What religious society could fulfill the purpose for which it was established when deprived of the right even to hold such real property as is indispensable to its object? Is not religion being shackled and fettered when it is forbidden to have colleges for the teaching of its children, charitable institutions for the care of its needy, hospitals for its sick, means of affording a fitting livelihood to its ministers? Is not placing of obstacles in the way of leading the religious life a violation of the individual's right to embrace and profess any religion? By what power other than that of the tyrant can the state decree such spoliation?

The Church in the eyes of Catholics is the house of God, the holiest spot on earth. Consequently the feelings of Mexicans have been outraged by the sacrilegious profanation, destruction and alienation of places of worship left to them up to now. Every religious man regards the church as the place where the most solemn acts bearing both on this present life and on the life to come, are performed; a church building is indispensable for the exercise of religion. There can be no religious freedom where the church buildings are left in the hands of those not belonging to the clergy and faithful, or where they are not the property of religious organizations.

The church buildings in Mexico, as throughout the Christian world, belong to the Catholic incorporated bodies (dioceses, parishes, religious communities, etc.), because they have been built and supported by their funds, or because they have been accepted by way of gift from those who erected them.

All this is so obvious that the Constitution of 1857, which snatched from the Catholics so many rights, not only did not deprive them of this right, but expressly recognized it (art. 27); and the Laws of Reform did not go to the extent generally supposed, for they merely nationalized the places of public worship of the suppressed regular orders and did not restrict the right to acquire in absolute ownership new places of worship.

We accordingly protest against the double outrage perpetrated in this ar-

ticle against Catholics, whereby we are deprived of property rights in, and the right to acquire, places of worship. We also protest against the violation of religious freedom which such action entails. We protest, too, against the wrong done us in wresting from us ownership of our asylums and other institutions devoted to education and charity, on the ground that even the Constitution of 1857 authorizes corporations and institutions dependent upon religious associations to acquire and administer such buildings as may be immediately and directly destined for the service and purposes of the said institutions (art. 27, as amended 4 May 1901), and because, moreover, many of these properties are held by private individuals. We protest, furthermore, against the spoliation of episcopal residences, rectories, and seminaries, ownership of which is likewise sanctioned by law (art. 100 of Law of 5 Feb. 1861, art. 27 of the Federal Constitution, and art. 14 of the Organic Law of 1874).

Article 130, which here follows, contains, it is clear, such a series of limitations and restrictions as to make "religious freedom" a mere travesty:

I. The Federal authorities shall have the exclusive power to exercise in matters of religious worship and outward ecclesiastical forms such intervention as by law authorized. All other officials shall act as auxiliaries to the Federal authorities.

II. The Congress shall not enact any law whatsoever establishing or forbidding religion.

III. Marriage is a civil contract. Marriage and all other acts relating to the civil status of individuals shall appertain to the exclusive jurisdiction of the civil authorities, in the manner and form by law provided, and they shall have the force and validity given them by said laws.

IV. The law recognizes no juridical

personality in the religious institutions known as churches.

V. The ministers of religious creeds will be considered as persons exercising a profession, and shall be directly subject to the laws enacted on the matter.

VI. The State legislatures shall have exclusive power of determining the maximum number of ministers of religious creeds, according to the needs of each locality.

VII. Only a Mexican by birth may be a minister of any religious creed in Mexico.

VIII. No ministers of religious creeds shall, either in public or private meetings, nor in acts of worship or religious propaganda, criticize the fundamental laws of the country, the authorities or the government in general, they shall have no vote, nor be eligible to office, nor shall they be entitled to assemble for political purposes.

IX. Before dedicating new temples of worship for public use, permission shall be obtained from the Department of the Interior, and the opinion of the governor of the respective State shall be previously heard on the subject. Every place of worship shall have a person charged with its care and maintenance who shall be legally responsible for the faithful observance of the laws controlling religious practices within the said place of worship, and for all the objects used for purposes of worship.

X. The caretaker of each place of public worship, together with ten citizens of the place, shall promptly advise the municipal authorities as to the person charged with the care of the said place of worship. The outgoing minister shall, in every instance, give notice of any change, for which purpose he shall be accompanied by the incoming minister and ten other citizens of the place. The municipal authorities, under penalty of dismissal and a fine, not exceeding one thousand pesos for each breach, shall be responsible for the exact performance of this provision; they shall keep a register of the place of worship and another of the caretakers thereof, subject to the same penalties as above provided. The municipal authorities shall likewise give notice to the Department of the Interior, through the state governor, regarding the opening to public use of a new place of worship, as well as of any change in the caretakers. Personal gifts may be received in the interior of places of public worship.

XI. Under no conditions shall studies carried on in institutions devoted to the professional training of ministers of religious creeds be ratified or be granted any other dispensation of privilege which shall have for its purpose the ratification of these studies for courses in official institutions. Any authority violating this provision shall be punished as a criminal and all such dispensations of privilege shall be null and void, and shall invalidate wholly and entirely the professional degree towards the obtaining of which the infraction of this provision may in any way have contributed.

XII. No periodical publication which, either by reason of its program, its title, or merely because of its general tendencies, is of a religious character, shall comment upon any political affairs of the nation, nor publish any information regarding the acts of the authorities of the country or of private individuals, in so far as the latter have to do with public affairs.

XIII. Every kind of political association whose name shall bear any word or indication relating to any religious belief is hereby strictly forbidden. No assemblies of any political character shall be held within places of public worship.

XIV. No minister of any religious creed may inherit, either on his own behalf or by means of a trustee or otherwise, any real property occupied by any association of religious propaganda or with religious or charitable purposes. Ministers of religion are incapable legally of inheriting from ministers of the same religious creed or from any private individual to whom they are not related by blood within the fourth degree.

XV. All real and personal property pertaining to the clergy or to religious institutions shall be governed in so far as their acquisition by private parties is concerned, in conformity with article 27 of this Constitution.

XVI. No trial by jury shall ever be granted for the infraction of any of the preceding provisions.

Is there anyone who, after reading the above quotation, will not ask in amazement: "What has become of religious freedom?"

The Federal authorities empowered to intervene in matters of religious and outward ecclesiastical forms; the clergy considered as persons exercising a profession and subject to the laws enacted with reference to the exercise of professions; the places of worship the property of the nation; and neither Catholics nor anyone else authorized to build new churches! What is there left of freedom to worship God? Is this not tantamount to destroying the very essence of religious organization, in itself independent of the State? Is it not subjecting to public authority the conscience of the individual and his relations with God? Is it not to enslave to the power of the State not only the Church and the clergy, but also all Catholics, all men who profess any religion whatever? Is not this tyranny?

In the rest of the article still further evidence is given of the slavery to which religion and religious observances are reduced. Thus, paragraph II says: "Marriage is a civil contract." This is a dogmatic definition; and if the state may not establish or prohibit by law any religion whatever, it has as little right to define dogmas by law. We Catholics and with us all Christian denominations, believe that marriage is a religious contract. And yet we are forbidden to teach this belief, even though at the same time we exhort and even direct the Faithful to obey the law so far as the civil effects of this contract are concerned. This prohibition appears in paragraphs VIII and XII which provide that neither in the pulpit, nor in the press nor in any other way may the fundamental laws of the nation be censured. To the state

legislatures paragraph V gives the power to determine the maximum number of priests which may exist in their respective jurisdictions; and paragraph VII establishes, for the exercise of the priestly office, the requisite of Mexican citizenship by birth. By means of these provisions the state projects itself into the internal management of the Church; it is not the function of the civil government but of the religious community through its own appropriate agencies, and in Catholicism we, the bishops, are that agency, to determine the number of clergymen needed; and to that appropriate agency alone belongs the right of seeking its clergy among whomsoever it believes desirable, whether alien or citizen.

Moreover, these latter limitations operate to the ignominious exclusion of the priestly office. Why are not the other professions limited either in number or in nationality? Why exclude foreigners from the clergy, even to the extreme of offending the nations to which they belong? What is aimed at is to make impossible in Mexico the life of the priest. This is clearly shown by the provisions depriving priests of their political rights and even of the right of inheritance conceded to all men. The priest is subjected to special tribunals, dependent upon the government, for any infraction of this irreligious legislation, while any other delinquent has the right to be tried by tribunals of the people. And, as obviously there cannot be religion without its ministers, each attack of this sort on the clergy is an attack upon religion itself and the right to profess it.

On the basis of what we here set forth, we protest against such violation of religious freedom and of the rights of the Church and against all other evidences of such violations contained in the Constitution of February 5 of this year; and we declare that we shall not recognize as valid any act or decree, even though issued by any person of our several dioceses, whatever be his ecclesiastical rank, which shall be contrary to this protest or declaration.

We have duly met our painful obligation, and before closing this document, we wish to make a statement inspired by all the sincerity with which our honorable and lofty calling inspires us. Since there does not now exist a unity of faith in Mexico, we Catholics have not sought, nor have we had the right to seek, to impose religious unity by law, for the very reason that we have respected liberty; and it is our wish, and our right, that the law shall not be hostile to us in such a manner as to favor unbelief and irreligion. We do not seek to amass wealth; we cannot assent to the snatching from our hands whatever the faithful have committed to our care for the advancement of religion, and for their own good, as well as for our support. Neither priest nor prelate seeks civil power; but it is indeed our common and lawful desire that our Catholic citizens should not find themselves deprived of this right and thus be pariahs in their own native land. We yield to no one in longing for the improvement of the condition of the poor and toward this end no one in Mexico has labored harder than we, nor was anyone laboring for it before us. But we are not the enemies of the rich man, because he is wealthy, nor do we accuse him of injustice in keeping the goods which he possesses. We are firmly convinced that only when a sound democracy prevails will our land enjoy a stable and lasting government, a government which will respect, balance and adjust the rights of all, and give to each his due. When the National Catholic party was formed, it was able to count upon our approval and good-will because its purpose was to work honorably and in accordance with the law, for the promotion of all these ideals of justice, humanity and patriotism.

It will be seen that there is no injustice in all we have set forth, nothing unwarranted, nothing smacking of the oppressor, nothing opposed to democracy, and finally, nothing that can be thought an obstacle to the common welfare. God grant that all Mexicans may be persuaded of the truth of what we say, learn to tolerate each other's opinions and to respect each other's rights, above all in civil affairs, and thus hasten the dawn of that real peace for which we have all longed! In that day no government will find the Church in its way except for the purpose of enhancing the greatness of the Mother Country through its moral power.

B. STATEMENTS OF E. PORTES GIL AND ARCHBISHOP LEOPOLDO RUIZ Y FLORES, 22 JUNE 1929

1. The Government [E. Portes Gil]

I have had conversations with Archbishop Ruiz y Flores and Bishop Pascual Diaz. These conversations took place as the result of public statements made by Archbishop Ruiz on May 2 and a statement made by me on May 8.

Archbishop Ruiz and Bishop Diaz informed me that the Mexican bishops have felt that the constitution and laws, particularly the provision which requires registration of ministers and the provision which grants separate states the right to determine the maximum number of ministers, threaten the identity of the Church, giving the state the control of its spiritual offices.

They assure me that the Mexican bishops are animated by sincere patriotism and that they desire to resume public worship if this can be done consistently with their loyalty to the Mexican Republic and their consciences.

They stated that it could be done if the Church could enjoy the freedom within the law to live and to exercise its spiritual offices.

I am glad to take advantage of this opportunity to declare publicly and very clearly that it is not the purpose of the constitution, nor of the laws, nor of the government of the Republic to destroy the identity of the Catholic Church or of any other, nor to interfere in any way with its spiritual functions.

In accordance with the oath of office which I took when I assumed the Provisional Government of Mexico to observe and to cause to be observed the Constitution of the Republic and the laws derived therefrom, my purpose has been at all times to fulfill honestly that oath and see that the laws are applied without favor to any sect and without any bias whatever, my administration being disposed to hear from any person, be he dignitary of some church or merely a private individual, any complaints in regard to injustices arising from undue application of the laws.

With reference to certain provisions of the law which have been misunderstood, I also take advantage of this opportunity to declare:

1) That the provision of the law which required the registration of ministers does not mean that the government can register those who have not been named by a hierarchical superior of the religious creed in question or in accordance with its regulations;

2) With regard to religious instruction, the constitution and laws in force definitely prohibit it in primary or higher schools whether public or private, but this does not prevent ministers of any religion from imparting its doctrines within the church confines to adults and their children, who may attend for that purpose;

3) That the constitution as well as the laws of the country guarantee to all residents of the Republic the right of petition and therefore the members of any church may apply to the appropriate authorities for amendment, repeal or passage of any law.

2. The Church [Archbishop Leopoldo Ruiz y Flores]

Bishop Diaz and I have had several conferences with the President, the results of which are set forth in the statement which he has issued today.

I am glad to say that all conversations have been marked by a spirit of mutual good-will and respect. As a consequence of the statement made by the President, the Mexican clergy will resume religious services pursuant to the laws in force.

I entertain the hope that resumption of religious services may lead the Mexican people, animated by a spirit of mutual good-will, to cooperate in all moral efforts made for the benefit of all people of our fatherland.

C. CONSTITUTIONAL AMENDMENT OF ARTICLE III ON EDUCATION BY THE CHAMBER OF DEPUTIES AND SENATE OF THE UNITED STATES OF MEXICO, 1 DECEMBER 1934

Article 3 of 1917 Constitution:

Instruction is free: that given in public institutions of learning shall be secular. Primary instruction, whether higher or lower, given in private institutions shall likewise be secular.

No religious corporation nor minister of any religious creed shall establish or direct schools of primary instruction.

Private primary schools may be established only subject to official supervision.

Primary instruction in public institutions shall be gratuitous.

Amended Article 3:

Education imparted by the state shall be socialist, and, in addition, shall exclude every religious doctrine, shall combat fanaticism and prejudice, and to this end the school will organize its teaching and activities so as to permit the creation in the young of a rational and exact concept of the universe and of social life.

Only the state—Federation, States, Municipalities—shall impart primary, secondary or normal education. Private persons who desire to impart education in any of these three grades may be authorized to do so provided, in each case, that the following rules be complied with:

1) The activities and teaching of the private establishment, without any exception, must be adjusted to the precepts of the initial paragraph of this article, and shall be in charge of persons who, in the opinion of the state, have sufficient professional preparation, acceptable morality, and ideology in harmony with these precepts. Under this provision, religious corporations, ministers of any religion, stock companies whose activities are exclusively or chiefly educational, and associations or societies directly or indirectly affiliated with the propagation of any religious creed, shall not in any manner intervene in primary, secondary or normal schools, nor give them economic support.

2) The formation of plans, curricula and methods of teaching is in every case an affair of the state.

3) Private establishments cannot function unless they have obtained, in each case before beginning to function, the express authorization of the public power.

4) The state can revoke, at any time, any authorization granted. Against such revocation there shall be no recourse or court action whatever.

These same rules apply to education of every type or grade imparted to laborers or peasants.

Primary education shall be compulsory, and imparted gratuitously by the state.

The state, at its discretion, can withdraw at any time official recognition of validity granted to studies made in private establishments.

The Congress of the Union, for the purpose of unifying and coördinating education throughout the Republic, shall promulgate laws that may be necessary—to distribute the social function of education among the Federation, the States and the Municipalities; to fix the economic contributions corresponding to this public service; and to prescribe penalties for functionaries who themselves do not comply or who fail to compel others to comply with provisions binding on them, as well as for anyone who disobeys such provisions.

31. *Pope Pius XI: Encyclical Letter, "Divini Redemptoris," on Atheistic Communism, 19 March 1937*

Encyclical Letter of His Holiness Pius XI on Atheistic Communism (London: The Catholic Truth Society, 1937), *passim.*

I. THE promise of a redeemer brightens the first page of the history of mankind, and the confident hope aroused by the promise softened the keen regret for a paradise which had been lost. It was this hope that accompanied the human race on its weary journey, until in the fullness of time the expected Savior came to begin a new universal civilization, the Christian civilization, far superior even to that which up to this time had been laboriously achieved by certain more privileged nations.

Nevertheless, the struggle between good and evil remained in the world as a sad legacy of the original fall. Nor has the ancient tempter ever ceased to deceive mankind with false promises. It is on this account that one convulsion following upon another has marked the passage of the centuries, down to the revolution of our own days. This modern revolution has actually broken out or threatens almost everywhere, and it exceeds in amplitude and violence anything yet experienced in the preceding persecutions launched against the Church. Entire peoples find themselves in danger of falling back into a barbarism worse than that which oppressed the greater part of the world at the coming of the redeemer.

This all too imminent danger, venerable brethren, as you have already surmised, is bolshevistic and atheistic communism, which aims at upsetting the social order and at undermining the very foundations of Christian civilization. . . .

II. The Communism of today, more emphatically than similar movements in the past, poses as the savior of the poor. A pseudo-ideal of justice, of equality and fraternity in labor impregnates all its doctrine and activity with a deceptive mysticism, which communicates a zealous and contagious enthusiasm to the multitudes entrapped by delusive promises. This is especially true in an age like ours, when unusual poverty has resulted from the unfair distribution of the goods of this world. This pseudo-ideal is even boastfully advanced as if it were responsible for a certain economic progress. As a matter of fact, when such progress is at all real, its true causes are quite different, as for instance the intensification of industrialism in countries which were

formerly almost without it, the exploitation of immense natural resources by inhuman methods, and the use of the most brutal pressure on the workers to perform very heavy labor at a low wage.

The doctrine of modern Communism, which is often concealed under the most seductive trappings, is in substance based on the principles of dialectical and historical materialism previously advocated by Marx, of which the theorists of bolshevism claim to possess the only genuine interpretation. According to this doctrine there is in the world only one reality, matter, the blind forces of which evolve into plant, animal, and man. Even human society is nothing but a kind or form of matter, evolving in the same way. By a law of inexorable necessity and through a perpetual conflict of forces, matter moves towards the final synthesis of a classless society. In such a doctrine, as is evident, there is no room for the idea of God; there is no difference between matter and spirit, between soul and body; there is neither survival of the soul after death nor any hope of a future life. Insisting on the dialectical aspect of their materialism, the Communists claim that the conflict which carries the world towards its final synthesis can be accelerated by man. Hence they endeavor to sharpen the antagonisms which arise between the various classes of society. Thus the class-struggle with its consequent violent hate and destruction takes on the aspect of a crusade for the progress of humanity, and all obstacles whatever to their violent and systematic efforts must be annihilated as hostile to the human race.

Communism, moreover, strips man of his liberty, on which the spiritual rules of conduct depend, robs human personality of all its dignity, and removes all the moral restraints that check the eruptions of blind impulse.

Since according to Communism, human personality is, so to say, a mere wheel in the machine of the universe, the natural rights which spring from it are denied to individuals and attributed to the community. In man's relations with other individuals, besides, Communists hold the principle of absolute equality, rejecting all divinely constituted hierarchy and authority, including the authority of parents. What men call authority and subordination is derived from the community as its first and only source. Nor is the individual granted any property rights over material goods or the means of production, for inasmuch as these are the source of further wealth, their possession would give one man power over another. Precisely on this score, all forms of private property must be eradicated, for they are at the origin of all economic enslavement.

Refusing to human duties any sacred character, such a doctrine logically makes of marriage and the family a purely artificial and civil institution, the outcome of a specific economic system. There exists no matrimonial bond of a juridico-moral nature that is not subject to the whim of the individual or of the community. Naturally, therefore, the notion of an indissoluble marriage-tie is repudiated. Communism is particularly characterized by the rejection of any link that binds woman to the family and the home, and her emancipation is proclaimed as a basic principle. She is withdrawn from the family and the care of her children, to be thrust instead into public life and collective production under the same conditions as man. The care of home and children then devolves upon civil society. Finally, the right of education is denied to parents, for it is conceived as the exclusive prerogative of the community, in whose name and by whose mandate alone parents may exercise this right.

What would be the condition of a human society based on such materialistic tenets? It would be a community with no other authority than that derived from the economic system. It would have only one mission: the production of material things by means of collective labor, so that the goods of this world might be enjoyed in a paradise where each would "give according to his powers" and would "receive according to his needs." Communism recognizes in the community the right, or rather, unrestricted power, to draft individuals for the labor of the community with no regard for their personal welfare; so that even violence could be legitimately exercised to dragoon the recalcitrant against their wills. In the Communistic commonwealth, morality and law would be nothing but a derivation from the existing economic order, purely earthly in origin and unstable in character. In a word, the Communists claim to inaugurate a new era and a new civilization which is the result of blind evolutionary forces culminating in a "society without God."

When all men have finally acquired the mentality necessary for this utopia of a classless society, the political state, which is now conceived by Communists merely as the instrument by which the proletariat is oppressed by the capitalists, will have lost all reason for its existence and will "wither away." However, until that happy consummation is realized, the state and the powers of the state furnish Communists with the most efficacious and most extensive means for the achievement of their goal.

Such, venerable brethren, is the new gospel which bolshevistic and atheistic Communism offers the world as the glad tidings of deliverance and salvation! It is a system full of errors and illusions. It is in opposition both to reason and to divine revelation. It subverts the social order, because it means the destruction of its foundations; because it ignores the true origin, nature, and purpose of the state; because it denies the rights, dignity, and liberty of human personality. . . .

Meanwhile the sorry effects of this propaganda are before our eyes. Where Communism has been able to assert its power—and here we are thinking with special affection of the people of Russia and Mexico—it has striven by every possible means, as its champions openly boast, to destroy Christian civilization and the Christian religion by banishing every remembrance of them from the hearts of men, especially of the young. Bishops and priests were exiled, condemned to forced labor, shot and done to death in inhuman fashion; laymen suspected of defending their religion were vexed, persecuted, dragged off to trial, and thrown into prison. . . .

This, unfortunately, is what we now behold. For the first time in history we are witnessing a struggle, cold-blooded in purpose and mapped out to the least detail, between man and "all that is called God." Communism is by its nature anti-religious. It considers religion as "the opium of the people" because the principles of religion which speak of a life beyond the grave dissuade the proletariat from the dream of a paradise which is of this world.

But the law of nature and its author cannot be flouted with impunity. Communism has not been able, and will not be able, to achieve its objectives even in the merely economic sphere. It is true that in Russia it has been a contributing factor in rousing men and materials from the inertia of centuries, and in obtaining by all manner of means, often without scruple, some measure of material success. Nevertheless we know from reliable and even very recent testimony that not even there, in spite of slavery imposed on millions of men, has Communism reached its promised goal. After all,

even the sphere of economics needs some morality, some sense of moral responsibility, which can find no place in a system so thoroughly materialistic as Communism. Terrorism is the only possible substitute, and it is terrorism that reigns today in Russia, where former comrades in revolution are exterminating each other. Terrorism, having failed despite all to stem the tide of moral corruption, cannot even prevent the dissolution of society itself.

In making these observations it is no part of our intention to condemn the peoples of the Soviet Union as a whole. For them we cherish the warmest paternal affection. We are well aware that not a few of them groan beneath the yoke imposed on them by men who in very large part are strangers to the real interests of the country. We recognize that many others were deceived by fallacious hopes. We blame only the system, with its authors and abettors who considered Russia the best-prepared field for experimenting with a plan elaborated years ago, and who from there continue to spread it from one end of the world to the other. . . .

But God has likewise destined man for civil society according to the dictates of his very nature. In the plan of the creator, society is a natural means which man can and must use to reach his destined end. Society is for man, not man for society. This must not be understood in the sense of liberalistic individualism, which subordinates society to the selfish use of the individual; but only in the sense that by means of an organic union with society and by mutual collaboration the attainment of earthly welfare is placed within the reach of all. Further, it is society which affords the opportunities for the development of all the individual and social gifts bestowed on human nature. These natural gifts have a value surpassing the immediate interests of the moment, for in society they reflect the divine perfection, which would not be true were man to live alone. But on final analysis, even in this latter function society is made for man, that he may recognize this reflection of God's perfection, and refer it in praise and adoration to the creator. Only man and not society in any form is endowed with reason and a free will subject to the moral law.

Man cannot be exempted from his divinely imposed obligations toward civil society, and the representatives of authority have the right to coerce him when he refuses without reason to do his duty. Society, on the other hand, cannot defraud man of his God-granted rights, the most important of which we have indicated above, or make their use impossible. It is therefore according to the dictates of reason that all earthly things should be for the use and benefit of man, and so, through him, be referred to the creator. This accords with the words of the apostle of the gentiles, who writes to the Corinthians on Christian salvation: "All things are yours, and you are Christ's, and Christ is God's." While Communism impoverishes human personality by inverting the terms of the relation of man to society, to what lofty heights is man not elevated by reason and revelation! . . .

In view of this organized common effort towards peaceful living, Catholic doctrine vindicates to the state the dignity and authority of a vigilant and provident defender of those divine and human rights on which the sacred Scriptures and the fathers of the Church insist so often. It is not true that all have equal rights in civil society. It is not true that there exists no lawful social hierarchy. Let it suffice to refer to the encyclicals of Leo XIII already cited, especially to that on political authority, and to the other on the Christian constitution of states. In these documents the Catholic will find

the principles of reason and the faith clearly explained, and these principles will enable him to defend himself against the errors and perils of a communistic conception of the state. The enslavement of man despoiled of his rights, the denial of the transcendental origin of the state and its authority, the horrible abuse of public power in the service of a collectivistic terrorism, are the very contrary of all that corresponds with natural ethics and the will of the creator. Both man and civil society derive their origin from the creator, who has mutually ordained them one to the other. Hence neither can be exempted from their correlative obligations, nor deny or diminish each other's rights. The creator himself has regulated this mutual relationship in its fundamental lines, and it is by an unjust usurpation that Communism arrogates to itself the right to enforce, in place of the divine law based on the immutable principles of truth and charity, a partisan political programme derived from the arbitrary human will and filled with hatred. . . .

But the enemies of the Church, though forced to acknowledge the wisdom of her doctrine, accuse her of having failed to act in conformity with her principles, and from this conclude to the necessity of seeking other solutions. The utter falseness and injustice of this accusation is shown by the whole history of Christianity. To refer only to a single typical trait, it was Christianity that first affirmed the real and universal brotherhood of all men of whatever race and condition. This doctrine she proclaimed by a method, and with an amplitude and conviction, unknown to preceding centuries; and with it she potently contributed to the abolition of slavery. Not bloody revolution, but the inner force of her teaching made the proud Roman matron see in her slave a sister in Christ. It is Christianity that adores the son of

God, made man for love of man, and become not only the "son of a carpenter" but himself a "carpenter." It was Christianity that raised manual labor to its true dignity, whereas it had hitherto been so despised that even the moderate Cicero did not hesitate to sum up the general opinion of his time in words of which any modern sociologist would be ashamed: "All artisans are engaged in sordid trades, for there can be nothing ennobling about a workshop. . . ."

It may be said in all truth that the Church, like Christ, goes through the centuries doing good to all. There would be today neither socialism nor Communism if the rulers of the nations had not scorned the teachings and maternal warnings of the Church. On the bases of liberalism and laicism they wished to build other social edifices which, powerful and imposing as they seemed at first, all too soon revealed the weakness of their foundations, and today are crumbling one after another before our eyes, as everything must crumble that is not grounded on the one corner stone which is Christ Jesus. . . .

IV. This, venerable brethren, is the doctrine of the Church, which alone in the social as in all other fields can offer real light and assure salvation in the face of communistic ideology. But this doctrine must be consistently reduced to practice in everyday life, according to the admonition of St. James the Apostle: "Be doers of the word and not hearers only, deceiving your own selves." The most urgent need of the present day is therefore the energetic and timely application of remedies which will effectively ward off the catastrophe that daily grows more threatening. We cherish the firm hope that the fanaticism with which the sons of darkness work day and night at their materialistic and atheistic propaganda will at least serve the holy purpose of stimulating the sons of light to a like and even greater zeal for the honor of the divine majesty. . . .

As in all the stormy periods of the history of the Church, the fundamental remedy today lies in a sincere renewal of private and public life according to the principles of the Gospel by all those who belong to the fold of Christ, that they may be in truth the salt of the earth to preserve human society from total corruption. . . .

Nevertheless we cannot deny that there is still much to be done in the way of spiritual renovation. Even in Catholic countries there are still too many who are Catholics hardly more than in name. There are too many who fulfill more or less faithfully the more essential obligations of the religion they boast of professing, but have no desire of knowing it better, of deepening their inward conviction, and still less of bringing into conformity with the external gloss the inner splendor of a right and unsullied conscience, that recognizes and performs all its duties under the eye of God. We know how much our divine Saviour detested this empty pharisaic show, he who wished that all should adore the Father "in spirit and in truth." The Catholic who does not live really and sincerely according to the faith he professes will not long be master of himself in these days when the winds of strife and persecution blow so fiercely, but will be swept away defenseless in this new deluge which threatens the world. And thus, while he is preparing his own ruin, he is exposing to ridicule the very name of Christian. . . .

For, in reality, besides commutative justice, there is also social justice with its own set obligations, from which neither employers nor working men can escape. Now it is of the very essence of social justice to demand from each individual all that is necessary for the common good. But just as in the living organism it is impossible to provide for the good of the whole unless each single part and each individual member is given what it needs for the exercise of its proper functions, so it is impossible to care for the social organism and the good of society as a whole unless each single part and each individual member—that is to say, each individual man in the dignity of his human personality—is supplied with all that is necessary for the exercise of his social functions. If social justice be satisfied, the result will be an intense activity in economic life as a whole, pursued in tranquillity and order. This activity will be proof of the health of the social body, just as the health of the human body is recognized in the undisturbed regularity and perfect efficiency of the whole organism. . . .

If, therefore, we consider the whole structure of economic life, as we have already pointed out in our encyclical *Quadragesimo anno,* the reign of justice and charity in social-economic relations can only be achieved when professional and interprofessional organizations, based on the solid foundations of Christian teaching, constitute, under forms adapted to different places and circumstances, what used to be called guilds. . . .

See to it, venerable brethren, that the faithful do not allow themselves to be deceived! Communism is intrinsically wrong, and no one who would save Christian civilization may give it assistance in any undertaking whatsoever. Those who permit themselves to be deceived into lending their aid towards the triumph of Communism in their own country will be the first to fall victims of their error. And the greater the antiquity and grandeur of the Christian civilization in the regions where Communism successfully penetrates, so much more devastating will

be the hatred displayed by the Godless. . . .

It must likewise be the special care of governments to provide for their citizens those conditions of life without which the state itself, however sound its constitution, is in danger of collapse; and particularly to secure employment for fathers of families and for young people. To achieve this end demanded by the pressing needs of the common welfare, the wealthy classes must be induced to assume those burdens without which human society cannot be saved nor they themselves remain secure. However, measures taken by the state with this end in view ought to be of such a nature that they will really fall upon those who actually possess more than their share of capital resources, and who continue to accumulate them to the grievous detriment of others.

The state itself, mindful of its responsibility before God and society, should be a model of prudence and sobriety in the administration of the commonwealth. Today more than ever the acute world crisis demands that those who dispose of immense funds, built up on the sweat and toil of millions, keep singly in mind the common good and make every effort to promote it. Public officials and state employees are obliged in conscience to perform their duties faithfully and unselfishly, imitating the brilliant example of distinguished men of the past and of our own day, who with unremitting labor sacrificed themselves for the good of their country. In international trade relations let all means be sedulously employed for the possible removal of those artificial barriers to economic life which are the effects of distrust and hatred. All must remember that the peoples of the earth form but one family in God.

At the same time the state must

allow the Church full liberty to fulfill her divine and spiritual mission, and this in itself will be an effectual contribution to the rescue of nations from the dread torment of the present hour. Everywhere today there is an anxious appeal to moral and spiritual forces; and rightly so, for the evil we must combat is at its origin primarily an evil of the spiritual order. From this polluted source the monstrous emanations of the communistic system flow with satanic logic. Now, the Catholic Church is undoubtedly pre-eminent among the moral and religious forces of today. Therefore the very good of humanity demands that her work be allowed to proceed unhindered. . . .

32. *Political Constitution of the Portuguese Republic, 11 April 1933*

Political Constitution of the Portuguese Republic (Lisbon: National Incorporation of Publicity, 1957), *passim.*

. . . 4. The Portuguese nation is an independent state. Its sovereignty recognizes in the internal sphere morality and law as the only limitations; in the international field it recognizes only those limitations which are derived from conventions or treaties freely entered into, or from customary law freely accepted. It is the duty of the nation to co-operate with other states in preparing and adopting measures making for peace among people and for the progress of mankind.

Portugal advocates arbitration as a means of settling international disputes.

5. The Portuguese state is a unitary and corporative republic founded upon the equality of all its citizens in the eyes of the law, upon the free access for all classes to the benefits of civilization, and upon the participation of all the constituent forces of the nation in its administrative life and in the making of laws.

Equality before the law implies the right to be employed in public service according to ability or services rendered; it also involves no recognition of privilege of birth, nobility, title, sex or social position, save only the distinction due to women by reason of their nature and in the interest of the family; in regard to the obligations and benefits of citizens, it involves those differences imposed by diversity of circumstances or arising out of natural conditions.

6. It is the duty of the state:

I) To promote the unity and establish the juridical order of the nation by defining and enforcing respect for the rights and guarantees of morality, justice or the law, in the interest of the individual, of families, and local autonomous and public or private bodies;

II) To co-ordinate, stimulate and direct all social activities in order to promote a proper harmony of interests within the lawful subordination of private interests to the general good;

III) To strive to improve the conditions of the least favored social classes, endeavoring to secure for them a standard of living compatible with human dignity;

IV) To protect public health. . . .

8. Portuguese citizens shall enjoy

the following rights, liberties and individual guarantees:

I) The right to life and personal safety;

Ia) The right to work within the terms prescribed by law;

II) The right to good name and reputation;

III) Liberty and inviolability of religious beliefs and practices, on the ground of holding which nobody may be persecuted, deprived of a right or exempted from any obligation or civic duty. Nobody shall be compelled to answer questions concerning the religion he professes, except in a legally conducted census;

IV) The free expression of thought in any form;

V) Freedom of teaching;

VI) The inviolability of residence and the privacy of correspondence as may be determined by law;

VII) Freedom of choice of profession or nature of work, art or trade, subject to such legal restrictions as may be necessary in the interests of public welfare and to monopolies which, by law, can only be granted by the state and administrative bodies for reasons of recognized public utility;

VIII) Nobody shall be deprived of personal liberty or arrested without being charged except for cases coming under paragraphs 3 and 4 hereof;

IX) Nobody shall be sentenced for a criminal offense unless there is an existing law which declares the act or omission to be punishable;

X) To prepare a case in defense, the accused being given the necessary guarantees to this end both before and after being formally charged;

XI) Nobody shall be punished by imprisonment for an unlimited term or by death, except however, as regards the latter, during a state of war with a foreign country, in which case the sentence must be carried out in the theater of war;

XII) There shall be no confiscation of goods nor can any personal punishment be inflicted except upon the delinquent;

XIII) Nobody shall suffer imprisonment for failure to pay costs or stamp duties;

XIV) Freedom of meeting and association;

XV) The right of property and its transmission during life or by death, as provided by civil law;

XVI) Freedom from the payment of taxes not decreed in accordance with the constitution;

XVII) The right to reparation for all actual damage in accordance with the provisions of the law, which may prescribe pecuniary reparation for damages of a moral character;

XVIII) The right of making representation or petition, claim or complaint, to sovereign or other public authority, on matters affecting personal rights or the general good;

XIX) The right of resistance to any order which may infringe individual guarantees, unless legally suspended, and of repelling by force private aggression when recourse to public authority is impossible;

XX) Sentences for criminal offenses shall be open to revision, and the right of an indemnity from the state for loss and damage shall be assured to the convicted person or his heirs by measures to be defined by law.

The enumeration of the above rights and guarantees shall not exclude any others derived from the constitution or the law, it being understood that citizens should always exercise them without injuring the rights of third parties, or damaging the interests of society or moral principles.

Special laws shall govern the exercise of the freedom of expression of opinion, education, meeting and of association. As regards the first item, they shall prevent, by precautionary or restrictive measures, the perversion of public opinion in its function as a social force, and shall protect the character of citizens, who, when libelled or abused in a periodical publication, shall have the right to have a correction or reply inserted in the same, free of charge, without prejudice to any other right or to such proceedings as may be determined by law.

Imprisonment without formal charge is permitted in cases of *flagrante delictu* and in cases of the following actually committed, prevented or attempted crimes: those against the safety of the state; the counterfeiting of money, bank-notes and government bonds; willful homicide; burglary or robbery; larceny, fraud or embezzlement, when perpetrated by a habitual criminal; fraudulent bankruptcy; arson; the manufacture, possession, or use of explosive bombs and other similar appliances.

Except in the cases specified in the preceding paragraph, imprisonment in a public jail, or detention in a private residence, or institution for lunatics, is only permitted on a written order from the competent authorities, and shall not be continued on the accused offering proper bail or bond in regard to residence, when allowed by law.

The exceptional safeguard of *habeas corpus* may be used against an abuse of authority in the circumstances prescribed in a special law.

9. No one shall be prejudiced in his situation or permanent employment by virtue of the obligation to undergo military service or in consequence of his services in the civil defense of the territory.

10. The state shall bestow distinctions of honor or rewards on those citizens who distinguish themselves by reason of personal merit or civic or military deeds, and likewise on foreigners when there is an international interest; the law prescribing the orders, decorations, medals and diplomas which may be used for this purpose. . . .

12. The state shall insure the constitution and protection of the family as the source of preservation and development of the race, as the first basis of education, discipline and social harmony, and as the foundation of all political and administrative order through family grouping and representation in parish and on town councils.

13. The constitution of the family is based upon:

I) Marriage and legitimate offspring:

II) Equality of rights and duties of husband and wife in regard to the maintenance and education of their legitimate children;

III) The obligation to register the marriage and birth of children.

14. With the object of protecting the

family it is the duty of the state and local bodies:

I) To encourage the establishment of separate homes under healthy conditions, and the institution of the family household;

II) To protect maternity;

III) To adjust taxation to the legitimate obligations of the family, and to promote the adoption of a family wage;

IV) To assist parents in the discharge of their duty of instructing and educating their children, and to co-operate with them by means of public institutions for education and correction, or by encouraging private establishments having the same objects;

V) To take all measures necessary to prevent the corruption of morals. . . .

16. It is the duty of the state to authorize, unless otherwise provided by law to the contrary, all corporative, collective, intellectual or economic bodies, and to promote and assist their formation.

17. The principal aims of the corporative bodies, referred to in the preceding article, shall be scientific, literary or artistic, or physical training, relief, alms, or charity; technical improvement or solidarity of interests.

18. Foreigners domiciled in Portugal may be members of the corporative organizations referred to, on such conditions as may be determined by law; they shall not be allowed a share in the exercise of the political rights granted to these bodies.

19. It is the particular privilege of families to elect the parish councils.

20. In the corporative organization, all branches of the nation's activities shall be represented through their association in the corporative organizations, and it shall be their duty to participate in the election of town councils and provincial boards and the constitution of the Corporative Chamber.

21. Under the political organization of the state the parish councils shall elect the town councils which in turn shall elect the provincial boards. Local autonomous bodies shall be represented in the corporative chamber.

22. Public opinion is a fundamental part of the policy and administration of the country; it shall be the duty of the state to protect it against all those influences which distort it from the truth, justice, good administration, and the commonweal.

23. The function of the press is of a public nature and for that reason it may not refuse to insert any official notices of normal dimensions on matters of national importance sent to it by the government.

24. Civil servants are for the service of the community and not for that of any party or association of private interests; it is their duty to respect the authority of the state and cause others to do so. . . .

26. Planned interruption of public services or of those of interest to the community shall involve the dismissal of the offenders, without prejudice to any other liability at law. . . .

28. All citizens are bound to lend their services and co-operation to the state and local bodies as established by law and to contribute towards public expenditure according to their means.

29. The economic organization of the nation must provide the maximum production and wealth for the benefit of society, and shall create a collective existence from which shall flow power to the state and justice to its citizens.

30. The state shall conduct its economic relations with other countries according to the principle of proper co-operation, without prejudice to the

commercial advantages to be obtained from any particular country, or the necessity for protection against external threats or attacks.

31. It shall be the right and duty of the state to co-ordinate and control economic and social life with the following objects:

    I) To establish a proper balance of the population, of professions, of occupations, of capital and of labor;

    II) To protect the national economic system from agricultural, industrial and commercial ventures of a parasitic nature, or those incompatible with the higher interests of human life;

    III) To secure the lowest price and the highest wage consistent with fair remuneration for other factors of production, by means of improved technical methods, services and credit;

    IV) To develop the settlement of the national territories, to protect emigrants and to regulate emigration.

32. The state shall encourage those private economic activities which are the most profitable, relative costs being equal, but without detriment to the social benefit conferred and to the protection due to small home industries.

33. The state may only intervene directly in the management of private economic ventures when it has to finance them and for the purpose of securing a larger measure of social benefit than would otherwise be the case.

State undertakings carried on for profit, even if working on the basis of free competition, are likewise subject to the provisions laid down in the latter part of the present article.

34. The state shall promote the formation and development of the national corporative economic system, taking care to prevent any tendency among its constituent bodies to indulge in unrestricted competition with each other, contrary to their own proper aims and those of society, and shall encourage them to collaborate as members of the same community.

35. Property, capital and labor have a social function in the field of economic co-operation and common interest, and the law may determine the conditions of their use or exploitation in accordance with the community aim in view.

36. Labor, whether unskilled, skilled, or technical, may be associated with an undertaking in any form that circumstances render advisable.

37. Only economic corporations which are recognized by the state may conclude collective labor contracts, in accordance with the law, and those made without their intervention shall be null and void.

38. Disputes arising out of labor contracts shall be the concern of special tribunals.

39. In their economic relations with each other, neither capital nor labor shall be allowed to suspend operations with the object of imposing their respective claims.

40. Obstacles will be placed in the way of the accumulation of posts in private enterprises, as being contrary to public economy and morality.

41. The state shall promote and encourage community concerns and provident, co-operative, and mutual benefit institutions.

42. Education and instruction are obligatory and are the concern of the family and of public or private institutions in co-operation with the same.

43. The state shall officially maintain primary, secondary middle and high schools, and institutions for advanced education.

Elementary primary instruction is

obligatory and may be given at home, or in private or state schools.

The arts and sciences shall be encouraged and their development, teaching and dissemination favored, provided that respect is maintained for the Constitution, the authorities and the co-ordinating functions of the state.

The instruction provided by the state, in addition to aiming at physical fitness and the improvement of intellectual faculties, has as its object the formation of character and of professional ability as well as the development of all moral and civic qualities, the former according to the traditional principles of the country and to Christian doctrine and morality.

No permission shall be required for the teaching of religion in private schools.

44. The establishment of private schools on the lines of the state schools shall be free, but subject to state inspection; schools may be subsidized by the state or authorized to grant diplomas if their *curricula* and the standard of their teaching staff are not inferior to those of the corresponding public institutions.

45. The Catholic religion may be freely practiced, in public or in private, as the religion of the Portuguese nation. The Catholic Church shall enjoy juridical personality and may organize itself in conformity with canon law and create thereunder associations or organizations, the juridical personality of which shall equally be recognized. The relationship between the State and the Catholic Church shall be one of separation, with diplomatic relations maintained between the Holy See and Portugal by means of reciprocal representation, and concordats or agreements entered into in the sphere of the *padroado* (patronage) and where other matters of common interest are, or need to be, regulated.

46. The state shall also insure free-

dom of worship and organization for all other religious faiths practiced on Portuguese territory, their outward manifestations being regulated by law, and it may grant juridical personality to associations constituted in conformity with the creeds in question.

These provisions shall not apply to creeds incompatible with the life and physical integrity of the human person and with good behavior, or to the dissemination of doctrines contrary to the established social order.

47. The state may not assign to any other purpose any chapel, building, or article belonging to a religious body.

48. Public cemeteries shall be secular in character and ministers of any religions may freely practice their respective rites therein.

49. The public domain of the state shall comprise the following:

I) Mineral deposits, medicinal mineral springs and other natural wealth below the surface;

II) Sea waters and their shores;

III) Lakes, lagoons, and watercourses navigable to ships or rafts, their respective beds or channels, and also any others recognized by special decree to be of public utility as suitable for the production of electric power, national or regional, or for irrigation;

IV) Dikes opened up by the state;

V) The air over the land beyond such limits as the law fixes in favor of the owner of the surface;

VI) Railways of public interest of any kind, public highways and roads;

VII) Territorial areas reserved for military defense;

VIII) Any other property placed

by law under the regime of public domain.

The authority of the state over the property of the public domain and the use of it by citizens shall be governed by law and by the international conventions concluded by Portugal, without prejudice to the prior rights of the state and the acquired private rights of individuals. The latter rights, however, shall be subject to expropriation as may be determined by the public interest and upon payment of reasonable indemnity.

Rocks and common earths, and materials commonly employed in building are expressly excepted from the natural riches specified in (I) above.

The state shall undertake the demarcation of those private lands which abut on any property of public domain.

50. The administration on the mainland and on the adjacent islands of property owned by the state in a private capacity pertains to the Ministry of Finance, except when it is expressly attributed to any other ministry.

51. No state property or rights which affect its prestige or the more important national interests may be alienated.

52. Artistic, historical and natural monuments, and artistic objects officially recognized as such, are under the protection of the state, and their alienation in favor of foreigners is prohibited. . . .

71. Sovereignty is vested in the nation; its representatives are the head of the state, the national assembly, the government and the courts of justice.

72. The chief of the state is the president of the republic elected by the nation. . . .

83. The president of the republic shall perform his functions in conjunction with the council of state, composed of the following members:

    I) President of the council of ministers;

    II) President of the national assembly;

    III) President of the corporative chamber;

    IV) President of the supreme court of justice;

    V) Procurator general of the republic;

    VI) Ten public men of outstanding ability, appointed for life by the chief of state.

84. The council of state shall be obliged to discharge the following functions:

    I) To decide on the suitability of candidates to the presidency of the republic, for the purpose of provision in § 1 of article 73;

    II) To assist the chief of state when exercising certain of the functions assigned to him by paragraphs 4, 5, 6 of article 81 and § sole of article 87.

    III) To deliver its opinion, in the manner laid down by § 1, of article 80, in all emergencies threatening the life of the nation and whenever the president of the republic deems it necessary to summon it. . . .

102. There shall be a corporative chamber, equal in length of term with the national assembly, composed of representatives of local autonomous bodies and social interests, the latter being those of an administrative, moral, cultural and economic order; the law shall designate those bodies on which such representation falls, the manner of their selection and the duration of their mandate.

When vacancies occur in offices whose holders as such have a seat in the corporative chamber, the representation of such offices devolves upon those who properly substitute them according to law or by statute. The same principle applies to cases of impediment.

Except in the case mentioned in the preceding paragraph, vacancies occurring in the corporative chamber shall be filled in the same manner as the original officer was appointed.

The provisions of article 89 and its subsections shall apply to the members of this chamber; but the action envisaged in b), c), and d), of that article shall be taken on the authority, or by the decision, of the president. The amount of the remuneration mentioned in e) (of article 89) and the conditions on which it is granted shall be regulated by law.

103. It is the duty of the corporative chamber to report and give its opinion on all proposals or draft bills and on all international conventions or treaties submitted to the national assembly, before discussion thereof is commenced by the latter.

The report shall be given within thirty days or within such period as the government or the assembly shall fix if the matter concerned is considered urgent.

Should the time limit referred to in the preceding subsection expire before the report has been sent to the national assembly discussion may proceed immediately.

If the corporative chamber, while advising on general grounds the rejection of a bill, recommends that it be replaced by another, the government or any deputy may adopt the bill in question and it shall then be considered jointly with the original bill, independently of further reference to the corporative chamber. If the latter suggests alterations of a detail in a proposal or bill, the national assembly may decide that a vote be taken first on the text proposed by the corporative chamber and any deputy may always move such amendments as his own.

104. The corporative chamber shall function in plenary sessions or in committees and sub-committees.

There will be committees for administrative, moral, cultural and economic questions and sub-committees for specialized questions within each committee.

When the matter under discussion so requires, two or more committees or sub-committees may meet jointly.

The president of the council, the minister of corporations, and the ministers and under-secretaries of state concerned, or their representatives, may take part in the discussion of proposals or bills, as also may a Deputy in the case of a bill which he has originated.

Sessions of the committees and sub-committees of the corporative chamber shall not be held in public, but plenary sessions may be.

105. The government may consult the corporative chamber on enactments to be published or on draft bills to be presented to the national assembly; it may decide that the work of the committees or sub-committees shall continue or take place during adjournments, interruptions or intervals between legislative sessions; and it may request the convocation of all or any of the committees or sub-committees in order to make a communication to them.

The discussion of draft bills in the national assembly shall not be dependent on fresh reference to the corporative chamber if the latter has already been consulted by the government.

During the legislative session of the national assembly the corporative chamber may suggest to the government such measures as it considers advisable or necessary.

106. The provisions of article 86 apply to the corporative chamber, except insofar as concerns the verification of powers. This duty shall be entrusted to a special commission elected by the

chamber, and in article 101 a) and b) the respective committees and sub-committees shall also enjoy the facilities conferred by article 96 on the members of the national assembly. . . .

116. The exercise of judicial functions belongs to the ordinary courts and special tribunals.

The supreme court of justice and the judicial courts of first and second instance are the ordinary courts, and they shall have such material and territorial jurisdiction as is determined by law.

117. The establishment of special courts with exclusive jurisdiction to try a certain category of crime or certain categories of crimes, is forbidden, unless the crimes are fiscal or social by nature or are against the safety of the state.

118. The state shall be represented in the courts by the public attorney.

119. Judges of the ordinary courts are appointed for life, and cannot be removed; the conditions of their appointment, promotion, dismissal, suspension, transfer and nomination outside the cadre shall be fixed by law and they may not accept any other office of profit from the government; this shall not however prejudice their being requisitioned for permanent or temporary commissions.

120. Judges shall not be held re-sponsible for the judgments pronounced by them, except in cases specified by law.

121. The sittings of the courts shall be public, except in special cases prescribed by law, and whenever publicity would be contrary to good order, the interests of the state, or morality.

122. In the execution of their decisions and judgments, the courts shall have a right to the collaboration of other authorities whenever required.

123. In cases submitted for judgment the courts may not apply laws, decrees or any other ordinances which transgress the provisions of this constitution or violate the principles herein contained.

The organic or formal constitutional illegality of ordinances promulgated by the president of the republic may only be called into question by the national assembly either on its own initiative or on that of the government, and the national assembly shall determine the effects of such constitutional illegality, without prejudice however to situations created by *causae judicatae*.

124. As a means of preventing and suppressing crime, penalties and precautionary measures shall be introduced for the protection of society and as far as possible for the social rehabilitation of the offender.

33. *The Constitution of the Republic of Eire,* 29 December 1937

From *The Original Irish and English Texts of the Constitution of Eire* (Dublin: Government Publication Office, 1945).

IN THE name of the most holy Trinity, from whom is all authority and to whom, as our final end, all actions both of men and states must be referred,

We, the people of Eire,

humbly acknowledging all our obligations to our divine Lord Jesus Christ, who sustained our fathers through centuries of trial,

gratefully remembering their heroic and unremitting struggle to regain the rightful independence of our nation,

and seeking to promote the common

good, with due observance of prudence, justice and charity, so that the dignity and freedom of the individual may be assured, true social order attained, the unity of our country restored and concord established with other nations,

do hereby adopt, and give to ourselves this constitution.

1. The Irish nation hereby affirms its inalienable, indefeasible, and sovereign right to choose its own form of government, to determine its relations with other nations, and to develop its life, political, economic and cultural, in accordance with its own genius and traditions.

2. The national territory consists of the whole island of Ireland, its islands and the territorial sea.

3. Pending the re-integration of the national territory, and without prejudice to the right of the parliament and government established by this constitution to exercise jurisdiction over the whole of that territory, the laws enacted by that parliament shall have the like area and extent of application as the laws of *Saorstát Eireann* and the like extra-territorial effect. . . .

6. All powers of government, legislative, executive and judicial, derive, under God, from the people, whose right it is to designate the rulers of the state and, in final appeal, to decide all questions of national policy, according to the requirements of the common good. . . .

40. All citizens shall, as human persons, be held equal before the law.

This shall not be held to mean that the state shall not in its enactments have due regard to differences of capacity, physical and moral, and of social function. . . .

The state guarantees liberty for the exercise of the following rights, subject to public order and morality:

The right of the citizens to express freely their convictions and opinions.

The education of public opinion being, however, a matter of such grave import to the common good, the state shall endeavor to ensure that organs of public opinion, such as the radio, the press, the cinema, while preserving their rightful liberty of expression, including criticism of government policy, shall not be used to undermine public order or morality or the authority of the state.

The publication or utterance of blasphemous, seditious or indecent matter is an offense which shall be punishable in accordance with the law.

Laws regulating the manner in which the right of forming associations and unions and the right of free assembly may be exercised, shall contain no political, religious or class discrimination.

41. The state recognizes the family as the natural primary and fundamental unity group of society, and as a moral institution possessing inalienable and imprescriptible rights, antecedent and superior to all positive law.

The state, therefore, guarantees to protect the family in its constitution and authority, as the necessary basis of social order and as indispensable to the welfare of the nation and the state.

The state pledges itself to guard with special care the institution of marriage, on which the family is founded, and to protect it against attack.

No law shall be enacted providing for the grant of a dissolution of marriage.

No person whose marriage has been dissolved under the civil law of any other state but is a subsisting valid marriage, under the law for the time being in force within the jurisdiction of the government and parliament established by this constitution, shall be capable of contracting a valid marriage within that jurisdiction during the lifetime of the other party to the marriage so dissolved.

42. The state acknowledges that the

primary and natural educator of the child is the family and guarantees to respect the inalienable right and duty of parents to provide, according to their means, for the religious and moral, intellectual, physical and social education of their children.

Parents shall be free to provide this education in their homes or in private schools or in schools recognized or established by the state.

The state shall not oblige parents in violation of their conscience and lawful preference to send their children to schools established by the state, or to any particular type of school designated by the state.

The state shall, however, as guardian of the common good, require in view of actual conditions that the children receive a certain minimum education, moral, intellectual and social.

The state shall provide for free primary education and shall endeavor to supplement and give reasonable aid to private and corporate educational initiative and, when the public good requires it, provide other educational facilities or institutions with due regard, however, for the rights of parents, especially in the matter of religious and moral formation.

In exceptional cases, where the parents for physical or moral reasons fail in their duty towards their children, the state as guardian of the common good, by appropriate means, shall endeavor to supply the place of the parents but always with due regard for the natural and imprescriptible rights of the child.

43. The state acknowledges that man, in virtue of his rational being, has the natural right, antecedent to positive law, to the private ownership of external goods.

The state, accordingly, guarantees to pass no law attempting to abolish the right of private ownership or the general right to transfer, bequeath, and inherit property.

The state recognizes, however, that the exercise of the rights mentioned in the foregoing provisions of this article ought, in civil society, to be regulated by the principles of social justice.

The state, accordingly, may, as occasion requires, delimit by law the exercise of the said rights with a view to reconciling their exercise with the exigencies of the common good.

44. The state acknowledges that the homage of public worship is due to almighty God. It shall hold his name in reverence, and shall respect and honor religion.

The state recognizes the special position of the holy Catholic Apostolic and Roman Church as the guardian of the faith professed by the great majority of the citizens.

The state also recognizes the Church of Ireland, the Presbyterian Church in Ireland, the Methodist Church in Ireland, the Religious Society of Friends in Ireland, as well as the Jewish Congregations and the other religious denominations existing in Ireland at the date of the coming into operation of this constitution.

Freedom of conscience, and the free profession and practice of religion are, subject to public order and morality, guaranteed to every citizen.

The state guarantees not to endow any religion.

The state shall not impose any disabilities or make any discrimination on the ground of religious profession, belief or status.

Legislation providing state aid for schools shall not discriminate between schools under the management of different religious denominations, nor be such as to affect prejudicially the right of any child to attend a school receiving public money without attending religious instruction at that school.

Every religious denomination shall have the right to manage its own affairs, own, acquire, and administer property, moveable and immoveable, and maintain institutions for religious or charitable purposes.

The property of any religious denomination or any educational institution shall not be diverted save for necessary works of public utility and on payment of compensation.

45. The state shall strive to promote the welfare of the whole people by securing and protecting as effectively as it may a social order in which justice and charity shall inform all the institutions of the national life.

The state shall, in particular, direct its policy towards securing:

That the citizens (all of whom, men and women equally, have the right to an adequate means of livelihood) may through their occupations find the means of making reasonable provision of their domestic needs.

That the ownership and control of the material resources of the community may be so distributed among private individuals and the various classes as best to subserve the common good.

That, especially, the operation of free competition shall not be allowed so to develop as to result in the concentration of the ownership or control of essential commodities in a few individuals to the common detriment.

That in what pertains to the control of credit, the constant and predominant aim shall be the welfare of the people as a whole.

That there may be established on the land in economic security as many families as in the circumstances shall be practicable.

The state shall favor and, where necessary, supplement private initiative in industry and commerce.

The state shall endeavor to secure that private enterprise shall be so conducted as to insure reasonable efficiency in the production and distribution of goods and to protect the public against unjust exploitation.

The state pledges itself to safeguard, with special care, the economic interests of the weaker sections of the community and, where necessary, to contribute to the support of the infirm, the widow, the orphan, and the aged.

The state shall endeavor to insure that the strength and health of workers, men and women, and the tender age of children shall not be abused and that citizens shall not be forced by economic necessity to enter avocations unsuited to their sex, age or strength.

34. *The Lateran Treaty and Concordat Between the Holy See and Italy, 11 February 1929*

From *The Homiletic and Pastoral Review,* XXIX (September, 1929), 338-340; XXX (October, 1929), 76-81; XXXI (November, 1929), 179-185.

A. THE TREATY OF THE LATERAN, 11 FEBRUARY 1929

CONSIDERING that the Holy See and Italy have recognized the desirability of eliminating every cause of dissent between them and of reaching a definitive settlement of their mutual relations in conformity with justice and with the dignity of both high contracting par-ties, a settlement which—while assuring to the Holy See permanently a position *de facto* and *de jure* which shall guarantee its absolute independence for the fulfillment of its high mission in the world—would enable the Holy See to consider the "Roman Question," which arose in 1870 with the annexation of Rome to the Kingdom of Italy under the dynasty of Savoy, as settled in a final and irrevocable manner;

And considering that in order to secure to the Holy See absolute and visible independence and to guarantee its unquestionable sovereignty also in international matters, it has been found necessary to constitute, under particular conditions, the Vatican City (*la Città del Vaticano*) and to recognize the full ownership of the Holy See and its exclusive and absolute, sovereign jurisdiction over it.

His Holiness and Supreme Pontiff Pius XI, and His Majesty Victor Emmanuel III, king of Italy, have resolved to conclude a treaty and nominated for that purpose two plenipotentiaries, namely:

On behalf of His Holiness, His Eminence the Most Reverend Cardinal Pietro Gasparri, His Holiness' secretary of state, and on behalf of His Majesty Victor Emmanuel, His Excellency the Cavaliere Signor Benito Mussolini, prime minister and head of the government;

Who, having exchanged their respective full powers and found them to be in good and due form, have agreed to the following articles:

1. Italy recognizes and reaffirms the principle contained in art. 1 of the statute of the kingdom of 4 March 1848, according to which the Catholic Apostolic and Roman Religion is the sole religion of the state.

2. Italy recognizes the sovereignty of the Holy See in international matters as being an attribute inherent in its nature and in conformity with its tradition and the requirements of its mission in the world.

3. Italy recognizes the full ownership, absolute power, and sovereign jurisdiction of the Holy See over the Vatican as it is constituted now with all its appurtenances and endowments, thus creating for the special ends and

under the conditions stated in the present Treaty, the Vatican City.

The boundaries of the said city are indicated on the plan which forms the first annex to the present treaty and is an integral part thereof.

It is, however, agreed that St. Peter's Square, while being a part of the Vatican City, shall continue to be normally open to the public and subject to the police power of the Italian authorities; this power shall cease to operate at the foot of the steps to the basilica which continues to be devoted to public worship. The Italian authorities shall, therefore, abstain from ascending the steps and approaching the basilica unless their intervention is asked for by the competent authority.

Whenever the Holy See may consider it necessary to interrupt temporarily, for some particular purposes, the free traffic of the public in St. Peter's Square, the Italian authorities shall withdraw, unless invited by the competent authority to do otherwise, beyond the external lines of the Bernini Colonnade and their prolongation.

4. The sovereignty and exclusive jurisdiction of the Holy See over the Vatican City, which Italy recognizes, implies that no interference on the part of the Italian Government can be exercised in it and that there cannot be any other authority there than that of the Holy See.

5. For the purpose of the execution of the provisions contained in the preceding article before the present treaty enters into force, the territory forming the Vatican City shall be freed from any burden and from possible occupants by the care of the Italian Government. The Holy See shall provide for closing the access thereto, enclosing the open part of it with the exception of St. Peter's Square.

Moreover, it has been agreed that with regard to the buildings there existing which belong to religious institutions and bodies, the Holy See shall make arrangements as to its relations to them directly, without involving the Italian state in the matter.

6. Italy shall provide, by means of appropriate agreements with the interested parties, that the Vatican City shall be assured of an adequate water supply of its own. She shall furthermore provide for connection with the state railways by means of a railway station to be constructed in the Vatican City on the spot as indicated on the annexed map and by allowing the railway carriages belonging to the Vatican to circulate on the Italian railways. She shall further provide for direct connection with other states also of telegraphic, telephonic, radio-telegraphic, radio-telephonic and postal services of the Vatican City. And she shall also provide for the co-ordination of other public services.

All this will be effected at the expense of the Italian state within one year from the entry into force of the present treaty. The Holy See shall, at its own expense, make arrangements about the existing means of access to the Vatican and about others which it may deem necessary to provide in the future.

Further agreements shall be concluded between the Holy See and the Italian state regarding the circulation in the territory of the latter of land vehicles and aircraft belonging to the Vatican City.

7. The Italian government undertakes not to permit the construction in the territory adjacent to the Vatican City of such new buildings which might be able to overlook it and shall for the same end provide for the partial demolition of those already existing at the Porta Cavaleggeri, and along the Via Aurelia and the Viale Vaticano.

In conformity with the rules of international law aircraft of any kind are forbidden to fly over the territory of the Vatican.

In the Piazza Rusticucci and in the zone adjoining the colonnade whereto the extra-territoriality mentioned in art. 15 does not extend, any alteration in buildings or streets which might be of interest to the Vatican City shall be made by common agreement.

8. Considering the person of the supreme pontiff to be sacred and inviolable, Italy declares that any plot against him, or any incitement to commit such, shall be punishable with the same penalties as are enacted for a plot or incitement to commit the same against the person of the king.

Offenses and public insults committed in Italian territory against the person of the supreme pontiff by speeches, acts or writings shall be punished as if offenses and insults against the person of the king.

9. In accordance with the rules of international law all persons having permanent residence in the Vatican City are subject to the sovereignty of the Holy See. Such residence shall not be forfeited by the mere fact of dwelling temporarily elsewhere, unless accompanied by loss of domicile in the Vatican City or by other circumstances proving the abandonment of the said residence.

If ceasing to be subject to the sovereignty of the Holy See, those persons mentioned in the preceding paragraph who shall not be regarded—according to the provisions of the Italian law and independently from the factual circumstances referred to above—as possessing some other citizenship, shall be considered in Italy without question as Italian nationals.

To these persons, while subject to the sovereignty of the Holy See, the provisions of the Italian law shall be applicable within the territory of the Kingdom of Italy even in matters in which personal law should be observed (unless they are covered by legal provisions emanating from the Holy See) or, in the case of persons having a foreign nationality, the law of the state to which they belong.

10. The dignitaries of the Church and the persons belonging to the papal court who shall be indicated in a list to be agreed between the high contracting parties, shall always and in every case—even if they are not citizens of the Vatican—be exempted from military service so far as Italy is concerned, from the duty to be jurors and from any service of a personal nature.

This provision shall be also applicable to regular officials declared by the Holy See to be indispensable, who are employed permanently and with a fixed salary in the offices of the Holy See, and also to those employed in the departments and offices mentioned in arts. 13, 14, 15 and 16, which are situated outside the Vatican City. These officials shall be indicated in another list to be agreed as above, which list will be annually brought up to date by the Holy See.

The ecclesiastics who by reason of their office shall participate outside the Vatican City in the execution of the acts of the Holy See shall not, for that reason, be subject to any hindrance, investigation or molestation on the part of the Italian authorities.

Any foreigner invested with an ecclesiastical office at Rome shall enjoy the personal guarantees appertaining to Italian citizens according to the laws of the Kingdom of Italy.

11. The central bodies of the Catholic Church are exempt from any interference on the part of the Italian state (except as provided in Italian law with regard to the acquisition of property by juridical persons and to the conversion of real estate).

12. Italy recognizes the right of legation to the Holy See, active and passive, according to the general rules of international law. The envoys of the foreign governments to the Holy See shall continue to enjoy in the kingdom all prerogatives and immunities appertaining to diplomatic agents under international law, even if their states have no diplomatic relations with Italy.

It is understood that Italy engages to leave free always and in every case the correspondence of all states—including belligerent—with the Holy See and vice versa, as well as the access of the bishops of the whole world to the Apostolic See.

The high contracting parties undertake to establish normal diplomatic relations between themselves by accrediting an Italian ambassador to the Holy See and a papal nuncio to Italy, who shall be the *doyen* of the diplomatic corps in accordance with the customary law recognized by the Congress of Vienna in its Act of 9 June 1815. In consequence of the recognized sovereignty and without prejudice to the provisions of art. 19 below, the diplomats of the Holy See and the couriers sent in the name of the supreme pontiff shall enjoy in the territory of the kingdom, even in time of war, the same treatment as enjoyed by diplomats and diplomatic couriers of other governments according to the rules of international law.

13. Italy recognizes the full ownership of the Holy See over the patriarchal basilicas of S. Giovanni in the Lateran, Santa Maria Maggiore and S. Paolo with their annexed buildings. The state transfers to the Holy See the free management and administration of the said Basilica of S. Paolo with its dependent monastery; moreover, it gives to the Holy See the capital corresponding to the sums set aside annually for the said basilica in the budget of the ministry of education. It has been also agreed that the Holy See remains full proprietor of the edifice of

S. Callisto, adjoining Sta. Maria in Trastevere.

14. Italy recognizes the full ownership of the Holy See over the papal Palace of Castel Gandolfo with all its endowments, appurtenances, and dependencies as they are already in the possession of the Holy See, and also the obligation to cede [to the Holy See]—into similar full ownership and within six months after the coming into force of present treaty—the Villa Barberini in Castel Gandolfo, together with all its endowments, appurtenances and dependencies.

In order to round off the real property owned by the sacred congregation of Propaganda Fide and by other ecclesiastical institutions, which is situated on the northern side of the Janiculum Hill facing the Vatican palaces, the state engages to transfer to the Holy See and to the bodies indicated by the Holy See, all real estate situated in that area and belonging to the state or to third persons.

Finally, Italy shall transfer to the Holy See into full ownership the buildings of the former monasteries at Rome, attached to the Basilica of the Twelve Holy Apostles and to the churches of Sant' Andrea della Valle and S. Carlo ai Catinari with all their annexes and dependencies within one year after the entry into force of the present treaty and free of all occupants.

15. The property indicated in art. 13 and in the first and second paragraph of art. 14, as well as the palaces of the Dataria, the Cancellaria, the Sacred Congregation of Propaganda Fide in the Piazza di Spagna, the Palace of the S. Offizio and buildings adjacent, that of the Convertendi (at present the Congregation of the Eastern Church) in Piazza Scossacavalli, that of the Vicariato and those in which the Holy See may place in the future its other departments, while

forming part of the Italian state's territory, shall enjoy the immunities recognized by international law to the seats of diplomatic agents of foreign states. These immunities shall also be applicable to other churches, even outside Rome, during the time when the supreme pontiff shall take part in religious ceremonies in such churches without their being opened to the public.

16. The property mentioned in the three preceding articles as well as that in which the following pontifical institutions are housed: the Gregorian University, the Biblical, Oriental and Archeological Institutes, the Russian Seminary, the Lombard College, the two Palaces of Sant' Apollinare, and the House of SS. Giovanni and Paolo for the retreat of the clergy shall never be subject to any charges or expropriation on account of public utility without previous agreement with the Holy See and shall be exempt from all taxation, whether ordinary or extraordinary, by the state or by any other body.

It is left to the Holy See to provide for all the said edifices and real property indicated in the present article and in the three articles preceding at its will, without any authorization or consent of any Italian governmental, provincial, or communal authorities, who can rely with confidence on the noble artistic traditions of the Catholic Church.

17. The remunerations of whatsoever nature, due to the Holy See, by other central bodies of the Catholic Church, and by bodies administered directly by the Holy See to dignitaries, employees and other salaried people, even if not permanent, shall be exempt in Italian territory—as from 1 January 1929—from any tax to be paid either to the state or to any other body.

18. The treasures of art and science existing within the Vatican City and

in the Lateran Palace shall remain open to scholars and visitors, the Holy See reserving full freedom of regulating the admission of the public thereto.

19. The diplomats and envoys of the Holy See, the diplomats and envoys of the foreign governments accredited to the Holy See, and the dignitaries of the Church coming from abroad direct to the Vatican City and provided with passports of the states from which they come, and with due visas of papal representatives abroad, can proceed without any formalities across the Italian territory to the said city. The same applies to the aforementioned persons who, provided with regular pontifical passports, shall go abroad from the Vatican City.

20. Merchandise coming from abroad direct to the Vatican City or outside its boundaries to the institutions or offices of the Holy See, shall be admitted at any point of the Italian border and in any port of the kingdom for transit through Italian territory with full exemption from custom and import duties.

21. All the cardinals shall enjoy in Italy the honors due to princes of the blood; if resident in Rome, even outside the Vatican City, they shall be regarded, for all purposes, as its citizens.

During the vacancy of the pontifical see, Italy shall take special precautions that the free transit and access of cardinals across Italian territory to the Vatican be not hindered, and shall provide that their personal liberty is not impeded or limited.

Italy shall also take measures in her territory surrounding the Vatican City to prevent any acts that may in any way disturb the meetings of the conclave.

These provisions shall also apply to conclaves held beyond the boundaries of the Vatican City, and to councils presided over by the supreme pontiff or his legates, and with regard to bishops summoned to take part in them.

22. At the request of the Holy See, or through delegation (of authority) which can be made by the Holy See in each particular case or permanently, Italy shall provide in her territory for the punishment of offenses committed within the Vatican City, except when the delinquent shall have taken refuge in Italian territory, in which case he shall be proceeded against according to the provisions of the Italian laws.

The Holy See shall hand over to the Italian state persons who shall take refuge in the Vatican City while charged with acts committed in Italian territory which are considered as punishable by the law of both states.

Analogically, this provision shall be applicable with regard to persons who may have taken refuge within the buildings whose immunity has been stipulated in art. 15, unless those who have authority over the said buildings prefer to invite the Italian police to enter and arrest them.

23. The rules of international law shall apply to the execution in the kingdom of the sentences of the Vatican City's courts of law. The sentences and measures emanating from ecclesiastical authorities, which concern ecclesiastical or religious persons, deal with spiritual or disciplinary matters and have been officially communicated to the civil authorities, shall obtain legal validity and all due effects following from civil law without any further formalities being necessary.

24. With regard to the sovereignty belonging to it in international matters, the Holy See declares that it remains and shall remain outside all temporal rivalries between other states and shall take no part in international congresses summoned to settle such matters, unless the parties in dispute make jointly appeal to its mission of peace; in any case, however, the Holy See reserves

the right of exercising its moral and spiritual power.

Consequently, the Vatican City shall always and in any event be considered as neutral and inviolable territory.

25. A special convention, signed jointly with the present treaty, being an integral part thereof, provides for the liquidation of credits possessed by the Holy See towards Italy.

26. The Holy See considers that in the agreements signed today an adequate guarantee is given providing it with the requisite liberty and independence for the pastoral government of the Roman diocese, and of the Catholic Church in Italy and throughout the world; it declares the "Roman Question" finally and irrevocably settled and hence eliminated, and recognizes the Kingdom of Italy under the dynasty of the House of Savoy with Rome as the capital of the Italian State.

Italy, on her part, recognizes the State of the Vatican City under the sovereignty of the supreme pontiff.

The law of May 13, 1871, No. 214, and any other provisions contrary to the present treaty are hereby abrogated.

27. The present treaty shall be submitted to the supreme pontiff and to the king of Italy for ratification within four months after the signature thereof and shall enter into force by the fact of the exchange of ratifications.

B. CONCORDAT BETWEEN THE HOLY SEE AND ITALY, 11 FEBRUARY 1929

In the Name of the Most Holy Trinity:

From the beginning of the dealings between the Holy See and Italy for the purpose of settling the "Roman Question," the Holy See has proposed that the treaty concerning that question be accompanied as a necessary adjunct by a concordat intended to regulate the conditions of the Catholic religion and the Church in Italy.

Now that on this very day the treaty has been concluded and signed for the solution of the "Roman Question," His Holiness Pope Pius XI and His Majesty Victor Emanuel III, king of Italy, have resolved to make the concordat, and for that purpose they have named the same plenipotentiaries who were delegated to make the treaty, namely, on the part of His Holiness, His Eminence Cardinal Peter Gasparri, his secretary of state, and on the part of His Majesty, His Excellency Signor Benito Mussolini, prime minister and head of the government. The two plenipotentiaries, having exchanged their letters of appointment and having found them to have been executed in due form, have agreed on the following articles:

1. Italy, according to the intent of article 1 of the treaty, assures the Catholic Church the free exercise of its spiritual power, the free and public exercise of worship, and also of its jurisdiction in ecclesiastical matters conformable to the rules of the present concordat. Whenever necessary, Italy gives to the ecclesiastics, for the purpose of the acts of their spiritual ministry, the protection of its power. In consideration of the sacred character of the eternal city, the episcopal see of the supreme pontiff, center of the Catholic world and the goal of pilgrimages, the Italian government shall take care to stop at Rome everything that may be contrary to the said character.

2. The Holy See has free communication and correspondence with the bishops, the clergy and the whole Catholic world without any interference on the part of the Italian government. Likewise, in reference to all things concerning their pastoral ministry, the bishops have free communication and correspondence with their clergy and with all the faithful. Both the Holy See and the bishops can freely publish and

also post, in the interior and on the outside doors of the buildings destined for divine worship or at the offices of their ministry, the instructions, ordinances, pastoral letters, diocesan bulletins and other acts concerning the spiritual government of the faithful which they within the confines of their jurisdiction desire to publish. Such publications and posters, and in general all acts and documents relative to the spiritual government of the faithful, are not subject to fiscal burdens. The aforesaid publications, in so far as the Holy See is concerned, may be made in any language; those of the bishops shall be made in the Italian or Latin languages, but to the Italian text the ecclesiastical authority may join a translation into other languages. The ecclesiastical authorities may without any interference on the part of the civil authorities take up collections in the interior or at the entrance of the churches and in the buildings that are owned by them.

3. The students of theology—those making the two years' studies in preparation for theology with a view to studying for the priesthood, and the novices of religious institutes—may at their request delay from year to year until the twenty-sixth year of age the military service. The clerics who have been promoted to major orders, and the religious who have pronounced the vows, are exempt from military service, save in case of a general mobilization. In that event, the priests enter the armed forces of the state, but they retain the ecclesiastical garb in order that they exercise among the soldiers the sacred ministry under the jurisdiction of the military ordinary according to article 14. The other clerics and religious are by preference destined for the non-combatant services. In any case, even in a general mobilization, priests having the care of souls are dispensed from presenting themselves at the levy. The men thus dispensed are the ordinaries, the pastors, the vice-pastors and coadjutors, the vicars and the priests permanently appointed in charge of churches open to public worship.

4. The ecclesiastics and religious are exempted from jury service.

5. No ecclesiastic can be appointed or remain in an employment or office of the Italian state, or in institutions depending on the state, without the diocesan ordinary having declared that he has no objection (*nihil obstat*). The revocation of the *nihil obstat* deprives the ecclesiastic of the ability to continue to exercise the employment or office which he held. In every case apostate priests and those laboring under a censure shall not be given nor be retained in an assignment, office or employment, in which they come into immediate contact with the public.

6. The salaries and other payments which ecclesiastics receive for reason of their office are exempt from seizure to the same extent as the salaries and other payments of the employees of the state.

7. The ecclesiastics cannot be requested by the magistrates or other authorities to give information about persons or matters of which they obtained knowledge by reason of the sacred ministry.

8. In case an ecclesiastic or a religious is brought before the criminal court for some offense, the prosecutor of the state must immediately inform the ordinary of the diocese in whose territory the prosecutor exercises jurisdiction. He must promptly send official notice to the ordinary of the preliminary sentence and—if it takes place—of the final sentence of the court in the first instance as well as in the court of appeal.

In case of arrest, the ecclesiastic or religious is to be treated with due regard to his state and his rank in the Church.

In case of condemnation of an ecclesiastic or a religious, the prison term should, if possible, be served in places distinct from those of laical prisoners, unless the competent ordinary has reduced the condemned person to the laical state.

9. As a rule, the edifices open for divine worship are exempt from requisitions and occupation. If there be need of occupying a public place of worship for reason of grave public need, the authorities which proceed to take occupation must first come to an agreement with the ordinary, unless reasons of absolute urgency make previous agreement impossible. In such an emergency the authorities shall immediately inform the ordinary of their action. Except in case of urgent necessity, the public forces may not enter for the purpose of their functions into public places of worship without having first notified the ecclesiastical authorities.

10. For no reason at all may the authorities of the state demolish public places of worship, unless they have first come to an agreement with the competent ecclesiastical authorities.

11. The state recognizes the feast days established by the Church, which are the following: all Sundays, New Year's, the Epiphany, St. Joseph, Ascension, Corpus Christi, Sts. Peter and Paul, Assumption of our Lady, All Saints, Immaculate Conception, Christmas.

12. On Sundays and holydays of obligation, in churches in which a chapter officiates, the celebrant of the Conventual Mass shall chant a prayer for the welfare of the king of Italy and the Italian state, according to the rules of the sacred liturgy.

13. The Italian government shall inform the Holy See of the number of ecclesiastics which are to exercise the spiritual care of the military forces, as soon as this matter has been passed on by the government. The designation of those ecclesiastics to whom shall be entrusted the supreme direction of the spiritual care of the military forces (military ordinary, vicar, inspectors), shall be made confidentially by the Holy See to the Italian government. If the government has reason to object to the persons designated, it shall inform the Holy See, which shall designate others. The military ordinary shall be vested with the archiepiscopal dignity. The nomination of the military chaplains is to be made by the competent authorities of the Italian state from among the priests designated by the military ordinary.

14. The Italian troops of the air, land and naval services enjoy, in reference to their religious duties, the privileges and exemptions granted by canon law. The military chaplains have parochial rights over the men in military service. They exercise the sacred ministry under the jurisdiction of the military ordinary and his own curia. The military ordinary has jurisdiction also over the religious persons, men and women, assigned to military hospitals.

15. The military ordinary is president of the chapter of the Church of the Pantheon at Rome, constituting with the chapter the clergy to whom is entrusted the religious service at the said basilica. That clergy is authorized to attend to all the religious functions, even outside of Rome, which in conformity with the canonical rules are requested by the state or by the royal house. The Holy See agrees to confer upon all the canons of the chapter of the Pantheon the dignity of prothonotaries *ad instar* during their office. The nomination of all canons shall be made by the cardinal vicar of Rome upon presentation by His Majesty, the king of Italy; confidential notice of the pres-

entation shall be made previously by the king. The Holy See reserves to itself the right to transfer the *diaconia* of the Pantheon to some other church.

16. The Holy See and the Italian government shall by means of a mixed committee come to an agreement concerning the circumscription of the dioceses of Italy for the purpose of possibly making them coincide with the boundaries of the provinces of the state of Italy. It is understood that the Holy See shall erect the Diocese of Zara; that no part of the territory subject to Italy shall be under the jurisdiction of a bishop whose see is outside of Italian territory; and that no diocese of the Kingdom of Italy shall comprise districts belonging to another nation. The same principle shall apply to all parishes now existing or to be in future established near the borders of other countries. The modifications of the boundary lines of dioceses which may have to be made shall be done by the Holy See after reaching an agreement with the Italian government in the manner spoken of above, saving some minor rectifications of territory made necessary for the good of souls.

17. The abolishment of the dioceses resulting from the aforesaid redistribution shall be put in effect gradually as those dioceses become vacant. It is understood that the reduction of the dioceses does not mean the suppression of the titles of the dioceses nor of the cathedral chapters, which shall be preserved; but the suppressed dioceses shall be rearranged so that their sees shall correspond to those of the provinces. The said suppressions shall leave intact all the actual resources of the dioceses and of other ecclesiastical entities existing within the same, including the allowances now given by the Italian state.

18. If the ecclesiastical authorities decide to rearrange the parishes, either temporarily or definitively, by joining several parishes, either temporarily or definitively, by joining several parishes under one pastor with one or more assistant priests, or by putting into one parish house several priests, the state shall retain unaltered the financial allowances due to the parishes.

19. The choice of the archbishops and bishops belongs to the Holy See. Before the appointment of an archbishop or a bishop or of a coadjutor with the right of succession, the Holy See shall inform the Italian government of its choice to assure itself that the government has no reason of a political nature to raise against the appointment. The dealings on each side shall be conducted with the greatest care and in such a manner that the name of the one to be appointed does not become known until he is actually appointed.

20. Prior to taking possession of their dioceses, the bishops shall take an oath of fealty before the head of the state according to the following form: "Before God and his holy Gospels I swear and promise, as it behooves a bishop, fealty to the Italian state. I swear and promise to respect and to make my clergy respect the king and the government established according to the constitutional laws of the state. I swear and promise, moreover, that I shall not participate in any agreement nor assist at any meeting which may bring harm to the Italian state or to public order, and that I shall not permit my clergy similar participation. Being highly interested in the welfare and advantage of the Italian state, I shall seek to prevent every harm that may threaten it."

21. The appointment to ecclesiastical benefices belongs to the ecclesiastical authority. The appointments of men to parochial benefices shall be confidentially made known by the competent ecclesiastical authority to the Italian government, and the appoint-

ments may not take effect until thirty days after the said notification. Within that time the Italian government, where grave reasons are against the appointment, may manifest them privately to the ecclesiastical authority, who, in case the difference of opinion remains, shall refer the matter to the Holy See. If grave reasons arise that render the continuation of an ecclesiastic in a certain parochial benefice harmful, the Italian government shall communicate such reasons to the ordinary, who in harmony with the government shall take proper measures within three months. In case of difference between the ordinary and the government, the Holy See shall commit the solution of the question to two ecclesiastics of its own choice, who together with two delegates of the Italian government shall come to a definite decision.

22. Ecclesiastics who are not Italian citizens cannot be invested with benefices existing in Italy. The appointees to dioceses and parishes must be able to speak the Italian language. If necessary, coadjutors must be appointed to them who, besides Italian, understand and speak the language locally in use for the purpose of giving spiritual assistance in the language of the people according to the regulations of the Church.

23. Articles 16, 17, 19, 20, 21 and 22 do not apply to Rome and the suburban dioceses. It is also understood that, whenever the Holy See should proceed with a new adjustment of the said dioceses, the allowances made at present by the Italian State, either for the *mensa* [allowance for sustenance] or for other ecclesiastical institutes, must remain unchanged.

24. The *exequatur* and the *regium placet* are abolished, and also all nominations by the king in the matter of appointment to ecclesiastical benefices or offices throughout all Italy, saving the exceptions laid down in article 29 under the letter g.

25. The Italian state surrenders the sovereign prerogative of the royal patronage over major and minor benefices. Abolished are likewise the royalties from the major and minor benefices to the crown and the pensionable third in the provinces of the former Kingdom of the Two Sicilies. The burden connected with the above-mentioned rights rests on the state or its dependent administrations.

26. The appointment of men to major or minor benefices, and of persons who temporarily govern a vacant diocesan see or a benefice, takes effect from the date of the ecclesiastical appointment, which shall officially be made known to the government. The administration and the enjoyment of the income during vacancy shall be governed by the rules of canon law. In the case of bad administration, the Italian state, having come to an agreement with the ecclesiastical authority, can proceed to sequester the temporalities of the benefice, applying the net income in favor of the holder of the benefice, or, if there be none, in favor of the benefice.

27. The Basilicas of the Holy House at Loreto, of St. Francis at Assisi and of St. Anthony at Padua, together with the buildings and works attached, excepting only those of a purely laical character, shall be ceded to the Holy See, and their administration shall be freely in the hands of the Holy See. They shall be free from all interference by the state and from seizure, like all the other entities of whatever nature administered by the Holy See in Italy and the missionary colleges. Nevertheless, the Italian laws concerning the acquisition of property by moral bodies shall be applicable.

In reference to the goods at present belonging to the said sanctuaries, a mixed committee shall proceed with a repartition, in which regard must be had to the rights of third parties and to necessary endowments for the above-mentioned purely laical works.

In other sanctuaries where civil administrators exist, a free administration by ecclesiastical authority shall be substituted, saving, where the case occurs, the repartition of the goods according to the manner spoken of in the first paragraph of this article.

28. For peace of conscience, the Holy See grants complete condonation to all those persons who in consequence of the Italian laws that destroyed ecclesiastical property find themselves in possession of ecclesiastical goods. The Holy See shall issue to the ordinaries timely instructions to this effect.

29. The Italian state shall revise its legislation, in so far as ecclesiastical matters are concerned, in order to reform and complete and put it in harmony with the principles contained in the treaty between the Holy See and Italy and the present concordat. The two contracting parties agree to the following:

(a) Besides the juridical personality of the ecclesiastical entities already recognized as such by the present laws of Italy (the Holy See, dioceses, chapters, seminaries, parishes, etc.), that personality shall be accorded also to public churches open to divine worship which do not yet possess that character, including those which belonged to the suppressed ecclesiastical entities, with the assignment in reference to the latter of the income which actually is destined for each from the fund for the cult. Saving the disposition of article 27, the councils of administration, even when composed largely or entirely of laymen, shall not be permitted to interfere in the services of divine worship, and the appointment of the persons to such council shall be made by agreement with the ecclesiastical authority.

(b) The juridical personality of religious organizations with or without vows approved by the Holy See shall be recognized, provided they have their principal house in the Kingdom of Italy, and are there represented juridically and *de facto* by persons who possess Italian citizenship and are domiciled in Italy. Furthermore, in the case of associations which have their principal seat in foreign countries, the juridical personality shall be recognized of their religious provinces in Italy within the territory of the state and its colonies, when the above-mentioned conditions are realized. The juridical personality of the religious houses shall be recognized, if the particular rules of the individual orders attribute to the houses the capacity to acquire and possess. Finally, the juridical personality shall be recognized of the houses of the generals and the procurators of religious organizations of foreign organizations. The associations and religious houses which already possess juridical personality shall retain the same. The acts relative to the transfer of immovable property which the associations already possess from the actual holders of title to the associations themselves shall be free from every tax.

(c) Those confraternities which have no exclusive or principal purpose of divine cult are not subject to further transformation of their purposes and depend on the ecclesiastical authority in so far as their work and administration is concerned.

(d) The foundations of every kind for divine cult shall be admitted, provided it is certain that they correspond to the religious needs of the people and no financial burden to the state arises from them. This rule shall apply also to the foundations already existing.

(e) In the civil administration of the ecclesiastical property arising from the laws which upset the affairs of the Church, one-half of the members of administrative councils shall be designated by the ecclesiastical authority. The same shall apply to the funds for religion in the new Italian provinces.

(f) The acts done until now by ecclesiastical or religious entities without the observance of the civil laws can be recognized and made regular by the Italian state at the request of the ordinary to be presented within three years from the date that the present concordat goes into effect.

(g) The Italian government renounces the privileges of exemption from ecclesiastical jurisdiction of the Palatine clergy throughout Italy with the exception of those assigned to the Churches of the Holy Shroud at Turin, of the Superga, of the Sudario at Rome, and the chapels attached to the palaces where the sovereign and the royal princes live. In all other churches the appointment and provision of benefices and offices shall be governed by the rules contained in the above articles. A special committee shall provide for every palatine basilica or church an assignment of a sufficient endowment under the principles indicated for the goods of sanctuaries in article 27.

(h) The relief from taxes already granted by the Italian laws to some of the ecclesiastical entities shall remain in force; the purpose of divine worship or of religion is, in reference to the laws of taxation, to be held equal to the purposes of charity and education. . . .

(i) The use of the ecclesiastical or religious garb by seculars or by ecclesiastics and religious who by definitive order of the competent ecclesiastical authority have been deprived of the garb, and which order must be for the purpose of this article made known of-

ficially to the Italian government, is forbidden and punishable with the same penalties under which it is forbidden and punishable to wear the military uniform without authorization.

30. The ordinary and extraordinary administration of the goods belonging to any ecclesiastical institute or religious organization shall be carried on under the vigilance and control of the competent authority of the Church to the exclusion of all interference on the part of the Italian state and without obligation to submit the immovable property to seizure. The Italian state recognizes the capacity of ecclesiastical institutes and religious associations to acquire goods, saving the rules of the civil law concerning the acquisition of goods by moral bodies.

So long as no new agreements shall have been made ruling otherwise, the Italian state shall continue to supply the deficiencies of the income of ecclesiastical benefices by assignments which in quantity are to correspond as to their real value to the amount fixed by the laws actually in force. In consideration of this assistance, the administration of the patrimony of the said benefices shall, whenever the acts and contracts exceed mere administration, be done with the intervention of the Italian state, and in case of vacancy the consignment of the goods shall be made in the presence of a representative of the Government and two copies of the transaction shall be made.

To the aforesaid intervention of the state are not subject the *mensa episcopalis* in the suburban sees and the patrimonies of the chapters and parishes of Rome and of the said dioceses. Concerning the supplement to be given to these benefices by the government, the computing of the income which is to be paid to the beneficiaries from the said *mensæ* and patrimonies shall be based on a declaration given annually by the bishops for the suburban dioceses and by the cardinal-vicar for the city of Rome under their own responsibility.

31. The erection of new ecclesiastical entities or religious associations shall be made by the ecclesiastical authority according to the rules of Canon Law; their recognition for the purpose of the civil effects shall be given by the civil authority.

32. The recognitions and authorizations provided for in the present concordat and in the Treaty shall be given according to the rules established by the civil laws, which are to be put in harmony with the dispositions of the concordat and the Treaty.

33. To the Holy See is reserved the control of the catacombs existing in the territory of Rome and in other parts of the kingdom with the consequent burden of guarding, maintaining and conserving them. The Holy See can, therefore, while observing the laws of the state and safeguarding the eventual rights of third parties, proceed with necessary excavations and the transfer of the bodies of the Saints.

34. The Italian state being willing to restore to the matrimonial state, which is the basis of the family, the dignity conformable to the Catholic traditions of its people, accords to the sacrament of matrimony governed by canon law the civil effects.

The publications of marriage shall be made, not only in the parochial church, but also in the municipal building.

Immediately after the celebration of marriage, the pastor shall explain to the newly married couple the civil effects of marriage, and shall read to them the articles of the civil code about the rights and duties of married people, and shall make the record of the marriage, of which he shall within five days transmit a complete copy to the municipal building in order that it may be transcribed in the records of the civil state.

The cases concerning the nullity of marriage and the dispensation from the *matrimonium ratum non consummatum* are reserved to the competence of the ecclesiastical courts and offices.

The orders and sentences in these cases, after they have become final, shall be brought before the Supreme Tribunal of the Signatura, which shall investigate whether the rules of canon law relative to the competence of the judge, the summons and legitimate representation or refusal to appear of the parties have been observed.

The said final orders and sentences, with the relative decrees of the Supreme Tribunal of the Signatura, shall be sent to the court of appeals of the state competent in the respective territory, which, with the ordinances of the Chamber of the Council, shall make them effective in civil law and order that they be entered in the margin of the marriage records of the state.

In reference to mere separation of the married parties, the Holy See consents that these cases be judged by the civil courts.

35. For the high schools conducted by ecclesiastics or religious the law of the state prescribing the state examinations and the conditions are to be the same for candidates of the government and the Church schools.

36. Italy considers the teaching of the Christian religion according to the form of Catholic tradition the foundation and the crown of public instruction. Therefore, it consents that the religious teaching now given in the public elementary schools receive further development in the high schools, according to a program to be established by agreement between the Holy See and the state.

That teaching shall be imparted by teachers or professors, priests or religious, approved by the ecclesiastical authority, and subsidiarily by lay teachers and professors who are for the purpose approved by a certificate of fitness to be issued by the diocesan ordinary.

The recall of the certificate by the ordinary deprives the teacher without further formality of the right to teach.

For the religious instruction in public schools no other books shall be used than the text-books approved by the ecclesiastical authority. . . .

37. The directors of government associations for the physical education, for the pre-military instruction, for the [Fascist] *Avantguardisti* and the *Balilla,* shall arrange the schedules in such a way as not to impede on Sundays and holydays of obligation the fullfillment of the religious duties and to make possible religious instruction and assistance to the young people entrusted to their care. The directors of public schools shall do the same when gatherings of the pupils have been arranged for Sundays or holydays.

38. The appointment of professors at the Catholic University of the Holy Cross and the dependent Institute of Mary Immaculate is subject to the *nihil obstat* of the Holy See in order that the Holy See may assure itself that there is no objection to an appointment for reason of morals or religion.

39. The universities, major and minor seminaries (whether diocesan, interdiocesan or regional), the academies, colleges and other Catholic institutes for the formation and training of ecclesiastics, shall continue to depend exclusively on the Holy See without any interference on the part of the Ministry of Education of the state.

40. The doctor's degree in sacred theology conferred by a faculty approved by the Holy See shall be recognized by the Italian state. Likewise,

the certificates given in the schools of paleography, knowledge of archives, and diplomatic correspondence established at the library and archives in the Vatican City, shall be recognized by the state.

41. Italy authorizes in the kingdom and its colonies the use of honors of the papal knighthoods, provided the interested party presents the papal document of appointment and a written request to the state to have it recorded by the same.

42. Italy shall recognize by means of a royal decree the titles of nobility conferred by the popes even after 1870 and those which will be given in the future. Cases shall be pointed out in which the said recognition is not subject in Italy to the payment of a tax.

43. The Italian state recognizes the organizations which depend on the "Italian Catholic Action," inasmuch as these organizations at the command of the Holy See confine their activities to things altogether removed from every political party, and work under the immediate direction of the Catholic hierarchy for the diffusion of the knowledge and the practice of Catholic principles. The Holy See takes occasion from the stipulation of the present concordat to renew for all ecclesiastics and religious of Italy the prohibition to enroll in and to fight for any political party.

44. If in future some difficulty arises over the interpretation of the present concordat, the Holy See and Italy shall arrive at a friendly solution by mutual understanding.

45. The present concordat shall enter into force on the interchange of the ratifications at one and the same time with the treaty stipulated between the same high contracting parties, which treaty eliminates the "Roman Question."

At the moment that the present concordat becomes effective, the former concordats concluded with various Italian states shall cease to have any application. The Austrian laws and the laws, regulations and ordinances and decrees of the Italian state actually in force are, in so far as they are contrary to the dispositions of the present concordat, to be considered abrogated with the coming into force of the concordat.

In order to prepare for the execution of the present concordat, a committee composed of persons designated by the two contracting parties shall be appointed immediately after the signing of the concordat.

35. *Concordat Between the Holy See and the German Reich, 20 July 1933*

From *Church and State Through the Centuries*, trans. and ed. by Sidney Z. Ehler and John B. Morrall (Westminster, Maryland: The Newman Press, 1954), pp. 487-496.

HIS Holiness Pope Pius XI and the President of the German Reich, led by their common desire to consolidate and enhance the existing friendly relations between the Catholic Church and the state in the whole territory of the German Reich in a stable and satisfactory manner for both parties,

Have decided to conclude a solemn agreement which will supplement the concordats already concluded with some particular German States *(Laender)* and secure for the others the principles of a uniform treatment of the questions involved.

For this purpose

His Holiness Pope Pius XI has appointed as his plenipotentiary His Eminence the Most Reverend Cardinal Eugenio Pacelli, His Holiness' Secretary of State; and the President of the German Reich has appointed as plenipotentiary the Vice-Chancellor of the German Reich, Herr Franz von Papen; who, having exchanged their respective full powers and found them to be in due and proper form, have agreed to the following articles:

1. The German Reich guarantees freedom of profession and public practice of the Catholic religion. It recognizes the right of the Catholic Church to regulate and manage her own affairs independently within the limits of laws applicable to all and to issue—within the framework of her own competence —laws and ordinances binding on her members.

2. The concordats concluded with Bavaria (1924), Prussia (1929) and Baden (1932) and the rights and privileges of the Catholic Church recognized therein remain unchanged within the territory of the States *(Laender)* concerned. For the rest of the states the provisions of the present concordat shall be fully applicable. These provisions shall also be binding for the said three states in so far as they are relative to matters not regulated by the concordats concluded with those states, or in so far as they complete the arrangements already made.

In the future, concordats with the individual [German] states shall be concluded only in consultation with the government of the Reich.

3. In order to foster good relations between the Holy See and the German Reich, an apostolic nuncio will continue to reside, as hitherto, in the capital of the German Reich and an ambassador of the German Reich will reside with the Holy See.

4. The Holy See shall enjoy full freedom in its contact and correspondence with the bishops, clergy and all other members of the Catholic Church in Germany. The same applies to the bishops and other diocesan authorities in their contact with the faithful in all matters of their pastoral office.

Instructions, ordinances, pastoral letters, official diocesan gazettes, and other enactments concerning the spiritual guidance of the faithful, issued by the ecclesiastical authorities within the framework of their competence, may be published without hindrance and made known to the faithful in the ways heretofore usual.

5. The clergy enjoy in the discharge of their spiritual activities the same protection of the state as state officials. The state will proceed according to general provisions of its law in case of any outrage directed against the clergy personally or against their ecclesiastical character or in case of any interference with duties of their office and, if necessary, will provide official protection.

6. Clerics and religious are exempt from the obligation to undertake public offices and such obligations as are incompatible with their clerical or religious status. This applies particularly to the office of magistrate, membership of jury in law courts, membership of taxation committees or membership of the fiscal tribunal.

7. A member of the clergy can accept an official function or appointment in the state or in any publicly constituted corporation dependent on the state only after having received the *nihil obstat* of his diocesan ordinary, as well as that of the ordinary competent for the place where the seat of the corporation is situated. For important reasons in which the interests of the Church are involved, the *nihil obstat* can be withdrawn at any time.

8. The official income of the clergy is exempt from distraint to the same extent as the official salary of the civil servants of the Reich and of the states.

9. The judicial and other authorities cannot ask the clergy to give information about matters which have been entrusted to them while exercising the care of souls and which are consequently covered by the obligation of pastoral secrecy.

10. The wearing of clerical dress or of a religious habit by lay persons or by clerics or religious who have been forbidden to wear it on the strength of a final and valid decision of the competent Church authority—officially communicated to the state authorities—shall be punished by the state with the same penalties as the misuse of military uniform.

11. The present organization and delimitation of the Roman Catholic dioceses in the German Reich remains as it is. If, however, the rearrangement of a bishopric or of an ecclesiastical province, or any other changes in the delimitation of dioceses appear necessary in the future, they will be subject to an agreement with the government of the state concerned in case that they involve changes only with the boundaries of one German state *(Land)*. In case of rearrangement or changes which exceed the boundaries of one German state, the agreement is to be made with the Reich government, to whose care it shall be left to secure the consent of the state governments in question. The same applies to the establishment of new ecclesiastical provinces or alterations therein if these involve several German states. The foregoing provisions are not applicable to the shifting of boundaries which is made only with regard to the local care of souls.

In case of a wider reorganization within the German Reich, the Reich government shall consult with the Holy

See with a view to such regrouping of dioceses and to their delimitation.

12. Without prejudice to the provisions of article 11, ecclesiastical offices can be freely established and altered if no subsidy is asked for from the state funds. The co-operation of the state in establishing and changing the parish communities shall proceed according to rules which have been arranged with the diocesan bishops; the Reich government will endeavor to achieve a uniform formulation by the state governments of their rules as far as it is possible.

13. Catholic parishes, parish and diocesan associations, episcopal sees, bishoprics and chapters, religious orders and congregations, as well as institutions, foundations and property of the Catholic Church administered by ecclesiastical authorities, shall retain or acquire respectively juridical personality, recognized by the State according to the general provisions of civil law. They shall remain publicly recognized corporations as far as they have been such hitherto; the same rights may be granted to the others in accordance with the general law applicable to all.

14. As a rule, the Church has the right to appoint freely to all Church dignities and benefices without any co-operation on the part of the state or of the civil corporations, unless any other arrangement has been made in previous concordats mentioned in article 2. As far as the appointment to the episcopal sees is concerned, the arrangement reached with regard to the metropolitan see of Freiburg, in the diocese of the Upper Rhine, shall be applicable to the two suffragan bishoprics of Rottenburg and Mainz, as well as to the bishopric of Meissen. The same applies in the said two suffragan bishoprics as regards the appointments to the cathedral chapters and the settlement of the rights of patronage.

Furthermore, agreement has been reached on the following points:

(i) Catholic clerics who enjoy a spiritual office in Germany or exercise there a pastoral or educational activity, must:
(a) be German citizens;
(b) have obtained a school certificate (certificate of maturity) entitling them to study at a higher German school;
(c) have studied philosophy and theology for at least three years at a German state university, an academic ecclesiastical college in Germany or a papal high school in Rome.

(ii) The Bulls containing appointments of archbishops, bishops, coadjutors *cum iure successionis* or of a *prelatus nullius* will not be issued before the name of the selected person has been communicated to the *reichsstatthalter* in the state (*Land*) in question, and before it has been ascertained that there are no objections of a general political nature against such a person. The conditions laid down above under (i), par. (a), (b), (c), can be discarded by mutual agreement between Church and state.

15. Religious orders and congregations are not subject, on the part of the state, to any particular restrictions as far as their foundation, their various establishments, the number of their members and their qualifications (save, however, for the provisions of art. 15, par. 2), their pastoral or educational activity, their care of the sick and charitable work, the management of their affairs and the administration of their property are concerned.

Superiors of the religious orders who have their official residence within the

German Reich must have German citizenship. Provincials and superiors whose official residence is situated outside the German territory have the right of visitation of their establishments in Germany, even if they have a foreign citizenship.

The Holy See will see to it that the organization of the provinces of various religious orders, as regards their establishments in Germany, should be such as to avoid—so far as it can be done—the subordination of German establishments to foreign provincials. Exceptions therefrom may be admitted by mutual agreement with the Reich government, particularly in cases where the small number of establishments in Germany makes the formation of a German province impracticable or where special reasons exist for the maintenance of a provincial organization rooted in history and working well in practice.

16. Before taking possession of their diocese, the bishops shall take an oath of loyalty either between the hands of the *reichsstatthalter* in the state (*Land*) in question or between those of the president of the Reich, the formula of which shall be the following:

"Before God and on the Holy Gospels I swear and promise, as becomes a bishop, loyalty to the German Reich and to the *Land* of. . . . I swear and promise to respect the government established according to the constitution and to cause the clergy of my diocese to respect it. In the due solicitude for the welfare and the interests of the German Reich, I will endeavor, while performing the spiritual office bestowed upon me, to prevent anything which might threaten to be detrimental to it."

17. The property and all other proprietary rights of the publicly recognized corporations, institutions, foundations and associations of the Catholic Church will be guaranteed according to the common law of the state. No building used for public worship can be demolished under any pretext or for any reason whatsoever, except if a mutual agreement has been reached beforehand with the competent ecclesiastical authority.

18. Should the state payments in kind or money, which are made to the Catholic Church, whether based on law, contract, or any other special legal title, be discontinued, the Holy See and the Reich will proceed in due time beforehand to set up by amicable agreement the principles according to which the discontinuation is to be carried out. In this connection, a right derived from a legitimate traditional custom is to be considered as a special legal title. Such discontinuation, implying the cessation of a state payment or obligation, must be adequately compensated in favor of the claimant.

19. Catholic theological faculties in state universities shall be maintained. Their relationship to the Church authorities will be regulated by the provisions of the respective concordats and by the protocols annexed to them, with due regard to the ecclesiastical laws relative to these faculties. The Reich will endeavor to secure for all German Catholic faculties in question a uniform régime in accordance with the general spirit of the regulations concerned.

20. The Church has the right unless there is some other agreement, to establish theological and philosophical colleges for the training of clergy; if no state subsidies are claimed for these institutions, they will be dependent solely on the ecclesiastical authorities. The establishment, management and administration of seminaries and hostels for clerical students pertains exclusively, within the limits of the law applicable to all, to ecclesiastical authorities.

21. Catholic religious instruction in

primary, vocational, secondary and higher schools is a regular subject of tuition and is to be taught in accordance with the principles of the Catholic Church. In religious instruction the patriotic, civic and social consciousness and sense of duty will be particularly stressed and cultivated, as this is generally done in the school training. The teaching program of religious education and the selection of textbooks will be settled by agreement with the higher ecclesiastical authorities. These authorities will be given the opportunity to control, in harmony with the school authorities, whether pupils are receiving religious instruction in accordance with the teaching and requirements of the Church.

22. Mutual agreements shall be arrived at between the bishops and the governments of German states (*Laender*) with regard to appointment of the teachers of religion. Teachers who have been declared by the bishop unfit for the further exercise of their teaching function, either for pedagogical reasons or on account of their moral behavior, must not be employed as teachers of religion as long as the obstacle remains.

23. The maintenance of the existing Catholic confessional schools and the establishment of new ones is hereby guaranteed. In all localities where parents or guardians request it, Catholic primary schools will be established if the number of their prospective pupils, considered from the point of view of the local school conditions, appears to be sufficient for the establishment of a school corresponding to the standards prescribed by the state legislation.

24. Only members of the Catholic Church who can be trusted that they will correspond to the special requirements of a Catholic confessional school, can be employed as teachers in all Catholic primary schools. Within the framework of the general professional training of teachers, arrangements will be made to guarantee the education and training of Catholic teachers capable of fulfilling the special requirements of Catholic confessional schools.

25. Religious orders and congregations have the right to establish and run private schools within the limits of the general legislation and conditions laid down by law. The same qualifications as in state schools can be acquired in these private schools if they follow the teaching program prescribed for state schools. Members of religious orders and congregations are subject, with regard to their admission to teaching and to their employment in primary schools, to the general conditions applicable to all.

26. Pending a later and more detailed settlement of matters regarding matrimonial law, it is understood that a church wedding may precede the civil marriage ceremony not only in case of a grave illness of one of the fiancés which does not permit any delay, but also in case of great moral emergency (which, however, must be confirmed by the competent episcopal authority). In such cases, the parish priest is bound to report the matter at once to the registrar's office.

27. A special and exempt pastoral ministry is conceded to the officers, employees and men of the German army and to their families. An army bishop will be in charge of this pastoral care. His ecclesiastical appointment will be effected by the Holy See after contact has been made with the Reich government in order to select, by mutual agreement, a suitable candidate. The ecclesiastical appointment of military chaplains and other military clergy will be made by the army bishop after previous consultation with the competent authorities of the Reich. The army bishop can, however, appoint as military chaplains only such priests who have obtained, from their

ordinary, permission to engage in military pastoral work and who have obtained an appropriate certificate of fitness. Military chaplains have the rights of parish priests with regard to the troops and other army personnel assigned to their care.

An apostolic brief will be issued to regulate in detail the Catholic care of souls in the army. Regulations about the position of army chaplains as state officials will be issued by the Reich government.

28. The Church will be admitted to pastoral visits and to the holding of divine service in hospitals, prisons, and similar public institutions. If a regular care of souls, requiring the appointment of clergy as state or public officials, is introduced in such institutions, this will be made by agreement with the higher Church authorities.

29. Catholic members of non-German national minorities living within the Reich will not be placed in a worse status with regard to the use of their mother tongue in divine service, religious instruction and Church societies, than is the corresponding legal and practical position of the population of German origin and speech living in the territory of the corresponding foreign state.

30. On Sundays and Holy Days a prayer will be said for the welfare of the German Reich and its people in episcopal, parish, affiliated and conventional churches in the German Reich, immediately after the High Mass and according to the rules of the Church liturgy.

31. Catholic organizations and associations whose activity is devoted exclusively to religious, purely cultural and charitable purposes and which are, as such, subordinated to Church authorities, are protected as to their institution and activities.

Catholic organizations which, apart from religious, cultural or charitable purposes, have other tasks such as social or professional aims, shall also enjoy the protection of this article 31, paragraph 1, even though their organizations may be disposed in associations corresponding to states (*Laender*), provided they guarantee to develop their activities outside political parties.

It is reserved to the Reich government and the German episcopate to determine, by mutual agreement, the organizations and associations which fall within the provisions of this article.

In so far as the Reich and the states (*Laender*) take charge of sport and other youth organizations, care will be taken to enable their members to discharge regularly their Church duties on Sundays and Holy Days; and care will also be taken not to require them to do anything which would be incompatible with their religious and moral convictions and duties.

32. With regard to the special conditions existing in Germany and with regard to the provisions of the present concordat guaranteeing legislation to protect the rights and privileges of the Catholic Church in the Reich and its states (*Laender*), the Holy See will issue ordinances by which the clergy and the religious will be forbidden to be members of political parties or to be active on their behalf.

33. All matters regarding clerical persons or Church affairs which have not been mentioned in the preceding articles will be settled, for the sphere of the Church, according to canon law in force.

Should a divergence arise, in the future, as to the interpretation or application of any provision of this concordat, the Holy See and the German Reich will arrive at an amicable solution by mutual agreement. . . .

THE ADDITIONAL PROTOCOL

When signing the concordat concluded today between the Holy See and the German Reich, the undersigned, being duly empowered to do so, have formulated the following explanations which form an integral part of the concordat itself.

With regard to art. 3. In accordance with the exchange of notes between the apostolic nunciature in Berlin and the Reich foreign office on the 11th and 27th March respectively, the apostolic nuncio to the German Reich shall be the dean of the diplomatic corps accredited in Berlin.

With regard to art. 13. It is understood that the right of the Church to levy taxes is guaranteed.

With regard to art. 14, par. 2, sect. 2. It is understood that if objections of a general political nature exist, they shall be presented as soon as possible. Should they not be presented within twenty days, the Holy See will be entitled to believe that there are no objections against the candidate in question. Before an official announcement of the appointment is made, secrecy shall be kept about the candidates concerned. This article does not establish for the state a right of veto.

With regard to art. 17. In so far as buildings or land belonging to the state have been devoted to ecclesiastical purposes, they will continue to be devoted to them, with due regard, however, to the contracts which might have been concluded about them.

With regard to art. 19, sent. 2. The basis referred to consists, at the time when this concordat is being concluded, especially of the Apostolic Constitution *Deus scientiarum dominus* of 24 May 1931, and the Instruction of 7 July 1932.

With regard to art. 20. Hostels connected with high and secondary schools and administered by the Church will be recognized, from the taxation standpoint, as being in practice ecclesiastical institutions in the proper sense of the word, and as parts of diocesan organization.

With regard to art. 24. In so far as private institutions are able to satisfy, after the new regulations regarding the education of teachers, the generally applicable requirements of the state, the existing establishments of religious orders and congregations will be given due consideration in the accordance of recognition.

With regard to art. 26. A great moral emergency is considered as existing if the procuring in time of documents necessary for the wedding meets with obstacles which are either insuperable or whose removal would be disproportionately costly.

With regard to art. 27, sent. 2. Catholic army officers, personnel and men, as well as their families, do not belong to the local parish communities and are not to contribute to their maintenance.

With regard to art. 27, sent. 4. The apostolic brief will be issued in agreement with the Reich government.

With regard to art. 28. In urgent cases clergy shall be allowed to enter at any time.

With regard to art. 29. Since the Reich government has shown itself ready to make concessions with regard to non-German minorities, the Holy See declares—confirming hereby the principles which it has constantly maintained regarding the right of using the vernacular in the pastoral ministry, religious instruction and in the activities of Catholic associations—that it will keep in mind, when concluding future concordats with other countries, the inclusion in them of provisions of a similar value for the protection of the rights of German minorities there.

With regard to art. 31, par. 4. The principles laid down in par. 4 of this article are equally valid for the labor service (*Arbeitsdienst*).

With regard to art. 32. It is understood that the same provisions, regarding activity in political parties, will be enacted by the Reich for the non-Catholic confessions.

The conduct which has been stipulated as a duty for the German clergy and members of religious orders in art. 32 does not mean any restriction on their preaching and exposition of the dogmatic and moral teachings and principles of the Church, as it is their duty to do.

36. *Pope Pius XI: Encyclical Letter, "Mit Brennender Sorge," on the Church in Germany, 14 March 1937*

From the *Encyclical Letter of Pope Pius XI on "the Church in Germany"* (Washington: The National Catholic Welfare Conference, 1937), *passim.*

WITH deep anxiety and increasing dismay, we have for some time past beheld the sufferings of the Church, and the steadily growing oppression of those men and women who, loyally professing their faith in thought and deed, have remained true to her amidst the people of that land to which St. Boniface once brought the light and glad tidings of Christ and the kingdom of God.

This anxiety of ours has not been lessened by the accurate reports dutifully brought to us by the representatives of the most reverend episcopate, who came to visit at our sick-bed. They related much that is consoling and edifying about the struggle for religion that is being waged by the faithful, and yet, despite their love for their people and their fatherland, with every possible attempt to reach a dispassionate judgment, they could not pass over much that is bitter and sad. After receiving their accounts, we could say in great thankfulness to God: "I have no greater grace than this, to hear that my children walk in truth." But the frankness befitting our responsible apostolic office, and the desire to place before your eyes and those of the entire Christian world the actual facts in all their gravity, require us to add: A greater anxiety, a more bitter suffering

in our pastoral care, we have not, than to hear "many leave the way of truth."

In the summer of 1933, Venerable Brethren, we accepted the offer made by the government of the Reich to institute negotiations for a concordat in connection with a proposal of the previous year, and to the satisfaction of you all brought them to a conclusion with a solemn agreement. In this we were guided by the solicitude incumbent on us to safeguard the freedom of the Church in the exercise of her apostolic ministry in Germany and the salvation of the souls entrusted to her, and at the same time by the sincere wish of rendering an essential service to the progress and prosperity of the German people.

In spite of many serious misgivings at the time, we forced ourselves to decide that we should not withhold our consent. We wished to spare our faithful sons and daughters in Germany, so far as was humanly possible, the anxiety and suffering which, in the given circumstances, we would certainly have otherwise had to expect. Through our act we wished to prove to all, that seeking only Christ and the things of Christ, we do not refuse the hand of peace of mother Church to anyone who does not himself reject it.

If the tree of peace which we planted

with pure intention in German soil has not borne the fruit we desired in the interests of your people, no one in the wide world who has eyes to see and ears to hear can say today that the fault lies with the Church and her head. The lessons of the past years make it clear where the responsibility lies. They disclose machinations that from the beginning had no other aim than a war of extermination. In the furrows where we labored to plant the seeds of sincere peace, others were sowing, like the enemy in Holy Scripture, the tares of distrust, of discord, hatred, calumny, of secret and open enmity against Christ and his Church, an enmity in principle, fed from a thousand springs and working with every means at its disposal. With them and only with them, as well as with their open and silent supporters, lies the responsibility that now, instead of the rainbow of peace, the storm-clouds of destructive religious conflicts are visible on the German horizon.

We have not tired, Venerable Brethren, of portraying to the responsible guides of the destinies of your country the consequences that necessarily follow if such trends are left unhindered and much more if they are viewed with favor. We have done everything to defend the sanctity of a word solemnly pledged, to protect the inviolability of obligations, freely undertaken, against theories and practices which, if officially approved, must destroy all confidence and render valueless any word that might also be pledged in the future. When once the time shall have come to place before the eyes of the world these our endeavors, all right-minded persons will know where they have to look for those who kept the peace, and where for those who broke it. Everyone in whose mind there is left the least perception of the truth, in whose heart there is a trace of feeling for justice, will then have to admit

that in these grievous and eventful years after the signing of the concordat, in every word and in every action of ours, we have stood faithful to the terms of the agreement. But with amazement and deep aversion he will be obliged to admit that to change the meaning of the agreement, to evade the agreement, to empty the agreement of all its significance, and finally more or less openly to violate the agreement, has been made the unwritten law of conduct by the other party.

The moderation we have shown in spite of everything was neither dictated by considerations of human expediency nor motivated by unseemly weakness, but simply by the desire that we might not perchance tear up valuable wheat with the tares; by the intention not to pronounce judgment openly until minds were made ready for the inevitability of this judgment; by the determination not to deny definitively the good faith of others before the hard language of facts had torn away the coverings under which a systematic camouflage has been able and is able to disguise the attack on the Church. Even today, when the open campaign waged against the denominational school guaranteed by the concordat, when the nullification of the freedom of the vote for Catholics who should have the right to decide in the matter of education, shows the dreadful seriousness of the situation in a most important field of the Church's life and the unparalleled torment of conscience of believing Christians, our pastoral care for the salvation of souls counsels us not to leave unheeded even the slight prospects of return to a loyal adherence to a responsible agreement. In compliance with the prayers of the Most Reverend Episcopate, we shall not weary in the future also of pleading the cause of outraged right with the rulers of your people. Unconcerned with the success or failure of the day and obeying only our conscience and in accordance with our pastoral mission, we shall oppose an attitude of mind that seeks to stifle chartered right with open or covert violence. . . .

He who, in pantheistic vagueness, equates God with the universe, and identifies God with the world and the world with God does not belong to believers in God.

He who replaces a personal God with a weird impersonal Fate supposedly according to ancient pre-Christian German concepts denies the wisdom and providence of God, that "reacheth from end to end mightily and ordereth all things sweetly" and directs everything for the best. Such a one cannot claim to be numbered among those who believe in God. . . .

This God has given his commandments in his capacity as sovereign. They apply regardless of time and space, country or race. As God's sun shines on all that bear human countenance, so does his law know no privileges or exceptions. The rulers and the ruled, crowned and uncrowned, high and low, rich and poor, all alike are subject to his law. From the sum total of his rights as creator flows connaturally the sum total of his claims to obedience on the part of the individual and every kind of society. This claim to obedience comprehends every walk of life, in which moral questions demand a settlement in harmony with God's law and consequently the adjustment of transitory human legislation to the structure of the immutable law of God. Only superficial minds can lapse into the heresy of speaking of a national God, of a national religion; only such can make the mad attempt of trying to confine within the boundaries of a single people, within the narrow blood stream of a single race, God the creator of the world, the king and lawgiver of all peoples before whose greatness all peoples are small as a drop in the bucket.

The bishops of the Church of Christ set up "for the things that appertain to God" must be watchful that such pernicious errors, which are usually followed by more pernicious practices, find no foothold among the faithful. It is the holy duty of your office, as far as in you lies, to do everything to bring it about that the commandments of God shall be regarded and obeyed as the obligatory basis of morally ordered private and public life, that the sovereign rights of God, the name and the word of God, be not blasphemed; that the blasphemies—in word, writing and picture, at times countless as the sands by the sea—be made to cease; that over against the defying Promethean spirit of deniers, scorners and haters of God the propitiatory prayer of the faithful never falters but that, like incense, it may rise hour after hour to the Most High and stay his hand raised to punish.

We thank you, Venerable Brethren, your priests and all the faithful, who have done and continue to do their duty in defending the sovereign rights of God against the aggressive neo-paganism that unfortunately in many instances is favored in influential quarters. Our thanks are doubly sincere and coupled with admiration and approval of those who in the exercise of their duty were found worthy of making earthly sacrifices for God's sake and of enduring earthly suffering.

No belief in God will in the long run be preserved pure and genuine, if it is not supported by belief in Christ: "No one knows the Son, but the Father, but the Son and he to whom it shall please the Son to reveal him." "This is eternal life: that they may know You, the only true God and Jesus Christ, whom You have sent." Hence no one may say: I am a believer in God; that is religion enough for me. The words of the Savior allow no room for this kind of evasion. "Whosoever denies the Son, the same has not the Father. He that confesses the Son has also the Father."

The fullness of divine revelation has appeared in Jesus Christ, the incarnate Son of God. "God, Who at sundry times and divers manners spoke in times past to the fathers through the prophets, in the fulness of time hath spoken to us by his Son." The sacred books of the Old Testament are all God's Word, an organic part of his revelation. Corresponding to the gradual unfolding of the revelation, the dimness of the time preceding the full noon day of the redemption hovers over them. As is inevitable in the case of books of history and law, they are the reflections in many particulars of human imperfection, weakness and sin. Side by side with infinitely much that is high and noble, they relate the dissipation and worldliness that occurred time and again among the covenanted people who bore the revelation and promise of God.

Yet for every eye not blinded by prejudice and passion, out of the human failings, of which the Bible history speaks, shines forth all the more clearly the divine light of the work of salvation finally triumphant over all defects and sin. God's pedagogy of salvation develops on such a background oftentimes dark into perspectives that point the way, warn, fill with dread, elevate and make happy at the same time. Only blindness and pride can close their eyes to the treasures of instruction for salvation, that are in the Old Testament. He who wants to see the Biblical history and the wisdom of the Old Testament banished from the Church and school, blasphemes the Word of God, blasphemes the Almighty's plan of salvation, makes the narrow and limited mind of man judge over the divine plan of history. He de-

nies belief in the real Christ, who appeared in the flesh, who took his human nature from that people which was to nail him to the cross. He stands uncomprehendingly before the world-drama of the Son of God who opposed to the felony of his crucifiers the divine high-priestly action of the Redeemer's death and thus brought the Old Testament to its fulfillment and completion in the New, by which it is superseded.

The climax of revelation reached in the Gospel of Jesus Christ is definite, is obligatory for ever. This revelation knows no addition from the hand of man, above all, knows no substitution and no replacement by arbitrary "revelations" that certain speakers of the present day wish to derive from the myth of blood and race. Since Christ, the anointed, accomplished the work of redemption, broke the dominion of sin, and merited for us the grace of becoming children of God— since then no other name has been given under heaven to men, through which they can be saved, but the name of Jesus. No man, though all knowledge, all power, all outward might on earth should be embodied in him, can lay any other foundation than that which is already laid in Christ. He who sacrilegiously disregarding the yawning abyss of essential distinction between God and creature, between the God-Man and the children of men, dares to place any mortal, were he the greatest of all times, beside Christ, or worse, above him and against him, must be told that he is a false prophet, in whom the words of Scripture find terrible application: "He that dwells in heaven, shall laugh at them."

Belief in Christ will not be preserved true and genuine, if not supported and protected by belief in the Church, "the pillar and ground of the truth." Christ himself, God praised forever in the ages, has erected this pillar of faith. His command, to hear the Church, to hear his own words and commandments in the words and commandments of the Church, is meant for the men of all times and places. The Church founded by the Redeemer is one—for all peoples and nations. Beneath her vault, that like God's firmament arches over the whole earth, there is a place and home for all peoples and tongues; there is room for the development of all the particular qualities, points of excellence, missions and callings, that God has assigned to individuals and peoples. The heart of mother Church is wide and big enough to see in the development, according to God's purpose, of such special qualities and gifts rather the richness of variety than the danger of separation. She rejoices in the intellectual advancement of individuals and peoples. With the joy and pride of a mother she sees in their genuine achievements the fruits of education and progress, that she blesses and furthers whenever she can in conscience do so. But she knows, too, that limits are set to this freedom by the majesty of God's law that has willed and founded this Church one and indivisible in all essentials. He who touches this unity and indivisibility, takes from the Bride of Christ one of the diadems with which God himself has crowned her. He subjects her divine structure that rests on eternal foundations to the re-examination and remodeling of architects, to whom the heavenly Father has granted no plenipotentiary powers to build. . . .

In the final analysis every true and lasting reform has proceeded from the sanctuary; from men who were inflamed and driven by love of God and their neighbor. From their magnanimity and readiness to hearken to every call of God and to realize that call first of all in themselves, they grew in humility and in the conviction of their calling to be luminaries and renewers

of their times. When zeal for reform did not spring from the pure source of personal singleness of heart, but was the expression and outbreak of passionate frenzy, it caused confusion instead of bringing light, tore down instead of building up; and not seldom was the point of departure for errors more disastrous than were the evils that it was the intention or the pretended intention to correct. True, the spirit of God breathes where he will. He can raise up stones to prepare the way for his design. He chooses the instruments of his will according to his own plans, and not according to those of men. But he who founded his Church and called it into being in the storm of Pentecost, does not blast the foundation of the establishment he himself intended for salvation. Those who are moved by the spirit of God have of themselves the proper inward and outward attitude towards the Church, which is the precious fruit on the tree of the Cross, the Pentecostal gift of God's spirit to a world in need of guidance.

In your districts, Venerable Brethren, voices are raised in ever louder chorus urging men on to leave the Church. Among the spokesmen there are many who, by reason of their official position, seek to create the impression that leaving the Church, and the disloyalty to Christ the King which it entails, is a particularly convincing and meritorious form of profession of loyalty to the present state. With cloaked and with manifest methods of coercion, by intimidation, by holding out the prospect of economic, professional, civic and other advantages, the loyalty of Catholics and especially of certain classes of Catholic officials to their faith is put under a pressure that is as unlawful as it is unworthy of human beings. All our fatherly sympathy and deepest condolence we offer to those who pay so high a price for their fidelity to Christ and the Church. But here we reach the point of supreme importance, where it is a question of safety or destruction, and where consequently, for the believer the way of heroic fortitude is the only way of salvation. When the tempter or oppressor comes to him with the Judas-like suggestion to leave the Church, then, even at the cost of heavy, earthly sacrifices he can only reply in the words of the Savior: "Begone, Satan: for it is written: The Lord Your God you shall adore and him only shalt you serve." But to the Church he will say: You my Mother from the days of my childhood, my comfort in life, my intercessor in death, may my tongue cleave to my palate, if I, yielding to earthly enticements or threats, should turn traitor to the promises of my baptism. But to those who think that they can continue outward leaving of the Church with inward loyalty to the Church, let the Savior's words be earnest warning: "He that shall deny me before men, I will also deny him before my Father who is in heaven."

Belief in the Church will not be kept pure and genuine if it is not supported by belief in the primacy of the Bishop of Rome. At the very moment when Peter, foremost of all the apostles and disciples, confessed faith in Christ, the Son of the living God, the answer of Christ rewarding his faith and his confession was the word that speaks of the building of his Church, the one Church, and on Peter the rock. Belief in Christ, in the Church, in the primacy are thus connected in the holiest way. Real and lawful authority is everywhere the bond of unity, a source of strength, a security against disruption and dissolution, a pledge for the future; it is so in the highest and holiest sense in the case of the Church where alone to such authority the guidance of grace by the Holy Ghost and his assistance against which nothing can

prevail have been promised. When people who do not even agree on their faith in Christ hold before you as a thing to be desired or allure you with the picture of a German national church, know this: it is nothing but the denial of the Church of Christ, a manifest apostasy from the command to evangelize the whole world, to whose fulfillment only a universal church can be commensurate. The history of other national churches, their spiritual torpor, their attachment to or enslavement by earthly powers, shows the hopeless sterility that comes over every branch that separates itself from the living vine of the Church. To be on the alert right from the very start and to oppose an unflinching "No" to such sophistries, is to serve not only the purity of one's faith in Christ, but also the well-being and vital forces of one's people. . . .

Faith is the certain holding as true what God has revealed and through his Church proposes for belief, "the evidence of things that appear not." The joyous and proud confidence in the future of one's people, dear to everyone, means something quite different from faith in the religious sense. To play one off against the other, to try to replace one by the other, and thereupon demand to be recognized as a "believer" by the convinced Christian, is an empty play on words or a willful effacing of distinctions, or worse.

Immortality in the Christian sense is the continuance of the life of a man after temporal death, as a personal individual, to be rewarded or punished eternally. To designate with the word immortality the collective continued enjoyment of life in association with the continued existence of one's people on earth for an undetermined length of time in the future, is to pervert and falsify one of the principal truths of the Christian faith and strike at the foundations of every religious philosophy that demands a moral ordering of the world. If they do not want to be Christians, at least they should forego enriching the vocabulary of their unbelief from the Christian treasure of ideas.

Original sin is the inherited, though not personal, fault of the descendants of Adam, who sinned in him; loss of grace, and therewith loss of eternal life, with the propensity to evil that each one must combat and overcome by grace, penance, struggle and moral endeavor. The passion and death of the Son of God redeemed the world from the inherited curse of sin and death. Faith in these truths that today are clearly scorned in your country by the enemies of Christ belongs to the inalienable substance of the Christian religion. . . .

Grace, in the loose sense of the term, can be said to be everything that the creature receives from the creator. Grace in the proper and Christian sense of the word embraces, however, the supernatural manifestations of divine love, the loving kindness and working of God, whereby he raises men to that inward participation of life with himself, that is called in the New Testament sonship of God. "Behold what manner of charity the Father has bestowed upon us, that we should be called and should be the sons of God." The repudiation of this supernatural elevation of grace on account of the supposedly peculiar German type of being, is an error and an open challenge to a fundamental truth of Christianity. To put supernatural grace on the same level with the gifts of nature robs the vocabulary fashioned and sanctified by the Church. The pastors and guardians of God's people will do well to act with vigilance against this looting of the sanctuary and this work of confusing minds.

The moral conduct of mankind is grounded on faith in God kept true and pure. Every attempt to dislodge moral teaching and moral conduct from the rock of faith, and to build them on the unstable sands of human norms, sooner or later leads the individual and the community to moral destruction. The fool, who has said in his heart, there is no God, will walk the ways of corruption. The number of such fools, who today attempt to separate morality and religion, has become legion. They do not or will not see that by expelling confessional, i.e., clear and definite, Christianity from instruction and education, from the formation of social and public life, they are treading the ways of spiritual impoverishment and decline. No coercive power of the state, no mere earthly ideals, though they be high and noble in themselves, will be able in the long run to replace the final and decisive motives that come from belief in God and Christ. Take the moral support of the eternal and divine, of comforting and consoling belief in the rewarder of all good and the punisher of all evil, from those who are called on to make the greatest sacrifices, to surrender their petty self to the common weal, the result will be in countless instances not the acceptance, but the shirking, of duty. The conscientious observance of the ten commandments of God and the commandments of the Church—the latter are only the practical applications of the principles of the Gospel—is for every individual an incomparable schooling of systematic self-discipline, moral training and character formation—a schooling that demands much, but not too much. The God of kindness, who as lawgiver says: "Thou shalt," gives in his grace also the power to do. To disregard such profound and efficacious factors in moral training, or knowingly to bar their way to the field of popular education, is inexcusable cooperation in the religious undernourishment of the community. To hand over moral teaching to subjective human opinions that change with the trend of the time, instead of anchoring it to the holy will of the eternal God and to his commandments, is to open wide the door to the forces of destruction. Thus to have ushered in the betrayal of the eternal principles of an objective morality for the schooling of conscience, for the ennoblement of every sphere and branch of life, is a sin against the future of the people, whose bitter fruits the coming generations will taste.

It is part of the trend of the day to sever more and more not only morality but also the foundation of law and jurisprudence, from true belief in God and from his revealed commandments. Here we have in mind particularly the so-called natural law that is written by the finger of the creator himself in the tables of the hearts of men and which can be read on these tables by sound reason not darkened by sin and passion. Every positive law, from whatever lawgiver it may come, can be examined as to its moral implications, and consequently as to its moral authority to bind in conscience, in the light of the commandments of the natural law. The laws of man that are in direct contradiction with the natural law bear an initial defect that no violent means, no outward display of power can remedy. By this standard must we judge the principle: "What helps the people is right." A right meaning may be given to this sentence if understood as expressing that what is morally illicit can never serve the true interests of the people. But even ancient paganism recognized that the sentence, to be perfectly accurate, should be inverted and read: "Never is anything useful, if it is not at the same time morally good. And not because it is useful, is it morally good, but because it is morally good, it is also useful." Cut loose from this rule of morality,

that principle would mean, in international life, a perpetual state of war between the different nations. In political life within the state, since it confuses considerations of utility with those of right, it mistakes the basic fact that man as a person possesses God-given rights, which must be preserved from all attacks aimed at denying, suppressing or disregarding them. To pay no heed to this truth is to overlook the fact that the true public good is finally determined and recognized by the nature of man, with his harmonious coordination of personal rights and social obligations, as well as by the purpose of the community which in turn is conditioned by the same human nature. The community is willed by the creator as the means to the full development of the individual and social attainments, which the individual in give and take has to employ to his own good and that of others. Also those higher and more comprehensive values, that cannot be realized by the individual but only by the community, in the final analysis are intended by the creator for the sake of the individual, for his natural and supernatural development and perfection. A deviation from this order loosens the supports on which the community is placed, and thereby imperils the tranquillity, security and even the existence of the community itself.

The believer has an inalienable right to profess his faith and put it into practice in the manner suited to him. Laws that suppress or make this profession and practice difficult contradict the natural law. . . .

The Church, the guardian and exponent of the divine natural law, cannot do otherwise than declare that the registrations which have just taken place in circumstances of notorious coercion are the result of violence and void of all legality.

As the vice regent of him who said to the young man of the gospel: "If you will enter into life, keep the commandments," do we especially address fatherly words to youth. By a thousand tongues today a gospel is preached in your ears that is not revealed by your heavenly Father. A thousand pens write in the service of a sham Christianity that is not the Christianity of Christ. Day by day the press and the radio overwhelm you with productions hostile to your faith and Church and, with no consideration or reverence, attack what must be to you sacred and holy.

We know that many, very many, of you for the sake of loyalty to your religion and Church, for the sake of belonging to Church associations guaranteed by the concordat, have borne and still endure bitter days of misunderstanding, of suspicion, of contempt, of denial of your patriotism, of manifold injury in your professional and social life. We are aware that many an unknown soldier of Christ stands in your ranks, who with heavy heart but head erect bears his lot and finds comfort solely in the thought of suffering reproach for the name of Jesus.

Today, when new perils and conflicts threaten, we say to this youth: "If anyone preach to you a gospel, besides that which you have received" at the knees of a pious mother, from the lips of a Catholic father, from the education of a teacher true to his God and his church, "let him be anathema." If the state founds a state-youth to which all are obliged to belong, then it is—without prejudice to the rights of Church associations—an obvious, an inalienable right of the young men themselves, and of their parents responsible for them before God, to demand that this obligatory organization should be cleansed of all manifestations of a spirit hostile to Christianity and the Church, which, up to the re-

cent past and even at the present moment, place Catholic parents in hopeless conflicts of conscience, since they cannot give to the state what is demanded in the name of the state without robbing God of what belongs to God. . . .

We address a special word of recognition, encouragement and exhortation to the priests of Germany, on whom, in subordination to their bishops, there rests the task of showing the flock of Christ in a trying time and under difficult circumstances, the right paths, by precept and example, by daily sacrifice and apostolic patience. Be not weary, beloved sons and sharers in the holy mysteries, in following the eternal high priest, Jesus Christ, who bestows love and care like the good Samaritan. Keep yourselves day by day in conduct undefiled before God, in unremitting discipline and perfection, in merciful care for all entrusted to you, especially for those endangered, the weak and the wavering. Be the leaders of the faithful, the support of the stumbling, the teachers of the doubtful, the consolers of those who mourn, the unselfish helpers and counsellors of all. The trials and sorrows through which your people have passed since the war have left their mark on its soul. They have left behind conflicts and bitterness that can be healed only slowly, that can be overcome only in the spirit of unselfish and active charity. This charity, which is the indispensable armor of the apostle, especially in the world of the present day stirred up and distorted with hate, we pray and beg the Lord to bestow on you in superabundant measure. This apostolic love will make you, if not forget, at least forgive the many undeserved offenses that more plentifully than ever before are strewn in the path of your priestly ministration. This comprehending and merciful charity towards the erring, and even towards the contemptuous, does not mean and cannot mean, that you renounce in any way the proclaiming of, the insisting on, and the courageous defense of the truth and its free and unhindered application to the realities about you. The first and obvious duty the priest owes to the world about him is service to the truth, the whole truth, the unmasking and refutation of error in whatever form or disguise it conceals itself.

To Catholic religious of both sexes we likewise express our fatherly thanks, together with our utmost sympathy in the fate that, in consequence of regulations against the religious orders, has taken them out of the work of their chosen career, which they had loved and made rich in blessing. If individuals have fallen short and proved themselves unworthy, their misdeeds, punished by the Church herself, do not lessen the merits of the overwhelming majority, who, in unselfishness and voluntary poverty, were striving to serve their God and people in the spirit of sacrifice. The zeal, fidelity, striving after virtue, active charity and readiness to help on the part of the orders engaged in the ministry, hospitals and schools are, and remain, a praiseworthy contribution to private and public prosperity, to which undoubtedly a later and quieter time will accord more justice than the troubled present. We feel confident that superiors of religious communities will take occasion from their trials and difficulties to call down from the Almighty fresh blessing and fruitfulness on their heavy work through redoubled zeal, deepened life of prayer, holy earnestness in their vocation and religious discipline.

Before our eyes stands the countless throng of faithful sons and daughters, for whom the suffering of the Church in Germany and their own suffering has in no way diminished their devotion to the cause of God, their tender love for the father of Christendom, their obedience to their bishops and priests, their cheerful readiness, come what may, to remain true in the future to what they have believed and have received from their forefathers as a sacred inheritance. From a heart that is deeply moved we send them all our paternal greeting. . . .

Venerable Brethren, we are certain that the words which we address to you, and through you to the Catholics of the German Reich, in this decisive hour, will awaken in the hearts and actions of our loyal children the echo that answers to the loving solicitude of the common Father. If there is anything that we beseech of the Lord with particular fervor, it is this, that our words may also reach the ears and hearts of those who have already begun to allow themselves to be inveigled by the enticements and threats of those who take their stand against Christ and his holy Gospel and cause them to reflect. . . .

Just as other times of the Church, so will this be the harbinger of new advance and inward purification, if the readiness to suffer and confess the faith on the part of Christ's faithful is great enough to oppose to the physical violence of the persecutors of the Church the intransigence of inward faith, the inexhaustibleness of hope that rests on eternity, the commanding power of active charity. The holy seasons of Lent and Easter, that preach recollection and penance and direct more often than at other times the eyes of the Christian to the cross, but at the same time to the glory of the risen Christ, may they be for all and everyone of you a joyfully welcomed and eagerly used occasion to fill heart and mind with the spirit of heroism, patience and victory that shines forth from the cross of Christ.

Then, of this we are certain, will the enemies of the Church, who fancy that her hour has come, soon recognize that they rejoiced too soon and were too quick to dig her grave. Then will the day come when, instead of the too hasty songs of victory raised by the enemies of Christ, the *Te Deum* of liberation can rise to heaven from the hearts and lips of Christ's faithful; a *Te Deum* of thanks to the Highest; a *Te Deum* of joy, that the German people, even in its erring sons of today, has trodden the way of religious homecoming, that they once more bend the knee in faith purified by suffering before the king of time and eternity, Jesus Christ, and that they prepare to fulfill that calling which the designs of the eternal God point out to them, in the struggle against the deniers and destroyers of the Christian west, in harmony with all right-minded people of other nations.

He who searches the heart and reins is our witness, that we have no more heartfelt wish than the restoration of a true peace between Church and state in Germany. But if, through no fault of ours, there shall not be peace, the Church of God will defend her rights and liberties in the name of the Almighty, whose arm even today is not shortened. Trusting in him "We cease not to pray and beg" for you, the children of the Church, that the days of anguish may be shortened and that you may be found true in the day of searching; and we pray also for the persecutors and oppressors; may the Father of all light and all mercy grant them an hour of enlightenment, such as was vouchsafed to Paul on the road to Damascus, for themselves and all those who with them have erred and err. . . .

37. *Pope Pius XII: Efforts for Peace, 1939, 1945*

From *Pius XII and Peace, 1939-1944* (Washington, D.C.: The National Catholic Welfare Conference, 1944), pp. 8-13; *The Catholic Mind*, XLIV (February, 1946), 65-75. Reprinted with permission from *America*, The National Catholic Weekly Review.

A. CHRISTMAS ALLOCUTION OF
24 DECEMBER 1939

AMID the strife and tumult of varied world happenings, imperturbability of spirit is that real joy which resides in the power to withstand the storm through trust in God. We unite with Christ, principal and Fount of every grief and joy.

Where others lose themselves, where the waters of affliction and desperation submerge souls in cruelty, those who trust in Christ can do everything and, in harmony with order and the justification and magnificence of God, rise above the disorders and storms of the world with equal courage and order.

The indescribable disaster of war, which Pope Pius XI, with profound and extreme regret, foresaw and with the indomitable energy of his noble and most high spirit wished by all means to avert, has broken out and is now a tragic reality.

Before this tremendous war, an immense bitterness overcomes our souls, sad and troubled that this holy Feast of Christmas, this Feast of the Prince of Peace, must be celebrated to the funereal roar of cannon and under terror of flying war missiles, in the midst of menaces and dangers of armed navies.

It seems that the world has forgotten Christ's message of peace—the voice of reason. We of the Christian brotherhood have been obliged to see a series of irreconcilable acts, irreconcilable both in regard to international rights and to principles of national rights and to the most elemental sentiments of humanity, acts which show in what chaotic and vicious circles has the sense of justice been deviated from useful consideration.

In this category are premeditated aggressions against a small, laborious, and peaceful people on the pretext of a threat which neither exists, nor is desired, nor is possible.

Atrocities and illegal use of means of destruction even against non-combatants, refugees, old people, women and children and disregard of human dignity, liberty and life are acts which cry for the vengeance of God—as does ever more extensive and methodical anti-Christian and even atheistic propaganda, mostly among young people.

To preserve the Church and her mission among men from every contact with such anti-Christian spirit is our duty, and this is also our sacred and intimate wish as the father and teacher of the faith.

With anguished worry we are forced to contemplate the accumulating spiritual ruin before us—accumulating because of confusion of ideas which, more or less voluntarily, shades and distorts truth in the souls of many people, whether they be involved in war or not.

We, therefore, must regard with alarm the tremendous amount of work that will be necessary when a world tired of fighting wishes to restore peace, to break down the walls of aversion and hatred which have been built up in the heat of the strife.

Aware of the excesses to which that way of life leads, and of the political doctrines and acts which ignore the laws of God, when the disputes became critical we attempted, as you know, with every endeavor and to the last moment, to prevent the worst and

to persuade men in whose hands power lay and whose shoulders bore the grave responsibility, to abstain from armed conflict and so to save the world from incalculable disaster.

These efforts, and those coming from other influential and respected sources, failed to produce the hoped-for effect, chiefly because of deep and apparently irremovable distrust—distrust which had grown in recent years and which had raised insurmountable spiritual barriers.

The problems were not unsolvable, but this distrust, originating in a series of particular circumstances, stood in the way with almost irresistible force and to such an extent that there no longer was hope for promises made or for the maintenance of possible amicable conventions.

Finally, every effort to promote a peaceful solution became hopeless. There was nothing left but to try to lighten the burdens of war, although the effort to bring Christian charity to regions where the most urgent need of it would be felt was obstructed by difficulties not yet overcome.

With indescribable anguish, we watched this war initiated and proceeding in such unusual circumstances.

If up to now, excepting the blood-stained soil of Poland and Finland, the number of victims may be considered fewer than was feared, the total sorrows and sacrifices have reached such a point as to inspire great anxiety in those concerned with the future economic, social and spiritual condition of Europe, and not of Europe alone.

The more the war monster strives for, swallows and allots itself material means which are placed inexorably at the service of war needs, mounting from hour to hour, the more acute becomes the danger, for nations directly or indirectly struck by the conflict, of what we might call pernicious anemia, and they are faced with the pressing question: "How can an exhausted or weakened economy, at the end of the war, find means for economic and social reconstruction among difficulties which will be enormously increased, and of which the forces and artifices of disorder, lying in wait, will seek to make use in the hope of giving the final blow to Christian Europe?"

Such consideration of the present and future must cause much concern to the leaders and sane members of every people, even in the fever of the war, and cause them to examine the effects and reflect on the aims and justifiable ends of war.

We believe those who with watchful eyes consider these serious potentialities and the possibility of such an evolution of events will, notwithstanding war and its horrible accompaniments, hold themselves wholly prepared to define clearly, so far as they themselves are concerned, the fundamental points of a just and honorable peace at the opportune moment; and that they would not flatly reject opportunity for negotiations, whenever the occasion presents itself, with the necessary guarantees and security.

First. A fundamental condition of a just and honorable peace is to assure the right to life and independence of all nations, large and small, strong and weak. One nation's will to live must never be tantamount to a death sentence for another. When this equality of rights has been destroyed, injured or imperilled, the juridical order requires reparation whose measure and extent are not determined by the sword or selfish, arbitrary judgment, but by the standards of justice and reciprocal equity.

Second. That order, reestablished in such a manner, may be tranquil and durable—the cardinal principles of true peace—nations must be liberated from the heavy slavery of the race for armaments and from the danger that ma-

terial force, instead of serving to protect rights, become the tyrannical violator of them.

Conclusions of peace which failed to attribute fundamental importance to disarmament, mutually accepted, organic and progressive both in practice and spirit, and failed to carry out this disarmament loyally, would sooner or later reveal their inconsistency and lack of vitality.

Third. In any reordering of international community life it would conform to the rules of human wisdom for all parties concerned to examine the consequences of the gaps and deficiencies of the past; and in creating or reconstituting the international institutions, which have so lofty a mission and at the same time one that is so difficult and full of the gravest responsibilities, they should keep present before them the experiences which poured from the inefficacy or defective operation of similar previous projects.

And, since it is so difficult—one would be tempted to say almost impossible—for human weakness to foresee everything and assure everything at the time of the drafting of treaties of peace —when it is difficult to be entirely free from passions and bitterness—the establishment of juridical institutions, which serve to guarantee the loyal and faithful fulfillment of terms and, in case of recognized need, to revise and correct them, is of decisive importance for an honorable acceptance of a peace treaty and to avoid arbitrary and unilateral ruptures and interpretations of the terms of these treaties.

Fourth. A point which should draw particular attention if better ordering of Europe is sought, concerns the real needs and just demands of nations and of peoples as well as of ethnical minorities: demands which, if not always sufficient to form a strict right when there are recognized or confirmed treaties or other juridical titles which oppose them, deserve at all events benevolent examination to meet them in a peaceful way and, where it appears necessary, by means of equitable, wise and harmonious revision of treaties.

Once true equilibrium among nations is thus brought back and the basis of mutual trust is reestablished, many of the incentives to resort to violence would be removed.

Fifth. But even better and more complete settlements will be imperfect and condemned to ultimate failure, if those who guide the destinies of peoples, and the peoples themselves, do not allow themselves to be penetrated always more and more by that spirit from which alone can arise life, authority and obligation for the dead letter of articles in international agreements—by that spirit, namely, of intimate, acute responsibility that measures and weighs human statutes according to the holy, unshakeable rules of divine law; by that hunger and thirst for justice which is proclaimed as a beatitude in the sermon on the mount, and which has, as a natural presupposition, moral justice; by that universal love which is the compendium of and most comprehensive term for the Christian ideal, and therefore throws across also a bridge to those who have not the benefit of participating in our own faith.

We do not fail to recognize the grave difficulties which interpose themselves against the accomplishment of the aims which we have traced in broad outlines in a desire to lay foundations for, to put into effect and to preserve, a just international peace.

But if ever there were an aim worthy of the concourse of noble, generous spirits; if ever there arose a spiritual crusade which with new truth sounded the cry, "God wills it," it is truly that high aim and this crusade—to lead peoples back from the muddy gulf of material and selfish interest to the living fountain of divine law, which alone is powerful and gives that morality, nobility and stability of which a lack has been felt far too long, and which is gravely needed to repair the damage done to most nations, to humanity and to those ideals which are at the same time the real ends of peace based on justice and love.

We wait for and hope that all those who are united to us by the bond of faith, each at his post within the limits of his mission, will keep both mind and heart open, so that, when the hurricane of war ceases and is dispersed, there will rise up in every nation and among all peoples far-sighted and pure spirits, animated by courage, who will know how and will be able to confront the dark instinct of vile vengeance with the severe and noble majesty of justice—the sister of love and companion of all true wisdom.

Of this justice, which alone can create and assure peace, we and those who are listening to us know where to find a sublime example, intimate impulse and sure promise.

Let us go to Bethlehem. There we find lying in the manger the new-born "Son of Justice, Christ Our Lord," and by his side the Virgin Mary, the "Mirror of Justice" and the "Queen of Peace," with her holy guardian, Joseph, a just man. Jesus is the awaited of the Gentiles. The prophets called him this and sang his future triumphs.

B. CHRISTMAS ALLOCUTION OF 24 DECEMBER 1945

In the course of the last six years, venerable brethren and beloved sons, as this eve of our Lord's Nativity came around, we must all have felt keenly the sad contradiction between the spirit of holy joy and deep brotherly union in the service of God suggested by the beautiful Christmas season, and the lamentable spirit of vengeance and spite that prevailed throughout the world, between the sweet harmony of the "Gloria in excelsis Deo et in terra pax hominibus" and the discordant cries of hate amid the thunder of fratricidal war; between the suffused light of Bethlehem and the sinister glare of destructive fires; between the resplendent innocence radiating from the features of the heaven-sent Child and the mark of Cain which will long remain impressed on the countenance of our century.

What a sigh of relief, then, arose from all our hearts, as we heard that the gory conflict had ended, first in Europe, then in Asia! What fervent prayers had risen, during the long years of strife, to the throne of God, imploring him to shorten the days of affliction and stay the hands of those angels who hold the vials of God's wrath for the sins of men.

Now, by the mercy of God, the human family will begin once more to celebrate a Christmas without the terrors of war on land and sea and especially in the air any longer filling men's hearts with deadly anguish. For this turn of events let us all give humble thanks to our omnipotent Lord.

Peace on earth? True peace? No: Only the "post-war period," to use a sad but very pregnant term! How long will it take to cure the material and moral disorder, to close up so many wounds!

But yesterday men were scattering destruction, disaster, misery over vast territories; and today, when they must rebuild, men but faintly realize how much perspicacity and foresight, how much rectitude and good-will must go to the task of bringing the world back from physical and spiritual devastation and ruin to law, order and peace. So even this Christmas is still a time of expectancy, of hope and of prayer to the incarnate Son of God, that he, "The king of peace . . . whose face all

the earth desires to see close," may give to the world his peace. . . .

The Catholic Church, of which Rome is the center, is supra-national by its very nature. This has two implications, one negative and the other positive. The Church is a mother— *Sancta Mater Ecclesia*—a true mother, mother of all nations and all peoples no less than of all men individually. And precisely because a mother, she does not and cannot belong exclusively to this or that people, nor even more to one than to others but equally to all.

Since she is the mother, she cannot be a stranger anywhere; she dwells, or at least should, because of her nature, dwell among all peoples. Moreover, while the mother with her husband and children form a family, the Church, in virtue of a union incomparably more intimate, deeper and more perfect than is possible for the family, forms the mystical body of Christ. The Church is then supra-national because it is an indivisible, universal whole.

The Church is an indivisible whole because Christ, her head, is undivided and indivisible. Christ with his Church is—in the profound words of St. Augustine—*totus Christus,* the whole Christ. This wholeness of Christ, according to the saintly doctor of the Church, means the indivisible unity of the head with the body *in plentitudine ecclesiae,* in the fullness of the life of the Church, which brings together all places and all periods. Firmly established on such solid foundations, the Church, placed as she is in the center of the history of the whole human race, in the agitated and turbulent atmosphere of divergent energies and conflicting tendencies, is so far from being shaken—however much she be exposed to all forms of attacks on her indivisible integrity—that she actually diffuses from her own integral and coherent vitality ever new forces to heal and consolidate torn and divided mankind: forces of unifying divine grace, forces of the unifying spirit, for which all hunger, truths which are valid always and everywhere, ideals which are everywhere and always fresh.

From this it becomes clearer that a sacrilegious attack has been and is made against the *totus Christus,* the whole Christ, while at the same time a dastardly blow has been struck against the unity of mankind, whenever an attempt has been, or is made to put the Church, like a prisoner and slave, in the service of this or that particular people, to tie her up within the narrow confines of a single nation or on the other hand to ostracize her from any nation.

Such a mutilation of the Church's integrity has entailed and entails for the peoples who are victims of it—to a degree proportionate to its duration—the lessening of their real welfare and of their full vitality—but it is not merely that the individualism of nations and states has in these last centuries striven to break up the integrity of the Church, to weaken and hinder her unifying forces, those forces which nevertheless once had an essential part to play in the unification of western Europe. A musty liberalism strove to create, without the Church or in opposition to her, a unity built on lay culture and secularized humanism. Here and there—at once the result of its destructive force and the hostile reaction to it—totalitarianism supplanted it. In a word, what was the net result after a little more than a century of those strivings without—and often against—the Church? Human liberty buried; forced organizations; a world which for brutality and barbarity, for its achievement of destruction and ruin, but above all for its tragic disunity and insecurity has never known an equal.

At a time of stress such as ours still is, the Church, in her own interest and in that of mankind, should make every endeavor to use to the best advantage her undivided and indivisible integrity. She must be now more than ever supra-national. This spirit must pervade and inspire her visible head, the sacred college, all the activities of the Holy See, on which now more than ever there weigh grave responsibilities, not only for the present, but even more for the future. It is a question here of a spiritual factor, of having an accurate sense of the Church's supra-nationalism, and not measuring or determining it according to mathematical proportions or strictly on the basis of statistics giving the nationality of individuals.

During the long periods when, by the disposition of divine providence, the Italian nation, to a greater extent than the others, gave the Church her head and large numbers of collaborators in the central government of the Holy See, the Church as a whole has always kept its supra-national character intact. Indeed many factors contributed, precisely along this way, to preserve her from dangers which otherwise could easily have been more felt.

One might recall, to cite one example, the struggles for leadership of the national states of Europe and the great dynasties in past centuries. Ever since the reconciliation of church and state by the Lateran pacts, the Italian clergy as a whole, without any prejudice to natural and legitimate love of their country, have faithfully continued to support and promote the supra-national character of the Church. We hope and pray that they—and especially the younger clergy in Italy and throughout the Catholic world—may continue to do so: in any case the delicacy of the present situation calls for special care in safeguarding that supra-national character and indivisible unity of the Church.

She is supra-national because she extends the same love to all nations and peoples; she is also supra-national, as we have already said, because nowhere is she a stranger. She lives and grows in all countries of the world, and they all contribute to her life and growth. There was a time when ecclesiastical life, in its visible manifestations, flourished especially in the countries of old Europe, from which it flowed, like a majestic river, to what could then be called the outer limits of the world; today it appears rather as a sharing of life and energy between all the members of the Mystical Body of Christ on earth.

Not a few regions in other continents have long ago outlived the phase of missionary formation in their ecclesiastical development; they are governed by their own hierarchy and give spiritual and material benefits to the universal Church from which once they only received such benefits. Is there not revealed in this progressive enrichment of the supernatural and even natural life of mankind the true significance of the Church's supra-national character? She is not, because of this supra-national character, placed aloft as though suspended in an inaccessible and intangible isolation above the nations; for just as Christ was in the midst of men, so too his Church, in which he continues to live, is placed in the midst of the peoples.

As Christ assumed a real human nature, so too the Church takes to herself the fullness of all that is genuinely human, wherever and however she finds it, and transforms it into a source of supernatural energy.

Thus ever more fully is verified in the Church of today that phenomenon which St. Augustine praised in his *City of God:* The Church, he wrote, "recruits her citizens from all nations, and in every language assembles her community of pilgrims on earth; she is not anxious about diversities in customs, laws, institutions; she does not cut off or destroy any of these, but rather preserves and observes them. Even the differences in different nations she directs to the one common end of peace on earth, as long as they do not impede the worship of the one, supreme and true God."

Like a powerful lighthouse, the Church, in her universal integrity, casts her beam of light over those dark days through which we pass. No less obscure were those in which the great doctor of Hippo saw the world which he loved so dearly begin to founder. That light was then his comfort and, as it shone out, he greeted, in a prophetic vision, the dawning of a happier day. His love for the Church—it was no other than his love for Christ —was his consolation and his happiness.

God grant that all those who today, amid the sorrows and perils of their native land, endure sufferings like those of Augustine, may like him, find their solace and support in love of the Church, of that great universal home which according to God's promise will last to the end of time.

For our part we desire to make that home ever more solid, ever more attractive to all, without exception. Hence we desire to leave nothing undone that may reflect outwardly the supra-national character of the Church because it is the expression of her love for Christ, whom she sees and serves in the rich variety of her members scattered throughout the whole world.

At an hour like this, in which we celebrate the birth of him who came to reconcile men to God and to one another, we cannot let pass the opportunity of saying a word about the peace structure which the ruling classes in the state and in politics and economics have set themselves to erect. With an accumulation, hitherto perhaps never achieved, of experience, good-will, political insight and organizing talent, men have begun the preliminaries to the world peace settlement.

Never perhaps from the beginning of the world have statesmen found themselves faced with a task so gigantic and complex, because of the number, gravity and difficulty of the problems to be solved, so important for its effects in extent and in depth for good or for evil, as that of now restoring order, peace and prosperity to mankind after thirty years of world war, economic crises and incalculable destitution.

Exalted, formidable is the responsibility of those who set themselves to bring such a gigantic undertaking to a successful conclusion. It is not our intention to discuss the practical solutions that they may be able to apply to such thorny problems. We believe, however, that it belongs to our office, in continuation of our previous Christmas messages during the war, to indicate the fundamental moral prerequisites of a true and lasting peace; we shall reduce these to three short considerations:

1. The present hour calls imperiously for collaboration, good-will, reciprocal confidence in all peoples. Motives of hate, vengeance, rivalry, antagonism, unfair and dishonest competition must be kept out of political and economic debates and decisions. "Who can say," we may add, in the words of Sacred Scripture, "my heart is clean, I am pure from sin? Diverse weights and diverse measures, both are abominable before God." Anyone, then, who exacts the expiation of crime through the just punishment of criminals because of their misdeeds should take good care not to do himself what he denounces in others as misdeeds or crime. One who seeks reparations should base his claim on moral principles, respect for those inviolable natural rights which remain valid even for those who have surrendered unconditionally to the victor. One who asks for security in the future should not forget that its only true guarantee lies in one's own internal force—that is, in safeguarding the family, children, labor, in fraternal charity, the outlawing of all hate, all persecution, all unjust vexation of honest citizens, in loyal concord between state and state, between people and people.

2. To secure this, men must everywhere forego the artificial creation, through the power of wealth, of arbitrary censorship, onesided judgments and false assertions, of a so-called public opinion which sways the ideas and will of the electorate like reeds shaken by the wind. Let due heed be paid to the true and overwhelming majority of men, made up of those who live honestly and peacefully by their own labor in their own family circle, and who desire to do the will of God. In their eyes, disputes for more advantageous frontiers and the scramble for the treasure of the earth, even if not of necessity and *a priori* unjust in themselves, are at least always a dangerous venture which cannot be entered on without the risk of causing an accumulation of death and ruins. The vast majority of good fathers and mothers of families want to protect and safeguard the future of their own children against the pretensions of every policy of brute force, against the arbitrary totalitarianism of the powerful state.

3. The force of the totalitarian state. The whole surface of the globe, reddened with the bloodshed in these terrible years, cries aloud the tyranny of such a state.

The fabric of peace would rest on a tottering and ever-threatening base if an end were not put to such totalitarianism, which lowers man to the state of a mere pawn in the game of politics, a cipher in economic calculations. With a stroke of the pen it changes the frontiers of states; by a peremptory decision it deprives a people's economy—always part of its life as a nation—of its natural outlets; with ill-concealed cruelty it, too, drives millions of men, hundreds of thousands of families, in the most squalid misery, from their homes and lands, tears them out by the roots and wrenches them from a civilization and culture which they had striven for generations to develop.

It also sets arbitrary bounds to the necessity and right of migration, and to the desire to colonize. All this constitutes a policy contrary to the dignity and welfare of the human race.

And yet by divine right it is not the will or the power of fortuitous and unstable vested interests, but man in the framework of the family and of society, who by his labor is lord of the world. Consequently this totalitarianism fails by what is the only measure of progress, namely the progressive creation of ever more ample and better conditions in public life to ensure that the family can evolve as an economic, juridic, and moral and religious unit.

Within the confines of each particular nation as much as in the whole family of peoples, state totalitarianism is incompatible with a true and healthy democracy. Like a dangerous germ it infects the community of nations and renders it incapable of guaranteeing the security of individual peoples. It constitutes a continual menace of war.

The future peace structure aims at outlawing from the world every aggressive use of force, every war of aggression. Who could not greet such an intention enthusiastically, especially in its effective realization?

But if this is to be something more than a beautiful gesture, all oppression and all arbitrary action from within and without must be banned.

In the face of this accepted state of affairs, there remains but one solution: a return to God and to the order established by him.

The more the veil is lifted from the origin and increase of those forces which brought about the war, the clearer it becomes that they were the heirs, the bearers and continuers of errors of which the essential element was the neglect, overthrow, denial and contempt of Christian thoughts and principles.

If, then, the root of the evil lies here, there is but one remedy: to go back to the order fixed by God also in relations between states and peoples; to go back to a real Christianity within the state and among states. And let it not be said that this is not realism in politics. Experience should have taught all that the policy guided by eternal truths and the laws of God is the most real and tangible policy. Realistic politicians who think otherwise pile up only ruins.

And now, lastly, our gaze, which has wandered, if only for a moment, over the present state of the world, must pause once again on the masses, still immense, of war prisoners. As we get ready to pass in quiet, interior joy and fervent prayer the holy feast of Christmas, which reaffirms and ennobles, with century-old and undiminished harmony, the bonds of the human family, and invites to the domestic hearth, as to a sacred rite, even those who habitually live lone away from it, we remember with profound sorrow all those who, although the end of the war has been proclaimed, must this year again pass the beautiful season in a foreign land and feel, on the night of rejoicing and peace, the torment of their uncertain lot and of their separation from parents, wives, children, brothers, sisters, all their dear ones.

And while we wish to pay the tribute of just recognition and praise to those authorities and to those organizations and individuals who have striven to alleviate and to abbreviate their sorrowful condition, we cannot conceal the pain we felt when, in addition to the sufferings inevitably accruing from the war, we heard of others which were almost on purpose inflicted on prisoners and deported people; when, in some instances, we saw their captivity prolonged without reasonable cause; when the yoke of imprisonment, of itself oppressive, was aggravated by hard and unjustified labor, or when, in unconscionable disregard for standards set up by international conventions and by the still more sacred standards of Christian and civil conscience, they were refused in an inhuman way the treatment due to the vanquished.

To these children, still held in prison, may our Father's message be carried on the wings of the Christmas angels. May they receive and be comforted by our wish—shared by all who cherish the sense of man's brotherhood—to see them regularly and speedily restored to their anxious families and to their normal peace-time occupations. And we are certain that we voice the sentiments of all right-thinking men when we extend that wish to include those political prisoners, men, women, and youths, at times exposed to dire sufferings, against whom no accusation of crime or violation of the law can be brought, but, at most, only their past political views.

We shall include with affectionate solicitude also those missionaries and civilians in the Far East who in consequence of recent grave events are living in affliction and danger. There is an obvious natural obligation that these unfortunate victims be treated in a humane manner. Indeed, we consider that much-desired pacification and concord among peoples could not be better initiated than by their liberation and as far as possible by their fair, proper and equitable rehabilitation. . . .

C. VIEW ON THE SPIRITUAL POWER OF THE CHURCH AND CONTEMPORARY THEORIES OF STATE POWER, 2 OCTOBER 1945

For the first time since the moment when it pleased the Lord, who is supreme judge of all justice among men, to constitute us his representative and vicar, have we today, beloved sons, the opportunity—after hearing the exhaustive and learned report on the activity of this Sacred Tribunal, delivered by your worthy dean—to express our gratitude and our thoughts without our voice being drowned by the tumult of weapons and their sinister rumblings. Shall we venture to say that we have peace? Not yet, alas! With the Lord's help it may be, at least, its dawn. However, as soon as the violence of the fighting has stopped, there returns the rule of justice, the task of which consists in the restoration, by means of its judgments, of the order which has been shattered and disturbed. For enormous is that judicial dignity and power which has to be elevated above all passions and prejudices and, at the same time, has to reflect the justice of God himself in both deciding controversies and repressing offenses.

Such is, indeed, the purpose of all jurisdiction, the mission of all judicial power, ecclesiastical or secular. A rapid and superficial look at the law and the practice of the courts of law might lead to the impression that there are only secondary differences between the ecclesiastical and civil rules of procedure, differences similar to those which may exist between the administration of justice in two states belonging to the same juridical family. They both seem to have the same immediate purpose, namely to secure the operation of law and to safeguard the rights which are based upon law and contested or broken in particular cases, by means of juridical sentences, or, speaking more precisely, through jurisdiction exercised by competent authorities established under law. In both systems, too, we find law courts of various degrees; in both, the procedure follows the same main principles: it requires the case to be placed before the tribunal, a summons, the examination of witnesses, the communication of documents, the questioning of the parties, the termination of the proceedings, the judgment, the right of appeal.

And yet, this great similarity, both external and internal, must not obscure the profound difference which exists betwen the two systems with regard (1) to their origin and nature; (2) to their object; (3) to their purpose. Today, we shall limit ourselves to speaking of the first of these three points, reserving the treatment of the other two to future years, if it so please the Lord.

The judicial power is an essential part and a necessary function of the two perfect societies, the church and the state. Therefore the question of the origin of the judicial power inside each of them is identical with the question of the origin of power and authority in general. This is why it is sometimes believed that other similitudes, besides those already noted, and even more profound, can be found between the two powers. It is interesting to see how the adherents of various modern conceptions regarding the state power have adduced—in order to confirm and support their own views—the supposed analogies between the civil and the ecclesiastical powers. This applies not only to the so-called "totalitarianism" and "authoritarianism" but also to their opposite pole, the modern democracy. But, in reality, such deeper similarities do not exist in any of the three cases as a brief survey will easily demonstrate.

It is undeniable that one of the vital exigencies of any human community, consequently also of the Church and the state, consists in the permanent assurance of unity in the diversity of their members.

"Totalitarianism," however, can certainly not satisfy this exigency because it allows the state power to assume an undue extension, and to determinate, and to fix, both in substance and in form, every field of activity, so that it compresses all legitimate manifestation of life—personal, local and professional—into a mechanical unity or collectivity under the stamp of nation, race or class.

We have already pointed out, in our Christmas Radio Message of 1942, the particularly deplorable consequences of this theory and practice with regard to the judicial power, due to their suppressing the equality of all before the law, and to their leaving judicial decisions to the whim of changeable collective instinct.

Besides, who could ever think that such erroneous interpretations which violate human rights so flagrantly could have determined the origin or influence the action of ecclesiastical tribunals? This is not the case and can never be, for it is contrary to the very nature of the social authority of the Church, as we are going to see subsequently.

However, the above mentioned fundamental exigency is also far from being satisfied by that other concept of civil authority, which may be called "authoritarianism," for the latter excludes the citizens from all effective participation in, or influence upon the formation of the will of the society. Consequently, it splits the nation into two categories, the rulers and the ruled, and the mutual relationship between the two either becomes purely mechanical, being governed by force, or has no more than a biological basis.

Who, therefore, would not realize that in this manner the very nature of state power is completely perverted? The truth is that state power should tend, both in itself and through the exercise of its functions, to make of the state a true community, intimately united in a final purpose which is the common good. In the said system, however, the notion of the common good becomes so unstable and appears so obviously as a misleading mask for the unilateral interests of the rulers that a frantic legislative "dynamism" excludes all juridical security and so destroys a basic element of every true judicial order.

Such a false dynamism can never submerge and suppress the essential rights recognized in the Church to the individual persons, both physical and juridical. The nature of ecclesiastical authority has nothing in common with this "authoritarianism"; the latter can, therefore, claim no point of resemblance to the hierarchical constitution of the Church.

It remains to examine the democratic form of government, in which some would like to find a closer similitude to the power of the Church. Undoubtedly, wherever true democracy exists in theory and practice, it satisfies that vital requirement of every sound community to which we have referred above. However, the same applies, or could apply, under the same conditions, also to the other legitimate forms of government.

Certainly the Christian Middle Ages, which were particularly imbued with the spirit of the Church, proved by the abundance of their flourishing democratic communities not only that the Christian faith is able to produce a genuine and true democracy but also that it is the only durable foundation for democracy. A democracy without an accord of spirits, at least as to the fundamental maxims of life—and, above all, as to the rights of God, the dignity of the human person and the respect due to the honest activity and liberty of the person—would be defective and unsound even in its political aspect. If, therefore, the people depart from the Christian faith or do not hold it resolutely as the principle of civil life, even democracy is easily altered and deformed, and in the course of time is liable to fall into a one-party "totalitarianism" or "authoritarianism."

On the other hand, if we keep in mind the favorite thesis of democracy —which has been expounded in all ages by outstanding Christian thinkers —namely, that the original subject of civil power derived from God is the people (not the "masses"), then the distinction between the Church and even the democratic state becomes increasingly clear.

The ecclesiastical power is, indeed, essentially different from the civil power, and hence its judicial power is also different from that of the state.

The origin of the Church, unlike the origin of the state, is not to be found in natural law. The most complete and accurate analysis of the human person offers no ground for the conclusion that the Church, like civil society, was naturally bound to come into existence and to develop. Its existence is derived from a positive act of God beyond and above the social nature of man, though in perfect accord with it; therefore, the ecclesiastical power—and consequently also the corresponding judicial power of the Church—is born of the will and act by which Christ founded His Church. It remains true, however, that once the Church was constituted, as a perfect society, by the act of the Redeemer, not a few elements of resemblance to the structure of the civil society sprang from her very nature.

In one point, however, the fundamental difference between the two is particularly manifest. The establishment of the Church as a society was not effected from below, as was the case in the origin of the state, but from above; that is to say that Christ Who in His Church set up on earth the Kingdom of God which he had announced and destined for all men and all times, did not vest in the community of the faithful the mission of master, priest, and pastor which he had obtained from his Father for the salvation of mankind, but He transmitted and communicated it to a college of apostles or messengers, selected by himself, in order that they, by their preaching, by their priestly ministry, and by the social authority of their office, bring into the Church the multitude of the faithful to be sanctified, enlightened and led to the full maturity of followers of Christ.

Examine the words by which he communicated to them their powers: the power to offer sacrifice in remembrance of him, the power to forgive sins, the promise and the bestowal of the supreme power of the keys upon the person of Peter and the persons of his successors, the communication to all apostles of the power to bind and loose. Finally, meditate over the words with which Christ, before his ascension, transmitted to the same apostles the universal commission which he had received from the Father. Is there anything in all this which can leave room for doubt or equivocation? The whole history of the Church, from her beginning to our own day, does not cease to echo those words and give the same testimony with a clearness and precision that no prevarication can disturb or obscure. And all these words, all these testimonies proclaim as if with one voice that in the ecclesiastical power the essence, the central point according to the express will of Christ,

and hence according to divine law, is the commission which he gave to the ministers of the work of salvation in the community of the faithful and in the whole human race.

Canon 109 of the Code of Canon Law has put this marvellous edifice in a clear light and in monumental relief: "Those who are admitted to the ecclesiastical hierarchy are chosen, not by the consent or at the call of the people or of the secular power; but they are established in the various grades of the power of order by sacred ordination; in the supreme pontificate, by the divine law itself upon fulfillment of the condition of legitimate election and the acceptance thereof; in the other grades of jurisdiction, by canonical mission."

"Not by the consent or at the call of the people or of the secular power"; the faithful or the secular power may, during the course of the centuries, have participated often in the designation of those upon whom ecclesiastical offices were to be conferred; and to all of them, including the supreme pontificate, the son of the humblest workingman's family is eligible equally with the descendant of a noble stock. However, in reality the members of the ecclesiastical hierarchy have always received and do receive their authority from above and are responsible for the exercise of their mandate immediately to God only, to whom alone the Roman pontiff is subject, or, as far as the other grades are concerned, to their hierarchical superiors. But they have no account to render either to the people or to the civil power except, of course, for the opportunity, given to any of the faithful, of presenting in due form to the competent ecclesiastical authority, or even directly to the supreme power in the Church, their petitions and recourses, especially if the petitioner or the institutor of the recourse is prompted by motives which are connected with his personal responsibility for his own or other persons' spiritual welfare.

Two principal conclusions are to be deduced from the statements which we have made:

1. In the Church—unlike the state—the primordial subject of power, the supreme judge, the highest court of appeal, is never the community of the faithful. Therefore, in the Church, as founded by Christ, there does not exist and cannot exist any popular tribunal or judicial power deriving from the people.

2. The question of the extent and scope of ecclesiastical power also presents itself in a manner entirely different from that of state power. What is decisive for the Church in the first place is the will of Christ, Who could give her, according to His wisdom and goodness, means or powers of greater or lesser extent but always the minimum which is necessarily required by her nature and purpose. The power of the Church embraces man entirely, both his internal and external life, in order to lead him to the attainment of his supernatural destiny, so that he is completely subject to the law of Christ, which the Church has been constituted by her divine founder to guard and to execute both in the external forum and in that of conscience, the internal forum. Consequently this power is a full and perfect one, though far removed from that "totalitarianism" which neither admits nor recognizes due regard for the clear and inalienable dictates of a sound conscience and which does violence to the laws of individual and social life written in the hearts of men. In fact the Church, wielding her power, does not aim to enslave the human person, but to assure its liberty and perfection, redeeming it from the deficiencies, errors, aberrations in spirit and in heart, which sooner or later always end in dishonor and servitude.

The sacred character of the ecclesiastical jurisdiction which comes from its divine origin and from its being part of the hierarchical power of the Church should inspire you, beloved sons, with a high esteem of your office and spur you on to fulfill your austere duties with a lively faith, unwavering rectitude and ever vigilant zeal. But, behind the veil of this austerity, what splendor reveals itself to the eyes of one who is able to see in the judicial power the majesty of justice whose every activity tends to make the Church, the Spouse of Christ, appear "wholly and without blemish" before her Divine Spouse and before mankind. . . .

VI. *The Modern Popes Speak*

IN THE first half of the twentieth century the popes continued the tradition established by Pope Leo XIII of issuing numerous encyclical letters on subjects concerning faith and morals, as well as on particular problems relating to Catholic life in contemporary society. Popes in previous ages had employed this method of expressing Christian principles, but in modern times the procedure has become a more typical characteristic of papal policy. Its effectiveness in co-ordinating Christian thought and bringing the Catholic position before the attention of the world, has been repeatedly proved.

The wide range of subjects treated in modern papal encyclicals might well be a subject of special study. One example of each pope's writing, however, can supply some insight into the influence of the historical development of the Church on the contemporary scene.

One of the main characteristics of Pope Benedict XV's short reign of seven years was his far-seeing ENCYCLICAL LETTER ON MISSIONS AND A NATIVE CLERGY (*No. 38*) of 30 November 1919. This document has been termed the *magna carta* of the contemporary mission movement. Missionary work, the pope said, is the obligation of every Catholic. Not enough is being done; new seminaries for the foreign missions are to be established. The pope spoke out strongly against associating Christianity with any national government, and he unequivocally affirmed that a native clergy is the "one great hope of new missions." Native clergies are not to be mere auxiliaries of the foreign missionary, but rather they are to be equal partners destined one day to take over the work of the Church in their native land.

Pope Pius XI continued his predecessor's interest in the missions, worked to develop both a native clergy and a native lay apostolate in the missions, to dissociate the faith from charges of being a white man's religion based on European culture, and to emphasize that Catholic dogma and worship should be adopted to local culture. The pope asked that the Gospel "on being introduced into any new land not destroy or extinguish whatever its people possess that is naturally good, just or beautiful . . . whatever there is in the native customs that is not inseparably bound up with superstition and error will always receive kindly consideration and, when possible, will be preserved intact." In this spirit the Congregation for the Propagation of the Faith submitted a new policy for mission activity which was approved on 8 December 1939. The age-old controversy over "CHINESE RITES" (*No. 39*) was finally laid to rest, and the Holy See approved what Ricci had advocated in the seventeenth century, namely, that Chinese ceremonies are only civil acts of reverence for ancestors, and that they demonstrate love of one's native country or courtesy toward one's neighbor. The expansion of Catholic missions in the modern period, despite the disruptions of the times, has proceeded at such a pace under dedicated apostolic missionaries, the support of the laity, and the centralized direction of the Holy See, that Pius XII declared the proportion of contemporary missionary endeavor was "perhaps never witnessed before in the annals of Catholic missions."

Pope Pius XI's scholarly background is apparent in the wide range of subjects discussed in his thirty encyclicals. Throughout the seventeen years he ruled the Church he planned on a grand scale with courage and precision to re-state the ancient truths of Catholicism in terms of an apostolate keyed to the demands of the age. He modernized administration and techniques wherever he saw the need. Through all his endeavors runs the theme, repeated again and again, that only the reign of Christ the King will bring peace to mankind. A restoration of such a Christian way of life was to be accomplished by Catholic Action, i.e., organized religious activity by lay associations under the direction of the hierarchy. The modern Catholic has the obligation to act in the *milieu* in which God has placed him. When Italian Catholic Action was under attack by Fascists, the pope spoke out bravely against this persecution of "the apple of his eye" in an ENCYCLICAL LETTER IN DEFENSE OF CATHOLIC ACTION (*No. 40*) on 29 June 1931. Here is contained the core of the thought and aspiration of the intrepid Pius XI.

Pope Pius XII was called the chief pastor and teacher of all Catholics and a considerable part of the world in a more direct way than any pope since the earlier ages of the Church. His voluminous writings on spiritual, cultural, political, and social problems cover many aspects of contemporary life both in general principles and often in minute detail. There seemed to be no professional group, no subject of concern to modern man, which did not command his attention. His DISCOURSE ON THE WORLD COMMUNITY (*No. 41*) of 6 December 1953 reavealing, for example, his support of a tolerant world-wide society was a most vital clarification of the Church's position.

Pius XII's pontificate was another step in the return of the papacy, begun under Pope Leo XIII, as the living sign of the true, good, and charitable in human endeavor. He was the pope of peace; he was an archi-tect of the contemporary reunion of the spiritual and the secular. In order to effect such a reconciliation Pius XII wrote his ENCYCLICAL LETTER ON THE MYSTICAL BODY OF CHRIST (*No. 42*) on 29 June 1943. This major document is, perhaps, the basic synthesis of his over-all outline of the Chris-tian way of life. In this letter traditional doctrine is assembled and pre-sented to modern man as a summary of the nature of the Church as the Mystical Body of Christ, and its relation to Jesus Christ, founder of and sustainer of His society in the world. With such an appreciation of the true nature of the Church, Pius XII believed, man could go forward to deepen supernatural life in all areas. The liturgical movement begun in the previ-ous century was now officially recognized anew by Pius XII. He advanced it through drastic reforms and changes which were aimed at bringing peo-ple in contact with the divine mystery in the Church, the actual reality of the sacramental world. Modern man cannot get to the heart of the prob-lems of the world or the task of Christianity without realizing that he can-not live a complete life until he lives in the world of the sacraments. Here is the meeting point of the world of the resurrection with the very world where all men must live, suffer, and die. Louis Bouyer succinctly points out this purpose when he says:

. . . For the divine Mystery to dominate the world and so to redeem man who is in it, does not mean simply that some or other clerical politics are successful, or that some bargain is made with a state for a convenient arrangement of the affairs of the Church, nor even that some large segment of the population is persuaded to acknowledge the value of Christianity to some lesser or greater extent. The divine Mystery is to dominate the world and to redeem the men who are in it by taking the world as it is, filled with sin and sufferings and death, by making sin into a starting-point for penitence, and by making of suffering and death the authentic way of the Cross of Jesus himself.

38. *Pope Benedict XV: Encyclical Letter, "Maximum Illud," on Missions and a Native Clergy, 30 November 1919*

From *The Catholic Mind,* XVIII (8 May 1920), 167-181. Reprinted with Permission from *America,* The National Catholic Weekly Review.

THE great and sublime mission which our Lord Jesus Christ, just before re-turning to the Father, entrusted to his disciples in these words, "Go into the whole world and preach the Gospel to every creature," was certainly not to terminate with the death of the apos-tles, but to endure through the medium of their successors until the end of time, that is, as long as there should be men to be saved by the teaching of the truth. And in fact since that day when they "went forth and preached everywhere," so that "their sound hath gone forth into all the earth and their words unto the ends of the world," the holy Church of God, remembering the divine command, has never ceased through the centuries to send out continually heralds and ministers of the divine Word to announce the tidings of eternal salvation brought to the human race by Jesus Christ.

Wherefore, during the first three centuries of Christianity, when the fury of the persecutions let loose from hell seemed as if it would stifle the growing Church in blood, the Gospel was proclaimed and resounded to the extreme confines of the Roman empire. And when peace and liberty were then given to the Church, very great was the progress that she made in the apostolate throughout the whole world, especially by the aid of men distinguished for zeal and sanctity. Gregory the Illuminator enlightened Armenia with the light of the Gospel; Victorinus, Styria; Frumentius, Ethiopia; Patrick made a conquest of the Irish for the faith; Augustine of the English; Columba and Palladius of the Scots; then Clement Willebrod, the first Bishop of Utrecht, evangelized Holland; Boniface and Ansgar brought to the Church of Jesus Christ the peoples of Germany, and Cyril and Methodius the Slavs. Extending still further the scope of the apostolate, William de Rubruck penetrated with the torch of the Gospel among the Mongolians; Blessed Gregory the Tenth sent missionaries to China, and the sons of St. Francis soon afterwards established a flourishing Christian Church, which was subsequently destroyed by persecution. When the New World was discovered, a crowd of apostolic men, amongst whom was prominent the noble figure of Bartholomew Las Casas, the glory of the distinguished Dominican Order, devoted themselves to the defense and the conversion of the poor natives; while St. Francis Xavier, worthy in

truth to be compared to the apostles, after having worked so energetically in India and Japan for the glory of God and the salvation of souls, died on the borders of China, towards which he had been making, as if opening up by his death the way for a new evangelization of those immense regions, where members of so many distinguished religious orders and missionary congregations, eager to propagate the faith, were to exercise the apostolate amidst many vicissitudes. Finally, Australia, the latest discovered continent, and the interior of Africa, recently explored with great boldness and persistence, received messengers of the Christian faith, and now there is no island in the vast Pacific Ocean so remote that it has not experienced the zealous activity of our missionaries, amongst whom have been many who, whilst endeavoring to secure the salvation of their brethren, following the example of the apostles, reached the highest degree of sanctity, and not a few who, as martyrs, sealed their apostolate with the shedding of their blood.

Considering, then, the numerous and heavy labors undertaken by our brethren for the propagation of the faith, all their efforts, the proofs of their undaunted courage, we may well wonder at the numberless heathen who are still sitting in the shadows of death, for, according to recent statistics, their number amounts to a thousand million.

Taking therefore compassion on the sad fate of this multitude of souls, and as it has always been our nearest duty to extend to them the benefits of divine redemption, it is also with glad and grateful feelings that we watch the movement, inspired by the Holy Ghost, taking place throughout the Catholic world, for promoting and developing the missions. It is therefore to urge on and further this movement —a duty in keeping with our office and our dearest wishes—that after fervently imploring the Lord for light and assistance, we address to you, Venerable Brethren, this letter to exhort you, your clergy and your flocks, and to remind you how you can best serve this important cause.

This letter is first of all addressed to those who, either as bishops, apostolic vicars or prefects, have been placed at the head of the missions: as it is their first and direct care to propagate the faith, it is in them that the Church places her main hopes for expansion. We know their apostolic zeal, we know their difficulties and trials, chiefly these last years, in their efforts not only to remain at their posts, but also to extend the kingdom of God. It is because we know their loyalty to, and their love for, the Apostolic See, that we express our feelings to them as a father does to his sons. Let them, therefore, further the best interests of their priests and other assistants, by word and deed, encourage and urge them to better things. Whoever works in the Lord's vineyard, in whatever capacity, should be made to feel that the mission is ruled by a father, watchful, diligent and full of charity, keenly interested in all and everything, rejoicing in their success, sympathetic in their trials, encouraging and helpful in their good efforts and undertakings, and looking upon everything that concerns them as concerning himself. The condition and fate of the missions depend on their government, and the worst that could befall them would be to be ruled by men either incapable or unfit for the task. Whoever leaves his country, his nearest and dearest to propagate the Christian name, often exposes himself to long and dangerous journeys, joyfully keen on suffering the greatest trials to gather in a harvest of souls to Christ. If such men come under diligent rulers, whose prudence and charity they may benefit by in all things, their works will, no doubt, bear fruit;

if otherwise, it is much to be feared, that growing gradually tired of work and discomforts, they will finally give way to discouragement and disgust.

Then again, the first care of one who is at the head of a mission, is to extend the work and bring it to completion. For, as the whole country which lies within the limits of his mission is entrusted to his care, he must seek to work out the salvation of all those who inhabit that country. Hence when he has converted a few thousand out of an extensive population, he should not draw the line there and rest contented. He must, no doubt, foster, bring up and protect those whom Jesus Christ has begotten, nor should he allow them to drift and perish. But let him not imagine that he has done his duty, unless he strives with all his strength and without flagging to bring Christian truth and life within the reach of all the others, whose number is infinitely greater. In order then that the preaching of the Gospel should come within every one's hearing more successfully and quickly, he will find it useful to found other mission stations and centers, which will grow into so many seats of new vicariates and prefectures into which the same mission should be divided as soon as opportunities allow.

Here we must give due praise to all those apostolic vicars, whoever lay new foundations for the future kingdom of God in the way we have outlined: and when for this purpose they lacked a supply of men belonging to their own order, they never hesitated to call in and accept the assistance of other religious institutions.

On the other hand, how reprehensible would be the conduct of one who should look upon that portion of the Lord's field which was assigned to him, as his own property, which no one else would dare to touch. How severe would God's justice not be on him, chiefly if —as has happened too often—a small number of Christians were lost in the midst of a great number of heathen, and that he should refuse to accept proffered assistance to instruct them, though he and his clergy are unable to cope with the work. The head of a Catholic mission, for whom God's glory and the salvation of souls are nearest to his heart, calls in assistants if need be from everywhere to help him in his holy task, not caring whether they belong to another nation or to a different religious order as long as Christ be preached. Not only does he make use of men, but of nuns as well, for his schools, orphanages, hospitals, hostels and other charitable institutions, whom he knows are, with God's help, endowed with an extraordinary power to extend our faith.

For all this an efficient head of a mission does not lock himself up within his own limits, as though any other interests outside these were foreign to him; but under the impulse of Christ's charity, whose glory is his dearest interest, he tries to keep in touch and foster friendship with his neighboring colleagues. As a matter of fact, there are many interests common to the whole country which obviously can only be negotiated in common. Besides this it would be to the greatest profit of the missions were the various heads to gather at stated times for discussion and mutual encouragement.

Lastly, the main care of those who rule the missions should be to raise and train a clergy from amidst the nations among which they dwell, for on this are founded the best hopes for the Church of the future. Linked to his compatriots as he is by the bonds of origin, character, feelings and inclinations, the indigenous priest possesses extraordinary facilities for introducing the faith to their minds, and is endowed with powers of persuasion far superior to those of any other man. It thus frequently happens that he has access to where a foreign priest could not set foot.

But to obtain the expected results it is absolutely necessary to mold and build up an indigenous clergy in a way that is satisfactory. A raw and unfinished preparation, such as will allow one to be ordained, will not do by any means; but the training should be full, adequate in extent of studies and length of years, such as is given to priests of civilized nations. Neither should the indigenous priest be reared for the sole purpose of assisting foreign missionaries in subordinate ministry, but he must be fitted for his divine task, and rendered able one day to undertake with credit the administration of his own people. Indeed, as the Catholic Church of God is foreign to no nation, so should every nation yield its own sacred ministers to follow them as teachers of the divine law and spiritual leaders.

Wherever, therefore, there exists an indigenous clergy, adequate in numbers and in training, and worthy of its vocation, there the missionary's work must be considered brought to a happy close; there the Church is founded. And if ever persecution threatened her existence, her roots and foundations would have struck too deep to give any chance of success to hostile attacks. The Apostolic See has always urged the heads of the missions to look upon this grave duty with the care it deserves and to carry it out diligently: and of this the colleges recently erected in Rome to train priests of foreign nations, chiefly to the Oriental rite, afford clear evidence. Yet, notwithstanding, the Roman Pontiff's insistence, it is sad to think that there are still countries where the Catholic faith has been preached for several centuries, but where you will find no indigenous clergy, except of an inferior kind; sad to think that there are nations, who have fully seen the light of the Gospel, have reached such a degree of civilization as to possess men distinguished in every department of secular knowledge; who for many centuries have come under the salutary influence of the Gospel and the Church, and have yet been able to yield neither bishops to rule them, nor priests to direct them. Therefore, to all appearances, the methods used in various places to rear a clergy for the missions, have up to now been lame and faulty.

In order to remove this inconvenience, we order the Sacred Congregation of the Propagation of the Faith to establish wherever there is need, seminaries for the benefit of each country and several dioceses simultaneously, or to see to their foundation or to their proper management; and we enjoin on the Congregation to be particularly careful to watch the growth of the new clergy in vicariates and other missions.

And now we address you, beloved sons, tillers of the Lord's vineyard, in whose hands are directly placed the salvation of souls and the propagation of Christian wisdom. From the outset ever hold before your eyes the excellence and greatness of the dignity which informs our work. It is a divine task and one infinitely remote from the meanness of human interests, to light the torch to those sitting in the shadows of death, and open the gate of heaven to those who rush to their destruction. Holding therefore that these words of the Lord are addressed to each one of you: "Forget your people and your father's house," remember then that you are not to propagate the kingdom of men, but that of Christ; that you are not to enroll citizens into any country of this world, but that of the next. It would be regrettable indeed were any of the missionaries to be so forgetful of their dignity as to think more of their earthly than of their heavenly country, and were too much bent upon extending its earthly glory and power. This would indeed be a plague most deadly to their apostleship, which would kill in the preacher of the Gospel every activity for the love of souls, and would undermine his authority among the public. However barbarous and savage they be, men pretty easily understand what it is that the missionary expects from them, and they are very shrewd in detecting whether any of his expectations be at variance with their own spiritual advantage. Suppose him then to be in any way preoccupied in worldly interests, and instead of acting in everything like an apostolic man, to appear to further the interests of his own country, people will at once suspect his intentions, and may be led to believe that the Christian religion is the exclusive property of some foreign nation; that adhesion to this religion implies submission to a foreign country and the loss of one's own national dignity.

Some of the mission accounts, which have in recent years begun to spread, are very painful reading, as one finds there the anxiety not so much to extend the kingdom of God as to increase the power of the missionary's own country. We are surprised it does not occur to the writers to what extent the mind of the heathen is in danger of being thus repelled from religion. Not in this way does the Catholic missionary act, who is worthy of the name; but bearing perpetually in mind that he is the ambassador, not of his own country, but of Christ, he should so comport himself that everyone can recognize in him a minister of a religion which embraces all men that adore God in spirit and truth, is a stranger to no nation, and "where there is neither Gentile nor Jew, circumcision nor uncircumcision, Barbarian nor Scythian, bond nor free. But Christ is all and in all." Another danger which the missionary must carefully guard against is to seek no other profits but those of souls. But of this we need not say more. For how is one to seek only the glory of God as he should, and be ready to sacrifice his goods and his life to further that glory by calling others to wisdom, if one is actuated by the desire of lucre? Moreover, such a man would lose much of his authority over the Gentiles chiefly, as is natural, if the desire of acquisition should have degenerated into the vice of avarice; there is no stain more contemptible in the eyes of men and more unworthy of the kingdom of God. The good preacher of the Gospel will therefore follow in this matter also the Apostle of the Gentiles, who exhorted Timothy, though not him alone: "Having food and wherewith to be covered, with these we are content"; and the Apostle sometimes carried his love of abstention so far as to support himself with his own work, occupied as he was with the care of onerous duties.

It is understood that before undertaking his apostolic work, the missionary must undergo a thorough training, though it be sometimes objected that there is no need of so much learning for one who has to announce Christ to uncivilized nations. It is true that spiritual accomplishments are better adapted to the work of the salvation of souls than any literary equipment; yet if any one should be lacking in this he will often find that his deficiency is a hindrance to the successful exercise of his holy ministry. He is often without a library and far from learned men whom he could consult, yet he must answer questions, settle objections against the faith, and elucidate difficulties of an abstruse nature. The greater the misisonary's erudition, the greater the esteem in which he will be held, chiefly if he dwells among a nation which values mental accomplishments. In all this it would be too regrettable if the ministers of truth were overtaken by the ministers of error.

Hence, whilst ecclesiastical students, whom God should call, are trained for their apostolical expeditions, they must by all means be initiated into every department of knowledge, profane as well as sacred. This is what we wish to be done, as it behooves, in the Pontifical College of Urban for the Propagation of the Faith; and we order that the college should organize its own special staff for the teaching of the science of the missions.

One of the chief items of the missionary's equipment is evidently the language of the people to whose salvation he is destined to devote himself. He should not rest satisfied with a superficial knowledge, but it should be thorough enough for a fluent and elegant command. The missionary is at the service of all, the uneducated as well as the learned, and he ought to know what power a perfect command of the language gives to gain a sympathetic hearing from a crowd. Above all, a diligent missionary will not leave the duty of explaining the Christian doctrine to his catechist, but he must reserve to himself this department, not only as his own, but as the most important portion of his task; for no other reason was he sent by God but to preach the Gospel. He will sometimes be called upon, as the ambassador and interpreter of our holy religion, to approach influential men, or to address an educated body: how will he then preserve his dignity, if he cannot express himself in their own native language? This is what we have had particularly in view in founding a special house of studies in Rome for the spread of the Catholic name in the East, so that those who are preparing themselves for the apostolate in those countries may receive a serious grounding in the knowledge of Oriental languages and customs. As this institute seems to us to offer exceptional opportunities, we hasten to exhort all the superiors of religious orders whose work lies in the East to send there their recruits for the mission, so that they may avail themselves of its training.

But to one who wishes to qualify himself for apostolic work, there is one thing he must acquire before everything else, as being of the highest importance, it is, as we have said, sanctity of life. For whoever preaches God must be a man of God; who preaches hatred of sin must himself hate sin. It is chiefly among the Gentiles, who are led by sense more than by reason, that preaching by deeds is more efficient than by words. Granted, therefore, that the missionary be endowed with every quality of head and heart, versed in sciences, accomplished in every department of culture; if his accomplishments are not supported by innocence of life, they will be powerless instruments for the conversion of the people, nay more, they may become harmful to himself and to others.

Let him therefore be an example of humility, obedience, chastity, chiefly of piety, prayer and constant union with God, before whom he must fervently plead for the souls. The better united he is with God, the greater will be his share in Divine grace and assistance. Let him heed the Apostle's counsel: "Put on therefore, as the elect of God, holy and beloved, the bowels of mercy, benignity, humility, modesty, patience." It is by these virtues that truth finds an easy and straight access to the souls, and that all obstacles are removed; there is no obstinacy of will that can resist them. Hence a missionary, who like Jesus Christ is burning with charity and who is ready to number among the sons of God the most backward Gentiles as the children of redemption by the divine blood, is neither irritated by their roughness, nor is he roused by their moral perversity; he neither despises nor scorns them; he does not treat them harshly or bitterly, but he

will strive to attract them by all the good offices of Christian charity, to draw them all into the embrace of Christ, the good pastor. Holy Scripture gives on this subject food for meditation: "O how good and sweet is your spirit, O Lord, in all things! And therefore you chastise them that err, by little and little: and admonish them, and speak to them concerning the things wherin they offend, that leaving their wickedness, they may believe in you, O Lord. . . . But you, being master of power, judge with tranquility." What difficulties, annoyances and trials could make such an ambassador of Christ swerve from his resolve? None whatever: dear to God as must be one who has set himself such a sublime task, he will bravely face all hardships and difficulties, work, insults, poverty, hunger and even death however cruel, as long as he can snatch a soul from the mouth of hell.

Thus resolved and inspired, following in the footsteps of Christ the Lord and the apostles, the missionary will confidently buckle to his task, placing however the full measure of his confidence in God. It is as we have said, a work altogether divine to propagate Christian wisdom, for God alone can pierce through to the soul, to light up the mind with the glare of truth, warm the will in the flame of virtue, and endow man with the strength to follow and obey what he knows to be the good and the true. That is why, unless God stands by his minister, his efforts are vain. Let him nevertheless strain every nerve to carry out his resolve, relying on the assistance of divine grace, which never fails him who prays.

Here we must not omit to mention the women, who ever since the birth of the Christian religion, have lent their valuable assistance and given unstinted service to the preachers of the Gospel. Worthy of special mention and praise are those virgins who have consecrated themselves to God and gone to the missions in great numbers to devote themselves to the education of children, and to numerous works of mercy and charity; we wish that this commendation of their services may stir up their courage and enthusiasm in the service of holy Church. Let them, however, be convinced that the more they strive towards spiritual perfection, so much the more will their work yield abundance of results.

It is gratifying to address all those who by a special favor of the merciful God are in possession of the true faith, and share in its innumerable benefits. They should first of all consider by what sacred obligations they are bound to lend their support to the missions among infidels. "For [God] gave to every one of them commandment concerning his neighbor," which commandment is all the more urgent, as our neighbor is under a greater necessity. Who in fact stands in greater need of our brotherly assistance than the Gentile races which, in ignorance of God, are enslaved to blind and unbridled instincts, and live under the awful servitude of the evil one? Whoever therefore contributes, as far as in him lies, to enlighten them, chiefly by helping the missionaries, performs his duty in a work of the greatest moment, and acquits himself, in a manner most acceptable, of the debt of gratitude he owes to God for the grace of his own Faith.

Support can be given to the missions in three different ways, each answering the persistent requests of the missionaries themselves. The first, which is within everybody's reach, is to invoke God's protection. Again and again have we said that missionary undertakings are dry and barren, unless fecundated by divine grace, on St. Paul's own testimony: "I have planted, Apollo watered: but God gave the increase." To the acquisition of this grace there is but one way open, persevering and humble prayer, for as our Lord says: "Concerning anything whatsoever they shall ask, it shall be done to them by my Father." If ever such prayers remain unanswered, it cannot be so in this cause, than which there is none more sublime and more agreeable to God. As Moses, standing on the hill, raised his arms to secure divine assistance to the Israelites, battling with Amalec, so must all Christians give the assistance of their fervent prayers to the preachers of the Gospel exerting themselves in the Lord's vineyard. As the Apostleship of Prayer has been founded particularly for the better performance of this duty, we urgently recommend it to all the faithful, and with that none should fail to associate himself, all striving to take their share in the apostolic work if not by material assistance at least by their moral support.

Then, again, we must remedy the scarcity of missionaries. Great as it was, it has become appalling during the war, so much so that many portions of the Lord's vineyard have lost their laborers. It is for this that we make a special appeal, Venerable Brethren, to your devoted activities. You will do a deed most consonant with your love for your religion, if among your clergy and in your diocesan seminary, you carefully nurse the seeds of apostleship which you may discover in them. Do not be misled by appearances or moved by earthly reasons, as though the gift to the foreign missions were the loss to your diocese. Instead of one priest you might send abroad God will raise several priests to do useful work at home.

As to those who rule religious orders and congregations devoted to the missions, we pray and request them to destine to such an important work none but the choicest among their subjects, those who stand foremost for the innocence of their lives, the fervor of their piety and their zeal for souls. Then again when superiors know that their missionaries have successfully accomplished their task and converted some nation from unhallowed superstition to the Christian faith, and have founded there a church with sufficient prospects, they should transfer them, as Christ's forlorn hope, to some other nation to snatch it from Satan's grasp, willingly leaving to others whatever they have acquired for Christ, that they may carry on their work and improve it. Having in this way gathered, so to say, a rich harvest of souls, they will receive rich rewards of divine goodness for the institutions to which they belong.

Lastly, abundant resources are needed to keep up the missions, and their needs have greatly increased since the war by the loss of so many schools, hospitals, hostels and other free sources of income. We here appeal to all the faithful to exercise their liberality according to their means. For "he that has the substance of this world and shall see his brother in need and shall shut up his bowels from him: how doth the charity of God abide in him?" Thus speaks John the Apostle about those who suffer from material want. But how much more sacred becomes the obligation of the law of charity in this matter, where it is a question not only of relieving the poverty, destitution and other miseries of an infinite multitude of men, but also and chiefly of reconquering from Satan's proud dominion to the liberty of the children of God an incalculable number of souls. Hence, we wish Catholics liberally to assist those holy works organized for the support of the missions.

The first is known as the Propagation of Faith, so often praised by our predecessors; and to increase its usefulness in future, we order the Sacred Congregation to devote special atten-

tion to the propagation of the Christian faith. It must supply great resources to support missions already founded and those about to be established, but we are confident that the Catholic world will not allow its own to suffer from want in the dissemination of truth, when others are in abundance who work for the dissemination of error.

The second work we strongly recommend is that of the Holy Childhood, whose task it is to see that baptism be administered to the dying children of the faithful. This work is the more commendable, as it is open to the membership of children, who may thus learn to appreciate the gift of faith and to contribute their help to confer it on others. Neither must we omit to mention the Work of St. Peter which provides for the education and the upkeep of the indigenous clergy of the missions. We wish to call your careful attention to the regulation of our predecessor, Leo XIII, who stipulated that on the Feast of the Epiphany a collection should be made in all the churches of the world "to redeem African slaves" and that the collection should be sent to the Sacred Council of the Propagation of the Faith.

But that our wishes may be carried out with better security and success, you absolutely must, Venerable Brethren, direct, so to say, the training of your clergy towards the object of the missions. The faithful, as a rule, are willing and love to support apostolic men; but you must make a wise use of this inclination, for the great benefit of the missions. Know therefore it is our wish that in all Catholic dioceses of the world there be founded what we would call a Clerical Association of the Missions, to be placed under the authority of the Sacred Congregation of the Propagation of Faith to which we have given all necessary authority. Recently founded in Italy, it has rapidly spread to other countries; and as it has flourished with our support, we have munificently endowed it with pontifical indulgences. And for good reasons, for under its influence the activities of the clergy are excellently directed, not only to the work of inspiring the faithful with a zeal for souls, but also to carry on the various institutions which the Apostolic See has patronized for the benefit of the missions.

This is, Venerable Brethren, what we felt compelled to write to you about the propagation of the Catholic faith throughout the world. If, then, everyone acquits himself of his task, as it behooves him, the missionaries abroad and the faithful at home, we may cherish the fond hope of seeing the sacred missions reviving from the wounds and the ruin of the war. While the Lord's voice urges us as it once urged Peter: "Launch out into the deep," the fire of paternal charity presses us to drive into the Lord's embrace innumerable men. The Church is ever fed and strengthened by the Spirit of God; and the efforts of those apostolic men who have labored and are still laboring for her extension, cannot be without their fruits. Roused by their example many will henceforth arise who, supported by the piety and the munificence of the faithful, will gather unto Christ a cheerful harvest of souls. May the great Mother of God, the queen of the apostles, bless our common wishes by obtaining for the preachers of the Gospel the graces of the Holy Ghost. . . .

39. *Instruction of the Sacred Congregation of the Propagation of the Faith on "Chinese Rites," 8 December 1939*

From *Acta Apostolicae Sedis*, XXXII (1940), 24–26. Trans. by the Rev. Gregory Roettger, O.S.B.

IT HAS become increasingly evident that in the Far East certain ceremonies, which were originally connected with pagan religious worship, have now become nothing more than civil acts of reverence for the ancestors or a demonstration of love of one's country or courtesy towards one's neighbors.

For this reason the Sacred Congregation of the Propaganda had given instructions, with the approval of Pope Pius XI, and in accord with canon 22, to the Ordinaries of Manchuria and Japan in the years 1935 and 1936, adapting the conduct of the missionaries to the changed conditions.

Recently, on December 4, the eminent heads of this same Sacred Congregation met and discussed whether in other regions where the passage of time had effected similar changes of circumstances a like policy should be adopted.

After having carefully weighed all the evidence for and against and having asked the advice of prudent and experienced authorities, the eminent fathers have determined the following:

1. The Chinese government has repeatedly and openly declared that all are free to follow whatever religion they choose, and that it has no intention to make laws or issue ordinances about matters of religion. Wherefore, the ceremonies which are performed or prescribed by the public authorities in honor of Confucius are done not with the intention of giving him religious worship, but only to perpetuate the memory of this famous man and to respect the cultural traditions of the forefathers. It is, therefore, licit for

Catholics to take part in the acts of honor that are done before an image or a tablet of Confucius at Confucian monuments and in the schools.

2. For the same reason it is licit to place a picture or tablet of Confucius in the Catholic schools, especially when the authorities demand it, and to salute it with a head bow. If scandal is to be feared, the proper intention of the Catholics should be explained.

3. It may be tolerated that Catholic magistrates and pupils be present at public ceremonies which have the appearance of superstitious acts but at which they have been ordered to assist, provided that in accordance with canon 1258 they remain passive and exhibit only those signs of reverence which can justly be considered as mere civil honor.

4. Bowing of the head and other civil observances before the dead or their images and even before tablets bearing their name are to be considered licit and good.

The eminent heads also discussed the matter of the oath regarding Chinese rites which had been prescribed by Pope Benedict XIV in the Consti-

tution *Ex quo singulari* of 11 July 1742, which bound all missionaries in China and adjacent countries. Since such an oath is not in full accord with recent norms of action set down by the sacred congregation, since such an oath as an instrument of discipline seems superfluous in our times, since the heated controversies of former times over Chinese rites have died down, and finally since missionaries and other priests have no need for such a means to prompt their filial obedience to the Holy See, it has been decided that this oath need no longer be taken in China or in any other country in which it was in customary use. The precepts of this same pope which have not been changed by the recent instructions of the Holy See remain in force, especially the one forbidding disputations about the Chinese rites.

These opinions of the Eminent Fathers were presented to His Holiness, Pope Pius XII, by the undersigned cardinal prefect of the Sacred Congregation for the Propagation of the Faith [Pietro Cardinal Fumasoni-Biondi] in an audience of 7 December 1939. His Holiness deigned to approve and ratify them.

40. *Pope Pius XI: Encyclical Letter,*
"Non Abbiamo Bisogno,"
In Defense of Catholic Action, 29 June 1931

From *Church and State Through the Centuries*, trans. and ed. by Sidney Z. Ehler and John B. Morrall (Westminster, Maryland: The Newman Press, 1954), pp. 463-484.

. . . On several occasions, Venerable Brethren, in the most solemn and explicit manner and assuming entire responsibility for what we were saying, we have already protested against the campaign of false and unjust accusations which preceded the disbanding of the associations of the young people

and of the university students affiliated to Catholic Action. It was a disbanding which was carried out in such a way and by such methods as to give the impression that action was being taken against a vast and dangerous organization of criminals, although the young men and young women involved are certainly some of the best among the good, concerning whom we are happy and paternally proud to pay tribute still once more. It is noteworthy that even among the officers of the law charged to carry out these orders of suppression, there were many who were ill at ease and showed by their expressions and courtesies that they were almost asking pardon for obeying peremptory orders.

But, in sad contrast with the manner of acting of these officials, how many acts of brutality and of violence there have been, even to the striking of blows and the drawing of blood! How many insults in the press, how many injurious words and acts against things and persons not excluding ourself, have preceded, accompanied, and followed the carrying into effect of this lightning-like police order which in many instances, either through ignorance or malicious zeal, was extended to include associations and organizations not contemplated in the superior orders, such as the oratories of the little ones and the sodalities of the Children of Mary. And all this sad accompaniment of irreverences and of violences took place in the presence of and with participation of members of a political party, some of whom were in uniform, and were carried into effect with such a unison of action throughout all Italy and with such a passive acquiescence on the part of the civil authorities and the police as to make one necessarily suspect that some supreme authority had issued an instruction. It is easy to admit, and it was equally easy to have foreseen that the limits of these directions could and would have, almost necessarily, been exceeded. We must needs refer to these painful and distasteful things, because there has been an attempt made to have the public and the world at large believe that the disbanding of these associations which are so dear to us took place without

incidents and almost as if it were a normal proceeding.

But there have been other attacks on truth and justice on a larger scale. The inventions, falsehoods, and real calumnies diffused by the hostile press of the party, the only press which is free to say and to dare to say anything and is often ordered or almost ordered what it must say, were largely summarized in a message which was cautiously characterized as unofficial and yet was broadcast to the general public by the most powerful means of diffusion which exist at present.

The history of the documents prepared not in the service of truth, but in contempt of truth and of justice is a long and sad story. But we must affirm, with deep dismay, that in our many years of active life as librarian we have rarely seen an article so tendentious and so contrary to truth and justice in its references to this Holy See, to Italian Catholic Action, and particularly to the associations which have been so harshly treated. If we should be silent and if we should not contradict these things—that is to say if we should permit them to be believed —we should be much more unworthy than we already are to occupy this august apostolic chair; we should be unworthy of the filial and generous devotion of our dear children of Catholic Action, and especially of those dear sons and dear daughters—and, thanks be to God, they are numerous—who, because of religious loyalty to our invitations and directions, have suffered so much and are still suffering, thereby the more greatly honoring the school in which they have been reared and honoring also their divine Master and his unworthy vicar. They have borne such glorious witness by their Christian conduct, even in the face of threats and of violence, that there is no doubt on which side real dignity of character, true strength of mind, real courage, and education are displayed.

We shall try to be as brief as possible in correcting the facile assertions of the above mentioned wireless message, and we say "facile" in order not to be obliged to say impudent. Its authors imagined that the majority of the public would have no possibility of controlling its accuracy. We shall be brief also, because many times, especially of late, we have spoken on questions which now come up again, and our many words have reached you, Venerable Brethren, and through you they have reached also our dear children in Jesus Christ, as we trust also our words will reach them in this present letter.

Among other things, the above mentioned [wireless] message stated that the revelations of the hostile press of the [Fascist] party had been almost completely confirmed, at least in substance, by the *Osservatore Romano* itself. The truth is that the *Osservatore Romano* has, time after time, proved that the so-called revelations were either fabrications, or at least false in their interpretations of simple facts. It is sufficient to read without bad faith and with the modest capacity to understand.

The message further stated that it was ridiculous to try to make the Holy See appear as a victim in a country where thousands of travellers can testify to the respect shown to priests, prelates, the Church and religious functions. Yes, Venerable Brethren, the attempt unfortunately would be ridiculous, just as it would be ridiculous to break through an open door; because unhappily thousands of visitors who always abound in Italy and in Rome have sadly observed the irreverences, oftentimes of an impious and blasphemous character, and the acts of violence and vandalism committed against places, things, and persons throughout the country and in our very episcopal city; acts which have been repeatedly deplored by us after we had had sure and precise information about them.

The message denounces the "black ingratitude" of the priests, who are against the party which has been, so the message says, the guarantee of religious liberty throughout all Italy. The clergy, the bishops, and this Holy See have never failed to acknowledge everything that has been done during these years for the benefit and advantage of religion; indeed, they have on many occasions expressed their genuine and sincere appreciation. But we and the bishops and the clergy and all the faithful—in fact all citizens desirous of peace and order—have worried and suffered and are worrying and suffering in the presence of the systematic campaign all too quickly begun against the most reasonable and precious liberties of religion and of consciences such as were the attacks on Catholic Action and its different associations, especially those of the young. These attacks had their culmination in the police measures taken against the organizations in the manner to which we have already alluded. They were attacks and measures such as to lead one seriously to doubt whether the former benevolences and favors were indeed actuated by a sincere love and zeal for religion, or whether they were not rather due to pure calculation and to an ultimate goal of domination. And if the question of ingratitude is to be considered, it should be rather the ingratitude now shown towards the Holy See by a party and by a régime which, in the opinion of the whole world, from the fact of establishing friendly relations with the Holy See, both gained a prestige and a credit in the country and outside it, which some people deemed the favors on our part too great, and the trust and confidence which we reposed too full.

The police measures having been put into extreme effect with their accompaniments and consequences of acts of violence and of irreverence— acts which were unfortunately acquiesced in and connived at by the guardians of public order—we suspended the mission of our cardinal legate to the centenary celebration in Padua as well as the festive processions in Rome and in Italy. Such a decision was clearly within our competence, and we saw such grave and urgent reasons for it that it became a duty, although we were aware that this action would require heavy sacrifices on the part of the good people, and would cause perhaps a greater pain to ourself than to any other.

We know what happened in those places where our instructions did not arrive in time. "With the participation of the authorities," as the message reveals, some processions took place. But those "authorities" of the government and of the party were the selfsame persons who had already assisted or were about to assist, silently and inactively, at definitely anti-Catholic and decidedly anti-religious acts— which is something the message does not say. The message, on the contrary, asserts that there were local ecclesiastical authorities who considered themselves in a position "to pay no heed" to our prohibition. We do not know of any single local ecclesiastical authority who deserves the insult and the affront implied in these words. We do know, however, and we strongly deplore, the impositions, the threats, and the acts of force used or allowed to be used against local ecclesiastical authorities. We know of impious parodies of sacred processions, all of which were permitted to take place to the profound sorrow of the faithful and to the great amazement of those citizens who, de-

siring peace and order, were obliged to behold both peace and order undefended and even worse than undefended by those very persons who have both the solemn duty of defending them and a vital interest in doing so.

The message reiterates the argument which has been so often used in drawing a contrast between the situation in Italy and in other countries where the Church is really persecuted —"countries against which there have never been heard words spoken so strong as the words pronounced against Italy where religion has been restored." We have already said that we conserve, and shall still conserve a remembrance and an enduring gratitude for what has been done in Italy for the welfare of religion, a gratitude not lessened by the fact that, contemporaneously, a no less and perhaps greater benefit has accrued therefrom to the party and to the régime. We have stated and have repeated that it is not necessary, and would indeed sometimes be decidedly injurious to the ends desired, that everything should be heard and known which we and this Holy See, through our representatives and through our brothers in the episcopate, have to say and have to remonstrate wherever the interests of religion demand it, and in the measure which, in our judgment, the situation indicates, especially in those places where the Church is really persecuted.

As is well known, we have repeatedly and solemnly affirmed and protested that Catholic Action, both from its very nature and essence, "the participation and the collaboration of the laity with the apostolic hierarchy," and by our precise and categorical directions and orders is outside and above all party politics. We have also affirmed and protested our conviction that in all Italy our directions and orders have been faithfully obeyed and followed. The message says: "The assertion that Catholic Action has not had a true political character is absolutely false." On the discourtesy of these words we will not enlarge; and, if the case were not so lamentable, we should treat as ridiculous the untruthfulness and flippancy of what follows. Catholic Action, says the message, is a political party because it has banners, badges, identification cards and all the other external forms of a political party. But banners, badges, identification cards and other similar appurtenances are today the most common things in every country of the world for the most varied kind of associations and activities which have nothing and wish nothing, in common with politics, such as sports and professional organizations, civil and military clubs, commercial and industrial groups, even school-children, such as those organized exclusively in a religious way like the little ones who belong to the Crusaders of the Blessed Sacrament.

As for ourselves, we have already possessed, Venerable Brethren, information gathered long ago, as well as the results of a personal enquiry. Still, we felt it was our additional duty to secure new information, and to make new investigations. Here are the positive results. First of all, we have found out that while the Popular Party was still in existence, and before the new [Fascist] Party has asserted itself, it was decreed in 1919 that no one who had occupied a position of responsibility in the Popular Party could at the same time hold any directive office in Catholic Action. We have also found out, Venerable Brethren, that the cases of local ex-directors in the Popular Party who had subsequently become local directors in Catholic Action consist of four. We say four; and this infinitesimal number must be considered in the light of the fact that there are 250 diocesan committees, 4,000 sec-

tions of Catholic men, and more than 5,000 circles of Catholic youth. And we must add that in the four above cited instances the individuals concerned have never given any occasion for objection. Some of them are now sympathizers with the régime and the [Fascist] Party, and are favorably regarded thereby.

And we do not wish to omit mentioning another guarantee that Catholic Action abstains from politics, a reason well known to the bishops of Italy. Catholic Action has been, is, and will always be, dependent upon the episcopate, under your direction, under you who have always assigned its ecclesiastical assistants and have nominated the presidents of the diocesan committees. When the Popular Party was dissolved and passed out of existence, those who formerly belonged to Catholic Action continued to belong to Catholic Action, and they submitted themselves with perfect discipline to the fundamental law of Catholic Action, that is, abstention from every political activity. So did all those who on that occasion asked to be received as members. The régime and the party which seem to attribute such a fearful and feared strength to those who belong to the Popular Party for political reasons, should show themselves grateful to Catholic Action, which removed them precisely from that sphere and required them to make a formal pledge not to carry out any political activities, but to limit themselves to religious action.

The message asserts that Catholic Action was organized in a political way, and that it had nothing to do with "religious education and propaganda of the faith." Leaving aside the incompetent and confused manner in which the purposes of Catholic Action are thus described, all those who know and live the life of today will grant that there is no sort of initiative or activity, from the more spiritual and scientific bodies to the material and mechanical ones, which does not find the necessity of organization and of organized action. And the fact that an organization exists does not mean that very fact that the end and purpose of the organization is political.

"However," continues the message, "the strongest argument that can be used as justification for the destruction of the Catholic Circles of Youth is the defense of the state, which is no more than the simple duty of every government." There is no doubt of the solemnity and the vital importance of such a duty and of such a right. The first right is to do one's duty.

There still remain the circles of the Catholic young men, that same Catholic Youth which in the publications of the youth of the [Fascist] party and in the circular letters of the so-called leaders of the party are represented and held up to ridicule and scorn, with what sense of pedagogical responsibility, to say only this, any one may see, as a swarm of "rabbits," only fit to carry candles and to recite rosaries in sacred processions. This perhaps explains why they have been in these recent days so many times, and with such ignobility on the part of their assailants, attacked and maltreated even to the shedding of blood, and left undefended by those who could and should protect them.

If here is the strongest argument for the attempted "destruction," the word does not leave any doubt about the intentions, of the heroic and noble associations of young men of Catholic Action, you will see, Venerable Brethren, that we could and should congratulate ourselves on our position, since the incredible absurdity of this argument is very clear. But unfortunately we are obliged to repeat that "iniquity has lied to itself," and that the strongest argument for the desired destruction must

be sought in another field, for the battle which is now raging is not political, but moral and religious—essentially moral and religious.

It is necessary to close one's eyes to this truth and to set going the imagination in order to find politics where there is nothing but religion and morals, and to conclude, as does the message, that the absurd situation has been created of a strong organization at the orders of a "foreign Power, the Vatican, a thing which no government in this world would have permitted."

The documents of all centers of Catholic Action have been sequestered *en masse.* Correspondence that could be suspected to have some relation to the Associations affected, or even with those not affected, such as the oratories, continues to be intercepted and sequestered. Tell us, therefore, tell the country, tell the world, what documents and how many of them there are, which treat of politics woven and directed by Catholic Action with all this peril to the state! We venture to say that none such will be found, unless they are read and interpreted in accordance with preconceived and unfair ideas, which are contradicted fully by facts, by evidence and numberless proofs and witnesses. If and when there are any genuine documents found that are worthy of consideration, we shall be the first to take them seriously.

On the contrary, there will be found among the sequestered documents proofs and evidences literally numberless of the profound and consistent religious activity of all Catholic Action, and particularly so of the Associations of Youth and of University students.

In the presence of such facts and of such a documentation, with an eye and a hand on the reality of things, we say, as we have always said, that to accuse Italian Catholic Action of engaging in politics is a real and true calumny. The facts have demonstrated what was the real target aimed at when Catholic Action was struck, and what was the thing that was being prepared. Rarely has the fable of the wolf and the lamb been exemplified so strikingly; and history will recall it.

We, certain on the point of being concerned with and restricting ourselves to the field of religion, have never been able to believe that we could be considered as a "foreign power," especially by Catholics and by Italian Catholics. And thanks to this apostolic power which is now, unworthy though we be, entrusted by God to us, the good Catholics of all the world consider Rome as second country of each and every one of them. It is not so long ago that a statesman, who will remain certainly among the world's most celebrated men, a man neither a Catholic nor a friend of Catholicism, in a full political assembly said that he could not consider as a foreign power that authority which twenty million Germans revered, honored, and obeyed. To say then that "no government of the world would have permitted the continuance of the situation created in Italy by the existences of Catholic Action," it is necessary absolutely to ignore and to forget that in all other states of the world, as far as China, Catholic Action exists and lives, and the organization is even more highly developed than in Italy.

There is one first consideration and conclusion. From all which we have explained and still more from the events themselves as they have been evolving, it results that the so-called political activity of Catholic Action, the alleged manifest or disguised hostility of some of its partisans against the régime and the party, as well as its being also "the eventual refuge and haven of those refugees who, up to the present, have been spared" by the régime because they have sheltered under the banner of Catholic Action, and

similar accusations are nothing but a culmination of pretexts. We dare to say that even Catholic Action itself is only a pretext. That which was desired and that which was attempted is to tear away from the Church the young—all the young. So true is this, that after all the talk about Catholic Action, aim was taken only at the associations of the young. Nor were these attacks limited to associations of the young affiliated to Catholic Action. So far did this go that in many cases the grossness of the acts was recognized by the perpetrators themselves as a blunder.

This confirmation is made all the more explicit and categorical, we were almost about to say solemn and violent, by the individual who not only represents all, but who can do all, and who confirms it in official or quasi-official publications dedicated to the young, in interviews and in articles to be published abroad before they are published in Italy, and also, up to this very moment, by messages and by communications to representatives of the press.

Another reflection immediately and inevitably presents itself. No attention has been paid to our oft-repeated assurances and our protests. There has been no attention paid to your protests and assurances, Venerable Brethren, concerning the true nature of Catholic Action and its work, and concerning the sacred and inviolable rights of souls and of the Church.

We say "the sacred and inviolable rights of souls and of the Church," and this is the reflection which concerns us more than any other, being the most grave. We repeat: "The sacred and inviolable rights of souls and of the Church"; because this matter concerns the right of souls to procure for themselves the greatest spiritual good according to the teaching and under the formative work of the Church, the divinely appointed and sole mandatory of this teaching and of this work in that supernatural order which is established in the blood of the Redeemer and is necessary and obligatory for all of us if we are to share in the divine redemption. It concerns the right of souls so formed to share the treasures of the redemption with other souls, thus participating in the activities of the apostolic hierarchy.

It was in consideration of this double right of souls that we lately declared ourselves happy and proud to wage the good fight for the liberty of consciences, not indeed, as some, perhaps inadvertently, have represented us as saying, for "the liberty of conscience," which is an equivocal expression too often distorted to mean the absolute independence of conscience and therefore an absurdity in reference to a soul created and redeemed by God.

Besides, there is involved another right of the Church equally inviolable —the right to fulfill the imperative divine commission entrusted to her by her divine founder, to bring to souls, to bring to every soul, all the treasures of truth and good, doctrinal and practical, which he himself brought to the world.

And here we find ourselves confronted by a mass of authentic affirmations and no less authentic facts which reveal beyond the slightest possibility of doubt the resolve, already in great measure actually put into effect, to monopolize completely the young, from their tenderest years up to manhood and womanhood, for the exclusive advantage of a party and of a régime based on an ideology which clearly resolves itself into a true, a real pagan worship of the state—the "statolatry" which is no less in contrast with the natural rights of the family than it is in contradiction with the supernatural rights of the Church.

The Church of Jesus Christ has never contested the rights and the du-

ties of the state concerning the education of its citizens; indeed, we ourselves have recalled and proclaimed them in our recent Encyclical Letter on the Christian Education of Youth. Such rights and duties are unchallengable as long as they remain within the limits of the state's proper competence, a competence which in its turn is clearly indicated and determined by the role of the state; this role, though certainly not only bodily and material, is by its very nature limited to the natural, the terrestrial and the temporal.

The universal and divine mandate with which the Church of Jesus Christ has been incommunicably and exclusively commissioned by Jesus Christ himself, extends to the supernatural, the celestial, the eternal, and to that order of things which on the one hand is of the strictest obligation for every rational creature and which, on the other hand, must, by the very nature of things subordinate and co-ordinate to itself all else.

The Church of Jesus Christ is certainly acting within her mandate, not only when she puts into souls the first indispensable beginnings and elements of supernatural life, but also when she watches over the growth of this supernatural life according to the opportunities and the capacities, and in the ways and by the means which she deems suitable, even to the extent of preparing capable and efficient collaboration with the Apostolic Hierarchy.

It was Jesus Christ himself who laid the first foundation of Catholic Action, by choosing and educating the apostles and disciples as fellow-workers in his divine apostolate. And his example was at once followed by the first holy apostles as the sacred text itself proves.

Therefore it is an unjustifiable pretension and is, indeed, irreconcilable with the name and the profession of being a Catholic, to come to teach the Church and her head what is sufficient for the education and Christian formation of souls and for promoting, especially among the young, the application of the principles of the faith in social life. To this unjustifiable presumption is added very clear evidence of the absolute incompetence of the pretenders and their complete ignorance of the matters under discussion.

You know, Venerable Brethren, bishops of Italy, from your pastoral experience that it is a grave and disastrous error to believe and to make believe that the work of the Church done by Catholic Action and through Catholic Action is superseded and made superfluous by the religious instruction given in the schools and by the presence of chaplains in the Associations of Youth of the [Fascist] Party and of the régime. Both are certainly necessary. Without them the schools and the associations would inevitably and quickly become, by logical and psychological necessity, pagan things. Necessary therefore they are; but they are not sufficient. As a matter of fact, by such religious instruction and such ecclesiastical assistance from the chaplains, the Church of Jesus Christ can develop only a minimum of her spiritual and supernatural effectiveness, and even this minimum is attained amid surroundings and in environment which does not depend on the Church but are pre-occupied by many other kinds of teaching matters and by many other exercises in obedience to immediate superiors who are often little or not at all favorably disposed to religion, and who sometimes exercise a directly contrary influence both by their words and by the example of their lives.

A conception of the state which makes the rising generations belong to it entirely, without any exception, from the tenderest years up to adult life, cannot be reconciled by a Catholic either with Catholic doctrine or with the natural rights of the family. It is not possible for a Catholic to accept the claim that the Church and the pope must limit themselves to the external practices of religion, such as the Mass and the sacraments, and that all the rest of education belongs to the state.

The erroneous and false doctrines and maxims that we have just pointed out and deplored have cropped up many times during these last few years, and it is well known that we have never, with God's help, done any less than our apostolic duty in exposing them and in confronting them with the just claims of true Catholic doctrine, and with the inviolable rights of the Church of Jesus Christ and of the souls redeemed by his precious blood.

But notwithstanding the opinions and forecasts and suggestions which have come to us from many sources worthy of the greatest consideration, we have always refrained from formal and explicit condemnations, and have even gone so far as to believe possible and to favor compatibilities and co-operations which, to others, seemed inadmissible. We have done this because we thought, or rather we hoped in the possibility, that we had to deal only with exaggerated assertions and actions which called for no more than the censure of their individual authors, or which had come out of exceptional circumstances.

Therefore we must say, and do hereby say, that he is only a Catholic in name and by baptism, in contradiction to the obligations of that name and to the baptismal promises, who adopts and envelops a program with doctrines and maxims so opposed to the rights of the Church of Jesus Christ and of souls, and who also misrepresents, combats, and persecutes Catholic Action which, as is universally known, the Church and its head regard as very dear and precious.

You ask us, Venerable Brethren, in

view of what has taken place, what is to be thought about the formula of the oath which even little boys and girls are obliged to take, namely that they will execute orders without discussion from an authority which, as we have seen and experienced, can give orders against all truth and justice and in disregard of the rights of the Church and its souls, which are already by their very nature sacred and inviolable. Takers of this oath must swear to serve with all their strength, even to the shedding of blood, the cause of a revolution which snatches the young from the Church and from Jesus Christ, and which inculcates in its own young people hatred, violence, and irreverence without respecting, as recent occurrences have superabundantly proved, even the person of the pope.

When the question is posed in such terms, the answer from the Catholic point of view, as well as from a simple human point of view, is inevitably only one, and we, Venerable Brethren, do not wish to do otherwise than confirm the answer already given. Such an oath, as it stands, is unlawful.

It seems to us that such a means for those who have already received the membership card would be to make for themselves before God, in their own consciences, a reservation such as "Saving the laws of God and of the Church," with the firm proposal to declare also externally such a reservation if the need of it arose. Let the reservation just mentioned be included in the oath-formula. Better still, let the oath be dropped, seeing that an oath is an act of religion and that it is out of place on the membership-cards of a political party.

In everything that we have said up to the present, we have not said that we wished to condemn the [Fascist] Party as such. Our aim has been to point out and to condemn all those things in the program and in the activities of the party which have been found to be contrary to Catholic doctrine and Catholic practice, and therefore irreconcilable with the Catholic name and profession. And in doing this we have fulfilled a precise duty of our episcopal ministry towards our dear sons who are members of the party, so that their conscience may be at peace.

It is known by all who are familiar with the history of the country that anti-clericalism has had in Italy the importance and the strength conferred upon it by Masonry and Liberalism when these were the powers ruling Italy. But in our own day, on the occasion of the Lateran treaties, the unparalleled enthusiasm which united and overjoyed Italians would have left no room for anti-clericalism if it had not been evoked and encouraged on the very morrow of the treaty. During the recent occurrences, orders from high personages have switched anti-clericalism on or off, and this has been plain to all. There can be no doubt that a mere hundredth or even a thousandth part of the force used against Catholic Action will suffice to keep anti-clericalism in its place.

But other and very serious fears for the future concern us. At a meeting which was most official and most solemn, and was held immediately after these last acts were for us and for the Catholics of Italy and of all the world so sad and depressing, it was declared that "respect for the Catholic religion, and for its supreme head, is unchanged." But the respect which is "unchanged" is that same respect which we have already experienced. It is the respect which has had its expression in vastly extended and hateful police-measures, prepared in the deep silence of a conspiracy, and executed with lightning-like suddenness on the very vigil of our birthday which was the occasion of many acts of kindness and of courtesy towards us on the part of the Catholic world also. It is the respect which has expressed itself in violences and in irreverences permitted to be perpetrated without let or hindrance.

In the same context and in immediate relation with the "unchanged respect," there is an allusion to "refuges and protections" given to the still remaining opponents of the [Fascist] party, and "the directors of the 9,000 groups of Fascists in Italy" are ordered to direct their attention to this situation. But what is to be done if, as we have reason to believe, it has been decided that our Catholic young people must not meet, even silently, save at the cost of bitter punishment for their leaders?

If we have been well informed, it has been said recently that Catholic Action is now in the hands of the bishops, and that there is nothing to fear. And up to this point the statement is good, except for that phrase "nothing more," which seems to imply that hitherto there was indeed something to fear, and except also that word "now," as if before and from the beginning Catholic Action was not always essentially diocesan and dependent on the bishops, as we have above pointed out; and also for this, principally for this, we have always nourished the most certain confidence that our directions were observed. For this reason, next to the promised unfailing divine assistance, we remain, and we shall remain in the most serene confidence, even if tribulation—let us rather say the exact word—even if persecution shall continue and intensify. We know that you are, and you know yourselves that you are our brethren in the episcopate and in the apostolate. We know, and you know, too, Venerable Brethren, that you are the successors of those apostles whom St. Paul called, with words of towering sublimity, the

"Glory of Christ." You know that no mortal man, such as the head of a state or of a government, but the Holy Ghost himself has set you to rule in the Church of God.

Great also, and truly a measureless reason for hoping for the best is the immense chorus of prayers that the Church of Jesus Christ has offered up from all parts of the world to the divine founder of the Church and to his Blessed Mother for the Church's visible head, the successor of Peter, just in the same way as was done twenty centuries ago, when persecution assailed Peter himself.

In answer to prayer everything is definitely promised; and if the answer will not be the re-establishment of serene and tranquil relations, it will have its answer at any rate in Christian patience, in holy courage, in the infallible joy of suffering something with Jesus, and for Jesus, with the youth and for the youth so dear to him, until the hour hidden in the mystery of the divine heart, which will infallibly be the most opportune for the cause of truth and of good.

The Church of God, which wishes to take nothing from the state of that which belongs to the competence of the state, will cease to be asked for that which is of the Church's competence —the education and the Christian formation of youth, as this is hers, not through human favor, but by divine mandate. She must always claim it with an instance and intransigence which cannot cease or waver, because it does not come from human desire or design or from human ideas changeable in different times and places and circumstances, but from the divine and inviolable decree. And we are inspired also by faith and confidence to believe that good will undoubtedly come from the recognition of such a truth and of such a right.

Father of all the redeemed, and

vicar of that redeemer who, after having taught and commanded all to love their enemies, died pardoning those who were crucifying him, we are not and never will be the enemy of any one; nor will our true sons, those who wish to remain worthy of the name of Catholic. Yet Catholics will never be able to agree to adopt or to favor maxims or ways of thinking and of acting contrary to the rights of almighty God.

How preferable to this obstinate clash of minds and of wills would be a peaceful and tranquil union of thoughts and of sentiments. Such a union could not fail to translate itself into a fruitful cooperation of all for the true good and for the common good, and it would be rewarded by the sympathetic applause of the Catholics of all the world, instead of meeting, as at present, with universal blame and discontent.

41. *Pope Pius XII: Discourse on "The World Community,"* 6 December 1953

From *The World Community* (New York: The America Press, 1954), *passim.* Reprinted with permission from *America,* The National Catholic Weekly Review.

. . . It is not by chance that congresses are multiplying for the study of international questions, be they scientific, economic or political. The clear fact that relations between individuals of various nations and between nations themselves are growing in multiplicity and intensity makes daily more urgent a right ordering of international relations, both private and public; all the more so since this mutual drawing together is caused not only by vastly improved technological progress and by free choice but also by the more profound action of an intrinsic law of development.

This movement, then, is not to be repressed but fostered and promoted.

In this work of expansion, communities of states and peoples, whether already existing or only a goal to be achieved, have naturally a special importance. They are communities in which sovereign states, that is to say, states which are subordinate to no other state, are united into a juridical community to attain definite juridical ends.

It would give a false idea of these juridical communities to compare them to world empires of the past or of the present, in which different racial stocks, peoples and states become fused, whether they want it or not, into a single conglomeration of states.

In the present instance, however, states, remaining sovereign, freely unite into a juridical community.

In this connection, the history of the world, which shows a continuous succession of struggles for power, no doubt might make the establishment of a juridical community of free states seem almost utopian.

The conflicts of the past have too often been motivated by a desire to subjugate other nations and to extend the range of one's own power, or by the necessity of defending one's liberty and one's own independent existence.

This time, on the contrary, it is precisely the will to prevent threatening conflicts that urges men toward a supranational juridical community. Utilitarian considerations, which certainly carry considerable weight, point toward the working out of peace.

And finally, perhaps, it is precisely because of technological progress that this mingling of men of different nations has awakened the faith, implanted in the hearts and souls of individuals, in a higher community of men, willed by the Creator and rooted in the unity of their common origin, nature and final destiny.

These and other similar considerations show that advance toward establishing a community of peoples does not look, as to a unique and ultimate norm, to the will of the states, but rather to nature, to the Creator.

The right to existence, the right to respect from others and to one's good name, the right to one's own culture and national character, the right to develop oneself, the right to demand observance of international treaties, and other like rights, are exigencies of the law of nations, dictated by nature itself.

The positive law of different peoples, also indispensable in the community of states, has the office of defining more exactly the rights derived from nature and of adapting them to concrete circumstances; also of making other provisions, directed, of course, toward the common good, on the basis of a positive agreement which, once freely entered into, has binding force.

In this community of nations, then, every state becomes a part of the system of international law, and hence of natural law, which is both foundation and crown of the whole. Thus the individual nation no longer is—nor in fact was it ever—"sovereign," in the sense of being entirely without restrictions.

"Sovereignty" in the true sense means self-rule and exclusive competence concerning what has to be done and how it is to be done in regard to the affairs of a definite territory, always within the framework of international law, without however becoming dependent on the juridical system of any other state.

Every state is immediately subject to international law. States which

would lack this fullness of power, or whose independence of the power of any other state would not be guaranteed by international law, would not be sovereign.

But no state could complain about a limitation of its sovereignty if it were denied the power of acting arbitrarily and without regard for other states. Sovereignty is not a divinization of the state, or omnipotence of the state in the Hegelian sense, or after the manner of absolute juridical positivism.

There is no need to explain to you students of law how the setting up, maintenance and operation of a real community of states, especially one that would embrace all peoples, give rise to many duties and problems, some of them extremely difficult and complicated, which cannot be solved by a simple yes-or-no answer.

Such would be the question of race and origin, with their biological, psychological and social consequences; the question of language; the question of family life, with its relations, varying according to nation, between husband and wife, parents, the larger family group; the question of the equality or equivalence of rights in what regards goods, contracts and persons for the citizens of one sovereign state who either live for a short time in a foreign state or, retaining their own nationality, establish permanent residence there; the question of the right of immigration or of emigration, and other like questions.

The jurist, the statesman, the individual state, as well as the community of states should here take account of all the inborn inclinations of individuals and communities in their contracts and reciprocal relations: such as the tendency to adapt or to assimilate, often pushed even to an attempt to absorb; or contrariwise, the tendency to exclude and to destroy anything that appears incapable of assimilation; the tendency to expand, to embrace what is new, as on the contrary, the tendency to retreat and to segregate oneself; the tendency to give oneself entirely, forgetful of self, and its opposite, attachment to oneself, excluding any service of others; the lust for power, the yearning to keep others in subjection, and so on.

All these instincts, either of self-aggrandizement or of self-defense, have their roots in the natural dispositions of individuals, of peoples, of races and of communities, and in their restrictions and limitations. One never finds in them everything that is good and just. God alone, the origin of all things, possesses within Himself, by reason of His infinity, all that is good.

From what we have said, it is easy to deduce the fundamental theoretical principle for dealing with these difficulties and tendencies: within the limits of the possible and lawful, to promote everything that facilitates union and makes it more effective; to remove everything that disturbs it; to tolerate at times that which it is impossible to correct but which, on the other hand, must not be permitted to make shipwreck of the community from which a higher good is hoped for.

The difficulty rests in the application of this principle.

In this connection, we wish to treat with you who are happy to profess yourselves Catholic jurists, concerning one of the questions which arise in a community of peoples, that is the practical coexistence (*convivenza*) of Catholic with non-Catholic states.

Depending upon the religious belief of the great majority of citizens or by reason of an explicit declaration of law, peoples and member states of the international community will be divided into those that are Christian, non-Christian, indifferent to religion or con-

sciously without it, or even professedly atheist.

The interests of religion and morality will require for the whole extent of the international community a well-defined rule, which will hold for all the territory of the individual sovereign member-states of the international community. According to probability and depending on circumstances, it can be foreseen that this ruling of positive law will be thus enunciated:

Within its own territory and for its own citizens, each state will regulate religious and moral affairs by its own laws. Nevertheless, throughout the whole territory of the international community of states, the citizens of every member-state will be allowed to exercise of their own beliefs and ethical and religious practices, in so far as these do not contravene the penal laws of the state in which they are residing.

For the jurist, the statesman and the Catholic state arises here the question: can they give their consent to such a ruling when there is question of entering and remaining in an international community?

Now, in regard to religious and moral interests, a twofold question arises. The first deals with the objective truth and the obligation of conscience toward what is objectively true and good.

The second deals with the practical attitude of the international community toward the individual sovereign state and the attitude of the individual state toward the international community in what regards religion and morality.

The first question can hardly be a matter for discussion and legal ruling between the individual states and the international community, especially in the case of a plurality of different religious beliefs within the international community. On the other hand, the second question can be of extreme importance and urgency.

Now to give the right answer to the second question. Above all, it must be clearly stated that no human authority, no state, no community of states, whatever be their religious character, can give a positive command or positive authorization to teach or to do that which would be contrary to religious truth or moral good.

Such a command or such an authorization would have no obligatory power and would remain without effect. No authority may give such a command, because it is contrary to nature to oblige the spirit and the will of man to error and evil, or to consider one or the other as indifferent.

Not even God could give such a positive command or positive authorization, because it would be in contradiction to his absolute truth and sanctity.

Another question, essentially different, is this: could the norm be established in a community of states—at least in certain circumstances—that the free exercise of a belief and of a religious or moral practice which possesses validity in one of the member states, be not hindered throughout the entire territory of the community of nations by state laws or coercive measures?

In other words, the question is raised whether in these circumstances *non impedire* or toleration is permissible, and whether, consequently, positive repression is not always a duty.

We have just adduced the authority of God. Could God, although it would be possible and easy for him to repress error and moral deviation, in some cases choose the *non impedire* without contradicting his infinite perfection?

Could it be that in certain circumstances he would not give men any

mandate, would not impose any duty, and would not even communicate the right to impede or to repress what is erroneous and false? A look at things as they are gives an affirmative answer.

Reality shows that error and sin are in the world in great measure. God reprobates them, but he permits them to exist. Hence the affirmation that religious and moral error must always be impeded, when it is possible, because toleration of them is in itself immoral, is not valid absolutely and unconditionally.

Moreover, God has not given even to human authority such an absolute and universal command in matters of faith and morality. Such a command is unknown to the common convictions of mankind, to Christian conscience, to the sources of revelation and to the practice of the Church.

To omit here other scriptural texts which are adduced in support of this argument, Christ in the parable of the cockle gives the following advice: let the cockle grow in the field of the world together with the good seed in veiw of the harvest (Matt. 13, 24-30).

The duty of repressing moral and religious error cannot therefore be an ultimate norm of action. It must be subordinate to higher and more general norms, which in some circumstances permit, and even perhaps seem to indicate as the better policy toleration of error in order to promote a greater good.

Thus the two principles are clarified to which recourse must be had in concrete cases for the answer to the serious question concerning the attitude which the jurist, the statesman and the sovereign Catholic state is to adopt in consideration of the community of nations in regard to a formula of religious and moral toleration as described above.

First: that which does not correspond to truth or to the norm of morality objectively has no right to exist, to be spread or to be activated. Secondly: failure to impede this with civil laws and coercive measures can nevertheless be justified in the interests of a higher and more general good.

Before all else the Catholic statesman must judge if this condition is verified in the concrete—this is the "question of fact."

In his decision he will permit himself to be guided by weighing the dangerous consequences that stem from toleration against those from which the community of nations will be spared if the formula of toleration be accepted.

Moreover, he will be guided by the good which, according to a wise prognosis, can be derived from toleration for the international community as such, and indirectly for the member state. In that which concerns religion and morality he will also ask for the judgment of the Church.

For her, only he to whom Christ has entrusted the guidance of his whole Church is competent to speak in the last instance on such vital questions touching international life: that is, the Roman pontiff.

The institution of a community of nations, which today has been partly realized but which is striving to be established and consolidated upon a higher and more perfect level, is an ascent from the lower to the higher, that is, from a plurality of sovereign states to the greatest possible unity.

The Church of Christ has, in virtue of a mandate from her divine founder, a similar universal mission. She must draw to herself and bind together in religious unity the men of all races and of all times. But here the process is in a certain sense the contrary: she descends from the higher to the lower.

In the former case, the superior juridical unity of nations was and still is to be created. In the latter, the juri-

dical community with its universal end, its constitution, its powers and those in whom these powers are invested, are already established from the beginning, by the will and decree of Christ himself. The duty of this universal community from the outset is to incorporate all men and all races (cf. Matt. 28, 19) and thereby to bring them to the full truth and grace of Jesus Christ.

The Church, in the fulfillment of this her mission, has always been faced and is still faced in large measure by the same problems which the functioning of a community of sovereign states must overcome; only she feels them more acutely, for she is obligated to the purpose of her mission, determined by her founder himself, a purpose which penetrates to the very depths of the spirit and heart of man.

In this state of affairs conflicts are inevitable, and history shows that there have always been conflicts. There still are, and according to the words of the Lord, there will be till the end of time.

For the Church with her mission has been, and is, confronted with men and nations of marvelous culture, with others of almost incredible lack of civilization, and with all possible intermediate degrees: diversity of extraction, of language, of philosophy, of religious belief, of national aspirations and characteristics; free peoples and enslaved peoples; peoples that have never belonged to the Church and peoples that have been separated from her communion.

The Church must live among them and with them; she can never declare before anyone that she is "not interested." The mandate imposed upon her by her divine founder renders it impossible for her to follow a policy of non-interference or *laissez faire*.

She has the duty of teaching and educating in all the inflexibility of truth and goodness, and with this absolute obligation she must remain and work among men and nations that in mental outlook are completely different from each other.

Let us return now, however, to the two propositions mentioned above: and in the first place to the one which denies unconditionally everything that is religiously false and morally wrong. With regard to this point there never has been, and there is not now, in the Church any vacillation or any compromise, either in theory or in practice.

Her deportment has not changed in the course of history, nor can it change whenever or wherever, under the most diversified forms, she is confronted with the choice: either incense for idols or blood for Christ.

The place where you are now present, eternal Rome, with the remains of a greatness that was and with glorious memories of its martyrs, is the most eloquent witness to the answer of the Church. Incense was not burned before the idols, and Christian blood flowed and consecrated the ground.

But the temples of the gods lie in the cold devastation of ruins howsoever majestic; while at the tombs of the martyrs the faithful of all nations and all tongues fervently repeat the ancient creed of the apostles.

Concerning the second proposition, that is to say, concerning tolerance in determined circumstances, toleration even in cases in which one could proceed to repression, the Church—out of regard for those who in good conscience (though erroneous, but invincibly so) are of a different opinion —has been led to act and has acted with that tolerance, after she became the state Church under Constantine the Great and the other Christian emperors, always for higher and more cogent motives.

So she acts today, and also in the future she will be faced with the same necessity. In such individual cases the attitude of the Church is determined by what is demanded for safeguarding and considering the *bonum commune* on the one hand—the common good of the Church and the state in individual states; and on the other, the common good of the universal Church, the reign of God over the whole world.

In considering the "pro" and "con" for resolving the "question of fact," as well as what concerns the final and supreme judge in these matters, no other norms are valid for the Church except the norms which we have just indicated for the Catholic jurist and statesman.

The ideas we have set forth may also be useful for the Catholic jurist and statesman when, in their studies or in the exercise of their profession, they come in contact with the agreements (concordats, treaties, agreements, *modus vivendi,* etc.) which the Church (that is to say, for a long time now, the Apostolic See) has concluded and still concludes with sovereign states.

The concordats are for her an expression of the collaboration between the Church and the state. In principle, that is, in theory, she cannot approve complete separation of the two powers. The concordats, therefore, must assure to the Church a stable condition in right and in fact in the state with which they are concluded, and must guarantee to her full independence in the fulfillment of her divine mission.

It is possible that the Church and the state proclaim in a concordat their common religious conviction; but it may also happen that a concordat have, together with other purposes, that of forestalling disputes with regard to questions of principle and of removing from the very beginning possible matters of conflict.

When the Church has set her signature to a concordat, it holds for everything contained therein. But, with the mutual acknowledgment of both high contracting parties, it may not hold in the same way for everything.

It may signify an express approval, but it may also mean a simple toler-ance, according to those two principles which are the norm for the coexistence (*convivenza*) of the Church and her faithful with the civil powers and with men of another belief. . . .

42. *Pope Pius XII: Encyclical Letter, "Mystici Corporis" on the Mystical Body of Christ, 23 June 1943*

From *Mystici Corporis Christi* (New York: The Paulist Press, 1943), *passim.*

. . . That the Church is a body is frequently asserted in Sacred Scripture. "Christ," says the Apostle, "is the head of the body of the Church." If the Church is a body, it must be an unbroken unity according to those words of Paul: "Though many we are one body in Christ." But it is not enough that the body of the Church be an unbroken unity; it must also be something definite and perceptible to the senses, as our predecessor of happy memory, Leo XIII, in his Encyclical, *Satis cognitum,* asserts: "The Church is visible because she is a body." Hence they err in a matter of divine truth, who imagine the Church to be invisible, intangible, a something merely "pneumatological," as they say, by which many Christian communities, though they differ from each other in their profession of faith, are united by a bond that eludes the senses.

But a body calls also for a multiplicity of members, which are linked together in such a way as to help one another. And as in our mortal composite being when one member suffers, all other members share its pain, and the healthy members come to the assistance of those ailing; so in the Church the individual members do not live for themselves alone, but also help their fellows, and all work in mutual collaboration for their common comfort and for the more perfect building up of the whole body.

Again, as in nature a body is not formed by any haphazard grouping of members but must be constituted of organs, that is members that have not the same function and are arranged in due order; so for this reason above all the Church is called a body, that it is constituted by the coalescence of structurally united parts, and that it has a variety of members reciprocally dependent. It is thus the Apostle describes the Church when he writes: "As in one body we have many members, but all the members have not the same office: so we being many are one body in Christ, and everyone members one of another."

One must not think, however, that this ordered or "organic" structure of the Body of the Church contains only hierarchical elements and with them is complete; or, as an opposite opinion holds, that it is composed only of those who enjoy charismatic gifts—though members gifted with miraculous powers will never be lacking in the Church. That those who exercise sacred power in this body are its first and chief members, must be maintained uncompromisingly. It is through them, commissioned by the divine Redeemer himself, that Christ's apostolate as teacher, king, priest, is to endure. At the same time, when the fathers of the Church sing the praises of this Mystical Body of Christ, with its ministries, its variety of ranks, its offices, its conditions, its order, its duties, they are thinking not only of those who have received sacred orders, but of all those, too, who following the evangelical counsels pass their lives either actively among men or in the silence of the cloister, or who aim at combining the active and contemplative life according to their institute. They were thinking of those who though living in the world consecrate themselves wholeheartedly to spiritual or corporal works of mercy; as well as those who live in the state of holy matrimony. Indeed let this be clearly understood, especially in these our days: the fathers and mothers of families, and those who are spiritual parents through Baptism, and in particular those members of the laity who assist the ecclesiastical hierarchy in spreading the kingdom of the divine Redeemer, occupy an honorable, even though often lowly place in the Christian community. Under the impulse of God and with his help they can reach the peak of holiness; and such holiness, Jesus Christ has promised, will never be wanting to the Church.

Now we see how the human body is given its own means to provide for its own life, health and growth and for the same of all its members. Similarly the Savior of mankind out of his infinite goodness has provided in a marvelous way for his Mystical Body, endowing it with the sacraments; so that by so many consecutive graduated graces, as it were, its members should be supported from the cradle to life's last breath, and that the social needs of the Church might also be generously provided for. As all know, through the waters of Baptism those who are born into this world, being dead in sin, are not only born again and made members of the Church, but being stamped with a spiritual seal, they become capable and fit to receive the other sacraments. By the chrism of Confirmation, the faithful are given added strength to protect and defend the Church, their mother, and the faith she has given them. In the Sacrament of Penance a saving medicine is offered to the Church's members who have fallen into sin, not only to provide for their own health, but to remove from other members of the Mystical Body all danger of contagion or rather to afford them the tonic of virtuous example.

Nor is that enough; for in the Holy Eucharist the faithful are nourished and grow strong at the same table, and in a divine, ineffable way are brought into union with each other and with the divine head of the whole body. Finally, like a devoted mother the Church is at the bedside of those who are sick unto death; and if it be not always God's will that by the sacred anointing of the sick she restores health to this mortal body, yet she does minister supernatural medicine for wounded souls, and sends new citizens on to heaven to enjoy forever the happiness of God—new advocates assigned to her.

For the social needs of the Church, Christ has provided in a particular way by two sacraments which he instituted. Through Matrimony, when the contracting parties are ministers of grace to each other, provision is made for the external and properly regulated increase of Christian society and, what is of greater importance, for the correct religious education of the offspring, without which this Mystical Body would be in grave danger. Through Holy Orders men are set aside and consecrated to God, to offer in sacrifice the eucharistic victim, to feed the flock of the faithful with the bread of angels and the food of doctrine, to guide them in the way of God's commandments and counsels, to strengthen them with all the other supernatural helps. . . .

Only those are really to be included as members of the Church who have been baptized and profess the true faith and who have not unhappily withdrawn from body-unity or for grave faults being excluded by legitimate authority. "For in one Spirit," says the Apostle, "were we all baptized into one body, whether Jews or Gentiles, whether bond or free." As therefore in the true Christian community there is only one body, one Spirit, one Lord and one Baptism, so there can be only one faith. And so if a man refuse to hear the Church, let him be considered—so the Lord commands—as a heathen and a publican. It follows that those who are divided in faith or government cannot be living in one body such as this, and cannot be living the life of its one divine Spirit.

One must not imagine that the body of the Church, just because it bears the name of Christ, is made up during the days of its earthly pilgrimage only of members conspicuous for their holiness, or consists only of the group of those whom God has predestined to eternal happiness. It is the Savior's infinite mercy that allows place in his Mystical Body here for those whom he did not exclude from the banquet of old. For not every sin, however grave and enormous it be, is such as to sever a man automatically from the body of the Church, as does schism or heresy or apostasy. Men may lose charity and divine grace through sin and so become incapable of supernatural merit, and yet not be deprived of all life, if they hold on to faith and Christian hope, and illumined from above they are spurred on by the strong promptings of the Holy Spirit to salutary fear and by God are moved to prayer and penance for their sins. . . .

And first of all, by the death of our Redeemer, the New Testament took the place of the old law which had been abolished; then the law of Christ together with its mysteries, laws, institutions and sacred rites was ratified for the whole world in the blood of Jesus Christ. For, while our divine Savior was preaching in a restricted area— he was not sent but to the sheep that were lost of the house of Israel—the Law and the Gospel were together in force; but on the gibbet of his death Jesus made void the Law with its decrees, fastened the handwriting of the Old Testament to the cross, establishing the New Testament in his blood, shed for the whole human race. "To such an extent, then," says St. Leo the Great, speaking of the cross of our Lord, "was there effected transfer from the Law of the Gospel, from the Synagogue to the Church, from many sacrifices to one victim, that, as our Lord expired, that mystical veil which shut off the innermost part of the temple and its sacred secret from the main temple was rent violently from top to bottom. . . ."

If we closely consider all these mysteries of the cross, those words of the Apostle are no longer obscure for us, in which he teaches the Ephesians that Christ by his blood made the Jews and the Gentiles one, "breaking down the middle wall of partition . . . in his flesh" by which the two peoples were divided; and that he had made the old law void "that he might make the two in himself into one new man," that is the Church, and might reconcile both to God by the cross. . . .

That this Mystical Body which is the Church should be called Christ's, is proved, in the second place, from the fact that he must be universally acknowledged as its actual head. "He," as St. Paul says, "is the head of the body, the Church." He is the head from whom the whole body, perfectly organized, "grows and makes increase unto the edifying of itself. . . ."

However for the good of all we wish

to touch this point briefly. And first of all it is clear that the Son of God and of the Blessed Virgin is to be called the Head of the Church for his singular pre-eminence. For the head is in the highest place. But who is in higher place than Christ, God, who as the Word of the eternal Father must be acknowledged to be the "first born of every creature"? Who has reached more lofty heights than Christ, Man, who, though born of the Immaculate Virgin, is the true and natural Son of God, and thanks to his miraculous and glorious resurrection, a resurrection triumphant over death, has become the "first born of the dead"? Who finally has been so exalted as he, who as "the one mediator of God and men" has in a most marvelous manner linked earth to heaven, who raised on the cross, as on a throne of mercy, has drawn all things, to himself, who as the Son of Man, chosen from among countless, is the object of God's love beyond all men, all angels and all creation? . . .

Because Christ is so exalted, he alone by every right rules and governs the Church; and herein is yet another reason why he must be likened to a head. As the head is the "royal citadel" of the body—to use the words of Ambrose—and all the members, over which it is placed for their good, are naturally guided by it as being endowed with superior powers, so the divine Redeemer holds the helm of the universal state of Christians, and directs its course. And as a government of human society means merely this, to lead men to the end proposed by means that are expedient, just and helpful, it is easy to see how our savior, model and ideal of good shepherds, performs all these functions in a most striking way.

For while still on earth, he instructed us by precept, counsel and warning in words that shall never pass away, and will be spirit and life to all men of all times. Moreover he conferred a triple power on his apostles and their successors, to teach, to govern, to lead men to holiness. This triple power, defined by special ordinances, by rights and obligations, he made the fundamental law of the whole Church. . . .

But we must not think that he rules only in a hidden or extraordinary way. On the contrary, our divine Redeemer also governs his Mystical Body in a visible way and ordinarily through his vicar on earth. You know, Venerable Brothers, that after he had ruled the "little flock" himself during his mortal pilgrimage, when about to leave this world and return to the Father, Christ our Lord entrusted to the chief of the apostles the visible government of the entire community he had founded. He was all wise; and how could he leave without a visible head the body of the Church he had founded as a human society.

Nor against this may one argue, that the primacy of jurisdiction established in the Church gives such a Mystical Body two heads. For Peter in virtue of his primacy is only Christ's vicar; so that there is only one chief head of this Body, namely, Christ. He never ceases personally to guide the Church by an unseen hand, though at the same time he rules it externally, visibly through him, who is his representative on earth. After his glorious Ascension into heaven this Church rested not on him alone, but on Peter, too, its visible foundation stone. That Christ and his vicar constitute one only head is the solemn teaching of our predecessor of immortal memory, Boniface VIII, in the Apostolic Letter *Unam Sanctum;* and his successors have never ceased to repeat the same.

They, therefore, walk the path of dangerous error, who believe that they can accept Christ as the Head of the Church, while they reject genuine loyalty to his vicar on earth. They have taken away the visible head, broken the visible bonds of unity, and they leave the Mystical Body of the Redeemer in such obscurity and so maimed, that those who are seeking the haven of eternal salvation cannot see it and cannot find it.

What we have thus far said of the universal Church must be understood also of the individual Christian communities, whether Eastern or Latin, which go to make up the one Catholic Church. For they, too, are ruled by Christ Jesus through the voice of their own respective bishops. Bishops, then, must be considered as the nobler members of the universal Church, for they are linked in an altogether special way to the divine Head of the whole Body and so are rightly called "principal parts of the members of the Lord"; what is more, as far as one's own diocese is concerned, they each and all as true shepherds feed the flocks entrusted to them and rule them in the name of Christ. Yet in exercising this office they are not altogether independent, but are duly subordinate to the authority of the Roman pontiff; and although their jurisdiction is inherent in their office, yet they receive it directly from the same supreme pontiff. Hence, they should be revered by the faithful as divinely appointed successors of the apostles. To bishops, more than to the rulers of this world, even those in supreme authority, should be applied the sentence: "Touch not my anointed ones!" For bishops have been anointed with the chrism of the Holy Spirit. . . .

And now, Venerable Brothers, we come to that part of our explanation, in which we desire to make clear that the Body of Christ, which is the Church, should be called mystical. This word, used by many early writers, has the sanction of numerous pontifical documents. There are several reasons why it should be used; for by it we may distinguish the Body of the Church, which is a society whose head and ruler is Christ, from his physical Body, which born of the Virgin Mother of God now sits at the right hand of the Father and rests hidden under the Eucharistic veil; as well as from any ordinary body in the natural order, whether physical or moral. This latter distinction is of greater importance in view of modern errors.

In a natural body the principle of unity so unites the parts, that each lacks its own individual subsistence; on the contrary in the Mystical Body that mutual union, though intrinsic, links the members by a bond which leaves to each intact his own personality. Besides if we examine the relation existing between the several members and between the members and the head, in every physical, living body all the different members are ultimately destined to the good of the whole alone; while every moral association of men, if we look to its ultimate usefulness, is in the end directed to the advancement of all and of every single member. For they are persons. And so—to return to our theme—as the Son of the eternal Father came down from heaven for the salvation of us all, he likewise established the Body of the Church and enriched it with the divine Spirit to assure immortal souls attaining their happiness, according to the words of the Apostle: "All things are yours; but you are Christ's; and Christ is God's." For the Church exists both for the good of the faithful, and to give glory to God and Jesus Christ whom he sent.

But if we compare a Mystical Body to a moral body, here again we must notice that the difference between them is not slight, rather it is very considerable and very important. In the moral body, the principle of union is nothing more than the common end, and the common co-operation of all under authority for the attainment of that end; whereas in the Mystical Body, of which we are speaking, this collaboration is supplemented by a distinct internal principle, which exists effectively in the whole and in each of its parts, and whose excellence is such, that of itself it is vastly superior to whatever bonds of union may be found in a physical or moral body. This is something, as we said above, not of the natural but of the supernatural order. Essentially it is something infinite, uncreated: the Spirit of God, who, as the Angelic Doctor says, "numerically one and the same, fills and unifies the whole Church."

Hence, this word in its correct signification gives us to understand that the Church, a perfect society of its kind, is not made up of merely moral and juridical elements and principles. It is far superior to all other human societies; it surpasses them as grace surpasses nature, as things immortal are above all those that perish. Such human societies, and in the first place civil society, are by no means to be despised or belittled. But the Church in its entirety is not found within this natural order, any more than the whole of man is encompassed within the organism of our mortal body. The juridical principles, on which also the Church rests and is established, derive from the divine constitution given to it by Christ, and contribute to the attaining its supernatural end; but what lifts the society of Christians far, far above the whole natural order is the Spirit of our Redeemer who until the end of time penetrates every part of the Church's being and is active within it.

He is the source of every grace and every gift and every miraculous power. Just as our composite mortal body, for all its being a marvelous work of the creator, falls short of the eminent dignity of our soul, so the social structure of the Christian community, though eloquent of its divine architect's wisdom, remains still something inferior, when compared to the spiritual gifts which give it beauty and life and to their divine source.

From what we have thus far written and explained, Venerable Brothers, it is clear, we think how grievously they err who arbitrarily picture the Church as something hidden and invisible, as do they also who look upon it as a mere human institution with a certain disciplinary code and external ritual, but lacking power to communicate supernatural life. No; the Mystical Body of Christ is like Christ the head and exemplar of the Church; "Who is not complete, if only his visible human nature is considered, or if only his divine, invisible nature . . . but he is one through the union of both and one in both. . . ." Thus the Word of God took unto himself a human nature liable to sufferings, so that he might consecrate in his blood the visible society founded by him and "lead man back to things invisible under a visible rule."

For this reason we deplore and condemn the pernicious error of those who conjure up from their fancies and imaginary Church, a kind of society that finds its origin and growth in charity, to which they somewhat contemptuously oppose another, which they call juridical. But this distinction, which they introduce, is baseless.

For they fail to understand that the same reason that led our divine Redeemer to give to the community of men he founded the constitution of a society, perfect of its kind, containing all the juridical and social elements, namely that he might perpetuate on earth the saving work of redemption, was also the reason why he wished to be enriched with the heavenly gifts of the consoling Spirit. The eternal Father indeed wished it to be the "kingdom of the Son of his predilection"; but it was to be a real kingdom, in which all believers would make the obeisance of their intellect and will, and humbly and obediently model themselves on him, who for our sake "was made obedient unto death." There can, then, be no real opposition or conflict between the invisible mission of the Holy Spirit and the juridical commission of ruler and teacher received from Christ. Like body and soul in us, they complement and perfect each other, and have their source in our one Redeemer, who not only said, as he breathed on the apostles: "Receive the Holy Spirit," but also clearly commanded: "As the Father has sent me, so I send you"; and again: "He who hears you, hears me. . . ."

These juridical bonds far surpass those of any other human society, however exalted; and yet another principle of union must be added to them in those three virtues, which link us so closely to each other and to God: Christian faith, hope and charity. . . .

Corresponding to this love of God and of Christ there must be love of the neighbor. How can we claim to love the divine Redeemer, if we hate those whom he has redeemed with his precious blood, so that he might make them members of his Mystical Body? For that reason the beloved disciple warns us: "If any man say: I love God, and hate his brother, he is a liar. For he that loves not his brother whom he sees, how can he love God whom he sees not? And this commandment we have from God, that he who loves God love also his brother." Rather one should say that the more we become "members one of another," "mutually one of another," the closer we shall be united with God, with Christ; as on the other hand the more ardent the love that binds us to God and our divine head, the closer we shall be united to each other in the bonds of charity. . . .

This communication of the Spirit of Christ is the channel through which flow into all the members of the Church those gifts, powers and extraordinary graces found superabundantly in the head as in their source, and they are perfected day by day in these members according to the office they may hold in the Mystical Body of Jesus Christ. Thus the Church becomes, as it were, the filling out and complement of the Redeemer, while Christ in a sense attains through the Church a fullness in all things. Here we touch the reason why to the mind of Augustine the Mystical Head, which is Christ, and the Church, which on this earth as another Christ bears his person, constitute one new man, in whom heaven and earth are yoked together in perpetuating the cross's work of salvation: by Christ we mean the head and the body, the whole Christ.

We are well aware that many a veil shrouds this profound truth of our union with the divine Redeemer and in particular of the Holy Spirit's dwelling within our souls and impedes our power to understand and explain it. This mystery is enveloped in a darkness, rising out of the mental limitations of those who seek to grasp it. But we know, too, that well-directed and earnest study of this doctrine and the clash of diverse opinions and their discussion, provided love of truth and due submission to the Church be the arbiter, will open rich and bright vistas, whose light will help to progress in kindred sacred sciences. Hence we do not censure those who in various ways and with diverse reasonings strain every effort to understand and to clarify the mystery of this our marvelous union with Christ. But let all agree uncompromisingly on this, if they would not err from truth and from the orthodox teaching of the Church: to reject every kind of mystic union, by which the faithful would in any way pass beyond the sphere of creatures and rashly enter the divine even to the extent of one single attribute of the eternal Godhead being predicted of them as their own. And besides let all hold this as certain truth, that all these activities are common to the most Blessed Trinity, in so far as they have God as supreme efficient cause. . . .

Through the Eucharistic Sacrifice Christ our Lord wished to give special evidence to the faithful of our union among ourselves and with our divine Head, marvelous as it is and beyond all praise. For here the sacred ministers act in the person not only of our Savior but of the whole mystical Body and of everyone of the faithful. In this act of sacrifice through the hands of the priest, whose word alone has brought the immaculate Lamb to be present on the altar, the faithful themselves with one desire and one prayer offer it to the eternal Father,—the most acceptable victim of praise and propitiation for the Church's universal needs. And just as the divine Redeemer, dying on the Cross, offered himself as head of the whole human race to the eternal Father, so "in this pure oblation" he offers not only himself as head of the Church to the heavenly Father, but in himself his mystical members as well. He embraces them all, even the weak and ailing ones, in the tenderest love of his heart.

The Sacrament of the Eucharist is itself a striking image of the Church's unity, if we consider how in the bread to be consecrated many grains go to form one substance; and in it the very author of supernatural grace is given to us, so that through him we may receive the Spirit of charity, in which we are bidden to live now not our life but the life of Christ, and in all the members of his social body to love the Redeemer himself.

If in the sad and anxious days through which we are passing there are many who cling so firmly to Christ the Lord hidden beneath the Eucharistic veils that neither tribulation nor distress nor famine nor nakedness nor danger nor persecution nor the sword can separate them from his love, then undoubtedly holy Communion which once again in God's providence is much more frequented even from days of early childhood, may become a source of the courage that makes heroes out of Christians.

If the faithful, Venerable Brothers, in a spirit of sincere piety understand what has been written here and hold to it, it will be easier for them to escape the errors which arise from an irresponsible investigation of this difficult matter, such as some have made, and which are noised abroad not without seriously endangering Catholic faith and disturbing the peace of souls. For some there are who neglect the fact that the Apostle Paul has used metaphorical language in speaking of this doctrine, and failing to distinguish the physical from the social Body of Christ as they should, out of their fancy draw some deformed kind of unity. They want the divine Redeemer and the members of the Church to coalesce into one physical person and while they bestow divine attributes on man, they make Christ our Lord subject to error and to human inclination to evil. Catholic faith and the writings of the holy fathers reject such false teaching as impious and sacrilegious; to the mind of the Apostle of the Gentiles it is equally abhorrent. He brings Christ and his Mystical Body into a marvelously intimate union, it is true; but he distinguishes one from the other as bridegroom and bride.

Just as false and dangerous is the error of those who try to deduce from the mysterious union of all with Christ a certain unhealthy quietism. They would attribute the whole spiritual life of Christians and their progress in virtue exclusively to the action of the divine Spirit, setting aside and neglecting the corresponding work and collaboration which we must contribute to this action. No one of course can deny that the Holy Spirit of Jesus Christ is the one source of whatever supernatural power enters into the Church and its members. For "the Lord will give grace and glory," as the psalmist says.

But that men should continue consistently in their good works, that they advance generously in grace and virtue, that they strive earnestly to reach the heights of Christian perfection and at the same time do their best to stimulate others to gain the same goal,—all this the Spirit from above does not wish to bring about, unless men contribute their daily share of zealous activity. "For not on those who sleep but on the diligent," says St. Ambrose, "divine favors are conferred." In our mortal body the members are strengthened and grow through continued exercise; much more so is this true in the social Body of Jesus Christ, in which each member retains his own personal freedom, responsibility and principles of conduct. For that reason he who said: "I live, now not I, but Christ lives in me," did not at the same time hesitate to aver: "His [God's] grace in me has not yet been void, but I have labored more abundantly than all they: yet not I, but the grace of God with me." It is perfectly clear, therefore, that these false doctrines distort the mystery which we are considering and make it contribute not to the spiritual advancement of the faithful but to their tragic ruin.

The same result would follow from the opinions of those who assert that little importance should be given to the frequent confession of venial sins. Of far greater importance, they say, is that general confession which the Spouse of Christ surrounded by her children in the Lord makes each day by the mouth of the priest as he approaches the altar. It is true indeed, Venerable Brothers, that venial sins may be expiated in many ways which are to be highly commended. But to hasten daily progress along the path of virtue we wish the pious practice of frequent confession to be earnestly advocated. Not without the inspiration of the Holy Spirit was this practice introduced into the Church. By it genuine self-knowledge is increased, Christian humility grows, bad habits are corrected, spiritual neglect and tepidity are countered, the conscience is purified, the will strengthened, a salutary self-control is attained and grace is increased in virtue of the sacrament itself. Let those, therefore, among the young clergy who make light of or weaken esteem of frequent confession realize that what they are doing is foreign to the Spirit of Christ, and disastrous for the Mystical Body of our Savior.

There are others who deny any impetratory power to our prayers, and would spread abroad the idea that prayers offered to God in private should not be considered worth very much. Public prayers, they say, prayers that are made in the name of the Church, are those which really count, as they come from the Mystical Body of Jesus Christ. Such an opinion is false; for the divine Redeemer maintains closest union not only with his Church, which is his loved Spouse, but also with each and every faithful soul in it, and he longs to speak with them heart to heart, especially after Holy Communion. It is true that public prayers, prayers, that is, that are offered by mother Church, because of the dignity of the Spouse of Christ, excel any other kind of prayer; but no prayer, even the most private, lacks its own dignity and power, and all prayer is immensely helpful to the Mystical Body.

In that Body, thanks to the Communion of Saints, no good can be done, no virtue practiced by individual members without its contributing something also to the salvation of all. Similarly just because a man is a member of this Body, he is not forbidden to ask for himself particular favors even for this life, provided he is always resigned to the divine will. The members do not lose their own personality, and remain subject to their own individual needs. Moreover the common practice of the saints as well as ecclesiastical documents demonstrate how highly everyone should esteem mental prayer.

Finally some would have it, that our prayers should not be directed to the person of Jesus Christ, but rather to God, or to the eternal Father through Christ, since our Savior, as head of his Mystical Body, is only "mediator of God and men." But that, too, not only is opposed to the mind of the Church and to Christian usage but is false. For to speak exactly, Christ is head of the universal Church, as he exists at once in both his natures. Moreover he himself has solemnly stated: "If you shall ask me anything in my name, that I will do." Though it is true especially in the Eucharistic Sacrifice—in which Christ, at once priest and victim, exercises in an extraordinary way the office of conciliator—that prayers are very often directed to the eternal Father through the only-begotten Son; nevertheless it occurs, not seldom even in this sacrifice, that prayers to the divine Redeemer also are used. For, after all, every Christian must know full well that the man Christ Jesus is also the Son of God and God himself. . . .

But one may be deceived by the angel of darkness who assumes the appearance of an angel of light. Lest this happen, let this be the supreme law of our love: to love the Spouse of Christ as Christ wished her to be and as he purchased her with his blood. Hence not only should we cherish the sacraments with which holy mother Church sustains our life, the solemn ceremonies she offers for our solace and our joy, the sacred chant and liturgy by which she lifts our souls up to heaven, but the sacramentals too and all those exercises of piety which she uses to console the hearts of the faithful and gently to imbue them with the Spirit of Christ. It behooves us as sons to recompense her for this motherly goodness to us; but it is also our duty to respect the authority which she has received from Christ, and with which she brings unto captivity our understanding unto the obedience of Christ.

Thus we are commanded to obey her laws and her moral precepts, often hard enough to our fallen nature; through self-imposed mortification to bring this rebellious body to submission; at times we are warned to abstain even from harmless pleasures. Nor is it enough to love this Mystical Body for the glory of its divine Head and its celestial dowry. Our zealous love must follow it even as it appears in this mortal flesh of ours, made up, that is, of weak, human elements, although at times they are little fitted to the place of dignity which they occupy in this venerable body. . . .

Once the faithful try to live in this spirit of conscious faith, they will not pay due honor and reverence to the superior members of this Mystical Body, especially those who according to Christ's mandate will have to render an account of our souls, but they will take to their hearts those members who are the object of our Savior's special love: the weak, the mean, the wounded and the sick, who are in need of natural or supernatural assistance; children whose innocence is so easily exposed to danger these days and whose little hearts are as wax to be moulded; and finally the poor, in helping whom we touch, as it were, through his supreme mercy the very person of Jesus Christ.

For as the Apostle with good reason admonishes us: "Much more those that seem to be the more feeble members of the body, are more necessary, and such as we think to be the less honorable members of the body, about these we put more abundant honor." Conscious of the obligations of our high office, we deem it necessary to reiterate this grave statement today, when to our profound grief we see the bodily deformed, the insane and those suffering from hereditary disease at times deprived of their lives, as though they were a useless burden to society. And this procedure is hailed by some as a new discovery of human progress, and as something that is altogether justified by the common good. Yet what sane man does not recognize that this not only violates the natural and divine law written in the heart of every man, but flies in the face of every sensibility of civilized humanity? The blood of these victims, all the dearer to our Redeemer because deserving of greater pity, "cries to God from the earth." . . .

And so we desire that all who claim the Church as their mother, should seriously consider that not only the sacred ministers and those who have consecrated themselves to God in religious life, but the other members as well of the Mystical Body of Jesus Christ have the obligation of working hard and constantly for the upbuilding and increase of this body. We wish this to be remembered especially by members of Catholic Action who assist the bishops and priests in their apostolic labors—and to their praise be it said that they do remember—and also by those associates of pious unions who contribute their work to the same

end. Everyone is witness to the high seriousness and extraordinary importance of their energetic zeal especially in present circumstances.

In this connection we cannot pass over in silence the fathers and mothers of families, to whom our Savior has entrusted the most delicate members of his Mystical Body. We plead with them for the love of Christ and the Church to give the greatest possible care to the children confided to them, and to look to protecting them from the multiplicity of snares into which they can fall so easily today. . . .

While we want unceasing prayer to rise to God from the whole Mystical Body in common, that all the straying sheep may hasten to enter the one fold of Jesus Christ, yet we recognize that this step must come of their own free will; for no one believes unless he wills to believe. Hence they are most certainly not genuine Christians who against their belief are forced to go into a church, to approach the altar and to receive the Sacraments. The "faith without which it is impossible to please God" is a wholly free "submission of intellect and will." . . .

As we write these words, there passes before our eyes, alas, an almost endless throng of unfortunates for whom we mourn and weep; sick, poor, mutilated, widows, orphans, and many not infrequently languishing even unto death for their own bitter afflictions or those of their dear ones. From a father's heart we appeal to all who from whatever cause are plunged into grief, to lift their eyes in confidence to heaven, and to offer their sorrows to him who will one day reward them abundantly. Let them remember that their sufferings are not in vain, but will be to their great gain and that of the Church, if for this purpose they but take courage and bear them with patience. To make this intention more efficacious, the daily use of the offering made by the members of the Apostleship of Prayer will contribute very, very much; and we welcome this occasion to recommend that association highly, as one which is most pleasing to God.

There never was a time, Venerable Brothers, when the salvation of souls did not impose on all the duty of associating their sufferings with the torments of our divine Redeemer. But today that duty is clearer than ever when a gigantic conflict has set almost the whole world on fire, and leaves in its wake so much death, so much misery, so much sorrow. Today imposes with particular stress on everyone the duty to flee the vices and blandishments of the world, and to renounce the unrestrained pleasures of the body and that worldly frivolity and vanity, which contribute nothing to the Christian formation of the soul, nothing towards gaining heaven. Rather let those words of our immortal predecessor Leo the Great be deeply engraven in our minds, that Baptism has made us flesh of the Crucified One; and that beautiful prayer of St. Ambrose: "Carry me, Christ, on the cross, which is salvation to the wanderers, sole rest for the wearied, wherein alone is life for those who die." . . .

VII. *Intellectual and Spiritual Revival*

THE program inaugurated by Pope Leo XIII, of regaining culture for and through the Church, made marked headway during the first half of the twentieth century. Two world wars hastened a realization among men that a disintegrating secular culture had not supplied a viable synthesis for contemporary mechanical and scientific civilization. At the same time contemporary Catholics have not been able to present a comprehensive solution to current problems that has won the support of a majority of the world. Religious forces are still not strong and creative enough to bring about a renewal of Catholic life and culture that is in close contact with the spirit of the times.

Two attitudes of Catholics account in part for the measured revival. Through the course of seven centuries men have been steadily drawn away from the life and culture of the Church while religion followed its own departmentalized course of development. The task of making Catholic ideas and attitudes a cohesive part of all aspects of life would not, it appeared, be accomplished in a brief span of time. Secondly, Catholics grew accustomed to extolling the riches of the religious and cultural heritage of the Church. To influence effectively the contemporary age, more is necessary than enthusiastic training in and explanation of the incomparable Catholic heritage of an Augustine, Thomas, or Dante. Rather, as bearers of tradition, Catholics can contribute creatively to building up the kingdom of God in the twentieth century as their ancestors did at the end of the Roman empire, and in several periods of the middle ages. This also implies an understanding and appreciation of the age before an inner transformation of society can be realized.

The second spring that Newman foretold in 1852 began, however, to evidence some early fruits. One striking example was the English convert, Gilbert Keith Chesterton (1936), essayist in the grand tradition and master of the paradox, who with immense humor and intensity of experience announced repeatedly that religion is the very foundation and inner essence of life. Chesterton employed the light touch to explain profound truths. His THE CATHOLIC CHURCH AND CONVERSION (*No. 43*) deals with the process of conversion to the Catholic faith, and it draws upon the author's personal experience to point up the necessity of religion again playing a major role in the life of man.

An example of current theological thought (*No. 44*) is found in the writings of Bernard Häring's *The Law of Christ*. Emmanuel Cardinal Suhard, archbishop of Paris in the critical years during and following World War II, concerned himself with meeting the missionary needs of the Church in the de-Christianized industrial urban world of modern man. Suhard issued masterful pastoral letters to his flock, of which GROWTH OR DECLINE OF THE CHURCH (*No. 45*) of February 1947 is most typical. The French Cardinal asked who was going to infuse a soul into the compartmentalized modern civilization. In answer he attempted to turn the attention of contemporary man to the "profound nature of the Church as her dogma and her history reveal them to us." In his classic essay Cardinal Suhard anticipated in a striking way and by fifteen years the issues which Vatican Council II came to face.

In the political field the Sicilian priest, Don Luigi Sturzo (1959), stands out as one of the noblest figures of the times. Scholar and seminary professor, Don Sturzo entered into active politics and labored for progressive reforms, which included legal recognition of labor unions, woman suffrage, free education, housing needs of workers, agricultural stations, and progressive income taxes. In 1909 Sturzo formed the *Partito Populare,* a political party separate from the Church, which opposed the agitation of the Socialists and Communists. He was an outspoken opponent of Mussolini and Fascism, and an ardent defender of democracy; his party was the Italian forerunner of the present-day Christian Democratic parties of Western Europe. His courageous defense of morality, freedom, and democracy, and his creative proposals for a renewed participation by Christians in political life are described in THE CHRISTIAN DEMOCRATIC MOVEMENT (*No. 46*). Sturzo is an all too rare example, before World War II, of European Catholic understanding and appreciation of the ancient tradition of Christian democracy applied to modern problems. Following the wish of the Holy See, to which he was ever loyal, Sturzo was forced to withdraw from political life in 1922, and with the advent of Mussolini to power he went into exile in France, England, and the United States. The Christian Democratic movement of Europe following the war owed its inspiration to Don Sturzo, who had fathered the concepts which this political group has carried through as the main defense of freedom and democracy in Western Europe during the critical period of Communist aggression. Sturzo returned to his native Italy in triumph after the war, became an honorary member of the Italian senate, and continued to advise and counsel others until his death.

He was a confirmed opponent of statism in every form, and he never tired of advocating local autonomy and decentralization of government as protection against state monopoly, partnership or dominance in industrial and economic life.

The laity's participation in the mission of the Church has been of crucial importance to contemporary apostolic endeavors. Current ecclesiology has developed a deeper understanding of the organic position and activity of lay people in the Mystical Body of Christ. The role of the layman in the Church is placed in an integrated, vital unity by the French Dominican, Yves Congar, in his POSITION AND PROPER ROLE OF THE LAITY IN THE CHURCH (*No. 47*).

A new form of life of Christian perfection was recognized by Pope Pius XII on 2 February 1947 in his Apostolic Constitution PROVIDA MATER ECCLESIA (*No. 48*) when the Holy See sanctioned a consecration to God in Secular Institutes. Through these organizations Christians may bind themselves to acquire Christian perfection and carry out an apostolate in the world.

Another prophetic voice was that of Father Karl Adam, theological scholar and professor of theology in the University of Tuebingen. Dr. Adam gave long and careful study to the PRINCIPLES OF CHRISTIAN REUNION (*No. 49*) and supplied invaluable, scholarly, and prudent direction to the *Una Sancta* movement which was developing in Germany and on the continent. The ecumenical movement had made notable headway in the nineteenth and twentieth centuries, especially among Protestants, who looked for some principles of unity among themselves in spreading Christianity and making it more effective in the life of mankind. The movement to reunite the various separated national Orthodox Churches of the East with the Holy See has also gained momentum in recent years. Evidences of reconciliation and union between Eastern and Western Christians are growing steadily as cultural and political sources of separation are more thoroughly studied and understood. One of the leading contributors who is helping to bridge over the chasm between separated Christians through scholarly contributions is the Reverend Francis Dvornik, research scholar of the Dunbarton Oaks Foundation of Harvard University. His paper, THE ORIGIN OF THE EASTERN SCHISM (*No. 50*), delivered on 29 September 1956 at the First Unionist Congress at St. Procopius Abbey, is a model of unbiased analysis of the causes which led to separation and rupture.

The tragic and scandalous disunity among Christians—Catholics, Orthodox, and Protestants—is a serious hindrance to apostolic endeavor in mission territories. The Communist challenge to Christian existence has in a special way pointed up the immediacy of the problem and revealed clearly how closely the destiny of Christianity is linked with the problem of its world unity. The ecumenical movement opens a contemporary approach, sanctioned and encouraged by Vatican Council II, to that unity which was the prayer of the Lord and the ideal of Christianity since its inception.

The selections chosen here to represent contemporary intellectual and spiritual developments are not intended as inclusive or exclusive. They are merely one group of representative examples of the multiplying impulses, tendencies, and accomplishments of Catholic life today. Selections from such leading Catholic minds as Vonier, Maritain, Gilson, Dawson, Cardyn, La Grange, or Marmion would be equally valid. The selections chosen merely suggest some of the manifestations of the level which the contemporary Catholic revival has attained, and the challenge of future developments in the years ahead for the new generation of the people of God.

43. *Gilbert Keith Chesterton: The Catholic Church and Conversion, September 1926*

THE CATHOLIC faith used to be called the Old Religion; but at the present moment it has a recognized place among the new religions. This has nothing to do with its truth or falsehood; but it is a fact that has a great deal to do with the understanding of the modern world.

It would be very undesirable that modern men should accept Catholicism merely as a novelty; but it is a novelty. It does act upon its existing environment with the peculiar force and freshness of a novelty. Even those who denounce it generally denounce it as a novelty; as an innovation and not merely a survival. They talk of the "advanced" party in the Church of England; they talk of the "aggression" of the Church of Rome. When they talk of an extremist they are as likely to mean a ritualist as a socialist. Given any normal respectable Protestant family, Anglican or Puritan, in England or America, we shall find that Catholicism is actually for practical purposes treated as a new religion, that is, a revolution. It is not a survival. It is not in that sense an antiquity. It does not necessarily owe anything to tradition. In places where tradition can do nothing for it, in places where all the tradition is against it, it is intruding on its own merits; not as a tradition but a truth. The father of some such Anglican or American Puritan family will find, very often, that all his children are breaking away from his own more or less Christian compromise, regarded as normal in the nineteenth century, and going off in various directions after various faiths or fashions which he would call fads. One of his sons will become a socialist and hang up a portrait of Lenin; one of his daughters will become a spiritualist and play with a planchette; another daughter will go over to Christian Science and it is quite likely that another son will go over to Rome. The point is, for the moment, that from the point of view of the father, and even in a sense of the family, all these things act after the manner of new religions, of great movements, of enthusiasms that carry young people off their feet and leave older people bewildered or annoyed. Catholicism indeed, even more than the others, is often spoken of as if it were actually one of the wild passions of youth. Optimistic aunts and uncles say that the youth will "get over it," as if it were a childish love affair or that unfortunate business with the barmaid. Darker and sterner aunts and uncles, perhaps at a rather earlier period, used actually to talk about it as an indecent indulgence, as if its literature were literally a sort of pornography. Newman remarks quite naturally, as if there were nothing odd about it at the time, that an undergraduate found with an ascetic manual or a book of monastic meditations was under a sort of cloud or taint, as having been caught with a "bad book" in his possession. He had been wallowing in the sensual pleasure of Nones or inflaming his lusts by contemplating an incorrect number of candles. It is perhaps no longer the custom to regard conversion as a form of dissipation; but it is still common to regard conversion as a form of revolt. And as regards the established convention of much of the modern world, it is a revolt. The worthy merchant of the middle class, the worthy farmer of the middle west, when he sends his son to college, does now feel a faint alarm lest the boy should fall among thieves, in the sense of Communists; but has the same sort of fear lest he should fall among Catholics.

Now he has no fear lest he should fall among Calvinists. He has no fear that his children will become seventeenth-century Supralapsarians, however much he may dislike that doctrine. He is not even particularly troubled by the possibility of their adopting the extreme solfidian conceptions once common among some of the more extravagant Methodists. He is not likely to await with terror the telegram that will inform him that his son has become a Fifth-Monarchy man, anymore than that he has joined the Albigensians. He does not exactly lie awake at night wondering whether Tom at Oxford has become a Lutheran any more than a Lollard. All these religions he dimly recognizes as dead religions; or at any rate as old religions. And he is only frightened of new religions. He is only frightened of those fresh, provocative, paradoxical new notions that fly to the young people's heads. But amongst these dangerous juvenile attractions he does in practice class the freshness and novelty of Rome.

Now this is rather odd; because Rome is not so very new. Among these annoying new religions, one is rather an old religion; but it is the only old religion that is so new. When it was originally and really new, no doubt a Roman father often found himself in the same position as the Anglican or Puritan father. He too might find all his children going strange ways and deserting the household gods and the sacred temple of the capitol. He too might find that one of those children had joined the Christians in their *ecclesia* and possibly in their catacombs. But he would have found that, of his other children, one cared for nothing but the mysteries of Orpheus, another was inclined to follow Mithras, another was a Neo-Pythagorean who had learned vegetarianism from the Hindoos, and so on. Though the Roman father, unlike the Victorian father, might have the pleasure of exercising the *patria potestas* and cutting off the heads of all the heretics, he could not cut off the stream of all the heresies. Only by this time most of the streams have run rather dry. It is now seldom necessary for the anxious parent to warn his children against the undesirable society of the bull of Mithras, or even to wean him from the exclusive contemplation of Orpheus; and though we have vegetarians always with us, they mostly know more about proteids than about Pythagoras. But that other youthful extravagance is still youthful. That other new religion is once again new. That one fleeting fashion has refused to fleet; and that ancient bit of modernity is still modern. It is still to the Protestant parent now exactly what it was to the pagan parent then. We might say simply that it is a nuisance; but anyhow it is a novelty. It is not simply what the father is used to, or even what the son is used to. It is coming in as something fresh and disturbing, whether as it came to the Greeks who were always seeking some new thing, or as it came to the shepherds who first heard the cry upon the hills of the good news that our language calls the Gospel. We can explain the fact of the Greeks in the time of St. Paul regarding it as a new thing, because it was a new thing. But who will explain why it is still as new to the last of the converts as it was to the first of the shepherds? It is as if a man a hundred years old entered the Olympian games among the young Greek athletes; which would surely have been the basis of a Greek legend. There is something almost as legendary about

the religion that is two thousand years old now appearing as a rival of the new religions. That is what has to be explained and cannot be explained away; nothing can turn the legend into a myth. We have seen with our own eyes and heard with our own ears this great modern quarrel between young Catholics and old Protestants; and it is the first step to recognize in any study of modern conversation.

I am not going to talk about numbers and statistics, though I may say something about them later. The first fact to realize is a difference of substance which falsifies all the difference of size. The great majority of Protestant bodies today, whether they are strong or weak, are not strengthened in this particular fashion; by the actual attraction of their new followers to their old doctrines. A young man will suddenly become a Catholic priest, or even a Catholic monk, because he has a spontaneous and even impatient personal enthusiasm for the doctrine of virginity as it appeared to St. Catherine or St. Clare. But how many men become Baptist ministers because they have a personal horror of the idea of an innocent infant coming unconsciously to Christ? How many honest Presbyterian ministers in Scotland really want to go back to John Knox, as a Catholic mystic might want to go back to John of the Cross? These men inherit positions which they feel they can hold with reasonable consistency and general agreement; but they do inherit them. For them religion is tradition. We Catholics naturally do not sneer at tradition; but we say that in this case it is really tradition and nothing else. Not one man in a hundred of these people would ever have joined his present communion if he had been born outside it. Not one man in a thousand of them would have invented anything like his church formulas if they had not been laid down for him. None of them has any real reason for being in their own particular church, whatever good reason they may still have for being outside ours. In other words, the old creed of their communion has ceased to function as a fresh and stimulating idea. It is at best a motto or a war cry and at the worst a catch word. But it is not meeting contemporary ideas like a contemporary idea. In their time and in their turn we believe that those other contemporary ideas will also prove their mortality by having also become mottoes and catch-words and traditions. A century or two hence Spiritualism may be a tradition and Socialism may be a tradition and Christian Science may be a tradition. But Catholicism will not be a tradition. It will still be a nuisance and a new and dangerous thing.

These are the general considerations which govern any personal study of conversion to the Catholic faith. The Church has defended tradition in a time which stupidly denied and despised tradition. But that is simply because the Church is always the only thing defending whatever is at the moment stupidly despised. It is already beginning to appear as the only champion of reason in the twentieth century, as it was the only champion of tradition in the nineteenth. We know that the higher mathematics is trying to deny that two and two make four and the higher mysticism to imagine something that is beyond good and evil. Amid all these anti-rational philosophies, ours will remain the only rational philosophy. In the same spirit the Church did indeed point out the value of tradition to a time which treated it as quite valueless. The nineteenth-century neglect of tradition and mania for mere documents were altogether nonsensical. They amounted to saying that men always tell lies to children but men never make mistakes in books. But though our sympathies are traditional because they are human, it is not that part of the thing which stamps it as divine. The mark of the faith is not tradition; it is conversion. It is the miracle by which men find truth in spite of tradition and often with the rending of all the roots of humanity.

It is with the nature of this process that I propose to deal; and it is difficult to deal with it without introducing something of a personal element. My own is only a very trivial case but naturally it is the case I know best; and I shall be compelled in the pages that follow to take many illustrations from it. I have therefore thought it well to put first this general note on the nature of the movement in my time; to show that I am well aware that it is a very much larger and even a very much later movement than is implied in describing my own life or generation. I believe it will be more and more an issue for the rising generation and for the generation after that, as they discover the actual alternative in the awful actualities of our time. And Catholics when they stand up together and sing "Faith of our Fathers" may realize almost with amusement that they might well be singing "Faith of our Children." And in many cases the return has been so recent as almost to deserve the description of a Children's Crusade. . . .

44. *Bernard Häring, C.SS.R.: Human Freedom as the Basis of Morality, 6 June 1954*

From Bernard Häring, *The Law of Christ,* Volume I (Westminster, Maryland: The Newman Press, 1960). Chapter Four, pp. 99-108; 119-121; 208-213. Translated by Edwin G. Kaiser, C.PP.S.

I. WE RECOGNIZE the true nature of our freedom when we perceive values and experience the challenge of the morally good. Often we are brought to the keenest realization of our freedom by the very revolt of evil which we confidently trust we can resist and master. Freedom is not enunciated in the necessity of the Must, but in the Ought of the good, not in the triumph of sin, but in the temptation to embrace it. Freedom exists only in those profound depths of personality where the convictions are formed and positions taken, accepting the divine summons or revolting against it. In essence freedom is the power to do good. The power to do evil is not of its essence. Freedom is present only where there is the power to overcome evil. Indifference to good or evil is not a quality of liberty as such, but only of the finite and limited liberty of man. The power to do good, however, derives from the likeness of man to God, from the created participation in the divine freedom. When man is infallibly preserved from sin through the action of efficacious grace, he suffers no loss of liberty, but attains a superior power of freedom, which in itself transcends the normal condition of his finite nature.

Just as God is the Lord of the entire universe because he created it, so is man the ruler of the universe because God created him in his own likeness and placed him over it. "God created man to his own image: to the image of God he created him: male and female he created them. And God blessed them, saying: 'Increase and multiply and fill the earth, and subdue it, and rule over the fishes of the sea, and the fowls of the air, and all living creatures that move upon the earth.'" (GN 1:27f.). God is Lord and Creator of the world. He does not spend himself in creation and governance of the universe, but he celebrates his eternal Sabbath rest, his absolute blessedness apart from the world. In like manner the freedom of man is not spent in the task of ruling the world. If he is not completely absorbed in this mundane effort, if he is not taken up altogether in things of the world, but constantly raises his eyes to the Sabbath joy of God, then his freedom is safeguarded and preserved.

God's liberty is absolutely circumscribed only by his own great glory, for there can be no motive for his free acts outside himself. Analogously God's creature, man, made in the divine image, is constrained by nothing beyond his own freedom, for nothing altogether extrinsic to himself can determine or force his will.

Just as God transcends the world and yet preserves and governs it immanently, so in an analogous manner the free will of man transcends the composite of soul and body (only analogously, for there is no complete independence), and yet governs the entire body-soul structure with all the human urges and drives through the most intimate coordination with them. Similarly in the pattern of the divine causality, as God is the First Cause and has no cause outside himself moving him, so it is with man, though in an analogous and limited manner. Always dependent on God in all his acts, he is still a kind of first principle, a manner of "first cause." "He in himself is the cause that in one instance he becomes grain, in the other chaff."

Freedom is always fresh and new, always a creative beginning. It pertains to its essence that the free act is never univocally predetermined. But the free act itself, though on an entirely distinct level, is the first determining cause of the still undetermined movement of the will. It is really a new beginning, which is truly "creative" in so far as it is posited new and for the first time by the will. But it is not blind and irrational. Rather, as God creates according to the pattern of ideas, so also the creative new beginning in the free act decides according to motives, according to guiding ideas.

Human freedom is the capacity to take one's stand in accepting or rejecting God's call to us, but only by virtue of a participation in the divine freedom. The free human act produces itself, is a cause of itself (*causa sui*), though always dependently, for it depends on the First Cause. Even though absolutely speaking man himself in his voluntary act is the cause of his sin and the "first cause of the fall from grace," he can be so only by force of the actuation of his freedom to do good through the exercise of the causality which comes from the First Cause, God. Sin as defeat of freedom is a diminution of the sharing of divine freedom and therefore a lessening of human freedom itself. Conversely, the highest participation in the divine freedom is acting entirely under the influence of divine grace.

Altogether incomprehensible, especially to the science which relies solely on principles of natural causality, human liberty remains ever a great mystery, for it rests on the still greater mystery of God's own freedom. Most obscure in this mystery of human freedom is its participation on the one hand in the divine freedom and its

profound inviolability on the other. It partakes of God's freedom and yet is so highly esteemed by God himself and so utterly and inviolably its own that man can say no to God by force of the very freedom God grants him.

The grandeur of human freedom is manifested in the most exalted fashion when it surrenders entirely to the guidance of grace and thus becomes capable of saying *yes* to God, in filial obedient love in and through Christ. The dizzy height of freedom towering over the abyss of evil manifests itself in the terrifying and incomprehensible power of decision against Christ, which expels the Spirit of God, the loving source of liberty itself.

II. The power of freedom is effective on many levels, highly diversified in breadth and depth. Human freedom is greatly restricted in its scope by our biological and spiritual heritage and by our environment through the attraction of motives or ideals and the suggestion of lines of action. It is also circumscribed in many ways by the effects of our previous conduct and former free decisions.

The power of freedom is granted us only in germ. Its seeds implanted in us must grow from within through the development of person into personality. This growth and expansion is through the full exercise of the inherent capacity of the will tending to the good. Freedom in man is the power by which he transcends himself in his own act, attaining thereby—albeit gradually and progressively—a new and higher freedom. But neglect of the practice of true freedom (freedom in omission) or failure to exploit it fully will result in atrophy of liberty. If practiced only in the failure which is sin, it is progressively reduced to impotence for the good and ultimately impotence for true freedom altogether. On this point it is necessary to caution against any delusion arising from the force of passion in doing evil. It is true that freedom, if it is not to become impotent, must press the passions into its service. But the characteristic power of human freedom is to guide and direct them; its deepest impotence is to be overcome by them. Even though the utmost force of passion is manifested in evil, still the power of freedom itself is no greater than its practical capacity to channel the forces of passion into the good.

Freedom can be so far lost that the spirit becomes entirely the slave of base drives, free and responsible in its enslavement only because of prior voluntary decisions made when the capacity to choose the course of good was not yet vitiated. But still we must hold fast to the conviction that, so long as we are pilgrims on earthly sojourn, God will never deny the grace of returning to him. To everyone still possessed of normal mind and will he graciously grants the power to take the first step toward conversion. But a new guilt is always incurred if the sinner delays his conversion.

Freedom can also attain the stage in which man surrenders entirely to the guidance of the Spirit. "Now the Lord is the spirit; and where the spirit of the Lord is, there is freedom" (2 COR 3:17). There is no greater freedom than that of the children of God, who have freely risen above the impotence of sin, thrown off the shackles of the slavery of Satan, and voluntarily submitted to the law and yoke of Christ; who have liberated themselves from the selfish quest of self and from the law as a mere instrument of self-righteousness, and instead have placed themselves entirely in the service of the Kingdom of God. They have freed themselves from the universal law as the sole and ultimate norm of morality and without constraint of law have accepted the joyous responsibility of seeking what is most perfect in the

situation in which God has placed them; they have cast aside all desire of resisting the guidance of the Holy Spirit and have thus arrived at the very summit of freedom in obedient service to God.

Freedom is both a gift from the divine bounty and a divinely imposed task; it is both gift and burden. It is like a bud with the urge to blossom forth and ripen into rich fruit of virtue. But like the bud it can wither away, fail to blossom and ripen. Then the power of virtue is lost, and freedom becomes impotent. Freedom which makes man responsible for his actions is itself a noble trust committed to man, a tremendous responsibility.

III. God's freedom knows neither law nor limitation outside himself, but it would be rash to hold that it is in the slightest capricious or arbitrary. It is governed by the inviolable law of the sanctity of the divine essence. God's free will is under the sovereign law of divine love. Similarly human freedom, if it is true freedom in action, is not submission to the coercive pressure of external force, but self-fulfillment through inner love of the good in accordance with the pattern of the divine holiness which is the eternal law (*lex aeterna*) reflected in man's own nature (*lex naturalis*). Obviously God's freedom is infallibly effective in accordance with the law of his sanctity, whereas man on his earthly sojourn is in constant danger of lapsing from the lofty eminence of obedience to law and thereby marring the integrity of his liberty. But he is still free even in his defection from the integrity and ideal of freedom, free in breaking the hedge of freedom which is the law and lapsing into the slavery of license. The law is the warning which safeguards liberty. It grants liberty and imposes a task upon it: law is both gift and summons to duty. The more the Christian grows to maturity in the liberty of God's children, the more does the law of God unfold itself to him as a living safeguard of love. It is the hedge that encircles the golden center of love. Only those who possess the liberty of the children of God have real insight into the true nature of law, which in its depths is loving dialogue with God.

In the divine activity God's creative freedom is in accord with the pattern of his eternal ideas. Therefore human freedom, fashioned in the divine image, is all the greater the more man's activity is motivated by clear and evident ideals. Just as God himself cannot act outside himself without the light of his own love, so too man cannot exercise his freedom without motives. And as God in his free creative activity chooses from the infinite treasure of his eternal ideas, so man (analogously) within certain limitations chooses among a diversity of motives. He can elect from among various good motives, preferring one to another. He can choose between the evident good and the enticement of darksome passion, choose the illusory allurement of sheer pleasure and profit or follow the attraction of the morally good motives pleasing to God, often obscured by the vain pleasure of sense.

The crucial point in question regarding liberty is not whether the external act flows freely from the inner source (from the *actus elicitus,* the elicited act), but whether this inner source itself is pre-determined by the free will itself or by something else. The decisive question is this: is freedom unequivocally determined by the motives which press upon it, or does it transcend these very motives and remain free in choosing (though it cannot make any choice without motive)? The will is not necessitated. It determines itself in making its own final or ultimate decision, whether it permits itself to be drawn to the basically good and lofty or abandons itself to the illu-

sive splendor of self—self-glory or self-seeking. Once this final or ultimate decision has been made (i.e., the willed choice of what shall be the ultimate and decisive goal of life), the motives directing one's particular actions still leave room for freedom within their own area and according to their own scope of influence, so that the will is not necessitated by them, but itself selects from among them and directs them in accordance with the ultimate goal (assuming, of course, the limitations imposed by psychological laws).

If a motive thrusts itself upon the spirit of man with such insistence as to create an abnormal psychological tension which diverts the free will from every other possible alternative, then psychic coercion has removed the conditions of freedom. It is quite a different matter if the will with undivided force of freedom is motivated by a clear and lofty incentive. The more profound the motivation, the more potent is the freedom. In the choice and nurture of true ideals lies the final decision of freedom.

IV. From what we have just said, it is evident that any formation in obedience which merely domineers by means of imperatives, without furnishing insights and motivation, breaks the free will, at best "breaks it in," but does not truly educate it. Though liberty is in part a matter of exercise and use (of true freedom), it is still much more a matter of fostering motives with insight and love. This throws light upon the importance of meditation in the spiritual life. Education to obedience springing from the inmost source of liberty must be based on motivation rather than command. Even though at first the mind cannot provide an insight into the inmost nature of the good itself, still there must always be the wholesome motivation of noble authority and the gradual clarification of the intrinsic values and a growing perception of the worth of the commandment.

Genuine formation in obedience is without doubt also education in the law (in the established norm of the good), but it is even more initiation into liberty which goes beyond the universal law, into that liberty which is born of the insight into the good and of love for the good and for that which is always more perfect. Freedom unfolds its capacity as it exercises itself in obedience, but it must be obedience of the spirit. And this is impossible without the true spirit of independence and self-mastery. The spirit of true independence (virtue of freedom) reigns when the Christian acts even without bidding, when he possesses the disposition and will to obey even though there may be no mandate or precept. The spirit of obedience is marked by free initiative and acceptance of responsibility even without command.

V. Man's liberty is relatively narrow in the scope of its activity, though, as explained above, this scope can be significantly and gradually broadened. But it can likewise be restricted and narrowed through our own fault. Scope, impress, limit of freedom are all determined by one's own individual temperament, by the historic heritage, by the moral level of environment, by the surrounding communities. The "destiny" of man sets the bounds of his liberty, but it also determines the tasks and duties and broadens the scope of the free actions. Man must accept his destiny in freedom, bear up with it, and at the same time master it.

Freedom is effective not merely on the immediate level of decision or in actual intention (*intentio actualis*). In every moral act, besides the present actual free decision, in some way the prior decisions, the pre-determinations, the prejudices make themselves felt. The virtual intention (*intentio virtualis*) is the prolongation of previous decisions which are still effective in their influence until they are revoked or completely lose their dynamic power. Even in *conversion,* which is the act of renouncing or repudiating the past and revoking the prior false decisions of the will, they still may exert a very considerable influence as false attitudes or dispositions (examples are the lowering of esteem for true values due to mental dullness or partial blindness in this important area, superficiality in positive value judgments). Only steadfast and determined personal intervention will enable us to deprive these prior decisions of their force and render them impotent.

It is likewise true that previous decisions of our will often exert no influence on subsequent series of acts either because their effectiveness is suspended for the moment, even though the past may not have been actually repudiated or renounced, or—and this is usually the case—because they are not our present concern. However, for this very reason they can reassert themselves when the occasion arises, since the disposition and tendency (*habitus*) still persist. The unrevoked prior intention or attitude of mind which does not influence the subsequent acts is a habitual intention (*intentio habitualis*). But should it again become efficacious, it is no longer merely a habitual, but a virtual intention by which we again influence the subsequent acts.

We speak of a presumed intention or readiness of will (*intentio interpretativa*) in those instances of doubt when we have no evidence that the intention was ever actually made, but reasonably presume that it was. From the entire attitude of the individual concerned we have reason to assume that he would have made such an act (the actual intention) if the matter had been placed before him for decision, or that he actually did so. An interpretative intention is real and effective in so far as it is rooted in this attitude of the Christian and is expressed in acts corresponding to it.

VI. Man is directly accountable for the entire object of his free decision, whether it be through positive act or through failure to act. In fact, the consequences of omission can be as important and as far reaching as the effects of the positive acts, or acts of commission. Man is responsible, not merely for what he directly chooses or decides upon, but also for the other objects which are mediately or indirectly within his choice. In this way they fall within the scope of his intention. Responsibility, in fact, extends to much which is not included in his particular intention as means or end (*voluntarium in se* or *voluntarium directum*), but which is foreseen as a mere result of the act intended without being directly intended or sought (*voluntarium in causa* or *indirectum*).

An example: a drinker knows how he will act when he is under the influence of drink. He may indulge in profanity, resort to quarreling or fighting, engage in immoral conversation. Despite his attempt to assure himself as he takes his drinks, "I just want to enjoy a drink or two," he is still the voluntary cause responsible for all the resultant deviations in moral conduct precisely because he voluntarily makes himself their cause. He freely does the act and foresees, in a general way at least, the effects which will ensue. The guilt, however, and it is important not to overlook this point, is not so serious as the guilt of the premeditated offense. One who consciously seeks after a sinful object is far more culpable than one who is guilty as cause. The malice is greater in the former instance because there is a greater freedom of will in the choice of evil.

The mature man must have a keen realization of the profound and far-reaching influence of his moral conduct on his own personality as a whole and on the community, both in the immediate present and in the future. And if he does good or evil with this background of general knowledge, he also assumes the responsibility for his act and its consequences. He must bear the burden of blame for his bartering with evil and is responsible for the evil consequences of his acts, even though he may deplore them. However, the difference between deliberate choice of evil and the conscious but regretful acceptance of it in this form of package deal is quite apparent.

Responsibility for the consequences of such decisions is all the weightier the more certain and immediate is the consequence or effect which is foreseen, though not intended. The certainty is greater if the cause is direct (*causa per se*) than if it is indirect (*causa per accidens*). The effect is more immediate if the cause is a proximate or immediate cause (*causa proxima vel immediata*) than if it is only mediate or remote (*causa mediata vel remota*). There is a vast difference between an act which physically and necessarily produces an effect as its efficient cause and a moral impulse given to the free act of another.

One cannot entirely prevent one's own good or even one's obligatory acts from accidentally (*per accidens*) or remotely (*remote*) producing many evil effects. Some of these are physical, such as suffering and hardship; others are moral, as vexation and scandal to others (actions with double effect). Still there is an obligation in conscience to prevent the evil effects if one can do so without offending against what is right in the particular situation in which one is placed, or against the good which one is obliged to do. If the act as such and immediately (*per se et proxime*) produces an undesired evil effect, then only proportionately serious reasons (fulfillment of an obligation, attainment of a higher necessary good) can justify the act despite the evil effects. But all the circumstances must be seriously pondered. And under no condition may evil effects which in themselves are unlawful as ends of our action, be employed as means even for the attainment of a good end. Nor is it licit to will them or approve of them subsequently in the completion of the action. Moral evil may never be made the direct object of the deliberate free act of our will. . . .

DOCTRINE ON LIBERTY

The Church has defined as a dogma of faith that the children of Adam even after the fall are still in possession of moral freedom of choice. This means simply—neither more nor less —that the normal human being, at least in the decisive stages of his moral life, has at his disposal the measure of freedom of will necessary to decide for or against God, with such validity and earnestness that by God's own sanction eternal happiness or eternal loss depends on his free choice. As far as each particular action is concerned, however, we are often perplexed. Does it or does it not have this measure of freedom? It is impossible to form a clear and certain judgment on the moral maturity of many individuals of extremely elemental mentality or of the mentally ill or feeble-minded persons: are they sufficiently free to make a deliberate decision, such as is required for mortal sin? In other words, is the restricted scope of their free will such that they are still able to take a deliberate position in opposition to God, a position which God will judge with such stern disapproval as to respond to it by eternal rejection? Ultimately, only God can judge the individual. Our study and knowledge of psychology can and should serve to teach us to be mild and cautious in our judgment of our neighbor. It should help

us to do all we can by way of understanding and correcting ourselves and also others. We must make every effort to broaden the scope of moral freedom through control or elimination of the psychic disorders that hamper it. In the fundamental problem of the nature and degree of freedom essential for moral responsibility, the Church, not experimental psychology, has the authority to make the final decision.

We learn about the transcendent splendor and mystery of our liberty only through revelation: it is the exaltation of our freedom to a supernatural likeness to God in the liberty of his children. It is the divine dowry of Christ's own obedience unto death on the cross and the incipient revelation of Christ risen in his glory. It is the power to follow Christ, which is perfected and preserved in filial obedience to God, whose message of command to his children is expressed only through his deeds and gifts of love.

The freedom of the children of God is his noblest gift, and therefore it is also our most sacred obligation and bond of love.

I. That man is created in the "image and likeness of God" implies not only that his liberty is patterned on the divine, that it is participation in the divine freedom, but also that man's knowledge is like to God's and partakes of its splendor. Indeed, God's freedom is not blind, but essentially lucid and splendid. According to the measure in which man shares this infinite lucidity and splendor of divine knowledge, in the measure of his enlightenment by the divine knowing, can he be like to God through participation in his freedom. Man's likeness to God manifests itself in every conception of truth and every act of knowing, for there can be no truth except through participation in the eternal truth. A mere theoretic grasp of contingent realities, which is not directed to any action, is on the lowest rung of similarity to God. Next follows the knowledge of practical truth with power, a "power-conscious knowing" [hence patterned on God's creative mandate: "have dominion!" (GN 1:26)]. Higher is the philosophical knowledge of essences which with true insight into supreme causes and principles points to the ultimate source of all things, God, and shows how they all lead to God. Essentially the loftiest level of divine likeness in our knowledge is attained only through love. The summit is knowledge penetrated with love, engendering love, made dynamic in love. Such in its innermost reality is God's knowledge, for God is love! The second person in the most Holy Trinity is not just any word, but the Word breathing forth love. We can enunciate nothing more pertinent on the essence of the Word of God than this: the Word in eternal and necessary *élan vital* breathes forth the Spirit of love in union with the Father.

Moral religious knowledge, salutary knowledge or "science of salvation," therefore, reaches a singular depth of assimilation to God and participation in God. This cannot be said of the most exalted scientific understanding of the profane sciences unless their essential relation to God shines forth from them and awakens love for God. As a matter of fact, a simple peasant mother with her loving knowledge of God and of good has a much nobler cultural formation (in conformity with the image of God) than a "learned" sceptic. Moral-religious knowledge elevates man in the hierarchy of the divine likeness in proportion to the degree with which it is animated by the spirit of love and inspires us to love. The most brilliant theoretic moral knowledge is not on the same high level as the simple understanding of a saint who may be altogether illiterate. . . .

V. Already in the Old Testament the inspired writers incessantly stress the truth that God does not look so much to our exterior actions, the prayer of the lips, and sacrifice. Much more does he look to the "heart," to the genuine sentiment of love, of obedience, penance. Jahweh does not complain so much about the perverted actions of the Israelites as about their "hardened heart," about their adulterous, perverse dispositions (Is 6:9f.; 29:13; cf. MK 6:52; 8:17; 16:14; JN 12:39f.). The summit of the great Messianic prophecies is reached in God's promise to wash away the sins of his people, give to them a "new heart," and instill fear of him and love for him into their hearts (JER 32:40; 31:33; Is 51:7; Ez 36:26). "And I will give them one heart, and will put a new spirit in their bowels: and I will take away the stony heart out of their flesh, and will give them a heart of flesh" (Ez 11:19). God does not desire the rending of garments, but the inner sentiment of penance. "Rend your hearts, and not your garments" (JL 2:13).

Christ continues and fulfills the teaching of the Old Testament and in the sharpest contrast to the legalistic externalism of the Pharisees lays the greatest stress on the importance of the interior disposition, especially in his Sermon on the Mount (MT 5f.). It is not primarily the external deeds which offend God, but the very thoughts and desires, the inner sentiments and dispositions. On the contrary, "blessed are the pure of heart" (MT 5:8). The heart is the seat of disposition, above all the seat of love. Not merely our actions must be well ordered, but first of all the seat, the organ of love. The heart must be "pure," that is, it may not be filled with false love and defiled through perverse dispositions. Of its inmost nature the heart that is pure will turn to the true objects of its inner sentiments. Here in this life already it will look lovingly to God and in eternity will behold him face to face.

Whereas the Pharisees severely condemned the external infraction of petty human prescriptions, the Lord castigated the "evil heart," the base disposition, from which, as from a polluted spring, all evil flows (MT 15:18; MK 7:20ff.). Without good disposition every action of ours, even sacrifice and prayer, is worthless before God. Christ complains, as did the prophet (Is 29:13), about the cult which was mere lip service because it lacked the interior disposition and good will (MT 15:8). The most bitter reproach is St. Peter's accusation of Simon Magus: "Thy heart [disposition] is not right before God" (ACTS 8:21).

Stephen hurls the charge against the Jews that they are "uncircumcised in heart," a fact which accounts for their disbelief, their resistance to the Holy Spirit (ACTS 7:51). Conversion and acceptance of the faith presupposes change of disposition (MK 1:15: "Repent and believe in the gospel." *Metanoeîn,* the Greek word for *repent,* means an inner change of thinking, an utter interior reorientation). As Stephen, so Paul also demands, instead of external circumcision, "the circumcised heart," the inner disposition of penance and change of life (ROM 2:5, 29). A "pure conscience" and pure disposition are as inseparable as the two sides of a coin (1 TM 1:5). The very essence of imitation of Christ is to assume the inner spirit of Christ. "Have this mind in you which was also in Christ Jesus" (PHIL 2:5). The new inner spirit of the Christian is made possible, not merely through conformity with the example of Christ, but also and much more through the indwelling of Christ in us (ROM 8:10; EPH 4:17–24). Christ dwelling in us is the actual source of power for this renewal within us. This grace of Christ renewing our hearts from the depths is a challenge which we dare not ignore. Because we "have put on Christ" (GAL 3:27)

through a renewal of our whole inner selves, we are commanded in every action and above all in our inner sentiment "to put on the Lord Jesus Christ" (ROM 13:14; EPH 4:24; COL 3:10) with true effectiveness. The thought underlying the entire Gospel of John and his letters is that we are renewed in being, are "in love," and therefore we must take care that we "abide in love" (JN 15:9f.; 1 JN 2:17; 4:16), that the gift of love bestowed on us descend ever deeper and deeper into our hearts.

The doctrine on the fundamental meaning of right dispositions was always clearly taught by the Fathers and theologians. According to Augustine, "it is not the exterior accomplishment, but the moral disposition which plays the decisive role." "Change your disposition and the change in your actions will follow!" If you have mercy in your heart, God will accept your alms, even if you have nothing to offer with your hand." External violence cannot rob the virgin of the splendor of virginity, if only she remain pure in her resolution in her disposition. Patient endurance even exalts the glory of virginity. The disposition makes the will good or bad. "The right will is good love; perverted will is an evil love."

Scholastic theology places the primary stress on the clear explanation of the intention (*finis operantis*). Not the external action, but the inner intention plays the most important and decisive role. Similarly in scholastic teaching the infused virtues are more than the impulse toward external works. They are the most intimate dispositions. They are active powers of the heart. Medieval moral theology devotes special attention to the movements of the senses and the emotional or sensual impulses which are not deliberate movements of the will (*motus primo primi et secundo primi*). The opinion prevalent until the time of St.

Thomas that these sudden impulses were to be looked upon as sinful, even though they were not deliberate (either because of original sin or, according to the more common opinion, because of previous failure to discipline and restrain the inner dispositions), shows what importance was attached to those inner dispositions. And the very fact that since the time of St. Thomas the teaching has prevailed that these impulses are sinful only in so far as the will freely is responsible for them, merely serves to emphasize the importance of the free will in the deliberate cultivation of the good emotional impulses and the whole emotional structure.

The great medieval teachers of mystical doctrine place even greater emphasis than do the other theologians on the significance of disposition and inner attitude as opposed to mere external activity. And this is not quietism, not even in the case of Meister Eckhart. Theirs is a Biblical and Augustinian optimism. The "renewed heart," the "good tree," will manifest itself in good fruits, in sustaining the good effort through action and, above all, in steadfast endurance of trial and suffering. Scotus and his school stress interiority and all that relates to inner attitudes even more strongly than does Thomas. As one would expect, the Franciscan school with its doctrine of the primacy of love or will over intellect, places singular emphasis on the doctrine of interior disposition and spirit. As was Max Scheler in our time, so medieval mysticism and scholasticism in the Middle Ages were probing the depths of the most profound mystery of Christian morality of interiority when they described true love as "co-willing and co-loving with God." The child of God does not love merely because God loves and what God loves, but he loves with a divine love, with God's own love, by force of a love bestowed and infused by God. He dwells in the heart of God.

Whereas in scholastic moral theology, despite a sound appraisal of interior disposition, the orientation was toward law (the eternal law, the law of the Gospel, and the law of nature) and the ideal of right order, the *devotio moderna* (the main representatives were Gerson and Thomas à Kempis) was slanted even excessively toward the moral disposition or inner spirit. But there was a deep theological basis for the devotion in the interior dispositions of Christ as model of our own. This moral teaching bore rich fruit, in the practical order, in the inner reform of countless monasteries. However, in such devotion there is always the hazard of overemphasis of the inner disposition and inner spirit. Only too readily the ardent zeal for the kingdom of God and the right order in the world based on the divine law gives way to a very narrow concern for mere correctness of personal attitude of exclusive interest in one's own salvation.

VI. There is the sharpest contrast between the optimistic spirit of the Middle Ages and its noble striving for the fulfillment of a divine order in the universe and the pessimistic outlook of Luther with its denial of a well-ordered world and its condemnation of the aspirations of the human heart. His is a withdrawal from world responsibility (from the alleged "justice of works") into a "pure interiority" of the spirit where irresistible grace rules over the "totally depraved" heart of man. Such was the attitude of Luther in his quarrel with the Church that he considered obedience to her authority above all diametrically opposed to the genuine Christian attitude, as though true obedience to the Church is irreconcilable with the purest and loftiest dispositions and does not ultimately in its inner spirit turn to God (cf. MT 18:17f.). That all good conduct must be sustained by faith and be carried out with freedom and joy is simply the ancient Catholic traditional doctrine which Luther repeats according to his own concepts.

Kant's ethic is surely also an ethic of interiority, though his sense of value is no more than a shriveled and barren conscience of obligation. It is true that we agree with Kant in making the moral decision a free and deliberate act of will. But his moral world is still too threadbare for our taste. It has nothing of value but the "good will alone." Utterly arid and dour, this ethic of Kant derives primarily from his conception of God. For him every attitude toward God is meaningless since God cannot receive anything from us.

Ethic of interiority was dealt a severe blow by Hegel, who placed the summit of morality in the state and in consequence demanded of the individual as the greatest "interior achievement" complete submission to the ethic of the state. Though it is true that he did not theoretically reject human freedom and personal responsibility, in the last analysis such freedom is completely stifled by the world spirit (universal reason) incorporated in the state. If things came to such a pass in Germany that the individual gladly acquiesced in the moral decisions of the state in every conceivable problem of life, Hegel ultimately must share the responsibility. The state and submission to its decrees supplant the personal moral sense. Absolute submission is the only worthy "interior attitude." This is the legal docility toward the state, which has little in common, surely, with the inspired concept of the sacred pages. Little remains of the profoundly personal and truly interior.

Contemporary philosophical and sociological literature deals with an ethic of interiority (*Gessinungs-ethik*), but gives it a meaning quite different from

the traditional concept derived from the Biblical teaching about the "heart of man." The Biblically orientated ethic of interiority stresses the primacy of love as an inward acquiescence in the love of the Creator and Redeemer, whereas the idealistic ethic of interiority is largely a reflection of a defective grasp of the real order of things. Such an ethic must in great part be ascribed to an unsuspecting aloofness from the sociological or psychological realities, which consciously responsible conduct cannot neglect or ignore. Rightly does the sociologist Max Weber combat that false ethic of interiority which says: "The Christian does what is right and leaves the outcome to God," thus placing the responsibility for the evil consequences of "conduct flowing from pure dispositions" on the world, on the stupidity of others, or on the will of God who created them. Surely one must clearly realize that such a position is not in accord with the true and genuine Christian ethic of interiority. Christian ethics of the heart are indeed the very antithesis of the heartless and even unprincipled ethics of success, but they are in no wise irreconcilable with an ethic of responsibility. It is the very basic disposition, the love and loving acquiescence in that which is dear to the Divine Heart, which demands that we take the ordering of creation seriously, that we be concerned about the power of sin and the triumph of Christ to be revealed in the historic order. The history of Christian ethics of interiority, especially if we include in it also the Lutheran teaching on "utter inwardness," at least warns against the danger which it harbors.

In some way interiority can degenerate into a flight from the responsibility for the Kingdom of God—just as the ethic of responsibility, because of the narrowness and limitations of man, can deteriorate into an external ethic of success.

45. *Emmanuel Cardinal Suhard: Growth or Decline of the Church, February 1947*

From Emmanuel Suhard, *Growth or Decline* (St. Louis: Fides Publishers, 1950), pp. 23-33.

WHO is going to infuse a soul into this common civilization, into this world now compartmentalized? Who will infuse the soul into this sudden unity which has come about quicker than our thought, into this planetary humanism for which we were not prepared? Who will produce the synthesis of this new universe? Who will be its principle and its inspiration?

Unbelievers affirm that it will not be the Church, for the very simple reason that the Church is dying.

They say that the signs of her agony are visible enough. Consider the case of her numbers. The human race is increasing, Church membership is decreasing. Although always a minority she used to count, at least up to now, vast groups of faithful. Today what she herself calls "the apostasy of the masses" proves her failure. Through a thousand crevices she is dissolving and she sees whole peoples breaking away from her one after the other. Her decadence, they say, is even more notable in regard to her influence, her prestige and her friendships. Once the mistress of culture whose theology gave her a monopoly of it, once the center of power which she maintained by keeping the people in ignorance, she is now only a shadow of her old self. Divided into rival factions, discredited by her own sons, she is paying, in their eyes, the price of her infidelity to her origins and, in the eyes of the world, the penalty for her congenital archaism. She no longer holds the attention of men. Now, at last, they ask, what is left to her? What she always upheld: a "class" but recently the "ruling" class, and a liberal economy with which she identified herself. Allied with the capitalist system, she is collapsing with it. The Church is disappearing with a dying world.

Dying, she must not be counted on. But were she a living thing, then above all should she be put aside, for she is, they charge, the first enemy. The reason for her misconduct? Her ends are contrary to man, even worse, to modern humanism. Between them there is a divorce. The two systems are not only different, they oppose each other.

First, as to the conception of the universe, what does science teach us? It shows us its unity in space and duration. A dynamic continuity based on matter explains man and society. This becoming is not a haphazard one. It is a dialectical chain, an inevitable developing evolution which, through the constant progress of technique, will finally emancipate man from myths and servitudes, and will permit him, within a communal organization of mankind, "to possess the earth" to which he has a right. This is an optimistic ethic which believes in happiness, and, not satisfied with merely seeking it, writes its "summa" line by line by studying methodically its biological, psychological and sociological conditions.

Faced with these creative perspectives, what, they ask, has the Church to offer? A static and theistic universe, a dependent philosophy "frozen" in impossible dogmas, a negative *a priori* ethics over which a caste spirit hovers in jealous defiance of a science ever ready to dethrone God. As for the human person, they say, the Christian era has fashioned a model without force or beauty. Christianity has emasculated man. By offering him an avenue of escape into the next world, it detaches him from worldly tasks and turns him away from any fraternal participation in the City wherein he lives. Weak in battle, ineffective in action, timid in the face of adventure, the Christian, as a result of his "bourgeois" or repressed upbringing, is no companion. You cannot count on him to conquer the world.

With such a program how can the Church be other than a stranger in a world which believes in itself and enthusiastically devotes itself to the elaboration of a future at once more real and more beautiful? It is not astonishing that this conquest is taking place outside the Church, and even against her, to the extent that she opposes its success. No, modern man expects nothing from the Church in building the new world. He refuses and rejects this witness of a long dead past.

Here is where the believers have their say. They too have asked themselves the question. And their reply is clear: No, the Church is not dead. No, the new world will not come into being without her. But this is true only on certain conditions.

Here the hypotheses are divergent, not to say contradictory. The position of Catholics—and the numerous critiques to which they have devoted themselves in recent years—can be reduced, we believe, to two essential attitudes.

The first is to remain on the defensive. In their arguments they stand up to their opponents without flinching. The adherents of this attitude reply to aggressive atheism with a dogmatism of defense. It is not the Church which is in agony or at fault but the modern world—or simply the world—for it is "modern" only in our eyes. The problems to which it refers in order to justify its divorce from the Church are in no way original. They can be found in all past crises. "There is nothing new under the sun." The problems are the same, only their names change. The Church is not behind the times. It is man who sins or reasons badly. Like

all systems this one will have its day. Let the storm pass. Truth always triumphs in the end. The Church has known other crises, she is not afraid of this one.

The great danger the Church is running today, they say, is in wishing to adapt herself. She must resist this perpetual temptation. It is not for her to adapt her teaching but for civilizations to assimilate it. Let her strengthen therefore her intransigence. Let her turn a deaf ear to the deceptive appeals which the evil spirit already tried on the Savior. Today everything tends to make her forget her essential mission which is to give men, without concessions, the "words which do not pass." If she gives up this monopoly for a problematical growth she is done for. For the Church is not of this world. She is the kingdom of God. Far from trying the impossible task of bridging the gap which separates her from the world, she should steadfastly remain outside and above its successive fluctuations. The only attitude for the Church is to break with the world.

From a doctrinal point of view this should express itself by an integral return to traditional forms, reference to official texts which guarantee rectitude and strengthen her defenses. Above all, there must be no concessions, for they lead to surrender. Let there be only "truth" in all its hardness without flinching.

In action Catholics will remember that compromises win neither esteem nor advantage. Let them beware of premature co-operation. In union there is strength. The affirmation alone of their *credo,* of their membership among the people of God is worth more than rash advances. The Church will only come out of the crisis by refusing to establish herself in institutions. She is less afraid of Nero than of Constantine.

Those who criticize the Church for her lack of effectiveness in temporal affairs urge her to an exactly opposite reform. The Church—in the West—has not evolved with civil society. She has remained frozen in feudal forms which worked in times past. In our time instead of being fused with society as she was in the Middle Ages when the parish and the commune had the same extension and the same life, the Church is "absent" from the city. She hovers over humanity instead of being incarnate in its flesh and blood. In her message to men she has everything she needs, nay, more than she needs to animate the contemporary structures and to draw up plans for the future, but she does not use her resources. She lets strangers, or adversaries, take the decisive initiative on questions of doctrine, culture or action. When she acts or speaks it is often too late. In scientific research, social legislation, or humanism she has few innovators. It is not in this way that she will win the world to Christ. The Church still has time to hold her place—and even the first—in the formation of the future. But on one condition: She must become incarnate: "God became man in order that man become God." Then, and only then, will the Church come to life again.

The great majority of those who favor adaptation, this penetration of contemporary civilization, mean to respect formally the integral content of the faith. They do not soften their criticisms of the Church and the hierarchy, and the suggestions they propose bear upon many problems. As a result of their daily experiences with the de-Christianized masses, many apostles, both priests and laymen, have concluded that modifications—usually secondary, but pressing ones—are necessary for effective evangelization. They want a concrete and adapted religious teaching to replace the present preaching and catechizing which are too far from the Gospels. From theology, which is not a thing completed like

revelation, they want—without sacrificing anything—an attempt at synthesis and realism which will place the major dogmas of Christianity at the center and within the reach of the spiritual life of this century. They point out that worship and the form of the liturgy are often incomprehensible. For this reason the mass of the faithful and often the elite among Christians cannot enter into the great communal prayer. They practice—if they practice at all—a formalistic religion having no relation to the rest of their life. Will not the Church help them by facilitating the reception of the sacraments and giving them a better understanding of the sacred rites? They point out, too, that the independence of the laymen is often more verbal than real. Aware that the laity has reached its majority they claim for it more extensive responsibilities. Even financial matters, particularly insofar as they concern acts of worship, arouse a demand for reform.

It is clear from these appeals—and many others which we cannot consider here—that they all come down to the same request: the Church should adapt herself to the modern world if she wants to reconquer it.

Shall she remain rigid in order to safeguard all or shall she permeate all in order to win it to herself?

These are the two poles of Catholic opinion, at least in France.

Who is right? The answer is of great importance. It will determine the practical attitude of the majority of Catholics—for they have not taken sides. Attracted alike by these new values, and troubled to the point of distrust by so many deviations, they watch and wait, some, through timidity or tranquillity. Others, wholly sincere, do not know how to escape the dilemma which, on the collective level, constituted these two groups, and which on the personal level, torments their souls cruelly. For they belong to two worlds and know it. Loyal to both, they stand aloof. As citizens of the world they feel themselves a part of it and responsible for its destiny. As sons of God, they understand their mysterious incorporation in his church and their transcendent vocation. To avoid betrayal they refuse to choose and commit themselves.

Meanwhile, they observe the anxiety and suffer because of it. They see clearly that the world crisis reacts inevitably on the Church which has her roots in it. They do not fear for her and her final triumph. But they wonder how she can pull through the present and how they can help her. The mysticism of progress which seduces their contemporaries exerts upon them, without their realizing it, an influence, and perhaps an attraction. When they see their Church divided, and pulled in one direction and the other by her sons, between refusal and participation, shaken by conflicting currents, torn between the immutable and the present, her anxiety becomes their own; and, to avoid bewilderment, they take refuge either in prayer or in some form of diversion.

To stiffen, to adapt herself, or to wait? Who is right? What is the meaning of this crisis? What do these initiatives and anxieties signify? An agony or growing pains? An autumn or a springtime of the Church?

We have considered it our first duty to reply to this question which torments so many Catholic consciences, and to the accusations of our adversaries. As father and pastor of your souls we hear daily the appeal which rises from every horizon to this crossroads which is Paris. From the provinces and abroad, from intellectual and labor circles, from letters, reviews, congresses and private conversations, comes the same question, demanding a single clear decision. That is why this year we have chosen this crucial problem of our times for our pastoral letter. Our reply does not pretend, however, to solve everything.

Concerning the crisis we will say only this: insofar as it reveals a division among Catholics, it is an evil and ought to stop. The continuation of the mutual excommunications between brothers in Jesus Christ would constitute a scandal and an obstacle to going ahead. In proportion, however, as these parallel though opposite attitudes evidence an intense love of the Church they are a proof of her vitality, the sign of growing pains. This multiplication of ideas and undertakings is more reassuring than a stagnant satisfaction. We would like both to calm the anguish we observe among too many Catholics confronted with the times ahead, and to trouble the deceptive security into which too many of the faithful settle. We would like to show that both the only explanation of the present crisis and the only criterion of certitude and of action for the Christian today rest in the profound nature of the Church as her dogma and her history reveal them to us.

Far from concluding that the Church is in decline everything points to her growth.

46. *Luigi Sturzo: The Christian Democratic Movement (1815-1848; 1939-1946), 1 July 1946*

From Don Luigi Sturzo, *Nationalism and Internationalism* (New York: Roy Publishers, 1946), pp. 92-98, 124-130.

4, 1. . . . AT THE end of the Napoleonic wars Europe was in the process of bringing to maturity two great movements that were to cover the whole nineteenth century: one for constitutional regimes, among the bourgeois classes; the other for economic guarantees, among the working classes. The first of these movements gave origin to Liberalism; the other to Socialism.

When we speak of "liberalism" we must remember that in Europe there was not a single "liberalism" but various theoretical and practical forms, distinct in nationality (French, English, Italian, Spanish, and even German, Austrian, Hungarian liberalism) and in character (philosophical, religious, political, economic liberalism). Nor did socialism ever have a precise definition: its various phases are indicated by the names of their leaders (such as Saint-Simon, Fourier, Owen, Engels, Henry George, and the most famous of all, Karl Marx) or by their varying characteristics (Anarchical, Syndicalist, Communist, Christian Democratic) according to the prevalent economic and political pattern.

More than the working classes, it was really the bourgeoisie who, during the first half of the nineteenth century, kept gaining position in the economic and political fields in the name of liberty by inaugurating individualistic systems that facilitated their ascent. On the other hand the working masses were agitating and attempting to reorganize themselves in order to make headway against exploitation by a nascent capitalistic industry. It is necessary to keep in mind this dynamic process of the two principal classes of continental Europe in order to understand the role enacted by the authorities of the Catholic Church and by Catholics themselves from that time to the present day.

When one speaks of the Catholic Church it is necessary to avoid the error of attributing to bishops and popes every initiative made by the faithful of the local clergy, or of isolating popes and bishops from the faithful themselves. In the question that we are to examine we shall find individual, unauthorized initiatives (sometimes opposed at the time of origin) that afterward insert themselves into the general activity of Catholics and eventually obtain sanction; or else, other initiatives which in the beginning seem favored by ecclesiastic authorities and then gradually end by being merely tolerated, or opposed and even condemned. The Church, like every living, moral body, assimilates or rejects theories and practices of the earthly society, viewing them only from the point of view of Christian doctrine and morality. The historical developments deriving therefrom may be unwanted by the ecclesiastical authorities and can pervade society in an entirely autonomous manner.

The popes of the beginning of the nineteenth century, and many bishops too, were opposed to movements called liberal. In the Restoration and Holy Alliance period there prevailed the point of view of return to a prerevolutionary past. There was fear of liberty, and while admitting parliaments (as in France and Bavaria) they tried to restrict their functions and limit their importance. Still remembering the excesses of the French Revolution and the movements of the masses in revolt, some of them believed that by restoring the privileges of the nobles, clergy and monarchies, it was possible to hold in check the liberal groups and parties.

The effects of such a policy, directed by Vienna for the whole of Europe and agreed to by all the other powers, including England until Canning's arrival, were contrary to the trend of European interest and order. There were thirty years of conspiracies, revolts, repressions, civil wars. In 1830 France changed king and regime, and Belgium obtained her independence. In 1848 Sicily was the first to convene parliament on her own initiative and to proclaim on January 12 the revolt and war against the king of Naples. Pius IX, who had aroused the enthusiasm of the whole world for his nomination to pope in 1846 and for the political amnesty that followed it, granted his constitution. France ousted her king and proclaimed the Second Republic. There were uprisings in Munich, Prague, Berlin, Vienna, Budapest. Even the bourgeoisie was frightened and hastened to return to absolutism, except in Belgium and Piedmont.

In this period many Catholics had been for constitutional liberties in spite of the fact that often local ecclesiastical authorities were hostile: indeed, it would be impossible to understand the movements in Ireland, Belgium, France, Italy, the Rhineland, and Bohemia without taking into account the favorable attitude and initiative taken by eminent Catholics, the clergy, and laity.

The most noted of the Catholic leaders of the time was Daniel O'Connell in Ireland; to him is due the first political awakening of his island. His activity was not always pleasing to Rome; but he was admired as the champion of Catholicism and liberty.

The revolt of Belgium, its separation from Holland, and the constitutional form adopted were due to the masses and their leaders, who knew how to unite the national and Catholic spirit of the country to a profound feeling of liberty.

Another champion arose in Germany: the Westphalian priest, von Ketteler. He was a deputy to the Diet of Frankfurt in 1848, and there upheld the principle of liberty. Afterward, he, as the bishop of Mainz, espoused the Christian concept of property—the first indication of social laws that he later developed at Offenbach.

In France, the new movement for liberty was guided by the Abbé de Lamennais, with whom the youths Lacordaire and Montalembert had become associated. In 1832, Gregory XVI condemned some principles upheld by the newspaper they published, *l'Avenir* (although the pope did not mention it by name). Lamennais rebelled and ended outside of the Church; Montalembert and Lacordaire submitted and continued their political-social activity so that we find the latter a deputy to the Parliament of Paris in 1848, and the former in the House of Peers sustaining the political and social principles that were afterward to be those of Christian Democracy.

In the meantime there arose in France a first class youth who through his initiative and culture was to become an international figure: Frederic Ozanam. He was the first to give the real meaning of democracy and to affirm it in the difficult period between 1847 and 1853, not only from his professorial chair at the Sorbonne, but also through his newspaper and his organizational activity.

In Italy at that time the greatest proponent of liberty and democracy among Catholics was the Sicilian Theatine, Gioacchino Ventura, who after 1849 was forced to go into exile. His celebrated discourses in Rome on Daniel O'Connell (1847) and on the dead of Vienna (1848), his defense of the Sicilian revolt (1848) and his insistence that Pius IX should maintain the constitution, earned for him the hatred of reactionaries. Another great man, more famous than Ventura, and also a friend of Pius IX, was the philosopher who founded a religious congregation, the Abbé Antonio Rosmini Serbati, favorable to constitutional liberties and to the liberation of Italy from Austria. He, too, was persecuted by reactionaries.

Catholics, before 1848, headed an important intellectual, historical and literary movement which later became political. It was baptized Neo-Guelph because to the ideas of liberty and national independence they united an understanding with the papacy in an interstate Italian federation. The Abbe Vincenzo Gioberti was its exponent with his *The Primacy of Italians* and Cesare Balbo with his *The Hopes of Italy*. Both of them were later ministers of the Subalpine government. With the failure of the revolutionary uprisings of 1848 not only in Italy but also in all of Europe, and after Pius IX had gone into exile at Gaeta and had changed his policy, Neo-Guelphism fell as a political ideal. Liberal Catholics (among whom the greatest was Alessandro Manzoni, a poet and philosopher of international fame) joined the other liberal current without, however, renouncing their religious faith.

While the bourgeoisie in Europe was constructing the constitutional state—called Liberal from the prevalent current, but in fact a mixture of liberalism, conservatism and radicalism—the workers and peasant classes were held out of politics by lack of the right to vote, which was restricted at that time to income and tax-paying groups. The industrial workers had no guarantees of economic security, while the peasants were in wretched circumstances, oppressed by usury and in certain countries still wearing the chains of their traditional servitude to the soil.

Under such conditions two movements developed in Europe during the period: one for economic reform and the other for the political rights of the working classes. The latter asked for the political vote; the former appealed to revolt.

The year 1848 not only marked the political revolution of the bourgeoisie, it marked also the social-economic revolt of the masses. The Communist Manifesto bears that date; Marx emerges as the new prophet.

Another voice was contemporary to that of Marx; a voice certainly feebler and heard by few at the moment, but which had far-reaching effects—the voice of the Frenchman, Frederic Ozanam, for Christian Democracy. Ozanam was prepared to speak. In his commercial law course given at Lyons in 1839-40 he had already shown that he possessed a clear vision of the social problems of the time and the necessity for adequate, urgent measures. In his trips through Italy he came into contact with Gioacchino Ventura. Ozanam realized the necessity for Catholics to dedicate themselves to social and political reforms. His celebrated phrase was "On to the Barbarians." The modern barbarians were the working classes in revolt who were erupting into the political world. Catholics, he maintained, should support their claims.

Ozanam wrote in 1848: "Let us give up our repugnances and resentments and turn toward that democracy, that people that does not know us. Let us woo them not only with our preaching but with our good deeds. Let us help them, not only with those alms which make man obliged to man, but with our efforts to obtain from them institutions that will set them free and improve them."

And in September of the same year (year of struggles, hopes, delusions) when he was directing in Paris *l'Ère*

Nouvelle (The New Era), he wrote to his brother: "I have believed and still believe in the possibility of Christian Democracy; I do not even believe in anything else in the political field. . . ."

Ozanam was the prophet of the social activity of Catholics. Through him the term "Christian Democracy" entered into the consciousness of his followers—it matters not whether few or many, for it inspired far reaching social and political action.

Though Ozanam is known by many only as a great historical critic, a philosopher and the founder of the Society of St. Vincent de Paul (diffused over the whole world), those who have had faith in Christian Democracy place him in the top rank as their precursor. . . .

4, 6. "The People and Freedom Group" was founded in London in 1936 by some young people in agreement with Mrs. V. Crawford, a pupil of Cardinal Manning, and the author for the purpose of raising in Great Britain the voice of Christian Democracy and of educating youth to participate in national and international public life with moral and Christian perspectives. The People and Freedom groups are not political parties but nuclei of political action.

"People and Freedom" is Savonarola's motto: "People" means not only the working class but the totality of citizens, because all are to enjoy liberty and participate in government. "People" also means democracy; but democracy without freedom would be tyranny, just as freedom without democracy would become liberty only for some privileged class, never for the whole people.

The mottoes taken by the Group were: *magna est veritas et praevalebit,* against the lying propaganda of the Fascists; and *fiat justitia,* against the appeasement method of the democracies. When we remember that the first

group was founded in 1936, just when the Spanish Civil War had created an atmosphere of lies and injustice on both sides, the significance of the mottoes is better understood. The Group is formed of Catholics but has a Section of Friends of the Group in which Christian Democrats of all denominations participate.

The Group was against the Spanish War, and for the conciliation of both sides in order to avoid the creation of a Fascist-type dictatorship in Spain. To this end, it promoted a committee formed by representatives of various English political parties "for civil and religious peace in Spain." A convention was held in Paris, presided over by Wickham Steed, Jacques Maritain, and Madariaga. The proposal of conciliation was presented to Lord Halifax and G. Bonnet, the foreign ministers of England and France. All would have gone well, but Chamberlain refused to be an intermediary to Mussolini and preferred to sign the Mediterranean Pact with Italy, leaving Mussolini free in Spain.

Well known also is the opposition by "People and Freedom" to the *de jure* recognition of the Abyssinian conquest by Italy. A statement was made to Lord Halifax, with whom there was an exchange of interesting letters that document the unfortunate history of the affair.

The interest of the London "People and Freedom Group" in the Basque children brought to England, and later in the war refugees of various countries, has shown the usefulness of such a movement. This Group held the first assembly in London in favor of Occupied France, on 27 June 1940. It supported De Gaulle from the first, when in London there was still doubt as to what he represented. Interesting and significant is the use that the newspaper *People and Freedom,* published in London, is making of the principal figures of Christian Democracy and its historical development in the various countries.

Finally, in August, 1940, friends of the "People and Freedom Group" decided to form an "International Christian Democratic Union" to take the place of the secretariat of Paris. The union was to be more widely representative, including not only the parties but also political groups and social movements. The object of the union as defined by article 2 of the constitution was: "to create permanent bonds of solidarity between the Christian Democratic movements in the various nations, through association on the political plane, so as to combine their activities in the fight against the forces of materialism and totalitarian oppression and for the triumph of organic and parliamentary democracy in the government of states and as a means of assuring peace and solidarity among all men." It held its first assembly in London in January, 1941, with the support of Christian Democratic groups in England, France, Italy, Poland, Czechoslovakia, Holland, Belgium, Catalonia and the Basque Provinces. Many other general reunions were subsequently held.

The union was in favor of a real League of Nations, with political and juridical functions, with its own means for impeding effectively new recourses to arms. "People and Freedom" of London promoted an inquiry based on the motto, "A League of Nations Now," which had authoritative support. The defense of the Atlantic Charter against every *real politik* manipulation has been supported by the press and in timely discussions.

Italy has been the first country in which Christian Democracy was constituted on two bases—political and social-labor—both in the liberated zones and in those still occupied by the Germans. With the fall of Fascism in July,

1943, five parties of an anti-Fascist character emerged: the Socialist, the Christian-Democratic, the Communist, the Liberal, and the Actionist. In many cities committees of liberation were formed, composed of the representatives of the five parties (in some provinces six parties, the additional one of a local character), in order to confront the enemy, to avoid a resurgence of Fascism in any guise, and to prepare the constituent assembly which must decide the future regime of Italy.

The Christian Democratic Party was formed on the initiative (taken in May 1942) of the former members of the "Popular Party." There was no return to the former name. The members wanted to take up again the ancient tradition of Christian Democracy in order to mark more distinctly the party's personality with the public, and to bind themselves once again to all similar movements in Europe and elsewhere.

Christian Democracy makes more of an appeal to young people than did the name Popularism as they were rising out of the Fascist lethargy and reorienting themselves for new political battles. Popularism as a name did not take hold among the masses in spite of the success of the Popular Party, because the people preferred their ancient motto.

In all occupied countries the Christian Democrats participated in the movements of resistance; often they were the chief leaders. In France they were the first to oppose the Vichy policy, to resist making a moral theory of political conformity, and to prevent Catholics from being tied by certain hasty ecclesiastical declarations to the fate of Pétain's government. But that is not merely to the credit of the Christian Democrats, because even a certain number of Catholics of the right and bishops became aware of the danger for France and the Church in a Vichy

Government subject to the will of Berlin and the intrigues of the most discredited men in France, such as Laval, Maurras, Déat, and Doriot.

Stronger and more constant was the resistance of Catholics in Belgium, Holland, Luxembourg, Bohemia and Poland. Even in Germany and Austria (aside from the attitude taken by the bishops from the religious and moral point of view), the only passive resistance is due to Socialist and Christian Democratic groups.

In Latin America, at various times, tendencies toward Christian Democracy have been noted. In the social field there are not lacking labor unions or leagues and co-operatives promoted by Catholics. One of the most noted of the unions, in Buenos Aires, is promoted and directed by Bishop De Andrea.

On the political terrain, too, there are the Civic Union of Uruguay, the Popular Party of Argentina, Christian Democratic Party of Brazil, and the Christian Popular Party of Chile, all of which are inspired by the principles of Christian Democracy.

North America has not had any movements of Christian Democracy as in Europe. But the hierarchy and the Catholic press have favored labor unions, especially since the First World War, and have widely diffused the social theories of the papal encyclicals (particularly the *Quadragesimo Anno* of Pius XI) and the Catholic school of thought. The tradition of Cardinal Gibbons has never ceased. One of the best pioneers of social action was Monsignor John A. Ryan. During the war, Monsignor Francis J. Haas (before being named bishop) was chosen by President Roosevelt as chairman of the Fair Employment Practices Committee. The National Catholic Rural Life Conference is a social institution of great importance, and its executive secretary, Monsignor Luigi Ligutti, comes from a family in the Italian region of Friuli most closely tied to the Christian Democratic movement. The Antigonish co-operatives are well known in Canada and America too.

American political life differs widely from that of Europe. This writer has attempted to introduce "People and Freedom" groups here, but he has to recognize that the implementation of social ideas in the political field is very difficult, though Christian Democracy interests some intellectual and political quarters.

The first general elections which have taken place in continental Europe after the war have revealed the ripening of Christian Democracy in every country. In a few months the parties of such an ideology (though called by different names in each country) have achieved political leadership, emerging on top between the Leftist and Rightist parties. Before the war, Catholic parties, with their Christian Democratic wings, often led coalition governments in Holland, Belgium, and Luxembourg, but a Christian Democratic (or Social Christian) Party was never autonomous and as strong in those countries as it is now. In Italy, the Popular Party was strong enough (before Fascism) to win one-fifth of the seats in the lower chamber; but the Christian Democratic party (heir of the Popular Party) has now two-fifths of the seats in the constituent assembly, and its leader, Dr. Alcide de Gasperi, is the premier of the Government. In France the Christian Democrats, before the war, were comprised of three small groups: the "popular democrats" with sixteen deputies in the chamber of deputies; the "populars" of Alsace and Lorraine with fourteen deputies; and the "young republic" with four deputies. The Popular Republican movement has now one hundred and sixty-two deputies in the constituent assembly and as the leading party, Mr. Bidault, its leader, is the president of the government and the state.

Even in the occupied countries, Austria, Hungary, and Germany, the Christian Democratic parties (or People's parties) are the leading parties in most of the elections; a little setback is noted only in Czechoslovakia and that was due to the gain in the Communist party. In Poland the people's party is animated with the same ideals and aspirations as that of Western Christian Democracy even though the name of Christian Democracy was introduced there by another group which is probably still fighting for its autonomy.

The new position of political and governmental responsibility of the Christian Democratic parties in Europe during the coming year of reconstruction will test the strength, usefulness and the possibilities of a movement created by the people and for the people, and a movement which is popular in its structure and in its aim, truly democratic and fundamentally Christian.

47. *Yves Congar, O.P.: The Position and Proper Role of the Laity in the Church, 1953*

From Yves Congar, *Lay People in the Church,* trans. by Donald Attwater (Westminster, Maryland: The Newman Press, 1957), pp. 429-436.

THE laity (and monks as such) are not the subject of the acts by which the Church receives her structure as institution of salvation, which involve the exercise of apostolical powers; they are not the subject of the juridical mission constitutive of apostleship, which is carried out in various organs of apostolicity. In the gospels and Acts we see that the apostles, and those joined with them are appointed afterwards to exercise part of their ministry, partake of competences . . . that the other faithful do not share, competences that enable them to play the part in the building up of the church that St. Paul calls that of master-builders and of foundations. The faithful are indeed living stones and are all part of the temple; they are neither master-builders nor foundation, but rather are themselves built and based. There are gifts of authority and mediation in the Church and they are accorded to some members only. This is the hierarchical principle.

But apostolicity is an organic function, a service, a ministry. It is not an end in itself. It exists for the body and in the body; for the body, in somewhat the same way as the master-builder exists for the house; in the body in somewhat the same way as the foundations exist for the house once it is built. Foundations that are not organically part of the building do not make a house—they belong to an unfinished plan, or a ruin. All the stones are the house, and each one for itself makes the "act of the house," so to speak; some of them do this as foundation, but in order that all the others may be a house and not simply a formless mass of materials. The Church's hierarchical principle is of necessity accompanied by a communal principle.

These two principles are in no wise opposed, since the first is expressed in an organic function of a body wholly living throughout. Nothing is more noticeable than the persistence with which the Bible joins in the same passages mention of the functions or competences proper to the apostolic ministry with the affirmation of a life and spiritual quality in which all share. The Scriptures and tradition speak of the Church essentially as a living organism. She is the body of Christ; she is a city or a family all of whose members are active, though not all equal; if she is called a temple, it is a temple whose stones have life. All do not take part in the laying of the foundations and in directing the building, but all share in the dignity of the whole, in the functions that compose it and in the activities of its life.

In the Church's dignity. We are inclined to overlook this aspect, but the fathers were very conscious of it. As members of the body of Christ, the faithful share in his kingly and priestly dignity. There is in the world an order of inert existence, then an order of sensitive and perishable life, then an order of spiritual life; but beyond that there is an order of properly divine life, in and through the son of God made man, Jesus Christ. The name of Christian that every baptized person bears raises us to that height of dignity.

In the "body" each one fills a part determined by his vocation, by the gifts accorded him, and by his state and function. We have seen with what vigor this teaching of St. Paul and the fathers was taken up in the encyclical letter *Mystici Corporis*. Hierarchical functions alone assure the Church's structure as institution of salvation and, in that sense, they alone are essential to her existence pure and simple; but other functions enter into the concrete morphology of the Church and form part of her internal organization. The encyclical mentions charismatics (apparently in the modern sense of the word, which implies exceptional gifts); religious who make public profession of the evangelical counsels, whether in contemplative life or in the doing of works of spiritual

or corporal mercy; married people, fathers and mothers, godparents; all the members of the "order" of laity, and especially those who strive in Catholic Action.

Here we see, with the addition of a new category, the classic list of "ministries, grades, professions, states, orders and functions" (these words occur in the encyclical), of which tradition has always seen the body of Christ, the Church, to be made up (sometimes with the addition of preachers, widows and deaconesses). The Church is, then, presented to us as an organism in which certain functions ensure the existence of the institution and others ensure its perfection, in accordance with the will of God who bestows his gifts and his vocations as he pleases. So far as concerns its essential structure, the Church existed in the apostles, whose heirs and successors are the bishops; their priesthood is necessary to the institutional structure.

But from the beginning Jesus willed that, side by side with the apostles, there should be the seventy (or seventy-two) disciples, the holy women, and others. The list of the different "orders" of which mention has been made could be increased, or all could be reduced to two, religious life and life in the world; but in any case they too are necessary, not that the Church as institution may exist, but that she may fulfill her mission to the uttermost and fully carry out her work as body of Christ.

The lay function is necessary for the carrying out of this mission and work. Were it only a question of a receiving subject, a beneficiary, of the work of grace carried out by the priesthood, the monastic function would be enough. Monks are, one might say, mankind passing into a pure state in the Church, so offering themselves that Christ's life may inform them directly and wholly. But God's design is not that there should be only a Church here below, but rather a Church and a world, a Church with a mission to the world and making use of its resources; and at the last a kingdom, which each after its fashion will have prepared. The work of the mystical body involves the bringing together under Christ of all that the wealth of creation and the virtualities of mankind can achieve: the first Adam needs the Second Adam that he may be saved, but the Second Adam supposes the first, that he may save him and have something to reign over.

As for the Church's mission, it is fulfilled only if the gospel be declared to every creature, if creation with all its growth and increase be offered in Christ; it is not fulfilled in all its requirements and consequences unless there be a Christian influence opening the way to faith at the level of human structures, at work throughout civilization to turn it Christward.

These things can be done only by lay people, for they belong both to the world and to the Church in a way that is true neither of the clergy nor of the monks. And so the lay function as such is necessary to the Church's mission and to the economy of grace. Lay people are the proper and irreplaceable subject of some of the activities through which this mission and this work are accomplished in their fullness. We have seen how this, their own, mandate is determined by the providential circumstances of their mundane engagement; how it corresponds to the part of the Church's mission in which she acts through her spiritual "powers"; and how this mandate *ex spiritu, ex circumstantiis,* is confirmed by the hierarchical apostleship, which joins that of the laity to itself and therein finds its complement. We asked by what title lay people are the subject of functions by which the Church is con-

structed and how far they are necessary to her, and we find the answer is to a considerable degree positive. But that is not all. The laity also share, and fully, in the acts of the Church's life.

So far as its final determinations are concerned, that life reaches the body through the channel of apostolicity; but this is an organic function ordered by the Holy Spirit to the quickening of the whole body with the life of its head. Thus animated, the entire body is in the strongest sense of the word, concerned in the prophetical, priestly, apostolic, saving activity in which Christ takes those who are his as partners; the body is the true subject of all life in Christ, and is alone its adequate subject. This life is actualized in its fullness only in the totality of the body. And therefore, on the one hand, the Lord can be wholly found and truth fully known only in the fellowship of the whole; on the other, the hierarchical instances of apostolicity themselves, being what they are only in view of the body, can be exerted only in and with it.

That is a truth that we came upon at the end of all our inquiries, and principally under two forms, namely, the idea that the faithful are the *pleroma* of the hierarchy, and the idea of an association of communal principle with hierarchical principle. This is more particularly noticeable in the spheres of liturgical worship, of the life of faith, and of apostleship. There we find both duality and unity of subject. Duality, since the hierarchical priesthood and the magisterium are not at all a delegation by the people; the apostolic mission of the twelve, continued in the episcopal hierarchy, is complete and whole in itself; and yet there is a priesthood of the faithful, an infallibility of the believing Church, and an apostolic mission of all. Unity, since we have recognized that there is a sense in which the faithful with their clergy form one single subject of worship, of infallible faith and witness, and of apostleship. There is but one Lord, one Spirit, one Body; the Holy Spirit that quickens the hierarchical organs in order that the body may have life, and the Holy Spirit that quickens the whole body in order that it may do the works of that life, can only go together, if we may venture to put it so, for they are the same. As in the whole of creation, so in the Church, God goes from unit to unity through the many; he distributes his grace by communicating it to many individuals and he brings that many to unity in communion, in a kind of concelebration of the mystery of the same life. In so doing, God is only reflecting his own mystery in the Church, for everything in him is a proceeding from one principle, a communication to several, and a perfect communion in unity. *O beata Trinitas!*

The association of the laity with the hierarchy extends to a certain co-operation with it, at any rate at the level of execution, in the order of the juridical mission of which the hierarchy is the proper subject. We remember what we have found in the liturgy of worship, in teaching, in the apostolate and even in the regulation of God's household. There were the hierarchical power and acts coming from above, and the acts of life of the whole body from below; but also a sort of taking over of the second by the first which leads to, for instance, a liturgical worship of the Church as such, coming between properly sacramental acts and private personal prayer; or again, between apostleship, a certain "sharing" of the latter, and the instituted apostolate of Catholic Action. There were, too, the participations—however tenuous—in teaching authority and the functions of regulation. Thus the principle of association is found even in

institutions and is expressed canonically. But it is most fruitfully at work in the wider sphere of life, in an association of clergy with laity, wherein the priest energizes most effectively as spiritual man, as thoughtful and cultivated man, as apostolic man, his people's guide, joined with the faithful in seeking ways and means for the Church's well-being in the actual circumstances and events of history.

It is true that the development of ideas has worked rather against the combination of the communal principle with the hierarchical principle, and for an elaboration of the latter alone, especially in the West. For a long time the idea prevailed that hierarchical acts, sacramental celebrations in particular, were acts of the mystical body and that they could be accomplished only in the fellowship of the body. It became necessary to make it clear that their validity does not come from the body as such, but from on high. This necessary precision was secured at the beginning of a whole movement which developed the theology of hierarchical powers and means of grace—and therefore of the Church as institution—and it certainly contributed to the isolation of the hierarchical principle.

During the same era (eleventh and twelfth centuries), the old discipline that connected it clearly and effectively with the communal principle gave place to other usages. There was a change from priestly ordinations made for the service of a given church to ordinations "without title"; from episcopal elections with a lower clergy and people's element to elections reserved to the cathedral chapter; from canonizations made in various ways from below to canonizations reserved to the pope; from the idea of authority as guardian of tradition to that of authority as source of law; from communion bound up with the eucharistic celebration to communion out of Mass, from reserved hosts. These points could be illustrated by many references and the list could be easily lengthened: they all represent an impulse in the same direction, namely, towards isolated affirmation and exercise of the hierarchical principle.

In this matter there is considerable difference between the West and the East, which became so unhappily separated from one another at the time to which we have just referred. The West has tended to emphasize the hierarchical principle, the East the communal principle. The West looks at and stresses above all that there is only one principle and that the body receives from it: this can be seen in the idea of priesthood, in the theology of papal power, even in Mariology, wherein one can easily tend to make God's gifts a personally held privilege. . . .

The East, however, looks at and puts more stress on how all share that in which the hierarchical principle resides. But she does not deny the hierarchical principle, any more than the West entirely disregards the communal principle. The two are complementary, just as, fundamentally, the East and West are themselves complementary, having been providentially willed by God to be thus without separation, in a duality and fellowship which themselves form part of the concrete pattern of the Church.

Every idea ought to be both expressed and safeguarded in outward signs. For its proper expression in the Church, the union of our two principles has to have its significant signs, and there are no finer and better ones than those of the liturgy. As Pope Pius XI said to Dom Bernard Capelle, the liturgy is not simply "the Church's *didascalia";* beyond its defined ideas, it is the sacred ark wherein the spirit of the Church is kept and expressed. We have seen how at Mass all the forms of priesthood are operative in their mutual organic relationships and connexions. When priest and people assure one another that the Lord is with them and, thus assured, the priest says "let us pray," the hierarchical principle is effectually completed in the communal principle and the true nature of the mystical body is made manifest. The whole Mass is a wonderful expression and making real of the Church's symphonic unity, different members filling diverse roles in the oneness of the whole: one precants, another picks up the chant from his lips and continues it; one reads, another blesses; one consecrates, the other communicates; the priest, the deacon, the acolyte have their various offices and the service is made a whole only through their respective actions. . . .

48. *Pope Pius XII: Apostolic Constitution, "Provida Mater Ecclesia," on Secular Institutes, 2 February 1947*

From Salvador Canalo, *Secular Institutes and the State of Perfection* (Dublin: Scepter, Ltd., 1959), pp. 135-154.

WITH signal diligence and maternal affection our far-seeing mother the Church has striven continually to make those favored sons of her choice, who consecrate the whole of their lives to

Christ our Lord and follow him freely and resolutely in the way of the counsels, worthy of their godly purpose and supernatural vocation. How wisely she has always regulated their system of life, the repeated teaching and admonitions of popes, councils and fathers bear witness, and is splendidly proved by the unbroken course of the Church's history, as well as the whole tenor of canonical discipline up to the present time.

Undeniably, from earliest Christian times onward, the Church has busied herself with elucidating by her authoritative teaching the doctrine of Christ and the apostles, paramount and inspiring examples of perfection. With assurance she has taught by what system a life dedicated to perfection was to be led and duly regulated. So earnestly in her work and ministry did she spread and encourage wholehearted dedication and consecration to Christ, that the early Christians preferred to live spontaneously by the evangelical counsels, and thus became good soil ready for sowing and sure to yield abundant harvests. Within a short time, as can be easily proved from the apostolic fathers and more ancient ecclesiastical writers, so widespread and flourishing was the idea of perfection adopted that those who pursued it began to constitute a kind of rank and social group among the Christian communities, clearly recognized under various names—ascetics, celibates, virgins and so on—and winning approval and honor from many.

From ancient times until the compilation of canon law, in our own days, the Church, faithful to Christ her spouse and loyal to her own principles, had gradually worked out with sure and unfaltering steps under the guidance of the Holy Spirit what pertains to the state of perfection. For those who, under many different forms, willingly and wholeheartedly profess the life of perfection, she has ever shown maternal solicitude. In two respects she has markedly favored them in so holy an endeavor. In the first place she has not only accepted and recognized every single profession of perfection, always provided it was made in a public manner and witnessed on behalf of the Church, like that ancient and venerable blessing and consecration of virgins which used to be performed liturgically, but she has wisely confirmed such profession and zealously safeguarded it, according it many canonical prerogatives. Secondly, from the fourth century onward, the Church has directed her gracious favor and devoted care, rightly and deservedly, to that complete and truly public profession of perfection which is made in societies and communities established by her consent, her approval and her command.

It is plain to all how closely and essentially linked has been the history of the Church's holiness and of her universal apostolate with the history and annals of canonical religious life. By the grace of the Holy Ghost, that unfailing source of life, they have daily developed in amazing diversity and have been further strengthened by a new, ever deeper and more unshakable unity. No wonder then that even in the field of law the Church, firmly cleaving to the principle of action so clearly intimated by the far-seeing wisdom of God, should thus of set purpose have followed up and regulated the canonical state of perfection, so that she has rightly and deservedly been pleased to raise upon it the structure of Church discipline, as upon one of its chief cornerstones. Hence from the very first the public state of perfection has been counted among the three ecclesiastical states, and from it the Church has exclusively singled out the second order or rank of canonical persons. Truly a fact worth weighing with grave attention, for the other two orders of canonical persons—namely, clerics and laymen—are by divine law distinct in the Church. To this law ecclesiastical organization conforms, for the Church is a society hierarchically constituted and appointed. However, this intermediate class of religious, set between clerics and layfolk, yet comprising both, is wholly chosen for its close and exceptional relationship to the goal of the Church—namely, sanctification, which it pursues effectively by adequate means.

Moreover, to safeguard and strengthen this solemn and public profession of sanctity, the Church has recognized this canonical state of perfection only in those societies established and regulated by herself. In this matter her tendency is to demand even more stringent requirements, being satisfied only with religious institutes whose form and disposition she had in every instance not only again and again put to trial and weighed in the balance of doctrinal principles but had in very fact tested by actual experience. This is so rigorously and absolutely enforced by canon law that in no instance, not even by way of exception, may the canonical state of perfection be recognized unless profession of it be made in a religious institute approved by the Church. Finally, the canonical discipline regulating the state of perfection, insofar as it is a public state, has been wisely laid down by the Church. Thus, as far as clerical religious institutes are concerned, the institute takes the place of the diocese in those matters which have generally to do with the clerical life of the religious, and incorporation in an institute is judged equivalent to incardination in a diocese.

All legislation dealing with religious was carefully collated, assessed and accurately compiled in the code. The second book (part 2) was devoted to religious; and the canonical state of perfection, viewed again as a public state, was in many ways confirmed therein. Thus was wisely concluded the work of Leo XIII of happy memory, the Constitution *Conditae a Christo,* whereby congregations taking simple vows were admitted to the ranks of religious institutes properly so called; there seemed nothing further to add regarding the discipline of the canonical state of perfection. Yet the Church, with her proverbial magnanimity and maternal solicitude, deemed it fit to supplement her legislation on religious with a short codicil to round it off in a fashion suited to the times. She was pleased to accord certain societies—and they deserved well of her and frequently of civil society, too—a full measure of equality with the canonical state of perfection. These societies, though lacking some of the juridical requirements—for example, public vows—necessary to the complete canonical state of perfection, nevertheless in matters essential to the life of perfection are closely bound up with religious institutes properly so called, both by a strong resemblance and by a certain necessity.

The scope of these wise, prudent and benevolent regulations gave every encouragement to numberless souls desirous of leaving the world and embracing this newly established and truly canonical state given over to the winning of perfection. Now our Lord in his bountiful loving kindness, being no respecter of persons, has time and again invited all the faithful to the pursuit and practice of perfection, and that in all circumstances. Hence he has disposed according to the sublime design of his divine providence that also in the world, disfigured and distorted by so many vices never more apparent than in our own day, very many bands of chosen souls should have flourished and flourish still who burn with zeal for their own perfection. While remaining in the world they are able, through a special vocation from God, to devise new and unrivaled forms of association which particularly answer the needs of the times, and in which many can lead a life wholly conducive to the attainment of Christian perfection.

While with all our heart commending to the prudent and zealous care of spiritual directors the noble efforts in the realms of conscience (*in foro interno*) of souls striving for perfection, our present concern is with those associations which (*in foro externo*) are so designed as to lead their own members, as it were, by the hand, to a life of solid perfection. Nor is it a question here of each and every association which in all sincerity pursues perfection in the world, but only of those which by their internal structure, by the hierarchical form of their government, by their complete self-dedication (their only bond) which they require of their members properly so called in the profession of the evangelical counsels, and finally by reason of the exercise of the apostolate and Christian ministry, more nearly approach the canonical state of perfection—that is, as far as its substance is concerned. Especially do we refer to those societies whose members neither take public vows nor follow the religious community life but make use of other external forms.

These associations, hereafter to be known as Secular Institutes, began to be established in the first half of the last century. Nor were they without the special inspiration of divine providence. Their purpose was "to follow the evangelical counsels faithfully in the world, and to undertake those duties of charity which the religious institutes were almost or even absolutely prevented from carrying out, owing to the evils of the times." The first Institutes gave a good account of themselves. They proved conclusively by their work and deeds that, favored by this exceptional vocation from God and help of divine grace, they could assuredly achieve even in the world not only an inward but an outward consecration to the Lord, almost comparable to that of the religious life, and definite and effective enough for their purpose. This they accomplished through the stringent and prudent choice of their members, whose training entailed careful formation, long withal, and through the sufficiently firm yet flexible organization of their life. Thus they showed they could be regarded as a most timely instrument of apostolic penetration in secular life. For such manifold reasons, not infrequently "the Holy See commended these associations of the faithful not less than true religious congregations."

As time went on and these Institutes happily grew in number, it became increasingly clear in how many ways they could be turned to the effective support of the Church and of souls. They could well be applied to the earnest pursuit of perfection at all times and places. Many for whom the canonical life was not possible or feasible could join such Institutes. Through their daily contact with family life, professional circles and civil society, those whose lives were dedicated to sanctification could leaven the whole. Their manifold apostolate and Christian ministry could be turned to good use where priests and religious were forbidden or could make no headway. But, on the other hand, experience had shown that dangers and difficulties had not been wanting; in fact they had sometimes, even rather easily, beset this life of perfection. For it was a life led without the outward support of a religious habit; it was led freely, and lacked the supervision of diocesan bishops, whose notice it could easily escape, or of superiors who not infrequently dwelt a long way off. Discussion had also begun on the juridical nature of these Institutes, and on the mind of the Church in approving them. Here we think it timely to mention the Decree *Ecclesia Catholica,* published by the Sacred Congregation of Bishops and Regulars, and confirmed on 11 August 1889 by our predecessor of immortal memory, Leo XIII.

In this, praise and approval were not withheld from these Institutes. But it was declared that when the sacred congregation praised and approved these Institutes "it was pleased to praise and approve them not as religious institutes of solemn vows or as true religious congregations of simple vows but only as pious sodalities. In them, apart from such things as are demanded by the prevailing discipline of the Church, religious profession properly so called is not made. If any vows are taken they are deemed to be private, and not public—that is, accepted by a lawful superior in the name of the Church." Furthermore, as the same sacred congregation went on to say, these sodalities are praised and approved under this essential condition—namely, that they are fully and thoroughly known to their respective ordinaries, to whose jurisdiction they are wholly subject. These declarations of the Sacred Congregation of Bishops and Regulars were timely in that they helped to define the nature of these Institutes, and have governed their development and progress.

The Secular Institutes of this century have quietly increased in numbers and have assumed many forms, differing much from one another. Some are autonomous, others are linked in varying measures to religious institutes or societies. Nothing is said about them in the apostolic constitution *Conditae a Christo* which concerned itself only with religious congregations. Moreover, the Code of Canon Law has purposely omitted all references to these Institutes; as the time for framing laws

concerning them did not seem expedient, it left the matter for future legislation.

Time and again we turned these matters over, impelled by the consciousness of our duty and by the paternal love which we cherish for those souls who so generously pursue sanctity in the world. No less are we influenced by our determination to discriminate wisely and strictly between these societies. It is our resolve, moreover, to recognize as authentic only those Institutes which have as their genuine and avowed aim the life of perfection in all its fullness. We have to guard against the constant rise of fresh Institutes, the foundations for which are not infrequently insecurely and imprudently laid. Likewise, we have to frame special legislation which fully and aptly meets the nature, aims and requirements of those Institutes deemed worthy of our approval. For this reason it is our resolve and decree that similar measures to those which our predecessor of immortal memory, Leo XIII, so wisely and prudently effected to deal with congregations under simple vows through the apostolic constitution *Conditae a Christo,* should also be adopted in relation to secular institutes. At our command and under our direction, therefore, and after diligent examination by the Supreme Sacred Congregation of the Holy Office on all that falls within its jurisdiction, a general statute for Secular Institutes was drawn up and revised by the Sacred Congregation of Religious. In this present letter we give this statute our approval; and all that follows we decree and resolve and enact in virtue of our apostolic authority.

All these things having been set forth as above, we appoint the Sacred Congregation of Religious to put all these commands into execution, and grant all faculties needful and expedient so to act.

THE LAW GOVERNING SECULAR INSTITUTES

1. Societies, whether clerical or lay, whose members profess the evangelical counsels in the world as their aim, in order to attain Christian perfection and the full exercise of the apostolate, come under the special name of Institutes or Secular Institutes; thus are they clearly distinguished from other general associations of the faithful. Such Secular Institutes are subject to the laws of this Apostolic Constitution.

2. Since Secular Institutes neither allow the three religious public vows, nor impose community life, or living under the same roof, according to canon law, on their members:

a) By the law, *ex regula,* neither are they nor, strictly speaking, can they be described as religious institutes or societies of common life.

b) They are not bound by the law specific and proper to religious institutes and to societies of common life; nor can they invoke such law except when some prescription thereof, and especially if it obtain for societies not taking public vows, is, in exceptional cases, found legally suitable and applicable to themselves.

While observing the general norms of canon law which may concern them, Institutes are governed by the following prescriptions, as by law distinctive to them, and which will more precisely meet their specific character and condition:

a) By the general norms of this apostolic constitution, which can be said to constitute the statute proper to all Secular Institutes.

b) By the norms which the Sacred Congregation of Religious may decide to promulgate as necessity arises or experience dictates, whether by interpretation or by elaboration and application of the apostolic constitution, either for all or for some of these Institutes.

c) By individual constitutions, approved in accordance with the undermentioned articles (5-8), which prudently adapt the general and particular enactments of the law described in (a) and (b) to the aims, needs and widely differing circumstances of particular Institutes.

3. For any association of the faithful to be erected as a Secular Institute, in accordance with the articles following hereafter, it must have the undermentioned, as well as other common requirements:

With regard to the dedication of life and the profession of Christian perfection:

Persons who desire to be accounted members, in the stricter sense, of an Institute, in addition to those exercises of devotion and self-denial undertaken by all who aspire to a life of perfection, must resolutely direct themselves to acquiring perfection according to the following stipulations:

a) By profession of celibacy and perfect chastity genuinely made before God, and which is secured by vow, oath or consecration binding in conscience, according to the norm of the particular constitutions.

b) By a vow or promise of obedience, of such a nature that they bind themselves by a stable bond to dedicate themselves entirely to God and to works of charity or of the apostolate, and in all respects are always morally in the power and under the command of superiors, according to the norm of the particular constitutions.

c) By a vow or promise of poverty, in virtue of which they do not have the free, but a defined and restricted, use of temporal goods, according to the norm of the particular constitutions.

With regard to the incorporation of members in their own Institute and the bond arising therefrom:

The bond by which a Secular Institute and its members, properly so called, should be mutually joined together must be:

a) Stable, in accordance with the norm of the particular constitutions, either for life or for a set period, in which latter case it must be renewed at its expiration.

b) Mutual and comprehensive, so that, in accordance with the norm of the particular constitutions, the member hands himself wholly over to the Institute and the Institute takes care of and is responsible for him.

With regard to buildings and houses of the Institute held in common:

Even if Secular Institutes do not oblige their members to community life or to live under the same roof, according to the ruling of the law, nevertheless they should either of necessity or for convenience have one or several common houses in order that in them:

a) Those who exercise the authority of the Institute, the supreme in particular as well as the regional authority, may dwell.

b) Members can live or come together to receive and carry out instruction, to take part in the spiritual exercises, and for other reasons of a similar kind.

c) Members can be accommodated who, because of ill-health or for other reasons, cannot provide for themselves; or for whom it is deemed unwise to leave living privately, either alone or with others.

4. Secular Institutes come under the Sacred Congregation of Religious, excepting the rights of the Sacred Congregation for the Propagation of the Faith as set down in canon 252, paragraph 3, with reference to societies and seminaries whose aim is the foreign missions.

Associations whose whole object and function are not identical with the requirements in 1 (above), and those also which lack the essentials reviewed in 1 and 3 of this apostolic constitution, are governed by the law which affects associations of the faithful as in canon 684, and come under the Sacred Congregation of the Council, save for the prescription of canon 252, paragraph 3, with regard to missionary territories.

5. Bishops, but not vicars capitular or general, can establish Secular Institutes and erect them as moral persons, in accordance with canon 100, paragraphs 1 and 2.

However, bishops must neither establish these Institutes nor allow them to be established without consulting the Sacred Congregation of Religious, in accordance with canon 492, paragraph 1, and with the article which here follows.

6. When bishops, in accordance with 5 (above), make preliminary inquiries concerning the granting of permission for the erection of these Institutes, the Sacred Congregation of Religious must issue instructions (bearing in mind their own decisions in parallel matters) in accordance with their own norms governing the erection of purely diocesan congregations and societies of common life. In addition, measures heretofore or subsequently introduced by the same sacred congregation must be taken into account.

Once the bishops have obtained the permission from the Sacred Congregation of Religious they shall in no way be prevented from erecting the Institute freely and as of their own right. However, bishops must not neglect to inform officially the same sacred congregation that the erection has been put into effect.

7. Secular Institutes which have obtained the approval or the decree of praise from the Holy See become of pontifical right.

In order that Secular Institutes of diocesan right may obtain a decree of praise or approval, conditions similar to those required by the norms of the Sacred Congregation of Religious are required. Generally those conditions will be judged in the light of parallel decisions heretofore and hereafter taken by the same sacred congregation on behalf of congregations and societies of common life.

The procedure in granting the first, the renewed (if needs be) and the definitive approval of these Institutes and their constitutions shall be as follows:

a) The first discussion will take place in the consultative committee, under the presidency of His Excellency the secretary of the same sacred congregation or of his delegate. Beforehand the data will be prepared in the normal manner, and set forth with the appreciation and recommendation of at least one of the consultors.

b) Then the whole matter is submitted to the examination and decision of the full assembly of the sacred congregation, under the presidency of the cardinal prefect of the sacred congregation. Experts or the more experienced among the consultors should also be summoned, as necessity or expediency indicates.

c) The resolution of the assembly shall be made known by the cardinal prefect or by the secretary in audience with his Holiness the pope, and it shall be thus submitted to his supreme judgment.

8. In addition to their own laws, now prevailing or subsequently to be enacted, Secular Institutes are subject to diocesan ordinaries, according to the law governing nonexempt Congregations and Societies of common life.

9. The internal government of Secular Institutes can be hierarchic, following the pattern prevailing among religious institutes and societies of common life. This form of government, however, can only be instituted by the same sacred congregation if they, guided by their decisions promulgated in similar instances, deem such government to be conformable to the specific character, purpose and circumstances of those Institutes.

10. This apostolic constitution in no way alters the laws and obligations of Institutes already in existence, no matter whether they were established by bishops in consultation with the Holy See or approved direct by the Holy See. . . .

49. *Karl Adam: Principles of Christian Reunion, September 1947*

From Karl Adam, *One and Holy* (New York: Sheed and Ward, 1951), copyright 1951 Sheed & Ward, Inc., New York, pp. 1-6, 103-111.

1. WE CHRISTIANS have always found it an occasion of suffering that Christendom is divided into a Catholic and a non-Catholic part, a *corpus Catholicorum* and a *corpus Acatholicorum*. Wherever belief in the Son of God made man has remained alive, the Christian conscience has been pierced by the overwhelming reproach and accusation of the high Priest's prayer to the Father on the eve of his Passion: *Ut omnes unum sint*—"that they all may be one, as you, Father, in me and I in Thee!" He reproaches us for so cruel a wounding of his holy body the Church, and for letting centuries go by with these festering divisions among Christians unhealed. He laid on his disciples his new commandment that they should love one another. He formed

them into a united company by his own utterly self-giving love for men. And men who love him must answer today, as for centuries past, for the sin of scandalizing the non-Christian world with a shameful example of faction and conflict. "See how they love one another!" said the pagans of the first Christian centuries, when they beheld the loving unity of the early Christians. "See how little they love one another!" the modern pagans might and must say mockingly, as they become more and more conscious of the many deep divisions among Christians.

Even when the Reformation was a thing long established there were men who strove continually to realize that last and deepest desire of their Lord: *ut omnes unum sint.* We need only remember the efforts towards unity of Hugo Grotius (d. 1645) and Leibnitz (d. 1716) on the one side, of Bossuet, Bishop of Meaux (d. 1704) and the Franciscan Spinola, bishop of Wiener-Neustadt (d. 1695) on the other. These attempts all came to nothing. They were always thwarted by the fact that there were men on both sides who were not inspired simply by the one Spirit of the Lord, πνεῦμα ἅγιον, but by alien spirits, the πνεύματα of men, with their different aims and exigencies and desires, arising out of their various nationalities and cultures, their differences in temperament and in religious approach.

Must it always be so? Unity was our Lord's legacy to his disciples, attested in prayer before the face of the triune God and hallowed by the sacrificial death which he accepted for their sake. Is it further to remain for so many who love him an empty wish and a dead word, a reproach not only to us but to Christianity? Now, if ever, is the time to shake ourselves out of our spiritual torpor and religious indifference, and to plunge our consciences into the very heart of Jesus, into the ultimate depths

of the intentions bequeathed to us by the God-Man. We Christians have just passed through a time when religious disunity drove us to the very brink of the abyss. A set of godless men, hating Christ as the son of David, almost succeeded in rooting out from the German people not merely this or that Christian denomination but the very substance of Christianity itself. And this was because our people were unable to gather with closed ranks around the cross of our Lord and to confess with one heart and one mouth their *credo* in Jesus Christ.

After these bitter experiences a *rapprochement* between the Christian denominations—and ultimately a full, external reunion—can no longer be regarded, so far as Germans are concerned, as the desire of a few idealistic and far-seeing souls alone. For German Christianity it has become a vital question, a choice of "to be or not to be" for the Christian substance in our people, and so in the heart of Europe. We know that organized anti-Christianity lies in wait beyond our frontiers. We must recognize that there is in our midst something even more dangerous, carrying a far greater menace of ruin—the vacuum that has been left in the German soul: an emptiness, a fearful emancipation from all memories, traditions and ideals of Christianity, making room for every demon of heart and mind and preparing the soul to receive any and every gospel, not only the Gospel of the cross. How can German Christianity hold its ground against this anti-Christianity without and within, how can it arm itself against the gates of hell, when it is split to its very core? When, conscious of this disunity, it cannot even pray with a clear conscience to our Lord Jesus Christ? When it can no longer summon up the power to bear witness in one united confession to our Lord and Savior?

Today, then, the need, the longing and the clamor for unity have become the heritage of the Christian masses, as simple and elementary as any basic need. On all sides groups are forming whose one longing is for reunion. No longer is it thought that the fulfillment and realization of our Lord's longing that there should be one fold might be left solely to ecclesiastical leaders and their immediate subordinates. Pope and bishop, prelate and superior have certainly the heaviest responsibility for seeing that Christ shall not have prayed in vain. But this responsibility rests upon us too, upon us, Christian workers and peasants, officials and clergy, upon us, men and women, old and young. One single vast wave of longing for unity, of will to unity, must arise in German Christianity, must carry up and sweep along with it all our faith and all our devotion, and at last grow to a movement of such depth and breadth that even cold and indifferent Christians will be swept into it. Once this has happened, our will to unity will itself produce a way of accomplishing it.

Let me say at once that the way, seen as a whole, is wearisome and hard. A mere longing for unity is not enough. Each of us, in our different circumstances, must help to prepare for it. And it is surely true that we shall best show our loyalty to Jesus by refusing to let hindrances and difficulties keep us from seeking and following the road to unity. For there are hindrances and difficulties. Reunion is not a matter of simple goodwill only, but also of hard thinking and energetic action. More precisely, we need a kind of goodwill which is ready to abandon deep-seated prejudices and habits of thought for the sake of eternal truth, and is willing to go unconditionally to the very ground of truth itself.

The way is a way of blood and wounds, both for the Catholic and for the Protestant, though differently for each of them. It is only by surveying its approaches and its difficulties in the light of history that we can understand why we cannot as yet hope that all Christendom may be finally gathered into one in the near future and also why it was that our Lord prayed specially for unity and bequeathed it as a legacy to his disciples. It was made a special prayer and legacy of our Lord because it is, in the last analysis, God's affair. But it is nevertheless for us to prepare the way for the return within that unity of all who truly love Christ. . . .

3. In what follows we will point out the basic principles which, from the Catholic point of view, must animate and guide every attempt at understanding and which alone can make our efforts at reunion fruitful.

We may lay down, as our first principle, that every serious intention of understanding presupposes taking one's own Confession seriously: an underlying readiness to give a strict account of one's own religious Confession in full realization of one's responsibility before God. A man who has never taken his own church seriously will never take any other church seriously. He has no right to look towards another church if he has never taken the trouble to penetrate into the religious life and structure of his own Communion and to satisfy his religious needs there first. Religion is something so profound and so holy that of its very nature it obliges us in conscience to plumb the depths of our own Confession, to assay its whole content and know it in its entirety.

The history of Christianity has shown us that when the Enlightenment and German idealism had weakened or loosened the basic content of belief, the consequence was indifferentism, and this indifferentism led in turn to a complete loss of Christianity. The reunion of Christendom is an eminently religious matter. Therefore it demands an attitude of mind that searches for light and truth for the sake of religion.

If a man attains to this clarity within his own church, if he can say Yes with complete conviction to his own church, he may not think of leaving it for another, he may not become a Catholic. However objectively false, from the Catholic standpoint, his position may be, he is nevertheless subjectively bound to remain in it so long as his conscience compels him. For it is only the dictates of our own sovereign conscience that can transform an objective norm into a subjective duty. Every Christian must apply to himself the words of St. Paul: "the just man lives by faith." That is to say, only the man who lives according to the convictions of his conscience is truly just. When a convinced Protestant Christian lives thus in union with Christ, he stands also in a relationship to the Mystical Body of the Savior, of which indeed he had already become a member by the Sacrament of Baptism (cf. Encyclical, *Mystici Corporis*).

But where a man does not attain to this certainty of conscience, when an evangelical Christian finds that he has been mistaken, not indeed in Christ, but in his church, he finds himself, for the sake of truth, driven to leave his church in search of the true Church, and not to rest until he has found her. And he will find her, because the blessing of God, the strength and light of his grace, will certainly fall upon such single-minded and fervent struggles for the truth.

But in either case, whether his relationship to his original Communion turns out to be positive or negative, a joyful affirmation or a critical rejection, he must take that Communion seriously, both as to its functions and as to its demands on him. This attitude is the only one which corresponds to the high ideal presented to us by the reunion of Christendom.

We thus come to the second principle which will ensure reunion or at least allow us to hope for it. It is this: our striving for unity cannot be a matter of politics or culture or aesthetics or romanticism. It must be a religious movement. Wherever our concern is with religion, it is first and foremost God who is at work. Thus our movement must be primarily a movement of prayer. . . . There is only one place where we can find each other: the heart of Jesus. The way to unity is not from Peter to Christ but from Christ to Peter, not from the outer to the inner but from the inner to the outer. . . . It is only by starting from Christ, only in the light of his divine presence, free from all worldly attachments, that we shall be able to see eternal truth naked and sheer, free from earthly taint, untouched by the longings and passions of our own hearts. It is only standing before Christ that we breathe pure air. The men and things that surround us then stand no longer in our sight but in his. We no longer see them with our eyes, but with his. . . . Wherever we look we see the same thing: unity with Christ is the only possible foundation for the unity of Christians. It is only out of this inner unity with Christ that external unity, unity with Peter, will grow—when God wills and as God wills.

We touch here on our third principle. This common love in Christ must bring all those who are concerned in *Una Sancta* to do what they can, with passionate determination, to soften the antagonism that exists between believers of the two Churches. There is no question here of concealing or minimizing the real differences in doctrine. On the contrary, for the sake of truth these differences must be laid bare, for this is the only way to reveal the true religious intentions which ultimately lie behind them on both sides. But these doctrinal differences can be presented quite objectively, and indeed in a truly irenic form, directed towards mutual understanding. On the other hand, they can also be presented in an unreal and wounding form. Lutheran and Catholic controversial writing of the sixteenth and seventeenth centuries provides us with a shameful example. . . .

Trusting love, loving trust must be the animating principle of all our relations with each other, and especially of our religious literature and religious discussion. For where true love is, "love from a pure heart, and a good conscience, and an unfeigned faith," there, and only there, is the Holy Ghost. We pray God that this spirit of openness of heart and trusting love

may be active and fruitful also in those upon whom God's dispensation has laid the heavy duty of preserving the purity of the faith handed down by the Church. May they all keep for their guiding thread the prayer instituted by the Holy See for reunion with the Oriental churches: "We pray you, O Lord . . . keep us from any fault that might estrange us yet further."

To sum up: we must each take our own Confession seriously; we must each give ourselves unconditionally to Christ and his holy will; and, inspired by this love of Christ, we must each root out of ourselves all loveless prejudice, against those of the other faith. These tasks in the religious and moral order are the necessary *a priori* preliminaries to any union between us, to any approach between Catholics and Protestants if it is to bear fruit. . . .

50. *Francis Dvornik: The Origin of the Eastern Schism,* *29 September 1956*

From *The Proceedings of the First Unionistic Congress, September 28, 1956 to September 30, 1956* (Lisle, Illinois: St. Procopius Abbey, 1956), pp. 45-52.

THE disastrous events of the first half of our century have brought home to many Christians the harm caused by their division into a number of mutually conflicting bodies. The danger threatening not only Christianity, but indeed all religion, from the spread of materialistic philosophy, has increased the desire for a united Christian front against this danger. This has inspired the ecumenical movement among the leaders of the Protestant churches, and has induced many Catholic and Anglican thinkers to explore the possibilities of union with the Orthodox churches, which are nearest to them in doctrine and in religious discipline.

This has led many scholars today to study the causes which led up to the

separation of the Churches. The study of the eastern schism and its causes is important for all those Christians who seek a common basis of understanding in the ecumenical movement, the more so, since these same causes were also largely responsible for the disastrous cleavage of western Christianity during the Protestant Revolt.

One of the main causes of the estrangement between the Christian East and West lay in the difference in political theory which was growing steadily through the Middle Ages. Remote and strange though it may seem, this is extremely important. The earliest Christian political philosophers knew only the Hellenistic ideas on kingship, derived from the political speculation of ancient Greece and the Middle East. These ideas had already replaced and transformed the Roman republican constitution, and the first Christian political thinkers—Clement of Alexandria and Eusebius of Caesarea—adapted them to the principles of the Christian faith. Christian Hellenism deprived the emperor of his divine character, but made him the representative of God on earth, responsible both for the spiritual and the temporal welfare of his subjects and leading them to God. This, of course, implied as a sacred duty the direct intervention of the emperor in religious affairs, an intervention which was solicited and welcomed by the Church in the interest of the true faith. This political system cannot be termed caesaropapism, because the emperor, when intervening in ecclesiastical affairs, thought that he was exercising his duty and usurping nobody's rights. The bishops, for their part, only insisted firmly on their right to define the true faith. The whole history of the early Church becomes more comprehensible in the light of this struggle, from which the Eastern Church finally emerged victorious, despite the support lent by emperors to heretical doctrines. The right to define the true faith was expressly recognized as a prerogative of the Church and, from the ninth century on, the Emperors limited their interventions to the defense and enforcement of the Creed as defined by the Church.

This acceptance of an Hellenized Roman political ideology as a basis for Christian political speculation had important consequences for the development of the Church. Its organization was completely adapted to the political division of the empire so that the most important cities—Rome, Alexandria and Antioch—became also the leading Christian episcopal centers. The principles of adaptation to the political organization of the empire became so profoundly embedded in the minds of Eastern Christians that, when Constantinople became the capital of the empire, it seemed the most natural consequence that the new Rome should be given all the privileges of the old. Alexandria and Antioch willingly ceded precedence in the East to Constantinople. In the West, Rome's prestige was also due originally to the fact that it was the capital of the empire. As long as the emperors resided in that city, its bishops did not need to stress the apostolic foundation of their see and the primacy they derived from being the successors of St. Peter, the prince of the apostles. In fact this prerogative only began to be stressed by the bishops of Rome after the foundation and growth of Constantinople. Leo I's arguments against Constantinople's pretensions retained their validity during all the ensuing centuries of controversy between East and West. In this respect, however, the Romans, ever anxious to defend their primacy in the Church, were prone to overlook one important fact: the Easterners never had any intention of transferring the primacy from the old Rome to the new Constantinople. In their view the old Rome should always be given the place of honor in the empire and the primacy in the Church. The foundations of the empire were laid by Rome and in Rome. The Byzantines who regarded their empire as the continuation of that of Rome, would have cut the ground from under their own feet, if they had denied to Rome its primacy in the empire and in the Church. During all the centuries of controversy before the final consummation of the schism, Constantinople never claimed a primacy in the Church. All that the patriarchs of Constantinople claimed was a kind of primacy in the East, which had lost its important position in Christendom after the Arab conquests.

On the other hand, however, the easterners failed to show, in good time, a proper appreciation for the principle of apostolicity which was being so forcefully stressed by Rome. The eastern fathers had shown a particular lack of understanding for Roman apostolic claims when, in the year 453, they voted canon twenty-eight of the Council of Chalcedon, confirming Constantinople's second place in Church organization. Their intentions were in no wise hostile to the rights of Rome, but by overlooking the concept of apostolicity they gave Leo the Great the false impression that Roman primacy was being questioned. The Byzantine lack of understanding for the idea of apostolicity is best illustrated by the tardy spread of the legendary tradition connecting the Apostle Andrew with Byzantium. The city of Byzantium was mentioned at the end of the third century in the apocryphal story of St. Andrew's travels. But the Byzantines paid no attention to it before the beginning of the eighth century. Only then did the legend of the foundation of the Byzantine see by the Apostle Andrew take its rise. It spread during the ninth century, but was only officially accepted by the Byzantine church authorities in the tenth century. This failure in the East to appreciate the idea of apostolicity and this stress on the principle of adaptation to the political organization of the empire, were among the major causes of the growing lack of understanding between East and West and deserve special attention from the historians of the Schism.

We must next examine how the different development of political philosophy in East and West influenced the final rupture. Christian Hellenism permeated secular and ecclesiastical life in the East, although its political ideas also found acceptance in the Christian West. Roman bishops—until Gregory the Great at least—shared with the easterners the Hellenistic conception of kingship, regarding the emperor as divinely appointed to rule over the universe and recognizing his right to convoke general councils and to watch over religious orthodoxy. But the West had never shown the same enthusiasm for this political order as the East. The spirit of Roman republicanism had never perished completely in Rome and it influenced the great popes of the first centuries who were descended from the old Roman aristocratic and senatorial families. The fact that the emperors of the West seldom resided in Rome naturally enhanced the prestige of its bishops. This prestige grew in proportion as imperial authority and the empire itself slowly disintegrated in the West under the blows of the Germanic invaders. In these circumstances it was no wonder that, already before the collapse of the western empire, the Romans gradually transferred to their bishops prerogatives and titles proper to the emperors.

The Christianization of the Germanic nations made rapid progress thanks to the efforts of the Roman missionaries and enhanced accordingly the prestige of the Roman bishop. The growth of Church influence in political life in the West is best illustrated by the coronation orders introduced among the converted nations. In Christian Hellenism the role of the Church was very limited on the succession of new rulers. The order of succession and the ceremony of enthronement retained their secular character from the Roman constitution. Some of the ideas of Christian Hellenism were transmitted through Rome to the newly converted nations and assimilated to their political system. Yet the Roman Church, by modelling a coronation service on the rite for the consecration of bishops, unwittingly laid the foundations for the theory which was to develop further during the Middle Ages, namely that kingship was conferred by God through the Church. This basic idea of the superiority of spiritual over the temporal was something completely alien to the Christian Hellenism prevalent in the East.

In spite of this and in spite of frequent clashes between Rome and Constantinople in religious matters, the pope continued down to the beginning of the ninth century to recognize the authority of the emperor residing in Constantinople. This situation ended abruptly in the year 800, when Pope Leo III crowned Charlemagne Emperor. This was a precipitate action and we may well ask whether it would not have been better for the papacy to be content with the defeat of the Lombards who were threatening its liberty, and to retain the nominal supremacy of the one Roman emperor in Constantinople, rather than to fall into the arms of the victorious Franks. From the Byzantine point of view, the act was quite revolutionary and implied the disruption of the ideal Christian unity represented by the Roman empire.

It was fortunate for the papacy that Charlemagne's successors were rather weak partners for men like Hadrian I or Nicholas I, and that his empire could not maintain its unity. The prestige of the papacy, endowed by the Franks with secular power in Italy and disposing of the imperial crown, reached new heights. Nicholas I was able not only to strengthen his authority in Italy and to crush all attempts at independence in Gaul or France, but also to make a bold attempt to extend his direct jurisdiction over the eastern Church. This is the true significance of the conflict between Nicholas and the Patriarch Photius. The Byzantines defended spiritedly their autonomy in the ecclesiastical affairs. It seems strange to assert that this conflict provided a basis on which Roman and

Byzantine claims could have been enduringly reconciled and that it was Photius and his partisans who provided this basis. When condemned by the Patriarch Ignatius, they appealed to the Roman Patriarch, thus recognizing his primacy in a most telling way. The right to judge a patriarch was confirmed to the pope by the Council of 861 in which Ignatius was judged and deposed by the papal legates. It is a pity that the acts of that council have hitherto been ignored and misinterpreted by some writers of Church history. Their declarations express a reverence for the papacy—even as an instance of appeal against the Patriarch —which would have delighted the most fervent papalist. Never before had such words been heard in Constantinople. It is to be regretted that, in the hopes of obtaining more important concessions from Photius' opponents, this council was ignored in Rome and its acts declared null and void. Nicholas and his successors did not obtain further concessions and, in the defense of the autonomy of his church, Ignatius proved as stubborn and as adamant as Photius. The blame for this conflict should be laid on the intransigent diehards, who were to be found not only in Constantinople but also in Rome. In spite of the tempers aroused by this conflict in both cities, the damage was nothing like as great as is generally believed. The reconciliation effected at the council of 880 was sincere and Photius died in communion with Rome.

The rise of Frankish influence in the West also showed itself in the theological field. The Franks under Charlemagne had accepted the Spanish practice of adding to the Nicene Creed the word "Filioque," thus stressing the procedure of the Holy Ghost from the Father and the Son. Frankish theologians insisted that this addition to the creed should be accepted by all churches. The popes, although agreeing that the word "Filioque" accorded with the Western conception of the Trinity, protested against its addition to the creed. For they knew full well that any such initiative would be strongly opposed by the Easterners who regarded the Nicene Creed as untouchable. Nevertheless the Franks had some success in Rome and Formosus, a high Roman cleric, introduced this practice into Bulgaria, where he was sent as a missionary by Nicholas I. In this way Photius learned about the new practice and protested vehemently with the support of all his clergy. But because the papal legates had signed the Nicene Creed at the council of reconciliation in 880, without the "Filioque," and had agreed to the declaration that such an addition should not be permitted, the first phase of the dispute over the "Filioque" clause ended peacefully.

A new danger arose from Germany when Otto I, in a new bid to revive the Roman empire in the West, forced Pope John XII to crown him emperor in 962. In the following years German influence eliminated in Rome that of the native aristocracy who were more friendly to Byzantium. As a consequence, German theologians gradually imposed the addition of the "Filioque" clause in Rome also.

It is noteworthy that the new conflict between Rome and Byzantium under Pope Leo IX and the Patriarch Cerularius was not provoked by the acceptance of the "Filioque" clause in Rome. Yet it appears that, previously, the German popes who had accepted this addition to the creed, were not commemorated in Constantinople.

The new conflict had deep roots in the transformation which the western Church had undergone in the course of the preceding centuries thanks to the impact of Germanic ideology on the proprietorship of ecclesiastical institutions. Unable to grasp the old Roman legal conception that societies and organizations could own property, the Germanic nations continued after their Christianization, to vest ownership only in a person. The result of this conception was that churches and other ecclesiastical foundations, erected by nobles and kings, were regarded as the property of the founders, who then claimed the right to institute priests of their own choice. This marks a dangerous break with the old Roman law, which was still respected in Rome and throughout the Christian East. The consequences of this practice soon made themselves disastrously felt as western Christendom disintegrated into national churches ruled by kings and nobles.

The many consequent abuses provoked a reaction. While the Cluniac reformers were mainly concerned with monastic life, the reformers of Lorraine attacked the root of the troubles in the system of proprietary churches. Against the overwhelming influence of the laity in Church affairs they stressed the limitless character of papal supremacy over the whole Church. With Pope Leo IX the Lorraine reformists gained control of Rome and started to advocate uniformity of liturgical usage everywhere, in the interests of discipline and order. This new trend in the West spelled trouble for peaceful relations with the East. Already in 1028 the Cluniac reformers had prevented the conclusion of a compromise suggested to Pope John XIX by the Patriarch Eustathius, which involved recognition of the autonomy of the Byzantine church, but offered to recognize the basic primacy of Rome over the entire Christian Church.

It was unfortunate that Pope Leo IX had to choose his legates to the Byzantine emperor in 1054 among the most radical reformists who could not accept the right of other churches to follow their own customs. These men were intolerant of Church autonomy and insisted on the right of direct intervention of the pope in all matters throughout the Church. It was all the more unfortunate that Cardinal Humbert and his colleagues encountered in Constantinople an arrogant and ambitious patriarch with a profound dislike for the Latins. So it happened that their legacy, which was intended to conclude an alliance between the pope and the emperor against the Normans who threatened the interests of both in southern Italy, ended in a rupture which is still regarded, albeit wrongly, as the consummation of the eastern schism. The Byzantines were certainly amazed when they learned from Humbert's pamphlets and letters of the reformists' conception of papal primacy as conferring the right to intervene directly in all matters in all churches. They were equally amazed at the words of condemnation of their own liturgical and religious customs. The regrettable and precipitate action of the legates did not however imply that consummation of the schism. The bull they deposited on the altar of the Church of Saint Sophia proclaimed the excommunication of the patriarch himself, who had the good sense to condemn, not the western Church or the pope, but only the legate.

In spite of the bitterness which this incident left in both Constantinople and Rome, nobody thought of the churches as being in schism. The intercommunion of the faithful did not cease and the intellectuals of both sides were still able to discuss the differences in liturgy and in custom in a conciliatory atmosphere. This is particularly illustrated by the disputations which the western bishops had in Constantinople with their Greek confreres.

All this was happening despite the complete transformation of political ideology in Rome under the pontificate of Gregory VII. In his *Dictatus Papae*,

derived from the premises prepared by the reformists, the ultimate conclusion of the superiority of the spiritual power over the secular is found. The main documentation for this new conception of the papal primacy was sought by the Gregorian canonists in Pope Nicholas' decrees against Photius and Michael III, which were wrongly interpreted as implying that the pope had excommunicated an emperor. The investiture contest with the western emperors precluded the popes for some time from extending this new interpretation to the East. On the contrary, it appeared that a new period of good understanding between East and West was commencing when Urban II invited the West to help the eastern Christians in their struggle against the infidel Turks. The Pope and the Emperor Alexius hoped that the comradeship in arms, sealed with blood, would assure enduring amity between the Churches.

Unfortunately, the effects were contrary. So far only the intellectuals of both sides were aware of the differences existing between East and West. As long as the discussions were limited to the intellectuals, there was hope that an open breach could be avoided. The Crusade however brought these differences to the consciousness of the masses of western pilgrims and warriors and of the Greek populace. Both Greeks and Latins were bewildered at their new experiences. Misunderstandings and open conflicts resulted, mainly owing to the misbehavior of the Crusaders. Runciman rightly stresses the importance of this psychological factor which is often neglected by historians of the Crusades. The conflict arising from Bohemond's retention of Antioch, in contravention of the promise of the Crusaders to restore the city to the emperor, aggravated the situation. It was in this city that the first open schism occurred, when in the year 1100 a Latin patriarch was installed there against the Greek patriarch.

But even this was not yet final. Diplomatic contact between Rome and Constantinople continued to be maintained and disputations between intellectuals went on until the end of the twelfth century. The mutual animosity had however grown considerably during the Second and Third Crusades. This explains the disastrous course of the Fourth Crusade which ended with the capture of Constantinople in 1204 and the establishment of a Latin empire in the East. The last opportunity for a compromise was missed in 1206 by Innocent III. In desperation the Greek hierarchy offered to recognize the supremacy of Rome if it were allowed to retain its own patriarch and its own customs. The pope who had first deplored the excesses of the Crusaders, refused however to surrender the rights of the newly established Latin patriarch. The Greek bishops gathered in Nicaea and elected their own patriarch, thus giving definite confirmation to the schism. The conquest of Constantinople by the Latins could never be forgotten by the Greeks and its consequences overshadowed all other attempts at reunion, especially those made at the Councils of Lyons in 1274 and of Florence in 1439. Thenceforward both churches went their separate ways. The progress of the medieval papal theory, defined by Gregory VII and put into practice by Innocent III and Boniface VIII, deepened the gulf separating the two sections of Christianity, the more so as the Greeks adhere to their Christian Hellenism in determining the relations between Church and state. The excessive stress on the new ideology in the West contributed to the decline of the western Church in the fifteenth and sixteenth centuries which, in its turn, provoked the Reformation, splitting western Christianity again and more seriously. Thus Christendom became divided, so that it could not present a united front to danger.

Unity will be hard to achieve because the struggles and misunderstandings of past centuries are not easily forgotten. Nevertheless we must not abandon hope. The first step must be an unbiased analysis of the causes which led to separation and rupture. This will lead in its turn to a better understanding and mutual tolerance and this shall be the task of the scholars and theologians of the next generation.

VIII. *Communism and Church Unity*

No PERSON living in the modern world can fail to be conscious of the force of twentieth-century Communism and the challenge that this religio-political system presents to Christians today. The radical element of nineteenth-century Socialists who seized control in Russia in 1917 have declared themselves the heirs of Karl Marx's program of social revolution. They have encouraged radical elements in all countries of the world to form revolutionary parties and work under the banner of class struggle for the overthrow of parliamentary democracy, capitalism, and democratic-type international organizations. The success of Communism, especially after World War II when the Democracies united with Communist Russia to destroy Nazi and Fascist totalitarianism, has been a disillusioning shock to liberals. In some forty years over nine hundred million souls have come under Communist control. The people of the Democracies watched their former allies disregard international law and sweep nation after nation into the Communist camp. Economic conditions of under-developed nations, colonial policies of empires professing democracy, racial discrimination, and a blindness to the real aims of the former Russian allies, have all aided Communism in establishing totalitarian statism on a scale never before known in the history of the world.

The Communist movement is more than a revived cult of the worship of raw and absolute power, or a political, economic, and social form of statism. It is a movement as well, possessing a powerful and dedicated inner spirit which is crassly materialistic and anti-religious. For the first time since the split in the Church during the sixteenth century, an international movement has arisen aimed at winning the minds and hearts of all men. The Church was the first to grasp the reality of Communist intrigue and has repeatedly spoken out against this modern pagan revolution which is innately hostile to religion. The Holy See has warned against the horrors of Communist religious nihilism as blatant anti-religious campaigns were waged in Russia, Mexico, Spain, and after the war in the satellite nations of central Europe, in China, Korea, Viet Nam, Africa, South America; in short, wherever an inroad could be attempted. It has been stated that Communist persecutions of religion are the most effective in the history of the world, and that more Christians have suffered under this contemporary persecution than at any other time in the long history of the Church.

Documentary evidence of the CATHOLIC-COMMUNIST ENCOUNTER IN EAST EUROPE AFTER WORLD WAR II *(No. 51)* typifies the anti-religious excesses of Communists on every world front.

As the battle for men's souls waged through the critical years of the mid-century, and Pope Pius XII's pontificate came to an end in 1958, his successor, Angelo Cardinal Roncalli, patriarch of Venice, was raised to the papal throne as Pope John XXIII. The genial and astute new pope soon won the hearts of many people throughout the world with his open and loving appeal to all men of good will. Few popes in the long history of the Church enjoyed such universal popularity and sympathy. His first encyclical AD PETRI CATHEDRAM: ON SEEKING AND PROMOTING TRUTH, UNITY, AND PEACE *(No. 52),* of 29 June 1959, contained his calling of an ecumenical council of the universal Church to meet in Rome. This Second Vatican Council, the first since the incompleted first Vatican Council of 1870, was called to discuss anew the confrontation of the Church and the world, and the adapting of ecclesiastical discipline to the needs and conditions of the times. The long-standing rumors of an ecumenical council were thus realized. In the midst of Communist aggression, Pope John sought a new unity and devotion to Christian ideals as the foundation of any program of religious revival. This program was continued by his successor, Giovanni Battista Cardinal Montini, now Pope Paul VI, in 1963. The first decrees promulgated by Vatican Council II, as the beginning of the renewal of the Church, were the CONSTITUTION ON THE SACRED LITURGY of December 4, 1963 and the CONSTITUTION ON THE CHURCH, ON ORIENTAL CHURCHES, and on ECUMENISM *(No. 53)* of 21 November 1964.

One aspect of the ecumenical council especially attracted the attention of the world. It was the invitation of the Holy Father to Orthodox and Protestant Christians to participate as observers in the council. "Come, receive us," the pope declared in the words of St. Paul. "We have no other desire, no other wish. We ask nothing else from God save your salvation, your eternal happiness." To all Christian brethren separated from the see of Peter, he issued a moving Scriptural call: "I am your brother, Joseph."

Thus in the gigantic struggle of contemporary society the Church repeats the ageless plea of the Lord that all "may be made perfect in one." Only in this way will truth, peace, and harmony be achieved. Characterizing all men as brothers, Pope John addressed the Christian community in the words of St. Augustine:

Whether they like it or not, they are our brethren. They will cease to be our brethren only if they cease to say the "Our Father."
Let us love the Lord our God, let us love his Church: let us love him as a

father, her as a mother, him as a Lord, her as his handmaid; because we are children of his handmaid. But this marriage is fastened with bonds of great love; nobody can offend the one and be acceptable to the other. . . . What does it profit you not to have offended the father, who will not leave unpunished an offense given to the mother? . . . hold, therefore, dearly beloved, hold all of you with one mind God as your father, the Church as your mother. . . .

51. *Catholic-Communist Encounter in East Europe After World War II*

From *Communists Crush Churches in Eastern Europe* by Edward Meador (Boston: Forum Publishing Company); from *Communist-Christian Encounter in East Europe* (Indianapolis: School of Religion Press, 1956), pp. 420-425, 464, 472-473, 481-482, 516-522.

A. POLAND

1. *Pastoral Letter of the Polish Hierarchy on Church-State Relations, 24 April 1949*

BECAUSE the situation of the Church is growing worse and the carrying out of its apostolic mission is becoming more and more difficult, and because the hierarchy alone is blamed for this state of affairs, the truth must be told.

Church and state can reach harmony in education, family life, training of youth, public life. . . .

Is it not urgent to unite all forces to fight the misery left by the war, to work together in rebuilding our country. . . . After the moral destruction wrought by the war, what will help the country most: secularization or sanctification of the nation's spirit? Which is better for Poland: to break her up in rival sects or to strengthen her in one faith through one grace? Catholics, the critical hour for our Christian conscience has come.

In the worst years of bondage, the people felt the priests standing by as almost unique defenders and teachers. Polish priests built the first schools, opened the nation's eyes, provided books, founded libraries, hospitals, orphanages, the first cooperatives and savings banks. They were the first to teach hygiene. They brought the hard working people in their Sunday clothing before the altars of the Lord. They were the first to teach the people of the freedom of God's children and the high dignity of every worker and plowman.

Never before have the Polish people been closer to the priests, to the Church and to the altar. Their faithful eyes, prayerful lips, the overflowing churches, the besieged confessionals, the great response to all that is good is evidence.

Teaching the love of God, our clergy has not forgotten the love of its country. They combined the first with the second in such a wonderful manner that when the time came they could take the cross and themselves show how to die for the nation. They have taken their place at the head of the exiles, strengthening their faith in a higher justice, that of God. Too many priests have laid down their lives in this land for Poland to entertain any doubts as to whether their hearts love the nation.

When the enemy attacks, do not lose your peace of mind, remain at your posts as it befits you. Apply yourselves with zeal to teaching the Gospel, for that is your best and unique course of action. You know that you are not called upon to perform political work but to save human souls! Your works tend toward the country's peace, both when, at night, you go to the dying, when you strengthen the people in patience, as also when you defend the holy faith from sectarians and blasphemers, when you take your stand in the defense of crosses, of the Catholic schools which are being closed down, of prayer in the kindergarten!

You rightly believe that Poland does not need to be godless in order to be just to all! The defense of the faith, therefore, is not a political activity but the fulfillment of the obligation of religious vocation. Never were you so distant from political matters as today.

The Church recognizes the right of the family and the state to direct education at school; it also takes the stand that the education of a Catholic nation cannot take place without the active cooperation of the Church and the securing of its rights in the school and toward the school.

Catholic parents should have the right to choose their children's schools and should not be forced to send them to institutions where religion is altogether non-existent, or where education is based upon principles incompatible with Christian morality.

Religion in school cannot be a mere secondary subject; it must be the center of education, as a force whose value has been proven through the centuries.

The young Polish generation, which experienced the might of hatred in so many concentration camps, must believe in the values of the heart, for it must be prepared to build a just, loving Poland. Therefore, it should be educated in Christian principles of love and justice.

We await with confidence, after so many fruitless attempts, the triumph of the respect of a child's rights to God,

recognition of the Gospel's value, of the educational role of family and Church.

Remember, you are children of God. Shun treason toward your heavenly Father and your mother—the Church. Do not attend godless gatherings, do not raise your voice against your creator, do not renounce him who loved you to the death on the cross.

Face with courage and dignity the violent attacks against your conscience delivered by godless young elements, godless publications and associations! Do not mix with blasphemers and do not take part in their councils. Do not read godless literature and do not sing anthems which stir hatred, which are alien to our religious and national spirit.

Read diligently the holy Gospel, learn God's truths with zeal, pray fervently, defend your chastity and sobriety. Perform your service to Poland in such manner as not to abandon God's service. Remember that you will never build a better Poland by betraying God.

2. *Letter of the Primate, Cardinal Sapieha, to President B. Bierut, 16 February 1950*

Mr. President, the fight against the Church, against religion and against God himself in Poland is blatantly evident.

When we state this fact we desire one thing: that we shall not be asked to believe that this fight is not being waged at all. We ask at least this much of the consideration that is due to men: that the truth be told to them. Therefore either the deeds be openly acknowledged or the attitude adopted towards the Church should be changed. Should an acknowledgment follow, one would have to ask whether it is possible to take upon one's self the right to declare war on the Christian views and character of the nation. Poland never fought against the faith and religion of her citizens, or against the Catholic Church—which bears witness to one thing, namely, that the Church has never threatened the freedom of the national spirit.

The meeting at the Technical High School [in Warsaw], and the speeches delivered there by representatives of the Government and by various speakers, revealed the true intentions of the organizers of that meeting.

It is obvious that "putting an end to the abuses in Caritas" was not what mattered. One does not achieve such an aim by means of chicanery, by lavish receptions, by plying the clergy with drink at parties in the offices of district governors and in the premises of the council of state, by giving presents and similar bribery, for which so much money was spent that the limited budget of many a Caritas institution could be sufficiently provided for years to come. Who is going to believe that this waste of public funds was caused by solicitude for the poor?

A much bigger issue was at stake, namely, to disrupt and to sow discord among the clergy, and to make the clergy ridiculous in the public eyes; to oppose the clergy to the bishops and to create a jumping-off-board for detaching the clergy from the Holy See and from the unity of the Church, an objective to which much effort has been devoted for a very long time.

If these plans have not brought results, it is because you do not know the clergy. The clergy may have their faults, they may at first succumb to terror, but they will soon recognize violence and fraud and will turn their back on such behavior.

Propaganda has taken the liberty of making a distinction between the "reactionary clergy" and the "patriotic priests." We wish to remind you that in the years 1941-44 the German propaganda machine placed its hopes in the so-called "patriotic priests," and the people of Warsaw still remember it. Today we note a singular innovation in the press. We used to read about "the reactionary episcopate," but we read today about "the reactionary section of the episcopate." This is a new attempt, relying this time on "patriotic bishops." All these attempts can be reduced to one common denominator: they reveal the true countenance of the anti-Church activities.

Who will profit by the disruption of the Church? Most assuredly not Poland, who so many times in her tragic history has found the strength to survive in the unity of the Church, which united the whole nation.

Could the Church harm the people's Poland? If that Poland is to be truly a commonwealth of people, just and loving towards its citizens, if she does not violate their conscience and if she halts the fight against God, then such a Poland will truly deserve the full respect and support of all citizens.

The attitude of the Church towards the state will depend on the attitude of the state towards religion. If the state respects religion, who will dare to oppose the state? The state's anti-Church laws are today a source of accusations against the Government; when those laws disappear the long-desired peace will return.

All sorts of attempts have already been made to force the Catholic clergy to yield to the "modern reality." The bishops are being compelled to "recognize the People's Government"—as if the episcopate were a parliament. The episcopate holds itself and its clergy aloof from participation in political contentions. It is not for us to give approval to the actions of the Government. We have never done that, and we see no reason why we should do it now. The field of our activities is clearly-defined and well known. We desire to remain within it, convinced that our work will serve the realities of Poland.

On the other hand, we are astonished at the attempt to drag the clergy into politics and mass meetings, in direct contradiction to the argument of the party, that "priests should abstain from politics." First this attempt was made to turn the military chaplains into political agitators. This attempt met with no success. Now the attempt is being made to bring the whole of the clergy into politics, in order to incite them against the Episcopate.

Minister Wolski had the temerity to appeal the "mixed commission" [of representatives of the hierarchy and the Government, meeting in Warsaw] to the public meeting in the Technical High School on the question of an "agreement between Church and State," although he did not break off his negotiations with the bishop's committee. We are obliged to describe this unusual method of conducting negotiations as a demagogic move, prejudicial to the established method of conducting negotiations. At the same time it is an example of the lack of understanding of the internal life of the Church. The clergy may, by means of force, be brought to a mass meeting, as was done on January 30th, but they know well that nothing can happen in the Church through force.

Force was also used in appointing priests to offices in Caritas, although the clergy know that they may not accept any office from a lay authority without the permission of their bishops. Force was also used in trying to dissuade the clergy from obedience to the bishops when the bishops ordered the reading of their statement on Caritas.

The use of violence against the clergy is becoming an accepted method. Even if it should produce some results, it would hardly bring credit to the Government, for the Catholic people know their priests and are well aware to what

elements the Government has appealed. It must be stressed that more than a thousand priests who were brought to the Technical High School were deceived and assembled by violence and coercion. Those who delivered the lectures imposed on them, and those who participated in the discussion are men who had suffered from their experience in the war and in concentration camps, and who now find themselves in conflict with the law of the Church, or who are being blackmailed by the police because of the punishments hanging over them. To seek to establish a new order with the help of such people would mean to alienate the Catholics who constitute a majority of the nation.

Assuredly modern states have powerful means for disrupting the Church. We see what has been attempted against the Church in Hungary or in Czechoslovakia. Yet the outrages perpetrated there caused indignation through the whole of the civilized world.

The degradation of the high authority of the public administration became most evident when it was attempted to mobilize the clergy against the charitable activities of the Church. High government officials were reduced to the role of agents for bringing the clergy to Caritas meetings. The methods used were an insult to their human dignity and to the dignity of the state in whose name they were acting. County administrators, mayors of towns, and sometimes even the governors of provinces, ordered to bring priests to mass-meetings, would spend hours in irksome persuasion, often using threats and violence. What was most distressing was the obvious lies and blackmail used when other argument failed. All this was done to thousands of priests, all over Poland, often in the presence of the people, the servants of the Church and the domestic servants of the priests, who thus witnessed to what degradation the representatives of the state had sunk from their pedestal of authority. Even the men who carried out these orders did not always conceal their dislike of the ruthlessness of the orders. If today some priests are accused because, while defending their freedom against intruders, they used sharp words and, allegedly, "insulted the representatives of the state," one must take into account that these latter were insulted earlier, and a hundred times worse, by those who issued such instructions to them.

And what took place in Poland on the Friday and Saturday preceding February 12th, the day on which the statement of the episcopate on Caritas was to be read, surpasses all notions of legality and public order. Before the spectacle of such terror one feels offended, not only in one's dignity as a representative of the Polish clergy, but even in one's basic dignity as a human being. This was no longer the exercise of official functions, but a noisy riot of which the memory alone produces a humiliating feeling of shame that the state can sink to treating its citizens in this manner.

And all this is not considered to be a violation of the human conscience; it is even announced as being in conformity with binding decrees. But when a bishop exercises his authority with regard to the clergy and acts in defense of the discipline of the Church, the public prosecutor brings in legal actions and applies preventive measures against the bishop for an alleged infringement of the decree "On the Protection of the Freedom of Conscience and Faith." There can hardly be an example of a more glaring confusion of ideas.

Minister Wolski, in negotiating with the episcopate as your representative, Mr. President, is certainly aware of the nature of his actions. Being convinced that he acts in conformity with parlia-mentary procedures, we have refrained from appealing to you, Mr. President. Today, however, when the minister has appealed to the clergy to make "a concordat from the bottom," over the heads of the bishops, we no longer have any obligation to remain silent.

We therefore present our protests against the methods being used in conducting the negotiations. Minister Wolski, in spite of constant promises, never supplied in time the minutes of the meetings which had taken place. That delay hindered further discussions, and now the Minister has the audacity to charge the episcopate with responsibility for their slow progress. Other protests are aroused by the singular methods of seeking to intimidate the bishops. The minister has admitted that he seeks to bring a decisive pressure to bear upon the bishops by means of anti-Church laws. This method of constant intimidation has brought about an opposite result, and the episcopate has been continually confirmed in its conviction that the Government has no intention of keeping its word, but wants rather to confront the episcopate with *faits accomplis* against the freedom of the Church.

During the last conversation, on 19 December 1949, Minister Wolski undertook to send the outstanding minutes within four days, and a meeting of the mixed commission was to be arranged immediately afterwards. This was never done, and instead, during that period, the whole campaign against Caritas was prepared. Even on 23 January 1950, after that campaign had already begun, Minister Wolski received new proposals from the episcopate, and promised that he would immediately, on the following day, arrange a meeting of the sub-committee. This also did not take place, and instead the mass meetings began.

We are of the opinion that intimidation cannot be applied between two negotiating parties. We are the representatives of the Church, which sometimes submits to persecution for the sake of the truth, but does not ever change under threats. Even the most painful threats and the most prejudicial laws, therefore, will have no effect on our attitude on matters on which, on doctrinal grounds, we cannot yield.

Other protests are called forth by another peculiar argument, which Minister Wolski has used much too frequently. "Regulations already published," he used to say, "will not be implemented if the agreement is signed." The question arises: What exactly is the law, in the hands of the State? Is it a means of maintaining public order, or is it a means of intimidation? If today a minister of the Polish Republic proclaims that a law issued by the state may not be put into effect, what guarantee do we have that the Government will respect an agreement signed with the bishops?

Is it possible, in the light of these facts, to accuse the episcopate of delaying the negotiations and not desiring a real agreement with the state? And yet M. Wolski has had the audacity to do so. Although he knew only too well who was procrastinating and what was being prepared, he publicly accused the episcopate, laying the blame on the hierarchy of the Church.

Our letter on this occasion has not the character of a protest. It is not a declaration of grievances from the abused clergy or the slandered episcopate. Nor does our letter contain any request. Our letter is the voice of the conscience of the Polish nation, which speaks through us; and that voice is addressed to you, as president of the Republic, and is compelled to regard you, Mr. President, and your Government as responsible before God and before history for the fight against religion and against the Church in Poland.

3. *Polish Press Agency on Church-State Relations, 28 February 1950*

. . . The Government respects freedom of religion and of religious practices and scrupulously adheres to this attitude. Catholicism as a religious denomination is protected by law.

. . . In the interests of the state, and with the increasing support of the majority of the people and of the clergy, the Government has spared no effort to bring about a stabilization of relations with the Church through direct talks with the episcopacy. An indispensable condition for this highly desired stabilization is the discontinuation of all acts hostile to the Government, and loyalty on the part of the Polish episcopacy to the social system and the state interests of the People's Poland.

. . . The leading circles of the episcopacy failed even in such elementary loyalty as to consent to the use of the words "People's Poland" in the projected statement on Church-State relations.

. . . The episcopacy refuses to reconcile itself to the fact that power in Poland is now in the hands of the masses, that the form of government in which a handful of capitalists and landowners exploited and dominated the nation has been eliminated once and for all, and that the medieval privileges of the Church hierarchy—which have long since been removed in many European countries—cannot be maintained.

. . . The Government has never questioned the pope's jurisdiction in matters concerning the Roman Catholic religion. At the same time the Government, obviously enough, cannot shut its eyes to the fact that while the Vatican has no diplomatic relations with Poland, it stubbornly fosters such relations with the handful of reactionaries who call themselves the "London Government" and who are paid by foreign intelligence services.

. . . The Vatican has taken political measures to back the revisionist tendencies of the imperialists in the western zones of Germany and these measures coincide with the activities of warmongers. They are, therefore, aimed at Poland's most vital interests. Clearly, under such conditions, the execution by the Polish clergy of foreign orders issued by the Vatican on nonreligious matters cannot be reconciled with the interests and sovereignty of the Polish State.

That is why in this matter the Government proposed the following formula to the episcopacy: "Recognizing the pope as the competent authority of the Roman Catholic Church in religious matters, the episcopacy will in other matters be guided by the state interests of the People's Poland." Although such an attitude in no way violates the principles of the Catholic faith, the episcopacy rejected this proposition.

The introduction of Government control into the Caritas organization in order to end abuses, the waste of public property and criminal negligence, is unanimously looked upon today by public opinion as a step in the right direction of putting the administration of Caritas on a sound basis.

. . . The episcopacy's leading circles have . . . taken a stand against the decrees of Government authorities and they have tried to liquidate Caritas in order to exploit this fact in a political campaign against the People's Poland.

. . . Priests who, following the dictates of their own conscience, raised their voices in protest against the abuses of the Caritas organization and gave their support to the initiative of the Government, found themselves exposed to threats and severe reprisals on the part of some bishops.

. . . This is a game against the people and the state, which is determined to take part in the charitable work of Caritas . . . (Therefore) the great majority of the clergy refused to read from their pulpits the unprecedented statement on the Caritas affair released by the bishops.

. . . The attempts of the reactionary group of the Church hierarchy to bring political reprisals against honest and patriotic priests will encounter appropriate resistance and . . . can only lead to further isolation of the leading circles of the episcopacy.

. . . The Government is convinced that with the active support of the faithful and the proper understanding and continued active support of the enlightened clergy, relations between Church and State will eventually become stabilized. These relations will be based on full religious freedom and on the full recognition of the state interests of the People's Poland and of the achievements of the Polish people."

B. HUNGARY

1. *Josef Cardinal Mindszenty, Primate, on Confessional Education, 20 May 1946*

The Catholic Church founded the schools in this country which are the predecessors of the present schools. It was the Church which instituted schools of her own as early as the first centuries in the ancient Roman empire in order to protect the children from pagan influences by which they were taught idolatry and immoral mythological tales.

While the Church was most progressive in the matter of education, the state was slow in this activity and failed to establish schools until much later—in Hungary in the eighteenth century.

The Church has, however, still another much more compelling right to the education of youth than her historical right. Her educational mission springs from God himself. Perhaps this right is not acknowledged by those who do not believe in God and do not accept Christ and his Gospel. For you Catholics, however, it is an irrefutable law, since you have entered upon the inheritance of Christ. Before the Ascension, the Lord said to his disciples: "Go therefore, teach ye all nations." In the spirit of this commandment, the Church professed herself as the teacher of nationals.

The right of the Church to schools is entirely in concord with the right of parents to educate their children. What is incumbent upon the parents in all questions of natural life is incumbent upon the Church with regard to the supernatural life. Parents are prior to the state, and their rights were always and still are, acknowledged by the Church. The prerogative of parents to educate their children cannot be disputed by the state, since it is the parents who gave life to the child. They feed the child and clothe it. The child's life is, as it were, the continuation of theirs. Hence it is their right to demand that their children are educated according to their faith and their religious outlook.

It is their right to withhold their children from schools where their religious convictions are not only disregarded but even made the object of contempt and ridicule. It was this parental right which German parents felt was violated when the Hitler government deprived them of their denominational schools. The children came home from the new schools like little heathens, who smiled derisively or laughed at the prayers of their parents.

You Hungarian parents will likewise feel a violation of your fundamental rights if your children can no longer attend the Catholic schools solely because the dictatorial State closes down our schools by a brutal edict or renders their work impossible.

2. Last Pastoral Letter of Josef Cardinal Mindszenty on Government Abuses, 18 November 1948

For many weeks attempts have been made to state "resolutions" directed against me in all the townships and village communities of Hungary. I am being blamed for counter-revolutionary plots and activities hostile to the people, because of the Marian Celebration in 1947-48. It is complained that reconciliation between the Church and the State was frustrated and the demand is made that these "activities obnoxious to the people" should cease.

The goal of those "Days of Mary," celebrated in the Marian Year, was the deepening of the traditional Hungarian devotion for the holy Virgin and the strengthening of faith. Never were purely political matters made the subject of speeches on those occasions. The subjects were the virtues of the Mother of God, the ten commandments, human dignity, love and truth.

Those Marianic days attained their ends. The bishops of Hungary, who are the competent judges, testified to this in their letter of November 3rd. They identified themselves with me against those attacks which were launched against the Marian days. This same testimony is given also by the millions who represent public opinion in this country and against whose heroic patience, means had to be adopted which degrade those who employ them and which are in opposition to the principle of religious freedom guaranteed by democratic laws.

As to the legal significance of these "resolutions," it should be noted that no elections of local autonomous administrations have been held, in spite of many official promises, except in Budapest. Consequently all those decisions or "resolutions" which have been staged in counties, townships and villages lack any legal basis. The signatures to them are extorted by threats of loss of livelihood and freedom. The country is condemned to silence and public opinion has been made a mere frivolous jest. Democratic freedom in this country means that any opinion that differs from the official one is silenced. If a man dares to raise his voice in contradiction he is dismissed from his post because of his criticism of democracy, as many examples show, or he is punished in other ways. I feel the deepest sympathy with the sufferings of these people and compassion for every man who has fallen a victim of these measures. I was greatly impressed and deeply moved by many wonderful examples of unflinching courage and loyalty.

We asked the Government to publish those letters of mine to which such strong exception has been taken and to submit them to the judgment of public opinion in the whole world. But this has not been done. They continue to indulge in defamatory generalizations.

With regard to the fact that between Church and state—or perhaps we should say "Parties"—no agreement has yet been reached, it is well known that the Church was invited to negotiate an agreement only after a delay of three months, although she had publicly declared her willingness to enter into negotiations. At first it was announced that the questions pending between Church and state must be settled by mutual agreement. When, however, the Church was at last invited to negotiate, the main point—the problem of the schools—had been settled already by the state and the Church had to play the role of scapegoat.

I am looking calmly at this artificial whipping up of the waves. In the place where I stand, not by the grace of any party, but by the grace and confidence of the Holy See, such troubled waters are not an extraordinary phenomenon. This history proves.

Of my predecessors, two were killed

in action: two were robbed of all their possessions: one was taken prisoner and deported: one was assassinated: one exiled and one died after visiting and nursing victims of an epidemic.

Of all my predecessors, however, not one stood so bare of all means as I do. Such a systematic and purposeful propaganda of lies, time and again disproved but time and again repeated, has never been organized against the seventy-eight predecessors in my office. I stand for God, for Church, and for Hungary. This duty was imposed upon me by the fate of my nation which stands alone, an orphan in the whole world. As compared with the sufferings of my people, my own fate is of no importance.

I do not accuse my accusors. If I am compelled to speak out from time to time and to state the facts as they are, it is only the misery of my people which forces me to do so and the urge for truth.

I am praying for a world of truth and love. I am praying for those who, in the words of our Lord, "know not what they do."

I forgive them from the bottom of my heart.

3. *An Address Given by the Hungarian Minister of Public Worship and Instruction to the Party Committee, 7 June 1950*

We must start a vast work of enlightenment, and in the first place explain to our party colleagues and also to all workers that any father who sends his child to religion classes, places it in the hands of the enemy and entrusts his soul and thinking to the enemies of peace and imperialistic warmongers.

A part of our working people believes that participation of children in religious instruction is a private matter which has nothing to do with the political conviction of their parents. They are wrong. To send children to a reactionary pastor for religious instruction, is a political movement against the People's Democracy, whether intentional or not. Optional religious instruction in the schools is in this connection not yet the last possibility of realizing the democratic principles. We do not wish to change anything yet in the present order of optional religious instruction, but we emphasize that this order cannot present the clerical reaction with a free hand to agitate the children against the People's Democracy, to influence the children in the schools in a reactionary manner. So far, we have applied the principle of optional religious instruction too liberally, and this we shall also alter. Optional religious instruction cannot apply to technical and similar schools, even less so because the youth at these schools, if they wanted to, did attend religious instruction in the lower classes. No university has room for theological faculties any longer.

Logical consequence of the separation of State and Church is that the theological training of pastors is solely a Church concern and no responsibility of the State. The theological faculties must therefore be handed over to the churches. . . .

Already now I warn against any exaggeration, i.e., removing or branding every working person who sends his children to religious instruction in spite of our enlightenment. Probably we shall have to commence some propaganda against the participation of children in religious instruction, but we must not take administrative steps, and any threat of material disadvantage is not allowed.

The agreement with the Protestant churches is still in force and is working well. This agreement proves that the People's Republic assures complete religious freedom and that the churches, if they do not turn out to be accom-

plices of foreign and native reaction, can live in peace and fulfill their responsibility in the People's Democracy. But even in the Protestant churches there are reactionary efforts. In presbyteries in very many places 'Kulaks' are in the majority; a few Protestant pastors follow the Catholic reaction in connection with April 4th as their example, and the election of reactionary, formerly Horthy politicians, for leading offices of the Protestant churches shows that the reaction is still struggling to put its foot on these churches.

In carrying out the basic principles, religion within the party is no private matter, but we must make a difference between plain party members and party officials, and must not in any case make party membership dependent on the fact whether our party members are religious. In the first place, we must expect from our party officials, our leading men, that they do not send their children to religious instruction courses, do not take part in religious ceremonies and train their wives in the spirit of communistic conception.

Also, we must patiently endeavor to enlighten our members, and ensure through training and propaganda that they realize: "In going to Church, taking part in processions, sending our children to religious instruction, we unconsciously further the efforts of clerical reaction."

C. CZECHOSLOVAKIA

1. *Instructions to Communists, July 1942*

1. The Vatican: You are to undermine the authority of the Vatican by all means, especially by attacks in the press, compromising articles and news items.

2. To break down unity among the clergy, separate higher from the lower clergy, drive a wedge between bishops and clergy, also between the priests and their parishes.

3. Main principle: Do not deal directly with the higher clergy. This is reserved only to Dr. Cepicka, general secretary, and the Secretariat of the Communist party. Our experience shows that negotiations by the district action committees lead to compromises, which must be avoided.

4. The task of the Church Commission of the local committee of action is not to open co-operation or negotiation with the Roman Catholic Church, but to acquire authority to act without the Church and against the Church.

5. Closest co-operation with the Czechoslovak Church: Praise their bishops and give them highest honors in all state functions and celebrations.

6. Emphasize the frustration in the religious situation of today and the necessity for unity. In the first phase use the Czechoslovak Church as the instrument for unity; the Orthodox Church will take this place later (Prague will become a metropolitanate for the Russian Orthodox).

7. Attack the Catholic Church with all the usual weapons: unreasonableness of celibacy, economic power and wealth of the Church, the Church as a capitalist institution, moral delinquents, homosexual trials. . . .

2. *Aims of the Central Committee of the Czechoslovak Communist Party Against the Church*

1. Archbishops and bishops should be prevented from communicating with the Vatican otherwise than through the Government.

2. Pastoral letters must always have previous Government authorization.

3. Sermons of priests and all addresses to church associations should be censored and kept under rigid control.

4. The Czechoslovak Church and the Church of the Evangelical Brethren should be made state churches. The Catholic Church's property should be seized and distributed among national churches.

5. The Catholic clergy should be forced to join the National Church.

6. The Catholic clergy should be morally compromised, if necessary by means of woman agents.

3. *Law of 14 October 1949, Establishing the State Office for Church Affairs*

The National Assembly of the Czechoslovak Republic passes this law:

1. The state office for church affairs is established as a central office; it is in charge of a cabinet minister, who is appointed by the president of the Republic.

2. The purpose of the state office for church affairs is to take care that the church and religious life should develop in harmony with the constitution and principles of people's democratic order, and thus secure for everybody the right to freedom of confession guaranteed by the constitution, founded on principles of religious tolerance and equality of all confessions.

3. The functions in all church and religious affairs, which until now were performed by other central offices, are transferred to the state office for church affairs.

4. In Slovakia, the minister who is in charge of the state office for church affairs, performs his functions in principle through the Slovak office for church affairs, which is in charge of a representative appointed by the government.

5. The government shall disclose by a decree the detailed directions about the working and organization of the state office for church affairs, also about its functions.

6. This law shall become effective on the day of its publication; it shall be executed by all the members of the government.

4. *Law Passed by the National Assembly of the Czechoslovak Republic for the Economic Security of the Churches and Religious Societies by the State, 1 November 1949*

1. Personal salaries of clergymen: The state grants, according to the subsequent ordinances of this law, their personal salaries to clergymen of churches and religious societies, who function with the consent of the state as parish leaders in church administration, or in institutions for the education of the clergy. The state office may in exceptional cases after the previous agreement with the ministry of finance grant the personal salaries of clergymen who are otherwise occupied.

2. The consent of the state may be given only to clergymen who are Czechoslovak state citizens, are politically reliable and blameless, and fulfill also otherwise the general requirements of acceptance into the state service. The state office for church affairs may in cases worthy of a special consideration forego the requirements of state citizenship.

3. (1) The personal salary of clergymen consists of: a. fundamental pay, b. additional salary for higher dignitaries, c. reward for special functions.

(2) The government shall designate by a decree the sums of the fundamental pay, the methods and measures of its raising, the conditions of acknowledging the addition for higher dignitaries, and its limit, also the conditions for acknowledging the rewards for higher functions.

4. Compensation for traveling, moving and other expenses: Clergymen who have claim for personal salaries, have also claim for compensation on traveling, moving and other expenses according to the general directions.

5. The duty to teach religion: It is the duty of clergymen functioning as parish leaders to teach religion in schools without compensation, if religious instruction is not taken care of otherwise. The extent of this duty and its further arrangement shall be decided in agreement with the minister of schools, sciences, and art, by the minister who is directing the state office for church affairs.

6. Social allowances: Social additions, especially additions for minor children, pensions for clergymen and the members of their families are given according to the periodical directions valid for state employees. The details shall be fixed by the government.

7. Activity and appointment of clergymen: (1) Spiritual (preaching, etc.) activity in churches and religious societies may be performed only by persons who have for it the consent of the state and who take the oath. The contents of the oath will be disclosed by a government decree.

(2) Every appointment (election) of these persons requires the previous consent of the state.

(3) Vacant places must be occupied at the latest within 30 days. If this is not done, the state may take the necessary measures for securing the orderly course in the parish leadership, church administration or education of the clergy.

8. Material expenses: (1) The state covers, according to their accepted budget, the regular material expenses of churches and religious societies connected with divine service and other religious rites, also with church administration.

(2) The state gives in substantiated cases special help for extraordinary material expenses.

9. Budgets: (1) It is the duty of the representatives of churches and religious societies and the managers of church properties to prepare the budgets and financial statements, and

present them for approval to the state office for church affairs.

(2) The budgets for regular actual expenses are prepared according to actual needs, following the principles of state budget; the details will be decided by the state office for church affairs after agreement with the ministry of finance.

10. Property: (1) The state supervises the property of churches and religious societies.

(2) The representatives of churches and religious societies shall prepare an account of all movable and immovable property and property rights of the churches and religious societies, their constituent parts, units, institutions, endowments, church buildings, benefits and funds and shall present it within three months from the day on which this law becomes effective to the state office for church affairs. The details shall be worked out by the state office for church affairs.

(3) Any selling or mortgaging of the property of churches and religious societies requires the previous consent of the state government.

11. Elimination of obligations: (1) All the private and public patronates (endowments, etc.) of church building, benefits and other church institutions are transferred to the state.

(2) All the obligations to contribute toward the purposes of churches and religious societies, their constituent parts, units, institutions, endowments, church buildings, benefits and funds based on patronates or some other legal reasons and long time customs, shall cease to exist, with the exception of the obligations of the members of the churches and religious societies, based on the order recognized by the state.

12. Establishments for the training of clergymen: The schools of learning and institutions for the education of

the clergy are kept up entirely by the State.

13. Penalties: Actions or negligences contradicting the directions of this law or ordinances based on it are punished, if there is no question of criminal act, by the District National Committee as misdemeanors with a fine up to 160,000 Czechoslovak Crowns. In case of the impossibility to enforce the payment of the fine, a substitute punishment is meted out according to the degree of guilt, up to six months in prison.

14. Repeal of ordinances: All the ordinances which regulate the legal constitutions of churches and religious societies are repealed.

5. *Statement of Roman Catholic Clergy Against the Proposed Law, 14 August 1949*

Summary of the main points of the bishops' peace condition:

1. All measures restricting Mgr. Beran's personal freedom should be removed.

2. Government plenipotentiaries installed in the bishops' consistories or, as in the case of Slovakia, in the bishops' offices must be removed. By the latter the state has assumed the right to decide in matters of religious rites and worship and in matters of morals and faith.

"Already the work of these plenipotentiaries shows clearly the extent of their illegal activities." In some dioceses they claim the right exclusively to decide in all business of the Church and they illegally use official Church seals for their personal instructions.

3. The Catholic Action movement which "under a veil of seeking agreement between Church and state" was to bring disorder into the ranks of Czech and Slovak Catholics was rightly proclaimed by us as a movement of schism. We are of the opinion that a suitable

moment has now come to stop this enmity against the Church.

4. The idea of the Christian world will be respected and recognized in public life and education by both words and deeds.

5. The Government will recognize the spiritual authority of the Roman pope as supreme head of the Church as well as the right authority of the bishops in their obedience to the pope and Church orders.

6. All measures restricting and endangering religious freedom will be revoked.

We demand further that interference, violating Church rights, with the education of priests and juniors of the orders must cease. We protest against the cutting of contact between the bishops and the believers, and we protest against the silencing of our just defense against untrue accusations and measures of persecution. We protest against the persecution of priests for reading pastoral letters and for faithfully fulfilling their priestly duties. We protest against the continued publication of the so-called *Gazette* of the Catholic clergy, and we demand renewal of full freedom for the Catholic Press which has been stopped.

We call for a renewal of the freedom of meetings guaranteed by the constitution, and we especially protest against the fact that under various excuses priests are prevented from holding meetings among themselves and from making other expressions of religious life. We protest against the closing of Church schools, the requisitioning of Church and monastery buildings, and against all steps which limit religious freedom.

7. The bishops are willing to swear loyalty to the state on the terms of the existing arrangement between Czechoslovakia and the Vatican provided the Government stops attacking the Church, guarantees religious free-dom, and recognizes papal authority in Church affairs.

6. *Statement of the Czechoslovakian Hierachy Against the Law of 1 November 1949*

With the consent of all the Bishops, the whole clergy state that they do not accept the proposed new law dealing with the payment of personal and material expenses of the Church and religious organizations and that the entire vicariate decided to publish and submit to the Government of the Republic of Czechoslovakia this declaration (in which we list only the outstanding points):

1. The clergy gratefully admits that the Government of the Republic of Czechoslovakia recognizes as a fact that the economic and financial position of the clergy is not adequate to their education and their work for the common welfare and the supreme interests of the nation.

2. However, the suggested law aims to better the position of the clergy at the cost of their freedom and to bring the spiritual mission of the church into complete dependence on political agencies and interests. This can be seen in Paragraph 10 of the proposed law.

(Paragraph 10 of the proposed law reads: "The election or nomination of clergy receiving salaries or benefits in accordance with this law requires the prior approval of the state administration. The election or nomination of titular bishops, diocesan bishops, archbishops, as well as their coadjutors, apostolic administrators, army bishops and heads of individual churches requires prior approval of the proposed candidate by the Government. The Government may withhold approval on the ground of the political desirability of the candidates.")

Therefore the clergy declare that they will accept their church appointments only from the hands of free and unrestricted church superiors.

3. The proposed improvement in the position of the clergy and the material contributions to church objectives create an unfavorable impression, as if the church were to be satisfied in receiving compensation for its estates and property, which it lost against its will. This happened by one-sided action on the part of the state, without preliminary agreement with the Holy See.

4. The salaries of the clergy are to be raised at a time when, because of various economic difficulties, it is being considered to lower the wages of the workers and the insurance benefits of pensioned people. Under such conditions the clergy voluntarily relinquishes the benefits of the increases proposed in the new law and respectfully requests that the incomes of the workers and pensioners be retained at their present levels or, better still, improved.

5. A law such as this—which, in Paragraph 17, threatens destructive sanctions even for small violations—is at the most anti-social and unfair, and therefore it is necessary to reject it under all circumstances.

(Paragraph 17 of the proposed law states: "Actions or omissions contravening the provisions of this law or regulations issued under it shall be punished, in so far as it is not a matter punishable by a court, by a district national committee as an adminstrative misdemeanor with a fine not exceeding 100,000 crowns [$2,000]. An alternative sentence of imprisonment not exceeding six months shall be imposed simultaneously in case the fine is not collectable. Fines shall go to the state treasury.")

6. The clergy will be satisfied if, in agreement with the highest church dignitaries, the basic law be retained and in special cases adjusted, and if the repair of national church monuments will be financed and the Church needs satisfied.

(This was a reference to the state-church agreement of the eighteenth century laying down the terms for state financial aid to the Church in the old Austro-Hungarian Empire.)

7. It is particularly requested that the religious freedom of the people be completely respected and retained, as well as the freedom of priestly work and spiritual aims of the clergy, whose aim is the eternal and present welfare of our people.

D. DECREE OF THE SACRED CONGREGATION OF THE HOLY OFFICE ON JOINING OR SUPPORTING COMMUNIST PARTIES, 1 JULY 1949

This Sacred Supreme Congregation has been asked:

1. whether it is lawful to join Communist Parties or to favor them;

2. whether it is lawful to publish, disseminate, or read books, periodicals, newspapers or leaflets which support the teaching or action of Communists, or to write in them;

3. whether the faithful who knowingly and freely perform the acts specified in questions 1 and 2 may be admitted to the sacraments;

4. whether the faithful who profess the materialistic and anti-Christian doctrine of the Communists, and particularly those who defend or propagate this doctrine, contract *ipso facto* excommunication specially reserved to the Apostolic See as apostates from the Catholic faith.

The Most Eminent and Most Reverend Fathers entrusted with the supervision of matters concerning the safeguarding of faith and morals, having previously heard the opinion of the Reverend Lords Consultors, decreed in the plenary session held on Tuesday (instead of Wednesday), 28 June 1949, that the answers should be as follows:

To 1. *in the negative:* because Communism is materialistic and anti-Christian; and the leaders of the Communists, although they sometimes profess in words that they do not oppose religion, do in fact show themselves, both in their teaching and in their actions, to be the enemies of God, of the true religion and of the Church of Christ;

to 2. *in the negative;* they are prohibited *ipso iure* (cf. canon 1399 of the *Codex Iuris Canonici*);

to 3. *in the negative,* in accordance with the ordinary principles concerning the refusal of the sacraments to those who are not disposed;

to 4. *in the affirmative.*

And the following Thursday, on the 30th day of the same month and year, Our Most Holy Lord Pius XII, pope by divine providence, in the ordinary audience, granted to the Most Eminent and Most Reverend Assessor of the Sacred Office, approved of the decision of the Most Eminent Fathers which had been reported to him, and ordered the same to be promulgated officially in the *Acta Apostolicae Sedis.*

52. *Pope John XXIII: Encyclical, "Ad Petri Cathedram": On Seeking and Promoting Truth, Unity, and Peace, 29 June 1959*

From *Ad Petri Cathedram* (Rome: Vatican Press Office, 1959), *passim.*

3. . . . LET us speak of that unity which we especially desire, and with which the pastoral office committed to us by God is most closely linked. I mean the unity of the Church.

Of course, all know that the divine Redeemer founded a society that was to keep its unity till the end of time, according to the promise: "Behold I am with you all days even to the consummation of the world;" and that for this intention He prayed most fervently to his heavenly Father.

But this prayer of Jesus Christ, which surely was heard, and granted for his reverence: "That they all may be one as thou, Father, in me, and I in thee, that they also may be one in us," implants in us a comforting hope and gives assurance that eventually all the sheep who are not of this fold will desire to return to it; consequently, in accordance with the words of the same divine redeemer, "there will be one fold and one shepherd."

It was under the guidance of this comforting hope which encouraged us very much, that we publicly announced the plan to summon an ecumenical council, to which bishops from every part of the world will come to discuss matters important to religion.

The Council's chief business will concern the growth of the Catholic faith and the renewal along right lines of the habits of Christian people, and the adapting of ecclesiastical discipline to the needs and conditions of the present time.

That event will surely be a wonderful manifestation of truth, unity, and charity; a manifestation, indeed, which it is our hope that those who behold it, but who are separated from this Apostolic See, will receive as a gentle invitation to seek and find that unity for which Jesus Christ prayed so ardently to his heavenly Father.

We have already learned—and it was indeed a consolation to us—that quite recently in not a few communities separated from the Chair of blessed Peter, there has been aroused a certain sympathy of mind towards the faith and Catholic teaching. And considerable respect for this Apostolic See has arisen and daily increased as the study of truth destroys prejudices once held.

We also know that congresses have been held by nearly all those who, although in union neither with us nor with each other, call themselves Christians, with a view to uniting among themselves; and that they have set up councils to this end. This shows that they are experiencing a strong desire to reach at least some kind of unity.

It is beyond doubt that the divine Redeemer established his Church and endowed and strengthened it with a strong mark of unity. Otherwise—to use an absurd expression—if he had not done so, he would have done something completely contradictory to himself, in much the same way as nearly all philosophies, which depend on the whim of men's opinion, come into existence one after another in the course of time, are altered, and pass away.

But it is plain to all that this is opposed to the divine teaching authority of Jesus Christ who is "the way, the truth and the life."

This unity, however, venerable brethren and dear children—which, as we said, ought not to be something frail, uncertain, and unsteady, but something solid, firm and safe—if it is lacking in other groups of Christians, is not lacking in the Catholic Church, as all who carefully examine the question can easily observe.

It is a unity which is distinguished and adorned by these three marks: unity of doctrine, of government, of religious practice. It is a unity which is clearly visible to the gaze of all so that all can recognize and follow it.

It has this nature, we say, by the will of the divine founder, so that within it all the sheep may be gathered together into one fold, under the guidance of one shepherd; so that all the children may be invited into the one Father's house, founded on the cornerstone of Peter; and so that, as a result of it,

efforts may be made to link all peoples by this bond of brotherhood to the one kingdom of God, whose citizens, joined harmoniously together heart and soul while on earth, may eventually enjoy happiness in heaven.

For the Catholic Church ordains that all that has been divinely revealed must be firmly and faithfully believed; that is, what is contained in the Scriptures, or in oral or written tradition, and, from the time of the Apostles in the course of the centuries, has been approved and defined by the supreme pontiffs and the lawful ecumenical councils.

Whenever anyone has left this path, the Church using her maternal authority has never ceased to invite him back, again and again, to the right path. She indeed clearly knows and maintains that there is but one truth, and consequently that contrary "truths" cannot exist. She declares and bears witness to the saying of the Apostle of the Gentiles, "The powers we have are used in support of the truth, not against it."

There are quite a number of points that the Catholic Church leaves to the discussion of the theologians, both in so far as these points are not absolutely certain, and also, as the famous English writer John Henry Cardinal Newman noted, in so far as controversies of this kind do not tear asunder the unity of the Church, but rather greatly help (by striking new light out of the friction of the various opinions) to a deeper and better understanding of the dogmas, and level and strengthen the path to the attainment of that unity. (Newman, Difficulties of Anglicans, vol. 1, lect. X, p. 261 ff.)

However, that common saying, sometimes expressed in other terms and attributed to different authors, should be retained and approved: In essentials, unity; in doubtful matters, liberty; in all, charity.

Further, the unity of government in the Catholic Church is obvious to all. For just as the faithful are subject to their priests, and the priests to their bishops, whom "the Holy Ghost has placed . . . to rule the church of God," so each and all the bishops are subject to the Roman pontiff, who is regarded as the successor of St. Peter, whom Christ our Lord set as the rock and foundation of his Church, and to whom alone in a special manner he gave the power of binding and loosing whatever is on earth, and of strengthening his brethren, and of feeding the whole flock.

With regard to unity of religious practice, everyone knows that the Catholic Church from its earliest period down through the centuries has always had seven, neither more nor fewer, sacraments, received as a sacred legacy from Jesus Christ.

She has never ceased to dispense these throughout the Catholic world for the nourishing and fostering of the supernatural life of the faithful.

It is likewise known that in the Church is celebrated only one Sacrifice. This is the eucharistic sacrifice by which Christ himself, our salvation and our redeemer, daily sacrifices himself for us all in an unbloody manner but truly, as he did when hanging from the cross on Calvary; and thus in His mercy He pours out on us the immeasurable treasures of his grace.

Hence St. Cyprian with complete truth declares: "It is impossible for another altar to be set up or a new priesthood to be established apart from the one altar and the one priesthood."

However, as all are aware, that does not prevent the use and approval in the Catholic Church of various rites, by which she is displayed in greater beauty and, like the daughter of the King of Kings, seems to be dressed in varied robes.

That all may obtain this true and harmonious unity, the Catholic priest, when he is celebrating the eucharistic sacrifice, offers the spotless Victim to the most merciful God, interceding in the first place "for Thy holy Catholic Church, that Thou wouldst deign to give her peace and protection to unite and guide her the whole world over; together with Thy servant our pope, and all true believers who foster the Catholic and apostolic faith."

May this wondrous manifestation of unity, therefore, by which the unity of the Catholic Church stands forth for all to see—may these desires, these prayers by which she implores from God the same unity for all, move your mind and rouse it in a salutary manner. We say, your—for we are speaking to those who are separated from the Apostolic See.

Indulge this gentle longing we have to address you as brothers and sons; permit us to nourish that hope for your return, which we foster with sentiments of paternal love.

We are glad to address you with the same pastoral zeal with which Theophilus, Bishop of Alexandria, when an unhappy schism was rending the seamless garment of the Church, addressed his brethren and sons in these terms:

Let us, dearly beloved, as sharers in a heavenly invitation, each according to his degree, imitate Jesus, the guide and accomplisher of our salvation.

Let us embrace that humility of soul which uplifts, and that charity which unites us with God; and that sincere faith with respect to the divine mysteries.

Flee from division, shun discord . . . foster charity among yourselves: listen to Christ speaking, "in this will all men know that you are My disciples, if you have love one for another."

Note, we beg of you, that when we lovingly invite you to the unity of the Church we are inviting you, not to the home of a stranger, but to your own, to the Father's house which belongs to all. Permit us, then, longing for you all "with the tenderness of Jesus Christ" (Philip. I, 8), to exhort you to call to mind your ancestors "who preached God's work to you: contemplate the happy issue of the life they lived, and imitate their faith."

The noble ranks of the saints above, whom each of your races has sent before you into heaven, and those in particular who by their published writings handed down and explained clearly and accurately the teaching of Jesus Christ, seem to invite you by the example of their life to union with this Apostolic See, with which as a means of salvation your Christian community also was linked for so many centuries.

All those, therefore, who are separated from us, we address as brothers, using the words of St. Augustine:

Whether they like it or not, they are our brethren. They will cease to be our brethren only if they cease to say the "Our Father."

Let us love the Lord our God, let us love his Church: let us love him as a father, her as a mother, him as a Lord, her as his handmaid; because we are children of his handmaid. But this marriage is fastened with bonds of great love; nobody can offend the one and be acceptable to the other. . . . What does it profit you not to have offended the father, who will not leave unpunished an offense given to the mother? . . . Hold, therefore, dearly beloved, hold all of you with one mind God as your father, the Church as your mother.

But we direct our suppliant prayers for the protection of the Church and the extension of the fold and kingdom of Christ to the most gracious God, giver of heavenly lights and of all good things. And we urge that prayers may likewise be directed by all our dear brethren and children in Chirst.

The outcome of the future ecumenical council depends more, indeed, on all vying with each other in the ardor of their united prayers, than on human effort, industry and diligence. To take part in his prayerful appeal to God, we invite most lovingly those, also, who, though they are not of this fold, yet reverently worship God and with good will strive to keep his commandments.

May the divine entreaty of Christ increase and bring to fulfillment our hope and our intentions: "Holy Father, keep them in thy name whom thou hast given me, that they may be one as we also are. . . . Sanctify them in truth; thy word is truth. . . . Not for them only do I pray, but for them also who through their word will believe in me . . . that they may be made perfect in one. . . ."

We repeat these words in earnest prayer, along with the Catholic world united with us. We do so, inspired not only by a burning love for all nations, but also moved by the humility of spirit of the Gospel. For we know the lowliness of our own person, whom God, not by our merits but in his secret counsel, deigned to raise to the dignity of supreme pontiff.

Therefore, to all our brethren and all our children who are separated from this See of the Blessed Peter, we repeat these words: "I am . . . thy brother, Joseph."

Come; "receive us." We have no other desire, no other wish. We ask nothing else from God save your salvation, your eternal happiness.

Come; out of this so longed for and harmonious unity which brotherly love must foster and cherish, great peace will spring: that peace which "surpasses all our thinking," since it has its origin in heaven; that peace which Christ announced to men of good will by the choirs of angels who hovered above his crib, and which, after the institution of the Sacrament and Sacrifice of the Eucharist, he imparted with these words:

Peace I leave with you, my peace I give unto you; not as the world gives do I give unto you.

Peace and joy; joy also, for those who are really and effectively united with the mystical body of Jesus Christ, which is the Catholic Church, share in that life which flows into each single member from the divine head. And one account of that life, those who faithfully obey all the instructions and commandments of our redeemer, can enjoy even in this mortal life that happiness which is a foretaste and prophecy of the eternal happiness of heaven.

This peace, however, this happiness, while we travel amid the difficulties of this earthly exile, is still imperfect. For it is a peace not unruffled, not without its storms; it is an active peace, not a lazy or listless one. Further, it is a peace which makes war on all errors, however speciously these may be veiled in the guise of truth, and on the enticements and blandishments of vice.

It fights against the enemies of the soul, of whatever kind, who are capable of weakening, soiling and harming

innocence or our Catholic faith; and also against hatred, deceits and discord which can tear and wound it. For this reason, the divine Redeemer gave and entrusted to us the peace which is his.

Peace, then, which we must seek and towards which we must bend all our efforts, has to be, as we said, that which admits no errors nor compromise with those who hold them; the kind of peace which makes no concession to vice and which avoids all discord.

Those who pursue this peace must be ready to give up their own advantage and convenience for the sake of truth and justice, in accordance with the words: "Seek . . . first the kingdom of God and his justice. . . ."

Through the intercession of the blessed virgin Mary, queen of peace, to whose immaculate heart our predecessor of immortal memory Pius XII consecrated the whole human race, we make our earnest prayer to God that this unity in harmony, this true, active, fighting peace may be obtained, both for those who are our children in Christ, and also for all those who, though separated from us, yet cannot do other than love truth, unity and harmony. . . .

53. *Vatican Council II*

A. CONSTITUTION ON THE SACRED LITURGY, 4 DECEMBER 1963

From *Constitution on the Sacred Liturgy* (Collegeville, Minn.: The Liturgical Press, 1964), pp. 1-29.

THIS sacred Council has several aims in view: it desires to impart an ever increasing vigor to the Christian life of the faithful; to adapt more suitably to the needs of our own times those institutions which are subject to change; to foster whatever can promote union among all who believe in Chirst; to strengthen whatever can help to call the

whole of mankind into the household of the Church. The Council therefore sees particularly cogent reasons for undertaking the reform and promotion of the liturgy.

For the liturgy, "through which the work of our redemption is accomplished," [1] most of all in the divine

[1] Secret of the Ninth Sunday after Pentecost.

sacrifice of the eucharist, is the outstanding means whereby the faithful may express in their lives, and manifest to others, the majesty of Christ and the real nature of the true Church. It is of the essence of the Church that she be both human and divine, visible and yet invisibly equipped, eager to act and yet intent on contemplation, present in this world and yet not at home in it; and she is all these things in such wise that, in her the human is directed and subordinated to the divine, the visible likewise to the invisible, action to contemplation, and this present world to that city yet to come, which we seek.[2] While the liturgy daily builds up those who are within into a holy temple of the Lord, into a dwelling place for God in the Spirit,[3] to the mature measure of the fullness of Christ,[4] at the same time it marvelously strengthens their power to preach Christ, and thus shows forth the Church to those who are outside as a sign lifted up among the nations[5] under which the scattered children of God may be gathered together[6] until there is one sheepfold and one shepherd.[7]

Wherefore the sacred Council judges that the following principles concerning the promotion and reform of the liturgy should be called to mind, and that practical norms should be established.

Among these principles and norms there are some which can and should be applied both to the Roman rite and also to all the other rites. The practical norms which follow, however, should be taken as applying only to the Roman rite, except for those which, in the very nature of things, affect other rites as well.

Lastly, in faithful obedience to tradition, the sacred Council declares that holy Mother Church holds all lawfully acknowledged rites to be of equal right and dignity; that she wishes to preserve them in the future and to foster them in every way. The Council also desires that, where necessary, the rites be revised carefully in the light of sound tradition, and that they be given new vigor to meet the circumstances and needs of modern times.

I. GENERAL PRINCIPLES FOR THE RESTORATION AND PROMOTION OF THE SACRED LITURGY

A. THE NATURE OF THE SACRED LITURGY AND ITS IMPORTANCE IN THE CHURCH'S LIFE

God who "wills that all men be saved and come to the knowledge of the truth" (1 Tim. 2:4), "who in many and various ways spoke in times past to the fathers by the prophets" (Heb. 1:1), when the fullness of time had come sent his Son, the Word made flesh, anointed by the Holy Spirit, to preach the gospel to the poor, to heal the contrite of heart,[8] to be a "bodily and spiritual medicine,"[9] the Mediator between God and man.[10] For his humanity, united with the person of the Word, was the instrument of our salvation. Therefore in Christ "the perfect achievement of our reconciliation came forth, and the fullness of divine worship was given to us."[11]

The wonderful works of God among the people of the Old Testament were but a prelude to the work of Christ the Lord in redeeming mankind and giving perfect glory to God. He achieved his task principally by the paschal mystery

[2] Cf. Heb. 13:14.
[3] Cf. Eph. 2:21-22.
[4] Cf. Eph. 4:13.
[5] Cf. Is. 11:12.
[6] Cf. John 11:52.
[7] Cf. John 10:16.

[8] Cf. Is. 61:1; Luke 4:18.
[9] St. Ignatius of Antioch, *To the Ephesians*, 7, 2.
[10] Cf. 1 Tim. 2:5.
[11] *Sacramentarium Veronese* (ed. Mohlberg), n. 1265; cf. also n. 1241, 1248.

of his blessed passion, resurrection from the dead, and glorious ascension, whereby "dying, he destroyed our death and, rising, he restored our life."[12] For it was from the side of Christ as he slept the sleep of death upon the cross that there came forth "the wondrous sacrament of the whole Church."[13]

Just as Christ was sent by the Father, so also he sent the apostles, filled with the Holy Spirit. This he did that, by preaching the gospel to every creature,[14] they might proclaim that the Son of God, by his death and resurrection, had freed us from the power of Satan[15] and from death, and brought us into the kingdom of his Father. His purpose also was that they might accomplish the work of salvation which they had proclaimed, by means of sacrifice and sacraments, around which the entire liturgical life revolves.

Thus by baptism men are plunged into the paschal mystery of Christ: they die with him, are buried with him, and rise with him;[16] they receive the spirit of adoption as sons "in which we cry: Abba, Father" (Rom. 8:15), and thus become true adorers whom the Father seeks.[17] In like manner, as often as they eat the supper of the Lord they proclaim the death of the Lord until he comes.[18] For that reason, on the very day of Pentecost, when the Church appeared before the world, "those who received the word" of Peter "were baptized." And "they continued steadfastly in the teaching of the apostles and in the communion of the breaking of bread and in prayers . . . praising God and being in favor with all the people" (Acts 2:41-47).

From that time onwards the Church has never failed to come together to celebrate the paschal mystery: reading those things "which were in all the scriptures concerning him" (Luke 24:27), celebrating the eucharist in which "the victory and triumph of his death are again made present,"[19] and at the same time giving thanks "to God for his unspeakable gift" (2 Cor. 9:15) in Christ Jesus, "in praise of his glory" (Eph. 1:12), through the power of the Holy Spirit.

To accomplish so great a work, Christ is always present in his Church, especially in her liturgical celebrations. He is present in the sacrifice of the Mass, not only in the person of his minister, "the same now offering, through the ministry of priests, who formerly offered himself on the cross,"[20] but especially under the eucharistic species. By his power he is present in the sacraments, so that when a man baptizes it is really Christ himself who baptizes.[21] He is present in his word, since it is he himself who speaks when the holy scriptures are read in the Church. He is present, lastly, when the Church prays and sings, for he promised: "Where two or three are gathered together in my name, there am I in the midst of them" (Matt. 18:20).

Christ indeed always associates the Church with himself in this great work wherein God is perfectly glorified and men are sanctified. The Church is his beloved Bride who calls to her Lord, and through him offers worship to the Eternal Father.

12 Easter Preface of the Roman Missal.

13 Prayer before the second lesson for Holy Saturday, as it was in the Roman Missal before the restoration of Holy Week.

14 Cf. Mark 16:15.

15 Cf. Acts 26:18.

16 Cf. Rom. 6:4; Eph. 2:6; Col. 3:1; 2 Tim. 2:11.

17 Cf. John 4:23.

18 Cf. 1 Cor. 11:26.

19 Council of Trent, Session XIII, Decree on the Holy Eucharist, c. 5.

20 Council of Trent, Session XXII, Doctrine on the Holy Sacrifice of the Mass, c. 2.

21 Cf. St. Augustine, *Tractatus in Ioannem,* VI, n. 7.

Rightly, then, the liturgy is considered as an exercise of the priestly office of Jesus Christ. In the liturgy the sanctification of man is signified by signs perceptible to the senses, and is effected in a way which corresponds with each of these signs; in the liturgy the whole public worship is performed by the mystical body of Jesus Christ, that is, by the head and his members.

From this it follows that every liturgical celebration, because it is an action of Christ, the priest, and of his body which is the Church, is a sacred action surpassing all others; no other action of the Church can equal its efficacy by the same title and to the same degree.

In the earthly liturgy we take part in a foretaste of that heavenly liturgy which is celebrated in the holy city of Jerusalem towards which we journey as pilgrims, where Christ is sitting at the right hand of God, a minister of the holies and of the true tabernacle; [22] we sing a hymn to the Lord's glory with all the warriors of the heavenly army; venerating the memory of the saints, we hope for some part and fellowship with them; we eagerly await the savior, our Lord Jesus Christ, until he, our life, shall appear and we too will appear with him in glory.[23]

The sacred liturgy does not exhaust the entire activity of the Church. Before men can come to the liturgy they must be called to faith and to conversion: "How then are they to call upon him in whom they have not yet believed? But how are they to believe him whom they have not heard? And how are they to hear if no one preaches? And how are men to preach unless they be sent?" (Rom. 10:14-15).

Therefore the Church announces the good tidings of salvation to those who do not believe, so that all men may know the true God and Jesus Christ whom he has sent, and may be converted from their ways, doing penance.[24] To believers also the Church must ever preach faith and penance; she must prepare them for the sacraments, teach them to observe all that Christ has commanded,[25] and invite them to all the works of charity, piety, and the apostolate. For all these works make it clear that Christ's faithful, though not of this world, are to be the light of the world and to glorify the Father before men.

Nevertheless the liturgy is the summit towards which the activity of the Church is directed; at the same time it is the fount from which all her power flows. For the aim and object of apostolic works is that all who are made sons of God by faith and baptism should come together to praise God in the midst of his Church, to take part in the sacrifice, and to eat the Lord's supper.

The liturgy in its turn moves the faithful, filled with "the paschal sacraments," to be "one in holiness";[26] it prays that "they may hold fast in their lives to what they have grasped by their faith";[27] the renewal in the eucharist of the covenant between the Lord and man draws the faithful into the compelling love of Christ and sets them on fire. From the liturgy, therefore, and especially from the eucharist, as from a fount, grace is poured forth upon us; and the sanctification of men in Christ and the glorification of God, to which all other activities of the Church are directed as towards their end, is achieved in the most efficacious possible way.

But in order that the liturgy may be

22 Cf. Apoc. 21:2; Col. 3:1; Heb. 8:2.
23 Cf. Phil. 3:20; Col. 3:4.

24 Cf. John 17:3; Luke 24:27; Acts 2:38.
25 Cf. Matthew 28:20.
26 Postcommunion for both Masses of Easter Sunday.
27 Collect of the Mass for Tuesday of Easter Week.

able to produce its full effects, it is necessary that the faithful come to it with proper dispositions, that their minds should be attuned to their voices, and that they should cooperate with divine grace lest they receive it in vain.[28] Pastors of souls must therefore realize that, when the liturgy is celebrated, something more is required than the mere observation of the laws governing valid and licit celebration; it is their duty also to ensure that the faithful take part fully aware of what they are doing, actively engaged in the rite, and enriched by its effects.

The spiritual life, however, is not limited solely to participation in the liturgy. The Christian is indeed called to pray with his brethren, but he must also enter into his chamber to pray to the Father in secret;[29] yet more, according to the teaching of the apostle, he should pray without ceasing.[30] We learn from the same apostle that we must always bear about in our body the dying of Jesus, so that the life also of Jesus may be made manifest in our bodily frame.[31] This is why we ask the Lord in the sacrifice of the Mass that, "receiving the offering of the spiritual victim," he may fashion us for himself "as an eternal gift."[32]

Popular devotions of the Christian people are to be highly commended, provided they accord with the laws and norms of the Church, above all when they are ordered by the Apostolic See.

Devotions proper to individual Churches also have a special dignity if they are undertaken by mandate of the bishops according to customs or books lawfully approved.

But these devotions should be so drawn up that they harmonize with the liturgical seasons, accord with the sacred liturgy, are in some fashion derived from it, and lead the people to it, since, in fact, the liturgy by its very nature far surpasses any of them.

B. THE PROMOTION OF LITURGICAL INSTRUCTION AND ACTIVE PARTICIPATION

Mother Church earnestly desires that all the faithful should be led to that full, conscious, and active participation in liturgical celebrations which is demanded by the very nature of the liturgy. Such participation by the Christian people as "a chosen race, a royal priesthood, a holy nation, a redeemed people" (1 Pet. 2:9; cf. 2:4-5), is their right and duty by reason of their baptism.

In the restoration and promotion of the sacred liturgy, this full and active participation by all the people is the aim to be considered before all else; for it is the primary and indispensable source from which the faithful are to derive the true Christian spirit; and therefore pastors of souls must zealously strive to achieve it, by means of the necessary instruction, in all their pastoral work.

Yet it would be futile to entertain any hopes of realizing this unless the pastors themselves, in the first place, become thoroughly imbued with the spirit and power of the liturgy, and undertake to give instruction about it. A prime need, therefore, is that attention be directed, first of all, to the liturgical instruction of the clergy. Wherefore the sacred Council has decided to enact as follows:

Professors who are appointed to teach liturgy in seminaries, religious houses of study, and theological faculties must be properly trained for their work in institutes which specialize in this subject.

The study of sacred liturgy is to be ranked among the compulsory and

28 Cf. 2 Cor. 6:1.
29 Cf. Matthew 6:6.
30 Cf. 1 Thess. 5:17.
31 Cf. 2 Cor. 4:10-11.
32 Secret for Monday of Pentecost Week.

major courses in seminaries and religious houses of studies; in theological faculties it is to rank among the principal courses. It is to be taught under its theological, historical, spiritual, pastoral, and juridical aspects. Moreover, other professors, while striving to expound the mystery of Christ and the history of salvation from the angle proper to each of their own subjects, must nevertheless do so in a way which will clearly bring out the connection between their subjects and the liturgy, as also the unity which underlies all priestly training. This consideration is especially important for professors of dogmatic, spiritual, and pastoral theology and for those of holy scripture.

In seminaries and houses of religious, clerics shall be given a liturgical formation in their spiritual life. For this they will need proper direction, so that they may be able to understand the sacred rites and take part in them whole-heartedly; and they will also need personally to celebrate the sacred mysteries, as well as popular devotions which are imbued with the spirit of the liturgy. In addition they must learn how to observe the liturgical laws, so that life in seminaries and houses of religious may be thoroughly influenced by the spirit of the liturgy.

Priests, both secular and religious, who are already working in the Lord's vineyard are to be helped by every suitable means to understand ever more fully what it is that they are doing when they perform sacred rites; they are to be aided to live the liturgical life and to share it with the faithful entrusted to their care.

With zeal and patience, pastors of souls must promote the liturgical instruction of the faithful, and also their active participation in the liturgy both internally and externally, taking into account their age and condition, their way of life, and standard of religious culture. By so doing, pastors will be fulfilling one of the chief duties of a faithful dispenser of the mysteries of God; and in this matter they must lead their flock not only in word but also by example.

Transmissions of the sacred rites by radio and television shall be done with discretion and dignity, under the leadership and direction of a suitable person appointed for this office by the bishops. This is especially important when the service to be broadcast is the Mass.

C. THE REFORM OF THE SACRED LITURGY

In order that the Christian people may more certainly derive an abundance of graces from the sacred liturgy, holy Mother Church desires to undertake with great care a general restoration of the liturgy itself. For the liturgy is made up of immutable elements divinely instituted, and of elements subject to change. These not only may but ought to be changed with the passage of time if they have suffered from the intrusion of anything out of harmony with the inner nature of the liturgy or have become unsuited to it.

In this restoration, both texts and rites should be drawn up so that they express more clearly the holy things which they signify; the Christian people, so far as possible, should be enabled to understand them with ease and to take part in them fully, actively, and as befits a community.

Wherefore the sacred Council establishes the following general norms:

1. *General Norms*

Regulation of the sacred liturgy depends solely on the authority of the Church, that is, on the Apostolic See and, as laws may determine, on the bishop.

In virtue of power conceded by the law, the regulation of the liturgy within certain defined limits belongs also to various kinds of competent territorial bodies of bishops legitimately established.

Therefore no other person, even if he be a priest, may add, remove, or change anything in the liturgy on his own authority.

That sound tradition may be retained, and yet the way remain open to legitimate progress, a careful investigation is always to be made into each part of the liturgy which is to be revised. This investigation should be theological, historical, and pastoral. Also the general laws governing the structure and meaning of the liturgy must be studied in conjunction with the experience derived from recent liturgical reforms and from the indults conceded to various places. Finally, there must be no innovations unless the good of the Church genuinely and certainly requires them; and care must be taken that any new forms adopted should in some way grow organically from forms already existing.

As far as possible, notable differences between the rites used in adjacent regions must be carefully avoided.

Sacred scripture is of the greatest importance in the celebration of the liturgy. For it is from scripture that lessons are read and explained in the homily, and psalms are sung; the prayers, collects, and liturgical songs are scriptural in their inspiration, and it is from the scriptures that actions and signs derive their meaning. Thus to achieve the restoration, progress, and adaptation of the sacred liturgy, it is essential to promote that warm and living love for scripture to which the venerable tradition of both eastern and western rites gives testimony.

The liturgical books are to be revised as soon as possible; experts are to be employed on the task, and bishops are to be consulted, from various parts of the world.

2. *Norms Drawn from the Hierarchic and Communal Nature of the Liturgy*

Liturgical services are not private functions, but are celebrations of the Church, which is the "sacrament of unity," namely, the holy people united and ordered under their bishops.[33]

Therefore liturgical services pertain to the whole body of the Church; they manifest it and have effects upon it; but they concern the individual members of the Church in different ways, according to their differing rank, office, and actual participation.

It is to be stressed that whenever rites, according to their specific nature, make provision for communal celebration involving the presence and active participation of the faithful, this way of celebrating them is to be preferred, so far as possible, to a celebration that is individual and quasi-private.

This applies with especial force to the celebration of Mass and the administration of the sacraments, even though every Mass has of itself a public and social nature.

In liturgical celebrations each person, minister or layman, who has an office to perform, should do all of, but only, those parts which pertain to his office by the nature of the rite and the principles of liturgy.

Servers, lectors, commentators, and members of the choir also exercise a genuine liturgical function. They ought, therefore, to discharge their office with the sincere piety and decorum demanded by so exalted a ministry and rightly expected of them by God's people.

Consequently they must all be deeply imbued with the spirit of the liturgy, each in his own measure, and they must be trained to perform their functions in a correct and orderly manner.

To promote active participation, the

[33] St. Cyprian, *On the Unity of the Catholic Church,* 7; cf. Letter 66, n. 8, 3.

people should be encouraged to take part by means of acclamations, responses, psalmody, antiphons, and songs, as well as by actions, gestures, and bodily attitudes. And at the proper times all should observe a reverent silence.

The revision of the liturgical books must carefully attend to the provision of rubrics also for the people's parts.

The liturgy makes distinctions between persons according to their liturgical function and sacred orders, and there are liturgical laws providing for due honors to be given to civil authorities. Apart from these instances, no special honors are to be paid in the liturgy to any private persons or classes of persons, whether in the ceremonies or by external display.

3. *Norms Based upon the Didactic and Pastoral Nature of the Liturgy*

Although the sacred liturgy is above all things the worship of the divine majesty, it likewise contains much instruction for the faithful.[34] For in the liturgy God speaks to his people and Christ is still proclaiming his gospel. And the people reply to God both by song and prayer.

Moreover, the prayers addressed to God by the priest who presides over the assembly in the person of Christ are said in the name of the entire holy people and of all present. And the visible signs used by the liturgy to signify invisible divine things have been chosen by Christ or the Church. Thus not only when things are read "which were written for our instruction" (Rom. 15:4), but also when the Church prays or sings or acts, the faith of those taking part is nourished and their minds are raised to God, so that they may offer him their rational service and more abundantly receive his grace.

[34] Cf. Council of Trent, Session XXII, Doctrine on the Holy Sacrifice of the Mass, c. 8.

Wherefore, in the revision of the liturgy, the following general norms should be observed:

The rites should be distinguished by a noble simplicity; they should be short, clear, and unencumbered by useless repetitions; they should be within the people's powers of comprehension, and normally should not require much explanation.

That the intimate connection between words and rites may be apparent in the liturgy:

1) In sacred celebrations there is to be more reading from holy scripture, and it is to be more varied and suitable.

2) Because the sermon is part of the liturgical service, the best place for it is to be indicated even in the rubrics, as far as the nature of the rite will allow; the ministry of preaching is to be fulfilled with exactitude and fidelity. The sermon, moreover, should draw its content mainly from scriptural and liturgical sources, and its character should be that of a proclamation of God's wonderful works in the history of salvation, the mystery of Christ, ever made present and active within us, especially in the celebration of the liturgy.

3) Instruction which is more explicitly liturgical should also be given in a variety of ways; if necessary, short directives to be spoken by the priest or proper minister should be provided within the rites themselves. But they should occur only at the more suitable moments, and be in prescribed or similar words.

4) Bible services should be encouraged, especially on the vigils of the more solemn feasts, on some weekdays in Advent and Lent, and on Sundays and feast days. They are particularly to be commended in places where no priest is available; when this is so, a deacon or some other person authorized by the bishop should preside over the celebration.

Particular law remaining in force, the use of the Latin language is to be preserved in the Latin rites.

But since the use of the mother tongue, whether in the Mass, the administration of the sacraments, or other parts of the liturgy, frequently may be of great advantage to the people, the limits of its employment may be extended. This will apply in the first place to the readings and directives, and to some of the prayers and chants, according to the regulations on this matter to be laid down separately in subsequent chapters.

These norms being observed, it is for the competent territorial ecclesiastical authority mentioned in art. 22:2 to decide whether, and to what extent, the vernacular language is to be used; their decrees are to be approved, that is, confirmed, by the Apostolic See. And, whenever it seems to be called for, this authority is to consult with bishops of neighboring regions which have the same language.

Translations from the Latin text into the mother tongue intended for use in the liturgy must be approved by the competent territorial ecclesiastical authority mentioned above.

4. *Norms for Adapting the Liturgy to the Culture and Traditions of Peoples*

Even in the liturgy, the Church has no wish to impose a rigid uniformity in matters which do not implicate the faith or the good of the whole community; rather does she respect and foster the genius and talents of the various races and peoples. Anything in these peoples' way of life which is not indissolubly bound up with superstition and error she studies with sympathy and, if possible, preserves intact. Sometimes in fact she admits such things into the liturgy itself, so long as they harmonize with its true and authentic spirit.

Provisions shall also be made, when revising the liturgical books, for legitimate variations and adaptations to different groups, regions, and peoples, especially in mission lands, provided that the substantial unity of the Roman rite is preserved; and this should be borne in mind when drawing up the rites and devising rubrics.

Within the limits set by the typical editions of the liturgical books, it shall be for the competent territorial ecclesiastical authority mentioned in art. 22:2, to specify adaptations, especially in the case of the administration of the sacraments, the sacramentals, processions, liturgical language, sacred music, and the arts, but according to the fundamental norms laid down in this Constitution.

In some places and circumstances, however, an even more radical adaptation of the liturgy is needed, and this entails greater difficulties.

Wherefore:

1) The competent territorial ecclesiastical authority mentioned in art. 22:2 must, in this matter, carefully and prudently consider which elements from the traditions and culture of individual peoples might appropriately be admitted into divine worship. Adaptations which are judged to be useful or necessary should then be submitted to the Apostolic See, by whose consent they may be introduced.

2) To ensure that adaptations may be made with all the circumspection which they demand, the Apostolic See will grant power to this same territorial ecclesiastical authority to permit and to direct, as the case requires, the necessary preliminary experiments over a determined period of time among certain groups suited for the purpose.

3) Because liturgical laws often involve special difficulties with respect to adaptation, particularly in mission lands, men who are experts in these

matters must be employed to formulate them.

D. PROMOTION OF LITURGICAL LIFE IN DIOCESE AND PARISH

The bishop is to be considered as the high priest of his flock, from whom the life in Christ of his faithful is in some way derived and dependent.

Therefore all should hold in great esteem the liturgical life of the diocese centered around the bishop, especially in his cathedral church; they must be convinced that the pre-eminent manifestation of the Church consists in the full active participation of all God's holy people in these liturgical celebrations, especially in the same eucharist, in a single prayer, at one altar, at which there presides the bishop surrounded by his college of priests and by his ministers.[35]

But because it is impossible for the bishop always and everywhere to preside over the whole flock in his Church, he cannot do other than establish lesser groupings of the faithful. Among these the parishes, set up locally under a pastor who takes the place of the bishop, are the most important; for in some manner they represent the visible Church constituted throughout the world.

And therefore the liturgical life of the parish and its relationship to the bishop must be fostered theoretically and practically among the faithful and clergy; efforts also must be made to encourage a sense of community within the parish, above all in the common celebration of the Sunday Mass.

E. THE PROMOTION OF PASTORAL-LITURGICAL ACTION

Zeal for the promotion and restora-

[35] Cf. St. Ignatius of Antioch, *To the Smyrnians,* 8; *To the Magnesians,* 7; *To the Philadelphians,* 4.

tion of the liturgy is rightly held to be a sign of the providential dispositions of God in our time, as a movement of the Holy Spirit in his Church. It is today a distinguishing mark of the Church's life, indeed of the whole tenor of contemporary religious thought and action.

So that this pastoral-liturgical action may become even more vigorous in the Church, the sacred Council decrees:

It is desirable that the competent territorial ecclesiastical authority mentioned in art. 22:2, set up a liturgical commission, to be assisted by experts in liturgical science, sacred music, art, and pastoral practice. So far as possible the commission should be aided by some kind of institute for pastoral liturgy, consisting of persons who are eminent in these matters, and including laymen as circumstances suggest. Under the direction of the above-mentioned territorial ecclesiastical authority the commission is to regulate pastoral-liturgical action throughout the territory, and to promote studies and necessary experiments whenever there is question of adaptations to be proposed to the Apostolic See.

For the same reason every diocese is to have a commission on the sacred liturgy under the direction of the bishop, for promoting the liturgical apostolate.

Sometimes it may be expedient that several dioceses should form between them one single commission which will be able to promote the liturgy by common consultation.

Besides the commission on the sacred liturgy, every diocese, as far as possible, should have commissions for sacred music and sacred art.

These three commissions must work in closest collaboration; indeed it will often be best to fuse the three of them into one single commission. . . .

B. CONSTITUTION ON THE CHURCH, 21 NOVEMBER 1964

From *De Ecclesia:* The Constitution on the Church of Vatican Council II (New York: Paulist Press, 1965).

1) Christ is the Light of nations. Because this is so, this Sacred Council gathered together in the Holy Spirit eagerly desires, by proclaiming the Gospel to every creature (cf. Mk. 16, 15), to bring the light of Christ to all men, a light brightly visible on the countenance of the Church. Since the Church is in Christ like a sacrament or a sign and instrument of a very closely knit union with God and of the unity of the whole human race, it desires now to unfold more fully to the faithful of the Church and to the whole world its own inner nature and universal mission. This it intends to do following faithfully the teaching of previous councils. The present-day conditions of the world add greater urgency to this work of the Church so that all men, joined more closely today by various social, technical and cultural ties, might also attain full unity in Christ.

1. *The Mystery of the Church*

2) The Eternal Father, by a free and hidden plan of His own wisdom and goodness, created the whole world. His plan was to raise men to a participation of the divine life. God the Father did not leave to themselves the men fallen in Adam, but ceaselessly offered helps to salvation, for the sake of Christ, the Redeemer "who is the image of the invisible God, the first-born of every creature" (Col. 1, 15). All the elect, before time began, the Father "foreknew and predestined to become conformed to the image of His Son, that he should be the first-born among many brethren" (Rom. 8, 29). He planned to assemble in the holy Church all those who would believe in Christ. Already from the beginning of the world the foreshadowing of the Church took place. It was prepared in a remarkable way throughout the history of the people of Israel and by

means of the Old Covenant. In the present era of time the Church was constituted and, by the outpouring of the Spirit, was made manifest. At the end of time it will gloriously achieve completion, when, as is read in the Fathers, all the just, from Adam and "from Abel, the just one, to the last of the elect," will be gathered together with the Father in the universal Church.

3) The Son, therefore, came, sent by the Father. It was in Him, before the foundation of the world, that the Father chose us and predestined us to become adopted sons, for in Him it pleased the Father to reestablish all things (cf. Eph. 1, 4-5 and 10). To carry out the will of the Father Christ inaugurated the Kingdom of heaven on earth and revealed to us the mystery of that kingdom. By His obedience He brought about redemption. The Church, or, in other words, the kingdom of Christ now present in mystery, grows visibly through the power of God in the world. This inauguration and this growth are both symbolized by the Blood and Water which flowed from the open side of the crucified Jesus (cf. Jn. 19, 34), and are foretold in the words of the Lord referring to His death on the Cross: "And I, if I be lifted up from the earth, will draw all things to myself" (Jn. 12, 32). As often as the sacrifice of the cross in which Christ our Passover was sacrificed (I Cor. 5, 7) is celebrated on an altar, the work of our redemption is carried on, and, in the sacrament of the eucharistic bread, the unity of all believers who form one body in Christ (cf. I Cor. 10, 17) is both expressed and brought about. All men are called to this union with Christ, who is the light of the world, from whom we go forth, through whom we live, and to-

ward whom our whole life strains.

4) When the work that the Father gave the Son to do on earth (cf. Jn. 17, 4) was accomplished, the Holy Spirit was sent on the day of Pentecost in order that He might continually sanctify the Church, and thus, all those who believe would have access through Christ in one Spirit to the Father (cf. Eph. 2, 18). He is the Spirit of Life, a fountain of water springing up to life eternal (cf. Jn. 4, 14; 7, 38-39). To men, dead in sin, the Father gives life through Him until, in Christ, He brings to life their mortal bodies (cf. Rom. 8, 10-11). The Spirit dwells in the Church and in the hearts of the faithful, as in a temple (cf. I Cor. 3, 16; 6, 19). In them He prays on their behalf and bears witness to the fact that they are adopted sons (cf. Gal. 4, 6; Rom. 8, 15-16 and 26). The Church, which the Spirit guides in the way of all truth and which He unifies in communion and in works of ministry, He both equips and directs with hierarchical and charismatic gifts and adorns with His fruits (cf. Eph. 4, 11-12; I Cor. 12, 4; Gal. 5, 22). By the power of the Gospel He makes the Church keep the freshness of youth. Uninterruptedly He renews it and leads it to perfect union with its Spouse. The Spirit and the Bride both say to Jesus, the Lord, "Come!" (cf. Apoc. 22, 17).

Thus the Church is seen to be "a people made one with the unity of the Father, the Son and the Holy Spirit."

5) The mystery of the holy Church to manifest is its very foundation for the Lord Jesus set it on its course by preaching the Good News, that is, the coming of the Kingdom of God, which, for centuries, had been promised in the Scriptures: "The time is fulfilled, and the kingdom of God is at hand" (Mk. 1, 15; cf. Mt. 4, 17). This kingdom was clearly open to the view of men in the Word, in the work, and in the presence of Christ. The *Word* of the Lord may be compared to a seed which is sown in a field (Mk. 4, 14); those who hear the Word with faith and become part of the little flock of Christ (Lk. 12, 32), have received the Kingdom itself. Then, by its own power the seed sprouts and grows until harvest time (cf. Mk. 4, 26-29). The *Miracles* of Jesus also confirm that the Kingdom has already arrived on earth: "If I cast out devils by the finger of God, then the kingdom of God has come upon you" (Lk. 11, 20; cf. Mt. 12, 28). Before all things, however, the Kingdom is clearly visible in the very *Person* of Christ, of the Son of God and of the Son of Man, who came "to serve and to give His life as a ransom for many" (Mk. 10, 45).

When Jesus, who had undergone the death of the cross, had risen, He appeared as the one constituted as Lord, Christ and eternal Priest (cf. Act. 2, 36; Hebr. 5, 6: 7, 17-21), and He poured out on His disciples the Spirit promised by the Father (cf. Act. 2, 33). Hence the Church, equipped with the gifts of its Founder and faithfully guarding His precepts of charity, humility and self-sacrifice, receives the mission to proclaim and to establish among all peoples the Kingdom of Christ and of God and makes up the germ and beginning of that kingdom. While is slowly grows, the Church strains toward the completed Kingdom and, with all its strength, hopes and desires to be united in glory with its King.

6) In the old Testament the revelation of the Kingdom is often conveyed by means of metaphors. In the same way the inner nature of the Church is now made known to us in different images. Taken either from pastoral life or agriculture, sheep or cultivating the land, from building or even from family life and from husband and wife, the images receive preparatory shaping in the books of the Prophets.

The Church is a *Sheepfold*

whose one and necessary door is Christ (Jn. 10, 1-10). It is a flock of which God Himself foretold He would be the shepherd (cf. Is. 40, 11; Ex. 34, 11f), and whose sheep, although tended by human shepherds, are nevertheless ceaselessly led and nourished by Christ Himself, the Good Shepherd and the Prince of the shepherds, (cf. Jn. 10, 11; I Pet. 5, 4), who gave His life for the sheep (cf. Jn. 10, 11-16).

The Church the *Tillage or field* of God (I Cor. 3,9). On that land grows the ancient olive tree whose holy roots were the patriarchs and in which the reconciliation of Jews and Gentiles has been brought about and will be brought about (Rom. 11, 13-26). That land, like a choice vineyard, has been planted by the heavenly Cultivator (Mt. 21, 33-43; cf. Is. 5, 1f). The true vine is Christ, who gives life and the power to bear abundant fruit to the branches, that is, to us, who through the Church remains in Christ without whom we can do nothing (Jn. 15, 1-5).

Often the Church has also been called the *Building* of God (I Cor. 3, 9). The Lord Himself compared Himself to the stone which the builders rejected, but which was made into the cornerstone (Mt. 21, 42; cf. Act. 4, 11; I Pet. 2, 7; Ps. 117, 22). On this foundation the Church is built by the apostles (cf. I Cor. 3, 11), and from it the Church receives solidity and cohesion. This edifice has many names to describe it: the house of God in which dwells His *Family;* the dwelling of God in the Spirit (Eph. 2, 19, 22); the tabernacle of God among men (Apoc. 21, 3); and, especially, the holy *Temple.* This Temple, symbolized in sanctuaries of stone, is praised by the Holy Fathers and, not without reason, is compared in the liturgy to the Holy City, the New Jerusalem. As living stones we here on earth are built into it (I Pet. 2, 5). John sees this holy city

arrayed like a bride adorned for her husband, and coming down out of heaven from God when the world is made anew (Apoc. 21, 1f.).

The Church, further, "that Jerusalem which is above" is also called "our mother" (Gal. 4, 26; cf. Apoc. 12, 17). It is described as the spotless *Spouse* of the spotless Lamb (Apoc. 19, 7; 21, 2 and 9; 22, 17), whom Christ "loved and for whom He delivered Himself up that He might sanctify her" (Eph. 5, 26), whom He unites to Himself by an unbreakable covenant, and whom He unceasingly "nourishes and cherishes" (Eph. 5, 29), and whom, once purified, He willed to be cleansed and joined to Himself, subject to Him in love and fidelity. Finally He filled her with heavenly gifts for all eternity, in order that we may grasp the love of God and of Christ for us, a love which surpasses all knowledge (cf. Eph. 3, 19). While she is on pilgrimage here on earth the Church regards herself as an exile from the Lord so that she seeks and savors those things which are above, where Christ is seated at the right-hand of God, where the life of the Church is hidden with Christ in God until she appears in glory with her spouse (cf. Col. 3, 1, 4).

7) In the human nature united to Himself, the Son of God, by overcoming death through His own death and resurrection, redeemed man and transformed him into a new creation (cf. Gal. 6, 15; II Cor. 5, 17). By communicating His Spirit, Christ's brothers, called together from all nations, were mystically constituted as His Body.

In that Body the life of Christ is poured into the believers who, through the sacraments, are united in a hidden and real way to Christ who suffered and was glorified. Through Baptism we are formed in the likeness of Christ: "For in one Spirit we were all baptized into one body" (I Cor. 12, 13).

In this sacred rite a fellowship with Christ's death and resurrection is both symbolized and brought about: "For we were buried with Him by means of Baptism into death"; and if "we have been united with Him in the likeness of His death, we shall be so in the likeness of His resurrection also" (Rom. 6, 4-5). Really partaking of the body of the Lord in the breaking of the eucharistic bread, we are taken up into communion with Him and with one another. "Because the bread is one, we though many, are one body, all of us who partake of the one bread" (I Cor. 10-17). In this way all of us are made members of His Body (cf. I Cor. 12, 27), "but severally members one of another" (Rom. 12, 4).

As all the members of the human body, though they are many, form one body, so also are the faithful in Christ (cf. I Cor. 12, 12). So in the building up of Christ's Body a diversity of members and functions obtains. There is only one Spirit who, according to His own richness and the needs of the ministries, gives His different gifts for the welfare of the Church (cf. I Cor. 12, 1-11). Among these gifts the grace of the apostles is preeminent to their authority the Spirit Himself subjected even those who were endowed with charisms (cf. I Cor. 14). Giving the body unity through Himself and through His power and inner joining of the members, this same Spirit produces and urges love among the believers. From all this it follows that if one member endures anything, all the members suffer with it, and if one member is honored, all the members rejoice together with it. (cf. I Cor. 12, 26).

The Head of this Body is Christ. He is the image of the invisible God and in Him all things are grounded. He is before all creatures and in Him all things hold together. He is the head of the Body which is the Church. He is the beginning, the first born from the dead, that in all things He might have the first place (cf. Col. I, 15-18). By the greatness of His power He rules the things in heaven and the things on earth, and with His all-surpassing perfection and action He fills the whole body with the riches of His glory (cf. Eph. 1, 18-23).

All the members ought to be modelled on Him, until Christ be formed in them (cf. Gal. 4, 19). For this reason we, who have been made to conform with Him, who have died with Him and risen with Him, are taken up into the mysteries of His life, until we will reign together with Him (cf. Phil. 3, 21; II Tim. 2, 11; Eph. 2, 6: Col. 2, 12 etc.) While still pilgrims on earth, tracing in trial and in oppression the paths He trod, we are associated with His sufferings like the body is one with the Head, suffering with Him, that with Him we may be glorified (cf. Rom. 8, 17).

From Him "the whole body, supplied and built up by joints and ligaments, attains a growth that is of God" (Col. 2, 19). He continually distributes in His body, that is, in the Church, gifts of ministries in which, by His own power, we serve each other unto salvation so that, carrying out the truth in love, we might through all things grow unto Him who is our Head (cf. Eph. 4, 11-16. Gk.).

In order that we might be unceasingly renewed in Him (cf. Eph. 4, 23), He has shared with us His Spirit who, being one and the same in the Head and in the members, gives life to, unifies and moves the whole body in such a way that His work could be compared by the holy Fathers with the function that the principle of life, that is, the soul, fulfills in the human body.

Christ loves the Church as His bride; He is made the model of a man loving his wife as his own body; the Church, indeed, is subject to its Head (Eph. 23-24). "Because in Him dwells all the fulness of the Godhead bodily" (Col. 2, 9), He fills the Church, which is His body and the fulness, with His divine gifts cf. 1, 22-23) so that is may grow and attain to all the fulness of God (cf. Eph. 3, 19).

8) Christ, the one Mediator, established and ceaselessly sustains here on earth His holy Church, the community of faith, hope and charity, as a visible body through which He communicates truth and grace to all. But the society structured with hierarchical organs and the Mystical Body of Christ, are not to be considered as two realities, nor are the visible assembly and the spiritual community, nor the earthly Church and the Church enriched with heavenly things; rather they form one complex reality which combines a divine and a human element. For this reason, by no ordinary analogy, it is compared to the mystery of the incarnate Word. As the assumed nature inseparably united to the divine Word serves Him as a living organ of salvation, so, in a similar way, does the visible social structure of the Church serve the Spirit of Christ, who vivifies it, in the building up of the body (cf. Eph. 4, 15).

This is the one Church of Christ which in the Creed we profess as one, holy, catholic and apostolic, which our Savior after His Resurrection, gave to Peter to shepherd (Jn. 21, 17), and committed him and the other apostles to extend and direct with authority (cf. Mt. 28, 18, etc.), which He erected for all ages as "the pillar and mainstay of the truth" (I Tim. 3, 15). This Church, constituted and organized in the world as a society, subsists in the Catholic Church, which is governed by the successor of Peter and by the bishops in his communion, although many elements of sanctification and of truth may be found outside of its

visible structure, which, as gifts belonging to the Church of Christ, are forces impelling toward catholic unity.

Just as Christ carried out the work of redemption in poverty and oppression, so the Church is called to follow the same road that it might communicate the fruits of salvation to men. Christ Jesus, "though He was by nature God . . . emptied Himself, taking the nature of a slave" (Phil. 2, 6, 7), and "being rich, became poor" (II Cor. 8, 9) for our sakes. Thus, the Church, although it needs human resources to carry out its mission, is not set up to seek earthly glory, but to proclaim, even by its own example, humility and self-sacrifice. Christ was sent by the Father "to bring good news to the poor, to heal the contrite of heart" (Lk. 4, 18), "to seek and to save what was lost" (Lk. 19, 10). Similarly, the Church encompasses with love all those afflicted by human infirmity and recognizes in those who are poor and who suffer the image of its poor and suffering Founder. It does all it can to relieve their need and in them it strives to serve Christ. While Christ, holy, innocent and undefiled (Hebr. 7, 26) knew no sin (II Cor. 5, 21), but came to expiate only the sins of the people (cf. Hebr. 2, 17), the Church, embracing sinners in her bosom, at the same time holy and always in need of being purified, follows the endless way of penance and renewal. The Church, "like a pilgrim presses forward amid the persecutions of the world and the consolations of God" (14), announcing the cross and death of the Lord until He comes (cf. I Cor. 11, 26). By the power of the risen Lord it is given strength that it might, in patience and in love, overcome its sorrows and its challenges, both within itself and from without, and that it might reveal to the world, even though dimly, yet faithfully, the mystery of its Lord until finally, it will be manifested in full light.

2. *On the People of God*

9) At all times and in every nation God has given welcome to whomever fears Him and does what is right (cf. Acts 10, 35). It has pleased God, however, not to make men holy and save them merely as individuals, without mutual bond; rather has it pleased Him to make of them a people that acknowledges Him in truth and serves Him in holiness. He therefore chose the people of Israel as this people. With it He set up a covenant. Step by step He taught this people, making known in its history both Himself and the decree of His will and making it holy unto Himself. All these things, however, were done by way of preparation and as a figure of that new and perfect covenant, which was to be ratified in Christ, and of that fuller revelation which was to be given through the Word of God Himself made flesh. "Behold the days shall come, saith the Lord, and I will make a new covenant with the House of Israel, and with the House of Judah . . . I will give my law in their bowels, and I will write it in their heart, and I will be their God, and they shall be my people . . . For all of them shall know Me, from the least of them even to the greatest, saith the Lord" (Jer. 31, 34). Christ instituted this new covenant, the new testament, that is to say, in His Blood (cf. I Cor. XI, 25), calling together a people made up of Jew and Gentile, making them one, not according to the flesh but in the Spirit. This was to be the new people of God. For those who believe in Christ, who are reborn not from a perishable seed but from an imperishable, through the Word of the living God (cf. I Pet. 1, 23), not from the flesh but from water and the Holy Spirit (cf. Jn. 3, 5-6), and finally established as "a chosen race, a royal priesthood, a holy nation, a purchased people . . .

you who in times past were not a people, but are now the people of God" (I Pet. 2, 9-10).

That messianic people has Christ for its head, "Who was delivered up for our sins, and rose again for our justification" (Rom. 4, 25), and now, having won a name which is above all names, reigns in glory in heaven. The state of this people is that of the dignity and freedom of the sons of God, in whose hearts the Holy Spirit dwells as in His temple. Its law is the new commandment to love as Christ loved us. Its end is the kingdom of God, which has been begun by God Himself on earth, and which is to be further extended until it is brought to perfection by Him at the end of time, when Christ, our life (cf. Col. 3, 4), shall appear, and "creation itself will be delivered from its slavery to corruption into the freedom of the glory of the sons of God" (Rom. 8, 21). So it is that that messianic people, although it does not actually include all men, and at times may look like a small flock, is nonetheless a most certain seed of unity, hope and salvation for the whole human race. Established by Christ as a communion of life, charity and truth, it is also used by Him as an instrument for the redemption of all, and is sent forth into the whole world as the light of the world and the salt of the earth (cf. Mt. 5, 13-16).

Israel according to the flesh, which wandered as an exile in the desert, was already called the Church of God (cf. Num. 20, 4; Deut. 23, 1 sq). So the new Israel which, while living in this present age seeks of a future and abiding city (cf. Heb. 13, 14) is called the Church of Christ. For He has bought it for Himself with His blood (cf. Acts 20, 28), has filled it with His Spirit and provided it with those means which befit it as a visible and social union. God gathered together as one all those who in faith look upon Jesus as the author of salvation and the source of unity and peace, and established them as the Church, that for each and all it may be the visible sacrament of this saving unity. While it transcends all limits of time and national boundaries, the Church is destined to extend to all regions of the earth and so enters into the history of mankind. Moving forward through trial and tribulation, the Church is strengthened by the power of God's grace, which was promised to her by the Lord, so that in the weakness of the flesh she may not waver from perfect fidelity, but remain a bride worthy of her Lord, and moved by the Holy Spirit may never cease to renew herself, until through the Cross she arrives at the light that knows no setting.

10) Christ the Lord, the High Priest taken from among men (Heb. 5, 1-5), made the new people "a kingdom and priests to God the Father" (Apoc. 1, 6; 5, 9-10). The baptized, by the regeneration and the anointing of the Holy Spirit, are consecrated as a spiritual house and a holy priesthood, in order that through all the works of a Christian man they may offer spiritual sacrifices and proclaim the power of Him who has called them out of darkness into His marvelous light (cf. I Pet. 2, 4-10). Therefore, let all the disciples of Christ persevering in prayer and praising God (cf. Acts 2, 42, 47), present themselves as a living sacrifice, holy and pleasing to God (cf. Rom. 12, 1). Everywhere on earth let them bear witness to Christ and give an answer to those who seek an account of that hope of eternal life that is in them (cf. I Pet. 3, 15).

Though they differ from one another in essence and not only in degree, the common priesthood of the faithful and the ministerial or hierarchial priesthood are nonetheless interrelated: each of them in its own special way is a participation in the one priesthood of Christ. The ministerial priest, by the sacred power he enjoys, teaches and rules the priestly peoples; acting in the person of Christ, he performs the eucharistic sacrifice, and offers it to God in the name of all the people. But the faithful, in virtue of their royal priesthood, join in the offering of the Eucharist. They likewise exercise that priesthood in receiving the sacraments, in prayer and thanksgiving, in the witness of a holy life, and by self-denial and active charity.

11) It is through the sacraments and the exercise of the virtues that the sacred nature and organic structure of the priestly community is brought into actuality. Incorporated in the Church through baptism, the faithful are consecrated by the baptismal character to the worship of the Christian religion; reborn as sons of God they must confess before men the faith they have received from God through the Church. They are more perfectly bound to the Church by the sacrament of Confirmation; the Holy Spirit endows them with special strength so that they are more strictly obliged to spread and defend the faith, both by word and by deed, as true witnesses of Christ. Taking part in the eucharistic sacrifice, which is the source and crown of the whole Christian life, they offer the Divine Victim to God, and offer themselves along with It: Thus both by reason of the offering and through Holy Communion all act their proper part in this liturgical service, not indiscriminately but each in that way which is proper to himself. Strengthened at the holy table by the Body of Christ, they then manifest in a concrete way that unity of the people of God which is suitably symbolized and wondrously brought about by this most holy sacrament.

Those who approach the sacrament of Penance obtain pardon from the mercy of God for the offense committed against Him and are at the same time reconciled with the Church, which they have wounded by their sins, and which by charity, example, and prayer labors for their conversion. By the sacred anointing of the sick and the prayer of her priests the whole Church commends the sick to the suffering and glorified Lord, asking that He may lighten their suffering and save them (cf. Jas. 5, 15-16); she exhorts them, moreover, to contribute to the welfare of the whole people of God by associating themselves freely with the passion and death of Christ (cf. Rom. 8, 17; Col. 1, 24; II Tim. 2, 11-12; I Pet. 4, 13). Those of the faithful who are consecrated by Holy Orders are appointed in Christ's name to feed the Church with the Word and the grace of God. Finally, Christian spouses, in virtue of the sacrament of matrimony, whereby they symbolize and partake of of the mystery of that unity and fruitful love which exists between Christ and his Church (cf. Eph. 5, 32), help each other to attain to holiness in their conjugal life and in the rearing and education of their children. By reason of their state and rank in life they have their own special gift among the people of God (cf. I Cor. 7, 7). From the wedlock of Christians there comes the family, in which new citizens of human society are born, who in baptism are made children of God, by the grace of the Holy Spirit perpetuating the people of God through the centuries. The family is, so to speak, the domestic Church. In it parents should, by their word and example, be the first preachers of the faith to their children; they should encourage them in the vocation that is proper to each of them, fostering with special care the vocation to a sacred state.

Fortified by so many and such powerful means of salvation, all the faithful, whatever their condition or state, are called by the Lord, each in his own way, to that holy perfection whereby the Father Himself is perfect.

12) The holy people of God shares also in Christ's prophetic office; it spreads abroad a living witness to Him, especially by means of a life of faith and charity and by offering to God a sacrifice of praise, the tribute of lips which give praise to His name (cf. Heb. 13, 15). The entire body of the faithful, anointed as they are by the Holy One (cf. I Jn. 2, 20, 27), cannot err in matters of belief. They manifest this special property by means of the whole people's supernatural discernment in matters of faith when "from the bishops down to the last of the lay faithful" they show universal agreement in matters of faith and morals. That discernment in matters of faith is aroused and sustained by the Spirit of truth. It is exercised under the guidance of the sacred teaching authority, in faithful and respectful obedience to which the people of God accepts what is not just the word of men but truly the Word of God (cf. I Thess. 2, 13). Through it, the people of God adheres unwaveringly to the faith given once and for all to the saints (cf. Jud. 2), penetrates it more deeply with right thinking, and applies it more fully in its life.

It is not only through the sacraments and the ministries of the Church that the Holy Spirit sanctifies and leads the people of God and enriches it with virtues, but, "allotting his gifts to everyone according as He wills" (I Cor. 13, 11), He distributes special graces among the faithful of every rank. By these gifts He makes them fit and ready to undertake the various tasks and duties which contribute toward the renewal and building up of the Church, according to the words of the Apostle:

"The manifestation of the Spirit is given to everyone for profit" (I Cor. 12, 7). These charisms, whether they be the more outstanding or the more simple and widely diffused, are to be received with thanksgiving and consolation for they are especially suited to and useful for the needs of the Church. Extraordinary gifts are not to be rashly sought after, nor are the fruits of apostolic labor to be presumptuously expected from their use; but judgment as to their genuineness and proper use belongs to those who are appointed leaders in the Church, and to whose special competence it belongs, not indeed to extinguish the Spirit, but to test all things and hold fast to that which is good (cf. I Thess. 5, 12; 19, 21).

13) All men are called to belong to the new people of God. Wherefore this people, while remaining one and only one, is to be spread throughout the whole world and must exist in all ages, so that the decree of God's will may be fulfilled. In the beginning God made human nature one and decreed that all His children, scattered as they were, would finally be gathered together as one (cf. Jn. 11, 52). It was for this purpose that God sent His Son, whom He appointed heir of all things (cf. Heb. 1, 2), that He might be teacher, king and priest of all, the head of the new and universal people of the sons of God. For this, too, God sent the Spirit of his Son as Lord and Lifegiver. He it is who for the whole Church and each and every believer is the wellspring of their assembly unity in the teaching of the apostles and in fellowship, in the breaking of bread and in prayers (cf. Acts 2, 42).

So among all the nations there is but one people of God, which takes its citizens from every nation, making them citizens of a kingdom that is of a heavenly rather than of an earthly nature. All the faithful, scattered though they be throughout the world, are in communion with each other in the Holy Spirit, so that "he who occupies the see of Rome knows those afar as his members." Since the kingdom of Christ is not of this world (cf. Jo. 18, 36) the Church or people of God in establishing that kingdom takes nothing away from the temporal welfare of any people. Rather does it foster and adopt, insofar as they are good, the ability, riches and customs of each people. Taking them to itself it purifies, strengthens, elevates and consecrates them. In this the Church is mindful that she must work with and for that King to whom the nations were given for an inheritance (Ps. 71, 10; Is. 9, 4-7; Apoc. 21, 24). This characteristic of universality that adorns the people of God is a gift from the Lord himself. By reason of it, the Catholic Church strives constantly and with due effect to gather all humanity and all its possessions under Christ, its head in the unity of His Spirit.

In virtue of this catholicity each individual part contributes through its special gifts to the good of the other parts and of the whole Church. Through the common sharing of gifts and through the common effort to attain fulness in unity, the whole and each of the parts receive increase. Not only, then, is the people of God made up of different peoples, but in its inner structure also it is composed of various ranks. This diversity among its members arises either by reason of their duties, as is the case with those who exercise the sacred ministry for the good of their brethren, or by reason of their condition and state of life, as is the case with those many who enter the religious state and, tending toward holiness by a narrower path, stimulate their brethren by their example. Moreover, within the Church, particular Churches hold a rightful place; these Churches retain their own traditions without lessening the primacy of the Chair of Peter, which presides over the whole assembly of charity and protects legitimate differences, while at the same time assuring that such differences do not hinder unity but rather contribute toward it. Between all the parts of the Church there remains a bond of close communion whereby they share spiritual riches, apostolic workers and temporal resources. For the members of the people of God are called to share these goods in common, and concerning each of the Churches the words of the apostle hold good: "According to the gift that each has received, administer it to one another as good stewards of the manifold grace of God" (I Pet. 4, 10).

All men are called to be part of this catholic unity of the people of God which forecasts and promotes universal peace. And the Catholic faithful, all who believe in Christ, and indeed the whole of mankind belong to or are related to it in various ways. For all men are called by the grace of God to salvation.

14) This Sacred Council wishes to turn its attention firstly to the Catholic faithful. Basing itself upon Sacred Scripture and Tradition, it teaches that the Church, now sojourning on earth as an exile, is necessary for salvation. Christ, present to us in His Body, which is the Church, is the one Mediator and the unique way of salvation. In explicit terms He Himself affirmed the necessity of faith and baptism (cf. Mk. 16, 16; Jo. 3, 5) and thereby affirmed also the necessity of the Church, for through baptism as through a door men enter the Church. Whosoever, therefore, knowing that the Catholic Church was made necessary by Christ, would refuse to enter it or to remain in it, could not be saved.

They are fully incorporated in the society of the Church who, having the Spirit of Christ, accept her entire system and all the means of salvation given to her, and are united with her as part of her visible bodily structure and through her with Christ, who rules her through the Supreme Pontiff and the bishops. The bonds that bind men to the Church in a visible way are profession of faith, the sacraments and ecclesiastical government and communion. He is not saved, however, who, though part of the body of the Church, does not persevere in charity. He remains indeed in the bosom of the Church, but, as it were, only in a "bodily" manner and not "in his heart." All the Church's children should remember that their exalted status is to be attributed not to their own merits but to the special grace of Christ. If they fail moreover to respond to the grace in thought, word and deed, not only shall they not be saved but they will be the more severely judged.

Catechumens who, moved by the Holy Spirit, seek with explicit intention to be incorporated into the Church are by that very intention joined with her. With love and solicitude Mother Church already embraces them as her own.

15) The Church recognizes that in many ways she is linked with those who, being baptized, are honored with the name of Christian, though they do not profess the faith in its entirety or do not preserve unity of communion with the successor of Peter. For there are many who honor Sacred Scripture taking it as a norm of belief and a pattern of life, and who show a true apostolic zeal. They lovingly believe in God the Father Almighty and in Christ, the son of God and Saviour. They are consecrated by baptism, in which they are united with Christ. They also recognize and accept other sacraments within their own Churches or ecclesiastical communities. Many of them rejoice in an episcopate, celebrate the Holy Eu-

charist and cultivate devotion toward the Virgin Mother of God. They also share with us in prayer and other spiritual benefits, even in some true union, in the Holy Spirit, for to them, too, He gives His gifts and graces whereby He is operative among them with His sanctifying power. Some indeed He has strengthened to the extent of the shedding of their blood. In all of Christ's disciples the Spirit arouses the desire to be peacefully united, in the manner determined by Christ, as one flock under one shepherd. Mother Church never ceases to pray, hope and work that this may come about. She exhorts her children to purification and renewal so that the sign of Christ may shine more brightly over the face of the earth.

16) Finally, those who have not yet received the Gospel are related in various ways to the people of God. In the first place we must recall the people to whom the testament and the promises were given and from whom Christ was born according to the flesh (cf. Rom. 9, 4-5). On account of their fathers this people of election remains most dear to God, for God does not repent of the gifts He makes nor of the calls He issues (cf. Rom. 11, 28-29). But the plan of salvation also includes those who acknowledge the Creator. Among whom, in the first place are the Moslems, who, professing to hold the faith of Abraham, along with us adore the one and merciful God, who on the last day will judge mankind Nor is God far distant from those who in shadows and images seek the unknown God, for it is He who gives to all men life and breath and all things (cf. Acts 17, 25-28), and as Saviour wills that all men be saved (cf. I Tim. 2, 4). Those also can attain to salvation who through no fault of their own do not know the Gospel of Christ of His Church, yet sincerely seek God and moved by grace strive by their deeds to do His will as it is known to them through the dictates of conscience. Nor does Divine Providence deny the helps necessary for salvation to those who, without blame on their part, have not yet arrived at an explicit knowledge of God and with His grace strive to live a good life. Whatever good or truth is found among them is looked upon by the Church as a preparation for the Gospel. She knows that it is given by Him who enlightens all men so that they may finally have life. But often men, deceived by the Evil One, have become vain in their reasonings and have exchanged the truth of God for a lie, serving the creature rather than the Creator. Or some there are who, living and dying in this world without God, are left finally in a state of hopelessness. Wherefore to promote the glory of God and procure the salvation of all the aforementioned, and mindful of the command of the Lord, "Preach the Gospel to every creature" (Mk. 16, 16), the Church fosters the mission with care and attention.

17) As the Son was sent by the Father (cf. Jn. 20, 21), so He too sent the Apostles, saying: "Go, therefore, make disciples of all nations, baptizing them in the name of the Father and of the Son and of the Holy Spirit, teaching them to observe all things whatsoever I have commanded you. And behold I am with you all days even to the consummation of the world" (Mt. 21, 18-20). The Church has received this solemn mandate of Christ to proclaim the saving truth from the apostles and must carry it out to the very ends of the earth (cf. Acts 1, 8). Wherefore she makes the words of the Apostle her own: "Woe to me, if I do not preach the Gospel" (I Cor. 9, 16), and continues unceasingly to send heralds of the Gospel until such time as the infant churches are fully established and can themselves continue the work of evan-

gelizing. For the Church is compelled by the Holy Spirit to do her part that God's plan may be fully realized, whereby He has constituted Christ as the source of salvation for the whole world. By the proclamation of the Gospel she prepares her hearers to receive and profess the faith, prepares them for baptism, snatches them from the slavery of error and of idols and incorporates them in Christ so that through charity they may grow up into full maturity in Christ. Through her work, whatever good is in the minds and hearts of men, whatever good lies latent in the religious practices and cultures of diverse peoples, is not only saved from destruction but is also cleansed, raised up and perfected unto the glory of God, the confusion of the devil and the happiness of man. The obligation of spreading the faith is imposed on every disciple of Christ, according to his state. Although, however, all the faithful can baptize, the priest alone can complete the building up of the Body in the eucharistic sacrifice. Thus are fulfilled the words of God, spoken through His prophet: "From the rising of the sun until the going down thereof my name is great among the gentiles, and in every place a clean oblation is sacrificed and offered up in my name" (Mal. 1, 11). In this way the Church both prays and labors in order that the entire world may become the People of God, the Body of the Lord and the Temple of the Holy Spirit, and that in Christ, the Head of all, all honor and glory may be rendered to the Creator and Father of the Universe.

3. *The Hierarchical Structure of the Church and in particular the Episcopate*

18) For the nurturing and constant growth of the People of God, Christ the Lord instituted in His Church a variety of ministries, which work for the good of the whole body. For those ministers, who are endowed with sacred power, serve their brethren, so that all who are of the People of God, and therefore enjoy a true Christian dignity, working toward a common goal freely and in an orderly way, may arrive at salvation.

This Sacred Council, following closely in the footsteps of the First Vatican Council, with that Council teaches and declares that Jesus Christ, the eternal Shepherd, established His holy Church, having sent forth the apostles as He himself had been sent by the Father (Jn. 20, 21); and He willed that their successors, namely the bishops, should be shepherds in His Church even to the consummation of the world. And in order that the episcopate itself might be one and undivided, He placed Blessed Peter over the other apostles, and instituted in him a permanent and visible source and foundation of unity of faith and communion. And this teaching about the institution, the perpetuity, the meaning and reason for the sacred primacy of the Roman Pontiff and of his infallible magisterium, this Sacred Council again proposes to be firmly believed by all the faithful. Continuing in that same undertaking, this Council is resolved to declare and proclaim before all men the doctrine concerning bishops, the successors of the apostles, who together with the successor of Peter, the Vicar of Christ, the visible Head of the whole Church, govern the house of the living God.

19) The Lord Jesus, after praying to the Father, calling to Himself those whom He desired, appointed twelve to be with Him, and whom He would send to preach the Kingdom of God (Mk. 3, 13-19; Mt. 10, 1-42); and these apostles (Lk. 6, 13) He formed after the manner of a college or a fixed group, over which He placed Peter chosen from among them. He sent them first to the children of Israel and then to all

nations (Rom. 1, 16), so that as sharers in His power they might make all peoples His disciples, and sanctify and govern them (Mt. 26, 16-20; Mk. 16, 15; Lk. 24, 45-48; Jn. 20, 21-23), and thus spread His Church, and by ministering to it under the guidance of the Lord, direct it all days even to the consummation of the world (Mt. 28, 20). In this mission they were fully confirmed on the day of Pentecost (Acts 2, 1-26) in accordance with the Lord's promise: "You shall receive power when the Holy Spirit comes upon you, and you shall be witnesses for me in Jerusalem, and in all Judea and in Samaria, and even to the very ends of the earth" (Acts 1, 8). And the apostles, by preaching the Gospel everywhere (Mk. 16, 20), and it being accepted by their hearers under the influence of the Holy Spirit, gather together the universal Church, which the Lord established on the Apostles and built upon blessed Peter, their chief, Christ Jesus Himself being the supreme cornerstone (Apoc. 21, 14; Mt. 16, 18; Eph. 2, 20).

20) That divine mission, entrusted by Christ to the apostles, will last until the end of the world (Mt. 28, 20), since the Gospel they are to teach us is for all time the source of all life for the Church. And for this reason the apostles, appointed as rulers in this society, took care to appoint successors.

For they not only had helpers in their ministry, but also, in order that the mission assigned to them might continue after their death, they passed on to their immediate cooperators, as it were, in the form of a testament, the duty of confirming and finishing the work begun by themselves, recommending to them that they attend to the whole flock in which the Holy Spirit placed them to shepherd the Church of God (Act. 20, 28). They therefore appointed such men, and gave them the order that, when they should have died, other approved men would take up their ministry. Among those various ministries which, according to tradition, were exercised in the Church from the earliest times, the chief place belongs to the office of those who, appointed to the episcopate, by a succession running from the beginning, are passers-on of the apostolic seed. Thus, as St. Irenaeus testifies, through those who were appointed bishops by the apostle, and through their successors down to our own time, the apostolic tradition is manifested and preserved.

Bishops, therefore, with their helpers, the priests and deacons, have taken up the service of the community, presiding in place of God over the flock, whose shepherds they are, as teachers for doctrine, priests for sacred worship, and ministers for governing. And just as the office granted individually to Peter, the first among the Apostles, is permanent and is to be transmitted to his successors, so also the apostles' office of nurturing the Church is permanent, and is to be exercised without interruption by the sacred order of bishops. Therefore, the Sacred Council teaches that bishops by divine institution have succeeded to the place of the apostles, as shepherds of the Church, and he who hears them, hears Christ, and he who rejects them, rejects Christ and Him who sent Christ (cf. Lk. 10, 16).

21) In the bishops, therefore, for whom priests are assistants, Our Lord Jesus Christ, the Supreme High Priest, is present in the midst of those who believe. For sitting at the right hand of God the Father, He is not absent from the gathering of His high priests, but above all through their excellent service He is preaching the word of God to all nations, and is constantly administering the sacraments of faith to those who believe; by their paternal func-

tioning He incorporates new members in His body by a supernal regeneration, and finally by their wisdom and prudence He directs and guides the People of the New Testament in their pilgrimage toward eternal happiness. These pastors, chosen to shepherd the Lord's flock, are servants of Christ and stewards of the mysteries of God (cf. I Cor. 4, 1), to whom has been assigned the bearing of witness to the Gospel of the grace of God (cf. Rom. 15, 16; Act. 20, 24), and the ministration of the Spirit and of justice in glory (cf. II Cor. 3, 8-9).

For the discharging of such great duties, the apostles were enriched by Christ with a special outpouring of the Holy Spirit coming upon them (cf. Acts. 1, 8; 2, 4; Jn. 20, 23), and they passed on this spiritual gift to their helpers by the imposition of hands (cf. I Tim. 4, 14; II Tim. 1, 6-7), and it has been transmitted down to us in episcopal consecration. And the sacred council teaches that by episcopal consecration the fulness of the sacrament of Orders is conferred, that fulness of power, namely, which both in the Church's liturgical practice and in the language of the Fathers of the Church is called the high priesthood, the supreme power of the sacred ministry. But episcopal consecration, together with the office of sanctifying, also confers the office of teaching and of governing, which, however, of its very nature, can be exercised only in hierarchial communion with the head and the members of the college. For from the tradition, which is expressed especially in liturgical rites and in the practice of both the Church of the East and of the West, it is clear that, by means of the imposition of hands and the words of consecration, the grace of the Holy Spirit is so conferred, and the sacred character so impressed, that bishops in an eminent and visible way sustain the roles of Christ Himself as Teacher,

Shepherd and High Priest, and that they act in His person. Therefore it pertains to the bishops to admit newly elected members into the episcopal body by means of the sacrament of Orders.

22) Just as in the Gospel, the Lord so disposing, St. Peter and the other apostles constitute one apostolic colege, so the Roman Pontiff, the successor of Peter, and the bishops, the successors of the apostles, are joined together. Indeed, the very established in all parts of the world were in communion with one another and with the Bishop of Rome in a bond of unity, charity and peace, and also the councils assembled together, in which more profound matters were settled in common, after prudent deliberation on the opinion of the many, both of these factors are already an indication of the collegiate character and aspect of the episcopal order; and the ecumenical councils held in the course of centuries are also manifest proof of that same character. And it is intimated also in the practice, introduced in ancient times, of summoning several bishops to take part in the elevation of the newly elected to the ministry of the high priesthood. Hence, one is constituted a member of the episcopal body in virtue of sacramental consecration and hierachical communion with the head and members of the body.

But the college or body of bishops has no authority unless it is understood together with the Roman pontiff, the successor of Peter as its head. His power of primacy over all, both pastors and faithful, remains whole and intact. In virtue of his office, as Vicar of Christ and pastor of the whole Church, the Roman pontiff has full, supreme and universal power over the Church. And he is always free to exercise this power. The order of bishops, which succeeds to the college of apostles in teaching and ruling the Church and which gives this apostolic body continued existence, is also the subject of supreme and full power over the universal Church, provided we understand this body together with its head the Roman pontiff and never without this head. This power can be exercised with the consent of the Roman Pontiff. For Our Lord placed Simon alone as the rock and the bearer of the keys of the Church (Mt. 16, 18-19), and made him shepherd of the whole flock (Jn. 21, 15); it is evident, however, that the power of binding and loosing, which was given to Peter (Mt. 16, 19), was granted also to the college of apostles, joined with their head (Mt. 18, 18). This college insofar as it is composed of many, expresses the variety and universality of the People of God, but insofar as it is assembled under one head, it expresses the unity of the flock of Christ. In it, the bishops, faithfully recognizing the primacy and preeminence of their head, exercise their own authority for the good of their own faithful, and indeed of the whole Church, the Holy Spirit continually strengthening the organic structure and its harmony. This supreme power in the whole Church which this college enjoys, is exercised in a solemn way in an ecumenical council. A council is never ecumenical unless it is confirmed or at least accepted as such by the successor of Peter; and it is prerogative of the Roman pontiff to convoke these councils, to preside over them and to confirm them.—This same collegiate power can be exercised together with the pope by the bishops living in all parts of the world, provided that the head of the college calls them to collegiate action, or at least approves of or freely accepts the united action of the scattered bishops, so that it is thereby made a collegiate act.

23) This collegial union is apparent also in the mutual relations of the individual bishops with particular churches and with the universal Church. The Roman pontiff, as the successor of Peter, is the perpetual and visible principle and foundation of unity of both the bishops and of the faithful. The individual bishops, however, are the visible principle and foundation of unity in their particular churches, fashioned after the model of the universal Church, in and from which churches comes into being the one and only Catholic Church. For this reason the individual bishops represent each his own church, but all of them together and with the Pope represent the entire Church in the bond of peace, love and unity.

The individual bishops, who are placed in charge of particular churches, exercise their pastoral government over the portion of the People of God committed to their care, and not over other churches nor over the universal Church. But each of them, as a member of the episcopal college and legitimate successor of the apostles, is obliged by Christ's institution and command to be solicitous for the whole Church, and this solicitude, though it is not exercised by an act of jurisdiction, contributes greatly to the advantage of the universal Church. For it is the duty of all bishops to promote and to safeguard the unity of faith and the discipline common to the whole Church, to instruct the faithful to love the whole mystical body of Christ, especially its poor and sorrowing members and those who are suffering persecution for justice's sake (Mt. 5, 10), and finally to promote every activity that is of interest to the whole Church, especially that the faith may be spread and the light of full truth appear to all men. And this also is important, that by governing well their own church as a portion of the universal Church, they themselves are effectively contributing to the welfare of the whole Mystical Body, which is also the body of the churches.

The task of proclaiming the Gospel everywhere on earth pertains to the body of shepherds, to all of whom in common Christ gave His command, thereby imposing upon them a common duty, as Pope Celestine in his time recommended to the Fathers of the Council of Ephesus. From this it follows that the individual bishops, insofar as their own discharge of their duty permits, are obliged to enter into a community of work among themselves and with the successor of Peter, upon whom was imposed in a special way the great duty of spreading the Christian name. With all their energy, therefore, they must supply to the missions both workers for the harvest and also spiritual and material aid, both directly and on their own account, as well as by arousing the ardent cooperation of the faithful. And finally, the bishops, in a universal fellowship of charity, should gladly extend their fraternal aid to other churches, especially to neighboring and more needy dioceses in accordance with the venerable example of antiquity.

By divine Providence it has come about that various churches, established in various places by the apostles and their successors, have in the course of time coalesced into several groups, organically united, which, preserving the unity of faith and the unique divine constitution of the universal Church, enjoy thir own discipline, their own liturgical usage, and their own theological and spiritual heritage. Some of these churches, notably the ancient patriarchal churches, as parent-stocks of the Faith, so to speak, have begotten others as daughter churches, with which they are connected down to our own time by a close bond of charity in their sacramental life and in their mutual respect for their rights and duties. This variety of local churches with one common aspiration is splendid evidence of the catholicity of the undivided Church. In like manner the episcopal bodies of today are in a posi-

tion to render a manifold and fruitful assistance, so that this collegiate feeling may be put into practical application.

24) Bishops, as successors of the apostles, receive from the Lord, to whom was given all power in heaven and on earth, the mission to teach all nations and to preach the Gospel to every creature, so that all men may attain to salvation by faith, baptism and the fulfillment of the commandments (cf. Mt. 28, 18; Mk. 16, 15-16; Acts 26, 17sq.). To fulfill this mission, Christ the Lord promised the Holy Spirit to the Apostles, and on Pentecost day sent the Spirit from heaven, by whose power they would be witnesses to Him before the nations and peoples and kings even to the ends of the earth (Act 1, 8; 2, 1ff; 9, 15). And that duty, which the Lord committed to the Shepherds of His people, is a true service, which in sacred literature is significantly called *diakonia* or ministry (Acts 1, 17, 25; 21, 10; Rom. 2, 13; I Tim 1, 12).

The canonical mission of bishops can come about by legitimate customs that have not been revoked by the supreme and universal authority of the Church, or by laws made or recognized by that same authority, or directly through the success of Peter himself; and if the latter refuses or denies apostolic communion, such bishops cannot assume any office.

25) Among the principal duties of bishops the preaching of the Gospel occupies an eminent place. For bishops are preachers of the faith, who lead new disciples to Christ, and they are authentic teachers, that is, teachers endowed with the authority of Christ, who preach to the people committed to them the faith to be believed and put into practice, and by the light of the Holy Spirit illustrate that faith, bringing forth from the treasury of Revelation new things and old (Mt. 13, 52), making it bear fruit and vigilantly warding off any errors that threaten

their flock (2 Tim. 4, 1-4). Bishops, teaching in communion with the Roman pontiff, are to be respected by all as witnesses to divine and Catholic truth. When their bishop speaks in the name of Christ in matters of faith and morals, the faithful are to accept their teaching and adhere to it with a religious assent. This religious submission of mind and will must be shown in a special way to the authentic magisterium of the Roman pontiff, even when he is not speaking *ex cathedra;* that is, it must be shown in such a way that his supreme magisterium is acknowledged with reverence, the judgments made by him are sincerely adhered to, according to his manifest mind and will. His mind and will in the matter may be known either from the character of the documents, from his frequent repetition of the same doctrine, or from his manner of speaking.

Although individual bishops do not enjoy the prerogative of infallibility, they nevertheless proclaim Christ's doctrine infallibly whenever, even though dispersed through the world, but still maintaining the bond of communion among themselves and with the successor of Peter, and authentically teaching matters of faith and morals, they are in agreement on one position as definitively to be held. This is even more clearly verified when, gathered together in an ecumenical council, they are teachers and judges of faith and morals for the universal Church, whose definitions must be adhered to with the submission of faith.

And this infallibility with which the Divine Redeemer willed His Church to be endowed in defining doctrine of faith and morals, extends as far as the deposit of Revelation extends, which must be religiously guarded and faithfully expounded. And this is the infallibility which the Roman pontiff, the head of the college of bishops, enjoys in virtue of his office, when, as the supreme shepherd and teacher of all the faithful, who confirms his brethren in their faith (cf. Lk. 22, 32), by a definitive act he proclaims a doctrine of faith or morals. And therefore his definitions, of themselves, and not from the consent of the Church, are justly styled irreformable, since they are pronounced with the assistance of the Holy Spirit, promised to him in blessed Peter, and therefore they need no approval of others, nor do they allow an appeal to any other judgment. For then the Roman pontiff is not pronouncing judgment as a private person, but as the supreme teacher of the universal Church, in whom the charism of infallibility of the Church itself is individually present, he is expounding or defending a doctrine of Catholic faith. The infallibility promised to the Church resides also in the Body of Bishops, when that body exercises the supreme magisterium with the successor of Peter. To these definitions the assent of the Church can never be wanting, on account of the activity of that same Holy Spirit, by which the whole flock of Christ is preserved and progresses in unity of faith.

But when either the Roman pontiff or the Body of Bishops together with him defines a judgment, they pronounce it in accordance with Revelation itself, which all are obliged to abide by and be in conformity with, that is, the Revelation which as written or orally handed down is transmitted in its entirety through the legitimate succession of bishops and especially in care of the Roman pontiff himself, and which under the guiding light of the Spirit of truth is religiously preserved and faithfully expounded in the Church. The Roman pontiff and the bishops, in view of their office and the importance of the matter, by fitting means diligently strive to inquire properly into that revelation and to give apt expression to its contents; but they do not accept a new public revelation as pertaining to the divine deposit of faith.

26) A bishop marked with the fullness of the sacrament of Orders, is "the steward of the grace of the supreme priesthood," especially in the Eucharist, which he offers or causes to be offered, and by which the Church continually lives and grows. This Church of Christ is truly present in all legitimate local congregations of the faithful which, united with their pastors, are themselves called churches in the New Testament. For in their locality these are the new People called by God, in the Holy Spirit and in much fullness (cf. I Thes. 1, 5). In them the faithful are gathered together by the preaching of the Gospel of Christ, and the mystery of the Lord's Supper is celebrated, that by the food and blood of the Lord's body the whole brotherhood may be joined together. In any community of the altar, under the sacred ministry of the bishop, there is exhibited a symbol of that charity and "unity of the mystical Body, without which there can be no salvation." In these communities, though frequently small and poor, or living in the Diaspora, Christ is present, and in virtue of His presence there is brought together one, holy, catholic and apostolic Church. For "the partaking of the body and blood of Christ does nothing other than make us be transformed into that which we consume" (St. Leo Gt: Serm. 63, 7).

Every legitimate celebration of the Eucharist is regulated by the bishop, to whom is committed the office of offering the worship of Christian religion to the Divine Majesty and of administering it in accordance with the Lord's commandments and the Church's laws, as further defined by his particular judgment for his diocese.

Thus, by praying and laboring for the people, bishops make outpourings in many ways and in great abundance from the fullness of Christ's holiness. By the ministry of the word they communicate God's power to those who believe unto salvation (cf. Rom. 1, 16), and through the sacraments, the regular and fruitful distributions of which they regulate by their authority, they sanctify the faithful. They direct the conferring of baptism, by which a sharing of the kingly priesthood of Christ is granted. They are the original ministers of confirmation, dispensers of sacred Orders and the moderators of penitential discipline, and they earnestly exhort and instruct their people to carry out with faith and reverence their part in the liturgy and especially in the holy sacrifice of the Mass. And lastly, by the example of their way of life they must be an influence for good to those over whom they preside, refraining from all evil and, as far as they are able with God's help, exchanging evil for good, so that together with the flock committed to their care they may arrive at eternal life.

As vicars and ambassadors of Christ, bishops govern the particular churches entrusted to them by their counsel, exhortations, example, and even by their authority and sacred power, which indeed they use only for the edification of their flock in truth and holiness, remembering that he who is greater should become as the lesser and he who is the chief become as the servant (cf. Lk. 22, 26-27). This power, which they personally exercise in Christ's name, is proper, ordinary and immediate, although its exercise is ultimately regulated by the supreme authority of the Church, and can be circumscribed by certain limits, for the advantage of the Church or of the faithful. In virtue of this power, bishops have the sacred right and the duty before the Lord to make laws for their subjects, to pass judgment on them and to moderate everything pertaining to the ordering of worship and the apostolate.

The pastoral office or the habitual and daily care of their sheep is entrusted to them completely; nor are they to be regarded as vicars of the Roman pontiffs, for they exercise an authority that is proper to them, and are quite correctly called prelates, heads of the people whom they govern. Their power, therefore, is not destroyed by the supreme and universal power, but on the contrary it is affirmed, strengthened and vindicated by it, since the Holy Spirit unfailingly preserves the form of government established by Christ the Lord in His Church.

Since he is sent by the Father to govern his family, a bishop must keep before his eyes the example of the Good Shepherd, who came not to be ministered unto but to minister (Mt. 20, 28; Mk. 10, 45), and to lay down his life for his sheep (Jn. 10, 11). Being taken from among men, and himself beset with weakness, he is able to have compassion on the ignorant and erring (Heb. 5, 1-2). Let him not refuse to listen to his subjects, whom he cherishes as his true sons and exhorts to cooperate readily with him. As having one day to render an account for their souls, he takes care of them by his prayer, preaching, and all the works of charity, and not only of them but also of those who are not yet of the one flock, who also are commended to him in the Lord. Since, like Paul the Apostle, he is debtor to all men, let him be ready to preach the Gospel to all, and to urge his faithful to apostolic and missionary activity. But the faithful must cling to their bishop, as the Church does to Christ, and Jesus Christ to the Father, so that all may be of one mind through unity, and abound to the glory of God (II Cor. 4, 15).

27) Christ, whom the Father has sanctified and sent into the world, has through His apostles, made their successors the bishops partakers of His consecration and His mission. They have legitimately handed on to different individuals in the Church various degrees of participation in this ministry. Thus the divinely established ecclesiastical ministry is exercised on different levels by those who from antiquity have been called bishops, priests and deacons. Priests, although they do not possess the highest degree of the pontificate, and although they are dependent on the bishops in the exercise of their power, nevertheless are united with the bishops in sacerdotal dignity. By the power of the sacrament of Orders, in the image of Christ the eternal High Priest, they are consecrated to preach the Gospel and shepherd the faithful and to celebrate divine worship, so that they are true priests of the New Testament. Partakers of the function of Christ the sole Mediator, on their level of ministry, they announce the divine word to all. They exercise this function of Christ especially in the Eucharist liturgy or synaxis wherein, acting in the person of Christ and proclaiming His mystery, they join the offerings of the faithful to the sacrifice of their Head and, until the coming of the Lord, they represent and apply in the sacrifice of the Mass the one sacrifice of the New Testament, namely the sacrifice of Christ offering Himself once and for all to His Father as a spotless victim. For the sick and the penitents among the faithful, they exercise the ministry of alleviation and reconciliation and they present the needs and the prayers of the faithful to God the Father (Heb. 5, 1-4). Exercising within the limits of their authority the function of Christ as shepherd and Head, they gather together God's family as a brotherhood all of one mind, and lead them in the Spirit, through Christ, to God the Father. In the midst

of the flock they adore Him in spirit and in truth (Jn. 4, 24). Finally, they labor in word and doctrine, believing what they have read and meditated upon in the law of God, teaching what they have believed, and putting in practice in their own lives what they have taught.

28) Priests, prudent cooperators with the episcopal order, its aid and instrument, called to serve the people of God, constitute one priesthood with their bishop although bound by a diversity of duties. Associated with their bishop in a spirit of trust and generosity, they make him present in a certain sense in the individual local congregations, and take upon themselves his duties and burdens, and discharge them with a daily care. And as they sanctify and govern under the bishop's authority, that part of the Lord's flock entrusted to them, they make the universal Church visible in their own locality and bring an efficacious assistance to the building up of the whole body of Christ (Eph. 4, 12). Intent always upon the welfare of God's children, they must strive to lend their effort to the pastoral work of the whole diocese, and even of the entire Church. On account of this sharing in their priesthood and mission, let priests sincerely look upon the bishop as their father and reverently obey him. And let the bishop regard his priests as his co-workers and as sons and friends, just as Christ called His disciples now not servants but friends (Jn. 15, 15). All priests, both diocesan and religious, as regards Orders and ministry, belong to this body of bishops and priests, and serve the good of the whole Church according to their vocation and the grace given to them.

In virtue of their common sacred ordination and mission, all priests are bound together in intimate brotherhood, which naturally and freely manifests itself in mutual aid, spiritual as well as material, pastoral as well as personal, in their meetings and in communion of life, of labor and charity.

Let them, as fathers in Christ, take care of the faithful whom they have begotten by baptism and teaching (I Cor. 4, 15; I Pet. 1, 23). Becoming from the heart a pattern to the flock (I Pet. 5, 3), let them so lead and serve their local community that it may worthily be called by that name, by which the one and entire people of God is signed, namely, the Church of God (I Cor. 1, 2; II Cor. 1, 1). Let them remember by their daily life and interests to demonstrate a truly sacerdotal and pastoral ministry to the faithful and the infidel, to Catholics and non-Catholics, and that to all they bear witness to the truth and life, and as good shepherds go after those also (Lk. 15, 4-7), who though baptized in the Catholic Church have fallen away from the use of the sacraments, or even from the faith.

Because the human race today is growing more and more into a civic, economic and social unity, it is so much the more necessary that priests, by combined effort and aid, under the leadership of the bishops and the Supreme Pontiff, wipe out every kind of separateness, so that the whole human race may be brought into the unity of the family of God.

29) At a lower level of the hierarchy are deacons, upon whom hands are imposed "not unto the priesthood, but unto a ministry of service." For strengthened by sacramental grace, in communion with the bishop and his group of priests they serve in the diaconate of the liturgy, of the word, and of charity to the people of God. It is the duty of the deacon, according as it shall have been assigned to him by competent authority, to administer baptism solemnly, to be custodian and dispenser of the Eucharist, to assist at and bless marriages in the name of the Church, to bring Viaticum to the dying,

to read the Sacred Scripture to the faithful, to administer sacramentals, to officiate at funeral and burial services. Dedicated to duties of charity and of administration, let deacons be mindful of the admonition of Blessed Polycarp: "Be merciful, diligent, walking according to the truth of the Lord, who became the servant of all."

Since these duties, so very necessary to the life of the Church, can be fulfilled only with difficulty in many regions in accordance with the discipline of the Latin Church as it exists today, the diaconate can in the future be restored as a proper and permanent rank of the hierarchy. It pertains to the competent territorial bodies of bishops, of one kind or another, with the approval of the Supreme Pontiff, to decide whether and where it is opportune for such deacons to be established for the care of souls. With the consent of the Roman Pontiff, this diaconate can, in the future, be conferred upon men of more mature age, even upon those living in the married state. It may also be conferred upon suitable young men, for whom the law of celibacy must remain intact.

4. *The Laity*

30) Having set forth the functions of the hierarchy, the Sacred Council gladly turns its attention to the state of those faithful called the laity. Everything that has been said above concerning the People of God is intended equally for the laity, religious and clergy. But there are certain things which pertain in a special way to the laity, both men and women, by reason of their condition and mission. Due to the special circumstances of our time the foundations of this doctrine must be more thoroughly examined. For their pastors know well how much the laity contribute to the welfare of the entire Church. The pastors also know that they were not ordained by Christ to take upon themselves alone the entire salvific mission of the Church toward the world. On the contrary they understand that it is their noble duty to shepherd the faithful and to recognize their ministries and charisms, so that all according to their proper roles may cooperate in this common undertaking with one mind. For we must all "practice the truth in love, and so grow up in all things in Him who is head, Christ. For from Him the whole body, being closely joined and knit together through every joint of the system, according to the functioning in due measure of each single part, derives its increase to the building up of itself in love" (Eph. 4: 15-16).

31) The term laity is here understood to mean all the faithful except those in holy orders and those in the state of religious life specially approved by the Church. These faithful are by baptism made one body with Christ and are constituted the People of God; they are in their own way made sharers in the priestly, prophetical and kingly functions of Christ; and they carry out for their own part the mission of the whole Christian people, in the Church and in the world.

What specifically characterizes the laity is their secular nature. It is true that those in holy orders can at times be engaged in secular activities, and even have a secular profession. But they are by reason of their particular vocation especially and professedly ordained to the sacred ministry. Similarly, by their state in life, religious give splendid and striking testimony that the world cannot be transformed and offered to God without the spirit of the beatitudes. But the laity, by their special vocation, seek the kingdom of God by engaging in temporal affairs and by ordering them according to the plan of God. They live in the world, that is, in each and in all of the secular professions and occupations. They live in the ordinary circumstances of family and social life, from which the very web of their existence is woven. Today they are called there by God that by exercising their proper function and led by the spirit of the Gospel they may work for the sanctification of the world from within as a leaven. In this way they may make Christ known to others, especially by the testimony of a life resplendent in faith, hope and charity. Therefore, since they are tightly bound up in all types of temporal affairs it is their special task to order and to throw light upon these affairs in such a way that they may be made and grow according to Christ to the praise of the Creator and the Redeemer.

32) By divine institution Holy Church is ordered and governed with a wonderful diversity. "For just as in one body we have many members, yet all the members have not the same function, so we, the many are one body in Christ, but severally members one of another" (Rom. 12: 4-5). Therefore, the chosen People of God is one: "one Lord, one faith, one baptism" (Eph. 4: 5); sharing a common dignity as members from their regeneration in Christ; having the same filial grace and the same vocation to perfection; possessing in common one salvation, one hope and one undivided charity. There is, therefore, in Christ and in the Church no inequality on the basis of race or nationality, social condition or sex, because "there is neither Jew nor Greek: there is neither slave nor freeman: there is neither male nor female. For you are all 'one' in Christ Jesus" (Gal. 3: 28; cf. Col. 3: 11).

If therefore in the Church everyone does not proceed by the same path, nevertheless all are called to sanctify and have received an equal privilege of faith through the justice of God (cf. II Pt. 1: 1). And if by the will of Christ some are made teachers, pastors and dispensers of mysteries on behalf of others, yet all share a true equality with regard to the dignity and to the activity common to all the faithful for the building up of the Body of Christ. For the distinction that the Lord made between sacred ministers and the rest of the People of God bears within it a certain union, since pastors and the other faithful are bound to each other by a mutual necessity. Pastors of the Church, following the example of the Lord, should minister to one another and to the other faithful. These in their turn should enthusiastically lend their joint assistance to their pastors and teachers. Thus in their diversity all bear witness to the wonderful unity in the Body of Christ. This very diversity of graces, ministries and works gathers the children of God into one, because "all these things are the work of one and the same Spirit" (I Cor. 12:11).

Therefore, from divine choice the laity have Christ for their brother, who though He is the Lord of all, came not to be served but to serve (cf. Mt. 20: 28). They also have for brothers those in the sacred ministry who by teaching, by sanctifying and by ruling with the authority of Christ feed the family of God so that the new commandment of charity may be fulfilled by all. St. Augustine puts this very beautifully when he says: "What I am for you terrifies me; what I am with you consoles me. For you I am a bishop; but with you I am a Christian. The former is a duty; the latter a grace. The former is a danger; the latter, salvation" (1).

33) The laity are gathered together in the People of God and make up the Body of Christ under one head. Whoever they are they are called upon, as living members, to expend all their energy for the growth of the Church and its continuous sanctification, since this

very energy is a gift of the Creator and a blessing of the Redeemer.

The lay apostolate, however, is a participation in the salvific mission of the Church itself. Through their baptism and confirmation all are commissioned to that apostolate by the Lord Himself. Moreover, by the sacraments, especially holy Eucharist, that charity toward God and man which is the soul of all apostolate is communicated and nourished. Now the laity are called in a special way to make the Church present and operative in those places and circumstances where only through them can it become the salt of the earth (2). Thus every layman, in virtue of the very gifts bestowed upon him, is at the same time a witness and a living instrument of the mission of the Church itself "according to the measure of Christ's bestowal" (Eph. 4: 7).

Besides this apostolate, which certainly pertains to all Christians, the laity can also be called in various ways to a more direct form of cooperation in the apostolate of the hierarchy (3). This was the way certain men and women assisted Paul the Apostle in the Gospel, laboring much in the Lord (cf. Phil. 4: 3; Rom. 16: 3ff). Further, they have the capacity to assume from the hierarchy certain ecclesiastical functions that are to be performed for a spiritual purpose.

Upon all the laity, therefore, rests the noble duty of working more and more to extend the divine plan of salvation to all men of each epoch and in every land. Consequently, may every opportunity be given them so that, according to their abilities and the needs of the times, they may zealously participate in the saving work of the Church.

34. The supreme and eternal Priest, Christ Jesus, since He wills to continue his witness and service also through the laity, vivifies them in His Spirit and unceasingly urges them on to every good and perfect work.

For besides intimately linking them to His life and His mission, He also gives them a share in His priestly function of offering spiritual worship for the glory of God and the salvation of men. For this reason the laity, dedicated to Christ and anointed by the Holy Spirit, are marvelously called and wonderfully prepared so that ever more abundant fruits of the Spirit may be produced in them. For all their works, prayers and apostolic endeavors, their ordinary married and family life, their daily occupations, their physical and mental relaxation, if carried out in the Spirit, and even the hardships of life, if patiently borne—all these become "spiritual sacrifices acceptable to God through Jesus Christ" (I Pet. 2: 5). Together with the offering of the Lord's body, they are most fittingly offered in the celebration of the Eucharist. Thus, the laity, too, consecrate the world itself to God, insofar as adoring everywhere in holy activity.

35) Christ, the great Prophet, who proclaimed the Kingdom of His Father both by the testimony of His life and the power of his words, continually fulfills His prophetic office until the complete manifestation of glory, not only through the hierarchy who teach in His name and with His authority, but also through the laity whom therefore He made His witnesses and instructed by an understanding of the faith (*sensus fidei*) and the grace of the Word. (cf. Act. 2: 17-18; Apoc. 19: 10) so that the power of the Gospel might shine forth in their daily social and family life. They conduct themselves as children of the promise, and thus strong in faith and in hope they make the most of the present (cf. Eph. 5: 16; Col. 4: 5), and with patience await the glory that is to come (cf. Rom. 8: 25). Let them not, then, hide this hope in the depths of their hearts, but let them in the program of their secular life express it also by a continual conver-

sion and by wrestling "against the world-rulers of this darkness, against the spiritual forces of wickedness" (Eph. 6: 12).

Just as the sacraments of the New Law, by which the life and the apostolate of the faithful are nourished, prefigure a new heaven and a new earth (cf. Apoc. 21: 1), so too the laity go forth as powerful proclaimers of a faith in things to be hoped for (cf. Heb. 11: 1), when they courageously join to their profession of faith a life springing from faith. This evangelization, that is, this announcing of Christ by a testimony of life as well as by the spoken word, takes on a specific quality and a special efficacy in that it is carried out in the ordinary surroundings of the world.

In this undertaking great importance clearly attaches to that state of life that is sanctified by a special sacrament, namely, married and family life. For where Christianity pervades the entire mode of family life, and increasingly transforms it, one will find there both the practice and an excellent school of the lay apostolate. In such a home husbands and wives find their proper vocation in being witnesses of the faith and love of Christ to one another and to their children. The Christian family loudly proclaims both the present virtues of the Kingdom of God and the hope of a blessed life to come. Thus by its example and its witness it accuses the world of sin and enlightens those who seek the truth.

Consequently, even when preoccupied with temporal cares, the laity can and should perform a work of great value for the evangelization of the world. For even if some of them have to fulfill their religious duties on their own, when there are no sacred ministers or in times of persecution; and even if many of them devote all their energies to apostolic work; still it remains for each one of them to cooperate in the external spread and the dynamic growth of the Kingdom of

Christ in the world. Therefore, let the laity devoutly strive to acquire a more profound grasp of revealed truth, and let them insistently beg of God the gift of wisdom.

36) Christ, becoming obedient even unto death and because of this exalted by the Father (cf. Phil. 2: 8-9), entered into the glory of His kingdom. To Him all things are made subject until He subjects Himself and all created things to the Father that God may be all in all (cf. I Cor. 15: 27-28). Now Christ has communicated this royal power to His disciples that they might be constituted in royal freedom and that by true self-denial and a holy life they might conquer the reign of sin in themselves (cf. Rom. 6: 12) and by serving Christ in their fellow men they might by humility and patience lead their brethren to that King to serve whom is to reign. But the Lord wishes to spread His kingdom also by means of the laity, namely, a kingdom of truth and life, a kingdom of holiness and grace, a kingdom of justice, love and peace (4). In this kingdom creation itself will be delivered from its slavery to corruption into the freedom of the glory of the sons of God (cf. Rom. 8: 21). Clearly then a great promise and a great trust is committed to the disciples: "All things are yours, and you are Christ's, and Christ is God's (I Cor. 3: 23).

The faithful, therefore, must learn the deepest meaning and the value of all creation, as well as its role in the harmonious praise of God. They must assist each other to live holier lives even in their daily occupations. In this way the world may be permeated by the spirit of Christ and it may more effectively fulfill its purpose in justice, charity and peace. The laity have the principal role in the overall fulfillment of this duty. Therefore, by their competence in secular disciplines and by their activity, elevated from within by the grace of Christ, let them vigorously contribute their effort, so that created goods may be perfected by human labor, technical skill and civic culture for the benefit of all men according to the design of the Creator and the light of His Word; the goods of this world may be more equitably distributed among all men, and may they in their own way be conducive to universal progress in human and Christian freedom. In this manner, through the members of the Church, will Christ progressively illumine the whole of human society with His saving light.

Moreover, let the laity also by their combined efforts remedy the customs and conditions of the world, if they are an inducement to sin, so that they all may be conformed to the norms of justice and may favor the practice of virtue rather than than hinder it. By so doing they will imbibe culture and human activity with genuine moral values; they will better prepare the field of the world for the seed of the Word of God; and at the same time they will open wider the doors of the Church by which the message of peace may enter the world.

Because of the very economy of salvation the faithful should learn how to distinguish carefully between those rights and duties that are theirs as members of the Church, and those which they have as members of human society. Let them strive to reconcile the two, remembering that in every temporal affair they must be guided by a Christian conscience, since even in secular business there is no human activity which can be withdrawn from God's dominion. In our own time, however, it is most urgent that this distinction and also this harmony should shine forth more clearly than ever in the lives of the faithful, so that the mission of the Church may correspond more fully to the special conditions of the world today. For just as it must be admitted that the temporal sphere is governed by its own principles, since it is rightly concerned with the interests of this world, so also that unfortunate doctrine that attempts to build a society with no regard whatever for religion, and which attacks and destroys the religious liberty of its citizens, is rightly to be rejected.

37) The laity have the right, as do all Christians, to receive in abundance from their pastors the spiritual goods of the Church, especially the assistance of the word of God and of the sacraments. They should openly reveal to them their needs and desires with that freedom and confidence which is fitting for children of God and brothers in Christ. They are, by reason of the knowledge, competence or outstanding ability they may enjoy, permitted and sometimes even obliged to express their opinion on those things that concern the good of the Church. When occasions arise, let this be done through the organs erected by the Church for this purpose. Let it always be done in truth, in courage and in prudence, with reverence and charity toward those who by reason of their sacred office represent the person of Christ.

The laity should, as should all Christians, promptly accept in Christian obedience the decisions of their pastors, since they are representatives of Christ as well as teachers and rulers in the Church. Let them follow the example of Christ, who by His obedience even unto death, opened to all men the blessed way of the liberty of the children of God. Nor should they omit to pray for those placed over them, for they keep watch as having to render an account of their souls, so that they may do this with joy and not with grief (cf. Heb. 13: 17).

Let pastors recognize and promote the dignity as well as the responsibility of the laity in the Church. Let them willingly employ their prudent advice. Let them confidently assign duties to them in the service of the Church, allowing them freedom and room for action. Further, let pastors encourage lay people so that they may undertake tasks on their own initiative. Attentively in Christ, let them consider with fatherly love the projects, suggestions and desires proposed by the laity. However, let pastors respectfully acknowledge that just freedom which belongs to everyone in this earthly city.

A great many good things are to be hoped for from this familiar dialogue between the laity and their pastors: in the laity a strengthened sense of personal responsibility; a renewed enthusiasm; a more ready application of their talents to the projects of their pastors. The latter, on the other hand, aided by the experience of the laity, can more clearly and more aptly come to decisions regarding both spiritual and temporal matters. In this way, the whole Church strengthened by each one of its members, may more effectively fulfill its mission for the life of the world.

38) Each individual layman ought to stand before the world as a witness to the resurrection and life of the Lord Jesus and as a symbol of the living God. All the laity as a community and each one according to his ability must nourish the world with the fruits of the Spirit (cf. Gal. 5: 22). They must diffuse in the world that spirit which raises up the poor, the meek, the peace makers—those whom the Lord in the Gospel proclaimed blessed (cf. Mt. 5: 3-9). In a word, "as the soul is in the body, so let this spirit be in the Christian world" (9).

5. *The Universal Call to Holiness in the Church*

39) The Church, whose mystery is being set forth by this sacred synod, is believed to be indefectibly holy. Indeed Christ, the Son of God, who with the Father and the Spirit is praised as "uniquely holy," loved the Church as His bride, delivering Himself up for her that He might sanctify her (cf. Eph. 5, 25-26). He united her to Himself as His own body and enriched her with the gift of the Holy Spirit for God's glory. Therefore in the Church, everyone whether belonging to the hierarchy or being cared for by it, is called to holiness, according to the saying of the Apostle: "For this is the will of God, your sanctification" (I Thess. 4, 3; Eph. 1, 4). However, this holiness of the Church is unceasingly manifested, and must be manifested, in the fruits of grace that the Spirit produces in the faithful; it is expressed in many ways in individuals, who in their walk of life, tend toward the perfection of charity, thus causing the edification of others; in a very special way this (holiness) appears in the practice of the counsels, customarily called "evangelical." This practice of the counsels, under the impulse of the Holy Spirit, undertaken by many Christians, either privately or in a Church-approved condition or state of life, gives and should give in the world an outstanding witness and example of this same holiness.

40) The Lord Jesus, the divine Teacher and Model of all perfection, preached holiness of life to each and every one of His disciples of every condition. He Himself stands as the author and consummator of this holiness of life: "You therefore are the perfect, even as your heavenly Father is perfect" (Mt. 5, 48). Indeed He sent the Holy Spirit upon all men that He might move them inwardly to love God with their whole heart and their whole soul, with all their mind and all their strength (cf. Mk. 12, 30) and that they might love each other as Christ loves them (cf. Jn. 13, 34; 15, 12). The followers of Christ are called by God, not because of their works, but according to His own purpose and grace. They are justified in the Lord Jesus, because in the baptism of faith

they truly become sons of God and sharers in the divine nature and in this way are really made holy. Then too, by God's gift, they must hold on to and complete in their lives this holiness they have received. They are warned by the Apostle to live "as becomes saints" (Eph. 5, 3), and to put on "as God's chosen ones, holy and beloved, a heart of mercy, kindness, humility, meekness, patience" (Col. 3, 12), and to possess the fruit of the Spirit in holiness (cf. Gal. 5, 22; Rom. 6, 22). Since truly we all offend in many things (cf. Jam. 3, 2) we all need God's mercies continually and we all must daily pray: "Forgive us our debts" (Mt. 6, 12).

Thus it is evident to everyone, that all the faithful of Christ of whatever rank or status, are called to the fulness of the Christian life and to the perfection of charity; by this holiness a more human manner of living is promoted in this earthly society also. In order to reach this perfection the faithful must use their strength according to the measure they have received it, as a gift from Christ. They must follow in His footsteps and conform themselves to His image seeking the will of the Father in all things. They must devote themselves with all their being to the glory of God and the service of their neighbor. In this way, the holiness of the people of God will grow into an abundant harvest of good, as is admirably shown by the life of so many saints in the history of the Church.

41) In the various classes and differing duties of life, one and the same holiness is cultivated by all, who are moved by the Spirit of God, and who obey the voice of the Father and worship God the Father in spirit and in truth and follow Christ, poor humble and cross-bearing in order to be worthy of being sharers in His glory. Every person must walk unhesitatingly according to his own personal gifts and duties in the path of living faith, which arouses hope and works through charity.

In the first place, the shepherds of Christ's flock ought to carry out their ministry holily and eagerly, humbly and courageously in imitation of the eternal High Priest, the Shepherd and Guardian of our souls. If they fulfill this duty in this way it will be the principal means of their sanctification. Those chosen for the fulness of the priesthood are granted the ability by sacramental grace of exercising the perfect duty of pastoral charity in every form of episcopal care and service, be it prayer, sacrifice or preaching. Let them not fear to lay down their lives for their sheep, and let them promote greater holiness in the Church by their daily example—a pattern to their flock (I Pet. 5, 3).

Priests, who resemble the order of bishops form the spiritual crown of the bishops. They participate in the grace of their office through Christ, the eternal and unique mediator, and they should grow daily in their love of God and their neighbor by the exercise of their office through Christ, the eternal and unique Mediator. They should preserve the bond of priestly communion, and they should abound in every spiritual good and thus present to all men a living witness to God. All this they should do in emulation of those priests who often, down through the course of the centuries, left an outstanding example of the holiness in humble and hidden service. Their praise lives on in the Church of God. By their very office of praying and offering sacrifice for their own people and the entire people of God, keeping in mind what they are doing and imitating what they are handling, these priests, in their apostolic labors, rather than being ensnared by perils and hardships, should rather rise to greater holiness through these perils and hardships. They should ever nourish and strengthen their action from an abundance of contemplation, doing all this for the advantage of the entire Church of God. All priests, and especially those who are called "diocesan priests," due to the special title of their ordination, should keep continually before their minds the fact that their faithful loyalty toward and their generous cooperation with their bishop is of the greatest value in their growth in holiness.

Ministers of lesser rank are also sharers in the mission and grace of the Supreme Priest in a special way. In the first place among these ministers are deacons, who, in as much as they are dispensers of Christ's mysteries and servants of the Church, should keep themselves free from every vice and stand before men as personifications of goodness and friends of God (cf. I Tim. 3, 8-10 and 12-13). Clerics, who are called by the Lord and are set aside as His portion in order to prepare themselves for the various ministerial offices under the watchful eye of pastors, are bound to bring their hearts and minds into accord with this special election. They will accomplish this by their constancy in prayer, by their burning love, and by their recollection of whatever is true, just and of good repute, doing all things for the glory and honor of God. Besides these already named, there are also lay-folk, chosen of God and called by the bishop to give themselves completely to apostolic labors, working the Lord's field with much success.

Furthermore, Christian married couples and parents should follow their own proper path by faithful love. They should sustain one another in grace throughout the entire length of their lives. They should imbue their offspring, lovingly welcomed as God's gift, with Christian doctrine and the evangelical virtues. In this manner, they offer all men the example of unwearying and generous love; in this way they build up the brotherhood of charity; in so doing, they stand as the witnesses and cooperators in the fruitfulness of Holy Mother Church; by such lives, they are a sign and a participation in that very love, with which Christ loved His Bride and for which he delivered Himself up for her. A like example, but one given in a different way, is that offered by widows and single people, who are able to make great contributions toward holiness and apostolic endeavor in the Church. Finally, those who engage in labor—and frequently it is of a heavy nature—should better themselves by their human labors. They should be of aid to their fellow citizens. They should raise all of society, and even creation itself, to a better mode of existence. Indeed, they should imitate by their lively charity, in their joyous hope and by bearing one another's burdens, the very Christ who plied his hands with carpenter's tools and who in union with His Father, is continually working for the salvation of all men. In this, then, their daily work, they should climb even to the heights of holiness and apostolic activity.

May all those who are weighed down with poverty, infirmity and sickness, as well as those who must bear various hardships or who suffer persecution for justice sake—may they all know they are united with the suffering Christ in a special way for the salvation of the world. The Lord called them blessed in His Gospel and they are those whom "the God of all graces, who has called us unto His eternal glory in Christ Jesus, will Himself, after we have suffered a little while, perfect, strengthen and establish" (1 Pet. 5: 10).

Finally all Christ's faithful, whatever be the conditions, duties and circumstances of their lives and by means of all these things will daily increase in holiness, if they receive all things with faith from the hand of their heavenly Father and if they cooperate with the divine will. In this temporal service, they will manifest to all men the love with which God loved the world.

42) "God is love, and he who abides in love, abides in God, and God in Him" (I Jn. 4: 16). But, God pours out his love into our hearts through the Holy Spirit, who has been given to us (cf. Rom. 5: 5); thus the first and most necessary gift is love, by which we love God above all things and our neighbor because of God. Indeed, in order that love, as good seed may grow and bring forth fruit in the soul, each one of the faithful must willingly hear the Word of God and fulfill His Will, and must complete what God has begun by his own actions with the help of God's grace, by the use of the sacraments and in a special way the Eucharist, frequent participation in the sacred action of the liturgy, by application to prayer, self-abnegation, lively fraternal service and the constant exercise of all the virtues. For charity, as the bond of perfection and the fulfilling of the law, rules over all the means of attaining holiness and gives life to these same means. It is charity that guides us to our final end. It is the love of God and the love of one's neighbor that points out the true disciple of Christ.

Since Jesus, the Son of God, manifested His charity by laying down His life for us, so too no one has greater love than he who lays down his life for

Christ and His brothers (cf. I Jn. 3: 16; Jn. 15: 13). From the earliest times, then, some Christians have been called upon—and some will always be called upon—to give the supreme testimony of this love to all men, but especially to persecutors. By martyrdom a disciple is transformed into an image of his Master by freely accepting death for the salvation of the world—as well as his conformity to Christ in the shedding of his blood. The Church, then, considers martyrdom as an exceptional gift and as the fullest proof of love. Though few are presented such an opportunity, nevertheless all must be prepared to confess Christ before men in the midst of persecutions, which will never be lacking to the Church, to follow Him on the way of the cross.

Likewise, the holiness of the Church is fostered in a special way by the observance of the counsels proposed in the Gospel by Our Lord to His disciples. An eminent position among these is held by virginity or the celibate state (cf. I Cor. 7: 32-34). This is a precious gift of divine grace given by the Father to certain souls (Mt. 19: 11;I Cor. 7: 7), whereby they may devote themselves to God alone the more easily, due to an undivided heart. This perfect continency, for the sake of the kingdom of heaven, has always been held in particular honor in the Church as a sign and an incentive to charity, and as a special source of spiritual fecundity in the world.

The Church continually keeps before it the admonition of the Apostle that moved the faithful to charity, exhorting them to experience personally what was in Christ Jesus who "emptied Himself, taking the nature of a slave . . . becoming obedient to death" (Phil. 2: 7-8), and for our sakes "being rich, he became poor" (II Cor. 8: 9). Because the disciples must always offer an imitation of, and a testimony to, the charity and humility of Christ, Mother Church rejoices at finding within her bosom men and women who more closely follow and more clearly demonstrate the self-emptying of their Savior who, in their freedom as sons of God, take upon themselves the state of poverty, renounce their own wills and become subject of their own accord to another human for the love of God in the matter of perfection beyond the measure of the commandments, in order to be more fully like the obedient Christ.

Therefore, all the faithful of Christ are invited to strive for the holiness and perfection of their own proper state. Indeed they have an obligation to so strive. Let all then have care that they guide aright their own deepest sentiments of soul. Let neither the use of the things of this world nor attachment to riches, which is against the spirit of evangelical poverty, hinder them in their quest for perfect love. Let them heed the admonition of the Apostle to those who use this world; let them not rely on it, for this world, as we see it, is passing away (cf. I Cor. 7: 31ff).

6. *Religious*

43) The evangelical counsels of chastity dedicated to God, of poverty and of obedience are based upon the words and examples of the Lord. They were further commended by the apostles and Fathers of the Church, as well as by the learned doctors and pastors of souls. The counsels are a divine gift, which the Church received from its Lord and which it will always observe with the help of His grace. Church authority has taken care under the inspiration of the Holy Spirit, to interpret these evangelical counsels,

to regulate their practice and finally to build on them stable forms of living. Thus it has come about, that, as if on a tree which has grown in the field of the Lord, various forms of solitary and community life, as well as various religious families have branched out in a marvelous and multiple way from this divinely given seed. Such a multiple and miraculous growth augments both the progress of the members of these various religious families themselves and the welfare of the entire Body of Christ. These religious families give their members the support of a more firm stability in their way of life and a proven doctrine of acquiring perfection. They further offer their members the support of fraternal association in the militia of Christ and of liberty strengthened by obedience. Thus these religious are able to fulfill tranquilly and observe faithfully their religious profession and so spiritually rejoicing make progress on the road of charity.

From the point of view of the divine and hierarchical structure of the Church, the religious state of life is not an intermediate state between the clerical and lay states. But, rather, the faithful of Christ are called by God from both these states of life so that they might enjoy this particular gift in the life of the Church and thus each in one's own way, may be of some advantage to the salvific mission of the Church.

44) The faithful of Christ bind themselves to the three aforesaid counsels either by vows, or by other sacred bonds, which are like vows in their purpose. By such a bond, a person is totally dedicated to God, loved beyond all things. In this way, that person is referred to the honor and service of God under a new and special title. Indeed through Baptism a person dies to sin and is consecrated to God. How-

ever, in order that he may be capable of deriving more abundant fruit from this baptismal grace, he intends, by the profession of the evangelical counsels in the Church, to free himself from those obstacles, which might draw him away from the fervor of charity and the perfection of divine worship. By his profession of the evangelical counsels, then, he is more intimately consecrated to divine service. This consecration will be the more perfect, in as much as the indissoluble bond of the union of Christ and His bride, the Church, is represented by firm and more stable bonds.

Since the evangelical counsels which lead to charity join their followers to the Church and its mystery in a special way, the spiritual life of these people should then be devoted to the welfare of the whole Church. From this arises their duty of working to implant and strengthen the Kingdom of Christ in souls and to extend that Kingdom to every clime, to the extent of their capacities and in keeping with the proper type of their own vocation, through prayer or active works of the apostolate. It is for this reason that the Church preserves and fosters the special character of her various religious institutes.

The profession of the evangelical counsels, then, appears as a sign that can and ought to attract all the members of the Church to an effective and prompt fulfillment of the duties of their Christian vocation. Since the people of God have no lasting city here below, but look forward to one that is to come, the religious state, whose purpose is to free its members from earthly cares, more fully manifests to all believers the presence of heavenly goods already possessed here below. Furthermore, it not only witnesses to the fact of a new and eternal life acquired by the redemption of Christ, but it foretells the future

resurrection and the glory of the heavenly kingdom. The form of life which the Son of God accepted in entering this world to do the will of the Father and which He proposed to the disciples following him, this same state of life is accurately exemplified and perpetually made present in the Church. The religious state clearly manifests that the Kingdom of God and its needs, in a very special way, are raised above all earthly considerations. Finally it clearly shows all men both the unsurpassed breadth of the strength of Christ the King and the infinite power of the Holy Spirit marvelously working in the Church.

Thus, the state which is constituted by the profession of the evangelical counsels, though it is not the hierarchical structure of the Church, nevertheless, undeniably belongs to its life and holiness.

45) It is the duty of the ecclesiastical hierarchy to shepherd the people of God and lead them to abundant pastures; it should wisely regulate by law the practice of the evangelical counsels which fosters the perfection of love of God and love of neighbor in an outstanding manner. Furthermore, the hierarchy, following with docility the prompting of the Holy Spirit, accepts the rules presented by outstanding men and women and authentically approves these rules after further necessary adjustments. It also aids by its vigilant and safeguarding authority those institutes variously established for the building up of Christ's Body in order that these same institutes may grow and flourish according to the spirit of the founders. In order to more fully provide for the necessities of the entire flock of the Lord, any institute of perfection and its individual members may be removed from the jurisdiction of the local Ordinaries by the Supreme

Pontiff and subjected to himself alone. This is done in virtue of his primacy over the entire Church and in consideration of the common good. In like manner, these institutes may be freed from or committed to the charge of the proper patriarchical authority. The members of these institutes, in fulfilling their obligation to the Church due to their particular form of life, ought to show reverence and obedience to bishops according to the sacred canons. The bishops are owed this respect because of their pastoral authority in their own churches and because of the need of unity and harmony in the apostolate.

The Church not only raises the religious profession to the dignity of a canonical state by her approval, but even manifests that this profession is a state consecrated to God by the liturgical setting of that profession. The Church itself, by the authority given to it by God, accepts the vows of the newly professed. It begs aid and grace from God for them by its public prayer. It commends them to God, imparts a spiritual blessing on them and accompanies their self-offering by the Eucharistic sacrifice.

46) Religious should carefully keep before their minds the fact that the Church presents Christ to believers and non-believers alike in a striking manner daily through them. The Church thus portrays Christ in contemplation on the mountain, in His proclamation of the kingdom of God to the multitudes, in His healing of the sick and maimed, in His work of converting sinners to a better life, in His blessing of children and His goodness to all men, always obedient to the will of the Father who sent Him.

All men should take note that the profession of the evangelical counsels, though entailing the renunciation of certain values that are to be un-doubtedly esteemed, does not detract from a genuine development of human persons, but rather by its very nature is most beneficial to that development. Indeed the counsels, voluntarily undertaken according to each one's personal vocation, contribute a great deal to the purification of heart and spiritual liberty. They continually stir up the fervor of charity. But especially they are able more fully to mold the Christian man to that type of virginal and detached life, which Christ the Lord chose for Himself and which His Mother also embraced. This is clearly proven by the example of so many holy founders. Let no one think that religious have become strangers to their fellowmen or useless citizens of this earthly city by their consecration. For even though it sometimes happens that religious do not directly mingle with their contemporaries, yet in a more profound sense these same religious are united with them in the heart of Christ and spiritually cooperate with them. In this way the building up of the earthly city may have its foundation in the Lord and may tend toward Him, lest perhaps those who build this city shall have labored in vain.

Finally, this sacred Council encourages and praises the men and women, Brothers and Sisters, who in monasteries, or in schools and hospitals, or in the missions, adorn the Bride of Christ by their unswerving and humble faithfulness in their chosen consecration.

47) Let each of the faithful, therefore, carefully see to it that he persevere and ever grow in whatever vocation God has given him. Let him do this for the increased holiness of the Church, for the greater glory of the one and undivided Trinity, which in and through Christ is the font and the source of all holiness.

7. *Eschatological Nature of the Pilgrim Church and its Union with the Church in Heaven*

48) The Church, to which we are all called in Christ Jesus, and in which we acquire sanctity through the grace of God, will attain its full perfection only in the glory of heaven, when there will come the time of the restoration of all things (Acts 3, 21). At that time the human race as well as the entire world, which is intimately related to man and attains to its end through him, will be perfectly reestablished in Christ (Eph. 1, 10; Col. 1, 20; II Pet. 3, 10-13).

Christ, having been lifted up from the earth has drawn all to Himself (Jn. 12, 32). Rising from the dead (Rom. 6, 9) He sent His lifegiving Spirit upon His disciples and through Him has established His Body which is the Church as the universal sacrament of salvation. Sitting at the right hand of the Father He is continually active in the world that He might lead men to the Church and through it join them to Himself and that He might make them partakers of His glorious life by nourishing them with His own Body and Blood. Therefore the promised restoration that we are awaiting has already begun in Christ, is carried forward in the mission of the Holy Spirit and through Him continues in the Church in which we learn the meaning of our terrestrial life through our faith, while we perform with hope in the future the work committed to us in this world by the Father, and thus work out our salvation (Phil. 2, 12).

Already the final age of the world has come upon us (I Cor. 10, 11) and the renovation of the world is irrevocably decreed and is already anticipated in some kind of a real way; for the Church already on this earth is signed with a sanctity which is real although imperfect. However, until there shall be new heavens and a new earth in which justice dwells, the pilgrim Church in her sacraments and institutions, which pertain to this present time, has the appearance of this world that is passing and she herself dwells among creatures who groan and travail in pain until now and await the revelation of the sons of God (Rom. 8, 22 and 19).

Joined with Christ in the Church and signed with the Holy Spirit "who is the pledge of our inheritance" (Eph. 1, 14), truly we are called and we are sons of God (I Jo. 3, 1) but we have not yet appeared with Christ in glory (Col. 3, 4), in which we shall be like to God, since we shall see Him as He is (I Jo. 3, 2). And therefore "while we are in the body, we are exiled from the Lord (II Cor. 5, 6) and having the first-fruits of the Spirit we groan within ourselves (Rom. 8, 23) and we desire to be with Christ" (Phil. 1, 23). By that same charity however, we are urged to live more for Him, who died for us and rose again (II Cor. 5, 15). We strive therefore to please God in all things (II Cor. 5, 9) and we put on the armor of God, that we may be able to stand against the wiles of the devil and resist in the evil day (Eph. 6, 11-13). Since however we know not the day nor the hour, on Our Lord's advice we must be constantly vigilant so that, having finished the single course of our earthly life, we may merit to enter into the marriage feast with Him (Mt. 25, 1-13) and to be numbered among the blessed (Mt. 25, 31-46) and that we may not be ordered to go into eternal fire (Mt. 25, 41) like the wicked and slothful servant (Mt. 25, 26), into the exterior darkness where "there will be the weeping and the gnashing of teeth" (Mt. 22, 13 and 25, 30). For before we reign with Christ in glory, all of us will be made manifest "before the tribunal of Christ, so that each one may receive what he has won through the body, according to his works, whether good or evil" (II Cor. 5, 10) and at the end of the world "those who have done good shall come forth unto resurrection of judgment" (Jo. 5, 29; 25, 46). Reckoning therefore that "the sufferings of the present time are not worthy to be compared with the glory to come that will be revealed in us" (Rom. 8, 18; 2 Tim. 2, 11-12), strong in faith we look for the "blessed hope and the glorious coming of our great God and Saviour, Jesus Christ" (Tit. 2, 13) "who will refashion the body of our lowliness, conforming it to the body of His glory (Phil. 3, 21) and who will come "to be glorified in His saints and to be marveled at in all those who have believed" (2 Thess. 1, 10).

49) Until the Lord shall come in His majesty, and all the angels with Him (Mt. 25, 31) and death being destroyed, all things are subject to Him (I Cor. 15, 26-27), some of His disciples are exiles on earth, some having died are being purified, and others are in glory beholding "clearly God Himself triune and one, as He is"; but all in various ways and degrees are in communion in the same charity of God and neighbor and all sing the same hymn of glory to our God. For all who are in Christ, having His Spirit, form one Church and cleave together in Him (Eph. 4, 16). Therefore the union of the wayfarers with the brethren who have gone to sleep in the peace of Christ is not in the least interrupted, but on the contrary, according to the perennial faith of the Church, is strengthened by a communication of spiritual goods. For because those in heaven are more closely united with Christ, they establish the whole Church more firmly in holiness, lend nobility to the worship which the Church offers to God here on earth and in many ways

contribute to its greater edification (I Cor. 12, 12-27). For after they have been received into their heavenly home and are present to the Lord (II Cor. 5, 8), through Him and with Him and in Him they do not cease to intercede with the Father for us, showing forth the merits they won on earth through the one Mediator between God and man (I Tim. 2, 5), serving God in all things and filling up in their flesh those things which are lacking of the sufferings of Christ for His Body which is the Church (Col. 1, 24). Thus by their brotherly interest our weakness is greatly strengthened.

50) Fully conscious of this communion of the whole Mystical Body of Jesus Christ, the pilgrim Church from the very first ages of the Christian religion has cultivated with great piety the memory of the dead, and "because it is a holy and wholesome thought to pray for the dead that they may be loosed from their sins" (II Mach. 12, 46), also offers suffrages for them. The Church has always believed that the apostles and Christ's martyrs who had given the supreme witness of faith and charity by the shedding of their blood, are closely joined with us in Christ, and she has always venerated them with special devotion, together with the Blessed Virgin Mary and the holy angels. The Church has piously implored the aid of their intercession To these were soon added also those who had more closely imitated Christ's virginity and poverty, and finally others whom the outstanding practice of the Christian virtues and the divine charisms recommended to the pious devotion and imitation of the faithful.

When we look at the lives of those who have faithfully followed Christ, we are inspired with a new reason for seeking the City that is to come (Heb. 13, 14; 11, 10) and at the same time we are shown a most safe path by which among the vicissitudes of this world, in keeping with the state in life and condition proper to each of us, we will be able to arrive at perfect union with Christ, that is, perfect holiness. In the lives of those who, sharing in our humanity, are however more perfectly transformed into the image of Christ, God vividly manifests His presence and His face to men. He speaks to us in them, and gives us a sign of His Kingdom, to which we are strongly drawn, having so great a cloud of witnesses over us (Heb. 12, 1) and such a witness to the truth of the Gospel.

Nor is it by the title of example only that we cherish the memory of those in heaven, but still more in order that the union of the whole Church may be strengthened in the Spirit by the practice of fraternal charity (Eph. 4, 1-6). For just as Christian communion among way-farers brings us closer to Christ, so our companionship with the saints joins us to Christ, from whom as from its Fountain and Head issues every grace and the very life of the people of God. It is supremely fitting, therefore, that we love those friends and coheirs of Jesus Christ, who are also our brothers and extraordinary benefactors, that we render due thanks to God for them and "suppliantly invoke them and have recourse to their prayers, their power and help in obtaining benefits from God through His Son, Jesus Christ, who is our Redeemer and Saviour." For every genuine testimony of love shown by us to those in heaven, by its very nature tends toward and terminates in Christ who is the "crown of all saints," and through Him, in God Who is wonderful in His Saints and is magnified in them.

Our union with the Church in heaven is put into effect in its noblest manner especially in the sacred Liturgy, wherein the power of the Holy Spirit acts upon us through sacramental signs.

Then, with combined rejoicing we celebrate together the praise of the divine majesty; then all those from every tribe and tongue and people and nation (Apoc. 5, 9) who have been redeemed by the blood of Christ and gathered together into one Church, with one song of praise magnify the one and triune God. Celebrating the Eucharistic sacrifice therefore, we are most closely united to the Church in heaven in communion with and venerating the memory first of all of the glorious ever-Virgin Mary, of Blessed Joseph and the blessed apostles and martyrs and of all the saints.

51) This Sacred Council accepts with great devotion this venerable faith of our ancestors regarding this vital fellowship with our brethren who are in heavenly glory or who having died are still being purified; and it proposes again the decrees of the Second Council of Nicea, the Council of Florence and the Council of Trent. And at the same time, in conformity with our own pastoral care, we urge all concerned, if any abuses, excesses or defects have crept in here or there, to do what is in their power to remove or correct them, and to restore all things to a fuller praise of Christ and of God. Let them therefore teach the faithful that the authentic cult of the saints consists not so much in the multiplying of external acts, but rather in the greater intensity of our love, whereby, for our own greater good and that of the whole Church, we seek from the saints "example in their way of life, fellowship in their communion, and aid by their intercession." On the other hand, let them teach the faithful that our communion with those in heaven, provided that it is understood in the fuller light of faith, in no way weakens, but conversely, more thoroughly enriches the worship of adoration we give to God the Father, through Christ, in the Spirit.

PART 2. *The Church and the Contemporary Scene*   553

For all of us, who are sons of God and constitute one family in Christ (Heb. 3, 6), as long as we remain in communion with one another in mutual charity and in one praise of the most holy Trinity, are corresponding with the intimate vocation of the Church and partaking in foretaste the liturgy of consummate glory. For when Christ shall appear and the glorious resurrection of the dead will take place, the glory of God will light up the heavenly City and the Lamb will be the lamp thereof (Apoc. 21, 24). Then the whole Church of the saints in the supreme happiness of charity will adore God and "the Lamb who was slain" (Apoc. 5, 12), proclaiming with one voice: "To Him who sits upon the throne, and to the Lamb blessing, and honor, and glory, and dominion forever and ever" (Apoc. 5, 13-14).

8. *The Blessed Virgin Mary, Mother of God, in the Mystery of Christ and the Church*

I. INTRODUCTION

52) Wishing in His supreme goodness and wisdom to effect the redemption of the world, "when the fulness of time came, God sent His Son, born of a woman, . . . that we might receive the adoption of sons" (Gal. 4, 4).

"He for us men, and for our salvation, came down from heaven, and was incarnate by the Holy Spirit from the Virgin Mary." This divine mystery of salvation is revealed to us and continued in the Church which the Lord established as His Body. Joined to Christ the Head and in the unity of fellowship with all His saints, the faithful must in the first place reverence the memory "of the glorious ever Virgin Mary, Mother of our God and Lord Jesus Christ" (Gal. 4, 4-5).

53) The Virgin Mary, who at the message of the angel received the Word of God in her heart and in her body and gave Life to the world, is acknowledged and honored as being truly the Mother of God and Mother of the Redeemer. Redeemed in a more sublime manner by reason of the merits of her Son and united to Him by a close and indissoluble tie, she is endowed with the high office and dignity of being the Mother of the Son of God, by which account she is also the beloved daughter of the Father and the temple of the Holy Spirit. Because of this gift of sublime grace she far surpasses all creatures, both in heaven and on earth. At the same time, however, because she belongs to the offspring of Adam she is one with all those who are to be saved. She is "the mother of the members of Christ . . . having cooperated by charity that faithful might be born in the Church, who are members of that Head." Wherefore she is hailed as a pre-eminent and singular member of the Church, and as its type and excellent exemplar in faith and charity. The Catholic Church, taught by the Holy Spirit honors her with filial affection and piety as a most beloved mother.

54) Wherefore this Sacred Council, in expounding the doctrine on the Church, in which the divine Redeemer works salvation, intends to describe with diligence both the role of the Blessed Virgin in the mystery of the Incarnate Word and the Mystical Body, and the duties of redeemed mankind toward the Mother of God, who is mother of Christ and mother of men, particularly of the faithful. It does not, however, have it in mind to give a complete doctrine on Mary, nor does it wish to decide those questions which the work of theologians has not yet fully clarified. Those opinions therefore may be lawfully retained that are propounded in Catholic schools concerning her, who occupies a place in

the Church which is the highest after Christ and yet very close to us.

II. THE ROLE OF THE BLESSED MOTHER IN THE ECONOMY OF SALVATION

55) The Sacred Scriptures of both the Old and the New Testament, as well as venerable Tradition show the role of the Mother of the Savior in the economy of salvation in an ever clearer light and draw attention to it. The books of the Old Testament describe the history of salvation, by which the coming of Christ into the world was slowly prepared. These earliest documents, as they are read in the Church and are understood in the light of a further and full revelation, bring the figure of the woman, Mother of the Redeemer, into a gradually clearer light. When it is looked at in this way, she is already prophetically foreshadowed in the promise of victory over the serpent which was given to our first parents after their fall into sin (cf. Gen. 3, 15). Likewise she is the Virgin who shall conceive and bear a son, whose name will be called Emmanuel (cf. Is. 8, 14; Mich. 5, 2-3; Mt. 1, 22-23). She stands out among the poor and humble of the Lord, who confidently hope for and receive salvation from Him. With her the exalted Daughter of Sion, and after a long expectation of the promise, the times are fulfilled and the new Economy established, when the Son of God took a human nature from her, that He might in the mysteries of His flesh free man from sin.

56) The Father of mercies willed that the incarnation should be preceded by the acceptance of her who was predestined to be the mother of His Son, so that just as a woman contributed to death, so also a woman should contribute to life. That is true in outstanding fashion of the mother of Jesus, who gave to the world Him who is Life itself and who renews all things, and who was enriched by God with the gifts that befit such a role. It is no wonder therefore that the usage prevailed among the Fathers whereby they called the mother of God entirely holy and free from all stain of sin, as though fashioned by the Holy Spirit and formed as a new creature. Adorned from the first instant of her conception with the radiance of an entirely unique holiness, the Virgin of Nazareth is greeted, on God's command, by an angel messenger as "full of grace" (Lk. 1, 28), and to the heavenly messenger she replies: "Behold the handmaid of the Lord, be it done unto me according to thy word" (Lk. 1, 38). Thus Mary, a daughter of Adam, consenting to the divine Word, became the mother of Jesus. Embracing God's salvific will with a full heart and impeded by no sin, she devoted herself totally as a handmaid of the Lord to the person and work of her Son, under Him and with Him, by the grace of almighty God, serving the mystery of redemption. Rightly therefore the holy Fathers see her as used by God not merely in a passive way, but as freely cooperating in the work of human salvation through faith and obedience. For, as St. Irenaeus says, she "being obedient, became the cause of salvation for herself and for the whole human race." Hence not a few of the early Fathers gladly assert in their preaching: "The knot of Eve's disobedience was untied by Mary's obedience: what the virgin Eve bound through her unbelief, Mary loosened by her faith." Comparing Mary with Eve, they call her "the Mother of the living," and still more often they say: "death through Eve, life through Mary."

57) This union of the Mother with the Son in the work of salvation is made manifest from the time of Christ's virginal conception up to His death. It is shown first of all when

Mary, arising in haste to go to visit Elizabeth, is greeted by her as blessed because of her belief in the promise of salvation and the precursor leaped with joy in the womb of his mother (cf. Lk. 1, 41-45). This union is manifest also at the birth of Our Lord, who did not diminish His mother's virginal integrity but sanctified it, when the Mother of God joyfully showed her firstborn Son to the shepherds and Magi. When she presented Him to the Lord in the temple, making the offering of the poor, she heard Simeon foretelling at the same time that her son would be a sign of contradiction and that a sword would pierce the mother's soul, that out of many hearts thoughts might be revealed (cf. Lk. 2, 34-35). When the Child Jesus was lost and they had sought Him sorrowing, His parents found Him in the temple, taken up with the things that were His Father's business; and they did not understand the word of their Son. His Mother, however, kept these things to be pondered over in her heart (cf. Lk. 2, 41-45).

58) In the public life of Jesus, Mary makes significant appearances. This is so even at the very beginning, when at the marriage feast of Cana, moved with pity, she brought about by her intercession the beginning of miracles of Jesus the Messiah (cf. Jn. 2, 1-11). In the course of her Son's preaching she received the words whereby, in extolling a kingdom beyond the calculations and bonds of flesh and blood, He declared blessed (cf. Mk. 3, 35; Lk. 11, 27-28) those who heard and kept the word of God, as she was faithfully doing (cf. Lk. 2, 19-51). After this manner, the Blessed Virgin advanced in her pilgrimage of faith, and faithfully persevered in her union with her Son unto the cross, where she stood, in keeping with the divine plan (cf. Jn. 19, 25), grieving exceedingly with her only begotten Son, uniting herself with a maternal heart with His

sacrifice, and lovingly consenting to the immolation of this Victim which she herself had brought forth. Finally, she was given by the same Christ Jesus dying on the cross as a mother to His disciple, with these words: "Woman, behold thy son" (Jn. 19, 26-27).

59) But since it has pleased God not to manifest solemnly the mystery of the salvation of the human race before He would pour forth the Spirit promised by Christ, we see the apostles before the day of Pentecost "persevering with one mind in prayer with the women and Mary the Mother of Jesus, and with His brethren" (Acts 1, 14), and Mary by her prayers imploring the gift of the Spirit, who had already overshadowed her in the Annunciation. Finally, the Immaculate Virgin, preserved free from all guilt of original sin, on the completion of her earthly sojourn, was taken up body and soul into heavenly glory, and exalted by the Lord as Queen of the universe, that she might be the more fully conformed to her Son, the Lord of lords and the conqueror of sin and death.

III. ON THE BLESSED VIRGIN AND THE CHURCH

60) There is but one Mediator as we know from the words of the apostle, "for there is one God and one mediator of God and men, the man Christ Jesus, who gave himself a redemption for all" (1 Tim. 2, 5-6). The maternal duty of Mary toward men in no wise obscures or diminishes this unique mediation of Christ, but rather shows His power. For all the salvific influence of the Blessed Virgin on men originates, not from some inner necessity, but from divine pleasure and from the superabundance of the merits of Christ. It rests on His mediation, depends entirely on it and draws all its power from it. In no way does it impede, but rather does it foster the immediate union of the faithful with Christ.

61) Predestined from eternity to be the Mother of God by that decree of divine providence which determined the incarnation of the Word, the Blessed Virgin was on this earth the Virgin Mother of the Redeemer, and above all others and in a singular way the generous associate and humble handmaid of the Lord. She conceived, brought forth, and nourished Christ, she presented Him to the Father in the temple, and was united with Him by compassion as He died on the Cross. In this singular way she cooperated in the work of the Savior by her obedience, faith, hope and burning charity in giving back supernatural life to souls. Wherefore she is our mother in the order of grace.

62) This maternity of Mary in the economy of grace began with the consent she gave in faith at the Annunciation and sustained without wavering beneath the cross; it lasts until the eternal fulfillment of all the elect. Taken up to heaven, she did not lay aside this salvific duty, but by her constant intercession continued to bring us the gifts of eternal salvation. By her maternal charity, she cares for the brethren of her Son, who still journey on earth surrounded by dangers and difficulties, until they are led into the happiness of their true home. Therefore the Blessed Virgin is invoked by the Church under the titles of Advocate, Auxiliatrix, Adjutrix, and Mediatrix. This, however, is to be so understood that it neither takes away from nor adds anything to the dignity and efficaciousness of Christ the one Mediator.

For no creature could ever be counted as equal with the Incarnate Word and Redeemer. Just as the priesthood of Christ is shared in various ways both by the ministers and by the faithful, and as the one goodness of God is really communicated in different ways to His creatures, so also the unique mediation of the Redeemer does not exclude but rather gives rise to a manifold cooperation which is but a sharing in this one source.

The Church does not hesitate to profess this subordinate role of Mary. It knows it through unfailing experience of it and commends it to the hearts of the faithful, so that encouraged by this maternal help they may the more intimately adhere to the Mediator and Redeemer.

63) By reason of the gift and role of divine maternity, by which she is united with her Son, the Redeemer, and with His singular graces and functions, the Blessed Virgin is also intimately united with the Church. As St. Ambrose taught, the Mother of God is a type of the Church in the order of faith, charity and perfect union with Christ. For in the mystery of the Church, which is itself rightly called mother and virgin, the Blessed Virgin stands out in eminent and singular fashion as exemplar both of virgin and mother. By her belief and obedience, not knowing man but overshadowed by the Holy Spirit, as the new Eve she brought forth on earth the very Son of the Father, putting faith, not in the word of the ancient serpent, but unhesitatingly in that of God's messenger. The Son whom she brought forth is He whom God placed as the first-born among many brethren (cf. Rom. 3, 29), namely the faithful, in whose birth and education she cooperates with a maternal love.

64) The Church indeed, contemplating her hidden sanctity, imitating her charity and faithfully fulfilling the Father's will, by receiving the word of God in faith becomes herself a mother. By her preaching she brings forth to a new and immortal life the sons who are born to her in baptism, conceived of the Holy Spirit and born of God. She herself is a virgin, who keeps the faith given to her by her Spouse whole and entire. Imitating the mother of her Lord, and by the power of the Holy

Spirit, she keeps with virginal purity an entire faith, a firm hope and a sincere charity.

65) But while in the most holy Virgin the Church has already reached that perfection whereby she exists without spot or wrinkle, the followers of Christ still strive to increase in holiness by conquering sin (cf. Eph. 5, 27). And so they turn their eyes to Mary who shines forth to the whole community of the elect as the model of virtues. Piously meditating on her and contemplating her in the light of the Word made man, the Church with reverence enters more intimately into the great mystery of the Incarnation and becomes more and more like her Spouse. Since Mary takes a more intimate part in the history of salvation, she somehow unites and echoes the great dogmas of faith. When she is preached and venerated she calls the faithful to her Son and His sacrifice, and to love of the Father. Seeking after the glory of Christ, the Church becomes more like her exalted Type, and continually progresses in faith, hope and charity, seeking and doing the will of God in all things. Hence the Church in her apostolic work also, justly looks to her, who brought forth Christ, conceived of the Holy Spirit, born of the Virgin that through the Church He may be born and may increase in the hearts of the faithful also. The Virgin in her own life lived an example of that maternal love, by which it behooves that all should be animated who cooperate in the apostolic mission of the Church for the regeneration of men.

IV. THE CULT OF THE BLESSED VIRGIN IN THE CHURCH

66) Placed by the grace of God, as God's Mother, next to her Son, and exalted above all angels and men, Mary intervened in the mysteries of Christ and is justly honored by a special cult in the Church. Clearly from earliest times the Blessed Virgin is honored under the title of Mother of God, under whose protection the faithful took refuge in all their dangers and necessities. Hence after the Council of Ephesus the cult of the people of God toward Mary wonderfully increased in veneration and love, in invocation and imitation, according to her own prophetic words: "All generations shall call me blessed, because He that is mighty hath done great things to me" (Lk. 1, 48). This cult, as it always existed in the Church although it is altogether singular, differs essentially from the cult of adoration that is offered to the Incarnate Word, as well to the Father and the Holy Spirit, and it is most favorable to it. The various forms of piety toward the Mother of God, which the Church within the limits of sound and orthodox doctrine has approved, according to the conditions of time and place, and the nature and ingenuity of the faithful, bring it about that while the Mother is honored, the Son, through whom all things have their being (cf. Col. 1, 15-16) and in whom it has pleased the Father that all fulness should dwell (cf. Col. 1, 19), is rightly known, loved and glorified and all His commands are observed.

67) This most Sacred Council deliberately teaches this Catholic doctrine and at the same time admonishes all the sons of the Church that the cult, especially the liturgical cult, of the Blessed Virgin, be generously fostered, and the practices and exercises of piety, recommended by the magisterium of the Church toward her in the course of centuries be made of great moment, and those decrees, which have been given on previous occasions regarding the cult of images of Christ, the Blessed Virgin and the saints, be religiously observed. But it earnestly exhorts theologians and preachers of the divine word to abstain both from all false exaggerations as well as from a

too great narrowness of mind in considering the singular dignity of the Mother of God. Following the study of Sacred Scripture, the Holy Fathers, the doctors and liturgy of the Church, and under the guidance of the Church's magisterium, let them rightly illustrate the offices and privileges of the Blessed Virgin which always look to Christ, the source of all truth, sanctity and piety. Let them assiduously keep away from whatever, either by word or deed, could lead separated brethren or any other into error regarding the true doctrine of the Church. Let the faithful remember moreover that true devotion consists neither in sterile or transitory affection, nor in a certain vain credulity, but proceeds from true faith, by which we are led to know the excellence of the Mother of God, and we are moved to a filial love toward our mother and to the imitation of her virtues.

V. MARY, THE SIGN OF CREATED HOPE AND SOLACE TO THE WANDERING PEOPLE OF GOD.

68) In the interim the Mother of Jesus in the glory which she possesses body and soul in heaven, is the image and beginning of the Church as it is to be perfected in the world to come. Likewise she shines forth on earth, until the day of the Lord shall come (cf. II Pet. 3, 10), a sign of sure hope and solace to the wandering people of God.

69) It gives great joy and comfort to this holy and general Council that even among the separated brethren there are some who give due honor to the Mother of our Lord and Saviour, especially among the Orientals, who with devout mind and fervent impulse give honor to the Mother of God, ever virgin. Let the entire body of the faithful pours forth instant supplications to the Mother of God and Mother of men that she, who aided the beginnings of the Church by her prayers, may now, exalted as she is above all the angels and saints, intercede before her Son in the fellowship of all the saints, until all families of people, whether they are honored with the title of Christian or whether they still do not know the Saviour, may be happily gathered together in peace and harmony into one people of God, for the glory of the Most Holy and undivided Trinity.

C. DECREE ON ORIENTAL CHURCHES, 21 NOVEMBER 1964

PREAMBLE

1) The Catholic Church holds in high esteem the institutions, liturgical rites, ecclesiastical traditions and the established standards of the Christian life of the Eastern churches, for in them, distinguished as they are for their venerable antiquity, there remains conspicuous the tradition that has been handed down from the Apostles through the Fathers and that forms part of the divinely revealed and undivided heritage of the universal Church. This Sacred Ecumenical Council, therefore, in its care for the Eastern churches which bear living witness to this tradition, in order that they may flourish and with new apostolic vigor execute the task entrusted to them, has determined to lay down a number of principles, in addition to those which refer to the universal Church; all else is remitted to the care of the Eastern synods and of the Holy See.

2) The Holy Catholic Church, which is the Mystical Body of Christ is made up of the faithful who are organically united in the Holy Spirit by the same Faith, the same sacraments and the same government and who combining together into various groups

which are held together by a hierarchy, form separate churches or rites. Between these there exists an admirable bond of union, such that the variety within the Church in no way harms its unity; rather it manifests it, for it is the mind of the Catholic Church that each individual church or rite should retain its traditions whole and entire and likewise that it should adapt its way of life to the different needs of time and place.

3) These individual churches, whether of the East or the West, although they differ somewhat among themselves in rite (to use the current phrase), that is, in liturgy, ecclesiastical discipline, and spiritual heritage, are nevertheless, each as much as the others, entrusted to the pastoral government of the Roman Pontiff, the divinely appointed successor of St. Peter in supreme government over the universal Church. They are consequently of equal dignity, so that none of them is superior to the others as regard rite and they enjoy the same rights and are under the same obligations, also in respect of preaching the Gospel to the whole world (cf. Mark 16, 15) under the guidance of the Roman Pontiff.

4) Means should be taken therefore in every part of the world for the protection and advancement of all the individual churches and, to this end, there should be established parishes and a special hierarchy where the spiritual good of the faithful demands it. The Ordinaries of the different individual churches with jurisdiction in one and the same territory should, by taking common counsel in regular meetings, strive to promote unity of action and with common endeavor to sustain common tasks, so as better to further the good of religion and to safeguard more effectively the ordered way of life of the clergy.

All clerics and those aspiring to sacred orders should be instructed in the rites and especially in the principles that must be applied in interritual questions. The laity, too, should be taught as part of its catechetical education about rites and their rules.

Finally, each and every Catholic, as also the baptized of every non-Catholic church or denomination who enters into the fullness of the Catholic communion, must retain his own rite wherever he is, must cherish it and observe it, without prejudice to the right in special cases of persons, communities or areas, of recourse to the Apostolic See, which, as the supreme judge of interchurch relations, will, acting itself or through other authorities, meet the needs of the occasion in an ecumenical spirit, by the issuance of opportune directives, decrees or rescripts.

THE INDIVIDUAL CHURCHES OR RITES
PRESERVATION OF THE SPIRITUAL HERITAGE OF THE EASTERN CHURCHES

5) History, tradition and abundant ecclesiastical institutions bear outstanding witness to the great merit owing to the Eastern churches by the universal Church. The Sacred Council, therefore, not only accords to this ecclesiastical and spiritual heritage the high regard which is its due and rightful praise, but also unhesitatingly looks on it as the heritage of the universal Church. For this reason it solemnly declares that the churches of the East, as much as those of the West, have a full right and are in duty bound to rule themselves, each in accordance with its own established disciplines, since all these are praiseworthy from their venerable antiquity, more harmonious with the character of their faithful and more suited to the promotion of the good of souls.

6) All Eastern rite members should know and be convinced that they can and should always preserve their legitimate liturgical rite and their established way of life, and that these may not be

altered except to obtain for themselves an organic improvement. All these, then, must be observed by the Easterners themselves. Besides, they should attain to an ever greater knowledge and more exact use of them, and, if in their regard they have fallen short owing to contingencies of times and persons, they should take steps to return to their ancestral traditions.

Those who, by reason of their office or apostolic ministries, are in frequent communication with the Eastern churches or their faithful should be instructed according as their office demands in the knowledge and veneration of the rites, discipline, doctrine, history and character of the Easterners. To enhance the efficacy of their apostolate, congregations and associations of Latin rite working in Eastern countries or among Eastern faithful are earnestly counseled to found houses or even provinces of Eastern rite, as far as this can be done.

7) The patriarchate, as an institution, has existed in the Church from the earliest times and was recognized by the first ecumenical councils.

By the name Eastern patriarch, is meant the bishop to whom belongs jurisdiction over all bishops, not excepting metropolitans, clergy and people of his own territory or rite, in accordance with canon law and without prejudice to the primacy of the Roman Pontiff.

Wherever an Ordinary of any rite is appointed outside the territorial bounds of the patriarchate, he remains attached to hierarchy of the patriarchate of that rite, in accordance with canon law.

8) Though some of the patriarchates of the Eastern churches are of earlier and some of later date, nonetheless all are equal in respect of patriarchal dignity, without however prejudice to the legitimately established precedence of honor.

9) By the most ancient tradition of the Church the patriarchs of the Eastern churches are to be accorded exceptional respect, seeing that each is set over his patriarchate as father and head.

This Sacred Council, therefore, determines that their rights and privileges should be re-established in accordance with the ancient tradition of each of the churches and the decrees of the ecumenical councils.

The rights and privileges in question are those that obtained in the time of union between East and West; they should, however, be adapted somewhat to modern conditions.

The patriarchs with their synods are the highest authority for all business of the patriarchate, including the right of establishing new eparchies and of nominating bishops of their rite within the territorial bounds of the patriarchate, without prejudice to the inalienable right of the Roman Pontiff to intervene in individual cases.

10) What has been said of patriarchs is valid also, in harmony with the canon law, in respect to major archbishops, who are over the whole of some individual church or rite.

11) Seeing that the patriarchal office in the Eastern church is a traditional form of government, the Sacred Ecumenical Council ardently desires that new patriarchates should be erected where there is need, to be established either by an ecumenical council or by the Roman Pontiff.

EASTERN RITE PATRIARCHS
THE DISCIPLINE OF THE SACRAMENTS

12) The Sacred Ecumenical Council confirms and approves the ancient discipline of the sacraments existing in the Oriental churches, as also the ritual practices connected with their celebration and administration and ardently

desires that this should be re-established if there be need.

13) (The Minister of Confirmation) The established practice in respect of the minister of Confirmation that has obtained from the most early times among the Easterners should be fully restored. Therefore, priests validly confer this sacrament, using chrism blessed by a patriarch or a bishop.

14) All Eastern rite priests, either in conjunction with Baptism or separately from it, can confer this sacrament validly on all the faithful of any rite including the Latin; licitly, however, only if the regulations both of the common and the particular, local law are observed. Priests, also, of Latin rite, in accordance with the faculties they enjoy in respect of the administration of this sacrament, validly administer it also the faithful of Eastern churches; licitly if the regulations both of the common and of the particular law are observed.

15) (The Most Holy Eucharist) The faithful are bound to take part on Sundays and feast days in the Divine Liturgy or, according to the regulations or custom of their own rite, in the celebration of the Divine Office. That the faithful may be able more easily to fulfill their obligation, it is laid down that the period of time within which the precept should be observed extends from the Vespers of the vigil to the end of the Sunday or the feast day. The faithful are earnestly exhorted to receive Holy Communion on these days, and indeed more frequently—yes, even daily.

16) (The Minister of Penance) Owing to the fact that the faithful of the different individual churches dwell intermingled with each other in the same area or territory, the faculties for hearing confessions duly and without restriction given to priests of any rite by their own Ordinaries extend to the whole territory of him who grants them and also to the places and faithful of any other rite in the same territory, unless the Ordinary of the place has expressly excluded this for places of his rite.

17) (The Diaconate and Minor Orders) In order that the ancient established practice in the Eastern churches may flourish again, this Sacred Council ardently desires that the office of the permanent diaconate should, where it has fallen into disuse, be restored. The legislative authorities of each individual church should decide about the subdiaconate and the minor orders and the rights and obligations that attach to them.

18) (Mixed Marriages) To obviate invalid marriages when Eastern Catholics marry baptized Eastern non-Catholics and in order to promote fidelity in and the sanctity of marriage, as well as peace within the family, the Sacred Council determines that the canonical "form" for the celebration of these marriages is of obligation only for liceity; for their validity the presence of a sacred minister is sufficient, provided that what is by law to be observed is observed.

DIVINE WORSHIP

19) (The Sacred Seasons) It belongs only to an ecumenical council or to the Apostolic See to determine, transfer or suppress feast days common to all the Eastern Churches. On the other hand, to determine, transfer or suppress the feast days of any of the individual churches is within the competence not only of the Apostolic See but also of the patriarchal or archiepiscopal synod, due regard being had to the whole area and the other individual churches.

20) Until such time as all Christians are agreed on a fixed day for the celebration of Easter, with a view meantime to promoting unity among the Christians of the same area or nation,

it is left to the patriarchs or supreme authorities of a place to come to an agreement by the unanimous consent and combined counsel of those affected to celebrate the feast of Easter on the same day.

21) Individual faithful dwelling outside the area or territory of their own rite may follow completely the established custom of the place where they live as regards the law of the sacred seasons. In families of mixed rite it is permissible to observe this law according to one and the same rite.

22) (Divine Office) Eastern clerics and Religious should celebrate in accordance with the prescriptions and traditions of their own established custom the Divine Office, which from ancient times has been held in high honor in all Eastern churches. The faithful too should follow the example of their forebears and assist devoutly as occasion allows at the Divine Office.

23) (The Use of the Vernacular) It belongs to the patriarch with his synod, or to the supreme authority of each church with the council of the Ordinaries, to regulate the use of languages in the sacred liturgical functions and, after reference to the Apostolic See, of approving translations into the vernacular of texts.

RELATIONS WITH THE BRETHREN OF THE SEPARATED CHURCHES

24) The Eastern churches in communion with the Apostolic See of Rome have a special duty of promoting the unity of all Christians, especially Eastern Christians, in accordance with the principles of the Decree on Ecumenism of this Sacred Council, by prayer in the first place, and by the example of their lives, by religious fidelity to the ancient Eastern traditions, by a greater knowledge of each other, by collaboration and a brotherly regard for objects and feelings.

25) If any separated Eastern Chris-

tian should, under the guidance of the grace of the Holy Spirit, join himself to the unity of Catholics, no more should be required of him than what a bare profession of the Catholic Faith demands. Eastern clerics, seeing that a valid priesthood is preserved among them, should be permitted to exercise the Orders they possess on joining the unity of the Catholic Church, in accordance with the regulations established by the competent authority.

26) (*Communicatio in sacris:* Common participation in worship) Such *communicatio in sacris* as harms the unity of the Church or involves formal acceptance of error or the danger of aberration in the faith, of scandal and indifferentism, is forbidden by divine law. On the other hand, pastoral experience shows clearly that, as regards our Eastern brethren, there should be taken into consideration the different cases of individuals, where neither the unity of the Church is hurt nor are there verified the dangers that must be avoided, but where the needs of the salvation of souls and their spiritual good are impelling motives. For that reason the Catholic Church has always adopted and now adopts rather a mild policy, offering to all the means of salvation and an example of charity among Christians, through participation in the sacraments and in other sacred functions and things. With this in mind, "lest because of the harshness of our judgment we be an obstacle to those seeking salvation" and in order more and more to promote union with the Eastern churches separated from us, the Sacred Council lays down the following policy.

27) Without prejudice to the principles noted earlier, Eastern Christians who are in fact separated in good faith from the Catholic Church, if they ask of their own accord and have the right dispositions, may be admitted to the sacraments of Penance, the Eucharist

and the Anointing of the Sick. Further, Catholics may ask for these same sacraments from those non-Catholic ministers whose churches possess valid sacraments, as often as necessity or a genuine spiritual benefit recommends such a course and access to a Catholic priest is physically or morally impossible.

28) Further, without prejudice to the truth of those same principles, common participation by Catholics with their Eastern separated brethren in sacred functions, things and places is allowed for a good reason.

29) This conciliatory policy with regard to *communicatio in sacris* (participation in worship) with the brethren of the separated Eastern churches is put into the care and control of the local Ordinaries, in order that, by combined counsel among themselves and, if need be, after consultation also with the Ordinaries of the separated churches, they may by timely and effective regulations and directives direct the intercourse of Christians.

CONCLUSION

30) The Sacred Council feels great joy in the fruitful zealous collaboration of the Eastern and the Western Catholic churches and at the same time declares: All these directives of law are laid down in view of the present situation till such time as the Catholic Church and the separated Eastern Churches come together into complete unity.

Meanwhile, however, all Christians, Eastern as well as Western, are earnestly asked to pray to God fervently and assiduously, nay, indeed daily, that, with the aid of the most holy Mother of God, all may become one. Let them pray also that the strength and the consolation of the Holy Spirit may descend copiously upon all those many Christians of whatsoever church they be who endure suffering and deprivations for their unwavering avowal of the name of Christ.

"Love one another with fraternal charity, anticipating one another with honor" (Rom. 12, 10).

D. DECREE ON ECUMENISM, 21 NOVEMBER 1964

INTRODUCTION

1) The restoration of unity among all Christians is one of the principal concerns of the Second Vatican Council. Christ the Lord founded one Church and one Church only. However, many Christian communions present themselves to men as the true inheritors of Jesus Christ; all indeed profess to be followers of the Lord but differ in mind and go their different ways, as if Christ Himself were divided (cf. 1 Cor. 1, 13). Such division openly contradicts the will of Christ, scandalizes the world, and damages the holy cause of preaching the Gospel to every creature.

But the Lord of Ages wisely and patiently follows out the plan of grace on our behalf, sinners that we are. In recent times more than ever before, He has been rousing divided Christians to remorse over their divisions and to a longing for unity. Everywhere large numbers have felt the impulse of this grace, and among our separated brethren also there increases from day to day the movement, fostered by the grace of the Holy Spirit, for the restoration of unity among all Christians. This movement toward unity is called "ecumenical." Those belong to it who invoke the Triune God and confess Jesus as Lord and Savior, doing this not merely as individuals but also as corporate bodies. For almost everyone regards the body in which he has heard the Gospel as his church and indeed, God's church. All however, though in different ways, long for the one visible Church of God, a Church truly universal and sent forth into the world may be converted to the Gospel and so be saved, to the glory of God.

The Sacred Council gladly notes all this. It has already declared its teaching on the Church, and now, moved by a desire for the restoration of unity among all the followers of Christ, it wishes to set before all Catholics the ways and means by which they too can respond to this grace and to this divine call.

1. *Catholic Principles on Ecumenism*

2) What has revealed the love of God among us is that the Father has sent into the world His only-begotten Son, so that, being made man, He might by His redemption give new life to the entire human race and unify it (cf. 1 Jn. 4, 9; Col. 1, 18-20; Jn. 11, 52). Before offering Himself up as a spotless victim upon the altar, Christ prayed to His Father for all who believe in Him: "that they all may be one; even as thou, Father, are in me, and I in thee, that they also may be one in us, so that the world may believe that thou has sent me" (Jn. 17, 21). In His Church He instituted the wonderful sacrament of the Eucharist by which the unity of His Church is both signified and made a reality. He gave His followers a new commandment to love one another (cf. Jn. 13, 34), and promised the Spirit, their Advocate (cf. Jn. 16, 7), Who, as Lord and lifegiver, should remain with them forever.

After being lifted up on the cross and glorified, the Lord Jesus poured forth His Spirit as He had promised, and through the Spirit He has called and gathered together the people of the New Covenant, who are the Church, into a unity of faith, hope and charity, as the Apostle teaches us: "There is one body and one Spirit, just as you were called to the one hope of your calling; one Lord, one Faith, one Baptism" (Eph. 4, 4-5). For "all you who have been baptized into Christ have put on Christ . . . for you are all one in Christ Jesus" (Gal. 3, 27-28). It is the Holy Spirit, dwelling in those who believe and pervading and ruling over the Church as a whole, Who brings about that wonderful communion of the faithful. He brings them into intimate union with Christ, so that He is the principle of the Church's unity. The distribution of graces and offices is His work too (cf. 1 Cor. 12, 4-11), enriching the Church of Jesus Christ with different functions "in order to equip the saints for the work of the service, so as to build up the body of Christ" (Eph. 4, 12).

In order to establish this His holy Church everywhere in the world till the end of time, Christ entrusted to the College of the Twelve the task of teaching, ruling and sanctifying (cf. Mt. 28, 18-20, together with Jn. 20, 21-23). Among their number He selected Peter, and after his confession of faith determined that on him He would build His Church. Also to Peter He promised the keys of the kingdom of heaven (cf. Mt. 16, 18, together with Mt. 18, 18), and after His profession of love, entrusted all His sheep to him to be confirmed in faith (cf. Lc. 22, 32) and shepherded in perfect unity (cf. Jn. 21, 15-18). Christ Jesus Himself was forever to remain the chief cornerstone (cf. Eph. 2, 20) and shepherd of our souls (cf. 1 Petr. 2 25; Conc. Vaticanum I, Sess. IV (1870), *Constitutio Pastor Aeternus:* Coll. Lac. 7, 482 a).

Jesus Christ, then, willed that the Apostles and their successors—the bishops with Peter's successor at the head—should preach the Gospel faithfully, administer the sacraments, and rule the Church in love. It is thus, under the action of the Holy Spirit, that Christ wills His people to increase, and He perfects His people's fellowship in unity: in their confessing the one faith, celebrating divine worship in common, and keeping the fraternal harmony of the family of God.

The Church, then, is God's only flock; it is like a standard high lifted for the nations to see it (cf. Is. 11, 10-12): for it serves all mankind through the Gospel of peace (cf. Eph. 2, 17-18, together with Mc. 16, 15) as it makes its pilgrim way in hope toward the fatherland above (cf. 1 Petr. 3-9).

This is the sacred mystery of the unity of the Church, in Christ and through Christ, the Holy Spirit energizing its various functions. It is a mystery that finds its highest exemplar and source in the unity of the Persons of the Trinity: the Father and the Son in the Holy Spirit, one God.

3) Even in the beginnings of this one and only Church of God there arose certain rifts (cf. 1 Cor. 11, 18-19; Gal. 1, 6-9; 1 Jn. 2, 18-19), which the Apostle strongly condemned (cf. 1 Cor. 1, 11 sqq; 11, 22). But in subsequent centuries much more serious dissensions made their appearance and quite large communities came to be separated from full communion with the Catholic Church—for which, often enough, men of both sides were to blame. The children who are born into these communities and who grow up believing in Christ cannot be accused of the sin involved in the separation, and the Catholic Church looks upon them as brothers, with respect and affection. For men who believe in Christ and have been truly baptized are in real communion with the Catholic Church even though this communion is imperfect. The differences that exist in varying degrees between them and the Catholic Church—whether in doctrine and sometimes in discipline, or concerning the structure of the Church— do indeed create many obstacles, sometimes serious ones, to full ecclesiastical communion. The ecumenical movement is striving to overcome these obstacles. But even in spite of them it remains true that all who have been justified by faith in baptism are members of Christ's body (cf. Conc. Florentinum, Sess. VIII [1439], *Decretum Exultate Deo:* Mansi 31, 1055 A), and have a right to be called Christian, and so are with solid reasons accepted as brothers by the children of the Catholic Church (cf. S. Augustinus, In Ps. 32, Enarr. II, 29: PL 36, 299).

Moreover, some and even most, of the significant elements and endowments which together go to build up and give life to the Church itself, can exist outside the visible boundaries of the Catholic Church: the written word of God; the life of grace; faith, hope and charity, with the other interior gifts of the Holy Spirit, and visible elements too. All of these, which come from Christ and lead back to Christ, belong by right to the one Church of Christ.

The brethren divided from us also use many liturgical actions of the Christian religion. These most certainly can truly engender a life of grace in ways that vary according to the condition of each church or community. These liturgical actions must be regarded as capable to giving access to the community of salvation.

It follows that the separated churches (cf. Conc. Lateranense IV [1215] *Constitutio IVa;* Mansi 22,990; Conc. Lugdunense II [1274], *Professio fidei Michaelis Palaeologi;* Mansi 24,71 E. Conc. Florentinum, Sess. VI [1439], *Definitio Laetentur caeli:* Mansi 31, 1026 E.) and communities as such, though we believe them to be deficient in some respects, have been by no means deprived of significance and importance in the mystery of salvation. For the Holy Spirit has not refrained from using them as means of salvation which derive their efficacy from the very fullness of grace and truth entrusted to the Church.

Nevertheless, our separated brethren, whether considered as individuals or as communities and churches, are not blessed with that unity which Jesus Christ wished to bestow on all those who through Him were born again into one body, and with Him quickened to newness of life—that unity which the Holy Scriptures and the ancient Tradition of the Church proclaim. For it is only through Christ's Catholic Church, which is "the all-embracing means of salvation," that they can benefit fully from the means of salvation. We believe that Our Lord entrusted all the blessings of the New Covenant to the apostolic college alone, of which Peter is the head, in order to establish the one Body of Christ on earth to which all should be fully incorporated who belong in any way to the people of God. This People of God, though still in its members liable to sin, is ever growing in Christ during its pilgrimage on earth, and is guided by God's gentle wisdom, according to His hidden designs, until it shall happily arrive at the fullness of eternal glory in the heavenly Jerusalem.

4) Today, in many parts of the world, under the inspiring grace of the Holy Spirit, many efforts are being made in prayer, word and action to attain that fullness of unity which Jesus Christ desires. The Sacred Council exhorts all the Catholic faithful to recognize the signs of the times and to take an active and intelligent part in the work of ecumenism.

The term "ecumenical movement" indicates the initiatives and activities planned and undertaken, according to the various needs of the Church and as opportunities offer, to promote Christian unity. These are: first, every effort to avoid expressions, judgments and actions which do not represent the condition of our separated brethren with truth and fairness and so make mutual relations with them more difficult; then, "dialogue" between competent experts from different churches and communities. At these meetings, which are organized in a religious spirit, each explains the teaching of his communion in greater depth and brings out clearly its distinctive features. In such dialogue, everyone gains a truer knowledge and more just appreciation of the teaching and religious life of both communions. In addition, the way is prepared for cooperation between them in the duties of the common good of humanity which are demanded by every Christian conscience; and, wherever this is allowed, there is prayer in common. Finally, all are led to examine their own faithfulness to Christ's will for the Church and accordingly to undertake with vigor the task of renewal and reform.

When such actions are undertaken prudently and patiently by the Catholic faithful, with the attentive guidance of their bishops, they promote justice and truth, concord and collaboration, as well as the spirit of brotherly love and unity. This is the way that, when the obstacles to perfect ecclesiastical communion have been gradually overcome, all Christians will at last, in a common celebration of the Eucharist, be gathered into a single Church in that unity which Christ bestowed on His Church from the beginning. We believe that this unity subsists in the Catholic Church as something she can never lose, and we hope that it will continue to increase until the end of time.

However, it should be evident that,

when individuals wish for full Catholic communion, their preparation and reconciliation is an undertaking which of its nature is distinct from ecumenical action. But there is no opposition between the two, since both proceed from the marvelous ways of God.

Catholics, in their ecumenical work, must assuredly be concerned for their separated brethren, praying for them, keeping them informed about the Church, making the first approaches toward them. But their primary duty is to make a careful and honest appraisal of whatever needs to be done or renewed in the Catholic household itself, in order that its life may bear witness more clearly and faithfully to the teachings and institutions which have come to it from Christ through the hands of the Apostles.

For although the Catholic Church has been endowed with all divinely revealed truth and with all means of grace, yet its members fail to live by them with all the fervor that they should, so that the radiance of the Church's image is less in the eyes of our separated brethren and of the world at large, and the growth of God's kingdom is delayed. All Catholics must therefore aim at Christian perfection (cf. Iac. 1, 4; Rom. 12, 1-2) and, each according to his station, play his part that the Church may daily be more purified and renewed. For the Church must bear in her own body the humility and dying of Jesus (cf. 2 Cor. 4, 10; Phil. 2 5-8), against the day when Christ will present her to Himself in all her glory without spot or wrinkle (cf. Eph. 5, 27).

All in the Church must preserve unity in essentials. But let all, according to the gifts they have received, enjoy a proper freedom, in their various forms of spiritual life and discipline, in their different liturgical rites, and even in their theological elaborations of revealed truth. In all things let

charity prevail. If they are true to this course of action, they will be giving ever better expression to the authentic catholicity and apostolicity of the Church.

On the other hand, Catholics must gladly acknowledge and esteem the truly Christian endowments from our common heritage which are to be found among our separated brethren. It is right and salutary to recognize the riches of Christ and virtuous works in the lives of others who are bearing witness to Christ, sometimes even to the shedding of their blood. For God is always wonderful in His works and worthy of all praise.

Nor should we forget that anything wrought by the grace of the Holy Spirit in the hearts of our separated brethren can be a help to our own edification. Whatever is truly Christian is never contrary to what genuinely belongs to the faith; indeed, it can always bring a deeper realization of the mystery of Christ and the Church.

Nevertheless, the divisions among Christians prevent the Church from attaining the fullness of catholicity proper to her, in those of her sons who, though attached to her by Baptism, are yet separated from full communion with her. Furthermore, the Church herself finds it more difficult to express in actual life her full catholicity in all her bearings.

This Sacred Council is gratified to note that the participation by the Catholic faithful in ecumenical work is growing daily. It commends this work to the bishops everywhere in the world to be vigorously stimulated by them and guided by prudence.

2. *The Practice of Ecumenism*

5) The attainment of union is the concern of the whole Church, faithful and clergy alike. This concern extends to everyone, whatever his talent, whether it be exercised in his daily Chris-

tian life or in his theological and historical research. This concern itself reveals already to some extent the bond of brotherhood between all Christians and it helps toward that full and perfect unity which God in His kindness wills.

6) Every renewal of the Church is essentially grounded in an increase of fidelity to her own calling. Undoubtedly this is the basis of the movement toward unity.

Christ summons the Church to continual reformation as she goes her pilgrim way. The Church is always in need of this, in so far as she is an institution of men here on earth. Thus if in various times and circumstances there have been deficiencies in moral conduct or in church discipline, or even in the way that church teaching has been formulated—to be carefully distinguished from the Deposit of Faith itself—these can and should be set right at the opportune moment.

Church renewal has therefore notable ecumenical importance. Already in various spheres of the Church's life, this renewal is taking place. The Biblical and liturgical movements, the preaching of the world of God and catechetics, the apostolate of the laity, new forms of religious life and the spirituality of married life, and the Church's social teaching and activity— all these should be considered as promises and guarantees for the future progress of ecumenism.

7) There can be no ecumenism worthy of the name without a change of heart. For it is from renewal of the inner life of our minds (cf. Eph. 4, 24), from self-denial and an unstinted love that desires of unity take their rise and develop in a mature way. We should therefore pray to the Holy Spirit for the grace to be genuinely self-denying, humble, gentle in the service of others, and to have an attitude of brotherly generosity towards them. St.

Paul says: "I, therefore, a prisoner for the Lord, beg you to lead a life worthy of the calling to which you have been called, with all humility and meekness, with patience, forbearing one another in love, eager to maintain the unity of the spirit in the bond of peace" (Eph. 4, 1-3). This exhortation is directed especially to those raised to Sacred Orders precisely that the work of Christ may be continued. He came among us "not to be served but to serve" (Mt. 20, 28).

The words of St. John hold good about sins against unity: "If we say we have not sinned, we make Him a liar, and His word is not in us" (1 Jn. 1, 10). So we humbly beg pardon of God and of our separated brethren, just as we forgive them that trespass against us.

The faithful should remember that the more effort they make to live holier lives according to the Gospel, the better will they further Christian unity and put it into practice. For the closer their union with the Father, the Word, and the Spirit, the more deeply and easily will they be able to grow in mutual brotherly love.

8) This change of heart and holiness of life, along with public and private prayer for the unity of Christians, should be regarded as the soul of the whole ecumenical movement, and merits the name, "spiritual ecumenism."

It is a recognized custom for Catholics to have frequent recourse to that prayer for the unity of the Church which the Savior Himself on the eve of His death so fervently appealed to His father: "That they may all be one" (Jn. 17, 20).

In certain special circumstances, such as the prescribed prayers "for unity," and during ecumencial gatherings, it is allowable, indeed desirable that Catholics should join in prayer with their separated brethren. Such prayers in common are certainly an effective means of obtaining the grace of unity, and they are a true expression of the ties which still bind Catholics to their separated brethren. "For where two or three are gathered together in My name, there am I in the midst of them" (Mt. 18, 20).

Yet worship in common (*communicatio in sacris*) is not to be considered as a means to be used indiscriminately for the restoration of Christian unity. There are two main principles governing the practice of such common worship: first, the bearing witness to the unity of the Church, and second, the sharing in the means of grace. Witness to the unity of the Church very generally forbids common worship to Christians, but the grace to be had from it sometimes commends this practice. The course to be adopted, with due regard to all the circumstances of time, place, and persons, is to be decided by local episcopal authority, unless otherwise provided for by the Bishop's Conference according to its statutes, or by the Holy See.

9) We must get to know the outlook of our separated brethren. To achieve this purpose, study is of necessity required, and this must be pursued with a sense of realism and good will. Catholics who already have a proper grounding need to acquire a more adequate understanding of the respective doctrines of our separated brethren, their history, their spiritual and liturgical life, their religious psychology and general background. Most valuable for this purpose are meetings of the two sides—especially for discussion of theological problems—where each can treat with the other on an equal footing—provided that these who take part in them are truly competent and have the approval of the authorities. From such dialogue will emerge still more clearly what the situation of the Catholic Church really is. In this way too the outlook of our separated brethren will be better understood, and our own belief more aptly explained.

10) Sacred theology and other branches of knowledge, especially of an historical nature, must be taught with due regard for the ecumenical point of view, so that they may correspond more exactly with the facts.

It is most important that future pastors and priests should have mastered a theology that has been carefully worked out in this way and not polemically, especially with regard to those aspects which concern the relations of separated brethren with the Catholic Church.

This importance is the greater because the instruction and spiritual formation of the faithful and of religious depends so largely on the formation which their priests have received.

Moreover, Catholics engaged in missionary work in the same territories as other Christians ought to know, particularly in these times, the problems and the benefits in their apostolate which derive from the ecumenical movement.

11) The way in which the Catholic faith is expressed should never become an obstacle to dialogue with our brethren. It is, of course, essential that the doctrine should be clearly presented in this entirety. Nothing is so foreign to the spirit of ecumenism as a false irenicism, in which the purity of Catholic doctrine suffers loss and its assured genuine meaning is clouded.

At the same time, the Catholic faith must be explained more profoundly and precisely, in such a way and in such terms as our separated brethren can also really understand.

In ecumenical dialogue, when Catholic theologians join with separated brethren in common study of the divine mysteries, they should, while standing fast by the teaching of the Church, pursue the work with love for the truth, with charity, and with humility. When comparing doctrines with one another, they should remember that in Catholic doctrine there exists a "hierarchy" of truths, since they vary in their relation to the fundamental Christian faith. Thus the way will be opened whereby this kind of "fraternal rivalry" will incite all to have a clearer awareness and a deeper realization of the unfathomable riches of Christ (cf. Eph. 3, 8).

12) Before the whole world let all Christians confess their faith in God, one and three, in the incarnate Son of God, our Redeemer and Lord. United in their efforts, and with mutual respect, let them bear witness to our common hope which does not play us false. In these days when cooperation in social matters is so widespread, all men without exception are called to work together, with much greater reason all those who believe in God, but most of all, all Christians in that they bear the name of Christ. Cooperation among Christians vividly expresses the relationship which in fact already unites them, and it sets in clearer relief the features of Christ the Servant. Such cooperation, which has already begun in many countries, should be developed more and more, particularly in regions where a social and technical evolution is taking place. It should contribute to a just evaluation of the dignity of the human person, to the establishment of the blessings of peace, the application of Gospel principles to social life, and the advancement of the arts and sciences in a truly Christian spirit. Cooperation among Christians should also employ every possible means to relieve the afflictions of our times such as famine and natural disasters, illiteracy and poverty, lack of housing and the unequal distribution of wealth. All believers in Christ can, through such cooperation, be led to acquire a better knowledge and appreciation of one an-

other, and so is made smooth the road which leads to the unity of Christians.

3. *Churches and Ecclesial Communities Separated from the Roman Apostolic See*

13) We now turn our attention to the two chief types of division as they affect the seamless robe of Christ.

The first divisions occurred in the East, when the dogmatic formulae of Ephesus and Chalcedon were challenged, and later when ecclesiastical communion between the Eastern Patriarchates and the Roman See was dissolved.

Other divisions arose more than four centuries later in the West, stemming from the events which are usually referred to as "The Reformaton." As a result, many communions, national and confessional, were separated from the Roman See. Among those in which Catholic traditions and institutions in part continue to exist, the Anglican Communion occupies a special place.

These various divisions differ greatly from one another not only by reason of their origins, place and time, but still more in the serious matters of belief and church order. Therefore, without minimizing the differences between the various Christian bodies, and without overlooking the bonds between them which exist in spite of these differences, the Council proposes the following considerations for prudent ecumenical action.

I. THE SPECIAL POSITION OF THE EASTERN CHURCHES

14) For many centuries the Church of the East and that of the West each followed their separate ways though linked in a brotherly union of faith and sacramental life; the Roman See by common consent acted as guide when disagreements arose between them over matters of faith or discipline. Among other matters of moment, it is

a pleasure for this Council to remind everyone that there exist in the East many particular or local churches, among which the patriarchal churches hold first place, and many of which trace their origins back to the Apostles themselves. Hence a matter of primary concern and care among the Easterns, in their local churches, has been, and still is to preserve the family ties of common faith and charity which ought to exist between sister churches.

Similarly it must not be forgotten that from the beginning the churches of the East have had a treasury from which the Western Church has drawn extensively—in liturgical practice, spiritual tradition, and law. Nor must we undervalue the fact that it was the ecumenical councils held in the East that defined the basic dogmas of the Christian faith, on the Trinity, on the Word of God, Who took flesh of the Virgin Mary. To preserve this faith these churches have suffered and still suffer much.

However, the inheritance handed down by the Apostles was received with differences of form and manner, so that from the earliest times of the Church it was explained variously in different places, owing to diversities of genius and conditions of life. All this, quite apart from external causes, prepared the way for divisions arising also from a lack of charity and mutual understanding.

For this reason the Council urges all, but especially those who intend to devote themselves to the restoration of full communion between the Churches of the East and the Catholic Church, to give due consideration to this special feature of the origin and growth of the Eastern churches, and to the character of the relations which obtained between them and the Roman See before separation. They must take full account of all these factors and, where this is done, it will greatly contribute to the dialogue in view.

15) Everyone knows with what great love the Christians of the East celebrate the sacred liturgy, especially the Eucharistic Mystery, source of the Church's life and pledge of future glory, in which the faithful, united with their bishop, have access to God the Father through the Son, the Word made flesh, suffering, and glorified, and so, in the outpouring of the Holy Spirit, they enter into communion with the most holy Trinity, being made "sharers of the divine nature" (2 Petr. 1, 4). Hence, through the celebration of the Holy Eucharist in each of these churches, the Church of God is built up and grows in stature (cf. S. Ioannes Chrysostomos, *In Ioannem Homelia XLVI*, PG 59, 260-262.) and through concelebration, their communion with one another is made manifest.

In their liturgical worship, the Christians of the East pay high tribute, in beautiful hymns of praise, to Mary ever Virgin, whom the Ecumenical Synod of Ephesus solemnly proclaimed to be the Holy Mother of God, so that Christ might be acknowledged as being truly Son of God and Son of Man, according to the Scriptures. Many also are the saints whose praise they sing, among them the Fathers of the Universal Church.

The churches, although separated from us, yet possess true sacraments and above all, by apostolic succession, the priesthood and the Eucharist, whereby they are linked with us in closest intimacy. Therefore some worship in common (*communicatio in sacris*), given suitable circumstances and the approval of Church authority, is not merely possible but to be encouraged.

Moreover, in the East are to be found the riches of those spiritual traditions which are given expression especially in monastic life. From the glorious times of the holy Fathers, monastic spirituality flourished in the East, then later flowed over into the Western world, and there provided the source from which Latin monastic life took its rise and has drawn fresh vigor ever since. Catholics there are earnestly recommended to avail themselves of the spiritual riches of the Eastern Fathers which lift up the whole man to the contemplation of the divine.

The rich liturgical and spiritual heritage of the Eastern churches should be known, venerated, preserved and cherished by all. They must recognize that this is of supreme importance for the faithful preservation of the fullness of Christian tradition, and for bringing about reconciliation between Eastern and Western Christians.

16) From the earliest times the Eastern churches followed their own forms of ecclesiastical laws and custom, which were sanctioned by the approval of the Fathers of the Church, of synods, and even of ecumenical councils. Far from being an obstacle to the Churches unity, such diversity of customs and observances only adds to her comeliness, and is of great help in carrying out her mission, as has already been stated. To remove, then, all shadow of doubt, this Holy Synod solemnly declares that the churches of the East, while remembering the necessary unity of the whole Church, have the power and duty to govern themselves according to the disciplines proper to them, since these are better suited to the character of their faithful, and more for the good of their souls. The perfect observance of this principle which, for all its periodical neglect, is sanctioned by longstanding tradition, is one of the essential prerequisites for any restoration of unity.

17) What has just been said about the variety that can exist in the Church must also be taken to apply to the differences in theological expression of doctrine. In the study of revelation, East and West have followed different methods, and have developed differently their understanding and confession of God's truth. It is hardly surprising, then, if from time to time one tradition has come nearer to a full appreciation of some aspect of a mystery of revelation than the other, or has expressed it to better advantage. In such cases, these various theological expressions are to be considered often as mutually complementary rather than conflicting. Where the authentic theological traditions of the Eastern Church are concerned, we must recognize the admirable way in which they have their roots in Holy Scripture, and how they are nurtured and given expression in the life of the liturgy. They derive their strength too from the living tradition of the Apostles and from the works of the Fathers and spiritual writers of the Eastern churches. Thus they promote the right ordering of Christian life and, indeed, pave the way to a full vision of Christian truth.

All this heritage of spirituality and liturgy, of discipline and theology, in its various traditions, this Holy Synod declares to belong to the full Catholic and apostolic character of the Church. We thank God that many Eastern children of the Catholic Church, who preserve this heritage, and wish to express it more faithfully and completely in their lives, are already living in full communion with their brethren who follow the tradition of the West.

18) After taking all these factors into consideration, this Sacred Council solemnly repeats the declaration of previous councils and Roman Pontiffs, that for the restoration or the maintenance of unity and communion it is necessary "to impose no burden beyond what is essential" (Acts 15, 28). It is the Council's urgent desire that, in the various organizations and living activities of the Church, every effort

should be made toward the gradual realization of this unity, especially by prayer, and by fraternal dialogue on points of doctrine and the more pressing pastoral problems of our time. Similarly, the Council commends to the pastors and faithful of the Catholic Church to develop closer relations with those who are no longer living in the East but are far from home, so that friendly collaboration with them may increase, in the spirit of love, to the exclusion of all feeling of rivalry or strife. If this cause is wholeheartedly promoted, the Council hopes that the barrier dividing the Church between East and West will be removed, and that at last there may be but the one dwelling, firmly established on Christ Jesus, the cornerstone, who will make both one. (cf. Conc. Florentinum, Sess. VI (1439), *Definitio Laetentur* caeli: Mansi 31 1026 E.)

II. SEPARATED CHURCHES AND ECCLESIAL COMMUNITIES IN THE WEST

19) In the great upheaval which began in the West toward the end of the Middle Ages, and in later times too, churches and ecclesial communities came to be separated from the Apostolic See of Rome. Yet they have retained a particularly close affinity with the Catholic Church as a result of the long centuries in which all Christendom lived together in ecclesiastical communion.

However, these churches and ecclesial communities have different origins, and different convictions in matters of doctrine and the spiritual life. Since they vary considerably not only with us, but also among themselves, the task of describing them at all adequately is extremely difficult; and we have no intention of making such an attempt here.

Although the ecumenical movement and the desire for peace with the Catholic Church have not yet taken hold everywhere, it is our hope that ecumenical feeling and mutual esteem may gradually increase among all men.

It must however be admitted that in these churches and ecclesial communities there exist important differences from the Catholic Church, not only of an historical, sociological, psychological and cultural character, but especially in the interpretation of revealed truth. To make easier the ecumenical dialogue in spite of these differences, we wish to set down some considerations which can, and indeed should, serve as a basis and encouragement for such dialogue.

20) Our thoughts turn first to those Christians who make open confession of Jesus Christ as God and Lord and as the one mediator between God and men, to the glory of the one God, Father, Son and Holy Spirit. We are aware indeed that there exist considerable divergences from the doctrine of the Catholic Church concerning Christ Himself, the Word of God made flesh, the work of redemption, and consequently, concerning the mystery and ministry of the Church, and the role of Mary in the plan of salvation. But we rejoice to see that our separated brethren look to Christ as the source and center of Church unity. Their longing for union with Christ inspires them to seek an ever closer unity, and also to bear witness to their faith among the peoples of the earth.

21) A love and reverence for Holy Scripture which might be described as devotion, leads our brethren to a constant meditative study of the sacred text. For the Gospel "is the power of God for salvation to everyone who has faith, to the Jew first and then to the Greek" (Rom. 1, 16).

While invoking the Holy Spirit, they seek in these very Scriptures God, as it were speaking to them in Christ, Whom the prophets foretold, Who is the Word of God made flesh for us. They contemplate in the Scriptures the life of Christ and what the Divine Master taught and did for our salvation, especially the mysteries of His death and resurrection.

But while the Christians who are separated from us hold strongly to the divine authority of the Sacred Books, they differ from us—some in one way, some in another—regarding the relationship between Scripture and the Church. For according to Catholic belief, the authentic teaching of the Church has a special place in the interpretation and preaching of the written word of God.

But Sacred Scriptures provide for the work of dialogue an instrument of the highest value in the mighty hand of God for the attainment of that unity which the Savior holds out to all.

22) Whenever the sacrament of Baptism is duly administered as Our Lord instituted it, and is received with the right dispositions, a person is truly incorporated into the crucified and glorified Christ, and reborn to a sharing of the divine life, as the Apostle says: "You were buried together with Him in baptism, and in Him also rose again—through faith in the working of God. Who raised Him from the dead" (Col. 2, 12) (cf. Rom. 6, 4).

Thus Baptism establishes a sacramental bond of unity which links all who have been reborn by it. But of itself Baptism is only a beginning, an inauguration wholly directed toward the fullness of life in Christ. Baptism, therefore, envisages a complete profession of faith, complete incorporation in the system of salvation such as Christ willed it to be, and finally, completeness of unity which eucharistic communion gives.

Though the ecclesial communities which are separated from us lack the fullness of unity with us which should flow from Baptism and though we believe they have not retained the proper reality of the eucharistic mystery in its fullness, especially because of the absence of the sacrament of Orders, nevertheless when they commemorate His death and resurrection in the Lord's Supper, they profess that it signifies life in communion with Christ and look forward to His coming in glory. For these reasons, the subjects which should be subjects of dialogue are those of the Lord's Supper and the other sacraments, of worship, and of the Church's ministry.

23) The daily Christian lives of these brethren are nourished by their faith in Christ. They are strengthened by the grace of baptism and by hearing the word of God. This shows itself in their private prayer, their meditation on the Bible, in their Christian family life, and in the worship of community gathered together to praise God. Moreover, their form of worship not seldom displays notable features of the liturgy which they shared with us of old.

Their faith in Christ bears fruit in praise and thanksgiving for the good things received from the hands of God. Among them, too, is a strong sense of justice and a true charity toward others. This active faith has been responsible for many organizations for the relief of spiritual and material distress, the furtherance of the education of youth, the improvement of the social conditions of life, and the promotion of peace throughout the world.

While it is true that many Christians understand the moral teaching of the Gospel differently from Catholics, and do not accept the same solutions to the more difficult problems of modern society, nevertheless they share our desire to stand by the words of Christ as the source of Christian virtue, and to obey the command of the Apostle: "And whatever you do, in word or in work, do all in the name of the Lord Jesus

Christ, giving thanks to God the Father through Him" (Col. 3, 17). For that reason an ecumenical dialogue might start with discussion of the application of the Gospel to moral conduct.

24) Now that we have briefly set out the conditions for ecumenical action and the principles by which it is to be directed, we look with confidence to the future. This Sacred Council exhorts the faithful to avoid superficial and imprudent zeal, for these could only hinder real progress toward unity. Their ecumenical action must be fully and sincerely Catholic, that is to say, faithful to the truth which we have received from the Apostles and Fathers of the Church, in harmony with the faith which the Catholic Church as always professed, and at the same time directed toward that fullness to which Our Lord wills His Body to grow in the course of time.

It is the urgent wish of this Holy Council that the measures undertaken by the sons of the Catholic Church should in practice develop in step with those of our separated brethren. No obstacle must be placed to the ways of divine Providence or any limit set to the future inspirations of the Holy Spirit. The Council moreover professes its awareness that human powers and capacities cannot achieve this holy objective—the reconciling of all Christians in the unity of the one and only Church of Christ. It is because of this that the Council rests all its hope on the prayer of Christ for the Church, on our Father's love for us, and on the power of the Holy Spirit. "And hope does not disappoint, because God's love has been poured into our hearts through the Holy Spirit, who has been given to us" (Rom. 5, 5).